The Language and
Intercultural Communication
Reader

Language is key to understanding culture, and culture is an essential part of studying language. This reader focuses on the interplay between language and intercultural communication.

Reflecting the international nature of the field, this reader covers a wide range of language and cultural contexts: Arabic, Chinese, English (British, American, Australian and South African), Greek, Hebrew, Japanese, Samoan and Spanish. Divided into six parts, it covers: culture, language and thought; cultural approaches to discourse and pragmatics; communication patterns across cultures; teaching and learning cultural variations of language use; interculturality; and intercultural communication in professional contexts. With contributions written by eminent authorities in the field, as well as cutting-edge materials representing current developments, the book explores the breadth and depth of the subject, as well as providing an essential overview for both students and researchers.

Each part begins with a clear and comprehensive introduction and is enhanced by discussion questions, study activities and further reading sections. Alongside a comprehensive resource list, detailing important reference books, journals, organisations and websites, and an annotated glossary of key terms, the final section offers advice on how to carry out research in language and intercultural communication.

Zhu Hua is Reader in Applied Linguistics and Communication, Birkbeck College, University of London, UK. She recently co-edited *Language Learning and Teaching as Social Inter-action* (2007).

The Language and Intercultural Communication Reader

Edited by

Zhu Hua

Routledge
Taylor & Francis Group

LONDON AND NEW YORK

First published 2011
by Routledge
2 Park Square, Milton Park, Abingdon, Oxon, OX14 4RN

Simultaneously published in the USA and Canada
by Routledge
270 Madison Ave, New York, NY 10016

Routledge is an imprint of the Taylor & Francis Group, an informa business

Typeset in Perpetua and Bell Gothic by
Florence Production Ltd, Stoodleigh, Devon
Printed and bound in Great Britain by
The MPG Books Group

British Library Cataloguing in Publication Data
A catalogue record for this book is available from the British Library

Library of Congress Cataloging in Publication Data
The language and intercultural communication reader / edited by Zhu Hua.
       p. cm.
     Includes bibliographical references and index.
  1. Language and culture.   2. Intercultural communication.
  3. Sociolinguistics.   I. Hua, Zhu, 1970–
  P35.L28 2011
  306.44–dc22   2010032341

ISBN: 978–0–415–54912–7 (hbk)
ISBN: 978–0–415–54913–4 (pbk)

Contents

Acknowledgements

The editor would like to thank Louise Semlyen and her team at Routledge, in particular David Cox and Eloise Cook, for their support throughout the project. A special thank-you goes to Li Wei for his insight and help, both in the selection and editing of the material, to Brigid O'Connor for her proofreading and to Jiang Yan for her help with referencing. The edition of the *Reader* has benefited from a three-month research leave provided by the Department of Applied Linguistics and Communication, Birkbeck College.

The editor and publishers would like to thank the following copyright holders for permission to reprint material:

Whorf, B. (1956). The relation of habitual thought and behaviour to language. In J. B. Carroll (ed.), *Language, thought and reality: selected writings of Benjamin Lee Whorf* (pp. 134–59). Cambridge: Cambridge University Press. Reproduced with permission of Cambridge University Press.

Nisbett, R. (2003). Is the world made up of nouns or verbs? Selected from *The geography of thought* (Chapter 6, pp. 137–65). London: Nicholas Brealey Publishing. Reproduced with permission of Nicholas Brealey Publishing.

Samovar, L. A., Porter, R. E. & Stefani, L. A. (1998). Hofstede's value dimensions and Hall's high context/low context. Selected from *Communication between cultures* (3rd edn) (pp. 66–73, 79–81). Belmont: Wadsworth. Reproduced with permission of Wadsworth.

Scollon, R. & Scollon, S. W. (2001). Interpersonal politeness and power. Selected from *Intercultural communication* (Chapter 3, pp. 43–59). Malden, MA: Blackwell. Reproduced with permission of Blackwell.

Gu, Y. (1990). Politeness phenomena in modern Chinese. *Journal of Pragmatics*, 14, 237–57. Reproduced with permission of Elsevier.

Ide, S. (2005). How and why honorifics can signify dignity and elegance: the indexicality and reflexivity of linguistic rituals. In R. Lakoff & S. Ide (eds) *Broadening the horizon of linguistic politeness* (pp. 45–64). Amsterdam: John Benjamins. Reproduced with permission of John Benjamins.

Spencer-Oatey, H. (2002). Managing rapport in talk: using rapport-sensitive incidents to explore the motivational concerns underlying the management of relations. *Journal of Pragmatics*, 34, 529–45. Reproduced with permission of Elsevier.

Goddard, C. & Wierzbicka, A. (2004). Cultural scripts: what are they and what are they good for? *Intercultural Pragmatics*, 1(2), 153–66. Reproduced with permission of Mouton.

Blum-Kulka, S. & Olshtain, E. (1984). Requests and apologies: a cross-cultural study of speech act realisation patterns (CCSARP). *Applied Linguistics*. 5(3), 196–213. Reproduced with permission of Oxford University Press.

Katriel, T. (1986). Excerpts from *Talking straight: dugri speech in Israeli Sabra culture* (pp. 57–72). Cambridge: Cambridge University Press. Reproduced with permission of Cambridge University Press.

Nazzal, A. (2005). The pragmatic functions of the recitation of Qur'anic verses by Muslims in their oral genre: the case of Insha' Allah, "God's willing". *Pragmatics*, 15(2–3), 251–74. Reproduced with permission of International Pragmatics Association.

Sajavaara, K. & Lehtonen, J. (1997). The silent Finn revisited. In A. Jaworski (ed.), *Silence: interdisciplinary perspectives* (pp. 263–84). Berlin: Mouton de Gruyter. Reproduced with permission of Mouton.

Holliday, A. (1999). Small cultures. *Applied Linguistics*, 20(2), 237–64. Reproduced with permission of Oxford University Press.

Kasper, G. & Rose, K. (2002). Developmental patterns in second language pragmatics. Selected from *Pragmatic development in a second language* (pp. 125–57). Malden, MA: Blackwell. Reproduced with permission of Blackwell.

Mauranen, A. (2006). Signaling and preventing misunderstanding in English as lingua franca communication. *International Journal of the Sociology of Language*, 177, 123–50. Reproduced with permission of Mouton.

Sarangi, S. (1994). Intercultural or not? Beyond celebration of cultural differences in miscommunication analysis. *Pragmatics*, 4, 409–27. Reproduced with permission of International Pragmatics Association.

Nishizaka, A. (1995). The interactive constitution of interculturality: how to be a Japanese with words. *Human Studies*, 18, 301–26. Reproduced with permission of Springer Netherlands.

Higgins, C. (2007). Constructing membership in the in-group: affiliation and resistance among urban Tanzanians. *Pragmatics*, 17(1), 49–70. Reproduced with permission of International Pragmatics Association.

Clyne, M., Ball, M. & Neil, D. (1991). Excerpt from Intercultural communication at work in Australia: complaints and apologies in turns. *Multilingua*, 10, 251–73. Reproduced with permission of Mouton.

Schmidt, R., Shimura, A., Wang, Z. & Jeong, H. (1995). Suggestions to buy: television commercials from the U.S., Japan, China, and Korea. In S. Gass & J. Neu (eds), *Speech acts across cultures: challenges to communication in a second language* (pp. 285–316). Berlin: Mouton de Gruyter. Reproduced with permission of Mouton.

Bargiela-Chiappini, F. & Harris, S. (1996). Interruptive strategies in British and Italian management meetings. *Text*, 16(3), 269–97. Reproduced with permission of Mouton.

Márquez Reiter, R. & Placencia, M. (2004). Excerpt from Displaying closeness and respectful distance in Montevidean and Quiteño service encounters. Selected from R. Márquez Reiter & M. Placencia (eds), *Current trends in the pragmatics of Spanish* (Chapter 7, pp. 121–55). Amsterdam/Philadelphia: John Benjamins. Reproduced with permission of John Benjamins.

Every effort has been made to contact and acknowledge copyright owners. If any material has been included without permission, the publishers offer their apologies. The publishers would be pleased to have any errors or omissions brought to their attention so that corrections may be published at later printing.

The balance between a faithful reproduction of the original papers and the need to make a coherent collection within limited space has been achieved through the following editorial decisions and changes:

- The authors' original writing styles and conventions have been kept as much as possible.
- Minor textual omissions are indicated in the text with [. . .]. A brief note is provided in the square brackets where there is a substantial omission.
- The numbers for sections, subsections, examples, tables and figures are adjusted where appropriate in the *Reader* to make the selection coherent as a whole.
- The references and citations have been reformatted and adjusted.
- Where the selection comes from a monograph, cross-references to other chapters in the same monograph have been omitted where appropriate.

How to use the *Reader*

This *Reader* is aimed at advanced undergraduate and beginning postgraduate students on courses in intercultural communication, language learning and teaching, pragmatics and discourse analysis of a range of subjects, including languages and linguistics, TESOL, communication studies, cultural studies, anthropology and cross-cultural psychology. It can be used either on its own as a core course text or as a supplementary collection of key reading for other texts.

Special features of the *Reader* include the following:

- The general 'Introduction' outlines the main themes in the field of language and intercultural communication, paying particular attention to different disciplinary perspectives. It provides a broader context to the various papers selected for the *Reader*.
- The 'Introduction' to each part of the *Reader* aims to guide the student through the selected articles by giving a brief summary of each paper and highlighting its contributions to the field and links with other papers in the *Reader*. It can be read together with relevant sections in the general Introduction.
- 'Notes for students and instructors' are specially designed to facilitate the teaching and learning experience and aid classroom use. Each section consists of two types of exercise. 'Study questions' are aimed at a fairly basic level, to be used by the students themselves for checking comprehension and reviewing the key issues in each chapter. 'Study activities', on the other hand, are intended to be used, either in class by the instructors and students for discussion, or after class by the students to apply the key theoretical models or analytical frameworks to their own projects. The 'Further reading' sections contain additional sources of material for follow-up.
- The last chapter, 'Studying language and intercultural communication: methodological considerations', aims to provide guidance to students in their research activities and empirical studies. It summarises and compares the key research designs and data collection methods in the study of language and intercultural communication. The examples are drawn from the selected papers in the *Reader*, wherever possible, thus providing an opportunity to see methods or designs *in action*, as well as reviewing the methodological perspectives in each paper.

- A comprehensive 'Resource list' details important reference books, journals, corpora, organisations and websites.
- An annotated glossary of key terms in language and intercultural communication is provided, to which the student can refer in his or her studies.

The six parts of the *Reader* can be read in any order, although it is recommended that the Introduction be read first. Students are encouraged to think of the strengths and limitations that come with each perspective, as well as to compare from different perspectives. The rationale behind the selection of individual articles can be found in the general Introduction, as well as the Introduction at the beginning of each part.

ZHU HUA

INTRODUCTION
Themes and issues in the study of language and intercultural communication

INTERCULTURAL COMMUNICATION, as a field of enquiry, is concerned with how people from different cultural and ethnic backgrounds interact with each other, and what impact such interactions have on group relations, as well as individuals' identity, attitudes and behaviour. Although some would differentiate intercultural communication from cross-cultural communication (i.e. comparative studies of communication patterns in different cultures), more and more people now use intercultural communication as an umbrella term to include both interactions between people of different cultures and comparative studies of communication patterns across cultures.

Intercultural communication naturally entails the use of language. Many studies of intercultural communication are either oriented towards language use or focus on the interplay between cultural differences and language use. In what follows, I will review a number of themes in the field of language and intercultural communication. Under each theme, I will discuss the following:

• Who are the researchers?
• What are the key research questions?
• What are the context and purpose of the studies?
• What is the main disciplinary background?
• What does it have to say about the interplay of language and intercultural communication?

By doing so, I hope to map out the context and put things in perspective for each theme, which is echoed in the grouping and selection of the readings for this Reader and further explored in the introduction to each part of the *Reader*.

Theme 1: culture, language and thought

A fundamental theoretical question underlying the study of language and intercultural communication is the relationship between language, culture and cognition. It is a question that concerns many different fields of enquiry, from anthropology to cognitive science, and can be traced back to as early as the beginning of the twentieth century, when Franz Boas (1940) argued that one could not understand another culture without having direct access to its language. The widely acknowledged founder of the field of intercultural communication, Edward Hall, also made a strong claim that 'culture is communication and communication is culture' (1959, p. 191). The most often cited hypothesis on the relationship between language and culture, among various speculations and arguments, is perhaps the Sapir–Whorf hypothesis, also known as 'linguistic relativity'. The hypothesis suggests that thought is influenced by language, and at the same time it also influences language. Although the hypothesis does not concern culture directly and explicitly, many followers extend this hypothesis to the relationship between culture and language. For example, Gumperz & Levinson (1996, p. 1) state, 'culture, through language, affects the way in which we think, . . . especially our classification of the experienced world'.

Evidence supporting the existence of a close, two-way relationship between language and culture and between language and thought comes from several areas of enquiry, including vocabulary, syntax and cognitive studies (for a review, see Gumperz & Levinson, 1996; Kramsch, 2004; Risager, 2006). Apart from an often-cited example of elaborate words for different kinds of snow in Eskimo languages (cf. Pullman, 1991), how frequently a word is used in a language is also a key indicator of the importance of that concept or idea in the relevant culture (see key-word studies by Wierzbicka, 1997). In addition, recent work on ethnosyntax has gathered a growing body of evidence to suggest that the grammar and semantics of a language are entwined with the culture of its speakers (Enfield, 2002). An example of cultural differences in motion paths or the manner of action can be found in Slobin (2000). Some cross-cultural differences in cognition have also been identified. For example, it is claimed that some cultures tend to group by categories, whereas other cultures prefer groupings by relationship (Nisbett, 2003; a section is reproduced in this Reader).

However, not everyone agrees on the interrelationships between language, culture and thought. Many researchers argue for the existence of universality in grammar (Chomsky, 1965). Others, for example Berlin & Kay (1969), advocate universal patterns in colour terms. Among many prominent opponents of linguistic relativity is Steven Pinker (1994), who is adamant that no differences in thinking are linked with different languages.

Clearly, the interrelationships between language, thought and culture are subject to an ongoing debate, with evidence coming forward from different disciplines. The enquiry is critical to our understanding of how languages work in different cultural contexts and how to account for culture-specific communication styles. Many approaches and themes in language and intercultural communication relate, either explicitly or implicitly, to the broader question of the relationship between language, culture and cognition. One such example is the cultural value approach.

In order to understand the way people of different cultures communicate and behave, a number of scholars in the 1960s, 1970s and 1980s dedicated themselves to the categorisation of national cultures in terms of value and belief systems, referred to as cultural dimensions or value orientations. Working for IBM, the Dutch psychologist Geert Hofstede collected questionnaires from more than 100,000 IBM employees in forty countries and identified four cultural dimensions, including *individualism* vs. *collectivism, high-* vs. *low-power-distance, masculinity* vs. *femininity* and *high* vs. *low uncertainty avoidance*. Later, he added *long-term orientation* as a fifth dimension. Hofstede argued that people carry software-like 'mental programs', of which national culture is an important component (Hoftstede, 1991, 2001; also see Chapter 3 in this Reader for a review of his work). Other scholars following a similar approach include Fons Trompenaars and Charles Hampden-Turner (1998), Shalom Schwartz

(1992, 1994) and Kluckhohn & Strodtbeck (1961). Their work is also extended by the cross-cultural psychologist Harry Triandis (1990, 1995), who reconceptualised the dichotomy of individualism vs. collectivism.

Underlying the work of the cultural-value approach is an assumption that cultural values have a determining effect on an individual's style of communication. For example, people from an individualistic culture are often associated with an explicit or direct verbal communication style, and the wants, needs and desires of the speaker are embodied in the spoken message. In contrast, people from a collectivistic culture tend to communicate indirectly and within the group itself; interpersonal harmony and cooperation are important purposes of communication.

Over the years, cultural-value studies have been criticised for their essentialist and over-generalised view of culture, i.e. members of a cultural group are treated as the same, sharing definable characteristics, whatever the context may be (e.g. McSweeney, 2002). Nevertheless, the classification systems proposed by various scholars do act as a convenient tool in revealing the cultural differences in values and beliefs. The studies following this particular line of enquiry are still widely cited in business and organisation management studies and applied in intercultural training.

Theme 2: cultural approaches to discourse and pragmatics: theoretical considerations

Although the relevance of 'cultural membership' to the study of discourse involving speakers from different cultural and linguistic backgrounds seems obvious, it was not until the 1980s that the connection began to materialise in systematic analyses of the discourse patterns of speakers from different cultural and linguistic backgrounds. This was partly because discourse studies were, and still are, a very diverse field, and partly because those working in intercultural communication had relatively little knowledge of linguistic anthropology and sociolinguistics, two fields that provided much input and methodology to discourse-oriented approaches to intercultural communication. In fact, it is still true that many intercultural communication researchers look to psychology and sociology in developing general theories and models. Examples of earlier cultural approaches to discourse include Gumperz (1978, 1982), Gumperz & Tannen (1979) and Gumperz, et al. (1979). This body of work is part of so-called interactional sociolinguistics, which is concerned with how speakers signal and interpret meaning in interaction. It provides a framework for a close analysis of intercultural interaction and attributes breakdowns in intercultural communication to differences in discourse strategies and styles and/or the misinterpretation of contextualisation cues.

In the meantime, linguistic pragmatics, i.e. the study of language use in context, has made a significant impact on discourse-oriented intercultural communication studies, especially through the notions of politeness and face proposed by Goffman (1967), Lakoff (1973) and Brown & Levinson (1978). This line of enquiry, represented by Scollon & Scollon (2001b, one section of which is reproduced in this Reader), shares a similar approach with interactional sociolinguistics. However, instead of framing communication breakdown in terms of mismatches of contextualisation cues, the pragmatics approach uses the theoretical construct of *face* (namely, the positive social value a person claims for her or himself) and *politeness strategies* (the interactional strategies to address the hearer's positive and negative face) to account for intercultural differences in interaction.

Although the notions of politeness and face have inspired numerous subsequent studies of various languages to account for observed intercultural differences, their very universal appeal is under constant challenge. A number of studies, for example Matsumoto (1988, 1989), Ide (1989), Mao (1994), de Kadt (1998), Gu (1990, reproduced in this Reader), etc., have challenged the universalities of these notions and argued for culture- and language-specific renditions of these key notions. Some studies have also made an attempt to differentiate 'common-sense politeness', whereby politeness is associated with courtesy and good manners, from 'linguistic politeness', a technical term to describe whether and how speakers address the face-want in interactions (Ehlich, 1992). Watts (2003) further proposed the term 'politic behaviour' to describe both linguistic and non-linguistic behaviours that the participants construct as being appropriate to the ongoing social interaction.

Over the years, many alternative models or approaches have been proposed. Some studies, such as Li Wei (1996) and Ide (2005, reproduced in this Reader), advocate the use of local cultural terms to interpret a cultural phenomenon. Spencer-Oatey (2002, reproduced in this Reader), in her rapport-management model, has brought the interpersonal aspects of the notion of face (i.e. motivational concerns) into a clearer focus. Wierzbicka and her colleagues (Wierzbicka, 2003; Goddard, 2006) have also proposed a culturally and linguistically 'neutral' method, i.e. 'cultural scripts' written in 'natural semantic metalanguage', to describe cultural practices and thereby to ensure *like for like* comparison between cultural practices. Several scholars (e.g. Sharifian, 2005) have adopted the 'cultural schemas theory', which attempts to capture the cognitive processes underlying human behaviour for social interactions (for a review, see Nishida, 2005), in understanding cross-cultural differences in interaction.

Theme 3: communication patterns across cultures: empirical explorations

Whereas the works outlined in Theme 2 focus on providing theoretical accounts of the cultural approaches to discourse and pragmatics, an impressive number of empirical studies have emerged in the last three decades. These studies have examined various aspects of language use that may vary from one culture to another and from one language to another and can be grouped, very broadly, into the following types.

The first type is focused on comparing patterns of speech acts across cultures. Very often referred to as cross-cultural pragmatics – the study of speech acts by language users from different linguistic and cultural backgrounds – these studies investigate how speech acts or events, such as request, apology, greeting, refusal, persuasion, invitation, gift offering and acceptance, etc., are realised in different languages and to what extent a speaker's choice of linguistic politeness strategies is influenced by factors such as relative power, social distance and degree of imposition in a given culture. The first systematic cross-cultural and interlingual study is the CCSARP project reported in Blum-Kulka & Olshtain (1984, reproduced in this Reader). Blum-Kulka, House & Kasper (1989), Gass & Neu (1996), Wierzbicka (2003) and Hickey & Steward (2005), among others, contain comparative studies of a number of differing cultures.

The second type of empirical study of communication patterns across cultures is the ethnographic study of cultures. As perhaps the most used methodology in the study of language and intercultural communication, ethnography proves an effective tool for discovering, describing and interpreting culturally specific interaction patterns. (More discussion on ethnography can be found in the last chapter of the *Reader*; see also Blommaert, 1998.) There are a number of research monographs and studies that employ this methodology to study cultures in conversation and language use (e.g. Carbaugh, 2005; Katriel, 1986, reproduced in this Reader). Many popular cultural guidebooks also use this methodology in a broad sense; to name a few, *Watching the English: the hidden rules of English behaviour*, by Fox (2004); *Different games different rules: why Americans and Japanese misunderstand each other*, by Yamada (1997); *Understanding cultural differences: Germans, French and Americans*, by Hall & Hall (1990); *Encountering the Chinese: a guide for Americans*, by Hu & Grove (1991).

Given existing cross-cultural differences in many aspects of discourse and communication and increasingly widespread globalisation, how does someone living in two different cultures or speaking two or more languages deal with these potentially conflicting differences? This is the question addressed by the third type of study. A number of works, using personal narratives and/or in the form of autobiography, examine the impact of learning a new language or being bilingual on one's sociocultural identity. Written by linguists or culture experts, these works reveal the impact of immersion in two cultures on one's personal and professional life, as well as the creative and very often emotionally laden process of cultural adaptation (e.g., Hoffman, 1989; Besemeres & Wierzbicka, 2007; Bond, 1997). Ang (2001) reflects on the tension between Asia and the West by investigating the predicaments of Chineseness: in Taiwan she was different because she could not speak Chinese; in the West she was different because she looked Chinese.

The studies under this theme have not only made an important contribution to raising awareness of cultural differences in the way people communicate, but have also provided empirical evidence for the debate on the issue of the universality of human interaction.

Theme 4: teaching and learning cultural variations of language use

Traditional language-learning and -teaching approaches have often been criticised for failing to acknowledge the importance of culture (cf. Lado, 1957). Recent developments in language teaching and learning research have tried to incorporate a cultural dimension. There is, however, a risk of oversimplification or overgeneralisation: in Britain, the cultural dimension in language teaching and learning is very often reduced to what is known as the 3 Ss (namely, saris, samosas and steel bands) (Troyna & Williams, 1986) and 4 Fs (namely, food, fashion, festivals and folklore) in the USA (Banks, 2002). In contrast, a number of scholars have called for the integration of cultural values and practices in language teaching and learning. For example, Byram & Morgan (1994), Valdes (1986) and Kramsch (1993, 1998a) all discussed the ways in which the culture of the target language can be made explicit in the curriculum. Some recent studies look into Internet-mediated intercultural learning and teaching (e.g. Belz & Thorne, 2006; O'Dowd, 2007). A greater emphasis has been placed on teaching and learning culturally appropriate pragmatic strategies. Many current language-learning textbooks use cultural simulations, games, role-playing and drama to recreate the real-life situation. At a more theoretical level, there have been critical debates over the concept of 'native speaker' and the pedagogical challenges that a less native-speaker-centric approach would entail. Questions are asked about the nature of the second language (L2) user (e.g. Cook, 2002) and the role of 'authentic' language and 'native speaker' in language teaching (Cook, 1997; Kramsch, 1998b; Davies, 2004).

Learning to speak a language is not just about learning to produce grammatically correct sentences, but about learning what to say in a culturally appropriate way. The emerging and fast-developing field of second language pragmatics, also known as interlanguage pragmatics, is concerned with the development of pragmatic and discourse abilities by second-language learners (e.g. Kasper & Rose, 1999, 2002, a section of which is selected in this Reader; Bardovi-Harlig, 1999). Studies following this line of enquiry investigate developmental patterns in second language pragmatics; factors that contribute to the development of second language pragmatics, such as input, exposure and instruction; individual differences in second language pragmatic development, such as age, gender, motivation and social and psychological distance; and others. Recent years have also seen the debate on the problematic nature of the practice of measuring second-language learners' or bilingual speakers' pragmatic competence against monolingual native speakers' norms (e.g. Leung, 2005).

There is an increasingly common phenomenon in today's world, namely, lingua franca communication. It refers to interactions in which speakers do not share a native language. It is a result of globalisation and internationalisation. The field of lingua franca communication differs from interlanguage or second language pragmatics in that it does not treat the linguistic output of non-native speakers as an unfinished and developing product, but as a special form of language use. Therefore, it pays little attention to the learning process and does not measure language use against a native speaker's norm (e.g. Seidlhofer, 2004). A key feature of lingua franca communication is its heterogeneous nature (Meierkord, 2000; Firth, 2009), as it is very often the case that lingua franca participants speak the shared language with different degrees of proficiency (Mauranen, 2006, reproduced in this Reader). Heterogeneity is also reflected in the existence of several, and sometimes potentially conflicting, communicative norms that may be brought into lingua franca interaction by participants: whereas some participants may have acquired or adopted communicative norms regulating the language as a lingua franca to various degrees, others may follow norms of their own native languages while using a lingua franca. The contact and competition between the different communicative and cultural norms may result in the construction of a new cultural pattern, i.e. a lingua franca culture (Meierkord, 2000) or third space (Bhabha, 1994; Lo Bianco et al., 1999).

Theme 5: Reconceptualising cultural differences

As reviewed above, many predominant approaches in intercultural communication start with cultural memberships, assuming that differences between groups in terms of beliefs and practices are the cause of mis- or non-understanding in intercultural communication. However, as early as 1935, Bateson raised the issue of reifying cultures as discrete, separable entities in his book *Culture contact and schismogenesis* (Scollon & Scollon, 2001a). Bateson's challenge to the essentialist treatment of the concept of 'culture' is followed up by Drummond (1987), Clifford & Marcus (1986), Barth (1989), Street (1993), Thornton (1988), etc. These people, among others, questioned the simplest way of conceptualising cultures as memberships of different social groups.

Since the 1980s, many discourse analysts have adopted post-structural and post-modernist approaches to the relationship between culture and social behaviour, including language use, and have argued that, although discourse is influenced by social structures, it also impacts on social structures by negotiating, constructing or reinforcing the social and cultural perspectives and identities of the participants in social interaction (e.g. Gee, 1989, 1996, 1999; Fairclough, 1985, 1988, 1995). Many discourse studies that appeared in the late 1980s and 1990s followed this line of approach. An example is a special issue of *Pragmatics* (edited by Michael Meeuwis, 1994a) that includes works by Sarangi (1994, reproduced in this Reader), Day (1994),

Shi-xu (1994), Shea (1994) and Meeuwis (1994b) on the role of discourse and interaction in constructing the speaker's cultural or ethnic memberships. Other examples include Nishizaka (1995, reproduced in this reader) and Mori (2003). For the more recent developments, see a special issue of *Pragmatics* edited by Christina Higgins (2007).

An extension of this work is to see the outcome of intercultural encounters as a new, emerging set of cultural identities and values. Instead of taking intercultural communication as interactions between people of different cultural backgrounds, bringing with them their more or less static sets of values, identities and practices, the focus now is on the process of interaction and what the participants achieve from the experience in terms of new values, identities and practices (e.g. Holliday *et al.*, 2004; Riley, 2007). Using the framework provided by conversation analysis, Zhu Hua (2010) examines how 'interculturality' emerges through interactions among individuals with competing cultural conventions. She argues that cultural differences are neither prescribed nor static, and, instead, they are constructed through discursive practice. They may not always be relevant to mis- or non-understanding in intercultural interactions. Through a range of interactional resources, such as turn-taking, code-switching, address terms, topic management, repair, back-channelling, laughter etc., speakers constantly negotiate and reconstruct their sociocultural identities and ascribe their group memberships accordingly. Cultural differences are therefore a process rather than an end-product.

Related to the discursive nature of identity formation embodied in the interculturality approach, a recent interdisciplinary movement has proposed an alternative slant that goes one step further than interculturality. Represented by Gillespie (2006), Linell & Valsiner, (2009), Dervin & Riikonen (2009) and others, this approach advocates a dialogical turn in understanding the co-construction of 'in-between identities' and making sense of multiple selves by looking at the interplay between self and others.

Interculturality, as a new and developing research paradigm, provides an analytical concept that focuses on the emergent and dynamic nature of cultural differences. It takes intercultural encounters as instances of 'talk-in-interaction', and 'being intercultural' as a socially constructed phenomenon. It restores the speakers' or participants' agency as a central role in social construction, which is very often neglected in the earlier studies of intercultural communication.

Theme 6: intercultural communication in context

As a field that was born out of a concern for real-world problems, intercultural communication continues to be engaged with studies of intercultural encounters in the following areas:
    Different contexts include:

*   business (e.g. Bargiela-Chiappini & Harris, 1996, reproduced in this Reader; Bargiela-Chiappini & Harris, 1997; Bargiela-Chiappini, 2009; Ehlich & Wagner, 1995);
*   politics (e.g. Fetzer & Lauerbach, 2007; Harris *et al.*, 2006);
*   law (e.g. Eades, 2005, 2007; Kocbek, 2006; Mattila, 2006);
*   the media (e.g. Hinton, 2007);
*   health (e.g. Roberts & Sarangi, 2002; Roberts *et al.*, 2003; Roberts, 2007);
*   the workplace (e.g. Bardovi-Harlig & Hartford, 2005; Vine, 2004);
*   service encounters (e.g. Márquez Reiter & Placencia, 2004, reproduced in this collection);
*   marriage (e.g. Piller, 2007);
*   education (e.g. Brisk, 2008; Zhu Hua *et al.*, 2007).

Different genres include:

- small talk (e.g. Coupland, 2000);
- telephoning (e.g. Baker *et al.*, 2005; Luke & Pavlidou, 2002);
- jokes (e.g. Marra & Holmes, 2007; Vuorela, 2005);
- adverts (e.g. Schmidt *et al.*, 1995, reproduced in this Reader);
- job applications (e.g. Zhu Hua, 2007);
- business writing (e.g. Zhu, 2005);
- résumés and presentations (e.g. Pan *et al.*, 2002).

By looking at how intercultural communication takes place in a specific context, these studies explore the interplay of cultural and institutional factors, and sometimes genre, in shaping the way intercultural interactions are conducted. Many studies seek to identify culture-specific language use and communication patterns. They very often offer a cross-cultural and/or cross-linguistic comparison of the ways people communicate and thus contribute to our knowledge of cross-cultural differences in communicative patterns. The practical value of such studies is high, as many intercultural communication trainers use the results of these studies in their teaching programmes.

Recent years have seen a movement towards more critical analyses of multilingual interactions in multicultural workplaces and of how broader sociological issues of identity, power and racism, for example, are dealt with by participants themselves in real-life encounters (Riley, 2007).

Rationale behind the selection in this Reader

There were many challenges in selecting the articles for the present Reader. The first challenge came from the wide scope and the interdisciplinary nature of the field. There now exists a large body of published work on language and intercultural communication, scattered across a variety of disciplines and sub-fields. As a consequence, the existing studies vary in their theoretical and methodological orientations as well as practical implications. The second challenge is the balance between languages and cultures represented. Whereas some cultures and languages, such as Japanese and Chinese, seem to have received much attention in the field of intercultural communication, others remain under-explored. The third challenge is the balance between the classics and contemporary work. Although the classics are the foundation upon which the field expands and develops, the contemporary work represents current trends and indicates directions for future research. On top of these challenges, there are the usual issues that all publications need to deal with, such as space restrictions and the expectations and needs of users.

Bearing in mind these challenges, this Reader includes twenty-two chapters that are either influential articles in the field or representative of current developments in language and intercultural communication. The twenty-two articles are grouped into the six thematic parts, as discussed in the first part of this Introduction.

Part I, 'Culture, language and thought', includes some of the most influential theories and models on the fundamental question of the field, i.e. the relationship between language, culture and thought. A classic paper by Whorf and a recent one by Nisbett complement each other through their different approaches. The cultural-value studies reviewed by Samovar *et al.* offer an alternative theoretical perspective.

Part II, 'Cultural approaches to discourse and pragmatics: theoretical considerations', consists of five studies that aim to provide a theoretical account for cultural differences in language use, such as politeness, face, rapport and cultural scripts. The fact that most of the selected papers in this part base their arguments on the observations and data of East Asian languages and cultures is coincidental. The articles are included because of their influential status, not specifically because of the languages involved. Nevertheless, studies of East Asian languages generally have proved very fruitful in expanding certain theoretical models, such as the politeness theory, probably owing to the contrast between East Asian languages and cultures and European ones.

Part III, 'Communication patterns across cultures: empirical examples', consists of articles on a variety of speech acts and communication patterns across cultures. Particular effort is made to cover different languages and cultures.

Part IV, 'Teaching and learning cultural variations of language use', contains three different angles to language learning: Holliday's article raises a conceptual issue of the integration of culture into language teaching and the learning curriculum; Kasper and Rose's article focuses on the learner's perspective and the influence of the first language and culture on the learning of the second; and Mauranen's article treats second-language speakers as users rather than learners.

The articles in Part V, 'Interculturality', represent some of the recent developments in the field, from a primary focus on preconceived cultural differences to a position that sees cultural differences as something socially and discursively constructed through interaction.

The last part, Part VI, 'Intercultural communication in a professional context', includes applications of the study of language and intercultural communication in a range of *professional* contexts. Particular effort is made to incorporate a variety of contexts, languages and cultures.

More information on the individual articles is provided in the introduction to each part. Although every effort is made to ensure a good coverage of themes and a balance between classic and contemporary studies and between languages and cultures, many good articles cannot be included owing to space restrictions. Further reading and the Resource list provide additional references that the reader would find useful.

Intercultural communication is a highly multidisciplinary and interdisciplinary field in which language plays an important role. The study of language and intercultural communication focuses on the role of language in intercultural encounters, the complex relationship between language and cultural identities in the communication process, and the various cultural factors involved in the defining and differentiating of the linguistic behaviours of speakers and learners of different languages. It addresses some of the fundamental principles in human communication through an in-depth and systematic investigation of language use by speakers of different cultural backgrounds and orientations in real-life communicative contexts. Although its theoretical concerns include broader issues such as cultural cognition, identity and interculturality, it maintains a strong practical and professional interest, informing and influencing fields such as language teaching and learning, as well as business and organisational communication.

References

Ang, I. (2001). *On not speaking Chinese: living between Asia and the West.* London: Routledge.

Baker, C., Emmison, M. & Firth, A. (eds) (2005). *Calling for help. Language and social interaction in telephone helplines.* Amsterdam: John Benjamins.

Banks, J. (2002). *Cultural diversity and education: foundations, curriculum and teaching* (4th edn). New York: John Wiley and Sons.

Bardovi-Harlig, K. (1999). Exploring the interlanguage of interlanguage pragmatics: a research agenda for acquisitional pragmatics. *Language Learning*, 49, 677–713.

Bardovi-Harlig, K. & Hartford, B. (eds) (2005). *Interlanguage pragmatics. Exploring institutional talk*. London: Lawrence.

Bargiela-Chiappini, F. (ed.) (2009). *The handbook of business discourse*. Edinburgh: Edinburgh University Press.

Bargiela-Chiappini, F. & Harris, S. (1996). Interruptive strategies in British and Italian Management meetings. *Text*, 16(3), 269–97.

Bargiela-Chiappini, F. & Harris, S. (eds) (1997). *The languages of business: an international perspective*. Edinburgh: Edinburgh University Press.

Barth, F. (1989). The analysis of culture in complex societies. *Ethnos*, 54(3/4), 120–42.

Belz, J. & Thorne, S. (eds) (2006). *Internet-mediated intercultural foreign language education*. Boston, MA: Thomson Heinle.

Berlin, B. & Kay, P. (1969). *Basic color terms: their universality and evolution*. Berkeley: University of California Press.

Besemeres, M. & Wierzbicka, A. (eds) (2007). *Translating lives: living with two languages and cultures*. St Lucia, Queensland: University of Queensland Press.

Bhabha, H. K. (1994). *Location of culture*. London: Routledge.

Blommaert, J. (1998). *Different approaches to intercultural communication: a critical survey*. Plenary lecture, Lernen und Arbeiten in einer international vernetzten und multikulturellen Gesellschaft, Expertentagung Universität Bremen, Institut für Projektmanagement und Witschaftsinformatik (IPMI), 27–28 February 1998. Available online at: www.flw.ugent.be/cie/CIE/blommaert1.htm.

Blum-Kulka, S., House, J. & Kasper, G. (1989). *Cross-cultural pragmatics: requests and apologies*. Norwood, NJ: Ablex.

Blum-Kulka, S. & Olshtain, E. (1984). Requests and apologies: a cross-cultural study of speech act realisation patterns (CCSARP). *Applied Linguistics*, 5(3), 196–213.

Boas, F. (1940). *Race, language, and culture*. New York: Macmillan. Reprinted (1995). Chicago: University of Chicago Press.

Bond, M. (ed.) (1997). *Working at the interface of cultures: eighteen lives in social science*. London: Routledge.

Brisk, M. E. (ed.) (2008). *Language, culture, and community in teacher education*. New York: Lawrence.

Brown, P. & Levinson, S. (1978). Universals in language usage: politeness phenomena. In E. Goody (ed.), *Questions and politeness* (pp. 56–289). Cambridge: Cambridge University Press.

Byram, M., Morgan, C. *et al.* (1994). *Teaching-and-learning Language-and-culture*. Clevedon: Multilingual Matters.

Carbaugh, D. (2005). *Cultures in conversation*. Mahwah, NJ: Lawrence Erlbaum Associates.

Chomsky, N. (1965). *Aspects of the theory of syntax*. Cambridge: M.I.T. Press.

Clifford, J. & Marcus, G. E. (1986). *Writing culture*. Berkeley: University of California Press.

Cook, G. (1997). Language play, language learning. *ELT Journal*, 51(3), 224–31.

Cook, V. (ed.) (2002). *Portraits of the L2 user. Second language acquisition*. Clevedon: Multilingual Matters.

Coupland, J. (ed.) (2000). *Small talk*. London: Longman.

Davies, A. (2004). The native speaker in Applied Linguistics. In A. Davies & C. Elder (eds), *The handbook of applied linguistics* (pp. 431–50). Malden, MA: Blackwell.

Day, D. (1994). Tang's dilemma & other problems: ethnification processes at some multicultural workplaces. *Pragmatics*, 4, 315–36.

de Kadt, E. (1998). The concept of face and its applicability to the Zulu language. *Journal of Pragmatics*, 29, 173–91.

Dervin, F. & Riikonen, T. (2009). 'Whatever I am, Wherever I am, How does it Matter? . . . Why does it Matter?' Egocasting in-between identities. In Y. Abbas & F. Dervin (eds), *Digital technology of the self* (pp. 125–56). Newcastle upon Tyne: Cambridge Scholars Publishing.

Drummond, L. (1987). Are there cultures to communicate across? An appraisal of the 'culture' concept from the perspective of anthropological semiotics. In S. Battestini (ed.), *Georgetown University roundtable on languages and linguistics* (pp. 215–25). Washington, D.C.: Georgetown University.

Eades, D. (2005). Beyond difference and domination? Intercultural communication in legal contexts. In S. Kiesling & C. B. Paulston (eds), *Intercultural discourse and communication* (pp. 304–16). Malden, MA: Blackwell.

Eades, D. (2007). Understanding Aboriginal silence in legal contexts. In H. Kotthoff & H. Spencer-Oatey (eds), *Handbook of intercultural communication* (pp. 285–302). Berlin: Mouton.

Ehlich, K. (1992). On the historicity of politeness. In R. Watts, S. Ide & K. Ehlich (eds), *Politeness in language: studies in its history, theory and practice* (pp. 71–107). Berlin: Mouton de Gruyter.

Ehlich, K. & Wagner, J. (eds) (1995). *The discourse of business negotiation*. Berlin: Mouton.

Enfield, N. (ed.) (2002). *Ethnosyntax. Explorations in grammar & culture*. Oxford: Oxford University Press.

Fairclough, N. (1985). Critical and descriptive goals in discourse analysis. *Journal of Pragmatics*, 9, 739–93.

Fairclough, N. (1988). *Michel Foucault and the analysis of discourse*. CLSL Research Paper No. 10. Lancaster University.

Fairclough, N. (1995). *Critical discourse analysis: the critical study of language*. London: Longman.

Fetzer, A. & Lauerbach, G. E. (eds) (2007). *Political discourse in the media: cross-cultural perspectives*. Amsterdam: John Benjamins.

Firth, A. (2009). The lingua franca factor. *Intercultural Pragmatics*, 6(2), 147–70.

Fox, K. (2004). *Watching the English: the hidden rules of English behaviour*. London: Hodder.

Gass, S. & Neu, J. (eds) (1996). *Speech acts across cultures: challenges to communication in a second language*. Berlin: Mouton de Gruyter.

Gee, J. P. (1989). Literacy, discourse, and linguistics: essays by James Paul Gee. *Journal of Education*, 171(1), 1–176.

Gee, J. P. (1996). *Social linguistics and literacies: ideology in discourse* (2nd edn). Bristol, PA: Taylor & Francis.

Gee, J. P. (1999). *An introduction to discourse analysis: theory and method*. London: Routledge.

Gillespie, A. (2006). *Becoming other: from social interaction to self-reflection*. Greenwich, CT: Information Age Publishing, Inc.

Goddard, C. (ed.) (2006). *Ethnopragmatics: understanding discourse in cultural context*. Berlin: Mouton de Gruyter.

Goffman, E. (1967). *Interaction ritual: essays on face-to-face behaviour*. Garden City, NY: Anchor Books.

Gu, Y. (1990). Politeness phenomena in modern Chinese. *Journal of Pragmatics*, 14, 237–57.

Gumperz, J. (1978). The conversational analysis of interethnic communication. In E. Lamar Ross (ed.), *Interethnic communication* (pp. 13–31). Proceedings of the Southern Anthropological Society. Athens, GA: The University of Georgia Press.

Gumperz, J. (1982). *Discourse strategies*. Cambridge: Cambridge University Press.

Gumperz, J., Jupp, T. & Roberts, C. (1979). *Crosstalk*. Southall: National Council for Industrial Language Training.

Gumperz, J. & Levinson, S. (eds) (1996). *Rethinking linguistic relativity*. Cambridge: Cambridge University Press.

Gumperz, J. & Tannen, D. (1979). Individual and social differences in language use. In C. Fillmore, D. Kempler & W. Wang (eds), *Individual differences in language ability and language behaviour*. London: Academic Press.

Hall, E. T. (1959). *The silent language*. New York: Doubleday & Company. Reprinted in 1973, New York: Anchor Press.

Hall, E. T. & Hall, M. (1990). *Understanding cultural differences: Germans, French and Americans*. Yarmouth, ME: Intercultural Press.

Harris, S., Grainger, K. & Mullany, L. (2006). The pragmatics of political apologies. *Discourse & Society*, 17(6), 715–37.

Hickey, L. & Steward, M. (2005). *Politeness in Europe*. Clevedon: Multilingual Matters.

Higgins, C. (ed.) (2007). A closer look at cultural difference: 'Interculturality' in talk-in-interaction. A special issue of *Pragmatics*, 17(1), the whole issue.

Hinton, P. (2007). The cultural context of media interpretation. In H. Kotthoff & H. Spencer-Oatey (eds), *Handbook of intercultural communication* (pp. 323–40). Berlin: Mouton.

Hoffman, E. (1989). *Lost in translation: a life in a new language*. New York: Penguin Books.

Hofstede, G. (1991). *Cultures and organisations: software of the mind*. London: McGraw-Hill.

Hofstede, G. (2001). *Culture's consequences: international differences in work-related values* (2nd edn). Beverly Hills, CA: Sage.

Holliday, A., Hyde, M. & Kullman, J. (2004). *Intercultural communication: an advanced resource book*. London: Routledge.

Hu, W. & Grove, C. (1991). *Encountering the Chinese: a guide for Americans*. Yarmouth, ME: Intercultural Press.

Ide, S. (1989). Formal forms and discernment: two neglected aspects of linguistic politeness. *Multilingua*, 8(2/3): 223–48.

Ide, S. (2005). How and why honorifics can signify dignity and elegance: the indexicality and reflexivity of linguistic rituals. In R. Lakoff & S. Ide (eds), *Broadening the horizon of linguistic politeness* (pp. 45–64). Amsterdam: John Benjamin.

Kasper, G. & Rose, K. R. (1999). Pragmatics and SLA. *Annual Review of Applied Linguistics*, 19, 81–104.

Kasper, G. & Rose, K. R. (2002). *Pragmatic development in a second language*. Malden, MA: Blackwell.

Katriel, T. (1986). *Talking straight: dugri speech in Israeli Sabra culture.* Cambridge: Cambridge University Press.

Kluckhohn, F. & Strodtbeck, F. (1961). *Variations in value orientations*. New York: Row, Petersen.

Kocbek, A. (2006). Language and culture in international legal communication. *Managing Global Transitions*, 3(4), 231–47.

Kramsch, C. J. (1993). *Context and culture in language teaching*. Oxford: Oxford University Press.

Kramsch, C. J. (1998a). *Language and culture. Oxford introductions to language study*. Oxford: Oxford University Press.

Kramsch, C. J. (1998b). The privileges of the intercultural speaker. In M. Byram & M. Fleming (eds), *Language learning in intercultural perspective: approaches through drama and ethnography* (pp. 16–31). Cambridge: Cambridge University Press.

Kramsch, C. J. (2004). Language, thought and culture. In A. Davies & C. Elder (eds), *The handbook of applied linguistics* (pp. 235–61). Malden, MA: Blackwell.

Lado, R. (1957). *Linguistics across cultures*. Ann Arbor, MI: University of Michigan Press.

Lakoff, R. (1973). The logic of politeness: or minding your p's and q's. *Chicago Linguistics Society*, 8, 292–305.

Leung, C. (2005). Convivial communication: recontextualizing communicative competence. *International Journal of Applied Linguistics*, 15(2), 119–43.

Li Wei (1996). Chinese language, culture and communication. A non-contrastive approach. *Journal of Asian Pacific Communication*, 7(3&4), 87–90.

Linell, P. & Valsiner, J. (2009). *Rethinking language, mind, and world dialogically: interactional and contextual theories of human sense-making*. Charlotte, NC: Information Age Publishing.

Lo Bianco, J., Liddicoat, A. J. & Crozet, C. (eds) (1999). *Striving for the third place: intercultural competence through language education*. Melbourne: Language Australia.

Luke, K. K. & Pavlidou, T. (eds) (2002). *Telephone calls. Unity and diversity in conversational structure across languages and cultures*. Amsterdam: John Benjamins.

Mao, L. R. (1994). Beyond politeness theory: face revisited and renewed. *Journal of Pragmatics*, 21(5), 451–86.

Márquez Reiter, R. & Placencia, M. (2004). Displaying closeness and respectful distance in Montevidean and Quiteño service encounters. In R. Márquez Reiter & M. Placencia (eds), *Current trends in the pragmatics of Spanish* (pp. 121–55). Amsterdam/Philadelphia: John Benjamins.

Marra, M. & Holmes, J. (2007). Humour across cultures: joking in the multicultural workplace. In H. Kotthoff & H. Spencer-Oatey (eds), *Handbook of intercultural communication* (pp. 153–72). Berlin: Mouton.

Matsumoto, Y. (1988). Re-examination of the universality of face: politeness phenomena in Japanese. *Multilingua*, 8(2/3): 207–22.

Matsumoto, Y. (1989). Politeness and conversational universals – observations from Japanese. In P. Clancy (ed.), *Japanese/Korean linguistics*, II (pp. 55–67). Standford, CA: Center for Study of Language and Information.

Mattila, H. S. (2006). *Comparative legal linguistics*. Aldershot: Ashgate.

Mauranen, A. (2006). Signalling and preventing misunderstanding in English as lingua franca communication. *International Journal of the Sociology of Language*, 177, 123–50.

McSweeney, B. (2002). Hofstede's model of national cultural differences and their consequences: a triumph of faith – a failure of analysis. *Human Relations*, 55(1), 89–118.

Meeuwis, M. (ed) (1994a). Critical perspectives on intercultural communication. A special issue of *Pragmatics*, 4(3), the whole issue.

Meeuwis, M. (1994b). Leniency and testiness in intercultural communication: remarks on ideology and context in interactional sociolinguistics. *Pragmatics*, 4, 391–408.

Meierkord, C. (2000). Interpreting successful lingua franca interaction: an analysis of non-native-/non-native small talk conversations in English. Erfurt Electronic Studies in English (EESE). Retrieved on 10 March 2009 from www.linguistik-online.de/1_00/MEIERKOR.HTM.

Mori, J. (2003). The construction of interculturality: a study of initial encounters between Japanese and American students. *Research on Language and Social Interaction*, 36(2), 143–84.

Nisbett, R. (2003). *The geography of thought: how Asians and Westerners think differently . . . and why.* London: Nicholas Brealey Publishing.

Nishida, H. (2005). Cultural schema theory. In W. Gudykunst (ed.), *Theorizing about intercultural communication* (pp. 401–18). Thousand Oaks, CA: Sage.

Nishizaka, A. (1995). The interactive constitution of interculturality: how to be a Japanese with words. *Human Studies*, 18, 301–26.

O'Dowd, R. (ed.) (2007). *Online intercultural exchange: an introduction for foreign language teachers.* Clevedon: Multilingual Matters.

Pan, Y., Scollon, S. W. & Scollon, R. (2002). *Professional communication in international settings.* Malden, MA: Blackwell.

Piller, I. (2007). Cross-cultural communication in intimate relationships. In H. Kotthoff & H. Spencer-Oatey (eds), *Handbook of intercultural communication* (pp. 341–62). Berlin: Mouton.

Pinker, S. (1994). *The language instinct.* New York: W. Morrow and Co.

Pullman, G. K. (1991). *The great Eskimo vocabulary hoax and other irreverent essays on the study of language.* Chicago: The University of Chicago.

Riley, P. (2007). *Language, culture and identity: an ethnolinguistic perspective.* London: Continuum.

Risager, K. (2006). *Language and culture: global flows and local complexity.* Clevedon: Multilingual Matters.

Roberts, C. (2007). Intercultural communication in healthcare settings. In H. Kotthoff & H. Spencer-Oatey (eds), *Handbook of intercultural communication* (pp. 243–62). Berlin: Mouton.

Roberts, C. & Sarangi, S. (2002). Mapping and assessing medical students' interactional involvement styles with patients. In K. Spellman-Miller & P. Thompson (eds), *Unity and diversity in language use* (pp. 99–117). British Studies in Applied Linguistics 17. London: Continuum.

Roberts, C., Wass, V., Jones, R., Gillett, A. & Sarangi, S. (2003). Understanding communication in medicine: identification of components of communicative styles. *Medical Education*, 37, 192–201.

Sarangi, S. (1994). Intercultural or not? Beyond celebration of cultural differences in miscommunication analysis. *Pragmatics*, 4, 409–27.

Schmidt, R., Shimura, A., Wang, Z. & Jeong, H. (1995). Suggestions to buy: television commercials from the U.S., Japan, China, and Korea. In S. Gass & J. Neu (eds), *Speech acts across cultures: challenges to communication in a second language* (pp. 285–316). Berlin: Mouton de Gruyter.

Schwartz, S. H. (1992). Universals in the content and structure of values: theory and empirical tests in 20 countries. In M. Zanna (ed.), *Advances in experimental social psychology,* Vol. 25 (pp. 1–65). New York: Academic Press.

Schwartz, S. H. (1994). Are there universal aspects in the structure and contents of human values? *Journal of Social Issues*, 50(4), 19–45.

Scollon, R. & Scollon, S. W. (2001a). Discourse and intercultural communication. In D. Schiffrin, D. Tannen & H. E. Hamilton (eds), *The handbook of discourse analysis* (pp. 538–47). Malden, MA: Blackwell.

Scollon, R. & Scollon, S. W. (2001b). *Intercultural communication* (2nd edn). Malden, MA: Blackwell.

Seidlhofer, B. (2004). Research perspectives on teaching English as a lingua franca. *Annual Review of Applied Linguistics*, 24, 200–39.

Sharifian, F. (2005). The Persian cultural schema of shekasteh-nafsi: a study of complement responses in Persian and Anglo-Australian speakers. *Pragmatics and Cognition*, 13(2), 337–61.

Shea, D. P. (1994). Perspective and production: structuring conversational participation across cultural borders. *Pragmatics*, 4, 357–90.

Shi-xu (1994). Discursive attributions and cross-cultural communication. *Pragmatics*, 4, 337–56.

Slobin, D. (2000). Verbalised events. A dynamic approach to linguistic relativity and determinism. In S. Niemeier & R. Dirven (eds), *Evidence for linguistic relativity* (pp. 108–38). Amsterdam: John Benjamins.

Spencer-Oatey, H. (2002). Managing rapport in talk: using rapport-sensitive incidents to explore the motivational concerns underlying the management of relations. *Journal of Pragmatics*, 34, 529–45.

Street, B. V. (1993). Culture is a verb: anthropological aspects of language and cultural process. In D. Graddol, L. Thompson & M. Byram (eds), *Language and culture* (pp. 23–43). Clevedon, UK: BAAL and Multilingual Matters.

Thornton, R. (1988). Culture: a contemporary definition. In E. Boonzaier & J. Sharp (eds), *South African keywords: the uses and abuses of political concepts* (pp. 17–28). Cape Town: David Philip.

Triandis, H. C. (1990). Cross-cultural studies of individualism and collectivism. In J. J. Berman (ed.) *Cross-cultural perspective* (pp. 41–133). Lincoln, NB: University of Nebraska Press.

Triandis, H. C. (1995). *Individualism and collectivism*. Boulder, CO: Westview Press.

Trompenaars, F. & Hampden-Turner, C. (1998). *Riding the waves of culture: understanding diversity in global business* (2nd edn). New York: McGraw-Hill.

Troyna, B. & Williams, J. (1986). *Racism, education and the state: the racialisation of education policy.* Beckenham, UK: Croom Helm.

Valdes, J. M. (ed.) (1986). *Culture bound*. Cambridge: Cambridge University Press.

Vine, B. (2004). *Getting things done at work. The discourse of power in workplace interaction.* Amsterdam: John Benjamins.

Vuorela, T. (2005). Laughing matters: a case study of humour in multicultural business negotiations. *Negotiation Journal*, 21(1), 105–30.

Watts, R. (2003). *Politeness: key topics in sociolinguistics.* Cambridge: Cambridge University Press.

Wierzbicka, A. (1997). *Understanding cultures through their key words.* Oxford: Oxford University Press.

Wierzbicka, A. (2003). *Cross-cultural pragmatics: the semantics of human interaction* (2nd edn). Berlin: Mouton de Gruyter.

Yamada, H. (1997). *Different games different rules: why Americans and Japanese misunderstand each other.* New York: Oxford University Press.

Zhu Hua (2007). Presentation of self in application letters. In Zhu Hua, P. Seedhouse, Li Wei & V. Cook (eds), *Language learning/teaching as social (inter)action* (pp. 126–47). Mahwah, NJ: Lawrence Erlbaum.

Zhu Hua (2010). Language socialisation and interculturality: address terms in intergenerational talk in Chinese diasporic families. *Language and Intercultural Communication*, 10(3), 189–205.

Zhu Hua, Seedhouse, P., Li Wei & Cook, V. (eds) (2007). *Language learning/teaching as social (inter)action.* London: Palgrave Macmillan.

Zhu, Y.-X. (2005). *Written communication across cultures. A sociocognitive perspective on business genres.* Amsterdam/Philadelphia: John Benjamins.

INTRODUCTION: NOTES FOR STUDENTS AND INSTRUCTORS

Study questions

1   What is the study of language and intercultural communication about? Why is it important to investigate the interaction between language and intercultural communication?
2   What are the key questions in the study of language and intercultural communication?

Study activities

1   Reflect on your work experience, education or daily living. Is there any incidence of misunderstanding or non-understanding that may be the result of intercultural differences? Is there a particular intercultural communication theory or model that can account for or interpret what has happened?
2   Select a published study on language and intercultural communication and investigate what position/assumption it takes on the concept of culture, and whether the position impacts on the findings.

Further reading

For an introduction to intercultural communication, see:

Scollon, R. & Scollon, S. W. (2001). Discourse and intercultural communication. In D. Schiffrin, D. Tannen & H. E. Hamilton (eds), *The handbook of discourse analysis* (pp. 538–47). Malden, MA: Blackwell.
Piller, I. (2007). Linguistics and intercultural communication. *Language and Linguistic Compass*, 1(3), 208–26.

For the history of intercultural communication, see:

Chen, G.-M. & Starosta, W. J. (1998). *Foundations of intercultural communication* (Chapter 1). Needham Height, MA: Allyn & Bacon.

PART I

Culture, language and thought

Introduction to Part I

Zhu Hua

THE INTERRELATIONSHIP BETWEEN CULTURE, language and thought has been a topic of discussion for a long time. Some linguists argue that all human languages are structurally similar and can be accounted for in terms of universal grammars. However, apparent differences exist in most of the aspects, ranging from the writing system to the sound system, from vocabulary to sentence structure. For example, in some languages, such as French and German, most of the nouns have either a feminine or masculine gender, whereas in other languages, such as English or Chinese, gender is rarely marked. Similarly, some languages, such as English, classify number in nouns by singular or plural, whereas others, such as Arabic, have an additional category, i.e. dual (two). Why do some languages mark certain features, while others do not? Can these linguistic variations be explained in terms of one's habitual thinking process? If yes, to what extent? Does the existence or lack of a particular feature make a difference to the way people perceive reality? Or, put in another way, what is the relationship between language, thought and culture? This is a classical question that many researchers, from linguistic anthropology, cultural psychology, psychology, cognitive science, sociology of language etc., have attempted to answer since the beginning of the twentieth century. The three articles in this part represent three different perspectives that aim to bring about an understanding of the relationship between culture, language and thought.

Edward Sapir was an influential linguistic anthropologist at the beginning of the twentieth century. He believed that no two languages are sufficiently similar, because of the differences in the contexts in which different languages are used. His view was taken up by his student Benjamin Whorf. The reproduced article by Whorf (1956) presents his argument and views on the relationship between language and the habitual thinking process. In the article, he observes occasions in everyday life when language impacts on behaviour and provides many examples, some of which are still widely cited today. He also compares the way the concept of time is expressed in the Hopi language and standard American English. For example, in Hopi, there is not a plural form for nouns referring to time. Instead of saying 'they stayed ten days', the equivalent in Hopi is 'they stayed until the eleventh day' or 'they left after the tenth day'. In addition, all phase terms, such as summer, morning etc., are not nouns, but function as adverbs. The equivalent of 'this summer' is 'summer now' or 'summer recently' in Hopi. There is no 'tense' in the language either. Whorf argued that these examples serve as evidence for the so-called linguistic relativity hypothesis: that is, language structure controls thought. Nowadays, many researchers support a weaker version of the Sapir–Whorf hypothesis, which emphasises the bidirectional influence between language and thought, i.e. thought is influenced by language, and at the same time thought also influences language. However, not everyone agrees on the interrelationship between language and thought. Opponents of linguistic relativity are adamant that no differences in thinking are linked with differences in linguistic structures.

Nisbett's article (Chapter 2) represents a line of enquiry that is equally enlightening but very different from the linguistic relativity argument. As a cultural psychologist and cognitive scientist, Nisbett's work is concerned with identifying cultural differences in cognition, i.e. how people from different cultural backgrounds perceive and process things differently. In the selected article, Nisbett uses a number of examples and experiments to argue that some cultures prefer grouping by categories, while other cultures do so by relationship (readers may want to try the experiment themselves first, before they read the full text). The existence of these differences may be the result of different child-rearing practices in different cultures, as mentioned by Nisbett towards the end of the chapter.

Samovar *et al.*'s article (Chapter 3) reviews the dominant literature on cultural patterns, which have been the preoccupation of many anthropologists, social psychologists and communication scholars since the 1970s. Although this line of enquiry is not directly concerned with the relationship between culture, language and thought, its underlying assumption is relevant to the theme of this section. It assumes that the way people perceive, act and communicate is influenced by cultural patterns or orientations, which consist of beliefs, values, norms, attitudes and much more. Among a number of well-cited cultural patterns reviewed by Samovar *et al.*, Hofstede's four value dimensions and Hall's concept of high versus low context are of particular relevance to the study of language and intercultural communication, because of their implications for the way people from different cultures communicate.

Chapter 1

BENJAMIN WHORF

THE RELATION OF HABITUAL THOUGHT AND BEHAVIOR TO LANGUAGE

Human beings do not live in the objective world alone, nor alone in the world of social activity as ordinarily understood, but are very much at the mercy of the particular language which has become the medium of expression for their society. It is quite an illusion to imagine that one adjusts to reality essentially without the use of language and that language is merely an incidental means of solving specific problems of communication or reflection. The fact of the matter is that the "real world" is to a large extent unconsciously built up on the language habits of the group . . . We see and hear and otherwise experience very largely as we do because the language habits of our community predispose certain choices of interpretation.

—Edward Sapir[1]

THERE WILL PROBABLY BE GENERAL ASSENT to the proposition that an accepted pattern of using words is often prior to certain lines of thinking and forms of behavior, but he who assents often sees in such a statement nothing more than a platitudinous recognition of the hypnotic power of philosophical and learned terminology on the one hand or of catchwords, slogans, and rallying cries on the other. To see only thus far is to miss the point of one of the important interconnections which Sapir saw between language, culture, and psychology, and succinctly expressed in the introductory quotation. It is not so much in these special uses of language as in its constant ways of arranging data and its most ordinary everyday analysis of phenomena that we need to recognize the influence it has on other activities, cultural and personal.

The name of the situation as affecting behavior

I came in touch with an aspect of this problem before I had studied under Dr. Sapir, and in a field usually considered remote from linguistics. It was in the course of my professional work for a fire insurance company, in which I undertook the task of analyzing many hundreds of

Source: Whorf, B. (1956). The relation of habitual thought and behaviour to Language. In J. B. Carroll (ed.), *Language, thought and reality: selected writings of Benjamin Lee Whorf* (pp. 134–59). Cambridge: Cambridge University Press.

reports of circumstances surrounding the start of fires, and in some cases, of explosions. My analysis was directed toward purely physical conditions, such as defective wiring, presence or lack of air spaces between metal flues and woodwork, etc., and the results were presented in these terms. Indeed it was undertaken with no thought that any other significances would or could be revealed. But in due course it became evident that not only a physical situation *qua* physics, but the meaning of that situation to people, was sometimes a factor, through the behavior of the people, in the start of the fire. And this factor of meaning was clearest when it was a *linguistic meaning*, residing in the name or the linguistic description commonly applied to the situation. Thus, around a storage of what are called "gasoline drums," behavior will tend to a certain type, that is, great care will be exercised; while around a storage of what are called "empty gasoline drums," it will tend to be different—careless, with little repression of smoking or of tossing cigarette stubs about. Yet the "empty" drums are perhaps the more dangerous, since they contain explosive vapor. Physically the situation is hazardous, but the linguistic analysis according to regular analogy must employ the word "empty," which inevitably suggests lack of hazard. The word "empty" is used in two linguistic patterns: (1) as a virtual synonym for "null and void, negative, inert," (2) applied in analysis of physical situations without regard to, e.g., vapor, liquid vestiges, or stray rubbish, in the container. The situation is named in one pattern (2) and the name is then "acted out" or "lived up to" in another (1), this being a general formula for the linguistic conditioning of behavior into hazardous forms.

In a wood distillation plant the metal stills were insulated with a composition prepared from limestone and called at the plant "spun limestone." No attempt was made to protect this covering from excessive heat or the contact of flame. After a period of use, the fire below one of the stills spread to the "limestone," which to everyone's great surprise burned vigorously. Exposure to acetic acid fumes from the stills had converted part of the limestone (calcium carbonate) to calcium acetate. This, when heated in a fire, decomposes, forming inflammable acetone. Behavior that tolerated fire close to the covering was induced by use of the name "limestone," which because it ends in "stone" implies non-combustibility.

A huge iron kettle of boiling varnish was observed to be overheated, nearing the temperature at which it would ignite. The operator moved it off the fire and ran it on its wheels to a distance, but did not cover it. In a minute or so the varnish ignited. Here the linguistic influence is more complex; it is due to the metaphorical objectifying (of which more later) of "cause" as contact or the spatial juxtaposition of "things"—to analyzing the situation as "on" versus "off" the fire. In reality, the stage when the external fire was the main factor had passed; the overheating was now an internal process of convection in the varnish from the intensely heated kettle, and still continued when "off" the fire.

An electric glow heater on the wall was little used, and for one workman had the meaning of a convenient coathanger. At night a watchman entered and snapped a switch, which action he verbalized as "turning on the light." No light appeared, and this result he verbalized as "light is burned out." He could not see the glow of the heater because of the old coat hung on it. Soon the heater ignited the coat, which set fire to the building.

A tannery discharged waste water containing animal matter into an outdoor settling basin partly roofed with wood and partly open. This situation is one that ordinarily would be verbalized as "pool of water." A workman had occasion to light a blowtorch near by, and threw his match into the water. But the decomposing waste matter was evolving gas under the wood cover, so that the setup was the reverse of "watery." An instant flare of flame ignited the woodwork, and the fire quickly spread into the adjoining building.

A drying room for hides was arranged with a blower at one end to make a current of air along the room and thence outdoors through a vent at the other end. Fire started at a hot bearing on the blower, which blew the flames directly into the hides and fanned them along the room, destroying the entire stock. This hazardous setup followed naturally from the term "blower" with its linguistic equivalence to "that which blows," implying that its function necessarily is to "blow." Also its function is verbalized as "blowing air for drying," overlooking that it can blow other things, e.g., flames and sparks. In reality, a blower simply makes a current of air and can exhaust as well as blow. It should have been installed at the vent end to *draw* the air over the hides, then through the hazard (its own casing and bearings), and thence outdoors.

Beside a coal-fired melting pot for lead reclaiming was dumped a pile of "scrap lead"—a misleading verbalization, for it consisted of the lead sheets of old radio condensers, which still had paraffin paper between them. Soon the paraffin blazed up and fired the roof, half of which was burned off.

Such examples, which could be greatly multiplied, will suffice to show how the cue to a certain line of behavior is often given by the analogies of the linguistic formula in which the situation is spoken of, and by which to some degree it is analyzed, classified, and allotted its place in that world which is "to a large extent unconsciously built up on the language habits of the group." And we always assume that the linguistic analysis made by our group reflects reality better than it does.

Grammatical patterns as interpretations of experience

The linguistic material in the above examples is limited to single words, phrases, and patterns of limited range. One cannot study the behavioral compulsiveness of such material without suspecting a much more far-reaching compulsion from large-scale patterning of grammatical categories, such as plurality, gender and similar classifications (animate, inanimate, etc.), tenses, voices, and other verb forms, classifications of the type of "parts of speech," and the matter of whether a given experience is denoted by a unit morpheme, an inflected word, or a syntactical combination. A category such as number (singular vs. plural) is an attempted interpretation of a whole large order of experience, virtually of the world or of nature; it attempts to say how experience is to be segmented, what experience is to be called "one" and what "several." But the difficulty of appraising such a far-reaching influence is great because of its background character, because of the difficulty of standing aside from our own language, which is a habit and a cultural *non est disputandum*, and scrutinizing it objectively. And if we take a very dissimilar language, this language becomes a part of nature, and we even do to it what we have already done to nature. We tend to think in our own language in order to examine the exotic language. Or we find the task of unraveling the purely morphological intricacies so gigantic that it seems to absorb all else. Yet the problem, though difficult, is feasible; and the best approach is through an exotic language, for in its study we are at long last pushed willy-nilly out of our ruts. Then we find that the exotic language is a mirror held up to our own.

In my study of the Hopi language, what I now see as an opportunity to work on this problem was first thrust upon me before I was clearly aware of the problem. The seemingly endless task of describing the morphology did finally end. Yet it was evident, especially in the light of Sapir's lectures on Navaho, that the description of the *language* was far from complete. I knew, for example, the morphological formation of plurals, but not how to use plurals. It was evident that the category of plural in Hopi was not the same thing as in English, French, or German. Certain things that were plural in these languages were singular in Hopi. The phase of investigation which now began consumed nearly two more years.

The work began to assume the character of a comparison between Hopi and western European languages. It also became evident that even the grammar of Hopi bore a relation to Hopi culture, and the grammar of European tongues to our own "Western" or "European" culture. And it appeared that the interrelation brought in those large subsummations of experience by language, such as our own terms "time," "space," "substance," and "matter." Since, with respect to the traits compared, there is little difference between English, French, German, or other European languages, with the *possible* (but doubtful) exception of Balto-Slavic and non-Indo-European, I have lumped these languages into one group called SAE, or "Standard Average European."

That portion of the whole investigation here to be reported may be summed up in two questions: (1) Are our own concepts of "time," "space," and "matter" given in substantially the same form by experience to all men, or are they in part conditioned by the structure of particular languages? (2) Are there traceable affinities between (a) cultural and behavioral norms and (b) large-scale linguistic patterns? (I should be the last to pretend that there is anything so definite as "a correlation" between culture and language, and especially between ethnological rubrics such as "agricultural, hunting," etc., and linguistic ones like "inflected," "synthetic," or "isolating."[2] When I began the study, the problem was by no means so clearly formulated, and I had little notion that the answers would turn out as they did.

Plurality and numeration in SAE and Hopi

In our language, that is SAE, plurality and cardinal numbers are applied in two ways: to real plurals and imaginary plurals. Or more exactly if less tersely: perceptible spatial aggregates and metaphorical aggregates. We say "ten men" and also "ten days." Ten men either are or could be objectively perceived as ten, ten in one group perception[3]—ten men on a street corner, for instance. But "ten days" cannot be objectively experienced. We experience only one day, today; the other nine (or even all ten) are something conjured up from memory or imagination. If "ten days" be regarded as a group, it must be as an "imaginary," mentally constructed group. Whence comes this mental pattern? Just as in the case of the fire-causing errors, from the fact that our language confuses the two different situations, has but one pattern for both. When we speak of "ten steps forward, ten strokes on a bell," or any similarly described cyclic sequence, "times" of any sort, we are doing the same thing as with "days." *Cyclicity* brings the response of imaginary plurals. But a likeness of cyclicity to aggregates is not unmistakably given by experience prior to language, or it would be found in all languages, and it is not.

Our *awareness* of time and cyclicity does contain something immediate and subjective—the basic sense of "becoming later and later." But, in the habitual thought of us SAE people, this is covered under something quite different, which though mental should not be called subjective. I call it *objectified*, or imaginary, because it is patterned on the *outer* world. It is this that reflects our linguistic usage. Our tongue makes no distinction between numbers counted on discrete entities and numbers that are simply "counting itself." Habitual thought then assumes that, in the latter, the numbers are just as much counted on "something" as in the former. This is objectification. Concepts of time lose contact with the subjective experience of "becoming later" and are objectified as counted *quantities*, especially as lengths, made up of units as a length can be visibly marked off into inches. A "length of time" is envisioned as a row of similar units, like a row of bottles.

In Hopi there is a different linguistic situation. Plurals and cardinals are used only for entities that form or can form an objective group. There are no imaginary plurals, but instead ordinals used with singulars. Such an expression as "ten days" is not used. The equivalent statement is an operational one that reaches one day by a suitable count. "They stayed ten days" becomes "they stayed until the eleventh day" or "they left after the tenth day." "Ten days is greater than nine days" becomes "the tenth day is later than the ninth." Our "length of time" is not regarded as a length but as a relation between two events in lateness. Instead of our linguistically promoted objectification of that datum of consciousness we call "time," the Hopi language has not laid down any pattern that would cloak the subjective "becoming later" that is the essence of time.

Nouns of physical quantity in SAE and Hopi

We have two kinds of nouns denoting physical things: individual nouns, and mass nouns, e.g., "water, milk, wood, granite, sand, flour, meat." Individual nouns denote bodies with definite outlines: "a tree, a stick, a man, a hill." Mass nouns denote homogeneous continua without implied boundaries. The distinction is marked by linguistic form; e.g., mass nouns lack plurals,[4] in English drop articles, and in French take the partitive article *du, de la, des*. The distinction is more widespread in language than in the observable appearance of things. Rather few natural occurrences present themselves as unbounded extents; "air" of course, and often "water, rain, snow, sand, rock, dirt, grass." We do not encounter "butter, meat, cloth, iron, glass," or most "materials" in such kind of manifestation, but in bodies small or large, with definite outlines. The distinction is somewhat forced upon our description of events by an unavoidable pattern in language. It is so inconvenient in a great many cases that we need some way of individualizing the mass noun by further linguistic devices. This is partly done by names of body-types: "stick of wood, piece of cloth, pane of glass, cake of soap"; also, and even more, by introducing names of containers though their contents be the real issue: "glass of water, cup of coffee, dish of food, bag of flour, bottle of beer." These very common container formulas, in which "of" has an obvious, visually perceptible meaning ("contents"), influence our feeling about the less obvious type-body formulas: "stick of wood, lump of dough," etc. The formulas are very similar: individual noun plus a similar relator (English "of"). In the obvious case this relator denotes contents. In the inobvious one it "suggests" contents. Hence the "lumps, chunks, blocks, pieces," etc., seem to contain something, a "stuff," "substance," or "matter" that answers to the "water," "coffee," or "flour" in the container formulas. So with SAE people the philosophic "substance" and "matter" are also the naïve idea; they are instantly acceptable, "common sense." It is so through linguistic habit. Our language patterns often require us to name a physical thing by a binomial that splits the reference into a formless item plus a form.

Hopi is again different. It has a formally distinguished class of nouns. But this class contains no formal subclass of mass nouns. All nouns have an individual sense and both singular and plural forms. Nouns translating most nearly our mass nouns still refer to vague bodies or vaguely bounded extents. They imply indefiniteness, but not lack, of outline and size. In specific statements, "water" means one certain mass or quantity of water, not what we call "the substance water." Generality of statement is conveyed through the verb or predicator, not the noun. Since nouns are individual already, they are not individualized by either type-bodies or names of containers, if there is no special need to emphasize shape or container. The noun itself implies a suitable type-body or container. One says, not "a glass of water" but *kə • yi* "a water," not "a pool of water" but *pa • hə*,[5] not "a dish of cornflour" but *ŋəmni* "a (quantity of) cornflour," not "a piece of meat" but *sikʷi* "a meat." The language has neither need for nor analogies on which to build the concept of existence as a duality of formless item and form. It deals with formlessness through other symbols than nouns.

Phases of cycles in SAE and Hopi

Such terms as "summer, winter, September, morning, noon, sunset" are with us nouns, and have little formal linguistic difference from other nouns. They can be subjects or objects, and we say "at sunset" or "in winter" just as we say "at a corner" or "in an orchard."[6] They are pluralized and numerated like nouns of physical objects, as we have seen. Our thought about the referents of such words hence becomes objectified. Without objectification, it would be a subjective experience of real time, i.e. of the consciousness of "becoming later and later"— simply a cyclic phase similar to an earlier phase in that ever-later-becoming duration. Only by imagination can such a cyclic phase be set beside another and another in the manner of a spatial (i.e. visually perceived) configuration. But such is the power of linguistic analogy that we do so objectify cyclic phasing. We do it even by saying "a phase" and "phases" instead of, e.g., "phasing." And the pattern of individual and mass nouns, with the resulting binomial formula of formless item plus form, is so general that it is implicit for all nouns, and hence our very generalized formless items like "substance, matter," by which we can fill out the binomial for an enormously wide range of nouns. But even these are not quite generalized enough to take in our phase nouns. So for the phase nouns we have made a formless item, "time." We have made it by using "a time," i.e. an occasion or a phase, in the pattern of a mass noun, just as from "a summer" we make "summer" in the pattern of a mass noun. Thus with our binomial formula we can say and think "a moment of time, a second of time, a year of time." Let me again point out that the pattern is simply that of "a bottle of milk" or "a piece of cheese." Thus we are assisted to imagine that "a summer" actually contains or consists of such-and-such a quantity of "time."

In Hopi, however, all phase terms, like "summer, morning," etc., are not nouns but a kind of adverb, to use the nearest SAE analogy. They are a formal part of speech by themselves, distinct from nouns, verbs, and even other Hopi "adverbs." Such a word is not a case form or a locative pattern, like "des Abends" or "in the morning." It contains no morpheme like one of "in the house" or "at the tree."[7] It means "when it is morning" or "while morning-phase is occurring." These "temporals" are not used as subjects or objects, or at all like nouns. One does not say "it's a hot summer" or "summer is hot"; summer is not hot, summer is only *when* conditions are hot, *when* heat occurs. One does not say "*this* summer," but "summer now" or "summer recently." There is no objectification, as a region, an extent, a quantity, of the subjective duration-feeling. Nothing is suggested about time except the perpetual "getting later" of it. And so there is no basis here for a formless item answering to our "time."

Temporal forms of verbs in SAE and Hopi

The three-tense system of SAE verbs colors all our thinking about time. This system is amalgamated with that larger scheme of objectification of the subjective experience of duration already noted in other patterns—in the binomial formula applicable to nouns in general, in temporal nouns, in plurality and numeration. This objectification enables us in imagination to "stand time units in a row." Imagination of time as like a row harmonizes with a system of *three* tenses; whereas a system of *two*, an earlier and a later, would seem to correspond better to the feeling of duration as it is experienced. For if we inspect consciousness, we find no past, present, future, but a unity embracing complexity. *Everything* is in consciousness, and everything in consciousness *is*, and is together. There is in it a sensuous and a nonsensuous. We may call the sensuous—what we are seeing, hearing, touching—the "present" while in the nonsensuous the vast image-world of memory is being labeled "the past," and another realm of belief, intuition, and uncertainty "the future"; yet sensation, memory, foresight, all are in consciousness together—one is not "yet to be" nor another "once but no more." Where real time comes in is that all this in consciousness is "getting later," changing certain relations in an irreversible manner. In this "latering" or "durating" there seems to me to be a paramount contrast between the newest, latest instant at the focus of attention and the rest—the earlier. Languages by the score get along well with two tenselike forms answering to this paramount relation of "later" to "earlier." We can of course *construct and contemplate in thought* a system of past, present, future, in the objectified configuration of points on a line. This is what our general objectification tendency leads us to do and our tense system confirms.

In English the present tense seems the one least in harmony with the paramount temporal relation. It is as if pressed into various and not wholly congruous duties. One duty is to stand as objectified middle term between objectified past and objectified future, in narration, discussion, argument, logic, philosophy. Another is to denote inclusion in the sensuous field: "I *see* him." Another is for nomic, i.e. customarily or generally valid, statements: "We *see* with our eyes." These varied uses introduce confusions of thought, of which for the most part we are unaware.

Hopi, as we might expect, is different here too. Verbs have no "tenses" like ours, but have validity-forms ("assertions"), aspects, and clause-linkage forms (modes), that yield even greater precision of speech. The validity-forms denote that the speaker (not the subject) reports the situation (answering to our past and present) or that he expects it (answering to our future)[8] or that he makes a nomic statement (answering to our nomic present). The aspects denote different degrees of duration and different kinds of tendency "during duration." As yet we have noted nothing to indicate whether an event is sooner or later than another when both are *reported*. But need for this does not arise until we have two verbs: i.e. two clauses. In that case the "modes" denote relations between the clauses, including relations of later to earlier and of simultaneity. Then there are many detached words that express similar relations, supplementing the modes and aspects. The duties of our three-tense system and its tripartite linear objectified "time" are distributed among various verb categories, all different from our tenses; and there is no more basis for an objectified time in Hopi verbs than in other Hopi patterns, although this does not in the least hinder the verb forms and other patterns from being closely adjusted to the pertinent realities of actual situations.

Duration, intensity, and tendency in SAE and Hopi

To fit discourse to manifold actual situations, all languages need to express durations, intensities, and tendencies. It is characteristic of SAE and perhaps of many other language types to express them metaphorically. The metaphors are those of spatial extension, i.e. of size, number (plurality), position, shape, and motion. We express duration by "long, short, great, much, quick, slow," etc.; intensity by "large, great, much, heavy, light, high, low, sharp, faint," etc.; tendency by "more, increase, grow, turn, get, approach, go, come, rise, fall, stop, smooth, even, rapid, slow"; and so on through an almost inexhaustible list of metaphors that we hardly recognize as such, since they are virtually the only linguistic medium available. The nonmetaphorical terms in this field, like "early, late, soon, lasting, intense, very, tending," are a mere handful, quite inadequate to the needs.

It is clear how this condition "fits in." It is part of our whole scheme of *objectifying*— imaginatively spatializing qualities and potentials that are quite nonspatial (so far as any spatially perceptive senses can tell us). Noun-meaning (with us) proceeds from physical bodies to referents of far other sort. Since physical bodies and their outlines in *perceived space* are denoted by size and shape terms and reckoned by cardinal numbers and plurals, these patterns of denotation and reckoning extend to the symbols of nonspatial meanings, and so suggest an *imaginary space*. Physical shapes "move, stop, rise, sink, approach," etc., in perceived space; why not these other referents in their imaginary space? This has gone so far that we can hardly refer to the simplest nonspatial situation without constant resort to physical metaphors. I "grasp" the "thread" of another's arguments, but if its "level" is "over my head" my attention may "wander" and "lose touch" with the "drift" of it, so that when he "comes" to his "point" we differ "widely," our "views," being indeed so "far apart" that the "things" he says "appear" "much" too arbitrary, or even "a lot" of nonsense!

The absence of such metaphor from Hopi speech is striking. Use of space terms when there is no space involved is *not there*—as if on it had been laid the taboo teetotal! The reason is clear when we know that Hopi has abundant conjugational and lexical means of expressing duration, intensity, and tendency directly as such, and that major grammatical patterns do not, as with us, provide analogies for an imaginary space. The many verb "aspects" express duration and tendency of manifestations, while some of the "voices" express intensity, tendency, and duration of causes or forces producing manifestations. Then a special part of speech, the "tensors," a huge class of words, denotes only intensity, tendency, duration, and sequence. The function of the tensors is to express intensities, "strengths," and how they continue or vary, their rate of change; so that the broad concept of intensity, when considered as necessarily always varying and/or continuing, includes also tendency and duration. Tensors convey distinctions of degree, rate, constancy, repetition, increase and decrease of intensity, immediate sequence, interruption or sequence after an interval, etc., also *qualities* of strengths, such as we should express metaphorically as smooth, even, hard, rough. A striking feature is their lack of resemblance to the terms of real space and movement that to us "mean the same." There is not even more than a trace of apparent derivation from space terms.[9] So, while Hopi in its nouns seems highly concrete, here in the tensors it becomes abstract almost beyond our power to follow.

Habitual thought in SAE and Hopi

The comparison now to be made between the habitual thought worlds of SAE and Hopi speakers is of course incomplete. It is possible only to touch upon certain dominant contrasts that appear to stem from the linguistic differences already noted. By "habitual thought" and "thought world" I mean more than simply language, i.e. than the linguistic patterns themselves. I include all the analogical and suggestive value of the patterns (e.g., our "imaginary space" and its distant implications), and all the give-and-take between language and the culture as a whole, wherein is a vast amount that is not linguistic but yet shows the shaping influence of language. In brief, this "thought world" is the microcosm that each man carries about within himself, by which he measures and understands what he can of the macrocosm.

The SAE microcosm has analyzed reality largely in terms of what it calls "things" (bodies and quasibodies) plus modes of extensional but formless existence that it calls "substances" or "matter." It tends to see existence through a binomial formula that expresses any existent as a spatial form plus a spatial formless continuum related to the form, as content is related to the outlines of its container. Nonspatial existents are imaginatively spatialized and charged with similar implications of form and continuum.

The Hopi microcosm seems to have analyzed reality largely in terms of *events* (or better "eventing"), referred to in two ways, objective and subjective. Objectively, and only if perceptible physical experience, events are expressed mainly as outlines, colors, movements, and other perceptive reports. Subjectively, for both the physical and nonphysical, events are considered the expression of invisible intensity factors, on which depend their stability and persistence, or their fugitiveness and proclivities. It implies that existents do not "become later and later" all in the same way, but some do so by growing like plants, some by diffusing and vanishing, some by a procession of metamorphoses, some by enduring in one shape till affected by violent forces. In the nature of each existent able to manifest as a definite whole is the power of its own mode of duration: its growth, decline, stability, cyclicity, or creativeness. Everything is thus already "prepared" for the way it now manifests by earlier phases, and what it will be later, partly has been, and partly is in act of being so "prepared." An emphasis and importance rest on this preparing or being prepared aspect of the world that may to the Hopi correspond to that "quality of reality" that "matter" or "stuff" has for us.

Habitual behavior features of Hopi culture

Our behavior, and that of Hopi, can be seen to be coordinated in many ways to the linguistically conditioned microcosm. As in my fire casebook, people act about situations in ways which are like the ways they talk about them. A characteristic of Hopi behavior is the emphasis on preparation. This includes announcing and getting ready for events well beforehand, elaborate precautions to ensure persistence of desired conditions, and stress on goodwill as the preparer of right results. Consider the analogies of the day-counting pattern alone. Time is mainly reckoned "by day" (*taLk, -tala*) or "by night" (*tok*), which words are not nouns but tensors, the first formed on a root "light, day," the second on a root "sleep." The count is by *ordinals*. This is not the pattern of counting a number of different men or things, even though they appear successively, for, even then, they *could* gather into an assemblage. It is the pattern of counting successive reappearances of the *same* man or thing, incapable of forming an assemblage. The analogy is not to behave about day-cyclicity as to several men ("several days"), which is what *we* tend to do, but to behave as to the successive visits of the *same man*. One does not alter several men by working upon just one, but one can prepare and so alter the later visits of the same man by working to affect the visit he is making now. This is the way the Hopi deal with the future—by working within a present situation which is expected to carry impresses, both obvious and occult, forward into the future event of interest. One might say that Hopi society understands our proverb "Well begun is half done," but not our "Tomorrow is another day." This may explain much in Hopi character.

This Hopi preparing behavior may be roughly divided into announcing, outer preparing, inner preparing, covert participation, and persistence. Announcing, or preparative publicity, is an important function in the hands of a special official, the Crier Chief. Outer preparing is preparation involving much visible activity, not all necessarily directly useful within our understanding. It includes ordinary practicing, rehearsing, getting ready, introductory formalities, preparing of special food, etc. (all of these to a degree that may seem overelaborate to us), intensive sustained muscular activity like running, racing, dancing, which is thought to increase the intensity of development of events (such as growth of crops), mimetic and other magic preparations based on esoteric theory involving perhaps occult instruments like prayer sticks, prayer feathers, and prayer meal, and finally the great cyclic ceremonies and dances, which have the significance of preparing rain and crops. From one of the verbs meaning "prepare" is derived the noun for "harvest" or "crop": *na'twani* "the prepared" or the "in preparation."[10]

Inner preparing is use of prayer and meditation, and at lesser intensity good wishes and goodwill, to further desired results. Hopi attitudes stress the power of desire and thought. With their "microcosm" it is utterly natural that they should. Desire and thought are the earliest, and therefore the most important, most critical and crucial, stage of preparing.

Moreover, to the Hopi, one's desires and thoughts influence not only one's own actions, but all nature as well. This too is wholly natural. Consciousness itself is aware of work, of the feel of effort and energy, in desire and thinking. Experience more basic than language tells us that, if energy is expended, effects are produced. *We* tend to believe that our bodies can stop up this energy, prevent it from affecting other things until we will our *bodies* to overt action. But this may be so only because we have our own linguistic basis for a theory that formless items like "matter" are things in themselves, malleable only by similar things, by more matter, and hence insulated from the powers of life and thought. It is no more unnatural to think that thought contacts everything and pervades the universe than to think, as we all do, that light kindled outdoors does this. And it is not unnatural to suppose that thought, like any other force, leaves everywhere traces of effect. Now, when *we* think of a certain actual rosebush, we do not suppose that our thought goes to that actual bush, and engages with it, like a searchlight turned upon it. What then do we suppose our consciousness is dealing with when we are thinking of that rosebush? Probably we think it is dealing with a "mental image" which is not the rosebush but a mental surrogate of it. But why should it be *natural* to think that our thought deals with a surrogate and not with the real rosebush? Quite possibly because we are dimly aware that we carry about with us a whole imaginary space, full of mental surrogates. To us, mental surrogates are old familiar fare. Along with the images of imaginary space, which we perhaps secretly know to be only imaginary, we tuck the thought-of actually existing rosebush, which may be quite another story, perhaps just because we have that very convenient "place" for it. The Hopi thought-world has no imaginary space. The corollary to this is that it may not locate thought dealing with real space anywhere but in real space, nor insulate real space from the effects of thought. A Hopi would naturally suppose that his thought (or he himself) traffics with the actual rosebush—or more likely, corn plant—that he is thinking about. The thought then should leave some trace of itself with the plant in the field. If it is a good thought, one about health and growth, it is good for the plant; if a bad thought, the reverse.

The Hopi emphasize the intensity-factor of thought. Thought to be most effective should be vivid in consciousness, definite, steady, sustained, charged with strongly felt good intentions. They render the idea in English as "concentrating, holding it in your heart, putting your mind on it, earnestly hoping." Thought power is the force behind ceremonies, prayer sticks, ritual smoking, etc. The prayer pipe is regarded as an aid to "concentrating" (so said my informant). Its name, *na'twanpi*, means "instrument of preparing."

Covert participation is mental collaboration from people who do not take part in the actual affair, be it a job of work, hunt, race, or ceremony, but direct their thought and goodwill toward the affair's success. Announcements often seek to enlist the support of such mental helpers as well as of overt participants, and contain exhortations to the people to aid with their active goodwill.[11] A similarity to our concepts of a sympathetic audience or the cheering section at a football game should not obscure the fact that it is primarily the power of directed thought, and not merely sympathy or encouragement, that is expected of covert participants. In fact these latter get in their deadliest work before, not during, the game! A corollary to the power of thought is the power of wrong thought for evil; hence one purpose of covert participation is to obtain the mass force of many good wishers to offset the harmful thought of ill wishers. Such attitudes greatly favor cooperation and community spirit. Not that the Hopi community is not full of rivalries and colliding interests. Against the tendency to social disintegration in such a small, isolated group, the theory of "preparing" by the power of thought, logically leading to the great power of the combined, intensified, and harmonized thought of the whole community, must help vastly toward the rather remarkable degree of cooperation that, in spite of much private bickering, the Hopi village displays in all the important cultural activities.

Hopi "preparing" activities again show a result of their linguistic thought background in an emphasis on persistence and constant insistent repetition. A sense of the cumulative value of innumerable small momenta is dulled by an objectified, spatialized view of time like ours, but enhanced by a way of thinking close to the subjective awareness of duration, of the ceaseless "latering" of events. To us, for whom time is a motion on a space, unvarying repetition seems to scatter its force along a row of units of that space, and be wasted. To the Hopi, for whom time is not a motion but a "getting later" of everything that has ever been done, unvarying repetition is not wasted but accumulated. It is storing up an invisible change that holds over into later events.[12] As we have seen, it is as if the return of the day were felt as the return of the same person, a little older but with all the impresses of yesterday, not as "another day," i.e. like an entirely different person. This principle joined with that of thought-power and with traits of general Pueblo culture is expressed in the theory of the Hopi ceremonial dance for furthering rain and crops, as well as in its short, piston-like tread, repeated thousands of times, hour after hour.

Some impresses of linguistic habit in Western civilization

It is harder to do justice in few words to the linguistically conditioned features of our own culture than in the case of the Hopi, because of both vast scope and difficulty of objectivity—because of our deeply ingrained familiarity with the attitudes to be analyzed. I wish merely to sketch certain characteristics adjusted to our linguistic binomialism of form plus formless item or "substance," to our metaphoricalness, our imaginary space, and our objectified time. These, as we have seen, are linguistic.

From the form-plus-substance dichotomy the philosophical views most traditionally characteristic of the "Western world" have derived huge support. Here belong materialism, psychophysical parallelism, physics—at least in its traditional Newtonian form—and dualistic views of the universe in general. Indeed here belongs almost everything that is "hard, practical common sense." Monistic, holistic, and relativistic views of reality appeal to philosophers and some scientists, but they are badly handicapped in appealing to the "common sense" of the Western average man—not because nature herself refutes them (if she did, philosophers could have discovered this much), but because they must be talked about in what amounts to a new language. "Common sense," as its name shows, and "practicality" as its name does not show, are largely matters of talking so that one is readily understood. It is sometimes stated that Newtonian space, time, and matter are sensed by everyone intuitively, whereupon relativity is cited as showing how mathematical analysis can prove intuition wrong. This, besides being unfair to intuition, is an attempt to answer offhand question (1) put at the outset of this paper, to answer which this research was undertaken. Presentation of the findings now nears its end, and I think the answer is clear. The offhand answer, laying the blame upon intuition for our slowness in discovering mysteries of the Cosmos, such as relativity, is the wrong one. The right answer is: Newtonian space, time, and matter are no intuitions. They are recepts from culture and language. That is where Newton got them.

Our objectified view of time is, however, favorable to historicity and to everything connected with the keeping of records, while the Hopi view is unfavorable thereto. The latter is too subtle, complex, and ever-developing, supplying no ready-made answer to the question of when "one" event ends and "another" begins. When it is implicit that everything that ever happened still is, but is in a necessarily different form from what memory or record reports, there is less incentive to study the past. As for the present, the incentive would be not to record it but to treat it as "preparing." But *our* objectified time puts before imagination something like a ribbon or scroll marked off into equal blank spaces, suggesting that each be filled with an entry. Writing has no doubt helped toward our linguistic treatment of time, even as the linguistic treatment has guided the uses of writing. Through this give-and-take between language and the whole culture we get, for instance:

1. Records, diaries, bookkeeping, accounting, mathematics stimulated by accounting.
2. Interest in exact sequence, dating, calendars, chronology, clocks, time wages, time graphs, time as used in physics.
3. Annals, histories, the historical attitude, interest in the past, archaeology, attitudes of introjection toward past periods, e.g., classicism, romanticism.

Just as we conceive our objectified time as extending in the future in the same way that it extends in the past, so we set down our estimates of the future in the same shape as our records of the past, producing programs, schedules, budgets. The formal equality of the spacelike units by which we measure and conceive time leads us to consider the "formless item" or "substance" of time to be homogeneous and in ratio to the number of units. Hence our pro rata allocation of value to time, lending itself to the building up of a commercial structure based on time-pro rata values: time wages (time work constantly supersedes piece work), rent, credit, interest, depreciation charges, and insurance premiums. No doubt this vast system, once built, would continue to run under any sort of linguistic treatment of time; but that it should have been built at all, reaching the magnitude and particular form it has in the Western world, is a fact decidedly in consonance with the patterns of the SAE languages. Whether such a civilization as ours would be possible with widely different linguistic handling of time is a large question—in our civilization, our linguistic patterns and the fitting of our behavior to the temporal order are what they are, and they are in accord. We are of course stimulated to use calendars, clocks, and watches, and to try to measure time ever more precisely; this aids science, and science in turn, following these well-worn cultural grooves, gives back to culture an ever-growing store of applications, habits, and values, with which culture again directs science. But what lies outside this spiral? Science is beginning to find that there is something in the Cosmos that is not in accord with the concepts we have formed in mounting the spiral. It is trying to frame a *new language* by which to adjust itself to a wider universe.

It is clear how the emphasis on "saving time," which goes with all the above and is very obvious objectification of time, leads to a high valuation of "speed," which shows itself a great deal in our behaviour.

Still another behavioral effect is that the character of monotony and regularity possessed by our image of time as an evenly scaled limitless tape measure persuades us to behave as if that monotony were more true of events than it really is. That is, it helps to routinize us. We tend to select and favor whatever bears out this view to "play up to" the routine aspects of existence. One phase of this is behavior evincing a false sense of security or an assumption that all will always go smoothly, and a lack in foreseeing and protecting ourselves against hazards. Our technique of harnessing energy does well in routine performance, and it is along routine lines that we chiefly strive to improve it—we are, for example, relatively uninterested in stopping the energy from causing accidents, fires, and explosions, which it is doing constantly and on a wide scale. Such indifference to the unexpectedness of life would be disastrous to a society as small, isolated, and precariously poised as the Hopi society is, or rather once was.

Thus our linguistically determined thought world not only collaborates with our cultural idols and ideals, but engages even our unconscious personal reactions in its patterns and gives them certain typical characters. One such character, as we have seen, is *carelessness*, as in reckless driving or throwing cigarette stubs into waste paper. Another of different sort is *gesturing* when we talk. Very many of the gestures made by English-speaking people at least, and probably by all SAE speakers, serve to illustrate, by a movement in space, not a real spatial reference but one of the nonspatial references that our language handles by metaphors of imaginary space. That is, we are more apt to make a grasping gesture when we speak of grasping an elusive idea than when we speak of grasping a doorknob. The gesture seeks to make a metaphorical and hence somewhat unclear reference more clear. But, if a language refers to nonspatials without implying a spatial analogy, the reference is not made any clearer by gesture. The Hopi gesture very little, perhaps not at all in the sense we understand as gesture.

It would seem as if kinesthesia, or the sensing of muscular movement, though arising before language, should be made more highly conscious by linguistic use of imaginary space and metaphorical images of motion. Kinesthesia is marked in two facets of European culture: art and sport. European sculpture, an art in which Europe excels, is strongly kinesthetic, conveying great sense of the body's motions; European painting likewise. The dance in our culture expresses delight in motion rather than symbolism or ceremonial, and our music is greatly influenced by our dance forms. Our sports are strongly imbued with this element of the "poetry of motion." Hopi races and games seem to emphasize rather the virtues of endurance and sustained intensity. Hopi dancing is highly symbolic and is performed with great intensity and earnestness, but has not much movement or swing.

Synesthesia, or suggestion by certain sense receptions of characters belonging to another sense, as of light and color by sounds and vice versa, should be made more conscious by a linguistic metaphorical system that refers to nonspatial experiences by terms for spatial ones, though undoubtedly it arises from a deeper source. Probably in the first instance metaphor arises from synesthesia and not the reverse; yet metaphor need not become firmly rooted in linguistic pattern, as Hopi shows. Nonspatial experience has one well-organized sense, *hearing* —for smell and taste are but little organized. Nonspatial consciousness is a realm chiefly of thought, feeling, and *sound*. Spatial consciousness is a realm of light, color, sight, and touch, and presents shapes and dimensions. Our metaphorical system, by naming nonspatial experiences after spatial ones, imputes to sounds, smells, tastes, emotions, and thoughts qualities like the colors, luminosities, shapes, angles, textures, and motions of spatial experience. And to some extent the reverse transference occurs; for, after much talking about tones as high, low, sharp, dull, heavy, brilliant, slow, the talker finds it easy to think of some factors in spatial experience as like factors of tone. Thus we speak of "tones" of color, a gray "monotone," a "loud" necktie, a "taste" in dress: all spatial metaphor in reverse. Now European art is distinctive in the way it seeks deliberately to play with synesthesia. Music tries to suggest scenes, color, movement, geometric design; painting and sculpture are often consciously guided by the analogies of music's rhythm; colors are conjoined with feeling for the analogy to concords and discords. The European theater and opera seek a synthesis of many arts. It may be that in this way our metaphorical language that is in some sense a confusion of thought is producing, through art, a result of far-reaching value—a deeper esthetic sense leading toward a more direct apprehension of underlying unity behind the phenomena so variously reported by our sense channels.

Historical implications

How does such a network of language, culture, and behavior come about historically? Which was first: the language patterns or the cultural norms? In main they have grown up together, constantly influencing each other. But in this partnership the nature of the language is the factor that limits free plasticity and rigidifies channels of development in the more autocratic way. This is so because a language is a system, not just an assemblage of norms. Large systematic outlines can change to something really new only very slowly, while many other cultural innovations are made with comparative quickness. Language thus represents the mass mind; it is affected by inventions and innovations, but affected little and slowly, whereas *to* inventors and innovators it legislates with the decree immediate.

The growth of the SAE language—culture complex dates from ancient times. Much of its metaphorical reference to the nonspatial by the spatial was already fixed in the ancient tongues, and more especially in Latin. It is indeed a marked trait of Latin. If we compare, say, Hebrew we find that, while Hebrew has some allusion to not-space as space, Latin has more. Latin terms for nonspatials, like *educo, religio, principia, comprehendo*, are usually metaphorized physical references: lead out, tying back, etc. This is not true of all languages—it is quite untrue of Hopi. The fact that in Latin the direction of development happened to be from spatial to nonspatial (partly because of secondary stimulation to abstract thinking when the intellectually crude Romans encountered Greek culture) and that later tongues were strongly stimulated to mimic Latin, seems a likely reason for a belief, which still lingers on among linguists, that this is the natural direction of semantic change in all languages, and for the persistent notion in Western learned circles (in strong contrast to Eastern ones) that objective experience is prior to subjective. Philosophies make out a weighty case for the reverse, and certainly the direction of development is sometimes the reverse. Thus the Hopi word for "heart" can be shown to be a late formation within Hopi from a root meaning think or remember. Or consider what has happened to the word "radio" in such a sentence as "he bought a new radio," as compared to its prior meaning "science of wireless telephony."

In the Middle Ages the patterns already formed in Latin began to interweave with the increased mechanical invention, industry, trade, and scholastic and scientific thought. The need for measurement in industry and trade, the stores and bulks of "stuffs" in various containers, the type-bodies in which various goods were handled, standardizing of measure and weight units, invention of clocks and measurement of "time," keeping of records, accounts, chronicles, histories, growth of mathematics and the partnership of mathematics and science, all cooperated to bring our thought and language world into its present form.

In Hopi history, could we read it, we should find a different type of language and a different set of cultural and environmental influences working together. A peaceful agricultural society isolated by geographic features and nomad enemies in a land of scanty rainfall, arid agriculture that could be made successful only by the utmost perseverance (hence the value of persistence and repetition), necessity for collaboration (hence emphasis on the psychology of teamwork and on mental factors in general), corn and rain as primary criteria of value, need of extensive *preparations* and precautions to assure crops in the poor soil and precarious climate, keen realization of dependence upon nature favoring prayer and a religious attitude toward the forces of nature, especially prayer and religion directed toward the ever-needed blessing, rain—these things interacted with Hopi linguistic patterns to mold them, to be molded again by them, and so little by little to shape the Hopi world-outlook.

To sum up the matter, our first question asked in the beginning (p. 22) is answered thus: Concepts of "time" and "matter" are not given in substantially the same form by experience to all men but depend upon the nature of the language or languages through the use of which they have been developed. They do not depend so much upon *any one system* (e.g., tense or nouns) within the grammar as upon the ways of analyzing and reporting experience which have become fixed in the language as integrated "fashions of speaking" and which cut across the typical grammatical classifications, so that such a "fashion" may include lexical, morphological, syntactic, and otherwise systemically diverse means coordinated in a certain frame of consistency.

Our own "time" differs markedly from Hopi "duration." It is conceived as like a space of strictly limited dimensions, or sometimes as like a motion upon such a space, and employed as an intellectual tool accordingly. Hopi "duration" seems to be inconceivable in terms of space or motion, being the mode in which life differs from form, and consciousness *in toto* from the spatial elements of consciousness. Certain ideas born of our own time-concept, such as that of absolute simultaneity, would be either very difficult to express or impossible and devoid of meaning under the Hopi conception, and would be replaced by operational concepts. Our "matter" is the physical subtype of "substance" or "stuff," which is conceived as the formless extensional item that must be joined with form before there can be real existence. In Hopi there seems to be nothing corresponding to it; there are no formless extensional items; existence may or may not have form, but what it also has, with or without form, is intensity and duration, these being nonextensional and at bottom the same.

But what about our concept of "space," which was also included in our first question? There is no such striking difference between Hopi and SAE about space as about time, and probably the apprehension of space is given in substantially the same form by experience irrespective of language. The experiments of the Gestalt psychologists with visual perception appear to establish this as a fact. But the *concept of space* will vary somewhat with language, because, as an intellectual tool,[13] it is so closely linked with the concomitant employment of other intellectual tools, of the order of "time" and "matter," which are linguistically conditioned. We see things with our eyes in the same space forms as the Hopi, but our idea of space has also the property of acting as a surrogate of nonspatial relationships like time, intensity, tendency, and as a void to be filled with imagined formless items, one of which may even be called "space." Space as sensed by the Hopi would not be connected mentally with such surrogates, but would be comparatively "pure," unmixed with extraneous notions.

As for our second question (p. 22): There are connections but not correlations or diagnostic correspondences between cultural norms and linguistic patterns. Although it would be impossible to infer the existence of Crier Chiefs from the lack of tenses in Hopi, or vice versa, there is a relation between a language and the rest of the culture of the society which uses it. There are cases where the "fashions of speaking" are closely integrated with the whole general culture, whether or not this be universally true, and there are connections within this integration, between the kind of linguistic analyses employed and various behavioral reactions and also the shapes taken by various cultural developments. Thus the importance of Crier Chiefs does have a connection, not with tenselessness itself, but with a system of thought in which categories different from our tenses are natural. These connections are to be found not so much by focusing attention on the typical rubrics of linguistic, ethnographic, or sociological description as by examining the culture and the language (always and only when the two have been together historically for a considerable time) as a whole in which concatenations that run across these departmental lines may be expected to exist, and, if they do exist, eventually to be discoverable by study.

Notes

1 Reproduced from pp. 75–93, *Language, culture, and personality, essays in memory of Edward Sapir*, edited by Leslie Spier (Menasha, WI: Sapir Memorial Publication Fund, 1941). The article was written in the summer of 1939.

2 We have plenty of evidence that this is not the case. Consider only the Hopi and the Ute, with languages that on the overt morphological and lexical level are as similar as, say, English and German. The idea of "correlation" between language and culture, in the generally accepted sense of correlation, is certainly a mistaken one.

3   As we say, "ten at the *same time*," showing that in our language and thought we restate the fact of group perception in terms of a concept "time," the large linguistic component of which will appear in the course of this paper.

4   It is no exception to this rule of lacking a plural that a mass noun may sometimes coincide in lexeme with an individual noun that of course has a plural; e.g., "stone" (no pl.) with "a stone" (pl. "stones"). The plural form denoting varieties, e.g., "wines," is of course a different sort of thing from the true plural; it is a curious outgrowth from the SAE mass nouns, leading to still another sort of imaginary aggregates, which will have to be omitted from this paper.

5   Hopi has two words for water quantities; *kə • yi* and *pa • hə*. The difference is something like that between "stone" and "rock" in English, *pa • hə* implying greater size and "wildness"; flowing water, whether or not outdoors or in nature, is *pa • hə*; so is "moisture." But, unlike "stone" and "rock," the difference is essential, not pertaining to a connotative margin, and the two can hardly ever be interchanged.

6   To be sure, there are a few minor differences from other nouns, in English for instance in the use of the articles.

7   "Year" and certain combinations of "year" with name of season, rarely season names alone, can occur with a locative morpheme "at," but this is exceptional. It appears like historical detritus of an earlier different patterning, or the effect of English analogy, or both.

8   The expective and reportive assertions contrast according to the "paramount relation." The expective expresses anticipation existing *earlier* than objective fact, and coinciding with objective fact *later* than the status quo of the speaker, this status quo, including all the subsummation of the past therein, being expressed by the reportive. Our notion "future" seems to represent at once the earlier (anticipation) and the later (afterwards, what will be), as Hopi shows. This paradox may hint of how elusive the mystery of real time is, and how artificially it is expressed by a linear relation of past–present–future.

9   One such trace is that the tensor "long in duration," while quite different from the adjective "long" of space, seems to contain the same root as the adjective "large" of space. Another is that "somewhere" of space used with certain tensors means "at some indefinite time." Possibly however this is not the case and it is only the tensor that gives the time element, so that "somewhere" still refers to space and that under these conditions indefinite space means simply general applicability, regardless of either time or space. Another trace is that in the temporal (cycle word) "afternoon" the element meaning "after" is derived from the verb "to separate." There are other such traces, but they are few and exceptional, and obviously not like our own spatial metaphorizing.

10 The Hopi verbs of preparing naturally do not correspond neatly to our "prepare"; so that *na'twani* could also be rendered "the practiced-upon, the tried-for," and otherwise.

11 See, e.g., Ernest Beaglehole, *Notes on Hopi economic life* (Yale University Publications in Anthropology, no. 15, 1937), especially the reference to the announcement of a rabbit hunt, and, on p. 30, description of the activities in connection with the cleaning of Toreva Spring—announcing, various preparing activities, and finally, preparing the continuity of the good results already obtained and the continued flow of the spring.

12 This notion of storing up power, which seems implied by much Hopi behavior, has an analog in physics: acceleration. It might be said that the linguistic background of Hopi thought equips it to recognize naturally that force manifests not as motion or velocity, but as cumulation or acceleration. Our linguistic background tends to hinder in us this same recognition, for having legitimately conceived force to be that which produces change, we then think of change by our linguistic metaphorical analog, motion, instead of by a pure motionless changingness concept, i.e. accumulation or acceleration. Hence it comes to our naïve feeling as a shock to find from physical experiments that it is not possible to define force by motion, that motion and speed, as also "being at rest," are wholly relative, and that force can be measured only by acceleration.

13 Here belong "Newtonian" and "Euclidean" space, etc.

Chapter 2

RICHARD NISBETT

IS THE WORLD MADE UP OF NOUNS OR VERBS?

JORGE LUIS BORGES (1966), the Argentine writer, tells us that there is an ancient Chinese encyclopedia entitled *Celestial emporium of benevolent knowledge* in which the following classification of animals appears: "(a) those that belong to the emperor, (b) embalmed ones, (c) those that are trained, (d) suckling pigs, (e) mermaids, (f) fabulous ones, (g) stray dogs, (h) those that are included in this classification, (i) those that tremble as if they were mad, (k) those drawn with a very fine camel's hair brush, (l) others, (m) those that have just broken a flower vase, (n) those that resemble flies at a distance."

Though Borges may have invented this classification for his own purposes, it is certainly the case that the ancient Chinese did not categorize the world in the same sorts of ways that the ancient Greeks did. For the Greeks, things belonged in the same category if they were describable by the same attributes. But the philosopher Donald Munro (1969) points out that, for the Chinese, shared attributes did not establish shared class membership. Instead, things were classed together because they were thought to influence one another through *resonance*. For example, in the Chinese system of the Five Processes, the categories spring, east, wood, wind, and green all influenced one another. Change in wind would affect all the others—in "a process like a multiple echo, without physical contact coming between any of them." (p. 41). Philosopher David Moser (1996) also notes that it was similarity between classes, not similarity among individual members of the same class, that was of interest to the ancient Chinese. They were simply not concerned about the relationship between a member of a class ("a horse") and the class as a whole ("horses")(p. 171).

In fact, for the Chinese there seems to have been a positive antipathy toward categorization. For the ancient Taoist philosopher Chuang Tzu, ". . . the problem of . . . how terms and attributes are to be delimited, leads one in precisely the wrong direction. Classifying or limiting knowledge fractures the greater knowledge" (Mote, 1971, p. 102). In the *Tao Te Ching* we find the following dim view of the effects of relying on categories.

Source: Nisbett, R. (2003). Is the world made up of nouns or verbs? Selected from *The geography of thought* (Chapter 6, pp. 137–65). London: Nicholas Brealey Publishing.

The five colors cause one's eyes to be blind.
The five tones cause one's ears to be deaf.
The five flavors cause one's palate to be spoiled.

(Hansen, 1983, p. 108)

The lack of interest in classes of objects sharing the same properties is consistent with the basic scheme that the ancient Chinese had for the world. For them, the world consisted of continuous substances. So it was a *part–whole* dichotomy that made sense to them. Finding the features shared by objects and placing objects in a class on that basis would not have seemed a very useful activity, if only because the objects themselves were not the unit of analysis (Chan, 1967a, b; Hansen, 1983; Moser, 1996). Since the Greek world was composed of objects, an *individual–class* relation was natural to them. The Greek belief in the importance of that relation was central to their faith in the possibility of accurate inductive inferences: Learning that one object belonging to a category has a particular property means that one can assume that other objects belonging to the category also have the property. If one mammal has a liver, it's a good bet that all mammals do. A focus on the *one–many*, individual–class organization of knowledge encourages induction from the single case; a part–whole representation does not.

Categories vs. relationships in modern thought

Once again, we have a case of very different intellectual traditions in ancient Greece and ancient China, and once again we can ask whether the mental habits of ancient philosophers resemble the perception and reasoning of ordinary people today. We might expect, based on the historical evidence for cognitive differences and our theory about the social origins of them, that contemporary Westerners would (a) have a greater tendency to categorize objects than would Easterners; (b) find it easier to learn new categories by applying rules about properties to particular cases; and (c) make more inductive use of categories, that is, generalize from particular instances of a category to other instances or to the category as a whole. We might also expect that Easterners, given their convictions about the potential relevance of every fact to every other fact, would organize the world more in terms of perceived relationships and similarities than would Westerners.

Take a look at the three objects pictured in Figure 2.1. If you were to place two objects together, which would they be? Why do those seem to be the ones that belong together?

If you're a Westerner, odds are you think the chicken and the cow belong together. Developmental psychologist Liang-hwang Chiu (1972) showed triplets like those in the illustration to American and Chinese children. Chiu found that the American children preferred to group objects because they belonged to the "taxonomic" category, that is, the same classification term could be applied to both ("adults," "tools"). Chinese children preferred to group objects on the basis of relationships. They would be more likely to say the cow and the grass in the illustration go together because "the cow eats the grass."

Li-jun Ji, Zhiyong Zhang, and I (2002) obtained similar results comparing college students from the U.S. with students from mainland China and Taiwan, using words instead of pictures. We presented participants with sets of three words (e.g., panda, monkey, banana) and asked them to indicate which two of the three were most closely related. The American participants showed a marked preference for grouping on the basis of common category membership: Panda and monkey fit into the animal category. The Chinese participants showed a preference for grouping on the basis of thematic relationships (e.g., monkey and banana) and justified their answers in terms of relationships: Monkeys eat bananas.

A   B

What goes with this? A or B

Figure 2.1 Example of item measuring preference for grouping by categories vs. relationships.

If the natural way of organizing the world for Westerners is to do so in terms of categories and the rules that define them, then we might expect that Westerners' perceptions of similarity between objects would be heavily influenced by the degree to which the objects can be categorized by applying a set of rules. But if categories are less salient to East Asians, then we might expect that their perceptions of similarity would be based more on the family resemblance among objects.

To test this possibility, Ara Norenzayan, Edward E. Smith, Beom Jun Kim, and I (Norenzayan, 1999; Norenzayan et al., 2002) gave schematic figures like those shown in Figure 2.2 to Korean, European American, and Asian American participants. Each display consisted of an object at the bottom and two groups of objects above it. The participants' job was just to say which group of objects the target object seemed more similar to. You might want to make your own judgment about the objects in the illustration before reading on.

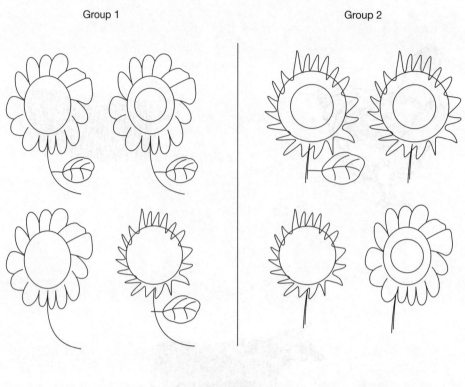

Target Object

Figure 2.2 Example of item measuring whether judgments of similarity are based on family resemblance or rules.

Most of the Koreans thought the target object was more similar to the group on the left, whereas most of the European Americans thought the object was more similar to the group on the right. The target object bears a more obvious family resemblance to the group on the left, so it's easy to see why the Koreans would have thought the object was more similar to that group, and on average they did so 60 percent of the time. But there is a simple, invariant rule that allows you to place the target object into a category that it shares with the group on the right. The rule is "has a straight (as opposed to curved) stem." European Americans typically discovered such rules and, 67 percent of the time, found the target object to be more similar to the group with which it shared the rule-based category. Asian American judgments were in between but more similar to those of the Koreans.

Categories are sometimes learned by applying rules to features. We come to know that rabbits are mammals because we are taught a rule that animals that nurse their young are mammals. (That's true for categories defined formally, in any case. Actually, most people probably learn what mammals are by ostention: "that rabbit is a mammal," "that lion is a mammal." The "folk" category that is learned is then induced from the common properties observed—fur-bearing, four-footed, etc.)

Explicit modeling or rule-making seems to be less characteristic of the causal explanations of East Asians than of Westerners. If Asians are less likely to use rules to understand the world, and less likely to make use of categories, they might find it particularly hard to learn categories by applying explicit rules to objects. In order to test this possibility, Ara Norenzayan and his colleagues (2002) showed color cartoon figures like those rendered in black and white in Figure 2.3 to East Asian, Asian American, and European American students at the University of Michigan. We told participants that they would be learning how to classify the animals as being either from Venus or from Saturn.

Figure 2.3 Example of cartoon animals used for study of ease of learning categories based on rules.

We told participants that an animal was from Venus if it had any three of five features: curly tail, hooves, long neck, mouth, and antennae ears.[1] Otherwise, the creature was from Saturn. The animal on the left at the top (seen as blue by participants) meets the criteria for being from Venus; the one on the right (seen as red) doesn't and has to be put in the Saturn category. After participants had learned how to classify animals correctly, we tested how much control they had over the categories by showing them new animals and seeing how fast and accurately they could classify them. The new animals included two types that resembled previously seen ones. Some animals were "positive matches": They looked like an animal participants had seen before during the training trials and they belonged to the same category in terms of the rules concerning their features. Other animals were "negative matches": They looked like an animal that had been seen before, but in terms of the rules, they belonged to a different category from the one seen in training. The animal on the lower left is a positive match for the one on the left above: It looks like the one categorized as being from Venus, and the rules also indicate that it is. The one on the lower right is a negative match: It looks like the Venus animal but the rules say it's not.

The Asian participants took longer to make their judgments about whether the animal was from Venus or Saturn than either the European Americans or Asian Americans. The three groups of participants were equally fast and equally accurate for the positive matches, for which both memory for the previously seen example and correct applications of the rules defining the category would produce the correct answer. But for the negative matches, which could be classified correctly only if the rules were remembered and applied correctly, Asian participants made twice as many classification errors as either European Americans or Asian Americans did. Categorization by rules seems not to come as easily to Easterners as to Westerners.

Which of the two arguments below, both ending in the conclusion "rabbits have enzyme Q in their blood," seems more convincing to you? Why?

(1)	(2)
Lions have enzyme Q in their blood	Lions have enzyme Q in their blood
Tigers have enzyme Q in their blood	Giraffes have enzyme Q in their blood
Rabbits have enzyme Q in their blood	Rabbits have enzyme Q in their blood

Most Westerners who have been asked this sort of question say that argument 2 is better (Osherson et al., 1990). They give as their reason some version of a "diversity" or "coverage" argument. Lions and tigers are rather similar animals in many ways, so they don't cover the mammal category, to which rabbits belong, very well. Lions and giraffes give better coverage of the mammal category because they're more different from each other. Now consider the arguments below, both ending in the conclusion "mammals have enzyme Q in their blood." Which seems more convincing to you?

(1)	(2)
Lions have enzyme Q in their blood	Lions have enzyme Q in their blood
Tigers have enzyme Q in their blood	Giraffes have enzyme Q in their blood
Mammals have enzyme Q in their blood	Mammals have enzyme Q in their blood

Again, most Westerners say the second argument is more convincing and give as their reason that the coverage of the mammal category is better for the second argument than for the first.

Incheol Choi, Edward E. Smith, and I (1997) gave problems like those above to Korean and American college students. Koreans, but not Americans, were more likely to prefer the second argument when the category was mentioned in the conclusion. For Koreans, the mammal category was not salient unless it was highlighted by actually referring to it. As a result, the diversity principle was more important to their inferences when they were explicitly reminded that the objects in question were mammals. One likely consequence of the low salience of categories for Easterners is that they do not fuel inductive inferences for Easterners as much as for Westerners.

Growing up in a world of objects vs. relationships

How is it possible that Easterners today have relatively little interest in categories, find it hard to learn new categories by applying rules about properties, and make little spontaneous use of them for purposes of induction? Why are they so much more inclined to consider relationships in their organization of objects than Westerners are? Surely not just because ancient Chinese philosophers had little use for categories and were more interested in part–whole relationships and thematic resemblances than in category-member classifications. It seems dubious that philosophers' concerns would have affected judgments about everyday objects even by their contemporaries. If relationships, and not categories, are relatively important to East Asians today, there must be factors that still operate in the socialization of children that prompt such different styles of perception and reasoning. Before looking for such factors, let's consider some important differences between categories and relationships.

Categories are denoted by nouns. It seems obvious that nouns would be easier for a young child to learn than verbs. All you have to do to learn that the animal you just saw is a "bear" is to notice its distinctive features—huge size, large teeth and claws, long fur, ferocious appearance—and you can store that object away with its label. The label is then available for application to any other object having that set of properties.

Relationships, on the other hand, involve, tacitly or explicitly, a verb. Learning the meaning of a transitive verb normally involves noticing two objects and some kind of action that connects them in some way. "To throw" means to use your arm and hand to move an object through the air to a new location. Merely pointing at the action does not guarantee that someone will know what you're referring to.

Because of their relative ambiguity, it's harder to remember verbs; verbs are more likely to be altered in meaning than nouns when a speaker communicates to another person or when one person paraphrases what another has said; and it's harder to correctly identify verbs than nouns when they're translated from one language to another. Moreover, the meaning of verbs, and other terms that describe relations, differs more across different languages than simple nouns do. "Verbs," says cognitive psychologist Dedre Gentner (1981, p. 168), "are highly reactive; nouns tend to be inert."

Given these differences between nouns and verbs, it is scarcely surprising that Gentner (1982) finds that children learn nouns much more rapidly than they learn verbs. In fact, toddlers can learn nouns at rates of up to two per day. This is much faster than the rate at which they learn verbs.

Gentner quite reasonably guessed that the large noun advantage would be universal. But it turns out not to be. Developmental psycholinguist Twila Tardif (1996) and others have found that East Asian children learn verbs at about the same rate as nouns and, by some definitions of what counts as a noun, at a significantly faster rate than nouns. There are several factors that might underlie this dramatic difference.

First, verbs are more salient in East Asian languages than in English and many other European languages (Gopnick & Choi, 1990; Tardif, 1996). Verbs in Chinese, Japanese, and Korean tend to come either at the beginning or the end of sentences and both are relatively salient locations. In English, verbs are more commonly buried in the middle.

Second, recall the father I overheard quizzing his child about the properties of pants. Western parents are noun-obsessed, pointing objects out to their children, naming them, and telling them about their attributes. Strange as it may seem to Westerners, Asians don't seem to regard object naming as part of the job description for a parent. Developmental psychologists Anne Fernald and Hiromi Morikawa (1993) went into the homes of Japanese and Americans having infants either six, twelve, or nineteen months old. They asked the mothers to clear away the toys from a play area and then they introduced several that they had brought with them—a stuffed dog and pig and a car and a truck. They asked the mothers to play with the toys with their babies as they normally would. They found big differences in the behavior of mothers even with their youngest children. American mothers used twice as many object labels as Japanese mothers ("piggie," "doggie"), and Japanese mothers engaged in twice as many social routines of teaching politeness norms (empathy and greetings, for example). An American mother's patter might go like this: "That's a car. See the car? You like it? It's got nice wheels." A Japanese mother might say: "Here! It's a vroom vroom. I give it to you. Now give this to me. Yes! Thank you."(Fernald & Morikawa, 1993, p. 653). American children are learning that the world is mostly a place with objects, Japanese children that the world is mostly about relationships.

Third, we know that naming objects that share a common set of properties results in infants' learning a category formed of objects sharing those features. Naming objects sharing features also prompts them to attend to features that would allow them to form other categories based on similar sets of properties. Developmental psychologists Linda Smith and her colleagues (Smith et al., 2002) randomly assigned seventeen-month-old children either to a control condition or to a condition in which, for nine weeks, they repeatedly played with and heard names for members of unfamiliar object categories that were defined by shape: for example, "cup." This taught the toddlers to attend to shape and to form categories for objects—even those seen outside the experimental setting—that could be grouped on the basis of some set of defining features. The result was that trained children showed a dramatic increase in acquisition of new object names during the course of the study.

Fourth, generic nouns (that is, category names) in English and other European languages are often marked by syntax. When the conversation turns to waterfowl, you can say "a duck," "the duck," "the ducks," or "ducks." The last term is a generic one, and the syntax tells you this. It's normally obligatory to indicate whether you're speaking about an object or a class of objects, though sometimes the context can do the job. But in Chinese and other Sinitic languages, contextual and pragmatic cues can be the only kinds of cues the hearer has to go on. The presence of a duck that has just waddled over from a pond to beg food, for example, would indicate that it is "the duck" one is talking about, rather than "a duck," "the ducks," or "ducks." Developmental psychologists Susan Gelman and Twila Tardif (Gelman & Tardif, 1998) studied English-speaking mothers and Mandarin Chinese-speaking mothers and found that, across a number of contexts, generic utterances were more common for the English-speaking mothers.

Finally, there is direct evidence that Eastern children learn how to categorize objects at a later point than Western children. Developmental psycholinguists Alison Gopnik and Soonja

Choi (1990) studied Korean-, French-, and English-speaking children beginning when they were one-and-a-half years old. They found that object-naming and categorization skills develop later in Korean speakers than in English and French speakers. The investigators studied means–ends judgments (for example, figuring out how to take things out of a container), and categorization, which they studied by showing children four objects of one kind and four of another, such as four flat, yellow rectangles and four small human figures, and telling them to "fix these things up," that is, put them together in some way that makes sense. English- and French-speaking toddlers mastered the means–end tasks and the categorization tasks at about the same age. Korean toddlers learned categorization almost three months later than means–end abilities.

Dispositions, stability, and categories

The ancient Greeks were fond of categories and used them as the basis for discovery and application of rules. They also believed in stability and understood both the physical and social worlds in terms of fixed attributes or dispositions. These are not unrelated facts, nor is it a coincidence that the ancient Chinese were uninterested in categories, believed in change, and understood the behavior of both physical and social objects as being due to the interaction of the object with a surrounding field of forces.

If the world is a stable place, then it is worthwhile trying to develop rules to understand it and refining the categories to which the rules apply. Many of the categories used to understand the world refer to presumed qualities of the object: hardness, whiteness, kindness, timidity. Easterners of course use such categories as well, but they are less likely to abstract them away from particular objects: There is the whiteness of the horse or the whiteness of the snow in ancient Chinese philosophy, but not whiteness as an abstract, detachable concept that can be applied to almost anything. In the Western tradition, objects have essences composed of mix-and-match abstract qualities. These essences allow for confident predictions about behavior independent of context. In the Eastern tradition, objects have concrete properties that interact with environmental circumstances to produce behavior. There was never any interest in discussing abstract properties as if they had a reality other than being a characteristic of a particular object.

Most importantly, the dispositions of objects are not necessarily stable for Easterners. In the West, a child who performs poorly in mathematics is likely to be regarded as having little math ability or perhaps even as being "learning disabled." In the East, such a child is viewed as needing to work harder, or perhaps her teacher should work harder, or maybe the setting for learning should be changed (Stevenson & Lee, 1996).

The obsession with categories of the either/or sort runs through Western intellectual history. Dichotomies abound in every century and form the basis for often fruitless debates: for example, "mind–body" controversies in which partisans take sides as to whether a given behavior is best understood as being produced by the mind independent of any biological embodiment, or as a purely physical reaction unmediated by mental processes. The "nature–nurture" controversy is another debate that has often proved to generate more heat than light. As evolutionary biologist Richard Alexander has pointed out, nearly all behaviors that are characteristic of higher order mammals are determined by both nature and nurture. The dichotomy "emotion–reason" has obscured more than it has revealed. As Hume said, "reason is and ought to be the slave of passion"; it makes sense to separate the two for purposes of analysis only. And it's been suggested that the distinction between "human" and "animal" insisted upon by Westerners made it particularly hard to accept the concept of evolution. In most Eastern systems, the soul can take the form of any animal or even God. Evolution was never controversial in the East because there was never an assumption that humans sat atop a chain of being and somehow had lost their animality.

Throughout Western intellectual history, there has been a conviction that it is possible to find the necessary and sufficient conditions for any category. A square is a two-dimensional object with four sides of equal length and four right angles. Nothing lacking these properties can be a square, and anything having those properties is definitely a square. Ludwig Wittgenstein (1953), in his *Philosophical investigations*, brought the whole necessity-and-sufficiency enterprise crashing to earth in the West.[2] Wittgenstein argued to the satisfaction (or rather, dismay) of even the most analytic of Western philosophers that establishing necessary and sufficient conditions for any complex or interesting category, such as a "game" or a "government" or an "illness," was never going to be possible. A thing can be a game even if it is not fun, even if played alone, even if its chief goal is to make money. A thing is not necessarily a game even if it is fun or is a nonproductive activity engaging several people in pleasurable interaction. Wittgenstein's sermon would never have been needed in the East. The pronouncement that complex categories cannot always be defined by necessary and sufficient conditions would scarcely have been met with surprise.

Is it language that does the job?

Given the substantial differences in language usage between Easterners and Westerners, is it possible that it is merely language that is driving the differences in tendency to organize the world in terms of verbs vs. nouns? Are the findings about knowledge organization simply due to the fact that Western languages encourage the use of nouns, which results in categorization of objects, and Eastern languages encourage the use of verbs, with the consequence that it is relationships that are emphasized? More generally, how many of the cognitive differences documented in this book are produced by language?

There are in fact a remarkable number of parallels between the sorts of cognitive differences discussed in this book and differences between Indo-European languages and East Asian languages. The parallels are particularly striking because East Asian languages, notably Chinese and Japanese, are themselves so different in many respects, yet nevertheless share many qualities with one another that differentiate them from Indo-European languages.

In addition to the practices already discussed—pointing and naming, location of verbs in sentences, marking of nouns as generic, and so on—there are several ways in which language usage maps onto differences in category usage.

The Western concern with categories is reflected in language. "Generic" noun phrases are more common for English speakers than for Chinese speakers, perhaps because Western languages mark in a more explicit way whether a generic interpretation of an utterance is the correct one (Lucy, 1992). In fact, in Chinese there is no way to tell the difference between the sentences "squirrels eat nuts" and "this squirrel is eating the nut." Only context can provide this information. English speakers know from linguistic markers whether it is a category or an individual that is being talked about.

Greek and other Indo-European languages encourage making properties of objects into real objects in their own right—simply adding the suffix "ness" or its equivalent. The philosopher David Moser (1996) has noted that this practice may foster thinking about properties as abstract entities that can then function as theoretical explanations. Plato actually thought that these abstractions had a greater reality than the properties of objects in the physical world. This degree of theorizing about abstractions was never characteristic of Chinese philosophy.

East Asian languages are highly "contextual." Words (or phonemes) typically have multiple meanings, so to be understood they require the context of sentences. English words are relatively distinctive, and English speakers in addition are concerned to make sure that words and utterances require as little context as possible. The linguistic anthropologist Shirley Brice Heath (1982) has shown that middle-class American parents quite deliberately attempt to decontextualize language as much as possible for their children. They try to make words understandable independent of verbal context and to make utterances understandable independent of situational context. When reading to a child about a dog, the parent might ask the child what the animal is ("A doggie, that's right") and who has a dog ("Yes, Heather has a dog"). The word is detached from its naturally occurring context and linked to other contexts where the word has a similar meaning.

Western languages force a preoccupation with focal objects as opposed to context. English is a "subject-prominent" language. There must be a subject, even in the sentence "It is raining." Japanese, Chinese, and Korean, in contrast, are "topic-prominent" languages. Sentences have a position, typically the first position, that should be filled by the current topic: "This place, skiing is good." This fact places an alternative interpretation on our finding that, after viewing underwater scenes, Americans start with describing an object ("There was a big fish, maybe a trout, moving off to the left") whereas Japanese start by establishing the context ("It looked like a pond"). While not obligatory from a grammatical standpoint, an idiomatic Japanese sentence starts with context and topic rather than jumping immediately to a subject, as is frequently the case in English.

For Westerners, it is the self who does the acting; for Easterners, action is something that is undertaken in concert with others or that is the consequence of the self operating in a field of forces. Languages capture this different sort of agency. Recall that there are many different words for "I" in Japanese and (formerly, at any rate) in Chinese, reflecting the relationship between self and other. So there is "I" in relation to my colleague, "I" in relation to my spouse, etc. It is difficult for Japanese to think of properties that apply to "me" (Cousins, 1989). It is much easier for them to think of properties that apply to themselves in certain settings and in relation to particular people. Grammar also reflects a different sense of how action comes about. Most Western languages are "agentic" in the sense that the language conveys that the self has operated on the world: "He dropped it." (An exception is Spanish.) Eastern languages are in general relatively nonagentic: "It fell from him," or just "fell."

A difference in language practice that startles both Chinese speakers and English speakers when they hear how the other group handles it concerns the proper way to ask someone whether they would like more tea to drink. In Chinese one asks, "Drink more?" In English, one asks, "More tea?" To Chinese speakers, it's perfectly obvious that it's tea that one is talking about drinking more of, so to mention tea would be redundant. To English speakers, it's perfectly obvious that one is talking about drinking the tea, as opposed to any other activity that might be carried out with it, so it would be rather bizarre for the question to refer to drinking.[3]

According to linguistic anthropologists Edward Sapir and Benjamin Whorf (1956), the differences in linguistic structure between languages are reflected in people's habitual thinking processes. This hypothesis has moved in and out of favor among linguists and psychologists over the decades, but it is currently undergoing one of its periods of greater acceptance. Some of our evidence about language and reasoning speaks directly to the Sapir–Whorf hypothesis.

Recall that Li-jun Ji, Zhiyong Zhang, and I (2002) examined whether language per se affects the way people categorize objects. We gave word triplets (for example, panda, monkey, banana) to Chinese and American college students and asked them to indicate which two of the three were most closely related. The Chinese students were either living in the U.S. or in China and they were tested either in English or in Chinese.

If the Sapir–Whorf hypothesis is correct, then it ought to make a difference which language the bilingual Chinese are tested in. They should be more likely to prefer relationships (monkey, banana) as the basis for grouping when tested in Chinese and more likely to prefer taxonomic category (panda, monkey) when tested in English. But there are different ways of being bilingual. Psycholinguists (Ervin & Osgood, 1954; Lambert et al., 1958) make a distinction between what they call "coordinate" bilinguals and "compound" bilinguals. Coordinate bilinguals are people who learn a second language relatively late in life and for whom its use is confined to a limited number of contexts. Mental representations of the world supposedly can be different in one language than in the other for such people. Compound bilinguals are people for whom the second language is learned early and is used in many contexts. Mental representations for such people should be fused, since the languages are not used for different functions or used exclusively in different settings. We tested both types of bilinguals. People from China and Taiwan could be expected to be coordinate bilinguals because they typically learn English relatively late, and its use is confined mostly to formal school contexts. People from Hong Kong and Singapore would be more likely to be compound bilinguals because they learn English relatively early and use it in more contexts. In addition, these societies, especially Hong Kong, are highly Westernized.

If language makes a difference to understanding of the world because different languages underlie different mental representations, we would expect to find the Sapir–Whorf hypothesis supported: The coordinate bilinguals, at least, should group words differently when tested in Chinese than when tested in English. If language makes a difference because structural features of the language compel different thinking processes, then we might expect even the compound bilinguals to group words differently when tested in Chinese than when tested in English. And, of course, if language is not important to cognitive tasks such as our grouping one, then we would expect no effect of language for either group.

The results could not have been more unequivocal. First, there were marked differences between European Americans tested in English and coordinate Chinese speakers tested in Chinese, whether in China or in the U.S. Americans were twice as likely to group on the basis of taxonomic category as on the basis of relationships. Mainland and Taiwanese Chinese tested in their native language were twice as likely to group on the basis of relationships as on the basis of taxonomic category, and this was true whether they were tested in their home countries or in the U.S. Second, the language of testing did make a big difference for the mainland and Taiwanese Chinese. When tested in English, they were much less likely to group on the basis of relationships. It thus appears that English subserves a different way of representing the world than Chinese for these participants.

But matters were quite different for compound bilinguals from Hong Kong and Singapore. First, their groupings were shifted in a substantially Western direction: They were still based on relationships more than on taxonomic category, but the preference was much weaker for them than for the coordinate Chinese and Taiwanese speakers. More importantly, it made precisely no difference for the compound speakers whether they were tested in Chinese or in English.

The results are clear in their implications. There is an effect of culture on thought independent of language. We know this because both the coordinate Chinese speakers and the compound Chinese speakers group words differently from Americans, regardless of language of testing. The differences between coordinate and compound speakers also indicate a culture difference independent of language. The compound speakers from Westernized regions are shifted in a Western direction—and to the same extent regardless of language of testing. There is also clearly an effect of language independent of culture—but only for the coordinate speakers from China and Taiwan. They respond very differently depending on whether they are tested in Chinese or in English.

A tentative answer to the Sapir–Whorf question as it relates to our work—and it must be very tentative because we have just been discussing a couple of studies dealing with a single kind of mental process—is that language does indeed influence thought, so long as different languages are plausibly associated with different systems of representation.

So there is good evidence that for East Asians the world is seen much more in terms of relationships than it is for Westerners, who are more inclined to see the world in terms of static objects that can be grouped into categories. Child-rearing practices undoubtedly play a role in producing these very different visions. East Asian children have their attention directed toward relationships, and Western children toward objects and the categories to which they belong. Language probably plays a role, at least in helping to focus attention, but probably also in stabilizing the different orientations throughout life. There appears to be nothing about the structure of language, though, that actually forces description in terms of categories versus relationships.

Notes

1   This experiment is based on procedures developed by Allen and Brooks (1991).
2   Skepticism about necessary and sufficient conditions was present, however, as early as the Scottish Enlightenment.
3   Twila Tardif (1996) pointed out this amusing language difference, arbitrary from an information-processing standpoint, but essential from a linguistic standpoint.

References

Allen, S. W. and Brooks, L. R. (1991). Specializing in the operation of an explicit rule. *Journal of Experimental Social Psychology*, General 120, 3–19.

Borges, J. L. (1966). *Other inquisitions 1937–1952*. New York: Washington Square Press.

Chan, W. T. (1967a). Chinese theory and practice, with special reference to humanism. In C. A. Moore (ed.), *The Chinese mind: Essentials of Chinese philosophy and culture* (pp. 11–30). Honolulu: East-West Centre Press.

Chan, W. T. (1967b). The story of Chinese philosophy. In C. A. Moore (ed.), *The Chinese mind: Essentials of Chinese philosophy and culture* (pp. 31–76). Honolulu: East-West Centre Press.

Chiu, L.-H. (1972). A cross-cultural comparison of cognitive styles in Chinese and American children. *International Journal of Psychology*, 7, 235–42.

Choi, I., Nisbett, R. E., and Smith, E. E. (1997). Culture, categorisation and inductive reasoning. *Cognition*, 65, 15–32.

Cousins, S. D. (1989). Culture and self-perception in Japan and the United States. *Journal of Personality and Social Psychology*, 56, 124–31.

Ervin, S. M. and Osgood, C. E. (1954). Second language learning and bilingualism. *Journal of Abnormal and Social Psychology*, 49, Supplement, 139–46.

Fernald, A. and Morikawa, H. (1993). Common themes and cultural variations in Japanese and American mothers' speech to infants. *Child Development*, 64, 637–56.

Gelman, S. A. and Tardif, T. (1998). A cross-linguistic comparison of generic noun phrases in English and Mandarin. *Cognition*, 66, 215–48.

Gentner, D. (1981). Some interesting differences between nouns and verbs. *Cognition and Brain Theory*, 4, 161–78.

Gentner, D. (1982). Why nouns are learned before verbs: Linguistic relativity vs. natural partitioning. In S. A. Kuczaj (ed.), *Language development: Vol. 2. Language, thought and culture*. Hillsdale, NJ: Lawrence Erlbaum.

Gopnik, A. and Choi, S. (1990). Do linguistic differences lead to cognitive differences? A cross-linguistic study of semantic and cognitive development. *First Language*, 10, 199–215.

Hansen, C. (1983). *Language and logic in Ancient China*. Ann Arbor: University of Michigan Press.

Heath, S. B. (1982). What no bedtime story means: Narrative skills at home and school. *Language in Society*, 11, 49–79.

Ji, L., Zhang, Z., and Nisbett, R. E. (2002). Culture, language and categorisation. Unpublished manuscript, Queens University, Kingston, Ontario.

Lambert, W. E., Havelka, J., and Crosby, C. (1958). The influence of language acquisition contexts on bilingualism. *Journal of Abnormal and Social Psychology*, 56, 239–44.

Lucy, J. A. (1992). *Grammatical categories and cognition: A case study of the linguistic relativity hypothesis*. New York: Cambridge University Press.

Moser, D. J. (1996). Abstract thinking and thought in ancient Chinese and early Greek societies. Unpublished PhD thesis, University of Michigan, Ann Arbor.

Mote, F. W. (1971). *Intellectual foundations of China*. New York: Knopf.

Munro, D. J. (1969). *The concept of man in Early China*. Stanford, CA: Stanford University Press.

Norenzayan, A. (1999). Rule-based and experience-based thinking: The cognitive consequences of intellectual traditions. Unpublished PhD thesis, University of Michigan, Ann Arbor, MI.

Norenzayan, A., Smith, E. E., Kim, B. J., and Nisbett, R. E. (2002). Cultural preferences for formal versus intuitive reasoning. *Cognitive Science*, 26, 653–84.

Osherson, D. N., Smith, E. E., Wilkie, O., Lopez, A., and Shafir, E. (1990). Category-based induction. *Psychological Review*, 97, 185–200.

Smith, L. B., Jones, S. S., Landau, B., Gershkoff-Stowe, L., and Samuelson, L. (2002). Object name learning provides on-the-job training for attention. *Psychological Science*, 13, 13–19.

Stevenson, H. W. and Lee, S. (1996). The academic achievement of Chinese students. In M. H. Bond (ed.), *The handbook of Chinese psychology* (pp. 124–42). New York: Oxford University Press.

Tardif, T. (1996). Nouns are not always learned before verbs: Evidence from Mandarin-speakers' early vocabularies. *Developmental Psychology*, 32, 492–504.

Whorf, B. L. (1956). *Language, thought and reality*. New York: Wiley.

Wittgenstein, L. (1953). *Philosophical investigations*. London: Macmillan.

Chapter 3

LARRY A. SAMOVAR, RICHARD PORTER, AND LISA A. STEFANI

HOFSTEDE'S VALUE DIMENSIONS AND HALL'S HIGH CONTEXT/LOW CONTEXT

Hofstede's value dimensions

HOFSTEDE (1980, 1991) has identified four value dimensions that have a significant impact on behavior in all cultures. These dimensions are individualism–collectivism, uncertainty avoidance, power distance, and masculinity and femininity. Hofstede's work was one of the earliest attempts to use extensive statistical data to examine cultural values. During the 1980s, he surveyed over a hundred thousand workers in multinational organizations in forty countries. After careful analysis, each country was assigned a rank of one through forty in each category, depending on how it compared to the other countries (see Table 3.1). The results yielded a clear picture of what was valued in each culture.

Individualism–collectivism

Although Hofstede is often given credit for investigating the concepts of individualism and collectivism, he is not the only scholar who has researched these crucial intercultural dimensions. Triandis (1990), for example, has derived an entire cross-cultural research agenda that focuses on these concepts. Therefore, we use Hofstede's work as our basic organizational scheme; we also examine the findings of Triandis and others. Although we speak of individualism and collectivism as if they are separate entities, it is important to keep in mind that all people and cultures have both individual and collective dispositions.

Individualism means that the individual is the single most important unit in any social setting, regardless of the size of that unit, and the uniqueness of each individual is of paramount value. According to Hofstede's findings, the United States, Australia, Great Britain, Canada, the Netherlands, and New Zealand tend toward individualism (see Table 3.1). Goleman highlights some of the characteristics of these and other cultures that value individualism:

> People's personal goals take priority over their allegiance to groups like the family or the employer. The loyalty of individualists to a given group is very weak; they feel

Source: Samovar, L. A., Porter, R. E. & Stefani, L. A. (1998). Hofstede's value dimensions and Hall's high context/low context. Selected from *Communication between cultures* (3rd edn) (pp. 66–73, 79–81). Belmont: Wadsworth.

Table 3.1 Ranking of forty countries or regions on individualism and collectivism*

Country or region	Ranking	Country or region	Ranking
Argentina	23	Japan	22
Australia	2	Mexico	29
Austria	18	Netherlands	5
Belgium	8	New Zealand	6
Brazil	25	Norway	13
Canada	4	Pakistan	38
Chile	33	Peru	37
Colombia	39	Philippines	28
Denmark	9	Portugal	30
Finland	17	Singapore	34
France	11	South Africa	16
Germany	15	Spain	20
Great Britain	3	Sweden	10
Greece	27	Switzerland	14
Hong Kong	32	Taiwan	36
India	21	Thailand	35
Iran	24	Turkey	26
Ireland	12	U.S.A.	1
Israel	19	Venezuela	40
Italy	7	Yugoslavia	31

* A high score means the country can be classified as collective; a lower score is associated with cultures that promote individualism.

Source: Adapted from Geert Hofstede (1980).

they belong to many groups and are apt to change their membership as it suits them, switching churches, for example, or leaving one employer for another.

(Goleman, 1990, p. 40)

In cultures that tend toward individualism, an "I" consciousness prevails: competition rather than cooperation is encouraged; personal goals take precedence over group goals; people tend not to be emotionally dependent on organizations and institutions; and every individual has the right to his or her private property, thoughts, and opinions. These cultures stress individual initiative and achievement, and they value individual decision making. When thrust into a situation that demands a decision, people from cultures that stress this trait are often at odds with people from collective cultures. This point is made by Foster:

At the negotiating table, differences in this dimension can clearly cause serious conflict. Individual responsibility for making decisions is easy in individualistic cultures; in group-oriented cultures this can be different. Americans too often expect their Japanese counterparts to make decisions right at the negotiating table, and the Japanese are constantly surprised to find individual members of the American team promoting their own positions, decisions, and ideas, sometimes openly contradicting one another.

(Foster, 1992, p. 267)

Collectivism is characterized by a rigid social framework that distinguishes between in-groups and out-groups. People count on their in-group (relatives, clans, organizations) to look after them, and in exchange for that they believe they owe absolute loyalty to the group. Triandis offers an excellent summary of this situation:

> Collectivism means greater emphasis on (a) the views, needs, and goals of the in-group rather than oneself; (b) social norms and duty defined by the in-group rather than behavior to get pleasure; (c) beliefs shared with the in-group rather than beliefs that distinguish self from in-group; and (d) great readiness to cooperate with in-group members.
>
> (Triandis, 1990, p. 52)

In collective societies such as those in Pakistan, Colombia, Venezuela, Taiwan, China, and Peru, people are born into extended families or clans that support and protect them in exchange for their loyalty. A "we" consciousness prevails: identity is based on the social system; the individual is emotionally dependent on organizations and institutions; the culture emphasizes belonging to organizations; organizations invade private life and the clans to which individuals belong; and individuals trust group decisions. Collective behavior, like so many aspects of culture, has deep historical roots. Look at the message of collectivism in these words from Confucius: "If one wants to establish himself, he should help others to establish themselves at first."

As is the case with all cultural patterns, collectivism influences a number of communication variables. Kim, Sharkey, and Singelis (1992), after studying the Korean culture, believe that traits such as indirect communication, saving face, concern for others, and group cooperation are linked to the collective orientation found in the Korean culture.

Numerous co-cultures in the United States can be classified as collective. Mexican Americans, for example, have most of the characteristics of collectivism mentioned by Triandis; and the research of Hecht, Collier, and Ribeau (1993) concludes that African Americans also have the characteristics of collective societies.

Triandis (1990, p. 48) estimated in 1990 that "about 70% of the population of the world lives in collective cultures." This fact alone should be sufficient motivation for members of other cultures to understand the perceptions and communication behaviors of these collective cultures. It is easy to imagine how differently cultures might approach the intercultural setting—whether that setting be a classroom or a factory. Knowing these and other differences in communication styles could facilitate successful intercultural communication.

Uncertainty avoidance

At the core of uncertainty avoidance is the inescapable truism that the future is unknown. Though we may all try, none of us can accurately predict the next moment, day, year, or decade. As the American playwright Tennessee Williams once noted, "The future is called 'perhaps,' which is the only possible thing to call the future." As the terms are used by Hofstede, *uncertainty* and *avoidance* indicate the extent to which a culture feels threatened by or anxious about uncertain and ambiguous situations.

High-uncertainty-avoidance cultures try to avoid uncertainty and ambiguity by providing stability for their members, establishing more formal rules, not tolerating deviant ideas and behaviors, seeking consensus, and believing in absolute truths and the attainment of expertise. They are also characterized by a higher level of anxiety and stress: people think of the uncertainty inherent in life as a continuous hazard that must be avoided. There is a strong need for written rules, planning, regulations, rituals, and ceremonies, which add structure to life. Nations with a strong uncertainty-avoidance tendency are Portugal, Greece, Peru, Belgium, and Japan (see Table 3.2).

At the other end of the scale we find countries like Sweden, Denmark, Ireland, Norway, the United States, Finland, and the Netherlands, which have a *low-uncertainty-avoidance* need. They more easily accept the uncertainty inherent in life and are not as threatened by deviant people and ideas, so they tolerate the unusual. They prize initiative, dislike the structure associated with hierarchy, are more willing to take risks, are more flexible, think that there should be as few rules as possible, and depend not so much on experts as on themselves, generalists, and common sense. As a whole, members of low-uncertainty-avoidance cultures are less tense and more relaxed—traits reflected in the Irish proverb "Life should be a dance, not a race."

As was the case with our first value dimension, differences in uncertainty avoidance affect intercultural communication. Imagine a negotiation session involving members from both groups. High-uncertainty-avoidance members would most likely want to move at a rather slow pace and ask for a greater amount of detail and planning. Some older members might also feel uncomfortable with young members of the group. There would also be differences in the level of formality with which each culture would feel comfortable. Low-uncertainty-avoidance

Table 3.2 Ranking of forty countries or regions on uncertainty avoidance*

Country or region	Ranking	Country or region	Ranking
Argentina	10	Japan	4
Australia	27	Mexico	12
Austria	19	Netherlands	26
Belgium	3	New Zealand	30
Brazil	16	Norway	28
Canada	31	Pakistan	18
Chile	6	Peru	7
Colombia	14	Philippines	33
Denmark	39	Portugal	2
Finland	24	Singapore	40
France	7	South Africa	29
Germany	21	Spain	9
Great Britain	35	Sweden	38
Greece	1	Switzerland	25
Hong Kong	37	Taiwan	20
India	34	Thailand	22
Iran	23	Turkey	11
Ireland	36	U.S.A.	32
Israel	13	Venezuela	15
Italy	17	Yugoslavia	5

* A low score means the country can be classified as one that does not like uncertainty; a high score is associated with cultures that do not feel uncomfortable with uncertainty.

Source: Adapted from Geert Hofstede (1980).

members would not become frustrated if the meeting was not highly structured. The negotiation process would see differences in the level of risk taking on each side. Americans, for example, would be willing to take a risk. As Harris and Moran (1996, p. 217) point out, "In light of their history, their perceptions of their rugged individualism, and the rewards of capitalism, Americans have embraced risk and are not risk avoidant."

Power distance

Another cultural-value dimension is *power distance*, which classifies cultures on a continuum of high- to low-power distance. The premise of the dimension deals with the extent to which a society accepts that power in relationships, institutions, and organizations is distributed unequally. Although all cultures have tendencies for both high- and low-power relationships, one orientation seems to dominate. Foster offers a clear and condensed explanation of this dimension:

> What Hofstede discovered was that in some cultures, those who hold power and those who are affected by power are significantly far apart (high power-distance) in many ways, while in other cultures, the power holders and those affected by the power holders are significantly closer (low power-distance).
>
> (Foster, 1992, p. 265)

This dimension is reflected in the values of the less powerful members of society as well as in those of the more powerful ones. People in *high-power-distance* countries such as India, Brazil, Singapore, Greece, Venezuela, Mexico, and the Philippines (see Table 3.3) believe that power and authority are facts of life. Both consciously and unconsciously, these cultures teach their members that people are not equal in this world and that everybody has a rightful place, which is clearly marked by countless vertical arrangements. Social hierarchy is prevalent and institutionalizes inequality.

We can observe signs of this dimension in nearly every communication setting. In schools that are characterized by high-power-distance patterns, children seldom interrupt the teacher, show great reverence and respect for authority, and ask very few questions. In organizations, you find a greater centralization of power, a large proportion of supervisory personnel, and a rigid value system that determines the worth of each job.

Low-power-distance countries such as Austria, Finland, Denmark, Norway, New Zealand, and Israel hold that inequality in society should be minimized. People in these cultures believe they are close to power and should have access to that power. To them, a hierarchy is an inequality of roles established for convenience. Subordinates consider superiors to be the same kind of people as they are, and superiors perceive their subordinates the same way. People in power, be they supervisors or government officials, often interact with their constituents and try to look less powerful than they really are. The powerful and the powerless try to live in concert.

Masculinity and femininity

Hofstede uses the words *masculinity* and *femininity* to refer not to men and women, but rather to the degree to which masculine or feminine traits prevail. *Masculinity* is the extent to which the dominant values in a society are male oriented and is associated with such behaviors as ambition, differentiated sex roles, achievement, the acquisition of money, and signs of manliness.

Table 3.3 Ranking of forty countries or regions on power distance*

Country or region	Ranking	Country or region	Ranking
Argentina	25	Japan	22
Australia	29	Mexico	2
Austria	40	Netherlands	28
Belgium	12	New Zealand	37
Brazil	7	Norway	34
Canada	27	Pakistan	21
Chile	15	Peru	13
Colombia	10	Philippines	1
Denmark	38	Portugal	16
Finland	33	Singapore	6
France	9	South Africa	24
Germany	30	Spain	20
Great Britain	31	Sweden	35
Greece	17	Switzerland	32
Hong Kong	8	Taiwan	19
India	4	Thailand	14
Iran	18	Turkey	11
Ireland	36	U.S.A.	26
Israel	39	Venezuela	3
Italy	23	Yugoslavia	5

* A low score means the country can be classified as one that prefers a large power distance; a high score is associated with cultures that prefer a small power distance.

Source: Adapted from Geert Hofstede (1980).

Ireland, the Philippines, Greece, South Africa, Austria, Japan, Italy, and Mexico are among countries that tend toward a masculine world view (see Table 3.4). In a masculine society, men are taught to be domineering and assertive and women nurturing. In Japan, for instance, despite the high level of economic development, the division of labor still finds most men in the role of provider and most women as, says Meguro (1988), "home-maker and breeder."

Cultures that value *femininity* as a trait stress caring and nurturing behaviors. A feminine world view maintains that men need not be assertive and that they can assume nurturing roles; it also promotes sexual equality and holds that people and the environment are important. Gender roles in feminine societies are more fluid than in masculine societies. Interdependence and androgynous behavior are the ideal, and people sympathize with the unfortunate. Nations such as Sweden, Norway, Finland, Denmark, and the Netherlands tend toward a feminine world view. As you might suspect, the acting out of gender roles influences communication. In masculine cultures, men do most of the talking and take an active role in decision making.

Some criticism has been leveled against Hofstede's work. First, since Hofstede's original study, numerous other studies have focused on individualism and collectivism; but the other three dimensions he studied lack what Draguns (1990, p. 368) called "systematic investigation." Second, because the people Hofstede surveyed were middle managers in large multinational organizations,

Table 3.4 Ranking of forty countries or regions on masculinity and femininity*

Country or region	Ranking	Country or region	Ranking
Argentina	18	Japan	1
Australia	14	Mexico	6
Austria	2	Netherlands	38
Belgium	20	New Zealand	15
Brazil	23	Norway	39
Canada	21	Pakistan	22
Chile	34	Peru	31
Colombia	11	Philippines	10
Denmark	37	Portugal	33
Finland	35	Singapore	24
France	29	South Africa	12
Germany	9	Spain	30
Great Britain	8	Sweden	40
Greece	16	Switzerland	5
Hong Kong	17	Taiwan	27
India	19	Thailand	32
Iran	28	Turkey	26
Ireland	7	U.S.A.	13
Israel	25	Venezuela	3
Italy	4	Yugoslavia	36

* A high score means the country can be classified as one that favors feminine traits; a lower score is associated with cultures that prefer masculine traits.

Source: Adapted from Geert Hofstede (1980).

most of his findings are work related. Third, many important countries and cultures were not included in Hofstede's study. For example, there were no Arab countries, and Africa was represented by only South Africa. Finally, Hofstede conducted his extensive study more than twenty years ago. Hence, many critics question the pertinence of his findings to the 1990s. We do not agree with this last charge. Although cultures change, we suggest that their deep structures are resistant to change. The values Hofstede studied were of those deep structures.

[. . .]

Hall's high-context and low-context communication

Hall (1976) offers us another effective means of examining cultural similarities and differences in both perception and communication. He categorizes cultures as being either high or low context, depending on the degree to which meaning comes from the settings or from the words being exchanged. The assumption underlying Hall's classifications is that "one of the functions of culture is to provide a highly selective screen between man and the outside world. In its many forms, culture therefore designates what we pay attention to and what we ignore" (1976, p. 74). The study of high-context and low-context cultures therefore offers us some insight into what people pay attention to and what they ignore.

The word *context*, as it is used by Hall and Hall, needs to be understood if one is to appreciate the link between context and communication. The Halls (1990, p. 6) define context as "the information that surrounds an event; it is inextricably bound up with the meaning of the event." They maintain that although all cultures contain some characteristics of both high and low variables, most can be placed along a scale showing their ranking on this particular dimension (see Table 3.5). The Halls define these two terms in the following manner:

> A high context (HC) communication or message is one in which most of the information is already in the person, while very little is in the coded, explicitly transmitted part of the message. A low context (LC) communication is just the opposite; i.e., the mass of the information is vested in the explicit code.
>
> (Hall, 1976, p. 79)

Table 3.5 Cultures arranged along the high-context and low-context dimension

High-context cultures
|
Japanese
|
Chinese
|
Korean
|
African American
|
Native American
|
Arab
|
Greek
|
Latin
|
Italian
|
English
|
French
|
American
|
Scandinavian
|
German
|
German–Swiss
|
Lower-context cultures

In *high-context* cultures (Native Americans, Latin Americans, Japanese, Chinese, and Korean), people are very homogeneous with regard to experiences, information networks, and the like. High-context cultures, because of tradition and history, change very little over time. These are cultures in which consistent messages have produced consistent responses to the environment. "As a result," the Halls (1990) say, "for most normal transactions in daily life they do not require, nor do they expect, much indepth, background information." Meaning, therefore, is not necessarily contained in words. In high-context cultures, information is provided through gestures, the use of space, and even silence. Meaning is also conveyed "through status (age, sex, education, family background, title, and affiliations) and through an individual's informal friends and associates." (Foster, 1992, p. 280)

In *low-context* cultures (German, Swiss, and American), the population is less homogeneous and therefore tends to compartmentalize interpersonal contacts. The Halls (1990, p. 7) say this lack of a large pool of common experiences means that "each time they interact with others they need detailed background information." In low-context cultures, the verbal message contains most of the information, and very little is embedded in the context or the participants. This characteristic manifests itself in a host of ways. For example, the Asian mode of communication is often indirect and implicit, whereas Western communication tends to be direct and explicit—that is, everything needs to be stated. Westerners are more prone to making very explicit statements and have little capability with nonverbal forms of expression (Servaes, 1988). High-context cultures tend to be more aware of their surroundings and their environment and do not rely on verbal communication as their main information channel. As an indicator of this, the Korean language contains the word *nunchi*, which means being able to communicate with the eyes. In high-context cultures, so much information is available in the environment that it is unnecessary to verbalize everything. For instance, statements of affection, such as "I love you," are rare because the message is conveyed by the context.

In addition to differences in nonverbal communication, there are other manifestations of high-context and low-context cultures that influence communication. For example, members of low-context cultures expect messages to be detailed, clear-cut, and definite. If there are not enough data, or if the point being made is not apparent, members of these cultures will ask very blunt, even curt, questions. They feel uncomfortable with the vagueness and ambiguity often associated with limited data. On the other hand, as the Halls (1990, p. 9) say, "High-context people are apt to become impatient and irritated when low-context people insist on giving them information they don't need."

Another problem is that people in high-context cultures perceive low-context people, who rely primarily on verbal messages for information, as less credible. They believe that silence often sends a better message than words, and anyone who needs words does not have the information. As the Indonesian proverb states, "Empty cans clatter the loudest."

Differences in this communication dimension can even alter how conflict is perceived and responded to. As Ting-Toomey has observed, the communication differences between high-context and low-context cultures are also apparent in the manner in which each approaches conflict. For example, because high-context cultures tend to be less open, they hold that conflict is damaging to most communication encounters. For them, Ting-Toomey (1997) says, "Conflict should be dealt with discreetly and subtly."

Harris and Moran (1996) summarize this dimension as follows:

Unless global leaders are aware of the subtle differences, communication misunderstandings between low- and high-context communicators can result. Japanese communicate by not stating things directly, while Americans usually do the opposite—

"spell it out." The former is looking for meaning and understanding in what is not said—in the nonverbal communication or body language, in the silences and pauses, in relationships and empathy. The latter places emphasis on sending and receiving accurate messages directly, usually by being articulate with words.

(Harris & Moran, 1996, p. 25)

References

Draguns, J. G. (1990). Normal and abnormal behaviour. In J. J. Berman (ed.), *Cross-cultural perspectives*. Lincoln: University of Nebraska Press.

Foster, D. A. (1992). *Bargaining across borders*. New York: McGraw-Hill.

Goleman, D. (1990). The group and self: new focus on a cultural rift, *New York Times*, December 22, 1990.

Hall, E. T. (1976). *Beyond culture*. Garden City, NY: Doubleday.

Hall, E. T. and Hall, M. R. (1990). *Understanding cultural differences: Germans, French and Americans*. Yarmouth, ME: Intercultural Press.

Harris, P. R. and Moran, R. T. (1996). *Managing cultural differences: leadership strategies for a new world of business*. Houston, TX: Gulf.

Hecht, M. L., Collier, M. J., and Ribeau, S. A. (1993). *African American communication: ethnic identity and interpretation*. Newbury Park, CA: Sage.

Hofstede, G. (1980). *Culture's consequences: international differences in work-related values*. Beverly, CA: Sage.

Hofstede, G. (1991). *Cultures and organisations: software of the mind*. London: McGraw-Hill.

Kim, M., Sharkey, W. F., and Singelis, T. (1992). Explaining individualist and collective communication—focusing on the perceived importance of interactive constraints. Paper presented at the Annual Convention of the Speech Communication Association, Chicago, October 1992.

Meguro, H. (1988). Address to the World Affairs Council, San Diego, CA, June 16, 1988.

Servaes, J. (1988). Cultural identity in East and West, *Howard Journal of Communications*, 1(2): 58–71.

Ting-Toomey, S. (1997). Managing intercultural conflicts effectively, in L. A. Samovar and R. E. Porter (eds), *Intercultural communication: a reader* (8th edn). Belmont, CA: Wadsworth.

Triandis, H. C. (1990). Cross-cultural studies of individualism and collectivism. In J. J. Berman (ed.), *Cross-cultural perspective*. Lincoln: University of Nebraska Press.

PART I: NOTES FOR STUDENTS AND INSTRUCTORS

Study questions

1   What is the empirical base of Whorf's argument that the linguistic label of the situation affects social behaviour?
2   Compare the grammatical patterns of Hopi and those of SAE and list three examples given by Whorf.
3   Discuss Whorf's view on the relationship between language and thought.
4   What examples or evidence does Nisbett use to argue that there are substantial differences in language usage between 'Easterners' and 'Westerners'? Compare them with Whorf's examples as in Question 2. Which ones do you think are more convincing and why?
5   Discuss Nisbett's view on the relationship between language and thought and compare his with Whorf's. What is your own take on the relationship?
6   Define Hofstede's four cultural dimensions and give examples in everyday life that reflect these cultural orientations.
7   What are the criticisms of Hofstede's work? Do you agree with them?
8   Define high context and low context and give examples in everyday life that reflect these cultural orientations.

Study activities

1   Translate the following sentences into any language(s) you know and then translate them back into English. Compare the sentences in English with the translation and then the version translated back into English. Discuss whether there are differences between different versions and why? Do the differences in linguistic structure impact on the way you think in a particular language? Relate your discussion to Whorf's argument.

   •   He likes her.
   •   It is 5 o'clock in the morning.
   •   Could you please lend me a hand?

2   Replicate Nisbett's study on bilingual Chinese/English speakers, but use bilingual speakers of different language pairs, for example English and Spanish. You need two groups of

bilingual speakers: one group with English as their first language and Spanish as their second language; the other group with Spanish as their first language and English as the second. Compare your findings with Nisbett's and discuss: (a) whether the language of the test makes any difference to the results; and (b) whether bilingual conditions make any difference to the results.

3   Select one of forty countries included in Hofstede's ranking of value dimensions. It could be your home country, or a country you or your friends know well. What is the ranking of the country in each dimension? Are they consistent with your own or your friends' experience? If yes, can you give examples? If not, why?

Further reading

On the relationship between language, culture and thought, see:

Kramsch, C. (2004). Language, thought and culture. In A. Davies & C. Elder (eds), *The handbook of applied linguistics* (pp. 235–61). Malden, MA: Blackwell.

Gumperz, J. & Levinson, S. (eds) (1996). *Rethinking linguistic relativity*. Cambridge: Cambridge University Press.

Criticism of the empirical base in Whorf's argument can be found in:

Pullman, G. K. (1991). *The great Eskimo vocabulary hoax and other irreverent essays on the study of language*. Chicago: The University of Chicago.

Counter-arguments towards linguistic relativity can be found in:

Pinker, S. (1994). *The language instinct: how the mind creates language*. New York: Harper & Row.

On cultural values, see:

Hofstede, G. (2001). *Cultural consequences* (2nd edn). Thousand Oaks, CA: Sage.

Hall, E. T. (1976). *Beyond culture*. Garden City, NY: Doubleday.

Criticism of Hofstede's model can be found in:

McSweeney, B. (2002). Hofstede's model of national cultural differences and their consequences: a triumph of faith—a failure of analysis. *Human Relations*, 55(1), 89–118.

The exchange of opinions between two differing – but both influential – proponents, featured in the following articles gives an insight into the logic and working process of the models:

Hofstede, G. (1996). Riding the waves of commerce: a test of Trompenaars' model of national culture differences. *International Journal of Intercultural Relations*, 20(2), 189–98.

Hampden-Turner, C. & Trompenaars, F. (1997). Response to Geert Hofstede. *International Journal of Intercultural Relations*, 21(1), 149–59.

PART II

Cultural approaches to discourse and pragmatics: theoretical considerations

Introduction to Part II

Zhu Hua

THIS PART OF THE *READER* CONTINUES TO explore the interplay between language and culture, but from a different angle. The central question addressed by the articles reprinted in this part is whether or not there are culturally specific patterns in language use, and if so, how should they be described and explained. The reproduced articles include some of the most influential theories and models in discourse analysis and pragmatics that are focused specifically on intercultural communication issues. Chapters 4–6 are on the politeness theory and the notion of face; Chapter 7 is on rapport management, and Chapter 8 on cultural scripts. While the authors of these articles start with the intention to account for cultural variations in language use, the theories and models they have developed have a universal appeal. Therefore, although the majority of the articles in this part use examples of communication patterns in East Asian cultures, the ideas put forward in these studies can be used in analysing discourse and pragmatics in other cultures as well.

The politeness theory, with the notion of face at its core, was proposed by Brown & Levinson (1978) to explain why people choose one particular linguistic form over another when they interact with each other, in their attempt to capture universals in language use. In Brown and Levinson's framework, every model person is assumed to possess a self-image and a desire to project it in public (i.e. face). They saw face as a sociopsychological construct consisting of two dimensions: the desire to be approved of by others (positive face) and the desire to be unimpeded in one's actions (negative face). The politeness theory has inspired numerous studies that have tried either to apply the theory to various cultures and languages or to refine, expand or challenge it. The first article in this part, by Scollon and Scollon, revisits and redefines the notions of face and politeness. They examine the influential factors in politeness/face systems from the perspective of interpersonal communication. What is of particular interest is that Scollon and Scollon choose to define the two sides of face as involvement vs. independence, rather than positive vs. negative. Their formulation may help to get round the potential problem of associating 'positive' politeness with something desirable and 'negative' politeness with something unwanted, a common confusion in applying Brown and Levinson's original framework. The term 'involvement' has been previously used by Tannen (1984) to refer to a type of conversational style, and it is different from the way it is used in Scollon and Scollon's article.

Although Brown and Levinson themselves acknowledge that their definition of face and classification of what constituted positive and negative faces should be subject to cultural elaboration to a certain extent, their theoretical framework has come under constant criticism for the apparent cultural bias. One problem has been the way face, originally a cultural notion, was reconstructed as a sociopsychological concept with binary choices. As Gu's article (Chapter 5) demonstrates, there are many different dimensions of face other than the positive and negative dichotomy that Brown and Levinson have postulated. What counts as politeness is therefore culture- and language-specific. The essential and different elements underlying the Chinese concept of *limao* (politeness) and the linguistic means of fulfilling the expectations of these key elements are discussed in detail in Gu's article.

In a similar vein, Ide's article (Chapter 6) challenges the universality of the politeness theory by arguing that Japanese honorifics (listed as a negative strategy in Brown and Levinson's framework) signify, not only politeness, but also the speaker's dignity and/or elegance and therefore serve as an integrated part of the language and culture rather than something that can be rectified or removed. She argues that a specific term, *wakimae*, should be used to incorporate the ritualistic aspect of language use, as in the case of honorifics. Her account of the notion of high context and its implications for linguistic relativity extend the articles in Part I.

Spencer-Oatey (Chapter 7) further extends the debate on the effectiveness of the politeness theory by proposing a rapport-management framework. She argues that it is important to consider the motivational concerns in interactions to take account of the situated socio-psychological context in which interactions occur. In her framework, face has two interrelated aspects: quality face (the desire to be evaluated positively) and social identity face (the desire for others to acknowledge and uphold their social identities or roles). The crucial difference between Spencer-Oatey's model and that of Brown and Levinson is that the former brings motivational concerns into clearer focus.

There is a risk of over-emphasizing the differences in studying cultural patterns in discourse and communication. Cultural variations exist and are important. Nevertheless, to account for the variations and differences, it is useful to have a framework or a tool that is relatively culturally neutral, free from language bias and applicable not only to one specific culture but to a range of different cultures. Such a framework or tool would allow meaningful comparisons, which are crucial to effective intercultural communication. Yet it has proved to be particularly challenging to develop such a framework, as the minute we start thinking and writing in a particular language, we cannot help bringing in a set of assumptions and ways of interpretation associated with that language. This may well be why many models that are developed on English language data are criticised for being 'Anglocentric' or 'terminologically ethnocentric', i.e. generalising on cultural and language practices on the basis of one's own or Anglo norms or practices. The concept of cultural scripts, as introduced in Chapter 8, is intended to express cultural norms, values and practices in a way free from cultural and language bias, yet at the same time being 'clear, precise and accessible' to cultural insiders and outsiders alike. The cultural scripts claiming to be culturally and linguistically neutral rely crucially on the employment of a set of simple, indefinable and universally lexicalised concepts such as *I, you, do, good, bad,* etc. Some examples of cultural scripts are provided in Chapter 8, alongside the authors' observations on what cultural scripts can do compared with other, more conventional approaches.

References

Brown, P. & Levinson, S. (1978). Universals in language use: politeness phenomena. In E. Goody (ed.), *Questions and politeness: strategies in social interaction.* New York: Cambridge University Press. Republished as (1987). *Politeness.* Cambridge: Cambridge University Press.

Tannen, D. (1984). *Conversational style: analyzing talk among friends.* Norwood, NJ: Ablex.

Chapter 4

RON SCOLLON AND
SUZANNE WONG SCOLLON

INTERPERSONAL POLITENESS
AND POWER

Communicative style or register

ON NATHAN ROAD IN TSIM SHA TSUI, one of Hong Kong's most crowded tourist and shopping areas, two men passed by a vendor of imitation Rolex watches.

Vendor (to first man):	Eh! Copy watch?
Vendor (to second man):	Rolex? Sir?

Both of the passers-by were Americans. The first was apparently a sailor from a US Navy ship in port at that time. This man was together with several other men who also looked like they might be American sailors. The second man the vendor of copy Rolexes spoke to was in his mid-fifties and dressed much more formally in a suit coat.

In speaking to these two men, the vendor of copy Rolexes made a shift in register or communicative style. When he spoke to the first man (who was quite a bit younger than the vendor) he used a very informal or familiar style. He addressed him with, "Eh!," and referred to the item for sale as a "copy watch." When he spoke to the second man (who was quite a bit older than the vendor) he used a more formal or deferential form of address, "Sir!," and referred to the item for sale as a "Rolex."

In this case the vendor used somewhat limited linguistic resources to signal that he had perceived a social difference between these two potential customers. This is very much like the example we gave above at the beginning of chapter 2, when Mr. Hutchins referred to his subordinate as Bill.

Linguists have used many different terms to refer to such shifts in linguistic form when those shifts are used to indicate changes in components of speech events or speech situations. Among linguists, the term "register" tends to be associated mostly with particular scenes, and "communicative style" tends to be associated with participants, though these are not clear distinctions in many cases. For example, a greeting might be given in a very informal way if you meet a friend casually on the street, but much more formally if the two of you are

Source: Scollon, R. & Scollon, S.W. (2001). Interpersonal politeness and power. In *Intercultural communication* (Chapter 3, pp. 43–59). Malden, MA: Blackwell.

participating in a board meeting. While the participants remain the same, the greeting will vary in register because of the different setting.

"Communicative style" is the term we prefer for this article on interpersonal politeness and power because it is a more general term than "register," used by most sociolinguists to refer to either personal identities or interpersonal relationships among participants. We would not say, for example, that Rebecca has an interesting register but we might say that she has an interesting communicative style. On the other hand we could say that Fiona is very good at choosing the appropriate register or communicative style for any situation. In other words, the term "communicative style" is less restrictive and can include the concept of register.

Face

The question of human psychological identity is a complex issue that goes beyond the study of communication into psychology, sociology, and philosophy. Nevertheless, there is an important aspect of identity that has been recognized as an essential element in all communication, [. . .] i.e., the interpersonal identity of the individuals in communication.

The concept of face is not new to Asian readers, who will recognize the term *mianzi* in Mandarin (*minji* in Cantonese, *mentsu* in Japanese, *chae myon* in Korean), where it carries a range of meanings based upon a core concept of "honor," but perhaps the way it is used in contemporary sociolinguistics and sociology will be somewhat different. The concept first was introduced by the Chinese anthropologist Hu in 1944, though the term had been used in English for at least several centuries before that. The American sociologist Erving Goffman (1967) based much of his work on interpersonal relationships on the concept of face.[1]

One of the most important ways in which we reduce the ambiguity of communication is by making assumptions about the people we are talking to. As the simplest example, when we begin talking to someone we try to speak to them in a language we know they will understand. In a monolingual speech community that is rarely a problem, but in the increasingly multilingual international business community it is becoming a major issue, to be solved right at the outset of communications.

We also make significant assumptions about what kind of a person the other person is and what kind of a person he or she would like us to think of him or her as being. When Mr. Hutchins called his subordinate colleague by his first name, Bill, he projected the assumption that there was a difference in status between them and he also projected that they both would agree to that difference in status by simply using the name Bill without further comment. Bill, in turn, projected that he accepted that difference in status and ratified that by calling his employer Mr. Hutchins.

Many aspects of linguistic form depend on the speakers making some analysis of the relationships among themselves. The choice of terms of address is one of the first of these recognized by sociolinguists. The watch vendor in Tsim Sha Tsui also recognized that different forms of address, "Eh!" or "Sir!", were appropriate in trying to catch the attention of two different potential customers. The study of face in sociolinguistics arose out of the need to understand how participants decide what their relative statuses are and what language they use to encode their assumptions about such differences in status, as well as their assumptions about the face being presented by participants in communication.

Within sociological and sociolinguistic studies face is usually given the following general definition: "*Face is the negotiated public image, mutually granted each other by participants in a communicative event.*" In this definition and in the work of sociolinguistics the emphasis is not so much on shared assumptions as it is on the negotiation of face. For our purposes we want to keep both aspects of face in mind. We believe that while there is much negotiation of face in any form of interpersonal communication, participants must also make assumptions about face before they can begin any communication.

We do not have to figure out everything from the beginning every time we talk to someone. Mr. Hutchins and Bill do not need to open up negotiations about their relationship each time they speak to each other. Just the fact that Mr. Hutchins is Bill's employer is sufficient information to know that they differ in status. Knowing that difference in status and how it is normally expressed in English, we can predict fairly accurately that Bill will say "Mr. Hutchins," and Mr. Hutchins will say "Bill."

Participants make certain unmarked assumptions about their relationships and about the face they want to claim for themselves and are willing to give to the other participants in any communicative situation. In addition to these unmarked assumptions, participants also undertake a certain amount of negotiation of their relationships as a natural process of change in human relationships. For example, if a person wants to ask a rather large favor of another person, he or she is likely to begin with the assumed relationship, but then he or she will begin to negotiate a closer or more intimate relationship. If such a closeness is achieved then he or she is likely to feel it is safer to risk asking for the favor than if their negotiations result in more distance between them.

In the field of sociolinguistics this combination of unmarked assumptions about the participants and their relationships with the negotiations about those assumptions is called the study of face. Such study also goes by the name of politeness theory.

The "self" as a communicative identity

One reason the term "face" is attractive in communicative studies is that it leaves open the question of who is the "real" person underneath the face which is presented in communication. That deeper question is ultimately a question of psychology or, perhaps, philosophy, and we will not go further into it. Nevertheless, it is important to point out now that there may be significant cultural differences in the assumptions made about the "self" that is involved in communication. The idea of "self" which underlies western studies of communication is highly individualistic, self-motivated, and open to ongoing negotiation. We believe that this concept of the "self" is not entirely appropriate as the basis for Asian communication. There is reason to believe that the "self" projected by Asians is a more collectivistic "self," one which is more connected to membership in basic groups such as the family or one's working group and which is taken to be more strongly under the influence of assumed or unmarked cultural assumptions about face.

The paradox of face: involvement and independence

Face is really a paradoxical concept. By this we mean that there are two sides to it which appear to be in contrast. On the one hand, in human interactions we have a need to be involved with other participants and to show them our involvement. On the other hand, we need to maintain some degree of independence from other participants and to show them that we respect their independence. These two sides of face, involvement and independence, produce an inherently paradoxical situation in all communications, in that *both* aspects of face must be projected simultaneously in any communication.[2]

The involvement aspect of face is concerned with the person's right and need to be considered a normal, contributing, or supporting member of society. This involvement is shown through being a normal and contributing participant in communicative events. One shows involvement by taking the point of view of other participants, by supporting them in the views they take, and by any other means that demonstrate that the speaker wishes to uphold a commonly created view of the world.

Involvement is shown by such discourse strategies as paying attention to others, showing a strong interest in their affairs, pointing out common in-group membership or points of view with them, or using first names. As we will indicate below, we might say such things as, "Are you feeling well today?" or, "I know just what you mean, the same thing happened to me yesterday," or, "Yes, I agree, I've always believed that, too." Any indication that the speaker is asserting that he or she is closely connected to the hearer may be considered a strategy of involvement.

Many other terms have been used in the sociolinguistic literature to present this concept. It has been called positive face, for example, on the basis of the idea of the positive and negative poles of magnetism. The positive poles of a magnet attract, and by analogy involvement has been said to be the aspect of communication in which two or more participants show their common attraction to each other.

Involvement has also been called solidarity politeness; again, for the reason that sociolinguists want to emphasize that this aspect of face shows what participants have in common. Any of these terms might be acceptable in some contexts, but we feel that the term "involvement" is clearest and creates the fewest analytical complications for the reader.

The independence aspect of face emphasizes the individuality of the participants. It emphasizes their right not to be completely dominated by group or social values, and to be free from the impositions of others. Independence shows that a person may act with some degree of autonomy and that he or she respects the rights of others to their own autonomy and freedom of movement or choice.

Independence is shown by such discourse strategies as making minimal assumptions about the needs or interests of others, by not "putting words into their mouths," by giving others the widest range of options, or by using more formal names and titles. For example, in ordering in a restaurant we might say, "I don't know if you will want to have rice or noodles," or in making the initial suggestion to go out for coffee we might say, "I'd enjoy going out for coffee, but I imagine you are very busy." The key to independence face strategies is that they give or grant independence to the hearer.

Independence has also been given various other names by researchers in sociolinguistics. It has been called negative politeness, as an analogy with the negative pole of a magnet, which repels. We prefer not to use this term, because technical or formal contrast between "positive" and "negative" can easily be forgotten, and readers can too easily begin to think of "positive politeness" as good and "negative politeness" as bad.

Another term which has been used as an attempt to get around the potential negative aspects of "positive" and "negative" politeness has been "deference politeness." We have used "solidarity" and "deference" in earlier writings, but find that some readers have a strong preference for one type of strategy or the other and, again, miss the point that *both* aspects of face must be projected simultaneously in any communication.

The most important concept to remember about face is that it is paradoxical. By that we mean the concept of face has built into it *both* aspects; involvement *and* independence must be projected simultaneously in any communication. It is always a matter of more or less, not absolute expression of just one or the other. A speaker must find just the right way of saying something which shows the degree to which he or she is involving the other participants and the degree to which he or she is granting independence to them.

The reason involvement and independence are in conflict is that emphasizing one of them risks a threat to the other. If I show you too much involvement, you are likely to feel that your independence is being threatened. On the other hand, if I grant you too much independence, you are likely to feel that I have limited your involvement.

Any communication is a risk to face; it is a risk to one's own face at the same time it is a risk to the other person's. We have to carefully project a face for ourselves and to respect the face rights and claims of other participants. We risk our own involvement face if we do not include other participants in our relationship. That is, if we exclude others, while that may increase our own independence, it at the same time decreases our own involvement. At the same time, if we include others, we risk our own independence face.

Looking at it from the other person's point of view, if we give too much involvement to the other person, we risk their independence face. On the other hand, if we give them too much independence, we risk their involvement.

The result of the double risk, the risk to involvement face and the risk to independence face of both the speaker and the hearer, means, therefore, that all communication has to be carefully phrased to respect face, both involvement face and independence face. This could be said another way: "*There is no faceless communication.*"

Politeness strategies of involvement and independence

Now that we have given you a general introduction to the concept of face in interpersonal communication, we hope that we can make this discussion clearer by giving a number of examples of actual linguistic strategies which are used to communicate these different face strategies.

The most extreme contrast between involvement and independence is the difference between speaking (or communicating) and silence (or non-communication). Any form of communication at all is somewhat on the side of involvement. In order to communicate at all, the participants must share some aspects of symbolic systems which they can interpret in shared ways. If I speak to you and you are able to answer me, we have already shared some small degree of involvement. As a result we would classify speech on the side of involvement, and silence (or better still, non-communication) on the side of independence.

Perhaps it is important to clarify that there are silences which can be interpreted as high involvement as well. We know that two people who share a very intimate situation can communicate to each other a high degree of involvement while remaining completely silent. That is why we have rephrased "silence" as "non-communication" above. It is the silence of non-communication to which we refer when we say it is at the independence end of the continuum. One grants (and claims for oneself) the highest level of independence by having no communication with the other.

Taciturnity and volubility are somewhat lesser extremes of non-communication and communication. Taciturnity means, simply, not talking very much. Volubility is the other side of the coin, "talking a lot." Both of these are highly relative terms. There is no absolute amount of speech which can be classed as taciturn or as voluble. The same is true for individuals; there are no absolutely taciturn or voluble individuals. Likewise there are no absolutely taciturn or voluble groups, or societies, or cultures.

Nevertheless, one aspect of the grammar of context is expectations of the amount of speech. For example, many religious rites or ceremonies are very restricted in the amount of incidental conversational or non-formal speech expected. In such a situation, a person who was speaking at all might be perceived as being very voluble. On the other hand, at a friendly dinner party among close friends, a person who was speaking, but not to any great extent, might be considered to be taciturn, because the expectations are for a good bit of conversational exchange.

Psychological studies of conversational exchanges and formal interviews have shown that the more talk there is, the more these exchanges are perceived as "warm" or "affiliative." In contrast, the less talk there is, the more they are perceived as "cold" or "non-affiliative." On the basis of this designation of "affiliative," we believe that it is best to consider more talk, volubility, to be an involvement strategy, and less talk, taciturnity, to be an independence strategy.

From the point of view of face relationships, we have said above that any communication is based on sharing a symbolic system, and that such a sharing is already to some degree an expression of involvement. Therefore, the question of what language to use is a crucial one in international business and government relationships as well as within bilingual or multilingual speech communities. If negotiations are conducted among participants using different languages (but, of course, with translators), this is a situation of lesser involvement or of higher independence than if negotiations are conducted using the same language. Therefore, it is a question of face relationships to decide whether discussions should go on in separate languages mediated by translators or whether they should go on in a common language. Naturally, of course, if the negotiations go on in the native language of one of the participants (or group of participants) that will tip the balance of involvement toward their side. It will give the other participants a sense of having their own independence limited, perhaps even unduly. At the same time, an insistence on the use of separate languages to overcome this problem can produce a sense of too great an independence, which can be felt as hostility or unwillingness to come to a common ground of agreement. The choice of language in discourse is not simply a matter of practical choice governed by efficiency of communication of information. Every such choice is also a matter of the negotiation of the face of the participants.

Linguistic strategies of involvement: some examples

There are many ways in which involvement can be shown through linguistic form. The examples which follow are just ten types which have been selected from English. While there is some disagreement among researchers about exactly which linguistic forms will be used in different languages to indicate these strategies, the examples here will give you a general idea of what we mean by linguistic strategies of involvement. (In these examples the letter "H" represents the "Hearer" to whom one is speaking, and "S" represents the "Speaker.")

1 Notice or attend to H:
   "I like your jacket."
   "Are you feeling better today?"
2 Exaggerate (interest, approval, sympathy with H):
   "Please be careful on the steps, they're very slippery."
   "You always do so well in school."
3 Claim in-group membership with H:
   "All of *us here* at City Polytechnic . . ."
4 Claim common point of view, opinions, attitudes, knowledge, empathy:
   "I know *just* how you feel. I had a cold like that last week."
5 Be optimistic:
   "I think we should be able to finish that annual report very quickly."

6   Indicate S knows H's wants and is taking them into account:
    "I'm sure you will all want to know when this meeting will be over."
7   Assume or assert reciprocity:
    "I know you want to do well in sales this year as much as I want you to do well."
8   Use given names and nicknames:
    "Bill, can you get that report to me by tomorrow?"
9   Be voluble.
10 Use H's language or dialect.

Linguistic strategies of independence: some examples

As in the case of involvement, there are many ways in which independence can be reflected linguistically. The ten types below have been selected from among the most common used in English. Again, "H" refers to the "Hearer" and "S" to the "Speaker."

1   Make minimal assumptions about H's wants:
    "I don't know if you will want to send this by air mail or by speedpost."
2   Give H the option not to do the act:
    "It would be nice to have tea together, but I am sure you are very busy."
3   Minimize threat:
    "I just need to borrow a little piece of paper, any scrap will do."
4   Apologize:
    "I'm sorry to trouble you, could you tell me the time?"
5   Be pessimistic:
    "I don't suppose you'd know the time, would you?"
6   Dissociate S, H from the discourse:
    "This is to inform our employees that . . ."
7   State a general rule:
    "Company regulations require an examination . . ."
8   Use family names and titles:
    "Mr. Lee, there's a phone call for you."
9   Be taciturn.
10 Use own language or dialect.

Politeness (or face) systems

We have said above that face relationships between and among participants consist of two elements: an unmarked set of initial assumptions and a series of negotiations in which those unmarked assumptions are either ratified or altered in some way. Under normal circumstances, face relationships remain fairly stable, and negotiation of the overriding relationship is relatively minor. When the assistant manager of a sales department meets with his or her manager, the relationship is not likely to change from meeting to meeting. Once it has been established at the beginning of employment in that position, it is likely to remain the same until one or the other moves to a different position.

We could describe such general and persistent regularities in face relationships as politeness systems. For example, Mr. Hutchins can be expected to always address Bill by his first name, and Bill is likely to always say "Mr." when speaking to Mr. Hutchins. Such a regular relationship indicates what we would call a politeness system, because both speakers in the system would use a certain fairly regular set of face strategies in speaking to each other.

There are three main factors involved which bring such a politeness (or face) system into being: power, distance, and the weight of the imposition.

Power (+P, −P)

In discussions of face or politeness systems, "power" refers to the vertical disparity between the participants in a hierarchical structure. In other words, Mr. Hutchins is above Bill in the hierarchical structure of their company. We would describe their relationship as +P (plus power) because Mr. Hutchins has special privileges (and, of course, responsibilities) over Bill, and Bill owes certain duties to Mr. Hutchins. In most business and governmental structures, the organization chart shows quite explicitly what the +P relationships are. As a result the language used between such participants is relatively predictable.

In contrast to such a situation, where there is little or no hierarchical difference between participants, we would consider that to be −P or an egalitarian system. Close friends generally share a −P relationship, since neither one is considered above the other. But the relationship does not have to be among close friends. Two people who have equivalent ranks in their own companies or their own organizations might have a −P relationship even though they do not know each other at all. In international protocols in both business and government, most communications are attempted at the same level so that −P relationships can be achieved. Company presidents talk to company presidents, assistant sales managers deal with other assistant sales managers, ambassadors talk to ambassadors, and clerks talk to clerks.

Distance (+D, -D)

The distance between two participants should not be confused with the power difference between them. Distance can be seen most easily in egalitarian relationships (−P). For example, two close friends would be classified as −D because of the closeness of their relationship. On the other hand, two governmental officials of different nations are likely to be of equal power within their systems but distant, +D.

Even within a single business organization, power (P) is not the same as distance (D). The head of the personnel office and his or her staff will have a hierarchical relationship (+P), but most likely will have a close (−D) relationship because they work together daily. Those same employees will have a hierarchical difference *and* a distance between them and the head of, say, the quality control department within the same company (+D, +P), because they rarely have contact with each other.

Weight of imposition (+W, −W)

The third factor that will influence face strategies is the weight of the imposition.[3] Even if two participants in a speech event have a very fixed relationship between them, the face strategies they will use will vary depending on how important the topic of discussion is for them. For example, if Bill is talking to Mr. Hutchins about a routine daily business matter, their face strategies will be quite predictable. On the other hand, if Bill has decided that today is the day to approach Mr. Hutchins about getting a promotion, he is likely to take on an extra-deferential tone and use a much higher level of independence strategies than he normally uses. Or on the other side of it, if Mr. Hutchins has to approach Bill with some rather bad news, perhaps that his position is going to be eliminated, he will use a much lower level of involvement than he customarily uses.

In other words, when the weight of imposition increases, there will be an increased use of independence strategies. When the weight of imposition decreases, there will be an increased use of involvement strategies.

From this you should be able to see that in relatively fixed interpersonal relationships, such as those within a business or some other organization, power (P) and distance (D) are not likely to change very rapidly or very frequently, and what is mostly under negotiation will have to do with the weight of imposition (W).

Because our focus is now on politeness or face systems and not on individual situational relationships, weight of imposition will not be a major factor in the discussion which follows. We will focus primarily on systems which develop through the variations in power and distance.

Three politeness systems: deference, solidarity, and hierarchy

Three main types of politeness system can be observed in many different contexts. These are based primarily on whether there is a power difference (+P or –P) and on the distance between participants (+D or –D). We have called them the deference politeness system, the solidarity politeness system, and the hierarchical politeness system.

Deference politeness system (–P, +D)

If a university professor named Dr. Wong from Hong Kong meets a university professor from Tokyo named Dr. Hamada, they are likely to refer to each other as "Professor Wong" and "Professor Hamada." In such a system they would treat each other as equals and use a relatively high concentration of independence politeness strategies out of respect for each other and for their academic positions. Such a system of mutual but distant independence is what we mean by a deference politeness system.

A deference politeness system is one in which participants are considered to be equals or near equals but treat each other at a distance. Relationships among professional colleagues who do not know each other well are one example.

The characteristics of this system are that it is:

1   symmetrical (–P), that is, the participants see themselves as being at the same social level;
2   distant (+D), that is, each uses independence strategies speaking to the other.

Such a face system can be sketched as in Figure 4.1.

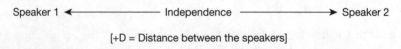

[+D = Distance between the speakers]

Figure 4.1 Deference politeness system

One could find deference politeness anywhere the system is egalitarian but participants maintain a deferential distance from each other. Much international political protocol is based on this system, where equals from each government meet but are cautious about forming unnecessarily close ties.

Solidarity politeness system (–P, –D)

When two close friends have a conversation with each other they exemplify a solidarity face system. There is a high level of involvement politeness strategies. There is no feeling of either a power difference (–P) or distance (–D) between them.

The characteristics of this solidarity face system are that it is:

1   symmetrical (–P), that is, the participants see themselves as being in equal social position;
2   close (–D), that is, the participants both use politeness strategies of involvement.

Such a face system can be sketched as in Figure 4.2.

Speaker 1 ◄——— Involvement ———► Speaker 2

[–D = Minimal distance between the speakers]

Figure 4.2 Solidarity politeness system

One could find solidarity politeness anywhere the system is egalitarian and participants feel or express closeness to each other. Friendships among close colleagues are often solidarity systems. For example, Professor Wong, who calls Professor Hamada "Professor" or "Doctor," might call a colleague in his own department with whom he works every day by some much more familiar name. Those familiar with North American business will recognize this pattern as one Americans adopt very quickly in business relationships, especially in sales and marketing.

Hierarchical politeness system (+P, ±D)

The third politeness system is hierarchical. In such a system the participants recognize and respect the social differences that place one in a superordinate position and the other in a subordinate position. This is the system of face in which Mr. Hutchins speaks "down" to his employee Bill, and Bill speaks "up" to his superior, Mr. Hutchins. The main characteristic of this system is the recognized difference in status, for which we are using the designation +P. It may be of much less significance whether or not there is distance between the participants. For our purposes we have considered this system to be either close or distant, +P or –P.

In such a face system the relationships are asymmetrical. By that we mean that the participants do not use the same face politeness strategies in speaking to each other. The person in the superordinate or upper position uses involvement strategies in speaking "down." The person in the subordinate or lower position uses independence strategies in speaking "up." Calling someone by his or her surname and title (Mr. Hutchins) is an independence strategy. Calling someone by his or her given name without a title (Bill) is an involvement strategy.

The characteristics of this hierarchical face system are that it is:

1   asymmetrical (+P), that is, the participants see themselves as being in unequal social position;
2   asymmetrical in face strategies, that is, the "higher" uses involvement face strategies, and the "lower" uses independence face strategies.

Such a face system can be sketched as in Figure 4.3.

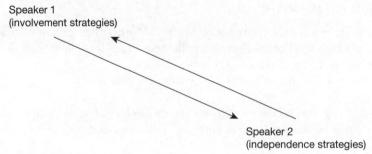

Speaker 1
(involvement strategies)

Speaker 2
(independence strategies)

Figure 4.3 Hierarchical politeness system

This sort of hierarchical face system is quite familiar in business, governmental, and educational organizations. In fact, it could be said to be the most common sort of organizational relationship, as indicated in tables of organization.

A sociolinguistic survey of many different communicative systems shows that the factors of power (or hierarchy) and distance may arise for many different reasons. In some societies or at some times in history, power differences (+P) arise based on differences in age, gender, wealth, hunting prowess, ability to entertain, education, physical strength or beauty, membership of particular families, or color of hair or skin. In fact, almost any element of human life which can be easily perceived by others has at some time or other been the basis for making hierarchical distinctions.

In the same way, distance (+D) can arise for perhaps all of the same factors. Members of one's family might be close (–D) while all others are distant (+D), or family members of one gender are close while those of the other gender might be distant. It has been said that Alpinists in Germany switch from the distant forms of the pronouns for "you" (the so-called V-forms) to the close forms (the so-called T-forms) of the pronouns when their climb brings them above the tree line. In some Asian business circles, late-night entertainment might bring out strategies of involvement indicating little distance (–D) which will then be reversed to the more normal distant (+D) strategies of independence in the next working day in the office.

We are most concerned that the reader understand the main properties of these three systems of face. Two of them are symmetrical: the deference system and the solidarity system. One of them is asymmetrical: the hierarchical system. In the first, all participants use on balance a greater proportion of independence face strategies. In the second, all participants use on balance a greater proportion of involvement face strategies. In the hierarchical face system, however, because it is asymmetrical, the participants use *different* face strategies; involvement strategies are used "downward" and independence strategies are used "upward."

Miscommunication

We have a friend who in learning Spanish could never get right the differences between the familiar set of pronouns and the formal set of pronouns. He found it difficult to remember when he should say, "*Usted*" ("you" formally), and when he should say, "*Tu*" ("you" informally). He simplified the whole system by just insisting on using the T-forms.

This, of course, presented a major problem for Spanish speakers in Mexico, where he was living at that time. As a foreigner he was expected to use the formal terms, the "*Usted*" forms of politeness. In other words, he was expected to use independence strategies of politeness. But he was not using them; he was using the T-forms, the involvement forms. In Mexican social terms there were only two contexts in which he could use the involvement forms: either if he was a very good friend or if he was trying to pick a fight (that is, if it was an attempt to assert power over the other). In other words, the solidarity system is used only among intimates.

Remember that when one participant uses involvement face strategies and the other uses independence strategies, the one using the involvement strategies is the *higher* of the two. When someone addresses you as Mr. Schneider and you answer back, "Juan," whatever your intentions might be, what he hears is the same thing we read above between Mr. Hutchins and Bill: we hear one person taking a higher position over the other. In the interpersonal world of Mexican conversations this sounded like trying to put someone down or to insult him or her by taking a superior position.

Our friend had thus presented our Mexican friends with a problem. Within their cultural interpretation of these face strategies, they expected a deference politeness system. When he used an involvement strategy, they had only two choices: (1) they could hear it as an insult, or (2) they could hear it as an expression of close and longstanding friendship. It should be noted that within that segment of Mexican society, at least at that time, it was quite normal for people to be relatively good friends for quite a few years before moving on to the stage of using the familiar pronouns or other involvement strategies. Those were reserved for close and old friends.

It is not surprising that our friend ran into both solutions to this problem. Many people befriended him, taking into consideration that his poor ability with the language was the cause of his misuse of pronouns and understanding that he only intended to show warmth and friendship. On the other hand, from time to time someone he did not know well took offense, and more than once he found himself with bruises as the result.

The point we wish to make with this anecdote is that miscommunication often arises, especially across the boundaries of discourses or discourse systems, because it is difficult to know in a new group, in a new language, or in a new culture how to express these rather subtle differences in face values. This analysis of face also tells us what sort of miscommunication arises. We can state it as a general rule: "*When two participants differ in their assessment of face strategies, it will tend to be perceived as difference in* power." If I use involvement strategies I expect to hear either reciprocal involvement (if I think it is a solidarity system, that is, $-P-D$) or independence (if I think it is a hierarchical system and I think I am in the higher position). If I think it is a solidarity system, and you use independence strategies, it sounds to me like you are putting yourself in a lower position and giving power over to me.

If I use independence strategies, I expect to hear reciprocal independence strategies (if I think it is a deference system and we have a level of mutual respect). But if you use involvement strategies back, what I hear is that you are trying to exert power over me.

To put it in the terms of our dialogue between Mr. Hutchins and Bill, if Bill answers back to Mr. Hutchins, "Sure, Jack, I can have it ready," we are certain that Mr. Hutchins will feel that something has gone wrong. And it is not just "something" that has gone wrong. He will feel that Bill is being insulting, trying to rise above his position, trying to usurp authority, or in some way trying to deny the authority structure.

We have said that face relationships consist of two elements: the initial unmarked assumptions and the ongoing negotiation in the interaction. Now we can say that where two or more participants fail to agree on what sort of face system they are using, they will feel the negotiation to be one over the dimension of power (P). This could also be worded conversely: where two or more participants fail to agree on the initial system of hierarchy (P), they will find it difficult to set a comfortable level of face strategies in their communications. Or to put it one final way: the calculation of the appropriate level of face strategies (or the appropriate face system) is always inextricably tied to the expression of the hierarchical system of relationship between or among the participants. We said earlier that there is no faceless communication. Now we would like to add to that there is no *non-hierarchical* communication. That is because any difference in sense of hierarchy gives rise to difficulties in selecting face strategies, and any miscalculation in face strategies gives rise to feelings of power differences.

It is for this reason that we have entitled this article "Interpersonal politeness and power." The characteristics of the communication of face make it inevitable that power (that is, hierarchy) is interrelated to politeness levels. Having said this we would like to make clear that we do not see power as existing only in face-to-face social interactions, nor do we see power as only a matter of interpersonal hierarchy. Power is also exercised between social groups, classes, and, in our terms, discourse systems in society. [. . .] While we have focused primarily on interpersonal power in this article, here we want to remind the reader that, overall, our goal is to show how differences in discourse system are not only differences in membership and identity, but also differences in relative positions of power.

Notes

1   Brown & Levinson (1978) introduced the theory of politeness strategies of face. Scollon & Scollon (1981, 1983, 1994) extended Brown and Levinson's theory to include the concept of global face systems.
2   Tannen (1984, 1989, 1990) has used the terms "involvement" and "independence" for the two competing face wants.
3   We use the symbol "W" for Brown and Levinson's "R" to indicate the weight of imposition.

References

Brown, P. and Levinson, S. (1978). Universals in language use: politeness phenomena. In Ester Goody (ed.), *Questions and politeness: strategies in social interaction*, New York: Cambridge University Press. Republished as (1987). *Politeness*. Cambridge: Cambridge University Press.
Goffman, E. (1967). *Interaction ritual*. Garden City, NY: Anchor Books.
Hu, H. C. (1944). The Chinese concept of "face". *American Anthropologist*, 46, 45–64.
Scollon, R. and Scollon, S. W. (1981). *Narrative, literacy and face in interethnic communication*. Norwood, NJ: Ablex.
Scollon, R. and Scollon, S. W. (1983). Face in interethnic communication. In J. Richards and R. Schmidt (eds), *Language and communication*, London: Longman.
Scollon, R. and Scollon, S. W. (1994). Face parameters in East–West discourse. In Stella Ting-Toomey (ed.), *The challenge of facework*. Albany: State University of New York Press.
Tannen, D. (1984). *Conversational style: analyzing talk among friends*. Norwood, NJ: Ablex.
Tannen, D. (1989). *Talking voices: repetition, dialogue and imagery in conversational discourse*. Cambridge: Cambridge University Press.
Tannen, D. (1990). *You just don't understand: women and men in conversation*. New York: William Morrow.

Chapter 5

YUEGUO GU

POLITENESS PHENOMENA IN MODERN CHINESE

Introduction: some explanatory remarks

THIS PAPER SEEKS TO DESCRIBE politeness phenomena in modern Chinese. It must be pointed out from the outset that it is intended to be illustrative rather than comprehensive.

Before going into detail, some clarification is in order. First, 'modern Chinese' is meant to refer to the officially standardized *pǔtōnghuà* 普通話 (literal translation, 'common language', i.e. the language used by the mass media and taught at schools and to foreign learners). Second, the data in this paper are accompanied by a transcription in *hànyǔ pīnyīn* 漢語拼音, the scheme for the Chinese phonetic alphabet, which was officially endorsed in 1958. Third, three ways of translating Chinese into English have been adopted: (a) word-for-word translation (abbreviated as WT), (b) literal translation (LT), and (c) free translation (FT). WT is used when no English equivalent is available or when LT or FT result in the loss of much of the flavour of the original. For instance, *bàidú* 拜讀 can be freely translated as 'to read' in English, but the speaker's self-denigration, an important feature of Chinese politeness, is lost. In the Chinese original, *bài* 拜 etymologically means 'to prostrate oneself', and *bàidú* implies that the speaker 'prostrates himself to read' the addressee's writing. In order to capture this implication of the word *bàidú* – prostrate oneself to read – WT is employed. LT is preferred when the English equivalent is easily available. For instance, the greeting formula *zǎoshang hǎo* is rendered thus: LT: 'good morning'. FT is the last resort when neither WT nor LT is sufficient.

Limao: a preliminary analysis

A historical survey

The most approximate Chinese equivalent to the English word 'politeness' is *lǐmào* 禮貌, which morphemically means 'polite appearance'. *Lǐmào* is derived from the old Chinese word *lǐ* 禮. To have a better understanding of the modern conception of *lǐmào*, it may be helpful to briefly review the classical notion of *lǐ* formulated by Confucius (551–479 BC), whose influence is still strongly felt today. Confucius lived at a time when the old slavery system had already

Source: Gu, Y. (1990). Politeness phenomena in modern Chinese. *Journal of Pragmatics*, 14, 237–57.

declined, and in an environment where there was constant war between feudal states. The former aristocratic social hierarchy was shattered, and chaos practically reigned over the land. One of the measures Confucius advocated taking to alter the situation was to restore *lǐ*. This *lǐ* does not mean politeness; it refers to the social hierarchy and order of the slavery system of the Zhou Dynasty (dating back to 1100 BC), which was regarded by Confucius as an ideal model of any society. In order to restore *lǐ*, it is necessary to *zhèngmíng* 正名, i.e. (WT) rectify names. Ming 名 (WT: name) in the Confucian sense encompasses, in contemporary terminology, sociological definitions and values of an individual's social roles and status. To *zhèngmíng* is to put each individual in his/her place according to his/her social position. This is important because,

> if *míng* is not properly rectified, *speech* cannot be used appropriately; if speech is not used appropriately, nothing can be achieved; if nothing is achieved, *lǐ* cannot be restored; if *lǐ* is not restored, law and justice cannot be exercised: and if law and justice are not exercised, people will not know how to behave.
>
> (Confucius, *zǐlù* 《子路》, quoted by Yang (1982: 160–61),
> translation and emphasis mine)

Thus speech had to be used appropriately in accordance with the user's status in the social hierarchy so that *lǐ* could be restored. For instance, a servant was required to call him/herself *núcai* 奴才 (LT: slave), while addressing his/her master as *dàren* 大人 (WT: great man) or *zhǔzi* 主子 (LT: master). Deviation from this usage, in Confucius' view, would disrupt the established social order, hence creating social chaos. An inferior's violation of this usage, at that time, would have been considered as being *fànshàng* 犯上 (LT: offending the superior). This was a serious breach of *lǐ*, which could result in the severe punishment of the offender.

Not until two or three hundred years after Confucius did the word *lǐ* designating politeness seem to be well established. This usage is found in the book *Lǐ Jì* 《禮記》 (*On Li*) compiled (reputedly) by Dai Sheng sometime during the West Han Dynasty. The volume opens with: 'Deference cannot not be shown', 'Speaking of *lǐ* [i.e. politeness], humble yourself but show respect to other'. Denigrating self and respecting other remain at the core of the modern conception of *lǐmào*.

The connection between *lǐ* (referring to social hierarchy and order) and *lǐ* (meaning politeness) is not difficult to see. From the servant's point of view, his use of *núcai* (slave) as a self-referring term and of *dàren* (great man) or *zhǔzi* (master) as an other-addressing term, is in accordance with *lǐ*, i.e. the inferior-vs.-superior relation between himself and his master; it is at the same time polite: he is humbling himself and respecting his master. It can be said, therefore, that it is *lǐ* (i.e. social hierarchy) that gives rise to *lǐ* (i.e. politeness), and that it is *lǐ* (i.e. politeness) that expresses and helps maintain *lǐ* (i.e. social hierarchy and order). Neustupny (1968, p. 412) comes closest to this when he observes: 'the function of which [polite behaviour] is primarily communication about vertical relations'.

The essence of *lǐmào* in New China

New China, that is, China since the founding of the People's Republic in 1949, has completed the job left over by Dr Sun Yat-sen and his followers of abolishing the feudal system (although it may not have been done as thoroughly as it is claimed to be). A new order of social structure and social relations among people has been introduced. This certainly has had some effect on politeness and its role in this new way of life. Its function of signalling social hierarchical relations has become obscure, and it seems to have assumed two new duties, viz. to enhance social harmony and to defuse interpersonal tension or conflict. Moreover, some honorifics have become obsolete (see the section on 'The self-denigration maxim' below).

What seems to have remained intact are the essential elements of politeness, or what counts as polite behaviour. There are basically four notions underlying the Chinese conception of *lǐmào:* respectfulness, modesty, attitudinal warmth and refinement. 'Respectfulness' is the self's positive appreciation or admiration of another concerning the latter's face, social status and so on. 'Modesty' can be seen as another way of saying 'self-denigration'. 'Attitudinal warmth' is the self's demonstration of kindness, consideration and hospitality to another. Finally, 'refinement' refers to the self's behaviour to another which meets certain standards.

Underneath the concept of *lǐmào* are two cardinal principles: sincerity and balance. Genuine polite behaviour must be enacted sincerely, and sincerely polite behaviour by itself calls for similar behaviour in return by others (the folk notion is *huánlǐ* 還禮, WT: to return politeness). The principle of sincerity may take the polite use of language far beyond sentential territory into conversation, since talk exchanges may be required to make sure that the principle is duly observed. The principle of balance breaks down the boundary of here-and-now conversation, predetermining follow-up talk exchanges long after the present conversation is terminated (see also the section on 'The balance principle: within and beyond transaction' below).

Some Chinese cultural anthropologists (e.g. Xu, 1981) observe that Western philosophers tend to pursue knowledge for the sake of it, whereas Chinese philosophers' (especially ancient ones) pursuit of knowledge is often motivated by moral or/and political goals. The Chinese conception of politeness is a good example. Dai's *Lǐ Jì* mentioned above is a treatise on politeness and rituals written for the purpose of attaining political goals. As a result, it is by no means descriptive (in the sense usually employed in linguistics); it is prescriptive: it aims to lay down rules of conduct. The four essential elements of politeness are basically derived from this book and handed down from one generation to another through formal or informal pedagogical channels. In the last ten years or so, the so-called 'beautification of speech' campaign has tried to revive the four elements as cultural heritage and explicitly appealed to the nation to abide by them (see Zhang et al., 1982). At least in the Chinese context, rules for politeness are moral maxims, the breach of which will incur social sanctions.

Note that the four elements need not co-occur to constitute *lǐmào.* In fact, behaviour which highlights one of them will usually be perceived as polite behaviour. Later in this paper these four notions will be elaborated into politeness maxims. Note also that polite behaviour can be verbal or nonverbal. Within polite verbal behaviour, being polite in content has to be distinguished from being polite in manner. For instance, it is possible in Chinese to criticize someone (i.e. being impolite in content) in a polite way (e.g. using indirect speech acts, hedges, politeness markers etc.).

Politeness: a functional approach

As its title suggests, this paper is not a treatise on all sorts of politeness systems (e.g. nonverbal rituals) in Chinese culture, but an account of politeness phenomena reflected in modern Chinese. The key issue is to illustrate how the consideration of politeness affects the Chinese language (i.e. as an abstract system) and language usage (i.e. the use of Chinese). My approach to the above issue is functional in the sense that politeness is studied through the way it manifests itself in interaction. This approach is, of course, not my invention. It is found in Brown and Levinson (1978, 1987) and in Leech (1977, 1983). Although I have drawn insights from their studies, I find some of their views unsuitable to account for Chinese data.

Brown and Levinson

Brown and Levinson's monograph can be seen in two ways. One is that it is a fairly thorough cross-cultural treatise on face-threatening acts (abbreviated hereafter as FTAs). The other is that it is a cross-cultural account of politeness phenomena by way of examining how politeness is employed to redress the performance of FTAs – recall the title of the monograph: 'Universals in language usage: Politeness phenomena'. Politeness is thus understood through its function. It is from the adoption of the second view that the ensuing comments are derived.

'Face', Brown and Levinson tell us, is 'the kernel element in folk notions of politeness' (1987, p. 62). This is indeed an off-record observation! It allows for more than one reading. (a) Face is the essential element of politeness. To be polite is to be face-caring. (b) Face and politeness hold a means-to-end relation between them. Since face is vulnerable to FTAs, it is politeness that anoints their performance to reduce, at least superficially, their poignancy so that face is made less vulnerable. Interpretation (a) is unlikely to be Brown and Levinson's understanding of the folk view of face and politeness. That to be polite is to be face-caring means that all FTAs are not polite, since they do not care for but threaten face; hence they are impolite acts. This conclusion is embarrassing to Brown and Levinson. For instance, on Brown and Levinson's view, 'formulaic entreaties' such as (1987, p. 96):

[12] $\begin{Bmatrix} \text{Excuse} \\ \text{Forgive} \\ \text{Pardon} \end{Bmatrix}$ me

[13]   Accept my thanks

count as bald-on-record FTAs. But it would be quite counter-intuitive to label them as being impolite. The Chinese equivalents to [12] and [13]:

(12')   duibu qǐ 對不起
          yuánliàng 原諒
          bāohan 包涵
(13')   jiēshòu wôde xièyi 接受我的謝意

are on the contrary intrinsically polite acts. Moreover, to claim, according to Brown and Levinson's theory, that (12') and (13') are acts threatening H's negative face also sounds quite counter-intuitive to the Chinese ear.

Interpretation (b) seems to be much closer to Brown and Levinson's position. In the cases of bald-on-record FTAs, politeness does not come into play. Politeness is called for when the performance of on-record FTAs is to be redressed. According to the direction of redress, politeness falls into two categories: positive politeness and negative politeness. The former is 'redress directed to the addressee's positive face, his perennial desire that his wants . . . should be thought of as desirable' (1987, p. 101). The latter is 'redressive action addressed to the addressee's negative face: his want to have his freedom of action unhindered and his attention unimpeded' (1987, p. 129).

Brown and Levinson's model is not suitable for Chinese data on the following accounts. First, the Chinese notion of negative face seems to differ from that defined by Brown and Levinson. For example, offering, inviting and promising in Chinese, under ordinary circumstances, will not be considered as threatening H's negative face, i.e. impeding H's freedom. This can be seen in the following illustration. A Chinese S will insist on inviting H to dinner (which implies that S will pay H's bill) even if H has already explicitly expressed his desire that S not do it. In this situation, a European will feel that S's act of inviting is intrinsically impeding, and that S's way of performing it is even more so. A Chinese, on the other hand, will think that S's act is intrinsically polite, and that the way S performs it shows that S is genuinely polite, for S's insistence on H's accepting the invitation serves as good evidence of S's sincerity. The Chinese negative face is not threatened in this case. Rather, it is threatened when self cannot live up to what s/he has claimed, or when what self has done is likely to incur ill fame or reputation.

Second, in interaction, politeness is not just instrumental. It is also normative. It may be preferable to treat face as wants rather than as norms or values, as Brown and Levinson have done, but it would be a serious oversight not to see the normative aspect of politeness. Failure to observe politeness will incur social sanctions. In the Chinese context, politeness exercises its normative function in constraining individual speech acts as well as the sequence of talk exchanges. That Brown and Levinson have failed to go beyond the instrumental to the normative function of politeness in interaction is probably due to the construction of their theory on two rational and face-caring model persons. A society, to be sure, consists of individuals, but it is more than a total sum of its individual constituents. Politeness is a phenomenon belonging to the level of society, which endorses its normative constraints on each individual.

Leech

Now let us turn to Leech's treatment of politeness. Whereas Brown and Levinson can be said to be interested in how politeness is used to redress the performance of FTAs, Leech is concerned with how politeness provides a missing link between the Gricean cooperative principle (CP) and the problem of how to relate sense to force (see Leech, 1983, p. 104). Leech distinguishes *relative politeness* from *absolute politeness*. Relative politeness highlights the fact that politeness is often relative to some norm of behaviour which is for a particular setting regarded as typical. Absolute politeness is seen as a scale or rather a set of scales, having a negative and a positive pole. At the negative pole is negative politeness, consisting of minimizing the impoliteness of impolite illocutions. At the positive pole is positive politeness, consisting of maximizing the politeness of polite illocutions (1983, pp. 83–4). The scales of absolute politeness are: cost-benefit, optionality, and indirectness (1983, p. 123).

Leech (1983) primarily deals with absolute politeness. Differing from Brown and Levinson, Leech emphasizes the normative (or regulative, to use Leech's favourite term) aspect of politeness (1983, p. 82)). This is brought out by his construction of politeness into the politeness principle and its maxims, which include the tact maxim, the generosity maxim, the approbation maxim, the modesty maxim, the agreement maxim and the sympathy maxim (1983, p. 132).

As is pointed out in the section on 'The essence of lǐmào in New China' above, the Chinese conception of politeness is to some extent moralized, which makes it more appropriate to analyse politeness in terms of maxims. This is the major reason for adopting Leech's theory of politeness as a basic framework for this paper. There are of course some reservations, of which the following, in view of this paper, deserve looking at in detail.

'Minimize' and 'maximize' are two key concepts in Leech's tact maxim and generosity maxim, which, for ease of reference, are reproduced below (Leech, 1983, p. 132):

(i) *tact maxim* (in impositives and commissives)
     (a) minimize cost to other [(b) maximize benefit to other]
(ii) *generosity maxim* (in impositives and commissives)
     (a) minimize benefit to self [(b) maximize cost to self]

What is exactly meant by 'minimize cost or benefit'? There are at least three different uses of the two terms in connection with politeness (not all found in Leech's book). Let us take 'minimize' as a sample for analysis (assuming that the same distinction applies to 'maximize'). Its first use, which is most likely to be prototypical in Leech's mind, is the move from the cost pole to the benefit pole on the cost–benefit scale (1983, p. 107):

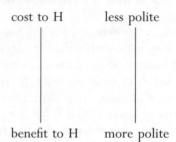

cost to H   less polite

[1] Peel these potatoes.
[2] Hand me the newspaper.
[3] Sit down.
[4] Look at that.
[5] Enjoy your holiday.
[6] Have another sandwich.

benefit to H   more polite

Minimizing cost to other (submaxim (a) of the tact maxim) means that, if S can afford to say [2] to H instead of [1], he should do so; and that, if S can afford to say [3] rather than [2], he should do so, etc. until probably [5], where the scale seems to change to the benefit of H. Note that this submaxim constrains what S requests H to do. For ease of reference, this first usage will be referred to as '*content-regulating minimization*' (or '*maximization*').

The second use of 'minimize' is represented in the following situation. If S has to ask H to peel the potatoes, he should ask H to peel as few potatoes as possible, hence minimizing H's cost. In this instance, the submaxim constrains the *degree* to which S requests H to do a certain act. This second usage will be referred to as '*manner-regulating minimization*' (or '*maximization*').

The third use of 'minimize' can be illustrated by the ensuing conversation, which actually took place between a lecturer of linguistics (A) and an overseas student (B):

[1] A: I can drop you in town if you like.
[2] B: It's very kind of you, but it will cause you some inconvenience, won't it?
[3] A: No, not at all. I'm going in that direction.
[4] B: Thank you very much.

A's polite offer [1] can be accounted for by either the tact maxim or the generosity maxim. By the tact maxim, A is maximizing benefit to B (i.e. content-regulating maximization: A has chosen to offer rather than not offer B a lift). By the generosity maxim, A is maximizing (in the content-regulating sense) cost to himself. In both cases, A is polite. Nevertheless, when B mentions the cost caused to A (see [2] above), who replies: 'No, not at all. I'm going in that direction' [3], clearly A is minimizing cost to himself. This goes against the generosity maxim, which requires A to maximize cost to himself. But note that this third use of minimization (or maximization) is different from the first two. It refers to the minimization (or maximization) operating at the conversational level: the minimization (or maximization) at this level only regulates speech behaviour, and does not alter the nature of the cost at the motivational level, i.e. A's offering B a lift is at A's cost, which is not minimized by A's saying [3]. *Speech-regulating minimization*, however, is by no means trivial: it makes it easier for B to accept A's offer. Speech-regulating minimization can therefore be seen as minimizing the debt B owes A due to A's maximization (at the motivational level) of benefit to B.

The advantage of distinguishing the above three uses of minimization or maximization is twofold. First, in Chinese culture (perhaps also in other cultures), speech-regulating minimization of cost in cornmissives and maximization of benefit received in impositives capture two politeness phenomena. If S offers H something, S will usually minimize by means of speech the cost which the offer incurs to him, and H will in turn maximize, also by means of speech, the benefit he receives from S's offer. Failure to observe speech-regulating minimization of cost can make a polite offer go foul. If A in the above conversation said the following instead of [3]: 'Oh, surely it costs petrol, time and energy to give you a lift to town', B would have some reason for believing that A was not making a polite offer at all. In Chinese culture, speech-regulating minimization of cost not only makes it easier for H to accept the offer, but also serves as important evidence of S's sincerity in making the offer.

Second, the distinction saves Leech's tact and generosity maxims from some embarrassment. As is shown above, speech-regulating minimization requires S to minimize cost to self. This runs counter to the generosity maxim. Speech-regulating maximization requires S to maximize benefit (to himself), which is at odds with the tact maxim. With the distinction we have made, Leech's two maxims can be made internally more coherent as follows:

The tact maxim (in impositives)

(i)   at the motivational level
      (a) minimize cost to other (including content- and manner-regulating senses)
(ii) at the conversational level
      (a) maximize benefit received.

The generosity maxim (in commissives)

(i)   at the motivational level
      (a) maximize benefit to other (including content- and manner-regulating senses)
(ii) at the conversational level
      (a) minimize cost to self

Leech's original versions of the two maxims are respectively other-centred and self-centred. This distinction is ignored, and is replaced by allocating impositives under the tact maxim and commissives under the generosity maxim. For further discussion of the two maxims see the section on 'The generosity and tact maxims and inviting' below.

Politeness principle and its maxims

In the section on 'The essence of lǐmào in New China', four essential notions underlying the Chinese conception of politeness are discussed. Elsewhere I have formulated, on the basis of them, seven politeness maxims (see Gu, 1985) which jointly give substance to the politeness principle (PP). In this paper, I shall concentrate on four of them, namely the self-denigration maxim, the address maxim, the tact maxim and the generosity maxim.

The PP can be understood as a sanctioned belief that an individual's social behaviour ought to live up to the expectations of respectfulness, modesty, attitudinal warmth and refinement. Note that the politeness principle and its maxims are to be cast in the vein of the Gricean doctrine of the CP and its maxims. Consequently some of the Gricean assumptions are taken for granted, namely that the politeness principle and its maxims are regulative and that they are subject to abuse and exploitation.

Mention has also been made of the principles of sincerity and balance (see the section on 'The essence of lǐmào in New China' above). They represent two socially sanctioned beliefs about the observance of the politeness principle. They, like the latter, are part of the politeness system (meaning 'total politeness phenomena as an interconnected whole') of Chinese culture.

The self-denigration maxim

This maxim consists of two clauses or submaxims: (a) denigrate self and (b) elevate other. This maxim absorbs the notions of respectfulness and modesty. The breach of submaxim (a), i.e. denigrate other, is perceived as being impolite or rude. The breach of submaxim (b), i.e. elevate self, is construed as being 'arrogant', 'boasting; or 'self-conceited'.

Let us first cite an introducing-each-other interaction to demonstrate this maxim. It is quite common among the Chinese to introduce each other by getting to know each other's names, particularly surnames. The following exchanges were held between a mainland Chinese (M) and a Singapore Chinese (S) (all literal translation):

[1]   M: nín guìxìng? 您貴姓
      M: Your precious surname?
[2]   S: xiǎodì xìng Lì. 小弟姓酈
      S: Little brother's surname is Li.
[3]   nín zūnxìng? 您尊姓
      Your respectable surname?
[4]   M: jiànxìng Zhāng. 賤姓章
      M: My worthless surname is Zhang.

When M refers to S's surname [1], he elevates it as 'precious surname', whereas in mentioning his own surname [4], he denigrates it by calling it 'worthless surname'. S, on his part, though he does not denigrate his surname in response to A's enquiry [2], denigrates instead himself as 'little brother' (implying that he is inferior to M). In his enquiry about M's surname, on the other hand, S elevates it as 'respectable surname' [3].

It may be of interest to note that this introducing-each-other interaction will differ from an English one under similar circumstances. The English tend to self-introduce, to start with the speaker's own name rather than ask for H's name, as the Chinese tend to do. The English practice can probably be explained as being motivated by the desire of avoiding potential face threat. The Chinese way, on the other hand, is more likely to be due to the constraint of the self-denigration maxim: to take the first chance to elevate other.

The concepts 'self' and 'other' in the maxim have wide extensions. Self or other's physical conditions, mental states, properties, values, attitudes, writing, spouse, family, relatives etc., all fall inside the sphere of self or other, and consequently the self-denigration maxim applies to them. Moreover, some acts such as visiting, reading etc., performed and referred to by self are also subject to the regulation of the maxim. When self pays a visit to other, his visiting is described by self as bàifáng 拜訪, or bàijiàn 拜見, or bàiwàng 拜望, or bàiyè 拜謁. The morpheme bài 拜, as is noted above, literally means 'to prostrate oneself at the foot of other'. The four verbs can be glossed (ignoring some nuances of difference among them) as 'to prostrate oneself to visit'. If self's visiting is a return visit, he huíbài 回拜 (WT: to return a prostration). Similarly, self's reading other's writing is bàidú (i.e. to prostrate self to read other's writing), and for self to say goodbye to other is bàibié 拜別 (i.e. to prostrate self to take leave of other).[1]

When self requests the pleasure of other's company, on the other hand, the former begs the latter to *shǎngguāng* 賞光 (WT: to bestow light), and the latter's presence is *guānglín* 光臨 (WT: light arrives). If self requests other to read his writing, he begs the latter to *cìjiào* 賜教 (LT: condescend to teach). or *fǔzhèng* 斧正 (LT: to use an axe to correct the blunders).

Table 5.1 summarizes some of the areas in which the self-denigration maxim usually operates, and the corresponding terms which have more or less lexicalized the self-denigration maxim.

Note that it is not something intrinsic in self's or other's surname, profession, writing, belongings etc. that is politeness-sensitive. Rather it is the acts of 'self-referring' and 'other-referring', i.e. acts of handling those attributes, that are politeness-sensitive, hence being regulated by the self-denigration maxim. By the term 'lexicalization of the self-denigration maxim' we do not mean that the maxim becomes an intrinsic element of the language system. The self-denigration maxim, like other politeness maxims, is extrinsic to the language system. However, since it constrains the use of language, it becomes frozen and 'soaked up' by the language system. Self-referring and other-referring acts, under the influence of the self-denigration maxim, give rise to the denigrative and elevative use of the expressions listed in Table 5.1. The denigrative expressions cannot be used to refer to other without being perceived as being rude or inappropriate, neither can the elevative expressions be used for self-description without being arrogant.

In ancient China, the distance between self-denigration and other elevation was much larger than that in modern China. Consequently, many classical terms sound either too denigrative or elevative to be used today. For instance, denigrative expressions like *núcai* 奴才 (LT: slave), *zúxià* 足下 (LT: footling), *xiǎode* 小的 (LT: small person), *dùnshǒu* 頓首 (WT: pressing the head to the ground), all referring to self, are obsolete. Elevative expressions such as *dàren* (LT: great person), *lǎoye* 老爺 (LT: master) etc., are rarely heard in contemporary Chinese.

A host of neutral expressions, i.e. neither denigrative nor elevative, however, have come into use, particularly since 1949, and particularly among younger generations. Now, denigrative and elevative expressions tend to be formal, while the neutral counterparts tend to be informal and are favoured by equals (for details see Gu, 1985). In the last few years, owing

Table 5.1 Lexicalization of the self-denigration maxim

Sphere of politeness	Self-denigration denigrative use	Other-elevation elevative use
Person	bǐrén 鄙人 (humble self)	nin 您 = *vous*
Surname	bìxìng, jiànxìng 敝姓,賤姓	zūnxìng, guìxìng 尊姓,貴姓
Profession	bēizhí 卑職 (humble job)	zūnzhí 尊職 (respectable job)
Opinion	yújiàn 愚見 (stupid opinion)	gāojiàn 高見 (great opinion)
Writing	zhuōzuò 拙作 (clumsy work)	dàzuò 大作 (big work)
Wife	nèizhù 內助 (domestic helper)	fūrén 夫人 (lady)
Offspring		gōngzǐ 公子 (refined son)
		qiānjīn 千金 (1,000 pieces of gold, i.e. daughter)
House	hánshè 寒舍	guìfǔ 貴府 (precious mansion)
School	bìxiào 敝校 (humble school)	guìxiào 貴校 (precious school)
		guìguó 貴國 (precious country)
Visit	bàifáng 拜訪	shǎngguāng 賞光

Note: This table is illustrative only. To save space only those terms appearing for the first time are translated.

to the speech beautification campaign, winds of change have begun to blow in the opposite direction. This can be seen most clearly in the resurrection of some classical deferential (i.e. elevative) terms, e.g. the honorific forms *lǎo* 老, *gōng* 公 and *wēng* 翁 (roughly meaning 'aged' and 'respectable' used in such formulae as surname + -*lǎo* (or *gōng* or *wēng*), to address aged and/or renowned figures.

The address maxim

The address maxim reads: address your interlocutor with an appropriate address term. This maxim is based on the notions of respectfulness and attitudinal warmth. To address one's interlocutor is not simply a matter of uttering some sounds to draw the interlocutor's attention. The act of addressing involves (a) S's recognition of H as a social being in his specific social status or role, and (b) S's definition of the social relation between S and H. It helps establish or maintain social bonds, strengthen solidarity, and control social distance.[2] In comparison with other maxims, the address maxim can be seen as being essentially an expression of linguistic politeness. A failure to use an appropriate address term is a sign of rudeness, or a signal of a breakdown of established social order. It is little wonder that the address system of modern Chinese is conventionalized to such an extent as to prevent hazardous misuse.

The term 'address' is used here as an umbrella term covering the vocative use of governmental titles, occupational titles, proper names, kinship terms and what can be called 'address politeness markers', which include honorifics and solidarity boosters (e.g. *tóngzhì* 同志, LT: comrade). These five major categories comprise the address system in modern Chinese.

Choice of an address term depends on the consideration of multiple variables. They include (1) kin or non-kin, (2) politically superior or inferior, (3) professionally prestigious or non-prestigious, (4) interpersonally familiar or unfamiliar, solidary or non-solidary, (5) male or female, (6) old or young, (7) on a formal or informal occasion, (8) family members or non-relatives, (9) in public or at home. Of these nine, (1), (5), (8) and (9) are binary opposites, whereas the remaining ones are scales.

It is impossible in this paper to do full justice to the complexity of the Chinese address system. Interested readers are referred to Gu (1985) and Chao (1976) for details. The following will focus on (1) some differences between Chinese and English address systems, (2) asymmetry in observing the address maxim, and (3) the connection between the use of address terms and the self-denigration maxim.

There are three noticeable differences between Chinese and English address systems which are likely to cause problems for cross-cultural communication. First, a Chinese proper name is arranged in the order of surname + (middle name) + given name. (The middle name today is optional. If there is a middle name, it cannot be used alone as an address term. It must be combined with the given name to form an address term.) An English proper name, however, is arranged in reverse order from the Chinese. This is a superficial difference. The real diversity lies in the use of various parts of a proper name as an address term. The Chinese surname is a non-kin public address term, and can be used alone by people outside the family, but the middle + given name and the given name are kin familial address terms. Family members of the same generation (e.g. siblings), can be on middle + given name terms. The older generation (e.g. parents) can use this combination to address the younger generations (e.g. sons and daughters). The given name is an address term reserved between lovers and occasionally used by parents.

In contrast, the English surname is non-kin and private, and, unlike the Chinese surname, cannot be used as an address term unless it is combined with other titles. The English first name (equivalent to the Chinese given name), on the other hand, is a non-kin public address term. These differences create problems for both parties when the Chinese and the English interact. For instance, Chinese intellectuals, particularly girls, studying in the U.K., will be considerably embarrassed when their English friends address them by their middle- + -given names, or worse still, by their given names, which are reserved for lovers.

Second, some Chinese kinship terms have extended and generalized usage, which is not the case with the English counterparts. For example, *yéye* 爺爺 (LT: grandpa), *nǎinai* 奶奶 (LT: grandma), *shūshu* 叔叔 (LT: uncle), *a'yi* 阿姨 (LT: aunt) etc. can be used to address people who have no familial relation whatever with the addresser. An English friend of mine once told me that she felt offended when, in her arranged visit to a pre-school centre, a group of Chinese children surrounded her, calling her *a'yi*, the use of which under such circumstances is perfectly polite in Chinese culture.

The third difference is that most occupational titles can be used as address terms in Chinese, but their English equivalents are not necessarily used in the same manner. This can be illustrated by the following talk exchange which actually occurred between a Chinese student (C) and an English lecturer (E):

[1] C: Teacher, how do you do?
[2] E: How do you do? Where do you teach?
[3] C: No, I'm not a teacher, I'm a student.

The English lecturer felt puzzled and asked me later on why that student told her that he was a teacher but at the same time denied it. The puzzlement is caused by the use of the word 'teacher' as an address term. The Chinese equivalent for 'teacher' is *lǎoshī* 老師, which is an address term. When C said [1] to E, C was using 'teacher' as an address term, which was interpreted by E as a self-introduction.

In unequal encounters (unequal not just in terms of political power, but also of profession, knowledge, age difference, kinship status and so on), it is usually the inferior who initiates talk exchanges by addressing the superior first. For example, a student meets his/her teacher on the way to school, and the following talk exchange may take place:

Student: lǎoshī, nin zǎo. 老師,您早
    (WT: teacher, you early.)   [nin = French *vous*]
    (LT: Teacher, good morning.)
Teacher: āi, zǎo. 唉,早
    (WT: āi, early) (LT: hi, morning)

If the inferior and the superior are both aware of each other's presence, but the former fails to initiate the greeting with an address term when it is necessary, the former's failure is construed as *bù dǒng lǐmào* 不懂禮貌 (LT: does not know how to be polite), or as a challenge to the latter's social position. If, on the other hand, the superior initiates conversation by addressing the inferior first, the talk exchange is clearly marked (it is assumed of course that the inferior is also aware of the superior's presence), and some implicatures will be generated along the line of explaining this markedness.

Another feature characteristic of the use of address terms in unequal encounters is that the inferior tends to choose those address terms which are more formal (a means of showing respect), whereas the superior favours those terms which are informal and which boost solidarity. Moreover, the superior can afford not to observe the address maxim, while the inferior will risk being rude if he opts out of the maxim.

The use of address terms also adheres to the self-denigration maxim. This is exemplified in the adoption of the downgraded view point in the use of kinship terms. Marriage and the birth of a child mark a turning-point in self's use of kinship terms. He starts, adopting his child's point of view, calling his siblings *bóbo* 伯伯 (LT: elder uncle), or *shūshu* 叔叔 (LT: younger uncle), or *dàgū* 大姑 (LT: elder aunt), or *xiǎogū* 小姑 (LT: younger aunt), and addressing his parents as *yéye* (LT: grandpa) and *nǎinai* (LT: grandma). Once self's child gets married and gives birth to a baby of his own, self begins adopting his/her grandchild's point of view and uses kinship terms in the way the latter does.

The self-denigration maxim also seems to be the cause of the asymmetry in the vocative use of some kinship terms. The Chinese kinship terms for siblings are an example. In Chinese, age difference is lexicalized: if A is B's *gēge* 哥哥 (i.e. elder brother) or *jiějie* 姐姐 (i.e. elder sister), B is not A's *gēge* or *jiějie*, but A's *dìdi* 弟弟 or *mèimei* 妹妹 (i.e. younger brother or sister). So the kinship terms for the siblings are not bilateral, but converse. The vocative use of the two pairs of kinship terms, however, are not converse, but asymmetrical: B can use *gēge* or *jiějie* to address A, but A does not normally use *dìdi* or *nèimei* to address B. Similarly, if A and B hold an uncle–nephew, or –niece relation, the nephew or niece can use *bóbo* or *shūshu* to address the uncle, but the use of *zhízi* 侄子 (i.e. nephew) or *zhínü* 侄女 (i.e. niece) as address terms will be inappropriate.

It may have been noted already that it is the kinship terms of the younger generation that are blocked in vocative use. The blocking is due to the constraint of the self-denigration maxim. In the Chinese familial hierarchy, the elder brother/sister or uncle/aunt is superior to the younger brother/sister or nephew/niece. The latter's vocative use of the former's kinship terms, therefore, is in conformity with the self-denigration maxim. But the former's use of the latter's kinship terms will be at odds with the maxim.

The generosity and tact maxims and inviting

In the section on Leech above, we have offered a modified version of Leech's generosity and tact maxims. In Chinese culture, these two maxims are underpinned by the notions of attitudinal warmth and refinement.

Leech notes about the two maxims (1983, p. 133):

> Bilaterality [i.e. between impositives and commissives] means that in practice, there is little need to distinguish the 'other-centred' Maxim of Tact from the 'self-centred' Maxim of Generosity.

In Chinese culture, however, the two maxims are complementary. This is because impositives and cornmissives are transactional (see also Gu, 1987): in view of the cost–benefit scale, S's impositives will be H's commissives, and S's cornmissives H's impositives. In impositives, S observes the tact maxim in performing them, while H observes the generosity maxim in responding (including perlocutionary response) to S's acts. In commissives, on the other hand, S observes the generosity maxim, whereas H observes the tact maxim.

A sample analysis of 'inviting' may serve to illustrate how the two maxims work. In Chinese, it is rare that a successful performance of inviting is realized in a single utterance. It more often than not takes several talk exchanges. It is therefore more appropriate to regard inviting as a transaction than a single speech act. The following is a case in point. It took place between A, a prospective mother-in-law, and B, a prospective son-in-law. A invites B to have dinner with A's family (word-for-word translation):

[1] A: míngtiān lái chi wǎnfàn(ar). 明天來吃晚飯啊
　　　　(tomorrow come eat dinner)

[2] B: bù lái(le), tài máfan. 不來了太麻煩
　　　　(not come too much trouble)

[3] A: máfan shénme(ya), 麻煩什麼呀
　　　　(trouble nothing)

[4] 　　 cài dōu shi xiànchěng(de) 菜都是現成的
　　　　(dishes all are ready-made)

[5] B: nà yěděi shāo(wa) 那也得燒哇
　　　　(that still cook)

[6] A: ni bù lái wǒmen yěděi chīfàn. 你不來我們也得吃飯
　　　　(you not come we all the same have meal

[7] 　　 yiding lái(ar), bù lái wǒ kě shēngqì(le). 一定來啊, 不來我可生氣啦
　　　　(must come not come I shall feel offended

[8] B: hǎo(ba), jiù suíbiàn yīdiǎn 好吧, 就隨便一點
　　　　(all right, just potluck)

[Note: The elements in parentheses are tone-softening markers. They create an overall attitudinal warmth of the transaction.]

This is a successful inviting-transaction. To a cultural outsider, A might appear downright imposing, while B would act hypocritically, i.e. making fake refusals. This, however, is far from being a correct picture of how participants (and cultural insiders) perceive the transaction. It is difficult to capture its complexity through an analysis of turn-taking, adjacency pairs or speech acts, all of which seem to be inadequate (for a rhetorical approach to the above transaction, see Gu (1987)). For the present argument, some structural features (or schemata) prototypical of the Chinese way of conducting an inviting-transaction will be discussed first. Then, 'sincerity', 'politeness' and 'face', which constitute much of the rationale underlying the transaction, will be considered.

My data indicate that the number of talk exchanges completing a successful inviting-transaction average three. A general pattern emerges:

(i) A: inviting
　　B: declining (giving reasons for doing so)
(ii) A: inviting again (refuting B's reasons, minimizing linguistically cost to self, etc.)
　　B: declining again (defending his/her reasons, etc.)
(iii) A: insisting on B's presence (refuting, persuading, minimizing linguistically cost to self)
　　B: accepting (conditionally or unconditionally)

Note that we are considering only those cases in which A sincerely invites B, and B wants to accept the invitation. Since B desires it, why does B not accept it immediately instead of going through this lengthy procedure? In Chinese culture, it is much easier to issue an invitation than to accept one. Although issuing an invitation places the inviter's face (positive face according to Brown and Levinson's distinction) at risk, it is intrinsically polite, since it manifests the inviter's observance of the generosity maxim, i.e. maximizing benefit to other (at the motivational level). Accepting an invitation, on the other hand, (1) renders the invitee indebted to the inviter, (2) goes against the tact maxim which requires the invitee to minimize cost to other, and (3) risks the invitee's face, for he might be seen as being greedy, if the inviter were in actual fact merely paying lip-service or issuing the invitation out of sheer consideration of formality. These three factors are at odds with the invitee's desire to accept it. A skilful invitee can use his language in such a way that s/he has her/his cake and eats it too. B's response [2] in the above conversation is such a tactful use of language:

[2] B: bù lái(le), tài máfan

Literally it means: 'No, I won't come. It is too much trouble for you to prepare the dinner'. *bù lái(le)* seems to decline A's invitation. *tài máfan* gives the reason for the declining. What is crucial is that this reason is derived from the consideration of the cost to A, a manifestation of B's observance of the tact maxim. It is, however, not a valid reason for declining an invitation. B's declining with an invalid reason derived from the tact maxim gives A sufficient evidence, together with other knowledge, to draw the following implicatures: (a) B would like to accept the invitation, (b) B declined it for the sake of politeness, (c) B might be protecting his own face from being seen as greedy, for he is uncertain that my inviting was sincere, and (d) B might be worried about the debt he would owe to me if he should accept the invitation.

It is not suggested that those implicatures are the only ones that A must draw, nor are they always as definite and clearly articulated as they are above. The point is that, whatever the implicatures are, they serve as a basis on which A formulates her language strategies for the second round of talk exchange. Let us look at A's conversational contribution [3] and [4].

[3] A: máfan shénme(ya).   (LT: No trouble at all)
[4]   cài dōu shì xiànchéng(de).   (LT: All dishes are ready-made)

[3] and [4] refute B's reason stated in [2], that is, it is not true that it is too much trouble to prepare the prospective dinner, since all dishes are ready-made. Note that what is stated in [2] can be actually true whereas what is claimed in [3] and [4] is false, and both A and B know it, and they know that they both know it. Here to utter truth or falsehood does not matter much. A Chinese host or hostess, who lays more than ten dishes on the table, will still claim, while showing the dishes to the guests, that there is nothing to eat (clearly false!). What is at issue is politeness. By refuting B's reason, A wishes to show that A sincerely wants B's presence. By minimizing cost to self (at the conversational level), that is, claiming that all dishes are ready-made, A makes it easier for B to accept the invitation.

In [5], [6] and [7], B and A continue exchanging arguments: B insists that he cannot come to the dinner because it is bothersome to A. A, on the other hand, argues that B's presence will not incur any extra cost, for the family has to have dinner anyway. A even 'threatens' that she would be offended if B should decline her invitation any longer.

The previous analysis serves to illustrate how 'face', 'politeness' (in terms of the generosity and tact maxims) and 'sincerity' interact with one another in shaping a transaction of issuing–accepting an invitation. Issuing and accepting an invitation place both the inviter's and the invitee's face at risk. For an inviter to issue an invitation is to present his positive face to the invitee for his approval (in Chinese folklore, the inviter requests the invitee to *shǎngliǎn* or *gěimiánzi*, both meaning 'give face', but the invitee can in theory refuse to accept the inviter's invitation, thus making the latter *diūliǎn* (LT: lose face). To accept an invitation is face-risking too, for the invitee may be seen as being greedy. In this face-risking transaction, the generosity and tact maxims and the principle of sincerity play the role of helping the transactors achieve their goals (the inviter's goal of getting the invitee to accept the invitation and the invitee's goal of satisfying the desire of accepting the invitation) without overtly hurting each other's face.

The balance principle: within and beyond transaction

Finally, let us turn briefly to the principle of balance. The underlying notions of this principle are *huánlǐ* (LT: return politeness) and *qiànrénqing* 欠人情 (LT: to be indebted). *Huánlǐ* means that, if S is polite to H, H ought to be polite to S. Unless it is superseded by other considerations, H ought to denigrate himself and elevate S if S denigrates himself and elevates H, and H ought to address S if S addresses him, etc. *Qiànrénqing* primarily refers to situations where impositives and commissives are involved. To continue with the inviting example, if S invites H, H is thus indebted to S, and H will in the near future, 'pay back' the debt, e.g. by inviting S. Thus, an initial S-inviting-H transaction calls for a follow-up H-inviting-S transaction in conformity with the principle of balance. This follow-up transaction may be carried out long after the initial S-inviting-H transaction has taken place. In this case, consideration of politeness is not just confined within one transactional boundary, but also provides a link between transactions.

Some further remarks

To conclude, the ensuing three points are worth noticing. First, as is pointed out in the introduction, 'modern Chinese' refers to the officially standardized Chinese. It does not belong to any specific speech community of a particular area. It is the language taught at schools and universities, and used in mass media. The politeness phenomena this paper captures can be said to be generally prevailing among the (fairly) educated. Second, at the most abstract level, politeness may indeed be a universal phenomenon, i.e. it is found in every culture. However, what counts as polite behaviour (including values and norms attached to such behaviour) is, as this paper attempts to demonstate, culture-specific and language-specific. Finally, in interaction, politeness fulfils normative as well as instrumental functions. Interactants can use politeness to further their goals (e.g. redress FTAs), but at the same time are constrained by it.

Notes

1 In modern Chinese, *bài* is seldom used alone as a one-morpheme word. Consequently, its denigrative sense discussed here is becoming more and more obscure.
2 A typical example of exploiting address terms to manipulate social distance is the official introduction of nationwide use of *tóngzhì* 同志 (LT: comrade) as an address term. It was meant to replace the use of governmental and occupational titles as address terms. Each was the other's *tóngzhì*, no matter what title or job he had. From 1949 to 1976, *tóngzhì* did to some extent prevail, but, since 1976, it has become less and less popular.

References

Brown, P. and Levinson, S. (1978). Universals in language usage: politeness phenomena. In E. N. Goody (ed.), *Questions and politeness* (pp. 56–289). Cambridge: Cambridge University Press.

Brown, P. and Levinson, S. (1987). *Politeness: Some universals in language usage*. Cambridge: Cambridge University Press.

Chao, Y. R. (1976). *Aspects of Chinese sociolinguistics*. Stanford, CA: Stanford University Press.

Dai, S. (1957). *On politeness and etiquette*. China Press.

Gu, Y. (1985). Politeness phenomena in modern Chinese. Unpublished M.A. dissertation, University of Lancaster.

Gu, Y. (1987). Towards a model of conversational rhetoric. Unpublished Ph.D. thesis, University of Lancaster.

Leech, G. N. (1977). Language and tact. LAUT Series A Paper 46. University of Trier.

Leech, G. N. (1983). *Principles of pragmatics*. London, New York: Longman.

Neustupny, J. V. (1968). Politeness patterns in the system of communication. Proceedings of the Eighth International Congress of Anthropological and Ethnological Science (pp. 412–19). Tokyo and Kyoto.

Xu, S. (1981). '区中西哲学的差异' ['On differences between Chinese and Western philosophy']. In Papers on social science, ed. by Shandong University.

Yang, Xian-ban (ed.) (1982). 中国哲学通史 [A general history of Chinese philosophy]. Beijing: People's University of China Press.

Zhang, J. et al. (eds) (1982). 札貌区言手册 [*A manual of polite expressions*]. Beijing Publishing Company.

Chapter 6

SACHIKO IDE

HOW AND WHY HONORIFICS CAN SIGNIFY DIGNITY AND ELEGANCE
The indexicality and reflexivity of linguistic rituals

HONORIFICS ARE KNOWN AS politeness markers in the languages that have them. However, the descriptions in the Western literature on the functions of honorifics were not felt by speakers of languages that employ honorifics to be satisfactory, either for academic or for general understanding. The goal of this paper is to try to make sense of the use and function of honorifics as fully as possible so as to explain how and why they can signify not only politeness but also the speaker's dignity and/or elegance. It is claimed that the indexing and reflexive functions of honorifics according to *wakimae* use have to be understood in a high-context culture where the speaker's viewpoint and the organization of speaking is different from what has been generally assumed in the discipline to date.

Can honorifics be abolished?

This article focuses on the use of linguistic forms characteristic of East Asian languages. It seems that the Thai language has a rich system of lexical varieties to show respect and humility. There are also complex varieties of person reference terms, which vary depending on the speaker's relationship to the hearer or the other people in the context of speaking. In contrast to English, these features show great similarity with the Japanese language. Thus, it appears to make sense to talk of East Asian languages, and to point to some things which have not been well dealt with in the frameworks of the linguistic and pragmatic traditions of Western oriented scholarship.

An incident which might illustrate the huge gap between the Western mind and the Eastern one occurred in 1997 when an economic crisis started in Thailand, and spread to all the East Asian countries including Korea. Japan was no exception. People all over the world watched to see how the Asians would cope with this economic crisis, as there was a possibility that it might trigger a worldwide economic collapse. One day, a journalist from *The Financial Times*, who had a Ph.D. in sociology from Cambridge University, came to my office for an interview. She felt that, if the honorific system were abolished from the Japanese language, this messy

Source: Ide, S. (2005). How and why honorifics can signify dignity and elegance: the indexicality and reflexivity of linguistic rituals. In R. Lakoff & S. Ide (eds), *Broadening the horizon of linguistic politeness* (pp. 45–64). Amsterdam: John Benjamin.

economical confusion could be resolved. She believed that language supports the infrastructure of a society. She presumed that the point of the system of honorifics was to ensure distance between interactants and it is also a system geared toward making information ambiguous and complicating its transmission. Therefore, if the system of honorifics were to be abolished from the society, it would make it easier for the Japanese to transmit information. This in turn would solve the complicated societal problems and economic crisis.

Japanese colleagues and students all laughed when told of this suggestion. While none knew how to explain what it was that this journalist had not understood, all knew that honorifics are essential. Language is not a tool like a pen, a typewriter, or a computer. The very way East Asians think and express and relate to others is tied to a system of language in which honorifics play an indispensable role. Therefore, East Asians cannot think of abolishing honorifics from their systems of language.

Honorifics were brought up by this journalist as the key hindrance for democratization of the society and efficient economic functioning. Behind this logic lies equating modernization and globalization with Westernization. To the extent East Asians become Westernized, they could have a better system, a better society, and a better world. In the face of such a proposition, it is necessary to stop and think whether language is really such a system that can or must be changed so that East Asian societies can operate in the Western way. Is it better for the world to Westernize, and does that mean sacrificing all of the varieties? There are quite a number of linguistic or pragmatic features around the world that cannot be accounted for if only Western theories of linguistics and pragmatics are followed.

It seems indisputable that the Western way of looking at language is basically somewhat different from the East Asian way. It seems that the Western way of looking at language is as something linear, which can be processed one piece after another in an alphabetic item-and-process approach. The way Western languages and Chinese are written highlights this difference, since Western languages are all written from left to right, and as an oversimplification it can be described such that each alphabet letter contributes to a whole, which could be said to have a space before and a space after each word. Chinese, in contrast, features characters, which work as a whole lexical unit, though they may relate to others in a variety of ways. It is easy to understand the alphabetic brain-frame as a mindset that lends itself to simple conceptualization, but some aspects of language cannot be explained within the framework of this kind of linear understanding of language. Some languages seem to require a sociolinguistic system of complex conceptualization.

Difference in speaking: the East and the West

This problem has been central for about a decade, ever since my article, "Formal forms and discernment: Two neglected aspects of linguistic politeness" appeared in *Multilingua* in 1989. The conclusion reached after all this time is that there are at least two essential aspects that must be incorporated if a fair account of the universals of linguistic politeness is to be given. The first is the difference in what it means to speak in the West and in the East. The second is that the organization of speaking must be considered in terms of hierarchical structures.

This first difference, that of what it means to speak in the West and in East Asia, is fundamental. This diversity is illustrated by a pioneering work by Linda Young called *Crosstalk and culture in Sino-American communication* (1994). Young realized that there are important differences in the way Americans speak English and the way Chinese speak English. What appears inscrutable to Westerners are Chinese discourse patterns that Chinese speakers use in English in crosstalk settings of business negotiations. For example, a summary statement of the main argument is delayed until the end, which is the reverse of an English discourse convention. She maintains that this is simply a consequence of the Chinese principle of pragmatics. She argued that such discourse phenomena could only be understood from the viewpoint of the Chinese cultural ideology of interpersonal interaction and the workings of the society.

This difference in the role of discourse in the East and the West can be highlighted by the popular saying in the West: "A man is as good as his word" and a Chinese philosopher's words that the "'Dao' (that is 'the ethical way') that can be spoken is not constant Dao," i.e. the ethical way cannot be expressed by speaking. This simple but contrasting cultural understanding of speaking gives a glimpse of the depth of the differences between what it means to speak in the West and the East.

However, it has been the trend up to now to base scholarship on the established assumptions of Western science, where the conviction that science is based on rationality emerged at the beginning of the sixteenth century, and sets a universal norm for accessing the value of cultural activity everywhere on the planet. The distinction of concern today is the outcome of the philosophical development in the civilizations in question, which can be traced back to their respective origins. The essential concepts in Western intellectual tradition, concepts such as "absoluteness," "transcendence," or "subjectivity," played no part whatsoever in the development of Asian cultures (Hall & Ames, 1995).

While in the West there is an absolute being which is supposed to have created individual beings, Asians do not assume such an entity or such an origin. The East Asian worldview goes back as far as the tenth century BC. The value system of yin and yang, which encompasses all objects and abstract concepts in the universe, has consistently endured despite changes in religion and philosophies over the 3,000 years of Chinese recorded history, spreading across neighboring countries, including Korea, Japan, Thailand, and others. According to this value system, every thing exists in relation to the other things. This differs greatly from the Western value of the individual as the central unit of society. In the Eastern world view, things exist in relation to others, for example, man and woman, parent and child, black and white, and so on. Herein lies a fundamental difference in the concept of "being," that is to exist, from the West, though it is assumed to be one of the foundations of cultural ideology both in the West and in the East.

As a medium of thinking, we have Buddhism and Christianity. While Buddhism views human beings as small, as nothing, Western political philosophy assumes that people were created by God. While in Buddhism, the world continues to exist, Christianity thinks of the world with limits.

This contrastive worldview of the East and the West, mediated by religion, gave rise to contrastive thinking prototypes by such people as the geologist Hideo Suzuki (1978), who characterized the Eastern prototype as "thinking in the forest." Such "thinking in the forest" means that the human viewpoint is that of a tree, surrounded by other trees, with no view to a horizon or vast expanses, but focused on the trees in the immediate vicinity. Such a perspective leads understandably to humility and caution in all things. An academic with the tree-in-the-forest perspective will hardly develop a theory of broad scope, but will rather focus on the precise technical discussion of the matter under investigation. The Western viewpoint can be characterized as that of the eagle soaring in the sky, alone, unfettered by its surroundings, with a perspective that spans all that is beneath it. The ultimate individual, the Western scholar, can pronounce sweeping and decisive judgments on problems surveyed from such heights.

In the Western way of thinking, there is nothing to obscure your perspective. In contrast, the way you conceive of the world in the East is as if your vision were hemmed in, as it is in the deep forest. The only things you can see are the things right in front of you. Therefore, in the East, you are very concerned with your relationship with whatever is around you. It is the tree-in-the-forest grasp of speech events.

Features of some East Asian languages: How can the complexity of person reference terms be explained?

When compared with English, Thai and Japanese share a number of characteristics with other East Asian languages. According to the *International encyclopedia of linguistics* (Bright, 1992), Thai is said to lack inflectional endings for number, person, and tense in the verb stems, but has extensive derivational compounding, the use of numerical classifiers, sentence final particles, widespread zero anaphora, and in addition, sociolinguistic factors are explicitly marked. Person reference terms are highly complex. That is, multi self-reference and addressee-reference terms are marked for the sex of the speaker, and the relationship of the speaker and the hearer.

Stylistic registers are lexically differentiated. Thus, there are various forms for the verb. Several variant forms, which are sociolinguistically chosen, are features of Thai, and the same can be said of Japanese. Figure 6.1 illustrates the Japanese case of self-reference and addressee-reference terms.

The personal pronoun for the first person reference is "I" in the Western languages, whoever you are, and whomever you are talking to. But in Japanese, and in Thai, the person reference terms are changed in many varieties of ways depending on the context. Varieties of lexical forms constitute sociolinguistic structures: the speaker's sex, age, role, or social ranking is one dimension, the formality of the context the other dimension. The latter is determined depending on the relationship between the speaker and the hearer, as well as the formality of the situation.

Table 6.1 shows the sociolinguistic structure of self and addressee reference terms.

Honorifics are another example of this kind of linguistic and pragmatic phenomenon. How can these linguistic and pragmatic phenomena be explained?

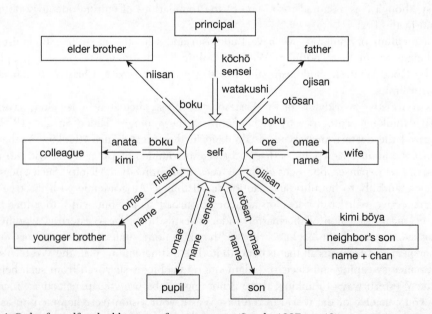

Figure 6.1 Rules for self and addressee reference terms (Suzuki 1987, p. 43)

Table 6.1 Sociolinguistic structure of self and addressee reference terms (Ide & Yoshida, 1999, p. 471)

| | | Speaker Adult | | | Young child | |
		Male	Female		Male	Female
Person	*Style*	*Male*	*Female*		*Male*	*Female*
First person Pronoun	Formal	*watakusi, watasi*	*watakusi, watasi*		None	*watasi*
	Normal	*boku*	*watasi, atasi*		*boku*	FN** + *tyan*
	Deprecatory	*ore*	None		*ore*	None
Second person Pronoun	Formal	*anata**	*anata**		(*kimi*)***	(*anata*)
	Normal	*kimi*	*anata*		FN + *kun* FN + *tyan*	FN + *kun* FN + *tyan*
	Deprecatory	*omae*	None		*omae*	None

* Not applicable in addressing superiors
** FN represents first name
*** () begins to appear around the age of five

Where can a framework to explain this difference be found? Why is it that East Asian languages have so many varieties of address terms? The richness in honorific forms is not unrelated to varieties of address terms. The discussion of these topics has as its goal the challenging of the Western perspective, which so clearly fails to give a fair account of the linguistic and pragmatic phenomena prevalent in East Asian societies.

In order to give an appropriate account of the sociolinguistic variables seen in the person referent terms in Thai and in Japanese, it is important to stop and think where the scholarship, or the science on which so much scholarship is based, actually came from. A great debt is owed to the scholarship that originated in the West. The academic disciplines created there naturally look at the phenomenon in question within their visible context. In the case of the study of language and language use, the frameworks to deal with such phenomena were established based on the worldview of Western people. Therefore, when an appropriate account of that which is unfamiliar in the Western context is to be given, there is simply no framework that encompasses such linguistic and pragmatic phenomena. When the journalist from *The Financial Times* suggested abolishing honorific use, it is obvious that this suggestion came from the perspective of Western society and Western languages. This paper attempts to show that what has been missing in the Western frameworks can be provided by independent thinking based on philosophical and historical developments in East Asia. This, it seems, may be a step towards a true understanding of the nature of human language and human interaction.

Two types of agreement

By returning to the differences in perspective between the East and the West, the deep-forest view versus the bird's-eye perspective, it is possible to gain a further understanding of the differences in what constitutes speaking in the East and the West. Figure 6.2 illustrates the differences in the speaker's positions.

When speaking in English, the speaker talks about the speech event, as it were, from a seat in the audience. As a consequence, speakers must observe themselves in the speech event as objective actors on the stage, distancing "me" on the stage and the speaking self as shown

Mary gave me this book.

(Mary ga watashi ni) kono hon (wo)
kurenta no yo.

English   Japanese

Figure 6.2 The speaker's position in speech event

in Figure 6.2. Therefore, a speaker has to describe the speech event objectively and say, "Mary gave me this book" in a full sentence. In contrast, in the speech event in Japanese, the speaker is on the stage with the audience, who are sitting on the same level as, and under the stage light with, the speaker, as shown in Figure 6.2. Therefore, the speaker shares the information with the hearer on the stage, and thus does not have to state what is obvious in the context. Thus, "*Kono hon kure ta no yo* (*kono* 'this' *hon* 'book' *kure* 'be given' *ta* 'PAST' *no* 'nominalizer particle' *yo* 'FINAL PARTICLE')" where there is no indication of the subject "Mary *ga*" (*ga* 'SUBJECT MARKER') nor an indirect object "*watashi ni*" (*watashi* 'I' *ni* 'DATIVE MARKER'), since both these items of information are obvious to the hearer, who is in the context of speaking. On the other hand, in Japanese there are two particles at the end of the utterance. One is "*no*," a particle to nominalize. This particle indexes the speaker's identity as a sweet female. Another sentence final particle "*yo*" at the end of the utterance asserts the speaker's attitude toward the information. If the equivalent utterance to English "*Mary ga kono hon wo watashi ni kure ta* (*wo* 'OBJECT MARKER')" were uttered, this would be considered pragmatically incorrect.

It might be useful to look at this in more detail. In speaking Japanese, the speaker is an element of the context on the stage, as illustrated in Figure 6.2. Therefore, the speaker shares the contextual information and the other factors relevant to the context with the hearer. Speakers carry on a complex analysis of a variety of factors while speaking: while thinking about the content of what to say, they also must recognize what kind of position or role they have, and index their identity. Next, they must recognize their relationship with the addressee, and index it by the choice of linguistic forms. Then, speakers must evaluate the extent to which the hearer shares the contextual information, because shared information does not need to be mentioned, as it is contained in the context. It is important for speakers to "agree" on the other contextual factors. For speakers of Japanese to express or to index such positions in the context is essential. This agreement is shown by appropriate modal expressions. In the

West, on the other hand, there is a tendency for speakers to situate their viewpoint in the audience and speak about what is going on on the stage from a seemingly objective perspective. This is not to say that they disregard the context completely, as such features as the T/V distinction show, but speakers do not show the multifaceted agreement with the context that speakers of Japanese so consistently do.

This illustrates a fundamental difference in linguistic and pragmatic phenomena in the East and the West. Although this and many other features are similar among languages in the East, and the points where they contrast are similar among many languages in the West, further illustrations will be drawn from Japanese and English as examples of the respective types of languages in the East and the West.

After gaining some insight into the importance of the difference in the speaker's position relevant to speaking itself, it seems probable that the difference in "agreement" may also have to do with the different levels at which the "agreement" takes place. In Japanese, it is the context of situation, meaning the speaker and the addressee as well as the formality of the setting, which determines the predicate forms, and this can be termed pragmatic modality. Agreement takes place in terms of *wakimae*, in terms of showing one's sense of self and relation to others, and takes place at the pragmatic level. In English, on the other hand, agreement occurs at the grammatical level, inasmuch as the subject determines the form of the predicate by establishing number, person, and gender. Such pragmatic level agreement as does exist in English is more a matter of lexical choice than of the language system, as incompatible choices are regarded as situationally inappropriate rather than as linguistically incorrect.

The organization of speaking

What has been discussed up to now about the differences between Eastern and Western speaking brings to mind the idea of Edward Hall (1966) on high context and low-context cultures. Since Japanese undoubtedly reflects the concept of a high-context culture, speakers of Japanese have to be more sensitive to context than people who speak in English. Therefore, the organization of speaking can be thought of as shown in Figure 6.3. When you speak in a high-contextual culture, you must take the context into account as part of the information of an utterance. Most of the analytic frameworks Western minds produced reflect a low-context culture. As soon as this basic difference is clear, it is obvious that speakers from high-context cultures will feel that "something is missing." It follows that a framework is needed that can take into account features essential when speaking in a high-context culture. In Figure 6.3, "The organization of speaking," there are three levels of communication. The first one is meta-communication, the second level is meta-pragmatics, and the third level is communication of propositions.

First, when you want to say something, you have to decide whether you should even say it or not. Every culture has rules about speaking and not speaking. In certain contexts, you evaluate your position and that of the person you are considering saying something to and decide that it would be better if you did not say it after all. For example, in Japanese, at a seminar in graduate school, students sit and listen to the professor or the fellow student's presentations, and they do not speak, even if they feel they have something they want to say. That is because it does not agree with the contextual norm, that is, with *wakimae*, as it applies in the seminar. So, not saying anything is a way of showing that the speaker's (or rather the non-speaker's) politeness conforms to the norm. One can, of course, show one's intention by a number of nonverbal behaviors, such as nodding to show that one agrees, or tilting one's head to show one's doubt.

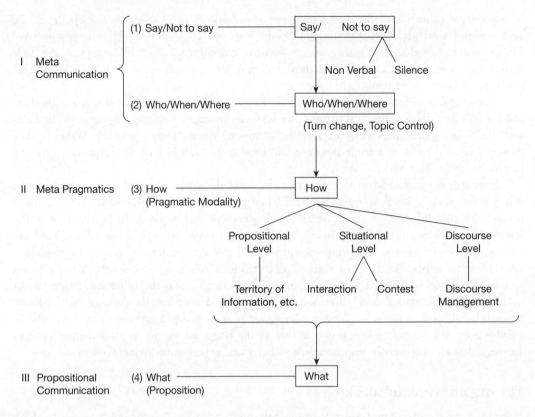

Figure 6.3 The organization of speaking

At the next level of speaking are the considerations of who is to speak, when to speak, and where to speak. Contextual information regarding the age, status, role, who has most knowledge, and many others are the factors that determine who speaks to whom, when, and where.

Another consideration involves the question of sequencing. How turn-taking is arranged means a lot. One can, of course, take one's turn, but it should be done within the shared knowledge of sense of place i.e. *wakimae* of the sequencing rules. If one breaks these rules, it gives a marked meaning, so it is always important to know when the appropriate time for one to speak has come. There are also rules regarding when and where one can interrupt or give back-channels, and who is to lead in topic selection. These and many other elements of a conversation are calculated with regard to the various contextual factors, factors that are shared among participants of the conversation in the speech event where the speaker and the hearer share the same context. In a high-context culture, the questions of speaking or not speaking, of who may say what to whom and when and where are all a part of the information exchanged as a meta-communication. One can give a meta-communicative message because there is shared knowledge of the context. When one follows this rule, it means that one has the appropriate reading of the contextual information and that is also the information one is expressing. And if one does not follow these rules, this intended deviation gives a special message beyond what is verbally communicated. This kind of communication reflecting the context of speaking plays a major role in communication and is absolutely essential in high-context cultures.

The next stage of speaking is the meta-pragmatic level. It is not the proposition alone that determines what to say, for there are a variety of ways to say the same thing, and therefore, how to say what one has to say is a question that is crucial in speaking in a high-context culture.

It turns out that there are three sub-levels of pragmatic modality: the propositional sub-level, the situational sub-level, and the discourse sub-level. First look at the propositional sub-level. In saying the same thing, in a high-context culture, one has to distinguish whether the information one is talking about is closer to oneself or the closer to the addressee (Kamio, 1997). Depending on one's judgment of this distinction, one can express the difference by means of modal expressions of evidentials. This is pragmatically obligatory.

The next level is the situational sub-level. Depending on the relationship of the speaker and the hearer and the formality of the situation, appropriate modal expressions must be selected. Essential modal expressions used for this sub-level are honorifics, person referent terms, and sentence final particles. This agreement to fit the context is just as obligatory as saying things grammatically correctly. If one fails to choose such modal expressions as honorifics appropriately, one may be criticized for the way one speaks. Matsumoto (1989, pp. 208–09) claims that there is no neutral predicate form in Japanese for the proposition sentence "Today is Saturday." One has to make obligatory choices for the predicate forms among plain, polite, or super-polite honorific forms according to context of speaking. In a high context culture, where the speaker is supposed to exercise the tree-in-the-forest perspective by paying attention to the immediate contextual matters, and to express the appropriate positions according to the expected norms of the society, i.e. *wakimae*, a person who fails to do so will be an awkward speaker, just as those who ignore grammatical rules in English are.

The next sub-level is the discourse. Appropriate devices such as constant back-channeling while listening make the conversation go smoothly. It is almost obligatory, as the lack of it would be regarded as the sign of disinterest or anger at the speaker. There are varieties of mitigating expressions or formulae to make the discourse pragmatically appropriate.

Finally, on the fourth level, having made decisions regarding all the other questions, one says what one wants to say, and that is the propositional content.

The organization of speaking as represented in Figure 6.3 shows the way to capture speaking in a high context culture. But scholarship up to now has focused primarily on level (4), the level of propositional content. Language use is bound to the context in a variety of ways from (1) to (3) levels. The rules for language use that have been discussed in terms of the speaker's intention are those we are familiar with such as the Grician Maxims, Speech Act Theory, and Linguistic Politeness Theories. However, little has been discussed regarding rules for linguistic form agreement with the context.

It is essential and very often obligatory in a high-context culture such as the Japanese culture to make appropriate choices of linguistic forms as are required by the context. It is often said among Japanese: "what that person says is right but the way the person says it is not acceptable." This saying reflects the importance of the meta-pragmatic level of speaking.

Politeness and pragmatic agreement

Honorifics have been mentioned as one of the linguistic forms that contribute to pragmatic modality in the organization of speaking. The use of honorifics makes the speech polite because of the linguistic role they play.

It seems that only some of the aspects of honorifics have ever been discussed in academic works. For example, the brilliant work "Ideologies of honorific language" by Judith Irvine (1998,

p. 62), for all its insight, still seems to fail to explain the essence of honorific use. She seems to claim, "grammatical honorifics accompany linguistic ideologies that specify that flattened affect, conventionality, and avoidance of engagement with the concrete or the sensory as appropriate ways to express respect for *others*." Her interpretation of the use of honorifics does not explain how they work as "dignity or elegance" markers for the speakers of languages that employ them. No Japanese could imagine that our language could get along without honorifics. Even a simple propositional sentence requires the choice between honorific or non-honorific predicate forms.

Honorifics work as linguistic politeness only when they are used in keeping with the context. In other words, the use of high honorific forms itself could be interpreted differently depending on the context of speaking. Thus, if a high honorific form is chosen inappropriately, that is in a context where a less polite honorific form is expected, it could imply "irony," "alienation," or any number of other meanings. If honorifics are not used in a context where they are expected, it means that the speaker has ignored or neglected politeness and appropriate behavior. Thus, just as grammatical agreement in Western languages require the agreement of the subject and the predicate form, it is the context of speaking that defines what constitutes agreement of the modal forms, and people in high-context cultures have a highly complex communicative competence regarding the structure of varieties of linguistic forms. It is this agreement that is at the heart of the concept called *wakimae*, an aspect of linguistic politeness that is totally unrelated to those with which analytical frameworks of linguistic politeness are already familiar. This concept differs rather strikingly from the linguistic politeness frameworks of Brown and Levinson (1978, 1987) or Leech (1983), which posit that speakers find their strategies in order to produce utterances in such a way as to save face of the interactants.

Perhaps explaining this from a different angle will aid in its clarification. Prevalent Western terms such as "common knowledge," "frames," "schema," or "script" all point to shared expectations in communication. *Wakimae* is the conceptual frame the members of the speech community share, and it is very often culturally defined. This kind of speaking is just like greetings or speech formulas in everyday language life that are used as rituals.

It is the ritual aspect that makes certain types of speech behavior polite. On first seeing somebody in the morning, one says a greeting like "Good morning." It is a ritualistic phrase intended to be uttered in the context of a first meeting early in the day. It is the situated practice to say "Good morning" in English speaking cultures, and "*Ohayoo*" in Japanese culture. It is a conventional practice. Everybody does it. Everybody knows that "Good morning" or "*Ohayoo*" are just a way of observing a ritualistic verbal exchange and indicating that the channels of communication are open. One could also say "Good morning" to one's daughter when she wakes up at 5 o'clock in the afternoon. In that case, it could ironically mean "you are a sleepy head," or "how in the world can you still be in bed when the sun is setting?". In this case, "Good morning" has a different meaning from "Good morning" uttered in the morning. It is not the exception, but the rule that linguistic forms and contexts have a matching relationship. In other words, linguistic forms do not stand by themselves. The forms and the situational context are in the relationship of co-occurrence. Speakers of a language where all belong to the same culture share the knowledge of the rules that match the linguistic forms and contextual situations in order to get along in the society. The system of "matching" between forms and context is not a one-to-one correlation made by calculations, rather it is a system whereby one form out of a number of options is matched in a complex way. It operates according to the dynamic super-system as the matching of the form and context are made dynamically so that new meaning is created from one moment to the next.

It might be useful to look at the way in which Japanese people acquire the appropriate use of honorifics. Up until they graduate from high school or college, they briefly learn how to use honorifics in the family, at school, or in the peer group. However, all they acquire is a rather superficial understanding of the forms and their uses. Once they become employed in a corporation, one of the first things they are trained in at many of corporations is the use of honorifics. They learn how to use honorifics to customers, or to other people they meet in business. In order to interact with people appropriately in the work place, they learn which linguistic forms to use in certain situational contexts. What they are learning is appropriate ritualistic behavior, because certain forms and certain situational practices are correlated, and the learning of this is the initiation ceremony for those newly employed in order to fit in in the society they will be working in. Therefore, the use of honorifics in Japanese society is not just an exercise in training people to respect certain other people in a certain way, or maintaining distance with certain people. It is first and foremost a way of learning the rules so that you can get along with language in the society to which you belong. It is not like leaning the rules to get a driver's license in a society where you have to drive a car. We learn the social rules by learning the rules concerning the use of linguistic forms, the core of which is honorific use.

Why is the use of honorifics polite?

Why is it that it is polite to use honorifics and formula? In other words, how does the pragmatics of ritualistic forms contribute to politeness? Ethologists have found that the basic wants of human beings are negative wants and positive wants. All human beings have the basic wants of negative face and positive face to be saved. Negative face has to do with the wants of a person not to be imposed on or hindered by others. On the other hand, positive wants have to do with the wants of every person that they want to be desirable to others. A way to achieve the satisfaction of negative wants is to do things indirectly. In order for the positive face wants to be satisfied, it is good to claim that the speaker's wants are the same as the hearer's wants.

The use of formal forms such as honorifics and formula can be viewed from this perspective. The use of formal forms according to the expected situational context is firstly accommodating to the positive face of the speaker and the hearer, because saying "Good morning" in the appropriate context, that is, in the morning, is an interactional behavior to establish common ground. Since it is uttered according to expected social behavior, it gives pleasure to both the speaker and the hearer by satisfying their positive face wants, giving both parties a sense of sharing. At the same time, since the speaker makes use of firmly established formula, it does not have a personal touch, and thus is a way of expressing things indirectly, which makes clear that it is a way to satisfy negative wants. Therefore, the use of rituals can be interpreted as the way to fulfill linguistic politeness with regard to both negative and positive face wants.

In Brown and Levinson's framework (1978, 1987), honorifics are treated under strategy No. 5, negative politeness. It means that the honorifics can be used as a strategy according to the speaker's intention using the speaker's rationality. It does not explain the most crucial aspect of this ritualistic use of honorifics. It is not the calculation of the speaker's intention that the honorific form is chosen to be appropriate to the context, but rather it is the employment of the set pattern of language use. People say "Good morning" in the morning, it just comes automatically in the context. This is an aspect of language use in high-context cultures, where there are many varieties of modal expressions, including honorifics, for saying the same thing. By now it should be obvious that it is highly "economical" to achieve linguistic politeness by linguistic rituals. Unlike Brown and Levinson's framework of politeness strategies, one does not have to calculate options, and one need only follow the rules for automatically matching the ritualistic forms and the context.

Honorifics are just one of a number of modal expressions. In Japanese, there is no grammatical agreement, like number, person, gender, or tense, but there is a pragmatic agreement between modal expressions and agreement with the context of the situation. While grammatical agreement is a strict kind with one-to-one agreement, pragmatic agreement is flexible. Several options of linguistic forms are often acceptable for one context. But there is a borderline of unacceptability such as that between *uchi* (in-group) and *soto* (out-group) that determines the use or non-use of formal forms.

While Brown and Levinson's (1978, 1987) framework of linguistic politeness and Leech's (1983) principle of politeness did not adequately cover the use of honorifics in the societies where they are used, Robin Lakoff's Rule of Politeness, published back in 1973, provided a foundation for the understanding and ultimately the incorporation of honorifics and all that they imply into pragmatic theory. Thirty years after its publication, it is now time to focus on Rule 1 of Robin Lakoff's linguistic politeness rules. It is this Rule 1, "Formality," which has not been touched upon in detail until today. Lakoff's outstanding insight into pragmatics led her to pinpoint the aspect of politeness that is made by the use of formal forms. In some societies, the choice of formal forms, formulaic expressions, and honorifics are the primary focus of linguistic politeness.

How can a universal principle of linguistic politeness be posited if, as Brown and Levinson did, this very important aspect of linguistic politeness in high-context societies is excluded? In order for linguistic politeness to be truly universal and balanced, it seems indicated that a universal principle of linguistic politeness should be proposed that incorporates this aspect of ritualistic language use, which can be called *wakimae*.

How honorifics express dignity and elegance

How and why can honorifics signify dignity and/or elegance? It has been shown that honorifics are formal linguistic forms that cannot be used independent of the context. They are basically ritualistic linguistic forms chosen to fit to the particular situational context. The use of honorifics functions as linguistic politeness because the fitting of the proper linguistic forms to the contextual factors makes the interactants feel secure in the interaction and the situation.

What does using honorifics accomplish? The use of honorifics expresses, or more precisely indexes, the appropriate relationship between the speaker and the hearer. It also indexes the formality of the situation. But honorifics do more than that. Honorifics can index the speaker's attributes. While honorific use for the interactants is geared to politeness for others, their usage to index the speaker's attributes is quite different in nature. It indexes the speaker's identity. People are judged as to what kind of person they are by the linguistic forms they choose. If honorifics are used appropriately according to the social norm, i.e. *wakimae*, a person is likely to be judged as a nice person.

What is the mechanism of the function of this language use? It is observed that female executives use more elaborate honorific forms than do women of lower status in the same corporation. This contradicts the popular belief that honorifics are supposed to be used by a person of lower status towards a person of higher status to show respect. What is the reason for this result that contradicts what people have always presumed? The findings show that women of higher status signify their dignity or elegance by using more elaborate, higher honorific forms than those used by lower status women (Ide & Inoue, 1992).

How can this reality be accounted for? Even though, in a democratic society, talking about varieties of language in terms of social class is somewhat taboo, it is a fact that there are dialects that differ on the basis of categories of social roles and status. Female executives are one case in point, since they are indexing their high status by the use of more elaborate honorifics.

Regional or geographical dialects are a familiar occurrence the world over. Osaka can serve as an example. People in Osaka, the second biggest city in Japan, speak in what is called the Osaka dialect. Listening to somebody speaking in Osaka dialect, one understands the referential meaning, but also that the speaker is from the Osaka area.

Parallel to this, people tend to have different dialects according to their social roles and status. The higher the social status of the speaker, the more elaborate the linguistic forms they are likely to use. Regardless of an individual's ability to employ the more elaborate honorifics, people in a speech community share at least passive communicative competence concerning their use. Just as people from the Osaka area are identified by their accent, hearers are able to categorize the social roles and status of speakers by the speech forms they use.

There are varieties of language that differ on the basis of geographical, social, gender, and generational differences in a society. To the extent that a society is complex, the same propositional content can be expressed in conjunction with varieties of linguistic forms that index social differences of the speaker. Since these linguistic forms cannot be omitted, some linguistic form must be chosen. And it is by this choice that speakers index their own attributes according to the social context. If one uses forms that signal the Osaka dialect, women's dialect, middle-class dialect, and young people's dialect, one indexes with great precision where one belongs in the society. The reading of the attributes of the speaker is possible only and if hearers share the sociolinguistic passive competence of varieties in the community. To the extent shared context is high, the reading of the speaker's attributes may be elaborated. People from Tokyo who do not share high context with the Osaka area, for example, find it difficult to distinguish between Osaka dialect and Kobe dialect, the dialect of the neighboring city.

It is very often the case that high-status people, such as executives in big corporations, use honorifics appropriately, not hypercorrecting, and with a relaxed tone. That variety of speech can be recognized as that of people of that social category. In this way, in the mind of the members of a speech community, the correlation between the type of speech and the type of person is widely recognized. The elaborate use of high honorifics indexes the features of the category of high-status persons. Since speakers who choose to use high linguistic forms are very often those who hold high positions and whose behavior exhibits dignity and elegance, this information is attached to the speaker of such speech. The speech itself does not have dignity or elegance, but the features of the people who make habitual use of that speech are reflected through their speech, offering metalinguistic meaning of dignity or elegance. This becomes possible owing to the reflexive capacity of language (Lucy, 1993, 1999). In this way, speakers are able to index their identity as persons of dignity and elegance.

Implication for linguistic relativity: concluding remarks

As has been emphasized, linguistic forms and contextual factors are closely connected in high-context cultures, where the speaker's vantage point is that of a tree-in-the-forest or on the stage, as seen in Figure 6.3, and thus limited to that which is in the immediate area. High-context cultures therefore require that speakers obligatorily pay attention to the contextual factors in the speech event in order to make the linguistic forms to be chosen agree with the relevant context.

The above statement does not entail that low-context cultures do not require appropriate linguistic choices according to situational context. For example, in English, when you want to leave, you say "May I please be excused?" to a person with authority over you, "I've got to be off now," to an equal, but perhaps "I'm out of here," to a close friend. The last option, said to a boss, could be grounds for disciplinary action or firing, because it is inappropriate for the situation. The levels discussed do exist in Western languages and cultures, too. These features have just been ignored, because they have to do with situations, and linguists have confined themselves to words, not people and situations. The choice of linguistic forms appropriate to situational contexts is a universal phenomenon. However, it has not been systematically investigated in the Western languages. One goal of investigating honorifics and some other linguistic phenomena in East Asian languages is to highlight these phenomena and shed light on what has been neglected in other languages, above all the Western languages.

What are the implications of this argument for the theory of linguistic relativity? It was stated above that the appropriate language use according to context can be found in English and many other languages, and therefore is universal. However, the focus should be made on the obligatory nature of systematic pragmatic agreement. The appropriate choice of predicate forms according to context for "Today is Saturday," for example, is automatic, just as the third person singular subject in English automatically takes "-s" morpheme. Slobin (1996, pp. 74–75) comments on Turkish narrative examples that have obligatory grammatical markings of evidentials, "We (English speakers) do have available optional lexical meaning for expressing notions that lie outside of the set of obligatory grammatical distinctions in a language." He further posits the aspect of "thinking for speaking" as the medium of language and thought, and says, "A 'verbalized event' is constructed on-line, in the process of speaking. Von Humboldt and Whorf and Boas were right in suggesting that the obligatory grammatical categories of a language play a role in this construction."

What have been discussed so far are pragmatic, not grammatical phenomena. But, as long as pragmatic constraints are obligatory, it can be claimed that honorifics and other modal expressions play distinct roles in the process of speaking. Having observed how linguistic forms are context saturated and pragmatic agreement is often obligatory, it becomes clear that language does not stand by itself but it is embedded in our everyday lives.

References

Bright, W. (ed.) (1992). *International encyclopedia of linguistics*. New York: Oxford University Press.

Brown, P. & Levinson, S. (1978). Universals in language usage: politeness phenomena. In E. N. Goody (ed.), *Questions and politeness: strategies in social interaction* (pp. 56–289). Cambridge: Cambridge University Press.

Brown, P. & Levinson, S. (1987). *Politeness: some universals in language usage*. Cambridge: Cambridge University Press.

Hall, E. (1966). *The hidden dimension*. New York: Fawcett.

Hall, D. & Ames, R. (1995). *Anticipating China: thinking through the narratives of Chinese and Western culture*. New York: State University of New York Press.

Ide, S. (1989). Formal forms and discernment: two neglected aspects of linguistic politeness. *Multilingua*, 8, 223–48.

Ide, S. & Inoue, V. (1992). Onna kotoba ni miru aidentiti [Identity in women's language]. *Gekkan Gengo*, 11, 46–48.

Ide, S. & Yoshida, M. (1999). Sociolinguistics: honorifics and gender differences. In N. Tsujimura (ed.), *The handbook of Japanese linguistics* (pp. 444–78). Oxford: Blackwell.

Irvine, J. (1998). Ideologies of honorific language. In B. Schieffelin, K. Woolard & P. Kroskrity (eds), *Language ideologies: practice and theory* (pp. 51–67). New York: Oxford University Press.

Kamio, A. (1997). *Territory of information*. Amsterdam and Philadelphia: John Benjamins.

Lakoff, R. (1973). The logic of politeness; or, minding your P's and Q's. In *Papers from the 9th Regional Meeting of the Chicago Linguistic Society* (pp. 292–305). Chicago: Chicago Linguistic Society.

Leech, G. (1983). *Principles of pragmatics*. London: Longman.

Lucy, J. (ed.). (1993). *Reflexive language: reported speech and metapragmatics*. Cambridge: Cambridge University Press.

Lucy, J. (1999). Reflexivity. In A. Duranti (ed.), *Language matters in anthropology: a lexicon for the millennium. Journal of Linguistic Anthropology*, 9(1–2).

Matsumoto, Y. (1989). Politeness and conversational universals: observations from Japanese. *Multilingua*, 2(2–3), 207–21.

Slobin, D. (1996). From "thought and language" to "thinking for speaking". In J. Gumperz & S. Levinson (eds), *Rethinking linguistic relativity* (pp. 70–96). Cambridge: Cambridge University Press.

Suzuki, H. (1978). *Shinrin no Shikou, Sabaku no Shikou* [*Thinking in the forest, thinking in the desert*]. Tokyo: NHK Books.

Suzuki, T. (1987). *Reflections on Japanese language and culture*. Tokyo: The Institute of Cultural and Linguistic Studies, Keio University.

Young, L. (1994). *Crosstalk and culture in Sino-American communication*. Cambridge: Cambridge University Press.

Chapter 7

HELEN SPENCER-OATEY

MANAGING RAPPORT IN TALK

Using rapport-sensitive incidents to explore the motivational concerns underlying the management of relations[1]

Introduction

M **ANY AUTHORS** (e.g. Watzlawick et al., 1967; Brown and Yule, 1983) have pointed out that an important macro-function of language is the effective management of relationships. In linguistics, this perspective on language use has been explored extensively within politeness theory, and as Fraser (1990) and Kasper (1990, 1996a, 1996b) explain, a number of different approaches have been taken towards linguistic politeness. Two of the most influential of these are Brown and Levinson's (1987 [1978]) face management model and Leech's (1983) conversational maxim approach. These approaches have stimulated a vast amount of research and resulted in extensive academic debate and controversy, with one perspective often pitted against another in terms of its effectiveness for explaining certain phenomena (e.g. Chen, 1993; Mao, 1994; Pavlidou, 1994).

This paper extends the debate by focusing on the social psychological component of the management of relations. It maintains that linguistic politeness (which is just one of the resources available for managing relations) should be studied within the situated social psychological context in which it occurs, and that it is therefore important for pragmaticists to consider the motivational concerns underlying the management of relations. The paper does not deal with the *process* of managing relations, nor with the strategies that can be used in this process; instead it focuses on fundamental motivational issues. It starts by identifying some key issues of controversy in politeness theory, and then draws on reports of authentic rapport-sensitive incidents to find out the relational management issues that people perceive in their everyday lives. It ends by presenting and arguing for a more elaborated motivational framework for understanding the management of relations than is currently available.

Issues of controversy in politeness theory

Face, maxims and/or rights

One key issue of controversy within politeness theory relates to the explanatory basis of people's 'polite' language use. According to Brown and Levinson (1987 [1978]), face is the key motivating

Source: Spencer-Oatey, H. (2002). Managing rapport in talk: using rapport-sensitive incidents to explore the motivational concerns underlying the management of relations. *Journal of Pragmatics*, 34, 592–45.

force for 'politeness'. They propose that each of us has a 'public self-image that every member wants to claim for himself' (Brown and Levinson, 1987 [1978], p. 61), and that this image or face can be maintained, enhanced or lost. They suggest that certain communicative acts, such as orders, requests, criticism and disagreements, inherently threaten the face needs of the interlocutors (such acts are labelled *face-threatening acts* for short), and that since it is in everyone's best interests to maintain each other's face, politeness involves selecting speech strategies that will minimize or eliminate such threats. Other linguists who propose a face-saving approach to politeness are Scollon and Scollon (1995).

Leech (1983), on the other hand, accounts for 'politeness' in terms of conversational maxims. He maintains that Grice's cooperative principle is constrained by the principle of politeness, in that what people say to achieve their illocutionary or discoursal goals may be modified by their desire to 'maintain the social equilibrium and the friendly relations which enable us to assume that our interlocutors are being cooperative in the first place' (Leech, 1983, p. 82). He proposes six interpersonal maxims (1983, p. 132), such as the *modesty maxim* (minimize praise of self; maximize dispraise of self) and the *agreement maxim* (minimize disagreement between self and other; maximize agreement between self and other), to account for the ways in which language use is constrained by social factors. Other authors who have also proposed a conversational maxim approach to politeness include Lakoff (1973) and Gu (1990).

A third perspective on 'politeness' is suggested by Fraser (1990; Fraser and Nolan, 1981). Fraser (1990, pp. 232–3) proposes the notion of a conversational contract:

> Upon entering into a given conversation, each party brings an understanding of some initial set of rights and obligations that will determine, at least for the preliminary stages, what the participants can expect from the other(s) . . . being polite constitutes operating within the then-current terms and conditions of the conversational contract.

So, for Fraser, politeness is associated with the fulfilment of conversational rights and obligations.

These three perspectives on why politeness occurs (because of face needs, social rules/maxims and conversational rights and obligations) are typically seen as alternative explanations (e.g. Fraser, 1990; Kasper, 1996b). However, Watts (1989, pp. 136–7) seems to link all three. He explains 'socially-agreed upon rules of politeness' in terms of interlocutor rights, and states that these are supplementary to the maintenance of mutual face wants. I agree with Watts and maintain that the three perspectives are complementary: that the politeness maxims proposed by Leech (1983) are best seen as pragmatic constraints that help manage the potentially conflicting face wants and sociality rights of different interlocutors.

Negative face, autonomy and/or cost–benefit considerations

A second issue of controversy in politeness theory revolves round why speech acts such as requests and orders are interpersonally sensitive. Brown and Levinson (1987 [1978]) explain it in terms of negative face. They maintain that face consists of two related aspects: positive face (a person's want to be appreciated and approved of by selected others, in terms of personality, desires, behaviour, values and so on) and negative face (a person's want to be unimpeded by others, the desire to be free to act as s/he chooses and not be imposed upon). They argue that directives are face-threatening because they impose on people's desire for autonomy, and thus threaten people's negative face.

Leech (1983, p. 132) similarly draws attention to the social sensitivity of impositives and commissives. However, whereas Brown and Levinson (1987 [1978]) link them with the question of autonomy, Leech links them with cost–benefit issues, and proposes the *tact maxim* (minimize cost to other; maximize benefit to other) and the *generosity maxim* (minimize benefit to self; maximize cost to self) to help manage them. Cost–benefit is a broader concept than autonomy, in that 'costly' messages may not only limit people's autonomy but may also involve time, effort, inconvenience, risk and so on. Thus cost–benefit incorporates the notion of autonomy.

Negative face and autonomous–associative orientation

Most of the criticisms of Brown and Levinson's (1987 [1978]) conceptualization of negative face have focused not so much on the distinction between desire for autonomy versus cost–benefit considerations, as on the relative importance of autonomy compared with 'social identity' (e.g. Matsumoto, 1988; Ide, 1989; Mao, 1994). For example, Matsumoto (1988, p. 405) argues as follows:

> What is of paramount concern to a Japanese is not his/her own territory, but the position in relation to the others in the group and his/her acceptance by those others. Loss of face is associated with the perception by others that one has not comprehended and acknowledged the structure and hierarchy of the group . . . A Japanese generally must understand where s/he stands in relation to other members of the group or society, and must acknowledge his/her dependence on the others. Acknowledgement and maintenance of the relative position of others, rather than preservation of an individual's proper territory, governs all social interaction.

In other words, Matsumoto's (1988) criticisms of Brown and Levinson (1987 [1978]) are twofold: that they have over-emphasized the notion of individual freedom and autonomy, and that they have ignored the interpersonal or social perspective on face.

In line with this, Mao (1994) suggests that two competing forces shape our interactional behaviour: the ideal social identity and the ideal individual autonomy. The ideal social identity motivates members of a community to associate themselves with each other and to cultivate a sense of homogeneity. The ideal individual autonomy, on the other hand, motivates members to preserve their freedom of action and to mark off separate and almost inviolable space. Mao (1994) labels the preference for one over the other 'relative face orientation', and points out that his distinction corresponds to a large extent to that between independent and interdependent construals of self (e.g. see Markus and Kitayama, 1991; Morisaki and Gudykunst, 1994; Ting-Toomey and Kurogi, 1998).

Similarly, Gu (1990) explains that, from a Chinese perspective, speech acts such as offers and invitations do not normally threaten the hearer's negative face (as Brown and Levinson (1987 [1978]) maintain); rather they are regarded as intrinsically polite. In fact, such acts are only intrinsically face-threatening if autonomy is assumed to be the desired valence of the dimension autonomy–association. But as Spencer-Oatey (2000) argues, it may not be valid to assume that such dimensions have universal valences; rather, in different circumstances, different options or points on the continuum may be favoured. So, for example, in societies or among individuals where association and involvement are valued positively, *failure* to make an offer or invitation could in fact be face-threatening.

Face and interpersonal/intergroup orientation

In defining face, many theorists seem to emphasize the personal or individual scope of face, using phrases such as *image of self* (Goffman, 1972), *self-image* (Brown and Levinson, 1987

[1987]), and *self-worth* (Ting-Toomey and Kurogi, 1998). Other theorists, however, point out that face concerns are not always personal; sometimes they can be group as well as individual concerns. Gao (1996, p. 96), for example, argues as follows:

> 'Face need' is not only a personal concern but, more important, a collective concern [. . .] face is more a concern to the family than to the person, and face-losing or face-gaining acts reflect both on persons themselves and on their families. To illustrate, one's failure threatens the face of the family; one's accomplishment, however, gains face for the family.

In line with this, Spencer-Oatey and Xing (2000), in a study of Sino-British business visits and meetings, found that, during one delegation visit, both British and Chinese business people seemed to orient towards each other in terms of group rather than individual needs and concerns when relationship and face issues arose during the visits.

So another issue of controversy relates to the focus of people's face concerns: are they personally oriented (i.e. oriented to the speaker and hearer as individual participants), are they group oriented (i.e. oriented to the speaker and hearer as group representatives), or a mixture of the two?

Rapport-sensitive incidents: reported issues of concern

Most of the concepts reported in the section on 'Issues of controversy in politeness theory' have emerged either from linguists' theoretical reflections, or else from analyses of linguistic data. However, as Fraser and Nolan (1981, p. 96) point out, no sentence or linguistic construction is inherently polite or impolite. Rather, politeness is a social judgement, and whether or not an utterance is heard as being polite is, to a large extent, in the hands (or ears) of the hearer (Fraser and Nolan, 1981, p. 96). This means that we cannot sensibly divorce linguistic politeness from the social context in which it occurs. If we are to understand how relations are managed, including the role of language in this process, we need to have insights into the social expectancies and judgements of the people involved. It is important, therefore, to include the interactants themselves as a source of data. In this section, I report a preliminary study that gathered information from participants about 'rapport-sensitive' incidents that they had experienced.

Data collection

A number of Chinese students (mostly recent arrivals in Britain) were asked to keep a record of 'rapport-sensitive' incidents, viz. incidents involving social interactions that they found to be particularly noticeable in some way, in terms of their relationship with the other person(s). This 'noticeable impact' could be either positive or negative (cf. Goffman's (1963, p. 7) concept of 'negatively eventful' and 'positively eventful' behaviour). So students were asked to record two types of incident: those that had some kind of particularly negative effect (i.e. interactions that made them feel particularly annoyed, insulted, embarrassed, humiliated and so on), and those that had some kind of particularly positive effect (i.e. interactions with other people that made them feel particularly happy, proud, self-satisfied and so on). The respondents recorded each incident on a record sheet, completing it in either Chinese or English, whichever they preferred. The record sheet is shown in Figure 7.1.

Name: Sex: M/F   Week No:

1) The setting:

2) Other people involved:

Gender		Age			Nationality				Relationship
M	F	Older	Similar	Younger	Chinese	English	Greek	Unknown	with you*

*Note: You can fill in this column with 'friend', 'classmate', 'teacher' etc. accordingly

3) The event and 4) Your reactions:

5) The reason for your reactions:

Figure 7.1 Record sheet

Fourteen students (six male and eight female) kept records of incidents, and a total of 73 incidents were reported (18 in Chinese and 55 in English). Of these, 14 did not involve interactions with other people and were discarded. This left 59 incidents for analysis: 41 of these were negative incidents, 17 were positive incidents, and 1 was mixed, in that it involved more than one person and the interaction effects were different for different people.

The purpose of collecting these data was *not* to try and obtain a large representative sample, and then to investigate the relative frequency of different types of rapport-management concern, nor to compare one nationality group with another. It was an exploratory study that aimed to identify the rapport-management issues that seem to be salient to people in authentic interactions, and thereby to gain insights into the fundamental concerns that give rise to the use of politeness/rapport-management strategies. It is very unlikely that one set of concerns underlie verbal behaviour, and another set of concerns underlie nonverbal behaviour, so although many of the incidents reflect concerns over general behaviour rather than specifically linguistic behaviour, I maintain that the incidents are equally relevant to politeness theory. Chinese students were used partly for social welfare reasons (an unusually large number had recently come to the university, and we were concerned about their adjustment), partly for convenience (a Chinese research student, Xiong Zhaoning, was available to collect the data) and partly for theoretical reasons (to help ensure that non-Western perspectives were included). The following sections describe the types of concern that seem to be reflected in the respondents' reports.

Incidents concerning face and/or rights

Several of the incidents were clearly described in terms of face concerns, in that the respondents reported a sense of humiliation, loss of credibility or similar kinds of feeling. The following incidents[2] illustrate this.

RESPONDENT J (MALE), INCIDENT 2

I often picked my nose when I had a lesson in the homework club. One day, when the teacher was giving a lecture, I started picking it again. An Indian/Pakistani student sitting beside me pointed out that what I was doing was very impolite. My face flushed instantly.

My face flushed because I thought what I had unconsciously done was something foreigners felt disgusting and it damaged my image in the eyes of others.

RESPONDENT G (MALE), INCIDENT 1

On Monday, we had reading class. Our teacher asked us to partner study together. My partner was a France girl, because my English was not well, so she looks very angry. Then she asked teacher to change the partner. I felt very terrible!

I think we are classmate, so we are friends, we should help each other. She couldn't to look down upon me. So I make my heart to study hard!

Other incidents were not described clearly in terms of face threat/loss, but were rather described in terms of rights and obligations. Rights were either referred to explicitly, or else some reference was made to what people should or should not do. It is possible that the incidents were regarded as threats to face as well as an infringement of sociality rights, but since there was no explicit mention of this, they are treated simply as infringements of sociality rights. The following incidents illustrate this.

RESPONDENT M (FEMALE), INCIDENT 1

On our way back from a theme park to the hotel, we felt hungry and went to a café for lunch. Initially, six of us all ordered hotdogs, which we hoped could warm us up a bit. But, the waitress came back and told us there were only 4 hotdogs left. And she suggested two of us have something else. Hearing this, one of the teachers said to us: 'I'm afraid two of you can't have hotdogs'. At the beginning, there's no response from the group. Then, two people agreed to order sandwiches. I was not happy about what the teacher had done.

In China, the relationship between teachers and students is supposed to be: students respect teachers while teachers are concerned about students, especially in the difficult situation. If the teacher didn't say that, we might be voluntary to have sandwiches for ourselves. But, she was a bit too selfish: only concerned about herself, but not us students.

RESPONDENT 1 (FEMALE), INCIDENT 2

One Saturday morning, I was going to prepare breakfast in the kitchen, but I could not find my dishcloth. I was wondering how it could vanish all of a sudden, so I asked a Greek girl, a flatmate of mine, 'Anna, have you seen my dishcloth?' She shrugged her shoulders and shook her head. I suddenly thought of the Greek boy, another flatmate. He might have thrown my cloth away, as he had done that before. Just as I was thinking, the boy came over. I asked him, 'You have thrown my dish cloth, haven't you?' He nodded and smiled in embarrassment, replying, 'I used it to wash the oven and it smelled awful.' I said with a frown, 'That was a new dishcloth.' 'I'll buy you a new one this afternoon,' he answered. 'This is not a question of who will buy it. The cloth is mine, so nobody but I have the right to decide if it should be thrown away,' I said.

I think we overseas students have the same right, though we are from different cultural backgrounds. Take this event as an example. I can easily buy a new dishcloth. This is not a matter of money but a matter of a person's independence. I should claim my right, even though this is a trivial thing. From then on, my personal belongings have never disappeared and I have a harmonious relationship with my flatmates as well. This is what an independent person should do. Only when you respect others, will they respect you.

Incidents concerning autonomy and/or cost–benefit considerations

Some of the reports focused clearly on cost-benefit issues, for example:

RESPONDENT N (FEMALE), INCIDENT 1

After we were driven outside, after we walked in the street – windy and cold night, at last we found a place sit in, a place where we could live. The friend's room was a small one, it had to accept four of us, and also our luggage. The friend was so kind. He knew we had urgent problem so he said 'come here, I can help you'. But it could make him problem – if his host know it he will be punished. But he still helped us. We were all grateful from our hearts.

We were driven outside by two bestial persons, and I looked for my other friends for help, but at last only one could help us and in fact he was not a close friend to me. In a short time, I felt the warm and cold from many people. My feel turned from surprising, angry, hopeless, and happy, grateful. It's true that there is kind man in world.

Others could be interpreted from either a cost–benefit or an autonomy–imposition perspective; for example:

RESPONDENT C (MALE) INCIDENT 2

Last Sunday, my English friend promised that he will visit my house this Sunday. But I waited for him from 8:00 am to 5:00 pm. There was nothing for wait. What is wrong with him? He forget this or made a joke for me?

I was very disappointed that my friend didn't visit my family. I think if he promised to visit my family, when he has some very important things to do that he couldn't come here, he could tell me. But he didn't do like this. It made me wasted a whole day to wait for him. I don't like this.

RESPONDENT B (FEMALE), INCIDENT 3

The agent promised me there'll be night shift during the holiday. So when I was on holiday I went to ask him everyday, he told me tomorrow. Every time I asked him 'Are you sure?' he said 'Sure'. One day, he's impatient in the end, he said 'OK, there was no work for you, OK?' I was offended.

If there was no work why he didn't tell me directly? And waste my time.

Often there seemed to be a general concern for equity or fairness; for example:

RESPONDENT B (FEMALE), INCIDENT 7

The Singapore lady is one of my friend's friends, that's the reason I chose to live in that house. She let the house from the owner and we let the room from her at a higher price. Because of the friend, although I knew she earned my money, I still lived there, but she didn't allow me to open the heating. I ask why people in all the other rooms could use the heating, why I couldn't. She said 'Everyone can open the heating except you'. I was irritated.

I know she is a very caustur [?] and vicious woman, but I still think she's excessive.

RESPONDENT M (FEMALE), INCIDENT 2

One evening, I got a call from a friend and we began to talk. While we were talking, I notice the hostess coming near me twice. It seemed she wanted to make a phone call. But, as my friend was speaking, I was not able to hang up the phone immediately. Then, the hostess shouted 'tell me after you finish it'. I was annoyed by what she said. I knew she was complaining about me. It seemed she had always been making fuss of trivial things since I mentioned that I was going to move out of this house later.

I always pay the full rent in time even though I quite often eat out. On top of that, I buy her flowers occasionally. However, having realised she wouldn't be able to get rents from me later, her attitude changed. According to the contract, our telephone bills are separate and I should have the right to make my phone call as a tenant, and that won't cost her a penny. What she did was unfair to me.

Incidents reflecting associative orientations

Several of the reports conveyed concerns over association issues; they expressed a desire for involvement or association rather than for autonomy or independence. The following incidents illustrate this.

RESPONDENT N (FEMALE), INCIDENT 8

My friends who lived with me since came here left this house – which is too far from school and too small also too expensive, but I stayed here. Because another friend of mine introduced it to me. She treated me well before. And the other people in this house are her friend. She promised me they could look after me as her done to me. But I was too disappointed my two friends leave me, we looked after each other like sisters. When the others (newly moved in) came back, they talked to each other, had supper together, looking like I was not here. I was tired and hungry, and no one noticed me. I moved from a warm family to a cold one. I had the sense of loss.

My friends treated me like their own sister. We lived in one house, the atmosphere was unity, but here was cool for me. Though, there were still three people lived with me, but it looked like only myself. And the house was too cold, as to I could (not) bear. That day I didn't have one meal, having nothing with me to eat, no one noticed me.

RESPONDENT J (MALE), INCIDENT 1

We (a group of students) were chatting the other day. I asked a girl who was strange to me, 'Where are you from?' She answered, 'Hong Kong'. I said, 'Oh, I'm a Chinese as well'. She responded immediately, 'No, I'm not a Chinese. I'm a Hong Kong-er and I wish Britain could take back Hong Kong.' Having heard that, I was very angry, but I didn't say anything.

I was angry because as a Chinese, she showed so little filial devotion that she even forgot her Mother (Motherland). I was silent because it's true that the economy in Hong Kong is experiencing some difficulties, but it isn't the fault of the Chinese government. It is the Southeast-Asian economic crisis and the massive withdrawal of foreign capital that have led to the depression in Hong Kong. One day when China becomes a powerful country, I'll say to her, 'Even though Mother can tolerate our remarks and acts, we children should never forget their mother, who has borne and brought them up.'

Incidents reflecting interpersonal and/or intergroup orientations

In terms of interpersonal versus intergroup orientation, several of the incidents show a clear intergroup orientation; for example:

RESPONDENT B (FEMALE), INCIDENT 8

One evening, I went to work in factory for night shift. I was late because the agency forgot to arrange the transport for me. To be reliable, I went to factory by taxi. It cost me much money, about a half of my wage that night. The supervisor didn't listen to my explanation. He asked me to leave for home, the words he said impressed me very much: 'Even whites late, I'll also ask them go back home'. I'm insulted.

I know he thought I'm a Chinese. He discriminate me. He thinks Chinese (maybe Colour) are not equal to White.

RESPONDENT L (FEMALE), INCIDENT 6

I once went to see a friend. I had to take a taxi since his house is somewhat remote. The taxi driver was an English man in his 50's. He mistook our destination because of my poor English pronunciation, and drove me to a street that I had never been to. After explaining laboriously where I would like to go, he finally understood me and drove me correctly to my friend's house. He just charged me for the right route and kept saying sorry to me.

Although it was my fault that led to the trouble, the driver time and again said that he should take the blame and he charged me fairly. The incident has convinced me that the English are civilised people; it reflects the degree of civilisation of a nation.

Other incidents reflected an intragroup orientation; for example:

RESPONDENT D (FEMALE), INCIDENT 3

It was happen in the afternoon. That day, my flat has fire alarm suddenly went off, in this situation. I had to go outside of the flat and my room lock was unlocked. So that my money were stolen by someone, who (is) from the same country with me. The problem is that I trust in him too much.

Even though, I'm very angry with him, I can do nothing to him, because he (is) from the same country.

(See also Respondent J, Incident 1, reported above.)

Yet others showed a mixture of interpersonal and intergroup orientation; for example:

RESPONDENT J (MALE), INCIDENT 4

The event took place in a Grammar lesson taught by Mary. When she was talking about the expression 'apologise for being late', a French student told Mary that she was not able to follow her explanation because it was different from what she had learned in school in France. Even though Mary explained it to her several times, she couldn't understand it. Then Mary had to move on and continue the lesson. As I was sitting next to her and I understood the expression, I wanted to give her a hand, so I said, 'I know its meaning'. But she simply turned her book to the other page. I was very angry with her at that moment.

Because I thought she was looking down upon me, or us Chinese. Wasn't I capable of sorting out such a minor grammar problem? I was really angry.

RESPONDENT F (FEMALE), INCIDENT 1

That was happened on the first day I worked in Macdonald's. That was the second job for me. I had worked in Burger King before that. The manager introduced my colleagues and asked me that what can I do for the first day. I said that I can do the till, that mean I can be the crew member work in front of the till, deal with the customers. The manager answer 'Can you? Are sure you can do that?' with doubt. I just felt 'Why you can't believe me, only because I am not native speaker and I am Chinese as well.'

The end of the story, I was working on the till. Normal employee must be work after 2 weeks, but I did that on my first day. I thought I must work harder than others, otherwise they might be look down at me.

I don't want to do things after other people. I must do everything well because I am other nationalities. I don't want anyone looking down at me I will do everything hard.

Fundamental rapport-management concerns: an elaborated framework

These incidents show that relational management is affected by at least the following:

- Concerns about both face and rights
- Concerns not only about autonomy but more broadly about cost–benefit
- Concerns about association as well as autonomy
- Variable orientations, including interpersonal, intergroup and intragroup.

Although many of the incidents reported above describe concerns over general behaviour rather than strictly linguistic behaviour, I maintain that they are nevertheless very relevant to politeness theory. They illustrate the fundamental types of issues that people get concerned about, and that people therefore need to pay attention to during verbal interaction if they are to 'maintain the social equilibrium and friendly relations' (Leech, 1983, p. 132). However, unlike politeness theory that takes language use as its starting point, I propose a model that starts with the management of relations and I call this a rapport-management model.

I suggest that the motivational force for rapport-management involves two main components: the management of face and the management of sociality rights. Face management, as the term indicates, involves the management of face needs and, following Goffman (1972, p. 5), I define face as 'the positive social *value* a person effectively claims for himself [sic] by the line others assume he has taken during a particular contact' [my emphasis]. I define sociality rights as the 'fundamental personal/social *entitlements* that a person effectively claims for him/herself in his/her interactions with others', and I suggest that they are derived primarily from personal/social expectancies and need to be handled appropriately. In other words, face is associated with personal/social value, and is concerned with people's sense of worth, credibility, dignity, honour, reputation, competence and so on. Sociality rights, on the other hand, are concerned with personal/social entitlements, and reflect people's concerns over fairness, consideration, social inclusion/exclusion and so on.

I suggest that face has the following two interrelated aspects:

1 *Quality face*: We have a fundamental desire for people to evaluate us positively in terms of our personal qualities; e.g. our competence, abilities, appearance etc. *Quality face* is concerned with the value that we effectively claim for ourselves in terms of such personal qualities as these, and so is closely associated with our sense of personal self-esteem.
2 *Social identity face*: We have a fundamental desire for people to acknowledge and uphold our social identities or roles, e.g. as group leader, valued customer, close friend. *Social identity face* is concerned with the value that we effectively claim for ourselves in terms of social or group roles, and is closely associated with our sense of public worth.

Similarly, I suggest that sociality rights have two interrelated aspects:

3   *Equity rights*: We have a fundamental belief that we are entitled to personal consideration from others, so that we are treated fairly: that we are not unduly imposed upon or unfairly ordered about, that we are not taken advantage of or exploited, and that we receive the benefits to which we are entitled. There seem to be two components to this equity entitlement: the notion of *cost–benefit* (the extent to which we are exploited, disadvantaged or benefitted, and the belief that costs and benefits should be kept roughly in balance through the principle of reciprocity), and the related issue of *autonomy–imposition* (the extent to which people control us or impose on us).

4   *Association rights*: We have a fundamental belief that we are entitled to association with others that is in keeping with the type of relationship that we have with them. These association rights relate partly to *interactional association/dissociation* (the type and extent of our involvement with others), so that we feel, for example, that we are entitled to an appropriate amount of conversational interaction and social chit-chat with others (e.g. not ignored on the one hand, but not overwhelmed on the other). They also relate to *affective association/dissociation* (the extent to which we share concerns, feelings and interests). Naturally, what counts as 'an appropriate amount' depends on the nature of the relationship, as well as sociocultural norms and personal preferences.

The components of the model, and their interrelationships, are shown diagrammatically in Table 7.1.

As can be seen, rapport management is conceptualized as having two motivational sources: concerns over face and concerns over sociality rights. Face, of course, is central to Brown and Levinson's (1987 [1978]) model; however, their model primarily emphasizes a personal or individual conceptualization of face, and so this model develops it by making the interpersonal or social component much more explicit. It thereby incorporates the important distinction between independent and interdependent perspectives that was suggested by Markus and Kitayama (1991) and developed by people such as Morisaki and Gudykunst (1994) and Ting-Toomey and Kurogi (1998). The model also takes account of the valid criticisms of people such as Matsumoto (1988), Ide (1989) and Mao (1994) that Brown and Levinson's model is too focused on individual autonomy.

The notion of sociality rights relates partly to Brown and Levinson's (1987 [1978]) concept of negative face but is not synonymous with it, in that it is broader in scope and is not limited to autonomy–imposition issues. It includes concerns about association as well as cost–benefit issues, and does not assume that autonomy/independence is always the preferred option. Moreover, sociality rights are not treated as face issues, in that an infringement of sociality rights may simply lead to annoyance or irritation, rather than to a sense of face threat or loss

Table 7.1 Components of rapport management

	Face management (personal/social value)	Sociality rights management (personal/social entitlements)
Personal/independent perspective	Quality face (cf. Brown and Levinson's positive face)	Equity rights (cf. Brown and Levinson's negative face)
Social/interdependent perspective	Social identity face	Association rights

Source: Spencer-Oatey, 2000, p. 15.

(although it is possible, of course, that both will occur). Similarly, a request for help, which could be regarded as an imposition or 'costly' act, may not in fact be regarded as an infringement of equity rights at all. On the contrary, it may be regarded as a boost to quality face, since the request shows trust in the other person's qualities (Turner, 1996, p. 4), or simply as an acknowledgement of association rights. I maintain, therefore, that it is important to separate the two concepts of face and sociality rights.

The following examples illustrate how participants can focus on different rapport-management concerns and how relational tensions can result when this happens.

Example 1: A Chinese professor visited a British university for one month in order to collect some data for his research. At the end of his visit, the Head of Department said to him 'We've enjoyed having you here, and hope you found your stay useful. I do hope we can keep in touch.' The professor gave a courteous reply, but inwardly he was disappointed that he had not been invited to give a guest lecture on his research. He wondered whether the staff in the department looked down on what he was doing, and decided it was not worth maintaining the contact. In fact, the Head of Department had been trying to be considerate – he wanted to give the professor the maximum opportunity to fulfil his research objectives, and simply wanted to avoid giving him any 'duties' that might distract him from that (i.e. he was focusing on the professor's personal cost–benefit equity rights). The professor, on the other hand, interpreted the lack of invitation as a threat to his quality face. After the professor returned to China, one of his junior colleagues asked him about his trip, including the question 'How many talks did you give on your research?' The professor found this extremely face-threatening and avoided giving a direct answer. He was afraid that if he admitted 'none', his reputation and standing in the department would go down (i.e. that he would lose social identity face).

Example 2: A delegation of Chinese business people visited a British company from whom they had bought some engineering products. During the first few days, a number of problems arose which they very much wanted to talk over with the British sales manager whom they had met in China. Unfortunately, however, he was away on a six week overseas trip, and was not returning until the Thursday evening prior to their departure the following Tuesday. They expected him to come and meet them immediately after his return, and when he did not do so on the Friday, they started asking to see him. This continued all over the weekend (when other British staff were accompanying them on excursions), and the British became irritated. They did not contact the sales manager, and it was Monday before he turned up. The Chinese visitors complained bitterly about this to their local interpreter. They thought the sales manager was their friend since they had hosted him in China, and thus felt that they had the right to see him immediately after his return (i.e. they were focusing on their association rights). The British, on the other hand, were concerned about the manager's personal equity rights – his need for some rest and refreshment after a long trip.

I am not claiming that these different motivational components are totally absent from Brown and Levinson's (1987 [1978]) model, but rather that an elaboration of them helps bring into clearer focus the different relational tensions that can occur when any of them are ignored or when participants focus on different rapport-management concerns.

Further developments

The motivational bases of rapport management described above need to be supplemented with a process perspective: an account of the dynamics of language use, including the factors influencing language production/interpretation. A comprehensive model thus needs to incorporate at least the following:

- the rapport orientations that people hold when interacting with others, including both their rapport-management goals (e.g. whether they want to enhance, maintain or challenge social relations), and their interactional orientations (interpersonal, intergroup or both; cf. Gudykunst and Kim, 1997).
- the role of contextual variables (e.g. participant relations, message content, social/ interactional roles and communicative activity)
- the role of pragmatic conventions (e.g. sociopragmatic conventions such as Leech's (1983) politeness maxims, and pragmalinguistic conventions; cf. Thomas, 1983)

It also needs to examine at least the following:

- the strategies available in a given language for conveying rapport-relevant information (e.g. whether honorifics exist in a given language or not)
- the different domains across which rapport-relevant information can be conveyed (e.g. the illocutionary domain which involves the performance/interpretation of speech acts, the discourse domain which concerns the discourse content and discourse structure of an interchange, the participation domain which concerns the procedural aspects of an interchange such as overlaps or inter-turn pauses, the stylistic domain which concerns the stylistic aspects on an interchange such as choice of tone, and the nonverbal domain which concerns the nonverbal aspects of an interchange such as gestures or other body movements).

Moreover, cultural differences need to be considered, and I suggest that there may be at least the following types of difference:

- There may be cultural differences in people's likely level of sensitivity to the varying rapport-management components. For example, people from some cultures (e.g. many Western societies) may be particularly concerned about personal rights while people in other societies (e.g. many East Asian societies) may be particularly concerned about social identity face (e.g. see Spencer-Oatey and Xing, 2000).
- People's conceptions of rights and obligations are likely to be culturally influenced. This is probably especially true of role-related rights and obligations (see, for example, *Respondent M Incident 1* above).
- Cultures may differ in their preferred strategies for mitigating potential threat to rapport. Strategy choice and use is an aspect that has not been dealt with at all in this paper, but is obviously a very important issue.

A detailed discussion of all these issues is beyond the scope of this paper; for a more extended description, see Spencer-Oatey (2000).

Finally, it is necessary to consider the extent to which face and sociality rights are distinct concepts: do they exist at two ends of a continuum, do they give rise to different types of affective reaction, or are they inextricably intertwined? The social psychologist Michael Bond (personal communication) maintains that 'face is too vague and metaphorical for social scientific use', and yet he also acknowledges that it is a very useful concept that needs to be elaborated. A major problem is that we do not know how to measure people's level of face sensitivity, except perhaps very indirectly by examining their use of language. However, if we could develop a way of independently measuring people's face sensitivity, as well as their sense of sociality rights, we could begin to unravel such questions. It is not difficult to measure the latter, but the former is far more challenging. Nevertheless, I believe it is definitely something worth working towards.

Notes

1   The author would like to thank Xiong Zhaoning for collecting the data reported in this paper.
2   The incidents that students reported in English (rather than Chinese) have not been corrected for their grammatical mistakes but are quoted verbatim.

References

Brown, G. and Yule, G. (1983). *Teaching the spoken language*, Cambridge: Cambridge University Press.
Brown, P. and Levinson, S. C. (1987). *Politeness. Some universals in language usage*. Cambridge: Cambridge University Press. [Originally published as Universals in language usage: politeness phenomenon. In E. Goody (ed.) (1978) *Questions and politeness: strategies in social interaction*. New York: Cambridge University Press.
Chen, R. (1993). Responding to compliments. A contrastive study of politeness strategies between American English and Chinese speakers. *Journal of Pragmatics*, 20, 49–75.
Fraser, B. (1990). Perspectives on politeness. *Journal of Pragmatics*, 14(2), 219–36.
Fraser, B. and Nolan, W. (1981). The association of deference with linguistic form. In J. Walters (ed.), *The sociolinguistics of deference and politeness* (pp. 93–111). The Hague: Mouton. [Special issue (27) of the *International Journal of the Sociology of Language*.]
Gao, G. (1996). Self and other: a Chinese perspective on interpersonal relationships. In W. B. Gudykunst, S. Ting-Toomey and T. Nishida (eds), *Communication in personal relationships across cultures* (pp. 81–101). London: Sage.
Goffman, E. (1963). *Behavior in public places*. New York: Free Press.
Goffman, E. (1972). *Interaction ritual: essays on face-to-face behavior*. Harmondsworth: Penguin.
Gu, Y. (1990). Politeness phenomena in modern Chinese. *Journal of Pragmatics*, 14, 237–57.
Gudykunst, W. and Kim, Y. Y. (1997). *Communicating with strangers. An approach to intercultural communication* (3rd edn). Boston: McGraw Hill.
Ide, S. (1989). Formal forms and discernment: two neglected aspects of universals of linguistic politeness. *Multilingua* 8(2/3), 223–48.
Kasper, G. (1990). Linguistic politeness – current research issues. *Journal of Pragmatics*, 14(2), 193–218.
Kasper, G. (1996a). Linguistic etiquette. In F. Coulmas (ed.), *Handbook of sociolinguistics* (pp. 374–85). Oxford: Blackwell.
Kasper, G. (1996b). Politeness. In J. Verschueren and J. O. Ostman (eds), *Handbook of pragmatics* (pp. 1–20). Amsterdam: John Benjamins.
Lakoff, R. (1973). The logic of politeness; or, minding your p's and q's. In *Papers from the Ninth Regional Meeting of the Chicago Linguistic Society* (pp. 292–305). Chicago: Chicago Linguistic Society.
Leech, G. N. (1983). *Principles of pragmatics*. London: Longman.
Mao, L. R. (1994). Beyond politeness theory: 'face' revisited and renewed. *Journal of Pragmatics*, 21, 451–86.
Markus, H. R. and Kitayama, S. (1991). Culture and the self: implications for cognition, emotion, and motivation. *Psychological Review*, 98, 224–53.
Matsumoto, Y. (1988). Reexamination of the universality of face: politeness phenomena in Japanese. *Journal of Pragmatics*, 12, 403–26.
Morisaki, S. and Gudykunst, W. B. (1994). Face in Japan and the United States. In S. Ting-Toomey (ed.), *The challenge of facework* (pp. 47–94). Albany: State University of New York Press.
Pavlidou, T. (1994). Contrasting German–Greek politeness and the consequences. *Journal of Pragmatics*, 21, 487–511.
Scollon, R. and Scollon, S. W. (1995). *Intercultural communication*. Oxford: Blackwell.
Spencer-Oatey, H. (2000). Rapport management: a framework for analysis. In H. Spencer-Oatey (ed.), *Culturally speaking. Managing rapport through talk across cultures* (pp. 11–46). London: Continuum.
Spencer-Oatey, H. and Xing, J. (2000). A problematic Chinese business visit to Britain: issues of face. In H. Spencer-Oatey (ed.), *Culturally speaking. Managing rapport through talk across cultures* (pp. 272–88). London: Continuum.
Thomas, J. (1983). Cross-cultural pragmatic failure. *Applied Linguistics*, 4(2), 91–112.
Ting-Toomey, S. and Kurogi, A. (1998). Facework competence in intercultural conflict: an updated face-negotiation theory. *International Journal of Intercultural Relations*, 22(2), 187–225.
Turner, K. (1996). The principal principles of pragmatic inference: politeness. *Language Teaching*, 29, 1-13.
Watts, R. J. (1989). Relevance and relational work: linguistic politeness as politic behavior. *Multilingua*, 8(2/3), 131–66.
Watzlawick, P., Bavelas Beavin, J. and Jackson, D. (1967). *Pragmatics of human communication. A study of interactional patterns, pathologies, and paradoxes*. London: Norton.

Chapter 8

CLIFF GODDARD AND ANNA WIERZBICKA

CULTURAL SCRIPTS
What are they and what are they good for?

THE TERM CULTURAL SCRIPTS refers to a powerful new technique for articulating cultural norms, values, and practices in terms which are clear, precise, and accessible to cultural insiders and to cultural outsiders alike. This result is only possible because cultural scripts are formulated in a tightly constrained, yet expressively flexible, metalanguage consisting of simple words and grammatical patterns which have equivalents in all languages. This is of course the metalanguage of semantic primes developed over the past 25 years of cross-linguistic research by the editors and colleagues in the natural semantic metalanguage (NSM) approach. [. . .] One recurrent theme is that the different ways of speaking of different societies are linked with and make sense in terms of different local cultural values, or at least, different cultural priorities as far as values are concerned. Cultural scripts exist at different levels of generality, and may relate to different aspects of thinking, speaking, and behaviour. [. . .]

The cultural scripts technique is one of the main modes of description of the broad project which can be termed ethnopragmatics (cf. Goddard, 2008). This refers to the quest, inaugurated in linguistics by Anna Wierzbicka (1985) in her article 'Different cultures, different languages, different speech acts: English vs. Polish', to understand speech practices from the perspective of the speakers themselves. For this purpose, the techniques of cross-cultural semantics are also essential because to understand speech practices in terms which make sense to the people concerned, we must be able to understand the meanings of the relevant culturally important words – words for local values, social categories, speech-acts, and so on. Important words and phrases of this kind often qualify for the status of cultural key words (Wierzbicka, 1997) [. . .] such as Spanish *calor humano* 'human warmth', Fulfulde *yaage* 'respect, deference', Korean *noin* 'respected old people', and Chinese *zìjĭrén* 'insider, one of us'. One of the attractions of the natural semantic metalanguage is that it can be used equally for writing cultural scripts and for doing 'cultural semantics', thus enabling us to draw out the connections between them.

It perhaps bears emphasizing that the cultural scripts approach is evidence-based, and that while not disregarding evidence of other sources (ethnographic and sociological studies, literature, and so on) it places particular importance on linguistic evidence. Aside from the semantics of cultural key words, other kinds of linguistic evidence which can be particularly

Source: Goddard, C. & Wierzbicka, A. (2004). Cultural scripts: what are they and what are they good for? *Intercultural Pragmatics*, 1(2), 153–66.

revealing of cultural norms and values include: common sayings and proverbs, frequent collocations, conversational routines and varieties of formulaic or semi-formulaic speech, discourse particles and interjections, and terms of address and reference – all highly 'interactional' aspects of language. From a data gathering point of view, a wide variety of methods can be used, including the classical linguistic fieldwork techniques of elicitation, naturalistic observation, text analysis, and consultation with informants, native speaker intuition, corpus studies, and the use of literary materials and other cultural products. Other methods such as role-plays, questionnaires, discourse-completion tasks, and the like, can also be fruitfully used.

As will be amply clear at this point, the cultural scripts approach is not trying to do something altogether new and different. Many of its concerns are shared by linguistic anthropology, ethnography of communication, and by aspects of cultural psychology (e.g. Hymes, 1962 [1968]; Gumperz and Hymes, 1986 [1972]; Bauman and Sherzer, 1974; Shweder, 1993). The chief contribution of the cultural scripts approach is an improved methodology to bear on these common concerns, a methodology which builds on two decades of research in cross-cultural semantics.

Semantic primes: the language of cultural scripts

The cultural scripts technique relies crucially on the metalanguage of empirically established semantic primes. Semantic primes are simple, indefinable meanings which appear to 'surface' as the meanings of words or word-like expressions in all languages. There are about 60 in them, listed using English exponents in Table 8.1. Comparable tables could now be given in a wide range of languages (in principle, in any language). It is impossible here to review the large body of detailed research which has gone into exploring the lexical and grammatical properties of semantic primes in many languages. It can be mentioned, however, that detailed 'whole metalanguage' studies have been carried out for English, Polish, Malay, Lao, Mandarin Chinese, Mbula, Spanish, Korean, and East Cree, and more selective studies on French, Italian, Russian, Amharic, Japanese, Ewe, Yankunytjatjara, and Hawaiian Creole English, among others; see the papers in Goddard and Wierzbicka (1994, 2002), as well as Yoon (2003), Maher (2000); Stanwood (1999); Amberber (2003, 2008); Junker (2003, 2008).[1]

The key claim is that the semantic primes expressed by English words like *someone/person, something/thing, people, say, words, true, do, think, want, good, bad, if, because*, among others, can be expressed equally well and equally precisely in other languages; and that, furthermore, they have an inherent universal grammar of combination, valency, and complementation which also manifests itself equally in all languages, albeit with language-specific formal variations. The universal mini-language of semantic primes can therefore be safely used as a common code for writing explications of word meanings and for writing cultural scripts, free from the danger of 'terminological ethnocentrism' (see below), with maximum clarity and resolution of detail, and in the knowledge that they can be readily transposed across languages. It offers a mechanism by which meaning can be freed from the grip of any single language. As the distinguished anthropologist Roy D'Andrade (2001, p. 246) remarks, the natural semantic metalanguage 'offers a potential means to ground all complex concepts in ordinary language and translate concepts from one language to another without loss or distortion in meaning'.

Some examples and observations

Consider the following set of three Anglo scripts (Wierzbicka, 2006a). They express the central Anglo value sometimes termed 'personal autonomy' [A], the consequent cultural inadvisability

Table 8.1 Table of semantic primes (after Goddard, 2002, p. 14)

Substantives:	I, YOU, SOMEONE/PERSON, SOMETHING/THING, PEOPLE, BODY
Relational substantives:	KIND, PART
Determiners:	THIS, THE SAME, OTHER/ELSE
Quantifiers:	ONE, TWO, SOME, ALL, MUCH/MANY
Evaluators:	GOOD, BAD
Descriptors:	BIG, SMALL
Mental/experiential predicates:	THINK, KNOW, WANT, FEEL, SEE, HEAR
Speech:	SAY, WORDS, TRUE
Actions, events, movement:	DO, HAPPEN, MOVE
Existence and possession:	THERE IS/EXIST, HAVE
Life and death:	LIVE, DIE
Time:	WHEN/TIME, NOW, BEFORE, AFTER, A LONG TIME, A SHORT TIME, FOR SOME TIME, MOMENT
Space:	WHERE/PLACE, HERE, ABOVE, BELOW, FAR, NEAR, SIDE, INSIDE, TOUCHING
Logical concepts:	NOT, MAYBE, CAN, BECAUSE, IF
Augmentor, intensifier:	VERY, MORE
Similarity:	LIKE (AS, HOW)

Notes: Primes exist as the meanings of lexical units (not at the level of lexemes); exponents of primes may be words, bound morphemes, or phrasemes; they can be formally, i.e. morphologically, complex; they can have different morphosyntactic properties, including word-class, in different languages; they can have combinatorial variants (allolexes); each prime has well-specified syntactic (combinational) properties.

of issuing overt directives [B], and the availability of a culturally approved alternative strategy, namely, presenting the addressee with a quasi-directive message in the guise of a *suggestion* [C]. Because they are framed exclusively in the controlled vocabulary and grammar of the natural semantic metalanguage, they can be readily transposed across languages, unlike words such as *autonomy, directive*, and *suggestion* which are the 'private property', so to speak, of the English language.

[A] [people think like this:]
    when a person is doing something
    it is good if this person can think about it like this:
        'I am doing this because I want to do it
        not because someone else wants me to do it'
[B] [people think like this:]
    when I want someone to do something it is not good if I say something like this to this person: 'I want you to do it, I think that you will do it because of this'
[C] [people think like this:]
    when I want someone to do something it can be good if I say something like this to this person: 'maybe you will want to think about it, maybe if you think about it you will want to do it'

Using these scripts as examples, one can make a number of observations about cultural scripts in general. The first is that societies are heterogeneous, and that not every member of Anglo culture would accept or endorse the scripts [A]–[C]. However, as indicated by the frame 'people think like this: . . .', the claim is that even those who do not personally identify with the content of a script are familiar with it, i.e. that it forms part of the interpretative backdrop to discourse and social behaviour in a particular cultural context. Cultural scripts are intended to capture background norms, templates, guidelines or models for ways of thinking, acting, feeling, and speaking, in a particular cultural context. While they explain a great deal about speech practices, they are not descriptions of behaviour as such.

Second, cultural scripts differ in their level of generality and can be interrelated in a variety of ways. Script [A] can be seen as one of the 'master scripts' of the mainstream Anglo culture. It does not concern speech, or even social interaction, as such, but captures a prevailing cultural attitude which has widespread ramifications across a range of cultural domains and practices. Scripts [B] and [C] spell out some of the consequences for social interaction. In the terminology of the ethnography of communication (Hymes, 1962), a master script such as [A] could be seen as stating a 'norm of interpretation', while [B] and [C] spell out more specific 'norms of interaction'.

Third, it can be seen that the scripts rely heavily on evaluative components such as 'it is good (bad) if . . .' and 'it is not good (bad) if . . .', or variants such as 'it can be good (bad) if . . .'. Another kind of framing component, useful for other scripts and in other contexts, concerns people's perceptions of what they can and can't do: 'I can say (think, do, etc.) . . .' and 'I can't say (think, do, etc.) . . .'. Also on the topic of the form of cultural scripts, it can be pointed out that the introductory 'when'-components and 'if'-components represent relevant aspects of social contexts. In scripts [A]–[C] these are very simple and schematic; in other scripts, they can be more complex. In particular, as shown by several contributions to this collection, they can contain certain language-specific 'semantic molecules', i.e. complex language-specific concepts, which are relevant to cultural construals of social context. For example, some Korean scripts make reference to the social category of *noin* (roughly) 'respected old people'; and some Chinese scripts make reference to the social category of *shúrén* (roughly) 'an acquaintance, someone known personally'.

Fourth, scripts [A]–[C] allow us to make the point that mere possession of a common language does not mean that people who use this language share all their cultural scripts and associated ethnopragmatic behaviour. There can be large regional and social variations, associated with significantly different histories and lived experiences of different speech communities. Jock Wong's study (2004) shows precisely that Anglo cultural scripts such as [A]–[C] are not shared by speakers of Singapore English. Conversely, several different contiguous languages in a 'speech area' can share many of the same cultural scripts, or variants of them, as shown by Felix Ameka and Anneke Breedveld's study of 'areal scripts' in West Africa (2004). Because they provide a fine-grained model of cultural description, scripts enable us to recognize and describe cultural change and variation.

Finally, this little set of Anglo scripts helps us to underscore the point that although English may be an incipient global language, it is by no means a culture-neutral language. On the contrary, it carries as much cultural baggage as any other (cf. Wierzbicka 2006a, 2006b). In general terms, this point may seem obvious. And it is certainly obvious, in an immediate practical sense, to millions of immigrants, refugees, business travellers, tourists, and English language-learners around the world; but oddly enough, there has been relatively little concrete work conducted into Anglo speech ways. There is a pressing need for more research of this kind, using investigative techniques which can 'de-naturalize' the pragmatics of Anglo English.

Cultural scripts compared with conventional 'universalist' approaches

By conventional 'universalist' approaches, we refer to the 'politeness theory' of Brown and Levinson (1978, 1987), to so-called Gricean and 'neo-Gricean' pragmatics (Grice, 1975; Levinson, 2000), and to the 'contrastive pragmatics' approach represented in the work of Shoshana Blum-Kulka and colleagues (Blum-Kulka et al., 1989; Blum-Kulka and Kasper, 1993). The first assumes a universal model of positive and negative face needs (generating positive and negative politeness strategies), the second adopts a set of universal maxims of communication said to be based on pure rationality, and the third assumes a universal inventory of speech-act types. Cultural variation is accommodated by way of differing weightings and 'realizations'. In our view, these models tend to greatly underestimate the cultural shaping of speech practices. Certainly the cultural scripts approach allows much finer granularity of description and much greater attention to cultural particularity.

A more serious critique of these avowedly universalist models, however, is the charge that they are Anglocentric, i.e. that they adopt as a baseline or template some aspect of Anglo norms or practices and attempt to generalize or adjust this to suit all others (cf. Ochs Keenan, 1976; Sohn, 1983; Matsumoto, 1988; Ide, 1989; Wierzbicka, 2003 [1991]; Clyne, 1994, pp. 176–201). The criticism is most readily illustrated with Grice's maxims such as 'say no more than is required' and 'avoid obscurity', which, as critics have often remarked, sound more like the ideals of an Anglo-American philosopher than the outcomes of the natural logic of human communication. The situation hardly improves when reformulated in terms of 'relevance', given that the term *relevance* itself, which is supposed to sum up the overriding principle of communication, is so culture-specific that it lacks equivalents even in most European languages, let alone in most of the languages of the world. Of course it is possible for a defender of relevance theory (or Grice's maxims, for that matter) to make light of the culture-specific nature of their central construct, but this merely illustrates ethnocentrism in action.

The fatal flaw of the 'contrastive pragmatics' approach is also easy to identify: the assumption that speech-act categories such as *request, apology*, and *compliment* are appropriate tools for describing languages and cultures which have no such indigenous categories. To use such words as cultural descriptors is clearly to engage in terminological ethnocentrism. By adopting 'non-emic' analytical categories, contrastive pragmatics foregoes the opportunity to represent the indigenous conceptualization of speech-acts in many, if not most, cultures of the world. As for Brown and Levinson's 'politeness theory', an increasing number of critics, especially from East Asia, have drawn attention to its 'individualist' character, which they see as betraying its Anglo origins. And of course, it too is flawed by terminological ethnocentrism, not only in its primary dichotomies of *positive face* and *negative face*, but also in its uncritical use of descriptors such as *direct* and *indirect*, not to mention quintessentially Anglo terms such as *imposition*. The central point is that terms which do not correspond to indigenous conceptualizations cannot articulate the perspective of a cultural insider. At best, they give a so-called 'observers' model' or 'outsider perspective'. Furthermore, because they are locked into the untranslatable vocabulary of a foreign language, they close off the description to the people concerned.

The accessibility and practicality of cultural scripts

[. . .]

From a methodological point of view, the accessibility of cultural scripts means that native speaker consultants can become involved in a very direct way with working and re-working them. In our experience, native speakers from different cultures are often surprisingly interested in engaging in this kind of collaborative work, especially those who have had direct personal experience of intercultural cross-talk and confusion. Of course, consultants need guidance and support in such work. It is no easy matter to learn to express one's ideas solely within the limited vocabulary and grammar of the natural semantic metalanguage. As Keith Allan (2001) has remarked, natural semantic metalanguage may be easy to read, but it can be difficult to write. But the intuitive accessibility of cultural scripts means that native speakers *can* at least read (or hear) them, that they can understand them, and that they can respond to them without the continual intervention and mediation of the analyst. Conventional technical approaches cast the 'Other' in the role of the object of description, never a co-interpreter or interlocutor. At the risk of using a PC term, cultural scripts are potentially empowering for native speaker consultants.

The accessibility and transparency of cultural scripts written in semantic primes give them a huge advantage over technical modes of description when it comes to real-world situations of trying to bridge some kind of cultural gap, with immigrants, language-learners, in international negotiations, or whatever. There is no need to begin with a 'tutorial' about collectivism vs. individualism, positive politeness vs. negative politeness, high context cultures vs. low context cultures, or other arcane academic concepts. Because cultural scripts 'interface' more or less directly with simple ordinary language – in any language – they can be practically useful for the purposes of cross-cultural education and intercultural communication (cf. Goddard, 2004).

[. . .]

Notes

1   For more on the theory and practice of NSM semantics, see Wierzbicka (1996, 1992), Goddard (1998), and Durst (2003). There is a comprehensive bibliography on the NSM homepage: www.une.edu.au/arts/LCL/disciplines/linguistics/nsmpage.htm.

References

Allan, K. (2001). *Natural language semantics*. London: Routledge.
Amberber, M. (2003). The grammatical encoding of thinking in Amharic. *Cognitive Linguistics,* 14(2/3), 195–220.
Amberber, M. (2008). The lexical exponents of semantic primes in Amharic. In Cliff Goddard (ed.), *Cross-linguistic semantics: metalanguage, scripts, and explications*. Amsterdam: John Benjamins.
Ameka, F. and Breedveld, A. (2004). Areal cultural scripts for social interaction in West African communities. *Intercultural Pragmatics,* (Special issue on 'Cultural scripts', edited by Cliff Goddard, and Anna Wierzbicka), 1(2), 167–87.
Bauman, R. and Sherzer, J. (eds) (1974). *Explorations in the ethnography of speaking.* London: Cambridge University Press.
Blum-Kulka, S., House, J. and Kasper, G. (eds) (1989). *Cross-cultural pragmatics: requests and apologies.* Norwood, NJ: Ablex.
Blum-Kulka, S. and Kasper, G. (eds) (1993). *Interlanguage pragmatics.* Oxford: Oxford University Press.
Brown, P. and Levinson, S. C. (1987). *Politeness: some universals of language use.* Cambridge: Cambridge University Press.
Brown, P. and Levinson, S. C. (1978). Universals in language usage: politeness phenomena. In E. Goody (ed.), *Questions and politeness: strategies in social interaction* (pp. 56–310). Cambridge: Cambridge University Press.
Clyne, M. (1994). *Intercultural communication at work.* Cambridge: Cambridge University Press.
D'Andrade, R. (2001). A cognitivist's view of the units debate in cultural anthropology. *Cross-Cultural Research,* 35(2): 242–57.
Durst, U. (2003). The natural semantic metalanguage approach to linguistic meaning. *Theoretical Linguistics,* 29(3): 157–200.

Goddard, C. (1998). *Semantic analysis: a practical introduction*. Oxford: Oxford University Press.

Goddard, C. (2002). The search for the shared semantic core of all languages. In C. Goddard & A. Wierzbicka (eds), *Meaning and universal grammar – theory and empirical findings. Vol. 1* (pp. 5–40). Amsterdam/Philadelphia: John Benjamins.

Goddard, C. (2004). 'Cultural scripts': a new medium for ethnopragmatic instruction. In M. Achard and S. Niemeier (eds), *Cognitive linguistics, second language acquisition, and foreign language teaching* (pp. 145–65). Berlin: Mouton de Gruyter.

Goddard, C. (ed.) (2008). *Cross-linguistic semantics*. Amsterdam: John Benjamins.

Goddard, C. and Wierzbicka, A. (eds) (1994). *Semantic and lexical universals – theory and empirical findings*. Amsterdam: John Benjamins.

Goddard, C. and Wierzbicka, A. (2002). *Meaning and universal grammar – theory and empirical findings*, Vols. I & II. Amsterdam/Philadelphia: John Benjamins.

Grice, P. (1975). Logic and conversation. In P. Cole & J. Morgan (eds), *Syntax and semantics: speech acts*. Vol. 3 (pp. 41–58). New York: Academic Press.

Gumperz, J. J. and Hymes, D. H. (eds) (1986 [1972]). *Directions in sociolinguistics. The ethnography of communication*. Oxford: Basil Blackwell.

Hymes, D. H. (1962 [1968]). The ethnography of speaking. Reprinted in Joshua Fishman (ed.), *Readings on the sociology of language* (pp. 99–138). The Hague: Mouton.

Ide, S. (1989). Formal forms and discernment: two neglected aspects of universals of linguistic politeness. *Multilingua*, 8(2/3): 223–48.

Junker, M.-O. (2003). A Native American view of the 'mind' as seen in the lexicon of cognition in East Cree. *Cognitive Linguistics*, 14(2/3): 167–94.

Junker, M.-O. (2008). Semantic primes and their grammar in a polysynthetic language: East Cree. In Cliff Goddard (ed.), *Cross-linguistic semantics*. Amsterdam: John Benjamins.

Levinson, S. (2000). *Presumptive meanings: the theory of generalized conversational implicatures*. Cambridge: MIT Press.

Maher, B. (2000). Le Gabbiette or the caged concepts of human thought. An Italian version of the natural semantic metalanguage. BA (Hons) thesis, Australian National University.

Matsumoto, Y. (1988). Reexamination of the universality of face: politeness phenomena in Japanese. *Journal of Pragmatics*, 12: 403–26.

Ochs Keenan, E. (1976). The universality of conversational postulates. *Language in Society*, 5: 67–80.

Shweder, R. A. (1993). Cultural psychology: who needs it? *Annual Review of Psychology*, 44: 497–523.

Sohn, Ho-min. (1983). Intercultural communication in cognitive values: Americans and Koreans. *Language and Linguistics*, 9: 93–136.

Stanwood, R. (1999). On the adequacy of Hawai'i Creole English. PhD dissertation, University of Hawai'i.

Wierzbicka, A. (1985). Different languages, different cultures, different speech acts: English vs. Polish. *Journal of Pragmatics*, 9: 145–78.

Wierzbicka, A. (1992). *Semantics: culture and cognition*. Oxford: Oxford University Press.

Wierzbicka, A. (1996). *Semantics, primes and universals*. Oxford: Oxford University Press.

Wierzbicka, A. (1997). *Understanding cultures through their key words*. Oxford: Oxford University Press.

Wierzbicka, A. (2003 [1991]). *Cross-cultural pragmatics* (expanded 2nd edn.). Berlin: Mouton de Gruyter.

Wierzbicka, A. (2006a). Anglo scripts against 'putting pressure' on other people, and their linguistic manifestations. In Cliff Goddard (ed.), *Ethnopragmatics. Understanding discourse in cultural context* (pp. 31–64). Berlin: Mouton de Gruyter.

Wierzbicka, A. (2006b). *English: meaning and culture*. New York: Oxford University Press.

Wong, J. (2004). Cultural scripts, ways of speaking and perceptions of personal autonomy: Anglo English vs. Singapore English. *Intercultural Pragmatics*, 1(2), 231–48.

Yoon, K.-J. (2003). Constructing a Korean natural semantic metalanguage. PhD thesis, Australian National University.

PART II: NOTES FOR STUDENTS AND INSTRUCTORS

Study questions

1 What does the concept of 'face' consist of? Scollon & Scollon refer to the two sides of 'face' as involvement vs. independence. Can you give examples of the involvement and independence?

2 What are the differences between 'politeness' and 'face' as linguistic phenomena and those as used in everyday life?

3 What are the three main factors in the politeness system? What are the different types of politeness system as classified by Scollon & Scollon?

4 Gu's article critically compares Western notions of face and politeness with the Chinese notions. What are Gu's main criticisms of Brown and Levinson's formulation of face and politeness?

5 What are the main features of honorifics in East Asian languages such as Japanese? Why are they an essential part of the languages involved?

6 What is *wakimae*? What is it for?

7 What is rapport management? What are its main components? What does the concept tell us that the politeness theory does not?

8 Define cultural scripts and explain what they are useful for?

9 According to Goddard & Wierzbicka, what do the three Anglo scripts on p. 125 tell us about cultural scripts? Do you agree?

10 What, in Goddard & Wierzbicka's opinion, are the pros and cons of cultural scripts, compared with conventional 'universalist' approaches? Do you agree?

Study activities

1 You are going to ask a favour from your friend, your lecturer and someone on the street. Write down the three extracts of conversation afterwards. Recorders can be used for more accurate and reliable transcription if you like.

(a) Go through the utterances one by one in each interaction and discuss what politeness strategies are employed by the speakers, using the classifications provided by Scollon & Scollon.

(b) Compare whether or not there are differences in the type and frequency of linguistic strategies between the three conversations. Relate your analysis to the three main influential factors of the politeness system identified by Scollon & Scollon.

2   Make a list of honorifics (i.e. words or expressions that convey respect when addressing or referring to someone) in your native language(s). These could be specific address terms, prefixes, suffixes etc. Please classify the list according to the following factors:

(a) distance

(b) power

(c) topic

(d) gender

(e) style of discourse (spoken vs. written, formal vs. informal).

Explain the general rules of using the honorifics in the language in terms of context and linguistic form. Are there culture- or language-specific rules or forms? Why? Relate your discussion to various cultural approaches and concepts in this part. Can the notions of politeness and face account for your observations?

3   Use the record sheet (Figure 7.1) in Spencer-Oatey's article to note five 'rapport-sensitive' incidents that take place either in English or other languages. What types of face concern do you think the recorded incidents reflect?

4   Following the examples of three Anglo scripts in Goddard & Wierzbicka's article, write cultural scripts for similar concepts or practice (i.e. personal autonomy vs. interdependence, directives, suggestion), from the perspective of a different culture. Compare the cultural scripts and discuss any similarities or differences. Comment on whether cultural scripts indeed achieve their aims, i.e. providing a mechanism to decode and capture a cultural practice with clarity, precision and accessibility across language.

Further reading

On politeness, see:

Brown, P. & Levinson, S. (1978). Universals in language use: politeness phenomena. In E. Goody (ed.), *Questions and politeness: strategies in social interaction*. New York: Cambridge University Press. Republished as (1987). *Politeness*. Cambridge: Cambridge University Press.

Cutting, J. (2002). *Pragmatics and discourse: a resource book for students*. London: Routledge.

Watts, R. (2003). *Politeness*. Cambridge: Cambridge University Press.

For empirical studies on the application of the politeness theory into different cultures and languages, see the *Journal of Pragmatics, Journal of Politeness Research, Intercultural Pragmatics, Multilingua*, among others.

On rapport management, see:

Spencer-Oatey, H. (ed). (2000). *Culturally speaking. Managing rapport through talk across cultures*. London: Continuum.

On cultural scripts, the following two books offer a comprehensive review of the origins and development of the approach in the last 20 years:

Wierzbicka, A. (2003). *Cross-cultural pragmatics* (2nd edn). Berlin: Mouton de Gruyter.

Goddard, C. (2006). *Ethnopragmatics: understanding discourse in cultural context*. Berlin: Mouton de Gruyter

The following special issue contains a number of studies applying the cultural scripts approach to cultures and languages other than English. The reprinted article in the *Reader* is the introduction to the special issue.

Goddard, C. & Wierzbicka, A. (eds) (2004). Cultural scripts. *A special issue of Intercultural Pragmatics*, 1(2).

PART III

Communication patterns across cultures: empirical examples

Introduction to Part III

Zhu Hua

CROSS-CULTURAL DIFFERENCES EXIST IN many aspects of discourse and communication. This part of the *Reader* focuses on culture-specific interactional strategies and patterns in language use (Chapters 9–11) and in nonverbal communication (Chapter 12). The goals of these papers are twofold: to discover language-specific patterns and in doing so, to address the issue of universality in speech acts. One common issue of concern in all the papers is the notion of directness vs. indirectness.

For anyone interested in carrying out a project in cross-cultural pragmatics, Chapter 9 is a good starting point. It introduces one of the very first systematic and influential investigations into the similarities and differences in the realisation patterns of the same speech acts across different languages. CCSARP (the Cross-Cultural Speech Act Realisation Patterns) project was set up to investigate cross-cultural and intralingual variation in the speech acts of requests and apologies in eight languages. The theoretical and methodological frameworks tried and tested in the different languages in the study have been applied to many subsequent empirical studies in cross-cultural pragmatics.

Chapter 10 describes a cultural way of speaking, i.e. *dugri* talk. Translated as straight or direct talk and sometimes referred to as 'Israeli directness of style', *dugri* talk, as the author argues, is central to the discourse of native-born Israelis of Jewish heritage. Using an enthnographic approach, the author compares *dugri* talk as a verbal ritual and discusses its forms and functions, as well as its cultural implications. In addition to its original methodology, readers may find it particularly interesting to note that the study demonstrates that 'directness' can mean different things and be accomplished differently in different cultures.

Chapter 11 occupies a special place in the studies of communication patterns. It looks at the use of Qur'anic verses as a communicative resource among Muslims and the interplay between religious, linguistic and cultural identities, a topic that has received relatively little attention in the literature. *Insha' Allah*, translated as 'God willing', implies that instead of being in control of the outcome, one is at the mercy of God – an Islamic belief embraced by Muslims. The author argues that the phrase, used in daily conversation, serves to mitigate one's commitment, to indirectly refuse or reject a request or invitation, to avoid undesirable consequences and to protect one's self-image. The data and the argument provide an interesting perspective on how the notion of indirectness is accomplished and negotiated in conversational interaction.

Chapter 12 discusses in depth the phenomenon of the frequent use of silence among Finnish people. It investigates whence the stereotypical view of 'the silent Finn' originates, both from the perspective of other cultures and that of the Finnish culture itself. The issue of particular interest to readers of this collection is how silence is perceived and what communicative goals it might achieve in conversation in different cultures, and why. The authors also raise the question of 'comparability' in cross-cultural studies of communicative patterns, a challenging yet important methodological issue in the field of intercultural communication.

Chapter 9

SHOSHANA BLUM-KULKA AND ELITE OLSHTAIN

REQUESTS AND APOLOGIES
A cross-cultural study of speech act realization patterns (CCSARP)[1]

Introduction

THE PAPER REPORTS ON AN ongoing project concerned with a cross-cultural investigation of speech act realization patterns. The goals of the project are to compare across languages the realization patterns of two speech acts—requests and apologies—and to establish the similarities and differences between native and non-native speakers' realization patterns in these two acts in each of the languages studied within the project. The theoretical and methodological framework for this investigation has been developed as a result of close collaboration among the participants of the project, who have all followed the same approach in data collection and data analysis. The paper will outline the theoretical framework for the project, present the methodology developed, and illustrate our procedures for analysis by giving examples from the data in some of the languages studied.[2]

Theoretical considerations

In recent years, the relevance of pragmatics has become increasingly clear to applied linguists. Though the scope of pragmatics is far from easy to define, the variety of research interests and developments in the field share one basic conern: the need to account for the rules that govern the use of language in context (Levinson, 1983). One of the basic challenges for research in pragmatics is the issue of universality: to what extent is it possible to determine the degree to which the rules that govern the use of language in context vary from culture to culture and from language to language? Answers to this question have to be sought through cross-cultural research in pragmatics. For applied linguists, especially for those concerned with communicative language learning and teaching, cross-cultural research in pragmatics is essential in coping with the applied aspect of the issue of universality: to what extent is it possible to specify the particular pragmatic rules of use for a given language, rules which second-language learners will have to acquire in order to attain successful communication in the target language?

The issue of universality is especially relevant in the context of speech act studies. A number of studies have established empirically (Cohen and Olshtain, 1981; Kasper, 1981;

Source: Blum-Kulka, S. & Olshtain, E. (1984). Requests and apologies: a cross-cultural study of speech act realisation patterns (CCSARP). *Applied Linguistics*, 5(3), 196–213.

House, 1982; Wolfson, 1981; Blum-Kulka, 1982; Thomas, 1983) that second language speakers might fail to communicate effectively (commit pragmatic failures), even when they have an excellent grammatical and lexical command of the target language. In part, second language speakers' pragmatic failures have been shown to be traceable to cross-linguistic differences in speech act realization rules, indicating in Widdowson's terms (Widdowson, 1978) that learners are just as liable to transfer "rules of use" (having to do with contextual appropriacy) as those of "usage" (related to grammatical accuracy).

The methodological framework set up for the study of requests and apologies is based on the assumption that observed diversity in the realization of speech acts in context may stem from at least three different types of variability: (a) intracultural, situational variability; (b) cross-cultural variability; (c) individual variability.[3] Thus, there might be systematic differences in the realization patterns of speech acts, depending on social constraints embedded in the situation. For example, requests addressed to superiors might tend, in a given culture, to be phrased in less direct terms than requests addressed to social inferiors, or vice versa. On another dimension, within the same set of social constraints, members of one culture might tend to express a request more or less directly than members of another culture. Finally, individuals within the same society might differ in their speech act realization patterns, depending on personal variables such as sex, age, or level of education. In order to investigate the nature of variability on each of these dimensions, and in order to be able to determine their relative role as compared with each other, we need to study speech act realization patterns in a variety of situations within different cultures, in cross-culturally comparable ways, across similar situations, preferably involving different types of individual. Furthermore, in order to establish the ways in which second language speakers' patterns of use differ from those of native speakers, we need to establish first how the different intra-cultural sources of variability (situational and individual) account for actual use in the two languages, the learner's native language and the learner's target language.

The goals of the project

The CCSARP project was initiated in a joint attempt to pursue this line of research. The project focuses on two speech acts (requests and apologies) in eight languages or varieties, divided among the participants as follows:

1   Australian English—Eija Ventola[4]
2   American English—Nessa Wolfson and Ellen Rintell
3   British English—Jenny Thomas
4   Canadian French—Elda Weizman
5   Danish—Claus Faerch and Gabriele Kasper
6   German—Juliane House-Edmondson and Helmut Vollmer
7   Hebrew—Shoshana Blum-Kulka and Elite Olshtain
8   Russian—Jenny Thomas

For each language, data are being collected from both native and non-native speakers. The goals of the project are:

1   To establish native speakers' patterns of realization with respect to two speech acts—requests and apologies—relative to different social constraints, in each of the languages studied (situational variability).

2   To establish the similarities and differences in the realization patterns of requests and apologies cross-linguistically, relative to the same social constraints across the languages studied (cross-cultural variability).

3   To establish the similarities and differences between native and non-native realization patterns of requests and apologies relative to the same social constraints (individual, native versus non-native variability).

The method used for data collection

In order to achieve the above-mentioned goals, we needed an empirical design that would allow us to account for cross-cultural variability, situational variability, and individual variability (of learners) in the realization patterns of the same speech acts.

Instrument

In order to ensure cross-cultural comparability, it was decided to obtain the data by the use of a controlled elicitation procedure. The instrument used is a discourse completion test, originally developed for comparing the speech act realization patterns of native speakers and learners (Blum-Kulka, 1982). The test consists of incomplete discourse sequences that represent socially differentiated situations. Each discourse sequence presents a short description of the situation, specifying the setting, the social distance between the interlocutors, and their status relative to each other, followed by an incomplete dialogue. Informants are asked to complete the dialogue, thereby providing the speech act aimed at in the given context.

In the following examples of test items, (1) is constructed to elicit a request, and (2) to elicit an apology.

1. AT A STUDENTS' APARTMENT

Larry, John's room-mate, had a party the night before and left the kitchen in a mess.

John: Larry, Ellen and Tom are coming for dinner tonight and I'll have to start cooking soon;
Larry: OK, I'll have a go at it right away.

2. AT THE PROFESSOR'S OFFICE

A student has borrowed a book from her teacher, which she promised to return today. When meeting her teacher, however, she realizes that she forgot to bring it along.

Teacher: Miriam, I hope you brought the book I lent you.
Miriam:
Teacher: OK, but please remember it next week.

From the answers given to (1) we can learn the preferences native speakers have for realizing a request for action among familiar equals; a cross-linguistic comparison of the answers provided for the same item will tell us whether there are differences in the type of strategy chosen to realize the act under the same social constraints across languages. From the answers to (2) we can tell whether speakers in a given culture consider it appropriate to apologize in the specific situation, and if they do, what strategies they use for realizing the act, as compared with members of other cultures.

Situational variation: The test is also designed to capture possible variability across social constraints. There are eight items eliciting requests, and eight items eliciting apologies, which vary on the social parameters of $\pm$ social distance and $\pm$ "dominance".[5]

Individual variation: Theoretically, it would be possible to capture individual variability along personal variables such as age, sex, level of education, type of occupation, etc., by seeking out different types of populations of informants in each language. In practice, our design at this stage allows for only one dimension of possible personal variance in native use (sex differences), and aims at an otherwise homogeneous population for both native and non-native speakers. On another level, individual variation is being studied by seeking out native and non-native informants for each of the languages studied.

Population

The group of informants for each language totals 400, and comprises an equal number of male and female university students in their second and third years of study in any subject but linguistics. Half of the informants are native speakers, and half non-natives.

Procedure

The first version of the discourse completion test in English, prepared in collaboration by the research team, was pilot-tested with a group of fifty native English speakers at the Hebrew University in Jerusalem. The goal of the pilot test was to establish the contextual appropriateness of the items in eliciting the speech acts under study, i.e. to check whether the completion items indeed elicited requests and apologies. Dialogues that did not prove to be sufficiently delimited contextually were slightly changed, and the resulting version was administered to another thirty-five native English-speaking students. This version proved to be reliable in eliciting the speech acts under study; it became the master version for the project and was distributed among the members of the research group for translation into each of the respective languages. In the process of translation, each researcher was free to introduce slight cultural and stylistic modifications, as long as the main features of the social context presented by each item remained intact. For example, the university teacher in (2) above is referred to in Hebrew as *marce* (lecturer), in the German version as *Professor* and in the English version as "teacher". In addition to such cultural modifications, it was also necessary to differentiate stylistically between different English versions of the test, so as to adapt the style to the different English dialects studied. To date, the test has been administered in seven target languages (except Russian) to two hundred native speakers and two hundred learners. The analysis of the results, now under way, is based on a coding scheme prepared in collaboration by the research team. In the following sections, we shall present the basic categories of the scheme, illustrating them with examples from actual data in different languages.

Designing the framework for cross-linguistic analysis of speech act patterns: the coding scheme

The analysis of the data yielded by the responses to the discourse completion test is based on an independent evaluation of each response according to a number of dimensions. These dimensions have been given operational definitions, presented in the form of a coding scheme.

The scheme comprises two main parts—one for apologies and one for requests—and each of these in turn is subdivided into relevant major categories for analysis, further subdivided into subclassifications.

The process of developing a coding scheme with its major categories and subclassifications is a major challenge for research of this kind. Originally, the categories were defined on the basis of general theoretical considerations and previous work in the field by members of the team. This scheme was then further modified and refined so as to fit the data yielded in the different languages. The main categories or dimensions of the scheme (as will be subsequently described) were kept constant, since they proved to be valid for analysing the data in the languages investigated. The sub-categories, however, are still undergoing modification as fresh data are coming in.

Requests

DEFINING UNITS FOR ANALYSIS

The unit of analysis for both requests and apologies in the discourse completion test is the utterance or sequence of utterances supplied by the informant in completing the test item, provided it realizes (or contains a realization of) the speech act under study.

The first problem in looking at the sequence is in deciding whether all of its parts are of equal importance or serve equal functions in realizing the speech act aimed at. In the procedure adopted, the problem is dealt with by analyzing the sequence into the following segments: (a) Address Term(s); (b) Head act; (c) Adjunct(s) to Head act.[6] The segmentation is meant to delimit the utterance(s) that constitute the nucleus of the speech act (the "Head act"), i.e. that part of the sequence which might serve to realize the act independently of other elements. For example, consider (3):

	A	B	C
3	Danny/	could you lend me £100 for a week/	I've run into problems with the rent for my apartment.(F)[7]

The sequence in (3) would be broken down into three parts:

a. "Danny" Address term
b. "Could you . . . etc." Head act
c. "I've run into problems . . ." Adjunct to Head act

The distinction between Address terms and Head acts is evident and hence will not be elaborated on any further here. The issue of separating Head acts from Adjuncts, on the other hand, is a more problematic one. Consider the following:

4   Between room-mates in a student apartment

	A	B
4a	A: Would you mind cleaning up the kitchen?/	You left it in a mess last night. (F)
	B: OK, I'll clean it up.	
4b	A: You left the kitchen in a mess last night.	
	B: OK, I'll clean it up.	

The point to be considered in contrasting (4a) and (4b) is that the same words (i.e., "you left the kitchen in a mess last night" (utterance B in (4a) and A in (4b)) might in one case serve only to strengthen or support an act realized by other verbal means, while in another case, this utterance constitutes the act itself. Thus, utterance B is redundant from a strictly illocutionary point of view in (4a), while the same utterance realizes the request in (4b). It follows that the segmentations in Head acts and Adjuncts is based on sequential, as well as contextual and functional criteria.

STRATEGY TYPES

Examples (4a) and (4b) illustrate different options in terms of the level of "directness" chosen for the realization of the request. There have been several attempts in theoretical, as well as empirical work on the speech act of request (Searle, 1975, 1979; Ervin-Tripp, 1976; House and Kasper, 1981; Blum-Kulka, 1984) to set up a classification of request strategies that would form a cross-linguistically valid scale of directness.

On theoretical grounds, there seem to be three major levels of directness that can be expected to be manifested universally by requesting strategies:

a. the most direct, explicit level, realized by requests syntactically marked as such, such as imperatives, or by other verbal means that name the act as a request, such as performatives (Austin, 1962) and 'hedged performatives' (Fraser, 1975);
b. the conventionally indirect level; procedures that realize the act by reference to contextual preconditions necessary for its performance, as conventionalized in a given language (these strategies are commonly referred to in speech act literature, since Searle (1975), as indirect speech acts; an example would be "could you do it" or "would you do it" meant as requests);
c. nonconventional indirect level, i.e. the open-ended group of indirect strategies (hints) that realize the request by either partial reference to object or element needed for the implementation of the act ("Why is the window open"), or by reliance on contextual clues ("It's cold in here").

On the basis of our empirical work on requests in different languages (House and Kasper, 1981; Blum-Kulka et al., 1983), we have subdivided these three levels into nine distinct sub-levels called "strategy types", that together form a scale of indirectness. The categories on this scale are expected to be manifested in all languages studied; the distribution of strategies on the scale is meant to yield the relative degree of directness preferred in making requests in any given language, as compared with another, in the same situation. The nine strategy types are presented in Table 9.1.

Requests are by definition face-threatening acts (Brown and Levinson, 1978); by making a request, the speaker impinges on the hearer's claim to freedom of action and freedom from imposition. The variety of direct and indirect ways for making requests seemingly available to speakers in all languages is probably socially motivated by the need to minimize the imposition involved in the act itself. One way in which the speaker can minimize the imposition is by preferring an indirect strategy to a direct one, i.e. by activating choice on the scale of indirectness. But even after the speaker has decided on the level of directness for performing the act, s/he still has a variety of verbal means available with which to manipulate the degree of imposition involved. As suggested by Faerch and Kasper (1984) such manipulations might take the form of either "internal" or "external" modifications. Internal modifications are achieved through devices within the same "Head act", while the external modifications are localized not within

Table 9.1 Request strategy types—definition of coding categories and tokens

Types	Tokens
1 Mood derivable The grammatical mood of the verb in the utterance marks its illocutionary force as a request.	(5) Leave me alone (S3, AUE)*
	(6) Clean up this mess, please (S1, BE)
2 Explicit performatives The illocutionary force of the utterance is explicitly named by the speakers.	(7) *Avekšex lo lehaxnot kan et haoto* (I'm asking you not to park the car here) (S11, H) (8) *Ich bitte Sie den Platz sofort freizumachen* (S11, G)
3 Hedged performative Utterances embedding the naming of the illocutionary force.	(9) *Tišma, hayiti roca levakeš mimxa šetakdim et haharcaa šelxa bešavua* (I would like you to give your lecture a week earlier) (S15, H)
4 Locution derivable The illocutionary point is directly derivable from the semantic meaning of the locution.	(10) Madam, you'll have to move your car (S11, AUE) (11) *Entschuldigen Sie, aber Sie müssen diesen Platz freihalten* (S11, G)
5 Scope stating The utterance expresses the speaker's intentions, desire, or feeling vis à vis the fact that the hearer do X.	(12) I really wish you'd stop bothering me (S3, AUE) (13) *Ich möchte von Ihnen in Ruhe gelassen werden* (S3, G)
6 Language specific suggestory formula The sentence contains a suggestion to X.	(14) Why don't you get lost? (S3, AUE) (15) How about cleaning up? (S1, AUE) (16) So, why don't you come and clear up the the mess you made last night!? (S1, BE) (17) *Wie wärs wenn Du die Küche aufräumen würdest?* (S1, G)
7 Reference to preparatory conditions Utterance contains reference to preparatory conditions (e.g. ability or willingness, the possibility of the act being performed) as conventionalized in any specific language.	(18) Could you clear up the kitchen, please? (S1, BE) (19) Would you mind moving your car, please? (S11, AUE)
8 Strong hints Utterance contains partial reference to object or to elements needed for the implementation of the act (directly pragmatically implying the act).	(20) You've left this kitchen in a right mess (S1, BE) (21) *Fahren Sie nicht auch in die gleiche Richtung!* (S7, G)
9 Mild hints[8] Utterances that make no reference to the request proper (or any of its elements) but are interpretable through the context as requests (indirectly pragmatically implying the act).	(22) I'm a nun (in response to the persistent boy, S3, AUE) (23) *Ich bin verheiratet und habe zwei kleine Kinder* (same situation as above, S3, G)

* Situation 3. Australian English. The key to the situations represented in the test is provided in Appendixes A and B.

the "Head act" but within its immediate context. In neither case does the modification affect the level of directness of the act, nor does it alter its propositional content. In the following, we shall outline the dimensions of both types of manipulation as captured by the coding scheme.

POINT OF VIEW OPERATION[9]

Many request realizations include reference to the requestor ("I" the speaker), the requestee ("you" the hearer), and the action to be performed. The speaker might choose different ways to refer to any of these elements, manipulating by his or her choice the perspective s/he wishes the request to take. For example, the difference between "could you do it" and "could we have it done" is one of perspective—"could you . . ." emphasizes the role of the hearer in the speech event, while "could we . . ." stresses that of the speaker. Given the fact that in requests it is the hearer who is "under threat", any avoidance in naming the addressee as the principal performer of the act serves to soften the impact of the imposition. We call this dimension of the analysis request perspective and distinguish between the following categories:

a. Hearer oriented
    (24) Could *you* tidy up the kitchen soon? (S1, BE)
b. Speaker oriented
    (25) Do you think *I* could borrow your notes from yesterday's class? (S1, AUE)
c. Speaker and hearer oriented
    (26) So, could *we* please clean up? (S1, AUE)
d. Impersonal (The use of people/they/one as neutral agents, or the use of passivation)
    (27) So it might not be a bad idea to *get it cleaned up*. (S1, AUE)

SYNTACTIC DOWNGRADERS

Mitigating the speech act of request might also be achieved by purely syntactic means (compare "Do it"/"Will you do it?"). Hence we included in the analysis a dimension of syntactic downgraders, which enabled us to account for language specific surface structure variations in form independently of strategy type. For example:

a. Interrogative
    (28) Could you do the cleaning up? (S1, BE)
b. Negation[10]
    (29) Look, excuse me. I wonder if you *wouldn't mind* dropping me home? (S7, AE)
    (30) Könnten Sie Ihr Referat *nicht schon nächste* Woche halten? (S15, G)
c. Past tense
    (31) Raciti levakeš dxiya (I wanted to ask for a postponement; S13, H)
    (32) Ich *wollte* mich erkundigen, ob noch etwas frei ist (S9, G)
d. Embedded "if" clause
    (33) I would appreciate it if you left me alone (S3, AUE)
    (34) Wie wäre es, wenn Du vorher die Küche aufräumtest? (S1, G)

The use of syntactic mitigation can indicate several different attitudes. For example, the speaker might wish to indicate that s/he is pessimistic with regard to the outcome of the request (certain negative usage) or that s/he feels hesitant about making the request (marked modals, such as "might" instead of "can"). Syntactic manipulations also serve as distancing elements (past tense) and as hedging devices (embedded "if" clause).

OTHER DOWNGRADERS

The phenomenon analyzed on this dimension relates to kinds of modification available to the speaker for achieving different effects of "softening" the act, a phenomenon widely discussed in speech act literature (Lakoff, 1973; Labov and Fanshel, 1977; Brown and Levinson, 1978). The classification we adopted is based on Edmondson (1981), Edmondson and House (1981), and House and Kasper (1981). The classification is a pragma-linguistic one, i.e., it attempts to capture the pragmatic functions played by various linguistic elements in the discourse. Examples of categories are:

a. Consultative devices. Elements by means of which the speaker seeks to involve the hearer and bids for his/her cooperation, in addition to other strategy types. Frequently these devices are ritualized formulae:
    (35) *Do you think* I could borrow your lecture notes from yesterday? (S5, BE)
b. Understaters. Elements by means of which the speaker minimizes parts of the proposition, such as the required action or object, as in:
    (36) Could you tidy up *a bit* before I start? (S1, BE)
    (37) Könntest du *bitte etwas* Ordnung schaffen? (S1, G)
c. Hedges. Elements by means of which the speaker avoids specification in making a commitment to the illocutionary point of the utterance, in naming the required action, in describing the manner in which it is to be performed, or in referring to any other contextual aspect involved in its performance:
    (39) It would really help if *you did something* about the kitchen (S1, AUE)
d. Downtoner. Elements by means of which the speaker modulates the impact his/her utterance is likely to have on the hearer, achieving the modulation via devices signalling the possibility of non-compliance:
    (40) Kannst du den Mist *vielleicht* mal eben *wegräumen?* (S1, G)
    (41) Tuxlu *ulay* lehasia oti? (Will you be able *perhaps* to drive me? (S7, H)

UPGRADERS

Besides the options for decreasing the impact of the speech act, speakers also have available means by which to increase its compelling force. This function of aggravating the request can again be achieved through internal modifications. For example:

a. Intensifiers. Elements by means of which the speaker over-represents the reality denoted in the propositions:
    (42) Clean up this mess, it's *disgusting* (S1, BE)
    (43) Hören Sie, Sie werden *unverschämt!* (S3, G)
b. Expletives. Lexical intensifiers by means of which the speaker explicitly expresses negative emotional attitudes:
    (44) You still haven't cleaned up that *bloody mess!* (S1, BE)
    (45) Mäch gefalligst Deine *Scheisse weg!* (S1, G)

ADJUNCTS TO THE HEAD ACT

The modifications analyzed so far are all internal, i.e., operate within the "Head act". In addition to or instead of internal modification, the speaker might also choose to support or aggravate the speech act by external modifications. External modification does not affect the utterance used for realizing the act, but rather the context in which it is embedded, and thus indirectly modifies illocutionary force (Faerch and Kasper, 1984). Our classification of Adjuncts to Head act draws heavily on Edmondson (1981), Edmondson and House (1981) and House and Kasper (1981).[11] Some of the categories are:

a. Checking on availability. The speaker prefaces his/her main speech act with an utterance intended to check if the precondition necessary for compliance holds true.

   (46) *Haim atem nosim lexivun hair?* veim ken, haim efšar lehictaref? (Are you going in the direction of the town? And if so, is it possible to join you?) (S7, H).

   (47) Entschuldingen Sie, wohnen Sie nichtauch in der x Strasse Wäre es möglich dass Sie mich mitnähmen? (S7, G)

b. Getting a precommitment. The speaker precedes the act by an utterance that can count as an attempt to obtain a precommital.

   (48) *Ata muxan la'asot li tova?* Ulay ata muxan lehašil lie et haršimot šelxa lexama yamin? (*Will you do me a favor?* Could you perhaps lend me your notes for a few days?) (S5, H).

   (49) *Könnten Sie mir whol einen grossen Gefallen tun?* Ihr Referat passt viel besser nächste Woche und . . . (S15, G)

c. Grounder. The speaker indicates the reasons for the request. (Grounders may precede or follow the Head act)

   (50) Judith, *I missed class yesterday*, could I borrow your notes? (S5, BE)

   (51) Excuse me, *I've just missed my bus and you live on the same road*. I wonder if I could trouble you for a lift? (S7, BE)

d. Sweetener. By expressing exaggerated appreciation of the hearer's ability to comply with the request, the speaker lowers the imposition involved.

   (52) *Yeš lax ktav yad nehdar,* efšar lekabel et haxomer lekama yamim? (You have beautiful handwriting, would it be possible to borrow your notes for a few days? S5, H)

e. Disarmer. The speaker indicates his/her awareness of a potential offense, thereby attempting to anticipate possible refusal.

   (53) Excuse me, *I hope you don't think I'm being forward*, but is there any chance of a lift home? (S7, BE)

f. Cost minimizer. The speaker indicates consideration of the "cost" to the hearer involved in compliance with the request.

   (54) Pardon me, but could you give me a lift, *if you're going my way*, as I just missed the bus and there isn't another one for an hour (S7, BE).

To summarize the procedure of analysis for request, consider (54) again:

> Pardon me, but could you give me a lift if you're going my way, as I've just missed the bus and there isn't another one for an hour (S7, BE).

This sequence would be coded as follows:

Dimension	Category	Element
1 Address term	Attention getter	"Pardon me"
2 Request perspective	Hearer dominant	"Could you"
3 Request strategy	Preparatory	"Could you give"
4 Downgraders	—	none
5 Upgraders	—	none
6 Adjuncts to Head act	1 Cost minimizer	"if you're going my way"
	2 Grounder	"as I've just missed"

Apologies

The speech act of apologizing is rather different from that of requesting, since apologies are generally post-event acts, while requests are always pre-event acts: requests are made in an attempt to cause an event or change one—apologies signal the fact that a certain type of event has already taken place (or the speaker might be aware of the fact that it is about to take place). By apologizing, the speaker recognizes the fact that a violation of a social norm has been committed and admits to the fact that s/he is at least partially involved in its cause. Hence, by their very nature, apologies involve loss of face for the speaker and support for the hearer, while requests might involve loss of face for both interlocutors.

There are three preconditions (see also Faerch and Kasper, 1984) which must hold true for the apology act to take place:

a.   S did X or abstained from doing X (or is about to do it).
b.   X is perceived by S only, by H only, by both S and H, or by a third party as a breach of a social norm.
c.   X is perceived by at least one of the parties involved as offending, harming, or affecting H in some way.

In order for the apology to materialize when these three preconditions exist, S must be aware of all the preconditions and infer the need for him/her to apologize. By performing the apology S pays tribute to the social norm (recognizes precondition (b)) and attempts to placate the hearer (recognizes precondition (c)).

If the violation has not yet been committed or if H is not as yet aware of it, S has various ways in which to break the news to H. In our study we have excluded such cases and have concentrated on situations in which the offense is known to both H and S.

STRATEGY TYPES

The linguistic realization of the act of apologizing can take one of two basic forms, or a combination of both:

a.   The most direct realization of an apology is done via an explicit illocutionary force indicating device (IFID),[12] which selects a routinized, formulaic expression of regret (a performative verb) such as: (be) sorry; apologize, regret; excuse, etc. The IFID fulfills the function of signalling regret (on the S's part) for X (the violation), and thus is intended to placate the H. Our earlier work on apologies (Olshtain and Cohen, 1984; Olshtain and Blum-Kulka, 1983) seems to indicate that for each language there is a scale of conventionality of IFID realizations. Thus, in English, the most common form is "(be) sorry", while in Hebrew the word "slixa", which means literally "forgiveness," is the most conventional realization of an apology. In our cross-cultural study we will develop a scale of conventionality for each language based on the data analysed. Table 9.2 presents coding categories for English apology IFIDs.
b.   Another way in which one can perform an apology (with or without an IFID) is to use an utterance which contains reference to one or more elements from a closed set of specified propositions. The semantic content of these propositions relates to the preconditions (mentioned earlier) which must hold true for the apology act to take place. Thus, an utterance which relates to: (a) the cause for X; (b) S's responsibility for X; (c) S's willingness to offer repairs for X or promise forbearance (that X will never happen again) can serve as an apology.

Table 9.2 Apology IFID types

Type (*performative verb*)	*Examples*
1 (be) sorry	(55) I'm sorry (that) I'm so late (S10, AUE)
2 excuse	(56) Excuse me for being late again (F)
3 apologize	(57) I apologize for coming late to the meeting (F)
4 forgive	(58) Forgive me for coming late (F)
5 regret	(59) I regret that I can't help you (F)
6 pardon	(60) Pardon me for interrupting (F)

In Olshtain and Cohen (1984) we suggest the notion of an "apology speech act set" to encompass the potential range of apology strategies, any one of which (i.e. an IFID or reference to preconditions (a)–(c)) may count as a realization of an apology. Thus, in addition to the IFID, the apology speech act set includes four potential strategies for performing the act of apologizing: (1) an explanation or account of the cause which brought about the offense; (2) an expression of the S's responsibility for the offense; (3) an offer of repair; (4) a promise of forbearance. In studying apologies, we are, therefore, concerned on the one hand with the selection of an IFID and on the other with an open-ended variety of utterances which must, however, contain reference to the specified set of propositions.

As we have seen so far, the difference in nature between requests and apologies is such that documentation of verbal realizations requires different criteria for each of these two speech acts. For requests, the continuum between direct and indirect means available for realizing the act includes for every language a finite set of conventional (indirect) strategies, which are realized in linguistically fixed ways. For apologies, on the other hand, there is no distinct set of mutually exclusive categories comparable with the request strategy types. Instead, we need to establish the presence or absence of the IFID and of each one of the four potential strategies which make up the speech act set. Accordingly, the general procedure for coding apologies used here is based on a series of independent, dichotomous questions: (a) does the utterance in question contain an IFID? (b) does it contain an explanation? (c) does it express S's responsibility? (d) does it convey an offer of repair? or (e) does it contain a promise of forbearance? If the answer to any of these questions is affirmative, then the utterance is assigned that category according to a list of sub-classifications. (See Table 9.2 for a sub-classification of IFIDs.)

Taking on responsibility: The first strategy analyzed is that of S's responsibility. In the attempt to placate H, S often chooses to take on responsibility for the offense which created the need to apologize. Such recognition of one's fault is face-threatening to S and intended to appease H. The sub-categories for this strategy may be placed on a continuum from strong self-humbling on S's part to a complete and blunt denial of responsibility. Thus, the acceptance of responsibility would be viewed by H as an apology, while denial of responsibility would be intended as S's rejection of the need to apologize. In our coding scheme we allow for various degrees of "taking on responsibility". Some of the sub-categories are:

a.   S expresses trait of self-deficiency (thus accepting responsibility)
    (61) I'm so forgetful (S4, AUE)
    (62) You know me, I'm never on time (S10, AUE)

b. Explicit self-blame
   (63) It's my fault/mistake (S12, AUE)
c. Denial of fault (rejecting the need to apologize)
   (64) It's not my fault that it fell down (S16, AUE)

Explanation, offer of repair, and promise of forbearance, the three strategies which have not yet been discussed in detail, are inherently situation-dependent and are therefore closely related to the type of violation which occurred. Thus, when S intends to justify the offense as resulting from external factors over which s/he has no (or very little) control, then an explanation or account of the situation fulfills the function of an apology. Such an explanation may be explicitly related to the offense or it may present the "state of affairs" in a general way, thus relating implicitly to the offense. In situations where the damage or inconvenience which affected H can be compensated for, S can choose to offer repair in a specified or general manner, intending this as an apology. Lastly, there are offenses for which S feels the need to promise forbearance. This, in a way, is also admitting responsibility without necessarily stating it explicitly. Examples of the coding categories for the three strategies discussed are:

a. Explanation or account of cause
   i   explicit: (65) The bus was late (S10, AUE)
   ii   implicit: (66) Traffic is always so heavy in the morning (F)
b. Offer of repair
   i   specified: (67) I'll pay for the damage (S12, AUE)
   ii   unspecified: (68) I'll see what I can do (S8, AUE)
c. Promise of forbearance
   (69) This won't happen again (S10, AUE)

APOLOGY INTENSIFICATION

Apology intensification can be brought about by any one of the following devices:

a. an intensifying expression within the IFID;
b. expressing explicit concern for the hearer—externally to the IFID;
c. using multiple strategies (± IFIDs and any one or more of the four other strategies).

These three different manners of intensification are not mutually exclusive and could all be used simultaneously.

The intensification which operates within the IFID is usually expressed via an intensifier, as seen in the following:

a. Intensification
   adverbials: (70) I'm *very* . . . sorry (S16, AUE)
   repetition (or double intensifier): (71) Ani *nora nora* mictaeret (I'm terribly, terribly sorry, S4, H)

Externally to the IFID, intensification can be brought about by an expression of concern for the hearer:

b. Concern for the Hearer
   (72) Have you been waiting long? (S6, AUE)

There are a number of different factors which affect the S's decision to apologize in order to further restore the H's face, even at high cost to S's face. Perhaps the most significant of these factors is the degree of violation or the seriousness of the offense, as perceived by S. Furthermore, there may be cultural, personal, and contextual elements that influence the decision to apologize, and affect the strategy selection. Culturally, for instance, coming late to a meeting might be perceived as a more serious offense in an American setting than in a comparable Israeli one, and therefore Americans, as a group, will tend to apologize more intensely in this situation. On the individual level, some people tend to apologize more than others.

On the contextual level, the physical setting may be such that an offense can be perceived as more or less serious. Thus, bumping into someone in a crowded bus might be viewed as a considerably lower offense than bumping into someone in an open space. Faerch et al. (1984) describe the degree of offense as being assessed in terms of the extent to which it violates norms of behavior in a given sociocultural structure and how it affects the interlocutors' role and relationship.

Social parameters of distance, power, and age might also contribute, within the cultural setting, to intensification of the apology. Thus, in some cultures, the need to apologize to an older person or to a superior may be very pronounced.

Conclusions

The CCSARP Project was initiated in an attempt to investigate intra-language and inter-language (cultural) variability in the realization patterns of requests and apologies, with special emphasis on the comparison between native and non-native usage. We would like to conclude this paper by considering some of the basic theoretical and empirical implications raised by this type of research.

One of the central issues in the study of speech acts in general is the question of universality: to what extent is it possible to reveal basic pragmatic features for given speech acts, expected to be manifested in any natural language? The analytical framework for the investigation of speech acts developed for this study is based on a series of working hypotheses regarding what constitutes possible candidates for universal features of requests and apologies.

For requests, three such working hypotheses regarding universal features guided our work: (a) in requesting behavior it is possible to distinguish among central phenomena such as strategy types as different from internal and external modification; (b) requesting behavior is inherently based on choices from a variety of options ranging from direct to indirect ones; (c) the scale of indirectness encompasses at least three main types of option (direct, conventionally indirect, and non-conventionally indirect).

For apologies, two working hypotheses are relevant: in apologies it is possible to delimit linguistic markers of pragmatic force (IFIDs); and (b) additionally (or alternatively) to IFIDs, apologies can be realized by reference to a set of specified propositions.

The above hypotheses have been translated into operational dimensions for data analysis. The classification of the CCSARP data along these dimensions is thus a constant challenge to the possible universality of the pragmatic feature captured by each dimension.

Another facet of the issue of universality relates to the degree and nature of possible cross-cultural variance in speech act realization. The use of the same empirical framework for the analysis of data from the CCSARP languages is expected to reveal this degree of variance. Thus, for example, the distribution of request strategy types for the situations represented by the test will enable us to determine general cultural preferences along the direct/indirect continuum. Furthermore, cross-linguistic comparison of the distribution of request strategy types along the same social parameters should reveal the differential effect of these parameters on strategy selection.

The nature of cross-linguistic variance is expected to be revealed by further analysis of the data, via the sub-classifications within each dimension. These sub-classifications represent a repertoire of pragma-linguistic options: languages might differ in the range of options included in the repertoire, in the degree to which these options are realized, and in the manner in which they combine to realize the speech act in actual use. It should be added that the full nature of language-specific pragma-linguistic features will probably be revealed only by further qualitative analysis of the request and apology data in each of the languages studied.

The analysis of CCSARP data so far seems to be in line with the basic assumptions underlying the study. Namely, on the one hand the phenomena captured by the main dimensions are validated by the observed data, and thus might be regarded as potential candidates for universality; on the other hand, the cross-linguistic comparative analysis of the distribution of realization patterns, relative to the same social constraints, reveals rich cross-cultural variability.

The CCSARP project, as outlined in this paper, is admittedly an ambitious undertaking. Hence a word of caution is called for: the phenomena captured by the analytical framework of the project are not to be regarded as an exhaustive description of requests and apologies, but rather as reflecting our present understanding of the speech acts studied. Subsequent stages of the project will, we hope, deepen this understanding.

Notes

1 CCSARP stands for Cross-Cultural Speech Act Realization Patterns. The project participants are: Shoshana Blum-Kulka, Hebrew University, Jerusalem; Claus Faerch, University of Copenhagen; Juliane House-Edmondson, University of Hamburg; Gabriele Kasper, University of Aarhus; Elite Olshtain, Tel Aviv University; Ellen Rintell, University of Massachusetts; Jenny Thomas, University of Lancaster; Elda Weizman, Hebrew University; Nessa Wolfson, University of Pennsylvania; Eija Ventola, University of Sydney; Helmut Vollmer, University of Ösnabrück.

2 Particular contributions to the presentation here were made by Claus Faerch, Gabriele Kasper, and Juliane House-Edmondson. For more details on the research design and methodology, see also Faerch and Kasper et al. (1984).

3 Two other variables that might influence choice of request strategy in context are: (a) the goal of the request and (b) the degree of imposition involved. Thus, it might be expected that requests for permission, since by definition they occur between unequals, will tend to be less direct than requests for action. The results of an ethnographic study on the language of requesting in Israel, based on close to 500 request tokens, showed requests for action as being the most direct, and requests for permission as the most indirect, with requests for goods and for information clustering in between the two extremes (Blum-Kulka et al., 1983). In the CCSARP project, the goal of the request is built into the description of the situation and hence can be taken into account in the analysis of the data, though at this stage it is not being manipulated systematically. Degree of imposition is a difficult variable to control for cross-culturally, since it might be the case that the same request, such as asking for a small loan, is considered in one culture more of an imposition than in another. In order to come to grips with this issue, we have been experimenting in Hebrew with a separate questionnaire, which contains the CCSARP project discourse sequences with completed dialogues. A group of judges has been asked to rate the degree of imposition involved in each request situation, presented to the judges in the form of questions such as "How difficult do you think it was to make the request?" and "How would you estimate the chances of the request being complied with?". The results indicate significant inter-situation variation in the ratings given by native speakers of Hebrew. The rating questionnaire is now in the process of being adapted for use in the other languages involved in the project.

4 The data have been analysed (so far) by Blum-Kulka and Olshtain.

5 The following role constellations are represented on the test: (a) [+ SD], [x > y]; (b) [− SD] [x = y]; (c) [− SD] [x > y]; and (d) [+ SD] [x < y].

6   The terms "Head act" and "Adjunct" have been introduced by Ervin Tripp and David Gordon in the coding manual for analyzing requests within the framework of the "Social Development and Communication Strategies Project" (David Gordon, personal communication).

7   The letter in parenthesis following the examples stands for data source: F—fabricated; AE—American English; AUE—Australian English; BE—British English; CF—Canadian French; D—Danish; G—German; H—Hebrew. S stands for number of situation on the discourse completion test. Thus, S3, AUE, means that the utterance in question was supplied by a native speaker of Australian English in completing the dialogue in situation 3.

8   For the distinction between Strong Hints and Mild Hints, see House and Kasper (1981) and also Wilson and Sperber (1981).

9   The notion of "point of view operations" here relates to the more general issue of the ways in which sentences in natural language embed certain aspects of the context of the situation. Fillmore (1971, 1975) has shown the different ways in which sentences encode such references to context, and Brown and Levinson (1978) have demonstrated how the deictic references can be manipulated for politeness functions in speech act realization. The term "point of view operations" is borrowed from Brown and Levinson.

10 Excluding clear propositional negation, such as "don't do it."

11 Edmondson et al. use the term "Supportive Move". The term "Adjunct" is preferred here, because it leaves room for the possibility of both aggravating and supporting external modifications of requests, instances of which occurred in the CCSARP data. For example, a threat added to a request would be an aggravating Adjust.

12 The term "illocutionary force indicating device" is taken from Searle (1969, p. 62).

Appendix A: Request situations

S1   A student asks his room-mate to clean up the kitchen which the other left in a mess.

S3   A girl tries to get rid of a boy pestering her on the street.

S5   A student asks another student to lend her some lecture notes.

S7   A student asks people living on the same street for a ride home.

S9   Applicant calls for information on a job advertised in a paper.

S11 A policeman asks a driver to move her car.

S13 A student asks a teacher for an extension for finishing a seminar paper.

S15 A university teacher asks a student to give his lecture a week earlier than scheduled.

Appendix B: Apology situations

S2   A university professor promised to return the student's term paper that day but didn't finish reading it.

S4   A student borrowed her professor's book, which she promised to return that day, but forgot to bring it.

S6   A staff manager has kept a student waiting for half an hour for a job interview because he was called to an unexpected meeting.

S8   The waiter in an expensive restaurant brings fried chicken instead of bœuf à la maison to a surprised customer.

S10 A notoriously unpunctual student is late again for a meeting with a friend with whom she is working on a joint paper.

S12 A driver in a parking lot backs into the hearer's car.

S14 The speaker offended a fellow worker during a discussion at work. After the meeting, the fellow worker mentions this fact.

S16 The speaker has placed a shopping bag on the luggage rack of a crowded bus. When the bus brakes, the bag falls down and hits another passenger.

References

Austin, J. (1962). *How to do things with words*. London: Oxford University Press.

Blum-Kulka, S. (1982). Learning to say what you mean in a second language: a study of the speech act performance of Hebrew second language learners. *Applied Linguistics*, III/1, 29–59.

Blum-Kulka, S. (1984). Interpreting and performing speech acts in a second language: a cross-cultural study of Hebrew and English in N. Wolfson and J. Elliot (eds), *TESOL and sociolinguistic research*. Rowley, MA: Newbury House.

Blum-Kulka, S., Danet, B. and Gerson, R. (1983). The language of requesting in Israeli society. Paper presented at the Language and Social Psychology Conference, Bristol.

Brown, P. and Levinson, S. (1978). Universals of language usage: politeness phenomena. In E. Goody (ed.), *Questions and politeness*. Cambridge: Cambridge University Press.

Cohen, A. D. and Olshtain, E. (1981). Developing a measure of socio-cultural competence: the case of apology. *Language Learning*, 31, 1.

Edmondson, W. (1981). *Spoken discourse. A model for analysis*. London: Longman.

Edmondson, W. and House, J. (1981). *Let's talk and talk about it*. Munich: Urban and Schwarzenberg.

Ervin-Tripp, S. (1976). Is Sybil there? The structure of some American English directives. *Language in Society*, 5/1, 25–66.

Faerch, C. and Kasper, G. (1984). Pragmatic knowledge: rules and procedures. *Applied Linguistics*, 5(3), 214–25.

Faerch, C., Kasper, G. et al. (1984). CCSARP—a project description. University of Copenhagen (mimeo).

Fraser, B. (1975). Hedged performatives. In P. Cole and S. L. Morgan (eds), *Syntax and semantics*, Vol. 3. New York: Academic Press.

Fillmore, C. (1971). Towards a theory of deixis. *The PCCLLU Papers*, 3/4, 219–41 (Department of Linguistics, University of Hawaii).

Fillmore, C. (1975). Santa Cruz lectures on deixis (1971). Indiana University Linguistics Club (mimeo).

House, J. (1982). Conversational strategies in German and English dialogues. In G. Nickel and D. Nehls (eds), *Error analysis. Constructive linguistics and second language learning* (Special Issue of IRAL). Heidelberg: Julius Groos.

House, J. and Kasper, G. (1981). Politeness markers in English and German. In F. Coulmas (ed.), *Conversational routine*. The Hague: Mouton.

Kasper, G. (1981). *Pragmatische Aspekte in der Interimsprache*. Tubingen: Gunther Narr.

Labov, W. and Fanshel, D. (1977). *Therapeutic discourse*. New York: Academic Press.

Lakoff, R. (1973). The logic of politeness: or minding your p's and q's. Proceedings of the Ninth Regional Meeting of the Chicago Linguistic Society.

Levinson, S. (1983). *Pragmatics*. Cambridge: Cambridge University Press.

Olshtain, E. and Blum-Kulka, S. (1983). Degree of approximation. Paper presented at Language Input in Second Language Acquisition Conference, Ann Arbor, Michigan.

Olshtain, E. and Cohen, A. (1984). Apology: a speech act set. In N. Wolfson and J. Elliott (eds), *TESOL and sociolinguistic research*. Rowley, MA: Newbury House.

Searle, J. (1969). *Speech acts—an essay in the philosophy of language*. London: Cambridge University Press.

Searle, J. (1975). Indirect speech acts. In P. Cole and S.L. Morgan (eds), *Syntax and semantics, Vol. 3: Speech acts*. New York: Academic Press.

Searle, J. (1979). *Expression and meaning*. Cambridge: Cambridge University Press.

Thomas, J. (1983). Cross-cultural pragmatic failure. *Applied Linguistics*, 4/2, 91–112.

Widdowson, H. (1978). *Teaching language as communication*. London: Oxford University Press.

Wilson, D. and Sperber, D. (1981). On Grice's theory of conversation. In P. Werth (ed.), *Conversation and discourse*. London: Croom Helm.

Wolfson, N. (1981). Compliments in cross-cultural perspective. *TESOL Quarterly*, 15/2.

Chapter 10

TAMAR KATRIEL

THE *DUGRI* RITUAL

THE *DUGRI* WAY OF SPEAKING IS embodied in a speech event that I have dubbed "the *dugri* ritual." In native terms, this event is referred to as *siha dugrit*, a *dugri* talk. A *dugri* talk is not just any encounter in which the *dugri* idiom is employed or in which utterances indexed as *dugri* are exchanged. A *dugri* talk is a distinct speech event with a sequential and motivational structure of its own. That Sabras themselves believe this to be true is shown, first, by references made to *siha dugrit*, as well as by the fact that informants clearly distinguished between speaking *dugri* and having a *dugri* talk. Thus, although a *dugri* talk implies *dugri* speech, speaking *dugri* does not necessarily imply the staging of a *dugri* talk. The consideration of a *dugri* talk, therefore, takes us beyond the single utterance or single speech-act level of analysis and involves the examination of larger discourse units and their episodic structure.[1]

Two typical enactments of the *dugri* ritual that appear in my data involve interactions in the workplace, that is, in a context that clearly relates to the social modality of *societas*, with its system of differentiated roles and statuses. In one case, an engineer in his early thirties told me at some length about a *dugri* talk he initiated with his boss. He started what he described as *siha dugrit* by declaring: "I want to speak to you *dugri*. I don't like the way this department is being run." In another case, a young faculty member of approximately the same age (whom some of his colleagues had independently identified as a *dugri* fellow) initiated what he referred to as a *dugri* talk with one of the senior professors in his department just as he was being put up for tenure, criticizing the way things were going in the department. He prefaced his list of complaints by saying that he wanted to voice his opinion before he got tenure so that no one could say he had been afraid to speak his mind before his job was secure. The forthcoming analysis should clarify what these two men were up to.

These examples could be easily multiplied. Let me mention a third example of the *dugri* ritual to which I myself was a witness, and which brought home to me its compelling force in a most vivid way. It occurred during a meeting between a group of university faculty and representatives of the Israeli Ministry of Education who had sought the academics' assistance in setting up some new extracurricular programs for elementary school children. In previous meetings, there had been fundamental differences of opinion between a number of the

Source: Katriel, T. (1986). Excerpts from *Talking straight: dugri speech in Israeli Sabra culture* (pp. 57–72). Cambridge: Cambridge University Press.

academics and the ministry people on the nature of the proposed programs and the kind of involvement expected from the former.

The meeting opened with a lengthy conciliatory speech by a ministry representative in which he acknowledged the validity of the academics' view that educational efforts should be directed toward the betterment of regular schooling, but pointed out the practical constraints under which the ministry operated, which had led them to plan the proposed programs. He expressed the need to bridge over differences and reach a working consensus.

One of the university professors, a first-generation Sabra, who had initially demanded a principled discussion of the cooperation proposed, changed the tone of the encounter by initiating a version of the *dugri* ritual. Using blunt language and a confrontational tone, she argued that the university should not play the role of educational contractor for the ministry and should become involved only with programs that called for and permitted the exploration and rethinking of educational issues and policies. She said that as long as children's regular schooling was allowed to be meaningless, there was no point in establishing extracurricular programs. She stressed that she had no problem helping those programs in her field of expertise and would do so if asked, but refused to share in the pretense that anything of substance was being done for the children. She concluded by saying that she would not lend her name to something she did not believe in.

The interesting point from the standpoint of this study is not just that this event provided me with a live, prototypical example of the *dugri* ritual as it will be characterized later, but that, familiar with my work, its initiator turned to me shortly after the event and, half triumphant, half embarrassed, said: "Well, there, I gave you an example of a *dugri* ritual." Neither she as initiator nor I as peripheral participant had been aware of this while it was happening, but both of us readily recognized it for what it was afterward, and could discuss our interpretations of it in the terms employed in the forthcoming analysis.

Notably, unlike the tenure situation, this case did not involve a clear-cut, hierarchical relationship but rather an attempt to prevent the incorporation of the academics into the educational establishment. It was a ritual act of confrontation, a ceremony of discord, performed in the culture's legitimatizing idiom: the idiom in which one's integrity and one's shared cultural world are reaffirmed. The use of *dugri* speech here, as in all other cases of its ritual enactment, served to counteract what in the Sabra culture is considered the tendency to gloss over interpersonal differences in the service of a false, superficial consensus, a concern with harmony in interpersonal relations at the expense of dealing with basic issues and matters of principle. Despite the discomfort caused by the confrontational tone, the *dugri* ritual was experienced as a moment of true contact, of unmasking, and was received as both legitimate and appropriate even by participants whose own style was a far cry from *dugri* speech.

It is not claimed that participants consciously recognize the ritual dimensions of a *dugri* talk. What I propose to do is to apply the ritual metaphor to the interaction referred to by my informants as a *dugri* talk so as to shed some light on what I perceive to be its ritual dimensions.[2] My focus, thus, differs from that of Turner in his study of the ritual process, with its emphasis on the high-profile, dramatic forms of expressive culture, in that it deals with everyday communicative practices that are not "officially" regarded as cultural performances by members. On the other hand, unlike other approaches geared to the everydayness of members' experience,[3] this study seeks to capture the more highly structured moments of life. It is these structured, repetitive, and affectively colored interaction sequences, experienced by cultural members in their everydayness, that are most readily amenable to analysis within a ritual framework.

In what follows, I try to show that the *dugri* ritual manifests a recognizable pattern of symbolic actions whose function includes the reaffirmation of participants' relationship to what can be considered a culturally sanctioned "sacred object," the Sabra image. A *dugri* talk can be seen as providing a context in which the meanings and values associated with *dugri* speech are encapsulated and dramatized. In particular, it is a context in which the image of the Sabra as the dauntless, morally driven, sincere New Jew is reaffirmed through a ritualized test of rebellious confrontation.

Thus, despite the discordant note associated with it, the *dugri* ritual manifests the functional nature of conflict as an integrative force in the life of individuals and groups. Simmel (1955, p. 19) expounds on the psychological satisfaction inherent in the act of opposition that "allows us to prove our strength consciously and only thus gives vitality and reciprocity to conditions from which, without such corrective, we would withdraw at any cost." Myerhoff's (1978, p. 184) account of a repetitive pattern of conflict among elderly Jews in California stresses both the psychological satisfaction associated with conflict and its bonding potential:

> To fight each other, people must share norms, rules, vocabulary, and knowledge. Fighting is a partnership, requiring cooperation. A boundary-maintaining mechanism—for strangers cannot participate fully—it is also above all a profoundly sociable activity.[4]

The agonistic behavior that constitutes the *dugri* ritual is perceived by members of the culture as a sign of engagement and commitment (the most frequently used native term being *ihpatijut*, which means concern with others or with public issues). It is conduct that is both self-assertive and communally oriented. As such, it is contrasted by cultural members to "silence" (in the sense of a failure to speak up, as in "I'll tell him *dugri*, I won't shut up") as well as with indifference (*lo ihpatijut*), which, as Simmel points out, is what both conflict and positive association should be conceptually distinguished from.

Given the potency of such ceremonial discords, it is no wonder that enactments of the *dugri* ritual tend to be so intensely remembered by participants in it, especially the initiators. Such events have often been reported to me spontaneously by friends and even casual acquaintances in rather emotional tones. The telling of the event carries its ritual import even beyond the context in which it was enacted, so that the initiator's sense of integrity is further reaffirmed and the sense of discomfort often associated with initiating conflict is alleviated.[5]

The form and function of a *dugri* talk

The forthcoming account of the *dugri* ritual utilizes Hymes's (1972) schema for the study of speech events, which was proposed as a heuristic input for ethnographic descriptions and includes the following components: message form, message content, setting, scene, participants, ends (further divided into goals and outcomes), key, channels, instrumentalities (or forms of speech), and norms of interaction and interpretation. These categories, though analytically distinguishable, often blend into each other in the description of actual speech events, as is the case at various points in the following account.

Participants

In broad terms, the initial relationship among participants in the *dugri* ritual is defined by their relative position, that is, by social-structural differences, rather than by a shared cultural core. In addition, participants must accept the Sabra culture's interpersonal ideology according to which the attempt to recreate *communitas* symbolically through direct, confrontational speech is an intelligible and legitimate interactional move. Indeed, a *dugri* talk can be seen as a way of effecting a ritualized transition from *societas* to a *communitas*-like state marked by a "back-stage" language of behavior. This implies the aforementioned twofold condition for participation: Participants must be linked through suspendable, social-structural bonds but at the same time must share the Sabra interpersonal ideology that guarantees the possibility of recreating the social modality of *communitas* within the ritual context.

The felicitous performance of the *dugri* ritual depends not only on the speaker's projection of a Sabra image but also on his ability to convey that image to the addressee, or at least to cast the addressee in the role of someone who can understand and accept it.[6] In contacts between the Sabra and outsiders to the culture who, unlike the non-Sabra parent generation, are neither familiar with nor inclined to accept the *dugri* idiom, the staging of the ritual is felt to be utterly inappropriate.

An example of a context in which the recreation of *communitas* through direct, confrontational, *dugri* speech is neither intelligible nor legitimate is that of diplomatic encounters. In fact, one of the opposites offered by informants for *dugrijut* was diplomacy. Diplomatic encounters probably stand at the farthest remove from *dugri* talks: Diplomacy has room neither for the *dugri* speaker's preference for clear-cut, unambiguous expression nor for his or her tolerance of a confrontational, direct approach. When this is forgotten or deliberately ignored, as seems to have been the case with former Defense Minister Ariel Sharon in one of his reported meetings with American Special Ambassador Philip Habib during the Lebanon War, the result can be confusing and disconcerting. In this case, the directness of the Sabra style seems to have been stretched beyond its customary bounds: The line between *dugrijut* and the "mere rudeness" from which my informants often tried to distinguish it—a line that is not always easy to draw—was blurred by the violation of a rule of participation. This made the rough edge of the talk more clearly noticeable.

Thus, a news headline in *Maariv* (July 23, 1982) reported that, "Habib needed medical treatment after a talk with Sharon." The subheading consisted of an anonymous citation stating that, "Habib was on the verge of a heart attack," apparently as a result of the fact that "Sharon employed a tough, resolute and blunt style." The body of the article stated:

> The protocol of the Habib–Sharon talk indicates that it was, indeed, not a routine conversation. The Minister of Defense, in his open and direct way of speaking, told the American intermediary what was on his mind, given the lack of progress in the negotiation which costs Israel human lives.

In fact, this conversation triggered what is known as a diplomatic incident as well as puzzlement at Israel's intentions and, possibly, a misinterpretation of its stance. In this as in other communicative contexts, the way things were said carried more weight than their actual content. This incident illustrates that the interpretations of the *dugri* style inside and outside of the Sabra culture often do not coincide. Thus, in the English-language daily newspaper of the same day, the *Jerusalem Post*, Wolf Bitzer reported that the American ambassador to Israel, Mr. Lewis, had complained on behalf of the U.S. government to Begin of Sharon's brusqueness with Habib. Begin apparently endorsed both the positions put forward by Sharon and the straightforward manner he had employed. The incident, according to this report, actually led to misunderstandings: Although he had been invited to Jerusalem by Sharon on Begin's behalf, Habib seemed to have interpreted Sharon's straight talk on that occasion as a signal that Israel had despaired of the diplomatic effort.

In discussing these issues with a couple of newcomers from the United States who resented the Sabras' directness, I noted a very interesting point in folk comparisons of Israeli and American patterns. The Americans' objection was not to the bluntness associated with *dugri* speech; they felt that, especially in discussions that would be classified as a *dugri* talk, the speaker, although claiming to be direct, was "hiding behind an impersonal facade," was not talking as one person to another. The *dugri* comments were made in the name of some general principle and were sometimes even prefaced by "Don't take it personally." I think these commentators captured an important aspect of the *dugri* ritual: Although it provides the initiator with a context for self-assertion, it is not the self-assertion of the individual qua individual; it is, rather, the principled defiance of the individual as the representative of an alternative, more valid point of view, of the individual as a paradigm-bearer. It was both startling and sobering for me to find out that the very cultural performance that epitomizes the Sabras' directness from the natives' point of view can be experienced as annoyingly indirect by at least some Americans, whose cultural interpretation of directness seems to include reference to interactants' orientation to their unique personalities (cf. Katriel and Philipsen 1981).

One more point: Although the *dugri* ritual marks an interactional shift of gears involving the social leveling of the participants, this does not imply an interactional symmetry between them. In fact, the ritual is organized in terms of two clearly differentiated interactional roles: The first is the role of the initiator, the person who has a protest to voice and who defines the situation as calling for the enactment of the *dugri* ritual, thereby challenging the addressee's position by expounding his or her views. This role involves personal choice and hence, by its very nature, implies a measure of self-expression. The second is the role of the respondent, the person whose position or paradigm is being challenged. The ritual is primarily the initiator's; the respondent's role is secondary. He or she contributes mainly by being attentive and thus facilitating the initiator's attempt to stage his or her "drama of character."

These observations concerning the structure of participation, which is typical of *dugri* rituals, bring out the nature of the role relationships associated with it. These role relationships cannot be comprehended in terms of Bernstein's (1964) distinction between positional versus personal social orientations. In the context of the *dugri* ritual, one set of positional relationships is suspended and another one invoked: What is suspended is a set of relationships pertaining to some domain of *societas*, and what is invoked is a set of relationships modeled on the liminal-state quality of *communitas*. In this ritually constructed, liminal-like order, participants play a representative role; they do not simply express their individual personalities. It is a relational domain akin to Bernstein's positional order in that it is grounded in a shared cultural norm. It is, however, unlike Bernstein's positional order in that the shared cultural norm is invoked precisely to engage in "elaborated" speech, speech oriented to the goals of clarification, the avoidance of misunderstanding, and the expression of divergent opinions. These features are associated with "elaborated" coding and personal relationships in Bernstein's work and not with limited, norm-oriented usage, characterized by implicit understandings that are invoked by set phrases, proverbs, and so on.

The poignancy of the ritual is greatest when the initiator has less power than the addressee in societal terms (the employee in the workplace, the son in the family), when no appeal can be made to institutional rights to warrant outspokenness. When the ritual is initiated by the more powerful person (the boss in the workplace, the father in the family), the enactment of the ritual implies that the initiator either cannot or refuses to appeal to his or her institutional rights.

In sum, whether a person's place in a hierarchy precludes outspokenness, or whether the person is unwilling or unable to mobilize his or her power-based right to speak, the *dugri* ritual is a culturally available format for sidestepping the bounds of *societas*. The confrontational encounter provides an arena for the assertion of character while at the same time being softened by the spirit of *communitas* upon which it is modeled. Its ritual containment prevents it from radically affecting participants' structural relations outside of the ritual framework, while it provides a forum for the airing of discontent and for affecting future action.

Setting

If the initiator wants to ensure that the *dugri* talk remains ritually contained, he or she enacts it in a private setting. This protects the respondent's interests, since the absence of onlookers softens the edge of the *dugri* talk. In taking this precaution, however, the initiator limits the audience for his or her own "drama of character," which has its own drawbacks. So, in choosing the setting for the staging of the ritual, both the initiator's and the respondent's interests come into play, and in making a choice the initiator indicates the degree to which they have been taken into account.

A *dugri* talk is a somewhat formal event and has to be set up in terms of time and place. It is not initiated casually. Typically, the initiator informs the respondent that he or she wishes to have a talk and will wait for an appropriate time or place to be suggested. This occurs when he or she is willing to oblige the respondent by limiting participation and conducting the talk in an inner office or the like. When no such consideration is intended, perhaps because it is not practicable (as in the meeting with the Ministry of Education people cited earlier), the ritual is enacted in a public domain, in view and hearing of other participants, who no less than the respondent become an audience for the initiator's message and self-dramatization.

Scene

My informants' characterization of the psychological setting of a *dugri* talk, as one calling for a corrective action, a protest, or a challenge, marks it as a rhetorical situation (Bitzer, 1968). This was revealed most clearly when they repeatedly cited two contexts in which they would not stage a *dugri* talk. The first one involved situations in which *dugri* speech would be ineffective, "would make no difference," or "would not change anything." The second one involved situations in which the informant had no stake: People said they would not bother to speak *dugri*, let alone initiate a *dugri* talk, if they "did not care" whether things would change or not. In this instance, what was missing was the sense of personal commitment and personal responsibility for shaping one's social world that is associated with the enactment of the *dugri* ritual.

A social situation is defined as rhetorical when it is interpreted as involving a rhetorical exigency, that is, in Bitzer's terms, an "imperfection marked by urgency" (1968, p. 386), which calls for a corrective rhetorical act. It is a rhetorical exigency because it is believed that it can be positively modified and that this modification requires or is assisted by the use of discourse. Thus, in order for a member of the culture to initiate the *dugri* ritual, he or she should:

1. Define the situation as involving a rhetorical exigency, that is, as requiring a remedy to be achieved through discourse.
2. Define the respondent as a rhetorical audience, one of a category of persons who "are capable of being influenced by discourse and of being mediators of change" (Bitzer, 1968, p. 387).
3. Feel a moral obligation and commitment to interpret the situation as one addressed to himself or herself.
4. Feel that he or she has the right to confront the respondent in demanding the correction of the situation.

The *dugri* ritual, then, can be regarded as a rhetorical act that seeks to function "as a fitting response to a situation which needs and invites it" (Bitzer, 1968, p. 386). It is predicated on a sense of communal participation interpreted both as an obligation and a right to have one's say and to influence one's social world in the direction one sees fit. The *dugri* ritual provides a way of doing so and a context for the self-dramatization of the person prepared to speak up. Therefore, even when the initiator does not really hope that much can be accomplished by a *dugri* talk (as was the case in all three examples cited at the beginning of the article), it is perceived as a link in a change-producing chain of actions in that it signals division and lack of consensus. The division is not only acknowledged but also intensified by the initiator's refusal to gloss over fundamental differences for the sake of maintaining the appearance of harmony, to "plaster the issues" (*letajeah et hadvarim*), as the prevailing metaphor has it. There is no expectation, however, that the ritual confrontation will lead to the resolution of these differences. In fact, persons who reported about *dugri* talks they had initiated indicated that they would have been confused and even embarrassed if the respondent had been readily persuaded. This would have meant that their "drama of character" had exceeded its stage. Immediate resolution thus implies a misjudgment. To know this is an important element of participant "competence," since to overdramatize one's "character" implies loss of face no less than underdramatizing it, which suggests that discussions of demeanor as an element of facework should be equally concerned with both aspects of self-presentation.

Message content

As noted earlier, in terms of its content the *dugri* ritual is a protest against a particular state of affairs the initiator perceives the addressee to uphold, and with which the initiator is dissatisfied. The *dugri* message involves an explicit verbalization of one's thoughts concerning a controversial issue as well as a commitment to deal with it, however uncomfortable and costly this may be in terms of participants' social relationships.

More often than not, the situation protested against in the *dugri* ritual is formulated as an issue related to the public good rather than to one's personal interest. It thus tends to be cast in moralistic terms and to deal with basic tenets and principles of moral and social life, with competing paradigms rather than with localized, particularized problems. The protest against "the way the department is being run" thus tends to challenge undemocratic management procedures, and the criticism of a university department becomes a defense of academic standards.

As noted earlier, differences of opinion that could be readily dealt with in discussion between the participants would not be proper candidates for a *dugri* ritual. This ritual, like the "griping ritual" studied elsewhere (Katriel, 1985), is not a problem-solving session, although it takes problematic issues as its topic. Whatever the subject of the *dugri* ritual, its underlying theme is the tension between dissensus and affiliation: The initiator, through an act of protest and self-assertion, disassociates himself from a given structural relationship or social paradigm while at the same time asserting a deeper affiliation with a more basic and more encompassing one.

The form in which this tension is expressed and resolved seems to be rooted as much in traditional Jewish culture as in a revolutionary orientation. The actualization of the individual in and through communal affiliation is a long-standing theme in Judaic culture as emerges, for example, from Robinson's (1964) discussion of the "corporate personality" in ancient Israel. A traditional ritual context in which this conception is dramatized is that of public prayer, whose symbolic structure has been insightfully analyzed by Prell-Foldes (1980). Jewish public prayer and the *dugri* ritual, in its very different but structurally parallel fashion, both demonstrate the possibility of interweaving individuality and communal affiliation in constituting members' sense of self.[7]

Message form

In this section I take the speech-event as the unit of analysis, sketching its internal, episodic organization. The explicitness and clarity of expression associated with the *dugri* code are also manifested in the form of the messages conveyed in a *dugri* talk. Speech exchanged in such talks seeks to avoid ambiguities and elaborate expressions that would render interpretation less immediate and clear-cut. This speech reflects both the attitude of "antistyle" and a stance of commitment, of standing behind one's words.

The sequential organization of a *dugri* ritual can, I believe, be fruitfully considered with reference to Turner's (1974, 1980, 1982) unit of a social drama, a unit of a particular type of agonistic behavior, divided into four phases: *breach*, which refers to the symbolic trigger of discord; *crisis*, a phase of acutely experienced division and disorientation; an ensuing phase of *redressive action* in which attempts are made to encompass the breach within the social order; and finally, *reintegration* when these attempts are successful or *schism* when they are not.

In staging a *dugri* talk the initiator ritually triggers a sequence of events that can be understood as a structural variant of a social drama. In fact, the *dugri* ritual can be viewed as involving a ritualization of the breach and crisis phases of a social drama. The breach in this case, in addition to the actual protest made, involves a rejection of what Goffman (1967) considers a basic interactional norm: interactants' implicit agreement to maintain their own and each other's face. That is, the breach of content is echoed by what on one level may be interpreted as a breach of form. The breach is legitimated in the name of another, higher set of norms—the norms mandating the communicative expression of sincerity, strength, courage, commitment, and so on. The latter values, articulated in the ritualized form of a *dugri* talk, dramatically illustrate the possibility of a competing sociocultural paradigm that involves a reinterpretation of the notion of face and suggests an alternative mode of human bonding.

This dramatization has an intense quality but is contained, encased in a ritual framework, not the outburst of the person blowing his top or the recklessness of the rebel burning bridges behind him. At the same time, the social drama sequel is not rounded off; it does not develop beyond the crisis phase, nor is it expected to. The ritual fulfills its function precisely by creating and culturally locating a state of crisis that remains unresolved. It thus both indexes the existence of conflict and capitalizes on it, suggesting the possibility of change within a culturally sanctioned framework.

There is a generally recognized pattern in the sequence of symbolic acts comprising the *dugri* ritual. As noted, a *dugri* talk tends to be prearranged in some way, often by the initiator's offer to have a talk with the respondent. When they get together the respondent, usually the more powerful person, may ask about the initiator's purpose or problem. In response, the initiator indicates that the discussion should be considered a *dugri* talk by saying: "I want to/I must/let me speak to you *dugri*," or "I want to be sincere with you," or the like. This use of *dugri* has a creative function. It establishes a ritual context within which direct talk is culturally sanctioned.

The respondent briefly signals agreement to enact the *dugri* ritual by indicating that the initiator can proceed. As noted, most of the ritual consists of the initiator voicing some protest. The respondent may make some counterclaims, but not vigorously: The respondent's position is well known; it is its challenge that is the issue.

Within the ritual context, there is no room for lengthy discussion of the issues brought up by the initiator: If such discussion follows, the ritual bounds have been overstepped. The ritual is terminated with a sense of relief, sometimes verbalized by the initiator's statement that, "I have done my part" and the respondent's reply, "OK, I've heard you." At times, particularly when there is a sense that one's interactant is not comfortable with the exchange, one of the participants may express gratitude at having been given an opportunity to speak (e.g., "Thank you for your frankness" or "I appreciate the fact that I could be frank"). This last step helps to bring participants back smoothly into the realm of *societas*, reaffirming the interactional norms applicable in it.

Instrumentalities

Several points should be made regarding the instrumentalities associated with *dugri* speech. The notion of *dugrijut*, a *dugri* talk in particular, is typically associated with spoken, face-to-face encounters. It involves directness in the sense of unmediated communication. Thus, as already mentioned, one of the common responses to my request to characterize talk that is not *dugri* was the notion of gossip: A person who does not stage a *dugri* talk when the occasion calls for it, it is claimed, is likely to end up speaking behind one's back. That is, a *dugri* talk is seen as employing the most direct, and therefore preferred, channel for conveying particular kinds of message.

There are interesting nonverbal concomitants to the enactment of a *dugri* talk. These came up most frequently in discussions of the *dugri* quality of various public figures. Informants listed a variety of nonverbal displays: For example, postural tendencies such as fidgeting while talking or shifty eyes tended to disqualify a person from being considered *dugri*.

The movements accompanying *dugri* speech can be described in terms of Laban's notation of movement analysis (Laban, 1966; Dell, 1970), which captures the qualitative aspects of movement referred to as its *Effort/Shape elements*. The most relevant parameters for delineating the quality of movement characteristic of the *dugri* ritual seem to be flow of tension, weight, and direction. In enacting the *dugri* ritual, speakers' movements tend to be free-flowing (rather than bound) and intense; they manifest the quality of strength (rather than lightness) on the weight dimension and the quality of directness in spatial orientation (focusing on each other). These elements of the Effort/Shape factor combined with the time factor of quickness or abruptness characterize the nonverbal signals attending *dugri* speech.

Both in its movement and in its verbal thrust, *dugri* speaking can be metaphorically regarded as a punch: It is direct, strong, and quick. Thus, a person who projects a resolute and sincere image in his or her verbal behavior, but whose nonverbal behavior is felt to undermine this claim, is not judged credible in the attempt to enact the *dugri* ritual. Similarly, a person who projects sincerity but speaks hesitantly and in a low-key manner, or whose posture is relaxed and noncommittal, is not likely to be judged as properly enacting the *dugri* ritual. The *dugri* speaker must signal through verbal expression, bodily posture, and eye contact, as well as tone of voice, that he or she is indeed sincere and resolute.

Key

In terms of its "key," that is, its feeling-tone or affective coloring, the *dugri* ritual can be characterized as an emotionally intense speech event: It is dominated by a sense of commitment, of "something important being at stake," as one informant put it, and also by the intensity accompanying confrontational exchanges. Despite the opposition and confrontation involved, the tone is one of contained, rather stylized, somewhat impersonal anger rather than the outburst that tends to accompany conflicts grounded in the clash of personal interests and incompatible desires.

Since the ritual roles of the participants are asymmetrical, they vary in the tone accompanying their respective performances: The initiator, as noted earlier, has to exude an air of resoluteness, sincerity, and defiance. The respondent, on the other hand, must maintain his or her composure and project the image of the forthright person who is prepared to accept criticism "without becoming personal about it," as one person put it. Thus, both participants, in their own way, pay homage to the image of the person of character. They do so by fulfilling complementary ritual roles marked by a reversal of tone.

Ends

Whatever point of view we adopt, the *dugri* ritual is a multifunctional affair. Its purposes pertain to the participants' psychic life, to their definition of their social task, to their definition of their cultural identity, and to their communal affiliation.

For the initiator, the ritual has a clear cathartic function: It provides a context in which to release pent-up frustrations and aggravations with respect to a structural social unit or relationship. It also provides a ritual context for conveying socially sensitive information as well as for publicly defining and clarifying one's position in an institutionalized social unit by asserting and publicizing issues that one has a right and an obligation to influence.

For the respondent, particularly in the more common cases in which he or she has power over the initiator, the *dugri* ritual is a cultural channel through which to obtain social information that may otherwise remain unavailable; at times, the *dugri* ritual can also allow the redefinition and clarification of social positions.

From the communal point of view, the *dugri* ritual reaffirms participants' cultural identities and communal affiliation. It encapsulates the whole spectrum of cultural meanings and values associated with *dugri* talk and suggests a model—more for than of—the ideal person and the ideal form of human relations.

The outcome of a *dugri* ritual is not a resolution of differences but a clarification of positions, especially the recognition of the existence and nature of the disagreement. Whereas the respondent may at times be disquieted and disoriented by the confrontation with an alternative conception, the initiator experiences a sense of relief at not having been "afraid to speak up." It is generally felt that for the initiator the main outcome of the ritual is a sense of increased confidence and control, the satisfaction that goes with self-assertion.

Genre

A *dugri* talk can be characterized as a conversational genre as distinguished from play, fictive, and static genres in the typology proposed by Abrahams (1976). It takes the form of a ritual confrontation marked by a high degree of interpersonal involvement. In conversational genres, according to Abrahams (p. 200),

> one person directs his expression in an interpersonal fashion to a limited number of others as part of everyday discourse. The speaker does not need to assume any involved character role to make his point. He, rather, is engaged in a spontaneous communicative relationship in which opportunities to introduce traditional devices of persuasion commonly arise.

The intensification of expression associated with the first, less formal types of conversational genre in Abrahams' scheme, of which a *dugri* talk is an example, is accomplished in this case through the stylization of the direct mode that colors and frames the flow of discourse. It may also be accompanied by colloquialisms and slang expressions functioning as intensifiers.

Celebrating a gesture of revolt, the *dugri* ritual is animated by a moral stance that favors action and a spirit of control over one's fate to a stance of passivity and the acceptance of one's circumstance. The activity/passivity contrast is very important in understanding Israeli culture. In dramatizing the choice of action over obedient restraint and acceptance (e.g., in silence), the *dugri* ritual provides a generic form through which members can reaffirm the cultural value attached to action that for them spells mastery, strength, and autonomy—hence, dignified survival. An intriguing conceptual link between action and conflict is pointed out by Turner (1982), who notes—in a completely different context—that the word *act* and the word *agon* (from which stem many conflict-related words such as *antagonism*) are etymologically related. It is in conflictual situations that a person's ability to act is brought to a head. Therefore, looking for a fight is a common way to test and reaffirm one's actional potential. In a sense, the *dugri* ritual as an agonistic ritual genre provides a safely circumscribed context for such a test.[8]

Norms of interaction

The performance of the *dugri* ritual is governed by two complementary interactional norms:

1. The initiator, having defined the situation (to himself and to others) as involving a rhetorical exigency, is expected to initiate the *dugri* ritual in an attempt to motivate the respondent to correct it.
2. The respondent, at the same time, is required to accept the *dugri* approach in good spirit and to refrain from interpreting it as a personal affront.

It should be stressed that the *dugri* ritual involves suspending or reinterpreting societal norms of "facework" and embracing an alternative set of interactional norms predicated on a cultural ideal of personal worth and on a culture-specific interpretation of the nature and role of "facework."

The normative force of the *dugri* ritual stands out when the respondent refuses to join the initiator in enacting the ritual, for example, when he or she acts insulted or loses composure in reacting to the threat to face involved. To members of the culture, such a response is highly unsatisfying. As informants repeatedly said, it indicates that the respondent is weak, that he or she cannot face the truth. Such a person is regarded as unwholesome. Moreover, by refusing to enact the *dugri* ritual, the respondent prevents the initiator from reaffirming his or her ideal version of the Sabra. That is, the respondent prevents the initiator from acting like—and therefore becoming —a wholesome person as defined by the culture. From the native's point of view, it is the respondent rather than the initiator who is felt to have violated a basic interactional norm.

In sum, an ideal *dugri* speaker should both speak *dugri* when this is called for and respond to *dugri* speech addressed to him or her in a fitting manner. Some of my informants made biting comments about Sabras who speak *dugri* but recoil when such speech is addressed to them. Whatever one's feelings about the *dugri* mode, the minimal requirement is to abide by its norms as both speaker and addressee, as the occasion arises.

[. . .]

Notes

1   In this article, I combine Turner's dramatistic, action-centered approach to the study of social life with Burke's dramatistic, linguistically centered approach. See Conquergood (1984) for a recent discussion of the basic affinities, as well as differences in emphasis, between these two seminal writers.

2   This is congruent with Goffman's (1967) approach to the study of interaction rituals; see Harre and Secord (1972) for a theoretical explication of this kind of move. In a later study, Harre (1976, p. xvi) points out the promise of such as focus while acknowledging its limitations:

> It is not our intention to suggest that the whole of social life can be exhausted by the application of the dramaturgical and liturgical models, nor that the uses of language are restricted to the acts and actions comprehended by them, but rather that those models and the action sequences they enable us to understand are characteristic of crucial moments in human lives.

3   For example, see Geertz (1973), Schneider (1980), and Schutz (1967).

4   See Tannen (1981) on the combativeness popularly associated with Jewish New York conversational style and Schiffrin (1984) on the use of argument as sociability among Philadelphia Jews. This seems to suggest that there may be a broader pattern at work there.

5   See Kochman's (1981) discussion of the self-assertion associated with Afro-American expressive style. Black self-assertion shares with *dugri* speech "the shift in focus from doing unto others to doing for oneself" (p. 124), but this shift has a different symbolic meaning in black culture: It is interpreted as the expression of feelings (rather than opinions) and is grounded in "the sanctity of individual feelings and the primary and independent status that feelings have within the culture" (pp. 123–4). The greater freedom of expression allowed in black culture (as compared with white American culture) results in greater confidence among blacks concerning their ability to manage anger and hostility at the verbal level without losing self-control, affects their handling of conflict situations, and is expressed in ritual insults such as "playing the dozens" (see Labov, 1972).

6   The poignancy of the Israeli identity problem is revealed in other expressive contexts as well. It has been illuminated in Oring's (1981) previously mentioned study of the *chizbat* (literally, "lie") of the *Palmah* prestate units. According to his analysis, the set of texts comprising the *chizbat* repertoire can be read as thematizing Israelis' profound unresolved conflict between the image of Sabra and the image of the Diaspora Jew. An example of a *chizbat* that involves a direct comment on the paradoxicality of the Sabra's preoccupation with character is the tale about the group of friends who, while sailing one night on the Lake of Galilee, dared one member to throw his fisherman's lamp into the water as a test of character, brushing aside his protest that it would be waste of a good lamp. However, when he finally conceded, the verdict came: "Hey, you've got no character. Anybody can influence you." The message is clear: The Sabra's need to prove his character undermines the validity of the proof itself. The paradox is built into the Sabra's situation.

7   Prell-Foldes stresses that this conception is incompatible with the modern view of the "psychological self," which sees the individual as pitted against society and self-actualization as the escape from communal constraints. Another study that examines basic cultural assumptions concerning the relationship between the individual and the community manifested in the communication patterns of a speech community is a study of the call–response pattern among black Americans (Daniel and Smitherman, 1976).

8   This also calls to mind Albert Camus's (1951) more general discussion of *l'homme révolté*. He describes the rebel as the person whose rejection of unwanted elements in his life is simultaneously an immediate and total reaffirmation of some part of his being. In Camus's account, rebellion is clearly associated with the semantic of identity. The rebel senses, dimly at first, that there is something within him that can serve as a basis for identification, even if for a moment, and this becomes an overpowering inner reality—so much so that the person becomes his rebellion, and any openness he may have had to compromise is exchanged for an all-or-none revolutionary orientation accompanied by a demand for a leveling of the hitherto unequals. This account is particularly useful in stressing the creative force of the act of rebellion: It not only reflects the actor's commitment but also helps to shape and strengthen it.

References

Abrahams, R. (1976). The complex relations of simple forms. In D. Ben-Amos (ed.), *Folklore genres*. Austin: University of Texas Press.

Bernstein, B. (1964). Elaborated and restricted codes: Their social origins and some consequences. In J. Gumperz and D. Hymes (eds), *The ethonography of communication*. Washington, DC: American Anthropological Association.

Bitzer, L. (1968). The rhetorical situation. *Philosophy and Rhetoric*, 1, 1–14.

Camus, A. (1951). *L'homme révolté*. Paris: Editions Gallimard.

Conquergood, D. (1984). Rhetoric and ritual: Implications of Victor Turner's dramaturgical theory for rhetorical criticism. Paper presented at the Western Speech Communication Convention, Seattle, Washington.

Daniel, J. and Smitherman, G. (1976). How I got over: Communication dynamics in the black community. *Quarterly Journal of Speech*, 62, 26–39.

Dell, C. (1970). *A primer for movement description*. New York: Dance Notation Bureau.

Geertz, C. (1973). *The interpretation of cultures*. New York: Basic Books.

Goffman, E. (1967). *Interaction ritual: Essays on face-to-face behaviours*. New York: Doubleday.

Harre, R. (ed.) (1976). *Life sentences: Aspects of the social role of language*. London: Wiley.

Harre, R. and Secord, P. (1972). *The explanation of social behaviour*. Totowa, NJ: Rowman & Littlefield.

Hymes, D. (1972). Models of the interaction of language and social life. In J. Gumperz and D. Hymes (eds), *Directions in sociolinguistics*. New York: Holt, Rinehart & Winston.

Katriel, T. (1985). Griping as a verbal ritual in some Israeli discourse. In M. Dascal (ed.), *Dialogue: An interdisciplinary approach*. Amsterdam: John Benjamins.

Katriel, T. and Philipsen, F. (1981). "What we need is communication": "Communication" as a cultural category in some American speech. *Communication Monographs*, 48, 301–17.

Kochman, T. (1981). *Black and white styles in conflict*. Chicago: University of Chicago Press.

Laban, R. (1966). *The language of movement*. Boston: Plays.

Labov, W. (1972). Rules for ritual insults. In W. Labov, *Language in the inner city* (pp. 297–354). Philadelphia: University of Pennsylvania Press.

Myerhoff, B. (1978). *Number our days*. New York: Dutton.

Oring, E. (1981). *Israeli humour: The content and structure of the 'chizbat' of the Palmah*. Albany: SUNY Press.

Prell-Foldes, R.-E. (1980). The reinvention of reflexivity in Jewish prayer: The self and community in modernity. *Semiotica*, 30–1(2): 73–96.

Robinson, H. W. (1964). *Corporate personality in ancient Israel*. Philadelphia: Fortress.

Schneider, D. (1980). *American kinship*. Chicago: University of Chicago Press.

Schutz, A. (1967). *The phenomenology of the social world*. Evanston, IL.: Northwestern University Press.

Schiffrin, D. (1984). Jewish argument as sociability. *Language in Society*, 13, 311-35.

Simmel, G. (1955). *Conflict and the web of group affiliations*. New York: New Press.

Tannen, D. (1981). New York Jewish conversational style. *International Journal of the Sociology of Language*, 30, 133–49.

Turner, V. (1974). *Dramas, fields and metaphors*. Ithaca, NY: Cornell University Press.

Turner, V. (1980). Social dramas and stories about them. *Critical Inquiry*, 7, 141–68.

Turner, V. (1982). *From ritual to theatre: The human seriousness of play*. New York: Performing Arts Journal Publications.

Chapter 11

AYMAN NAZZAL

THE PRAGMATIC FUNCTIONS OF THE RECITATION OF QUR'ANIC VERSES BY MUSLIMS IN THEIR ORAL GENRE
The case of *Insha' Allah,* "God's willing"

Introduction

THIS STUDY AFFORDS ONE the opportunity to study Muslims who happen to come from diverse cultural, ethnic, and linguistic backgrounds and their worldview through one of their discursive patterns. This study spares one the opportunity to see how the use of the Qur'an, the bedrock of Islam, as a communication resource provides Muslims with an opportunity to execute their action without staking their self-image or their interlocutor's. The significance of this study can be presented in four points: First, it points out the motivations and reasons that induce Muslims to invoke the recitation of Qur'anic verses in their ordinary discourse. Second, it underlies the multifaceted pragmatic functions that Muslims associate with the use of Qur'anic verses to further their own personal goals. Third, it underscores the significance that Muslims attach to the use of Qur'anic language as a communicative resource to guard against staking the self-image of their Muslim interlocutors. And fourth, it spares us the opportunity of minimizing misunderstanding in inter/cross-cultural communication by pointing out the different communicative practices that specific ethnic groups are inclined to use in invoking universal notions such as indirectness and politeness.

[The author reviewed the study on politeness and indirectness.]

Theoretical framework

The primary research questions that this study investigates thoroughly focus on the pragmatic functions of the recitation of some Qur'anic verses, primarily the recitation of *Insha' Allah* and the motivations that induce Muslims to enact such Qur'anic verses in a variety of social contexts. Since my analysis of the data presented in this paper is grounded in the Searlean framework for indirect speech act theory, I provided an overview of his theory and its overall significance to the type of data I am presenting in this paper.

Source: Nazzal, A. (2005). The pragmatic functions of the recitation of Qur'anic verses by Muslims in their oral genre: the case of Insha' allah, "God's willing". *Pragmatics*, 15(2–3), 251–74.

In accounting for the pragmatic meaning of the "illocutionary act" of any "speech act," John Searle (1969, p. 48) states:

> On the speaker's side, saying something and meaning it are closely connected with intending to produce certain effects on the hearer. On the hearer's side, understanding the speaker's utterance is closely connected with recognizing his intentions. In the case of literal utterances the bridge between the speaker's side and the hearer's side is provided by their common language.

The "common language" that Searle talks about underscores the pragmatic and sociocultural dimensions that conversational participants ought to have in order to minimize misunderstanding. This can potentially refer to the Qur'anic language that Muslims share in expressing their perception of the social world which they are part of. The tendency of some Muslims to enact Qur'anic verses in their ordinary conversation is an indication that this linguistic code is the common language that they share with one another. This linguistic code in this particular context is a restrictive linguistic code in the sense that it is only intelligible and accessible to those who are versed in and have an adequate knowledge of Qur'anic linguistics.

In the data analysis section, I point out how Muslims have a tendency to use certain communicative practices to either mitigate their commitments to carry out future actions or to express their perception of the social world that they are trying to make sense of. I also show how Muslims use certain linguistic devices not as a mere tool of communication to display their religious identity but rather as a social conduit to perform action, or to exert some influence on each other's attitude and behavior, and thus bringing about some change in the behavior of their interlocutors.

I attempt to show that the use of such a linguistic device is, in my opinion, a form of indirectness since the recitation of *Insha' Allah* (a) tentatively induces one to glean more than one particular interpretation from the same recitation itself, and therefore it (b) requires one to rely on some linguistic mechanisms to account adequately for the intended interpretation that the initiator wishes his/her addressee to infer from the enactment of the Qur'anic verses, *Insha' Allah*.

[The author reviewed John Searle's speech act theory and his notion of indirectness.]

The notion of indirectness that I am referring to in this paper is borrowed from Searle. In the following verbal exchange one can easily note that one of the spouses is able to mitigate the pragmatic force of his communicated utterance by being implicit in his refusal.

1. Wife: we ran out of milk and bread.
2. Hus: I have not finished my work at the university yet.

If we have to apply Searle's mechanism to the notion of indirectness that appears to manifest itself in the above exchange, we have first to show by the application of Searle's mechanism that there is a disparity between two distinct acts in the communicated utterance performed by the husband in line 2. Apparently, in the above exchange the wife has basically stated that they ran out of milk and bread and to that effect she expected her husband to respond positively to her indirect request in line 1.

If we pay closer attention to the husband's response in line 2, the wife is very likely to conclude that her husband's response is an implicit refusal of her request. The wife is able to establish such a disparity between what the husband has communicated in line 2 (the secondary illocutionary act) and what the husband in fact wishes his wife to glean from his assertion (the primary illocutionary act).

The wife is inclined to interpret her husband's response to contain much more information than the mere assertion of a state of affairs. Indeed, in saying, "I have not finished my work at the university yet," her husband is basically telling her that the preparatory condition of a commitment on his part doesn't obtain. In other words, he is not able to get milk and bread for her because he has not finished his work. Therefore, the primary point of her husband's utterance in line 2 is likely to be a mitigated rejection of her request in line 1. It would have been impolite and overbearing for the husband to be too explicit in rejecting his wife's request.

So by being indirect in his response, the husband appears to be able to mitigate the consequence of his unjustified action and at the same time to mitigate the consequences of his implicit rejection of his wife's request. As one can note, the issue at heart when one tries to account for the notion of indirectness or the speaker's intention hinges on one's ability to draw the line between the literal meaning (secondary) and the intended one (primary illocutionary act). Without being able to pin down such an important distinction, the process becomes quite slippery, particularly in accounting for the notion of indirectness.

Data analysis

The following is an English translation of an excerpt of an Arabic tape-recorded conversation in which the participants (two spouses: Husband is referred to hereafter as speaker H and wife is referred to hereafter as speaker W) use *Insha' Allah* as both a communicative resource and mitigating device for rejecting or turning down a request. That is to say, one of the major pragmatic functions of the recitation is used as an indirect speech act of rejection.

The discussion that transpires between the participants in the following tape-recorded material occurred as a result of the husband's reluctance to use his van on an impending trip from Albany, New York, to New Jersey. The wife wants to go to New Jersey to buy some items from an Arab market in Paterson, since she expects some company and wants to buy them some nice gifts. Apparently, H's reluctance to go on this trip has angered W who seems eager to go on this trip. It seems that H's reluctance is due to his apprehension that his van is too old and may break down on the highway. As we read the following excerpt, we realize that the debate between the spouses becomes so heated to the point that the wife accuses her husband of ruining everything. That is to say, the wife asserts that her husband's reluctance to use his van on that very day has apparently spoiled the atmosphere in her house. The most interesting instance in this tape-recorded interview is the instance in which the husband uses many Qur'anic verses, primarily the recitation of *Insha' Allah* in line 6, as a mitigating device to turn down his wife's request.

1 W. You ruined everything.
2 H. May God forgive you. I did not ruin anything.
3   Don't say you wanted to go. Say everything is in the hand of God.
4 W. Of course.
5 H. Don't say I want to go. Everything is in the hand of God and you
6   should not say you want to go. *You should say if God wills (Insha' Allah) that is all.*
7   I did not interfere or say anything and as you told me to warm up the van
8   which I did so that they could drive it instead of overusing their car
9 W. Our car is more spacious than theirs.
10 H. I started the van and warmed it up and gave it to them.
11 W. But why
12   Did you change your mind?

13 H.   I did not change my mind or said anything.
14 W.   You kept saying the van the van.

Before analyzing the participants' use of *Insha' Allah*, I would like to dwell on the talk (primarily the recitation of other Qur'anic verses that appear to be relevant to the recitation of *Insha' Allah*) that has preceded in order to provide the social context or matrix that has prompted the husband H to recite *Insha' Allah*. As we pay closer attention to what has transpired between the two spouses in the above tape-recorded conversation, we become more convinced that the participants seem to be aware of the pragmatic functions of the Qur'anic verses they are enacting.

It is rather obvious from the way the participants use these Qur'anic verses that they are aware of the fact they can be used to perform specific actions which are destined to produce some effect on the behavior of the participants. By virtue of that, the initiator appears to be able to mitigate the force and consequences of his/her action on the addressee, which may result in producing some influence on the addressee's behavior. Therefore, the enactment in and of itself is being used as a powerful strategy with which one participant exerts some influence on others' action and perception and at the same time skews one's understanding and perception of the social world in a way one would like it to be.

Such rationale seems to resonate with Austin's (1975) concept that one of the primary functions of language is the performance of action. Such an awareness of the performative aspect of language appears to manifest itself in the participants' use of certain communicative devices in the hope of bringing about an important change in one's behavior. This inclines us to conceive of language not merely as an entity with a referential function or a means of communication, but also as a tool with which one can change someone's attitude towards a particular state of affairs.

I attempt to show in the course of this analysis that H has enacted *Insha' Allah* skillfully to serve his own personal agenda. Let me first draw on W's statement in line 1, in which she expresses her frustration over H's refusal to go to New Jersey when she says, *"You ruined everything."* Of course, one is inclined to think that H must have done something appalling to have ignited speaker W's anger, otherwise W would not have accused speaker H of ruining everything.

Just to follow the stream of events as they unfold in the above excerpt, W's ultimate goal seems to be to induce H to go on this trip. In fact, W cannot go on this trip without the company of H. H knows very well that W eagerly wants him to use his van on this trip. However, H, for some reason, is hesitant to use his van probably on account that it is too old and it may break down on the way to New Jersey.

Another important point that needs to be emphasized here is how the use of Qur'anic verses empowers one conversational participant over the other, regardless of whether there is a disparity in the social status of the participants involved or not. The enactment of the recitation in and of itself appears to have empowered H over W. Speaker H remarks as he is responding to W's accusation by saying, *"Say everything is in the hands of God."*

The hearer (W) is likely to think that H's unequivocal acknowledgment of how our action lies in the hands of God is some sort of a double-edged sword. He can't possibly be giving her a lecture on the philosophy of Islam by his use of the word of God. He must be saying something else to her other than what the literal meaning of his use of the word of God implies. That is to say, H's use of the word of God has probably some important pragmatic functions. What H is trying to convey to W through his utterance is to prove W is wrong in her accusation of H's disinclination to use his van and probably to justify his unwillingness to use his van on the trip by deflecting the cause of what has happened on God.

Like that of all Muslims, H's action appears to be unrealistic particularly to a non-Muslim audience in terms of not being able to take a stance on this issue. What he has done so far is to show that we are all at the mercy of God and that no matter how hard we try everything is in God's hands and that everything depends on God's will. This may sound self-defeating to non-Muslims to surrender one's will or one's destiny to the existing circumstances. Of course, all Muslims are conscious of the fact that they are responsible for the actions they themselves intend to undertake but they strongly believe that their will is contingent upon God's will.

At this point, the distinctive role or pragmatic function of the recitation of the word of God by H, whether in line 2, 3, or 5, is probably to mitigate one's responsibility or commitment for whatever action one embarks upon. What H appears to be saying in his recitation of these Qur'anic verses in lines 2–3 and 5–6 is that while we are responsible for the actions we engage in, we are not always able to control the circumstances that determine our success or failure in executing these actions.

Now I come to the most important point, which is the interpretation of the recitation of *Insha' Allah*. It is worth mentioning that, based on the data that I analyzed so far, the recitation of the word of God, whether in lines 2–3 or 5, appears to function as a counterattack to W's accusation and possibly to mitigate H's commitment and responsibility for something.

The recitation of *Insha' Allah* in that particular instance (in line 6) appears to have a dual function: It functions as a countermove to W's accusation and an implicit turndown of W's initial request for H to use his van. H is probably trying to mitigate his commitment for the assignment that W is asking him to execute, which is carrying out her request.

As one can note, the recitation in and of itself constitutes an act of indirectness since the initiator may be enacting the recitation for more than one reason and by virtue of that the recitation leaves the recipient the strenuous task to work out which of these two distinct interpretations the initiator is trying to convey in reciting the word of God to his interlocutor.

The recitation of *Insha' Allah* that speaker H enacts in line 6 is an inseparable component of the initial talk (from lines 1 to 6). A thorough examination of what H has said in line 6 is likely to induce one to think that H is probably trying to convey a couple of things. Let's first take a closer look at H's response in line 6 in which he says, "*You should not say you want to go. You should say if God wills,* Insha' Allah *that is all.*"

Now the first question that arises in one's mind is whom H is talking to and in response to what? We ought to understand that what is at stake here is not what the spouses are talking about but rather the actions that H is ultimately performing in order to consummate his plan or to convince W that she is not behaving as a genuine Muslim would/should behave. This is indeed the focal point in this particular context. What H is doing by virtue of his recitation is a clear construction of his perception and an elaborate attempt on his part to dissuade W from holding firm onto her initial request.

I will ignore the first part of H's response in line 6 and focus on the second part since it is the part where H uses the recitation of *Insha' Allah*. Again, H appears to convey something in his performance of the recitation of *Insha' Allah*. W would probably resign herself to the fact that H's performance in line 6 is an assertive statement since the psychological state that is being expressed in that statement is a belief that H holds firmly about the contingency of one's action and it does not directly pertain to the accusation W has made against him.

In light of all this, the hearer (W) is probably inclined to say that if H's statement in line 6 does not pertain directly to the accusation made against him in line 1, then it must relate to something that the hearer (W) has said previously to H. Therefore, the hearer (W) is probably tempted to think that H's response appears to be relevant to the state of affairs that the hearer discussed with H previously (presumably W's initial request to use H's van). Of course, W would still assume that H is still cooperating since he is attending to the talk at hand whether explicitly or implicitly, and his assertive statement seems to address something that has been the cause of her accusation of him. Therefore, if H's statement in line 6 is not directly pointed at her accusation, then H is probably implying more than what he is saying in his statement (potentially one can consider it an assertion since H appears to be committed to the belief and truth of the expressed proposition or the state of affairs he is making).

W would be inclined to assume that H's response in line 6 could contain more than one important action. That is to say, H's response seems to represent a belief that Muslims are supposed to cherish wholeheartedly and that this belief deals with how the success or failure of one's actions is dependent on God's will. But the hearer (W) is likely to wonder the reasons for not using his van on the trip. W could then understand H's recitation as a speech act by way of which a primary act is produced and in that case a mitigated rejection. What could H's recitation of *Insha' Allah* (representative) imply if it is not directly about the accusation the hearer (W) has made against H in line 1? W is bound to realize that H's recitation of *Insha' Allah* is enacted to show that one is not really sure of one's action unless one has God's blessing. W is inclined to realize also that H's recitation of *Insha' Allah* appears to lessen his commitment for what he has been initially asked to do. W would probably arrive at this conclusion by drawing on several observations.

First, the hearer (W) would probably say that H's recitation (assertive) in line 6 does not directly pertain to the accusation W has made against H in line 1. Therefore, H's recitation probably refers to something else that the hearer (W) has previously asked H to do and H has shown a great deal of reluctance. W would be tempted to think that H's recitation of *Insha' Allah* has resulted from H's disinclination to use his van since if he is really committed to using his van, he would be much more explicit and forthcoming in his statement. Therefore, the hearer (W) is inclined to say that the primary point of H's recitation in line 6 is probably to turn down the hearer's (W) request, and his use of *Insha' Allah* in and of itself is probably done to mitigate his commitment or rejection.

As I said, W would arrive at this conclusion by drawing on the factual background information that is at her disposal and her knowledge that the preparatory condition on the acceptance of a request is contingent upon one's ability to perform the action predicated in the propositional content of any request. H's enactment of *Insha' Allah* has resulted from H's reluctance or inability to carry out an action or to mitigate his commitment for a specific action that he is not sure that he could carry it out without God's blessing.

H's recitation of *Insha' Allah* in line 6 differs from H's recitation of the word of God in the first two instances (in lines 2–3 and in line 5). W is likely to assume that H's recitation of *Insha' Allah* in line 6 could not possibly be a counter attack to the accusation she has made against H in line 1. Therefore, if it does not directly pertain to the accusation she has made against H, then it has to pertain indirectly to something that W has asked H to do or to a suggestion that pertains to H personally.

W is probably inclined to say that H is again trying to convey something else through his recitation of *Insha' Allah* other than saying that one's action is contingent upon God's will. W is likely to realize that H's recitation in line 6 does not pertain directly to the accusation. As a result of that, W is inclined to realize that the primary point of H's response in line 6 appears to differ from the literal point expressed in his recitation.

W is inclined to assume that, if the first two recitations of the word of God are performed to counter the accusation she has made against H, H's recitation in line 6 then must have been enacted for something other than the accusation she has made in line 1.

W would probably arrive at such a conclusion by relying on the following factors: First, W and H mutually share background information, whether linguistic or non-linguistic, about each other and the state of affairs they are talking about. Second, W knows very well that the main reason for her accusation of H is H's reluctance to commit himself for the impending trip which W is attempting to make happen. W is also inclined to assume that H's recitation of *Insha' Allah* appears to pertain to how the execution of a future action is dependent on God's blessing of that action rather than on the person who intends to execute or carry out that action. So if H's recitation is attending to such matters, then W is likely to think that the purpose of H's recitation is not only to counter W's accusation, but also to attend to W's initial request.

This sounds pretty bizarre and fatalistic to a non-Muslim audience. It is fatalistic in the sense that it is inconsistent with the accepted belief that man possesses a free will and has the ability to do whatever he/she determines to do, provided that the circumstances are propitious for the action to be executed. Of course, we all know that we have to work as assiduously as possible to achieve whatever action we wish to achieve. But it is fatalistic to leave one's freewill and action to be decided upon by one's creator.

The essential point of all this is that Muslims are inclined to enact these Qur'anic verses in the wake of unfavorable circumstances on account that the initiator could and would be in a position to mitigate his/her losses and as a result there are lots of payoffs to claim credit for. One of these payoffs is that the recitation is performed and enacted as a communicative resource which allows Muslims to mitigate the undesirable consequences of their offensive actions, whether in the form of turning down a request or failure to honor their commitment to carry out specific future actions. This allows those who resort to such a communication resource to safeguard themselves when being asked to honor certain commitments that they cannot fulfill.

The second payoff that Muslims gain by resorting to such a communication resource is that it protects the self-image of both the issuer of the recitation—if God wills, or *Insha' Allah*—and the addressee from further embarrassment or damage to one's face or self-image. Muslims are probably inclined to enact the recitation of *Insha' Allah* since by doing that they can avoid staking the self-image of each other and as a consequence they preserve the maintenance of face. Based on the analysis of the verbal exchanges that transpired between the participants, Muslims appear to be conscious of the merits of the enactment, particularly when their actions may have some adverse consequences on the self-image of their addressees. By virtue of performing the recitation, the initiator is opting for one of two possibilities, one of which has to do with mitigating his/her rejection of something like a request or an offer.

Analysis of excerpt #2

An implicit acceptance

1 G1: It is all right. Nothing has happened really.
2 H: This is the first time that I woke up on Saturday and I got out of bed and she
3   saw me dressed up and ready to go which was very unusual for me to do on a
4   Saturday or Sunday morning.
5 G2: It is okay really. May be there is no chance this time for us to go.
6 H: But for Ladies whether you make a right or a left turn it makes no difference
7   for them. You just never satisfy them.
8 G1: Laughter . . .

 9 G2: Because we were ready to go
10 H: She saw me dressed up as If I was going to work.
11   Don't you agree? So why do you blame me for what has happened?
12 G2: That's okay. May be there is no chance for us to go this time.
13 W: Samia wants to go there because she has lots of items to buy from there.
14 G2: Laughter
15 H: *If Gods wills and the weather is nice, we will definitely go either next week or some other*
         time.
16 W: We want meat also for the guests who are coming next week.
17 H: We will get meat also.
18 W: I don't want it. That's it.
19 H: It does not have to be this week. We can go next week.
20 W: The invitation is next week.
21 H: Change it. Postpone it. Every thing is possible.
22 W: I don't want to go next week. That's it.
23   Lapse of time. (5.0) Seconds.

Before analyzing the recitation of *Insha' Allah* in the above excerpt, I would like to provide an overview of what could have prompted and induced the husband (hereafter referred to as speaker H) to enact the recitation. In the above excerpt, the verbal exchange between the two spouses continues regarding the impending trip to New Jersey. Since the wife (hereafter referred to as speaker W) appears to be skeptical about H's intention and willingness to go on this impending trip, speaker H has feverishly tried to cast speaker W's skepticism away. As the data reveal, speaker W appears to be unconvinced with speaker H's rationale. For example in lines 2–3, speaker H tries to show his willingness and readiness for the impending trip to New Jersey.

So what speaker H is saying is that he was ready to go on this impending trip since he woke up on Saturday and got dressed up which he normally does not do. Of course, H's complaining is pointed and directed at speaker W because of her skepticism. In fact, one can easily note that speaker H is quite dismayed with the way speaker W is treating him. One can see that in their respective communicative actions in lines 6–7 and in line 11 in the above excerpt.

Now let me turn to the analysis of the recitation of *Insha' Allah* in order to find out the primary purpose and the motivation behind its enactment. The recitation of *Insha' Allah* in and of itself can be potentially considered a meaningful utterance whose interpretation seems to depend on the social context in which it is being expressed and partially on the participants involved in the verbal exchange. As we can note the recitation is a meaningful utterance since it imparts an important message for us to consider seriously. For instance, upon hearing it, the recipient treats it as a complete response, whether it implies a mitigating device for a rejection of something or a mitigating device for one's commitment to accept an invitation or carry out a request.

Therefore, besides its being a meaningful utterance, the performance of the recitation of *Insha' Allah* by speaker H is probably done intentionally to perform some sort of an action or a speech act in the Searlean terms. The purpose of H's recitation appears to mitigate his full commitment for using his van. One can argue that if H's real intention is to go on this trip and use his van, he could have said so explicitly. However, H has chosen not only to enact the recitation as a tactical strategy for the consummation of his own hidden agenda, but also to impose some conditions for his approval to use his van. Having said that, then it is very likely that H's recitation and the conditions that he attaches to his using his van are an implicit disinclination for using his van.

The question that arises in one's mind then is for what purpose has H enacted the recitation of *Insha'Allah*? One can probably assume that H's communicative action is carried out to induce W and the guests to believe that he wants to go on the impending trip, provided that the circumstances which are beyond his control would allow him to do so, and this is why his remarks in line 15 in the above excerpt seem to caution speaker W that unless the circumstances are propitious for this impending trip, he may not consider it seriously.

"If God wills and the weather is nice we will definitely go either next week or some other time."

Unless we pay closer attention to the communicative actions that occur in line 13 where W poses an indirect request to her husband (H) to use his van on that very day and in turn H responds to W's request in line 15 by invoking the recitation. W's statement in line 13 is, in my opinion, an implicit request in which she is trying to induce her husband to use his van by saying that one of the guests wants to buy some items from New Jersey. In turn, H's statement could be construed as saying, "I *will use my van*, Insha' Allah, *to go to New Jersey next week or some other time so long as the weather conditions permit.*"

Let me continue to ground my analysis in the Searlean framework so that I can make sense of the entire episode that involves W's statement (implicit request) in line 13 and H's recitation of *Insha' Allah* in line 15 in the above excerpt. The hearer (W) is very likely to say that she has made an implicit request to the speaker (H) and in response the speaker (H) responded as cooperatively as he conceives his utterance to be seemly for the occasion.

Furthermore, the hearer is inclined to say that the speaker's response falls short of being precise and definite. For example, the hearer is most likely to assume that the recitation of *Insha' Allah* coupled with the conditions that speaker H is talking about inclines the hearer to think that the speaker is not quite committed to carrying out the action predicated in the prepositional content of her request. The hearer is bound to think that H's communicative action in line 15 has conveyed more than one message.

Just as the person who speaks is likely to produce an utterance and in so doing that utterance is carried out probably to perform some sort of an action. The hearer is likely to say that the speaker is not interested in going on the trip today even though he appears to be willing to consider it seriously next week or some other time. In addition, the hearer is likely to think that if the speaker seems to be willing to go on this trip next week or some other time in the future, then what is the purpose of his enactment of the recitation?

The hearer knows very well that carrying out a future action requires that the person carrying out that specific action is able to do so. The hearer (W) is quite sure and certain that H is capable of carrying out the request since he possesses the ability and competence for the action to be carried out. But the hearer is inclined to infer that H's enactment of the recitation pertains directly or indirectly to his willingness and commitment for the impending trip. That is to say, for what purpose has H enacted the recitation if he is indeed committed to using his van on the impending trip? H could have committed himself without enacting the recitation. But the fact that he enacted the recitation has probably aroused W's curiosity about H's real commitment for the impending trip.

Since W and H are aware of what the recitation implies, the hearer is likely to infer that H's enactment of the recitation is probably performed to mitigate his commitment for the impending trip. Furthermore, the hearer is bound to say that the recitation of *Insha' Allah* along with conditions that H attaches to his going on this trip makes one question his real commitment. As we all know, the preparatory condition for the accomplishment of a request involves that the person carrying out such a request is able to do so and, based on H's statement in line 15, it is not obvious that he will do the expected action. As a consequence, the preparatory condition may not obtain since, by his recitation of *Insha' Allah*, H is not fully sure of his full commitment for the accomplishment of the request. Of course, the hearer is likely to arrive at this conclusion by drawing on her knowledge of the social context and her possession of the mutually shared background information that both W and H have at their disposal.

The hearer is inclined also to arrive at the conclusion that H's recitation of *Insha' Allah* has resulted from his being less certain of his full commitment for the impending trip. That is to say, the hearer (W) is inclined to understand H's statement in line 15 as some sort of commitment mitigated by the recitation of *Insha' Allah*.

My first reading and interpretation of H's recitation in line 15 induces me to think that it implies an implicit acceptance mitigated by the recitation. But then H's recitation and the conditions he attaches to his going and using his van on the impeding trip arouse one's curiosity about his genuine willingness and commitment for such a trip. H appears to mitigate his commitment for using his van when he says, "*If God wills and the weather is nice we will definitely go either this week or some other time.*" But if one takes a closer look at what precedes and follows H's recitation in line 15, one is hard pressed to assume that H's recitation in line 15 is a mitigated acceptance to use his van on this impending trip.

I am opting to claim that H's motivation for enactment of the recitation in line 15 is probably to mitigate his commitment for carrying out W's request based on the fact that he is not refusing to carry out W's request but rather attaches some conditions such as the weather factors and the time element to accepting W's implicit request in line 13. Therefore, one can infer that H's recitation of *Insha' Allah* is a mitigating commitment (which is an acceptance) of using his van next week. What prompted W to overreact angrily at H is his postponement of the trip, considering that W wants it on the same day whereas He wants it to be next week or in the near future? In the eyes of W, H appears to have shown no strong commitment to use his van. This has prompted H to enact recitation of *Insha' Allah* as a tactful strategy to mitigate his commitment for using his van. This inclines one to analyze the recitation in this particular instance as an implicit acceptance mitigated by the recitation for H's commitment for the impending trip.

One can say that the recitation of *Insha' Allah* in this instance (second excerpt) is solely performed and enacted as an implicit acceptance since its purpose is to mitigate H's commitment for carrying out W's request. In fact, the very reason for H's enactment of the recitation is probably to lessen his fear of the likelihood that he may not be able to use his van and that some circumstances may in fact undermine his ability to carry out such an action and therefore he invoked the recitation as a means or something to fall back on in the event that he can't honor his commitment. The recitation of *Insha' Allah* in the above excerpt appears to function as a mitigating device for accepting a request. Or it induces the hearer to think that the second pragmatic function of the recitation is that it implies an implicit acceptance.

In the following excerpt (excerpt #3) we will see that the enactment and performance of the recitation of *Insha' Allah* appears to function as a mitigating device of one's prediction of the future and it can have nothing to do with acceptance or rejection of a particular future action or an offer.

Analysis of excerpt #3

Mitigating a future commitment

The following is an English translation of an excerpt of an Arabic verbal exchange of an Egyptian couple who reside in Albany County, in New York State. This conversation was tape-recorded in the first week of April of 2001, at the residence of the participants. The debate between the spouses is focused on whether to settle in the U.S., or to go back to Egypt. While the wife seems to be eager to go back to her native country, the husband is quite pleased with the idea of making this country a home to his family.

1	H:	But people are sick because of the pollution
2	W:	My daughter wants to go back to Egypt because of the cold weather/climate here.
3	H:	No your daughter is not going back to Egypt because the weather there is polluted.
4		And she got sick because of that and she does not like it either.
5		So how do you say that your daughter wants to go back to Egypt?
6	W:	No, she does not want to settle here in the U.S.
7	H:	That is up to her.
8	W:	It is very clear that she does not want live here in America
9	H:	That is up to her really.
10	W:	It is better for here there.
11	H:	Do you want to go back to Egypt too.
12	W:	Insha' Allah *and with his permission* Insha' Allah.
13	H:	Insha' Allah.

The focal point of the debate between the spouses is whether to settle in America or go back to Egypt. As one can see in her communicative actions, the wife is eager to go back to Egypt for a variety of reasons. However, her husband, who seems much more grateful and pleased with living in America, disagrees with his wife. As a result, he prefers for his children to settle here and make this country their home.

As the debate between the spouses unfolds, there is an instance where the wife enacts *Insha' Allah* in response to her husband's request (the request is an inquiry made by the husband to find out whether his wife plans to settle in the U.S., or to go back to Egypt). This is an interesting instance for several reasons: First, it underlies the importance of the pragmatic functions of the recitation of *Insha' Allah*. Second, it underscores the significance that Muslims attach to the enactment of the recitation when confronting unfavorable circumstances. Third, it points out how the performance of the recitation in and of itself constitutes a communicative resource from which the initiator draws power and credibility to buttress the proposition he/she is expecting the addressee to act upon. That is to say, the enactment of the recitation seems to empower the initiator in producing some change in the addressee's mindset.

The enactment of the recitation in this particular instance differs from its enactment in the previous instances which I have already presented and in which the recitation is used as a mitigating commitment to carry out a future action and not as an implicit acceptance or rejection, as one has noted in the previous excerpt. In this particular instance, the enactment of the recitation by the wife in line 12 appears to have been performed as a mitigating device for the prediction that she is making in her statement in the same line—12.

As one can infer from the debate between the spouses, the wife is eager to settle in Egypt for several reasons. The enactment of the recitation can also be construed as a plea for God's blessings. Since the wife is eager to live in Egypt, she displays her need for God's blessing.

If one has to apply Searle's (1979) mechanism for indirect speech acts theory, then one has to follow the following steps: The husband has made a request to his wife and as a consequence the wife has adequately responded to her husband's request (facts about the conversation). The husband, having heard his wife's response, appears to be satisfied with his wife's response on account of their being Muslims and since it seems relevant to the discussion at hand (principles of conversational cooperation).

But the husband is very likely to say that his wife's response is not explicit enough to the question he posed to her in line 11 and therefore she must be trying to convey some important or extra information in her recitation of *Insha' Allah*. The expectation is that the wife could have responded positively or negatively and expressed her response in a clear-cut way. The fact that she has chosen to be implicit makes it obvious that she wishes her husband to glean a particular interpretation.

At this point, the hearer (H) is inclined to say that the wife's response is potentially and tentatively an indirect speech of predicting something or doing some sort of an action in the future, but because she is not sure of what the future carries for her she enacted the recitation as a way to mitigate her prediction of the future. The hearer (the husband) is very likely to say that the literal meaning of his wife's response does not explicitly attend to his question and therefore the wife's response must have been performed to imply something else other than the plea for God's will, since all believers particularly Muslims are conscious of God's blessing.

Based on the amount of background information that both spouses possess, they know that relocating from one city to another city is highly troublesome. The husband is probably aware that if his wife's real intention is not to live in America, then this requires a firm commitment on his wife's part. But he knows his wife well and realizes that the primary reason for her enactment of *Insha' Allah* is probably to mitigate the awesome responsibility (preparatory condition for making a future commitment or prediction) to carry out a future action which obviously requires the person who intends to carry out such an action or to honor such a commitment to have some valid evidence about the state of affairs that he/she is embarking upon. That is to say, the wife has to provide some sort of assurances that she will be relocating which is obviously not possible for her to do and this induced her to enact the recitation to mitigate her prediction of a future commitment.

Therefore, it seems obvious that the enactment of the recitation by the wife in the above instance has resulted from her apprehension that she may not live up to her prediction or commitment, otherwise she could have been much more explicit and forthcoming in her response. The main point is that the recitation in and of itself appears to have been performed as an action that could potentially be the primary act that the wife wishes to convey to her husband without directly and explicitly admitting that. As a consequence, one can assume that the wife's response could be construed as a short version of saying, "*I will live in Egypt,* Insha' Allah," which could be considered a prediction or commitment.

If she is making a prediction about some future action, then the preparatory condition requires that one has substantial evidence about the state of affairs that one is making prediction about. That is to say, if I predict that the stock market is likely to crash in 2003, I should provide some convincing reasons to buttress the proposition I am making, otherwise my prediction would not stand a chance or hold up. If she is embarking on predicting a future action, then she has to prove that she has the ability and capacity to carry out such action or predict the state of affairs of her prediction. Since the wife is not really sure of anything, she enacted the recitation as a means to mitigate the prediction she has made so that she would safeguard herself from any criticism or embarrassment from her husband in the event that she can't live up to her expectation.

Therefore, the enactment of the recitation of *Insha' Allah* in the above excerpt appears to have several payoffs that induce Muslims to draw on in situations where the stakes are high for them or when they want to maintain harmony and avoid social disputes. Furthermore, the enactment of the recitation by the wife in line 12 can be construed by others as a tactful strategy that the wife employs to guard against unnecessary embarrassment in the event that she would not be able to live up to her prediction. Moreover, the enactment of *Insha' Allah* appears to afford Muslims the opportunity to mitigate their commitment for whatever action they set out to achieve and at the same time to deflect their responsibility to achieve these actions on God's will.

Overall, the findings of data that I have presented in this paper indicate that Muslims have a proclivity to enact the Qur'anic verse *Insha' Allah* in certain circumstances where one is not sure of the outcome of one's action or in instances in which one finds himself or herself to be at the mercy of unforeseeable circumstances. In addition, the findings indicate that Muslims are inclined to invoke the same Qur'anic verse to accomplish one of several things. For instance, the recitation can be enacted in certain social contexts as an indirect speech act of rejection. This instance occurs when the addressee is not interested in carrying out the speaker's request or accepting an offer or invitation for some unknown reasons or for reasons that the addressee would not be privy to.

In enacting the recitation, the initiator is opting to mitigate the force of his/her communicative action, particularly if the intended action deals with a rejection to carry out the speaker's request or if the intended action is about turning down an invitation. So instead of rejecting the speaker's request flatly and directly, the addressee finds it fitting and seemingly to enact the recitation as a means to mitigate the force of rejecting the speaker's request or an invitation and by virtue of the enactment, the addressee lessens the consequences of his/her action.

Muslims are very much induced to the enactment of the recitation on the ground that there are lots of merits and payoffs for both participants (speaker and addressee) in the enactment of *Insha' Allah*. One of these payoffs is that the initiator of the recitation accomplishes his/her personal goals without incurring any cost or staking the addressee's self-image. Therefore, the recitation of *Insha' Allah* in and of itself is a communicative resource and its enactment functions as a mitigating device for the preservation of social harmony, the avoidance of undesirable consequences of one's actions, and the maintenance of the self-image of the participants.

It is highly important to point out that Muslims are probably inclined to enact the recitation of *Insha' Allah* since by doing that they can avoid staking the self-image of each other. Based on the analysis of the verbal exchanges that transpired between the participants, Muslims appear to be conscious of the merits of the enactment, particularly when their actions may have some adverse consequences on the self-image of their addressees.

It is worth mentioning that such an observation is consistent with Gudykunst's & Ting-Toomey's (1988, 1996) concept of self-image and maintenance of face cross-culturally. They claim that the concept of self-image and maintenance of face varies from one culture to another and that in individualistic cultures (i.e. American) the primary concern is the maintenance of one's face (self-image). In contrast, the primary concern in collectivistic cultures (i.e. Arab, Chinese, Japanese) is the maintenance of both the speaker's and his/her addressee's face. This appears to impose some restraints on the structure and content of the participants' communicative practices.

The third reason for the enactment of the recitation by Muslims is to mitigate one's commitment for whatever action one is asked to carry out. The addressee enacts the recitation in this particular instance not for rejecting the speaker's request but rather to mitigate the consequences of his/her being unable to honor the speaker's request. That is to say, the addressee is implicitly accepting the speaker's request but because he/she is not so sure of the circumstances, he/she is likely to enact the recitation of *Insha' Allah* as a means to mitigate commitment—his/her failure to carry out a particular action.

It is worth pointing out that the enactment of the recitation in the second instance seems to be tied up with the notion of fatalism that appears to manifest itself in the behavior of some Muslims. Even though the addressee is interested in carrying out the speaker's request, he/she is induced to enact the recitation, as a means to implicitly accept the request but at the same time leaves room for the possibility of one's being unable to carry out the request. Therefore, there appears to be some pragmatic functions for the enactment of *Insha' Allah* in both the first instance where the addressee appears to implicitly reject the speaker's request or in the second instance in which the addressee appears to implicitly accept the speaker's request but uses *Insha' Allah* to exonerate himself/herself from the responsibility for not being able to carry out the speaker's request.

The third payoffs that seem to induce Muslims to opt for the use of Qur'anic verses is that the enactment of Qur'anic verses increases and enhances the credibility of one's message since what one is citing represents the word of God, which Muslims passionately identify with and by virtue of that Muslims are inclined to use the recitation as a powerful strategy to produce some effect on their interlocutors' attitudes and behaviors.

Conclusion

What I have presented in this paper are the findings of a study conducted on the pragmatic functions of the use of Qur'anic verses as a communicative resource that Muslims are inclined to use to gain adherence for the assertions they make. The insightful thing about the use of Qur'anic verses is that the person who is reciting them is relying on God's credibility to appeal to his/her interlocutor's understanding and acceptance, whatever assertion he/she is making. Therefore, such a study is quite warranted on the basis that the use of such a communication resource has several pragmatic functions that are worth exploring since they underlie some of the values that Muslims embrace so passionately in their unshakable belief in the Qur'an.

The findings of this study have revealed that Muslims can resort to the use of this communicative strategy for a host of pragmatic functions. These pragmatic functions range from mitigating one's commitment for carrying out a future action or failing to honor one's commitment, to avoiding the effects and adverse consequences of one's specific action on others. In addition, the recitation appears to function as a confirmation of one's religious, linguistic, and cultural identity. Furthermore, the findings of this study underline the multifaceted functions that Muslims attach to and associate with the use of Qur'anic language. The import and significance that induce Muslims to use Qur'anic language in their oral genre emanate from their firm belief in the import and power of the Qur'an as the bedrock of Islam. And most importantly, Muslims seem to be able to exonerate themselves from the responsibility of rejecting directives or turning down offers, or avoiding staking the self-image of their recipients particularly when their action has undesirable consequences for their recipients.

References

Austin, J. L. (1975) *How to do things with words*. Cambridge: Harvard University Press.
Gudykunst, W. B. & Ting-Toomey, S. (1988) *Culture and interpersonal communication*. Newbury park, CA: Sage Publications.
Gudykunst, W.B. & Ting-Toomey, S. (1996) *Communicating in personal relationships across cultures*. Thousands Oaks, CA: Sage Publications.
Searle, J. (1969) *Speech acts: An essay in the philosophy of language*. Cambridge: Cambridge University Press.
Searle, J. (1979) *Expression and meaning*. Cambridge: Cambridge University Press.

Chapter 12

KARI SAJAVAARA AND JAAKKO LEHTONEN

THE SILENT FINN REVISITED

Introduction

O N   A   P O P U L A R   P O S T C A R D, each member nation of the European Union is
represented by a caricature of a characteristic stereotype such as German humour, British
cooking, and the sober Irishman. The perfect European is said to be 'as talkative as a Finn', and
this Finn is illustrated by a couple of people, their mouths closed with adhesive tape. The obvious
implication is that Finns are considered to be the least talkative among the Europeans. Similar
disparaging descriptions can also be found in some recent books about Europeans. Hill (1992,
pp. 182–3), for instance, gives Finns a special place among the silent 'Nordics': 'Finns are
the odd ones out . . . They tend to seem taciturn, partly a reflection of their difficulties in
communicating. Not only their language isolates the Finns from everyone else . . . they even
have problems in communicating among themselves.' In the same way, Lewis (1992) refers to
the shyness of the Finns and their unwillingness to open themselves up, which accentuates the
opacity of the culture, people's voluntary withdrawal from company, and their geographical
distance.

Finns also have similar characterizations of themselves. The difference between the
characterizations by Finns and those by non-Finns is in that, while foreigners flavour their
descriptions with some wit and humour, Finns themselves regard such descriptions of themselves
as deadly serious. In their own eyes, they *are* taciturn, stubborn, and slow backwoodsmen,
who live on the periphery of Europe, who do not speak, communicate, or show their feelings,
and whenever they open their mouths, they speak one of the most difficult languages of the
world.

In an earlier paper (Lehtonen & Sajavaara, 1985), an attempt was made to deal with the
problem of Finns being negatively stereotyped because of their frequent use of silence. Various
types of material were brought forward as evidence for the silence-bound behaviour of Finns
and the silence-related features of conversation among them. In the present paper, the problem
of the silent Finn is revisited on the basis of some more recent research. An attempt will be
made to answer the following questions: where does the stereotype of the silent Finn originate?;

Source: Sajavaara, K. & Lehtonen, J. (1997). The silent Finn revisited. In A. Jaworski (ed.) *Silence:
interdisciplinary perspectives* (pp. 263–84). Berlin: Mouton de Gruyter.

what are the reasons for such a stereotype?; and what are its consequences in interaction and intercultural communication?

National perception of self

Popular conceptions relating to national character are persistent. People have deeply embedded ideas about themselves as members of their reference groups, and the characteristics that they cite as typical of themselves and their fellow-members resist change. In Finland, people often talk about themselves as a nation whose members are practically incapable of communicating with each other and outsiders (see e.g. Greig, 1991, p. 342). The origin of this tendency is often ascribed to the isolated environment where Finns used to grow up and the peripheral location of the country on the northern outskirts of Europe. This self-effacing characteristic of Finns has been recorded by Bertolt Brecht in one of his plays, where he refers to Finns as a people who are silent in two languages (Finnish and Swedish, which are both national languages in Finland). Finns generally seem to find this characterization of themselves rather attractive.

It is by no means unexpected that the view of this national communicative handicap of Finns is extended to foreign language use in particular: Finns generally believe that their aptitude for learning foreign languages is not as good as that of other people. They easily picture themselves as people who have stiff tongues in hard heads.

Stereotypes are an important, and necessary, ingredient in cultural adaptability: they contribute towards the cognitive system's capacity to adjust to unexpected and unknown phenomena. It is also true that the proportion of cultural behaviour that is shared between people always exceeds the differences that distinguish them. What may turn out to be fatal in cross-cultural communication, however, is that 'negative stereotypes combined with negative collective self-esteem may lead to a vicious circle in which negative expectations result in negative perceptions and negative behaviours, or in the use of self-handicapping strategies which are handicapping for intercultural interaction as well' (Lehtonen, 1994b).

It is possible that the national image that Finns have of themselves may have been strengthened by the nationalistic movement in the late nineteenth and early twentieth century, when Finland was engaged in a fight for her independence: in that particular situation it was very important for Finns to emphasise the unique features of their nationality. The origins of such characterization can be traced significantly further back than this however. Daniel Juslenius, a bishop who is considered the originator of the Finnish nationalistic movement, wrote as early as 1700:

> [Finns] are very intelligent, to the extent that no other nationality could be any better than they are, unless they were diverted in their efforts of specialization by their being interested in far too many things. By now they have learnt to avoid this problem. It is to be hoped that they also learn to give up their reprehensible adoration of foreigners, their excessive consideration of their personal interests, and the under-estimation of them themselves.
>
> (Juslenius, 1987 [1700])

Stereotypical conceptualizations based on myths and misconceptions devoid of any true empirical foundation can also be found with established scholars. For his description of the history of Finnish, Lauri Hakulinen (1979, pp. 33–4), a well-known Finnish-language scholar, adopted certain characterizations from Hugo Bergroth, a Swedish-speaking teacher at the

University of Helsinki. Bergroth (1916) had made an attempt to explain why the way in which Finland Swedes spoke was more colourless, dry, and monotonous than that of Swedes living in Sweden. Sweden-Swedish speakers employ, according to Bergroth, the cords in the larynx with greater vigour and energy; a Finn is also slower and sulkier, while a Swede is more open and self-confident and has more temperament. In Hakulinen's opinion, Bergroth's characterization applies to the Finnish language and speakers of Finnish even better: they speak with a rather quiet voice, at a low pitch level, with little affect, with their mouths rather closed, because they do not move their lips a great deal, and with a mumbling overall style of expression arising from a lax execution of individual sounds.

Implying that characterizations of the above kind apply only to Finns would be highly misleading. Similar characterizations are often given of many other nationalities. In addition, the unforced flexibility that is typical of normal everyday uses of the mother tongue makes the efforts expended on the learning and use of foreign languages look particularly problematic, which again may result in misguided conclusions about the levels of energy required. Speaking one's mother tongue is normally easy, and there are mostly no problems in the execution of communicative objectives, while speaking a foreign language often exposes the speaker to hardships that tend to arise unannounced.

More recently it has not been customary to refer to national characteristics as an explanation for aspects of communicative behaviour. In the second edition of his book Hakulinen too adopts a slightly different angle: he predicts a change in the ways in which Finns speak as a result of 'alterations in the aesthetic and phonetic character of Finnish from a rustic dialectal level in a more positive direction', due to the spread of a conscious speech culture among educated people. Hakulinen's main argument is that education makes people 'better' speakers of a language. The same attitude is reflected, more popularly and from a different viewpoint, in regular complaints that people who appear in public, such as radio or TV announcers, cannot pronounce words or letters (sic!) correctly. Labelling of pronunciation and communicative style in this way may be a convenient way to label educated and non-educated (better and not-so-good) people (see also Milroy & Milroy 1985, p. 29ff.). It may have a destructive impact on the transference of communicative intentions if the label of lower education is also taken to be a signal of a lower level of intelligence.

A common concern in Finland is the question of what other people think about the inhabitants of the country. Here an entire nation behaves like an individual who has a low level of self-esteem. Persons who feel insecure and are not sure what sort of self-image they have are also more sensitive to picking up negative evaluations in their environment, and they tend to react to them with an irrational strength (see Lehtonen, 1993). Finnish media keep a keen eye on what is written about Finland and Finns abroad: journalists know that their readers are interested in the news about Finns who have been recognized abroad or in the news which throws a shadow of disrepute on Finland and her inhabitants. A reflection of this 'collective lack of self-confidence' is the constant demand for acknowledgement from the outside and for instances of international acclaim for the country's unique character. The whole world is seen from a perspective with Finland at its centre point: whatever is said about Finland and Finns is thought to attract everybody's attention throughout the world.

An element which is one of the major causes of misunderstanding in intercultural communication is a phenomenon called projected autostereotype. It is derived from a more general hypothesis of projected similarity: both parties assume that the other is thinking the same way and making the same assumptions about the situation (Lehtonen, 1991; see also Adler, 1986). In terms of a projected autostereotype, persons whose perception of their own culture is negative assume that the members of the neighbouring country see them in the same way, and the autostereotype is the stronger the closer the cultures are to each other and the more alike their external appearance. Swedes and Finns are next-door neighbours, and they 'wrongly' interpret each other's behaviour in just the same way as do the Germans and the Dutch, or the British and the Americans. The assumption based on the idea of projected autostereotype also explains why Finns accept the characteristic stereotype of Finland. The national image of Finland for Finns is largely built upon their assumptions about the way in which outsiders see Finland and Finns.

In 1987 a survey was carried out in Sweden which attempted to discover the way in which Swedes saw Finland (Laine-Sveiby, 1991). The informants were asked to pick out from a word-list those that they thought described Finns the best. The ten most common characteristics typical for Finns were vitality (36 per cent), taciturnity (30 per cent), power (28 per cent), discretion (24 per cent), violence (24 per cent), hospitality (23 per cent), cooperativeness (23 per cent), reliability (22 per cent), and purposefulness (22 per cent). The responses are characteristic of Swedish culture: each informant connects Finnish characteristics with features that are familiar, and the result is a number of discrepant characterizations constituting no uniform profile of Finns. Finns are like any other people with their virtues and vices.

Conceptions similar to those described above in terms of national characteristics also arise from observations of language behaviour. People's intuitions are often far removed from the actual state of affairs, since they are easily coloured by tradition, expectations, inferences, and pure belief. Observations on speech rate serve as an illuminating example (see Lehtonen & Sajavaara, 1985). The impression of slow speech rate, for instance, may be derived, not from actual speech rate, but from morphological or morphophonemic differences between the listener's and the speaker's variety of the language. The impression of slowness may also be due to pauses that are longer than they should be according to the (subconscious) experience of the listener. Since slow speech rate is also easily confused with slow rate of thinking, serious constraints on efficient interaction may be the result. Speakers, again, who are recognized as fast by listeners are not necessarily any faster than others: the impression may be derived from the same factors as above but in reverse order. Crown & Feldstein (1985) also argue for the relative nature of silence and speaking by providing statistical evidence of the fact that the amount of talk by a speaker is determined more by the silences of the listener than by the speaker.

Furthermore, there is a great deal of variability in each individual's speech behaviour. Nobody is a member of just one speech community (see Milroy, 1987; Fasold, 1990, pp. 235–8), and there is a great deal of variation in the ways in which one person uses the languages or language variants at his disposal in different contexts. The vernacular and the ways to communicate typical of it such as they have been acquired in childhood may have been pushed to the background in the process of the speaker's adoption through education of a more standard variety of communicative behaviour. Yet the vernacular may easily surface in situations where the speaker interacts with speakers of that variety, or when the monitoring of the speech chain misfires for one reason or another. In addition, peculiar forms of communicative behaviour may develop in interaction with specific groups of people. The shift from one form of expression to another mostly takes place automatically without any awareness of the change. The way in which the other party is approached is very important: a common language variety creates a bridge for further communication, while its absence may prove to be a serious handicap but is not necessarily fatal (for examples see e. g. Jordan & Fuller, 1975). Tannen (1986, 1989) cites numerous instances of failure that can be assigned to a missing common 'language'. The destructive impact of failure may even be greater when people speaking the same language do not realize that their respective codes are shared only partially.

National character as metaphor

Labelling people's communicative behaviour, one way or another, in general terms may be highly misleading. Scollon (1985, pp. 27–8) points out that 'differences in pausology lead to one set of attributions in one society and perhaps to a very different or conflicting set in another'. He argues that the problem lies with the process attribution, which he regards as 'essentially a culture-specific phenomenon' instead of a universal one. His conclusion is that 'if we are going to get any further in our understanding of the meaning of silence in conversation, we must first examine the metaphors generating our research and our conversational stance'.

National images are conglomerations of all the ideas, conceptions, illusions, and evaluations linked up with countries or nationalities, which are used when information and observations about these countries or nationalities are assessed and interpreted. Similar to other images, national images are ingredients in the knowledge structures of thinking and memory, necessary for the categorization of the surrounding reality in order to constitute it in terms of views of the reality that are easier to control. Like other images, a national image is a generalization embedded in memory that often exists trimmed of all the concrete information and experience that originally has given rise to this generalization. Such a generalization is constituted by knowledge and evaluations relating to a country's culture and experience, and to the information, from the media and elsewhere, about the country in question. All images share one and the same characteristic: they complement, or are substituted for, observations made of the reality around us. What we observe around us is, in many ways, a state of mind (cf. Bauman, 1992, p. vii). If the national image is negative, this negative imprint is easily transferred in people's minds to specific features, phenomena, and things relating to the country concerned. In the same way as sunglasses tint our view, the national image colours everything: negative expectations make the observer see negative features while positive ones remain in the background. The negative image supplies a meaning for whatever is done by the country and her inhabitants, and for the news that is received about it.

The major problem lies in the fact that for an average observer the cultural stereotype usually represents 'objective reality': it is how things stand. In cross-cultural communication, the potential breakdown of the communicative situation results from these conceptions being subconscious for the most part. People have the tendency not to be aware of the characteristics of their own culture that serve as the yardstick of their attributions, and they are also bound to think that people living in other cultures perceive the world in the same way as they do (Lehtonen, 1994a).

It is important to remember that stereotypes cannot be said to be based on illusory perceptions of reality. The behaviour that gives rise to them is true and real: it is the interpretation of the behaviour derived from misguided expectations resulting from a different cultural framework that leads the observer astray. Yet it may be necessary to reconsider the perceptual basis of attributions relating to national images to see to what extent they are 'social acts performed in discourse and not merely cognitions about social acts' (Edwards & Potter, 1995, p. 88).

Conceptualization of an ideal self may be seen as a facet of ego protection (see Lehtonen, 1994a). It may make sense to see others in a deprecatory light in order to boost one's own ego, and the discrepancy between what one considers oneself to be and what one wanted to be ideally may result – despite a certain degree of threat involved – in a positive conclusion: things can only turn out to be better in the future, because they cannot be worse than they are now.

Finland: a silent culture

The statement by Bertolt Brecht that Finns are silent in two languages can be considered just a cliché today. In their attitudes towards speech and silence, Finns share the overall tendencies with their Nordic neighbours: just like their fellow Scandinavians they are of the opinion that you speak only when you have something to say. If you do not have anything to say, you keep silent. Talkativeness is an indication of slickness, which serves as a signal of unreliability.

Since the main body of research in speech communication deals with Americans, it has become rather customary to compare the non-talkative Nordic communicator style with the kind of talkativeness that is characteristic of the majority of Anglo speakers in the United States. Talk and non-talk serve totally different objectives in these two cultures: while Americans make use of talk to gather information about the other party and to reduce uncertainty, Finns try to reach the same goal by making silent observations of the interlocutor. Representatives of southern and central European cultures become irritated, because they tend to assess their interlocutors by their skill in verbal argumentation and reasoning, and this is something that may be totally absent in situations with Finns. Germans may regard Finnish quietness and silence as reticence, reserve, and even aimlessness (Tiittula, 1993). Americans are often disoriented by this, but realize later on that the silence of Finns is not a signal to inform the interlocutor of willingness to retire. For an Arab this characteristic behaviour of a Finn may also be confusing: Arabs are liable to think that something is definitely wrong (Lewis, 1992, p. 139).

Descriptions that Finns immediately find familiar relate to North-American Indians (Scollon & Scollon, 1981). Representatives of Indian cultures would not find any problems in adjusting to behaviour typical of Finns, and Finns would regard their communicator styles as normal.

When Sallinen-Kuparinen (1987) asked Finns to describe themselves as communicators, many of them pointed out that it is talkativeness that is one of their weaknesses. This conclusion looks quite unexpected, but it can be interpreted against the way that Finns match themselves with an ideal communicator image: a good speaker for a Finn is one who can give expression to what he or she wants to say briefly and efficiently without talking too much and too profusely. Sallinen says that Finnish communicator style is clearly receiver-oriented. A Finn tries to avoid being the first speaker, and he prefers being a quiet listener who shows his respect towards the person having the floor through his non-interruptive behaviour. This manner of conduct in interactive situations may reflect a high level of appreciation for speech. The reasons that Finns give for their silences in this sense are labelled as 'negative politeness' by Greig (1991, pp. 233 ff.).

Nordic silence means retirement to solitude and non-communication, which makes it different from the kind of silence that is typical of Japan, Korea, and China. In these Asian high-context cultures non-talkativeness can mostly be described as active silence, which is expected to create the right kind of atmosphere and make the evaluation of the other party possible (see Gudykunst, 1989, p. 329). Even Finnish silence and Swedish silence are not exactly the same, which may result in a Swede interpreting a Finn's behaviour as an attempt to keep a certain distance from the interlocutor (Laine-Sveiby, 1991, p. 57).

If, as Gudykunst (1989, p. 336) points out, efficiency in intercultural contacts is a product of people's ability to forge new contacts with representatives of other cultures, Finns may be seriously handicapped by their silence-bound behaviour, which makes it rather difficult for them to open up and start communicating in such situations.

For people living outside the Nordic countries, these countries look very much alike. It is not rare that even people living in the Nordic countries themselves assume that these countries are culturally uniform. When looking at your neighbour from your own country, the picture may seem familiar, but it may also easily become threatening when the neighbouring country and her inhabitants are characterized by reference to features that you have regarded as typical for your own.

On Hofstede's (1991) cultural maps representing more than fifty national cultures, which are based on a statistical analysis of an extensive body of questionnaire data, Finland is grouped with the German-speaking countries. Hofstede summarizes his results in terms of a number of indices. The Power Distance Index, which relates to the expectations and conceptions in terms of power among people working in organizations, is 33 for Finland, while it is 35 for western Germany (on a scale from 11 for Austria to 104 for Malaysia). Along the Individuality–Collectivity Scale, Germany is given 67 points as against 63 for Finland (the top being 91 for the United States and the bottom 6 for Guatemala), and along the Uncertainty Avoidance Scale, Germany receives 65 points, Finland 59 (the extremes are 112 for Greece and 8 for Singapore). The only characteristic that links Finland up with Scandinavian culture is what Hofstede labels as masculinity. Scandinavian culture is characterized as the most feminine among the countries evaluated: Sweden receives 5 points, Norway 8, Denmark 16, and Finland 26, as against western Germany with 66 points, Switzerland with 70, and Austria 79 (Sweden is the bottom and Japan the top with 95 points). This implies that Finland is considered softer and more sensitive than the German-speaking countries but also more masculine than its Nordic neighbours. Swedes tend to regard Finns as too hard, while Germans regard them as too soft.

According to the conclusions made by Vaahterikko (1993) on the basis of interview data, Finnish company managers are closer to Germans and Spaniards than their British, French, or Dutch counterparts. They appreciate the same kinds of values. This may be due to the fact that both in Finland and in Spain people perceive themselves to be geographically distant from the major currents of European activities, and people are highly concerned about the loss of face (see e.g. Vaahterikko, 1993). The need of being accepted and a weak self-concept may be characteristic of cultural peripheries: similar tendencies are found in Canada as against the United States or in Iceland as against the rest of Scandinavia. According to Vaahterikko, Spain resembles Finland also in the sense that, similarly to Sweden for Finns, France is the coveted neighbouring country whose inhabitants are considered proud and arrogant, while Portugal is the country where people from Spain go to show off and give testimony to their high standard of living. Italy is the Finns' Norway for the Spaniards, a sympathetic country where everything is all right: it is not far, but far enough.

Several cultural phenomena have been described as typical for both Finns and Swedes. Swedes are bound towards melancholy and a taciturn disposition, and they are regarded as tedious partners in conversation (Hill, 1992). The phenomenon of painful silence is also found in Sweden, but there silence is mostly taken to be a positive phenomenon (Lundberg, 1991). Interaction in the country is characterized by a degree of reserve: people do not want to make public appearances, and they expect that other people will be polite to them and leave them in peace. They try to avoid loud conversation, accept extended pauses and long silences, do not interrupt other speakers, avoid criticizing other people, and do not like manifesting strong affections (Stedje, 1990). The Swedes are more silent and less talkative than other nations: they stick to the principle that you should not talk unless you have something to say (Daun, 1989). There are few nationalities that feel equal comfort when keeping silence. Finns cannot be considered talkative, but they too may feel that Swedes are rather uncommunicative.

The descriptions above are exactly the same as those that Finns are used to hearing and reading about themselves. These two neighbouring countries are competing with each other in many areas, notably in various sports, and in the area of speech communication and external communicator image the competition is as hard as anywhere else: the performances are equal but the styles are different.

In the 1980s many companies in Sweden had Finnish managers, which often resulted in cultural clashes. The way in which the Finns managed the companies looked austere to Swedes: the Finns made their decisions behind closed doors and dictated their decisions instead of applying the rules adopted for public relations in Sweden. At the same time, the Finns thought that their way of doing things was less bureaucratic and therefore more efficient. Swedes do not like the straightforward and direct way of decision-making that is typical of Finns. They expect there to be negotiation in order to take everybody's opinion into account. They cannot understand the different approach of their Finnish neighbours.

The interesting feature in the interpretation of the relative character of cultural behaviour is the fact that what is authoritarian to Swedes is experienced quite differently by Germans: Finnish managers are criticized by them for their exaggeratedly democratic attitudes and for their slow rate of decision-making. Along this dimension, Finnish culture seems to be somewhere between German and Scandinavian cultures.

It is possible to summarize a number of speech-related characteristics that are typical of Finnish or, more generally, Nordic culture. Many of the features reinforce the image of a silent culture held by west European or Anglo-Americans. The characteristics cannot be considered to be positive or negative as such: observers from some cultures regard them as strengths, while others take them to be weaknesses. The summary looks as follows (similar characterizations can also be found in Carbaugh (1995)):

1. It is typical of interaction in the Nordic countries that you speak only if you have got something to say. Competence is assessed in Finland on the basis of deeds, not of speech or speech behaviour.
2. All Nordic peoples share the characteristic of social reticence, i. e. unwillingness to appear in public and passive participation in situations where a large number of people are present. A Finn does not normally want to take the floor.
3. The approach adopted by Finns in new and unknown situations is that of passive information gathering: they observe the situation without saying anything, instead of using the active strategy of asking questions or the interactive strategy typical of Americans where the principle is that of speaking a great deal, which makes the other party talk about himself.
4. Finns respect the other party's privacy. They are not willing to open a discussion with a stranger, nor to disturb him. Finnish politeness is passive: it is considerate to let other people be in peace.
5. It is typical of Finns to respect the other person's opinion. An opinion constitutes part of a person's private self. If you question his opinion, you also question him as a human being. Argumentation in Finland is difficult because the questioning of other people's opinions is easily considered to be mud-slinging.
6. The right to listen is one of the basic features of Finnish communication. The listener has the right to listen, while the speaker has the obligation to talk. At school, the listener is the pupil, the speaker the teacher. In intercultural contacts the stranger is easily confused with the teacher.
7. Finnish listenership means quiet listening. Verbal or vocal backchannelling is not very common.
8. Silence is harmonious. Being together without speaking is accepted: it means relaxation.
9. Long pauses in discourse are common and acceptable: a speaker can pause without being threatened with the loss of floor; long switching pauses between interlocutors are usual. Speakers are given the right to speak, and there is not much simultaneous talk.

10. The impact of Finnish cultural traditions is also seen in the way in which Finns speak. Finnish culture is closed, and it is characterized by a high degree of uniformity. Its members are highly suspicious of anything that is foreign and different. The threshold to open up discussion with a stranger is very high.

11. Collective self-awareness is very strong, which results in an emphasis on aspects of the nation's cultural identity. Finns tend to take a reserved stand in situations of intercultural encounter and may be highly concerned about the saving of 'national face'. A way to avoid the loss of face arising from communicative failure is to be silent.

12. Disfluency may result from traditional methods of foreign language teaching. Finns who had their foreign language education in the old school system differ from their Nordic neighbours, at least when speaking Germanic languages. They tend to be highly dysfluent. Conscious control of language production consumes a great deal of cognitive capacity, which is liable to cause 'social non-fluency': this results in reduced social sensitivity, frozen nonverbal behaviour, and clumsy social participation. Many of the characteristics are quite different from what Finns do when speaking their mother tongue.

Observations of Finns as communicators

The main concern above has been the self-image of Finns, the way in which they see themselves as communicators and interactants in social situations. There is also a body of research now that deals with the way in which communication partners in other nationalities see Finns as foreign language users and communicators. Certain aspects of the results are relevant for the present discussion.

Questionnaires and interviews have been used by a number of Finnish researchers to deduce characteristics of foreign language use and communicative style among Finns, mainly in situations where they are interacting with their trade partners. Yli-Renko (1993) has gathered information about perceptions of Finns by a number of English-speaking and German-speaking interlocutors. Most informants accepted statements to the effect that Finns hesitate to use English or German, they approve of periods of silence in interaction, and appear to be reticent and tend to keep a certain distance from their interlocutors. About one half of the informants, however, did not accept arguments concerning Finns' inability to keep up interaction, high levels of hesitancy and apprehension, non-observance of partners, and high degree of monotony in foreign-language communicative situations.

The informants interviewed by Törnroos et al. (1991) listed the same depreciatory characteristics of Finns, but at the same time they also found a large number of commendatory ones that are not without an impact on communicative success: Finns are straightforward, easy to work with, open-minded, hospitable, sympathetic, and polite. Similar findings are also reported by Lehtonen (1993) on the basis of a study carried out among Estonians. A slightly different picture in terms of communicator style arises from reports of the way Chinese interactants experience Finns as communicators (Salo-Lee, 1994): the strengths of Finns are no different but the tendency to silence is no longer a problem. Silence is necessary for the evaluation of the partner and for the establishment of agreement, but even Chinese interlocutors experience Finns as reticent and distant: they appear stubborn and lack small words and expressions that are considered signals of friendliness and attention. Salo-Lee labels this kind of behaviour by Finns as social silence. Reticence was also reported as a characteristic of Finns by American exchange students who had spent a year in Finland (Mäkisalo, 1987).

Another characteristic of communicator style that is attached to Finns is directness, even bluntness (Salo-Lee, 1994; Tiittula, 1994). This comes up in interviews with Asians and Germans.

Bluntness may result from straightforward impoliteness, but it can also be a product of an inability to use various linguistic expressions such as downtoners, apologies, or polite requests. Since most of the information about Finns in this respect comes from situations where they are expected to use a foreign language, it is quite possible that what is experienced as bluntness actually is an effect of limitations in communicative competence in a foreign language. In their native communicative behaviour, many Finns, particularly if they have been enculturated in the eastern parts of the country, are famous for their indirect, ambiguous, and even incomprehensible practices.

A certain element of passivity and non-participation characterizes Finns in the studies surveyed for the present paper. These features come out strongly in Rusanen's (1993) study that is concerned with Finns in multinational workplaces: the Finn is normally a good listener but a poor speaker; he rarely opens up conversations, makes few initiatives, and seldom interferes in discussions. Finns could be characterized as friendly, quiet, hesitant, reticent, patient, and reliable. It is quite unexpected that in spite of the above characteristics, many of which are indicative of some reticence, Finns are regarded as sociable. This may be derived from a certain strength in the area of negotiating – instead of argumentation. Very interesting is Rusanen's finding that Finns are experienced as having no expression on their face. Here again we are dealing with situations where Finns are using foreign languages, which may explain the discrepancy with reports by Swedes (Laine-Sveiby, 1987) that Finns' nonverbal behaviour tends to be too open an indication of their feelings and attitudes.

To a Frenchman a Finn looks rather uncommunicative and withdrawn, while Japanese (and even Swedish) interlocutors may think that Finns tend to have too many gestures and they are too spontaneous. A German may think that as a negotiator a Finn is too conciliatory, taking too much time to reach an excessively democratic conclusion, whereas a Swede maintains that the way in which Finns present their case is too straightforward and blunt, and that as decision-makers Finns are authoritarian and too fast. The Finn's conduct may remain the same but the interpretation depends on the relative viewpoint of the observer.

Conclusion: Finnish silence: myth or reality?

A large number of characteristics have been listed as being indicative of Finns as a silent nation. Some of them originate through observations of Finns in interactional situations by foreigners, others are derived from experiences of Finns themselves. It would be certainly wrong to try and maintain that both groups of observers, both Finns and foreigners, have ended up having misguided conceptions about Finns as communicators. The conclusion is in any case that Finns have certain features in their communicative behaviour that strike the foreign observer as different. But at the same time, it must also be pointed out that the problem arises, in part at least, from the difficulties inherent in cultural perceptions: people make use of their own conceptual categories to organize their observations of the behaviour of others. The problem of having applicable concepts and categories arises when we are supposed to study conventions, norms, and behaviours cross-culturally.

The above comparability problem is aggravated in Finland through the tendency of labelling this or that communicative behaviour as better or communicatively more suitable than some other. Finns easily interpret their 'national' characteristics, true or assumed, that are considered to be different from those of members of certain (perhaps more prominent) nationalities as handicaps that they had better try and overcome. It is considered important to be alike with representatives of what is regarded as mainline international culture. Anything that is labelled as typical of this international culture is immediately adopted as a measuring stick for the future development of the nation, and what is considered characteristically Finnish is given a negative colouring. What is here labelled as Finnish silence represents a typical example of this tendency.

The respective proportions and particular forms of speech and silence are significant only as variables within a certain culture. They form part of the target-oriented behaviour of members of that culture and make sense only when interpreted within that specified context. If the features concerned are moved outside their domestic sphere and are given interpretations from the outside, it is understandable that the result is mis-guided. Yet one of the dilemmas in all this is that at the same time the insider is also incapable of seeing his or her true nature as a communicator. He too selects some features which he considers significant, and gives evaluations to his own behaviour in just these terms.

What is needed is a set of common denominators which could be used to assess the amount of talk and non-talk in the cultures to be compared. Such a set does not exist for the time being. Alternatively, the way in which a Finn talks could be compared with that of a member of another culture. So it could be maintained for instance that Finns speak less than Americans. Such a comparison is not however unproblematic: Finns may be less liable to intervene in public meetings and in classrooms but participate with vigour in discussions in pubs, at marketplaces, or in the sauna. It is not obvious where the measurement of the amount of talk should take place: in situations where the Finn is silent, or in those where he talks? Another notorious example is the observation that Finnish communicative behaviour lacks small talk, and what is found instead is silence. Yet here again the norm is brought in from the outside: the forms and topics of small talk in Finland are different, but it is not possible to say that there is less of it. When we observe a Finn's communicative behaviour in these terms, we are mostly concerned with a Finn as a user of a foreign language, which adds one more discrepancy: the comparison is always with native speakers of the target language using their mother tongue, and not with them as users of a foreign language.

The result of a comparison of the above kind also depends on who the other party is. As has been pointed out above, a Finn may be considered uncommunicative and quiet by representatives of certain cultures, while others may think that he/she is bound to excessive gestures and spontaneity.

All this means that an approach like Hofstede's through a grid based on attitudes towards other nationalities may have a relative value only. As such, Hofstede's indices tell us very little about the basic theme of the present paper: they can be taken to be indications of an overall positioning towards culture.

A great deal of research work remains to be done in the area of silence. A useful starting point was made by Saville-Troike's (1985) proposition for an etic grid for the study of silence in an 'integrated theory of communication'.

The terminology used may also be highly misleading depending on the type of culture that it is applied to. The American research tradition, for instance, includes the term 'tolerance of silence'. It is appropriate for the description of the affective impact of silence in a culture whose members are used to filling social silence with talk. A group of people can stand a certain period of silence, after which the silence is broken by means of behaviour that is acceptable in that particular culture. If, however, people are used to enjoying silence and relaxing by not having to talk even when they are in other people's company, tolerance of silence cannot easily be used to give an interpretation to the functions of social silence, and the absence of talk is given a wrong significance in terms of the culture concerned. The concept is no longer valid.

The application of concepts valid in one culture, where they may be highly pertinent and appropriate, to another cultural environment is often done under the assumption that the concepts used are universal. It is even possible to talk about conceptual imperialism (Lehtonen, 1994c). In the description of American speech behaviour a great deal of attention is paid to how active American speakers are. Activity is regarded as commendable, and it is considered one of the prerequisites of social success. Attitudes to taciturnity are characterized by, for instance, terms like 'communication apprehension', which means rather natural anxiety felt when public speech is expected. If, however, social success results from ways of conduct other than verbal activity, as is the case in many Asian countries or sometimes in Scandinavia, the correct measuring stick could be 'tolerance of talk'. In such cultures the right and obligation of speaking depends on the relative position of power that the person concerned has and on the interpretation of the requirements of the situation. The person concerned may feel as anxious as his or her American counterpart for exactly the same reasons – having to appear in public – but, in addition, he or she may be worried about taking the floor in a situation where it is not appropriate to say anything in his or her own culture.

Speaking is controlled in Finland, like elsewhere, by various situational norms such as silence in church, talking in the classroom when the teacher allows it, and constraints on 'chatter' at the dinner table. Finnish cultural behaviour also comprises a number of values and fundamental conceptions of appropriate behaviour which give an outsider an impression of a silent culture.

References

Adler, N. (1986). *International dimensions of organizational behaviour*. Boston, MA: Kent.

Bauman, Z. (1992). *Intimations of postmodernity*. London: Routledge.

Bergroth, H. (1916). *Finlandssvenska. Handledning till undvikande av provinsialismer i tal och skrift* [Finland Swedish: introduction to the avoidance of provincialisms in speech and writing]. Borgå: Holger Schildt.

Carbaugh, D. (1995). 'Are Americans really superficial?': Notes on Finnish and American cultures in linguistic action. In L. Salo-Lee (ed.), *Kieli ja kulttuuri oppimisessa ja opettamisessa* [Language and culture in learning and teaching] (pp. 53–60). Publications of the Department of Communication, University of Jyväskylä 12.

Crown, C. L. & Feldstein, S. (1985). Psychological correlates of silence and sound in conversational interaction. In Deborah Tannen & Muriel Saville-Troike (eds), *Perspectives on silence* (pp. 31–54). Norwood, NJ: Ablex.

Daun, Å. (1989). *Svensk mentalitet: ett jämförande perspektiv* [Swedish mentality: a comparative perspective]. Stockholm: Rabén & Sjögren.

Edwards, D. & Potter, J. (1995). Attribution. In Rom Harré & Peter Stearns (eds), *Discursive psychology in practice* (pp. 87–119). London: Sage.

Fasold, R. (1990). *The sociolinguistics of language*. Oxford: Blackwell.

Greig, F. E. (1991). Would you talk to a stranger? A multicultural study of self-report on initiating and maintaining conversation in a hypothetical travel encounter. Unpublished PhD dissertation, Georgetown University.

Gudykunst, W. B. (1989). Culture and the development of interpersonal relationships. In James A. Anderson (ed.), *Communication Yearbook 12* (pp. 315–54). Newbury Park, CA: Sage.

Hakulinen, L. (1979). *Suomen kielen rakenne ja kehitys* [The structure and development of the Finnish language] (4th edn). Helsinki: Otava.

Hill, R. (1992). *We Europeans*. Brussels: Europublications.

Hofstede, G. (1991). *Cultures and organizations*. London: McGraw-Hill.

Jordan, B. & Fuller, N. (1975). On the non-fatal nature of trouble: sense-making and trouble-managing in lingua franca talk. *Semiotica*, 13, 11–31.

Juslenius, D. (1987). *Aboa vetus et nova*. Transl. *Vanha ja uusi Turku*. By Tuomo Pekkanen & Virpi Seppälä-Pekkanen. Helsinki: Suomalaisen Kirjallisuuden Seura [originally published in 1700].

Laine-Sveiby, K. (1987). *Kansallinen kulttuuri strategiana: Suomi ja Ruotsi – eroja ja yhtäläisyyksiä* [National culture as a strategy: Finland and Sweden – differences and similarities]. Helsinki: Elinkeinoelämän valtuuskunta EVA.

Laine-Sveiby, K. (1991). *Företag i kulturmöten. Tre finländska företag och deras dotterbolag. En etnologisk studie* [Enterprises at cross-cultural meetings. Three Finnish enterprises and their daughters. An ethnographic study]. Edsbruk: Akademitryck.

Lehtonen, J. (1991). The role of national stereotypes in intercultural communication. In Edith Slembek (ed.), *Culture and communication* (pp. 175–85). Frankfurt a. M.: Verlag für interkulturelle Kommunikation.

Lehtonen, J. (1993). Suomalaisuus, Suomi-kuva ja kansainvälistymisen haasteet [Finnishness, image of Finland, and challenges of internationalization]. In Jaakko Lehtonen (ed.), *Kulttuurien kohtaaminen* [*Meeting of cultures*] (pp. 7–30). (Publications of the Department of Communication 9.) Jyväskylä: University of Jyväskylä.

Lehtonen, J. (1994a). Omakuva ja vieraskuva [Images of self and others]. In Olli Alho et al. (eds), *Ihminen ja kulttuuri* [*People and culture*] (pp. 41–65). Helsinki: Fintra.

Lehtonen, J. (1994b). *National attitudes as a self-protection strategy.* Proceedings of the SIETAR Europe 1994 Conference. Jyväskylä, Finland.

Lehtonen, J. (1994c). Vaikeneva suomalainen – myytti ja todellisuus [The silent Finn – myth and reality], *Tempus*, 5, 5–7.

Lehtonen, J. & Sajavaara, K. (1985). The silent Finn. In Deborah Tannen & Muriel Saville-Troike (eds), *Perspectives on silence* (pp. 193–201). Norwood, NJ: Ablex.

Lewis, R. D. (1992). *Mekö erilaisia? Suomalainen kansainvälisissä liikeneuvotteluissa* [*Finland – cultural lone wolf*]. Helsinki: Otava.

Lundberg, P. (1991) *Utbildning and träning för interkulturell kompetens* [*Education and training for intercultural competence*]. Lund: Studentlitteratur.

Mäkisalo, A. (1987). Suomalainen kommunikaatio ulkomaalaisen silmin [Finnish communication as seen by a foreigner]. Unpublished MA thesis, University of Jyväskylä.

Milroy, J. & Milroy, L. (1985). *Authority in language.* London: Routledge & Kegan Paul.

Milroy, L. (1987). *Language and social networks* (2nd edn). Oxford: Blackwell.

Rusanen, S. (1993). Suomalainen kansainvälisessä työyhteisössä [The Finn as a member of an international workplace]. In Jaakko Lehtonen (ed.), *Kulttuurien kohtaaminen* [*Meeting of cultures*] (pp. 31–76). (Publications of the Department of Communication 9.) Jyväskylä: University of Jyväskylä.

Sallinen-Kuparinen, A. (1987). Culture and communicator image. Paper presented at the Western Speech Communication Association Convention, Salt Lake City.

Salo-Lee, L. (1994). Suomalaiset ja kiinalaiset viestijöinä [Finns and Chinese as communicators: strengths and problems]. In Pekka Isotalus (ed.), *Puheesta ja vuorovaikutuksesta* [*On speech and interaction*] (pp. 103–14). Jyväskylä: Department of Communication, University of Jyväskylä.

Saville-Troike, M. (1985). The place of silence in an integrated theory of communication. In Deborah Tannen & Muriel Saville-Troike (eds), *Perspectives on silence* (pp. 3–18). Norwood, NJ: Ablex.

Scollon, R. (1985). Silence in the metaphor of malfunction. In Deborah Tannen & Muriel Saville-Troike (eds), *Perspectives on silence* (pp. 21–30). Norwood, NJ: Ablex.

Scollon, R. & Scollon, S. B. K. (1981). *Narrative, literacy, and face in interethnic communication.* Norwood, NJ: Ablex.

Stedje, A. (1990). Sprachliche Handlungsmuster und interkulturelle Kommunikation. In Bernd Spillner (ed.), *Interkulturelle Kommunikation* (pp. 29–39). Frankfurt a. M.: Peter Lang.

Tannen, D. (1986). *That's not what I meant: how conversational style makes or breaks relationships.* New York: William Morrow.

Tannen, D. (1989). *You just don't understand: women and men in conversation.* New York: William Morrow.

Tiittula, L. (1993). Stereotype in interkulturellen Geschäftskontakten, Manuscript.

Tiittula, L. (1994). *Kulttuurit kohtaavat* [*Meeting of cultures*]. Helsinki: School of Economics and Business Administration.

Törnroos, J.-Å., Berg, N. & Bergman, K. (1991). *Finlands image i Europa – europeiska företagsledares Finlandsbild* [*Finland's image in Europe – the image of Finland among European business managers*]. (Reports from the Faculty of Economics and Social Sciences A.342.) Åbo-Turku: Åbo Akademi/University.

Vaahterikko, P. (1993). Avoimet espanjalaiset ja kylmät suomalaiset [Open Spaniards and cold Finns]. *Tempus*, 8, 26–7.

Yli-Renko, K. (1993). *Intercultural communication in foreign language education.* (Research Reports, Faculty of Education A.168.) Turku: University of Turku.

PART III: NOTES FOR STUDENTS AND INSTRUCTORS

Study questions

1   What is CCSARP? What is its goal and theoretical and methodological framework?
2   Following the procedure explained on page 139 in Chapter 9, analyse the following requests:
    * Clean up this mess, it's disgusting.
    * It would really help if you did something about the kitchen.
    * Excuse me, I've just missed my bus and you live on the same road. I wonder if I could trouble you for a lift?
3   What is *dugri* talk? What is its cultural meaning? Why does the author regard it as a ritual?
4   Katriel in Chapter 10 follows Hymes' model in analysing the form and function of *dugri* talk in the Israeli culture. Can you summarise the main findings under each component such as participants, setting, scene, message content, message form, instrumentalities, key, ends, genre and norms of interaction?
5   What does *Insha' Allah* mean? What are the pragmatic functions of this phrase in conversation? Why, according to the author, does the wife of the Egyptian couple enact the recitation during the conversation on page 175?
6   The author of Chapter 11 lists some of the communication behaviours indicative of 'silent Finns'. What are they?
7   What implication do the stereotypes such as 'the silent Finn' have on intercultural communication?

Study activity

1   How does a Discourse Completion Test work? What are the pros and cons of this method of data collection? Please refer to the last chapter on Studying language and intercultural communication: methodological issues.
2   Design a Discourse Completion Test to elicit the speech act of request or apology using the situations provided in Appendix A and Appendix B in the article by Blum-Kulka & Olshtain. You can ask different groups of speakers to complete the test: English native speakers and non-native English speakers of a particular language, say, Spanish. In addition, you can ask native speakers of Spanish to complete the test in Spanish.

Analyse the data following the coding schemes provided in the article. Compare the different groups. Are there any differences among the groups? If so, what factors do you think contribute to the differences?

3   A speech event such as 'dugri talk' may be culture-specific, but it does not mean that such a speech event does not occur in other cultures. It may be more frequent and salient in some cultures than in others. Critically reflect on your home culture or the cultures you are familiar with and discuss how speakers from the culture(s) stage confrontational topics. Please give evidence or examples. What are the differences from dugri talk?

4   The concept of indirectness has been discussed from various perspectives. For example, in earlier discussions of cultural dimensions in Part I, both Hofstede and Hall in Chapter 3 talk about how cultural values such as power distance and high vs. low context can impact on the degree of indirectness in communication. In Part II, the notions of politeness and face are discussed in close association with indirectness. In this part, we have seen how people achieve indirectness by employing various communicative resources and interactional strategies. Discuss what indirectness is. Is it a means to achieve a communication goal or is it an end itself? Are there cross-cultural differences? Choose two cultures and investigate how indirectness is achieved through communication in these two cultures.

5   Similar to 'the silent Finn', we often hear phrases such as 'inscrutable Chinese', 'non-committal Japanese', etc. Choose a culture and look into the 'myths' or 'stereotypes' very often associated with it and answer the following questions: how does the stereotype originate and why? What do the myths and stereotypes suggest about the culture-specific communication patterns? What implications do they have on interaction and intercultural communication?

6   Many studies on speech acts are published in languages other than English. Choose a language other than English and carry out a literature review of the speech acts studies published in this language. Summarise the findings in bullet points. Are these findings similar to those on speech acts in English?

Further reading

The following two edited volumes contain a good collection of articles on various speech acts and cultures.

Blum-Kulka, S., House, J. & Kasper, G. (1989). *Cross-cultural pragmatics: requests and apologies.* Norwood, NJ: Ablex Pub. Corp.,
Gass, S. & Neu, J. (eds) (1996). *Speech acts across cultures: challenges to communication in a second language.* Berlin: Mouton de Gruyter.
Hickey, L. & Steward, M. (2005). *Politeness in Europe.* Clevedon: Multilingual Matters.

The following articles, among others, are widely cited:

Duranti, A. (1997). Universal and culture-specific properties of greetings. *Journal of Linguistic Anthropology,* 7(1), 63–97.
Maynard, S. (1986). On backchannel behaviour in Japanese casual conversation. *Linguistics,* 24, 1079–108.
Sifianou, M. (1993). Off-Record indirectness and the notion of imposition. *Multilingua,* 12(1), 69–79.
Carmen, G. (1996). Reprimanding and responding to a reprimand: a case study of Peruvian Spanish speakers. *Journal of Pragmatics,* 26, 663–97.

On nonverbal communication, see:

Hall, E. (1959). *The silent language.* New York: Doubleday & Company. Reprinted in 1973 by New York: Anchor Press.
Wharton, T. (2009). *Pragmatics and non-verbal communication.* Cambridge: Cambridge University Press.

PART IV

Teaching and learning cultural variations of language use

Introduction to Part IV

Zhu Hua

INTERCULTURAL COMMUNICATION OFTEN takes place between speakers who use a language other than their native languages. This part focuses on non-native speakers and second-language learners, and the related cultural issues in language teaching and learning.

Chapter 13 critically reviews how the concept of culture is represented in the language teaching curriculum and challenges the common practice of reducing culture to ethnicity and nationality in education. It argues for a 'small culture' approach in language education, in which the emphasis is on the process of interpreting commonalities shared by a small social grouping through activities, rather than prescribing groupings at the start. This article represents an important development in the field of language learning and teaching and extends the field of intercultural communication.

Chapter 14 provides a comprehensive overview of the research findings in second language pragmatics, focusing on developmental patterns of speech acts and pragmatics and discourse abilities in a second language. Commonalities shared among learners of various languages as well as language-specific patterns are discussed. In addition to the learning of English by learners of various language backgrounds, the chapter covers the learning of other languages such as Japanese, Brazilian Portuguese, Indonesian, etc. The speech acts under discussion include request, suggestion, refusal, greeting and apology. It could be read together with Chapter 8.

Despite its heterogeneous nature, lingua franca communication shows a remarkable cooperative feature, as most of the studies in the literature emphasise. Participants are often found to use various linguistic and non-linguistic means to make sense *in situ*. Examples of such resourcefulness include the use of various nonverbal means such as laughter to substitute verbal back-channels, and pauses to indicate topic changes, collaborative construction of turns and the use of code-switching. Chapter 15 by Mauranen investigates the variety of clarification and repair strategies with which lingua franca speakers signal and prevent misunderstanding. It also discusses the sources of misunderstandings in lingua franca situations and highlights the characteristics of lingua franca communication.

Chapter 13

ADRIAN HOLLIDAY

SMALL CULTURES

Introduction

THIS PAPER PRESENTS A NOTION of 'small' culture as an alternative to what has become the default notion of 'large' culture in applied linguistics and much social science and popular usage. Precise definitions will be developed through the paper, but in simple terms, 'large' signifies 'ethnic', 'national' or 'international', and 'small' signifies any cohesive social grouping. A 'small culture' approach thus attempts to liberate 'culture' from notions of ethnicity and nation and from the perceptual dangers they carry with them. This use of 'large' and 'small' is entirely my own; and throughout I will impose the distinction on current usages in the literature.

A motivation for differentiating a 'small' sense of culture is a concern with the way in which inter cultural issues in applied linguistics seem dominated by a 'large' culture approach. Within this approach, cultural differences in classroom and curriculum scenarios, the transportation of technologies from the English-speaking West, the general question of linguistic and cultural imperialism in global and professional spheres (e.g. Pennycook, 1994; Holliday, 1994a; Phillipson, 1992), and the learning of culture in language education (e.g. Byram and Morgan, 1994; Kramsch, 1993) have been placed around 'large' ethnic, national and international cultural differences. Large culture difference is also taken as the basic unit in influential cross-cultural management studies (e.g. Hofstede, 1991). In opposition, it can be argued that this large culture approach results in reductionist overgeneralization and otherization of 'foreign' educators, students and societies (Holliday, 1994b, 1997a, 1999). What is happening in applied linguistics is characteristic of a broader tendency within post–colonial and inter-ethnic discourses (e.g. Sarangi, 1995, pp. 10–14; Baumann, 1996).

Another motivation is that the two notions of 'culture' already seem to exist in both academic and popular usage but are often not recognized as distinct. It is therefore necessary to impose the 'large–small' distinction to clarify some of the confusion which has collected around 'culture'. It is not my intention to argue that 'culture' really means X rather than Y, but to clarify what we mean when we use the word in different ways for different purposes.

An orientation in my discussion is Berger and Luckmann's sociology of knowledge (1967). I will thus consider how 'culture' is socially constructed as a 'reality' in applied linguistics,

Source: Holliday, A. (1999). Small cultures. *Applied Linguistics*, 20(2), 237–64.

and the nature of the 'knowledge' which this construction precipitates. 'Culture' shall therefore be 'so-called' throughout. Borrowing Berger and Luckmann's sentiment (ibid., p. 14), quotation marks should be put around 'culture' whenever the term is used; but this would be 'stylistically awkward' and therefore not done unless the sense necessitates.

I shall first look at how large and small notions of culture relate to each other, then at the limitations of a large culture approach, followed by the merits of a small culture approach. In the last part I shall take an English language curriculum scenario as an example, and examine how cultural imperialism and culture learning may operate at the mezzo level of the institution. The nature of small culture formation and the role of ethnography will also be examined. Although this paper is about the use of 'culture' in applied linguistics, reference will be made to the 'parent' discussion within the social sciences. At the same time, what is said about applied linguistics will also be of relevance to social science, and to ethnography in particular.

Two Cultures

On asking both academics and non-academics what they mean by 'culture' one will invariably find that they first refer to 'large' entities such as British, Indonesian, Western or European cultures. However, at other times one may also hear people referring to 'small' entities such as hospital, research, family, office or organization cultures. When asked how these two types of culture relate to each other, some people say that the 'large' usage is the correct one and that the 'small' usage is metaphorical. Others say that the small cultures are 'sub-cultures'. Casual observation thus gives the impression that when asked, people will state 'large' culture, but will often use 'small' culture as an unmarked form.[1]

Between as well as within

It is important to distinguish between small culture and sub-culture. 'Sub-culture', although implying something small, seems to be essentially a large culture concept because it implies something within and subservient to a particular large ethnic, national or international culture. Within the Chicago school, sub-cultures have been defined as 'social groups which are perceived to deviate from the normative ideals of adult communities' (Thornton, 1997, p. 2). In the Birmingham school, where social deviance is perhaps less on the agenda, sub-cultures are still considered as elements in ideological tension with 'parent' or 'dominant' large cultures within which they exist (Gelder, 1997, p. 84–5). Such sub-sets of large cultures may indeed exist. Different to this notion of sub-cultures, small cultures do not necessarily have this Russian doll or onion-skin relationship with parent large cultures. For example, school, classroom, teacher and other education (small) cultures can extend beyond the boundaries of larger cultures (of say nation) where they are related to international education cultures (Holliday, 1994a, p. 29). There are secondary-school classrooms all over the world with very similar seating arrangements and teacher–student behaviour, despite national culture difference (Poppleton and Riseborough, 1990). That similarities between classrooms may be a result of global colonial or post-colonial European cultural influence does not denigrate their existence as real classrooms. Hence this conclusion to an ethnography of a girls' secondary school in Cairo:

> It is Egypt, it is the East, it is also a developing country. But it is also humanity. Beyond my initial fascination with the exotic protocol, drills, sounds and system, it became just an ordinary school. [. . .] I cannot count the times I felt myself transformed over six thousand miles and more than a decade away to the parochial school in

downtown San Francisco that I attended as a child. Superficially the two schools are vastly different. [. . .] Yet despite their specific features [one can] [. . .] join them together in the world community of schools.

(Herrera, 1992, pp. 80–1)

Clark and Ivanic give the similar example of 'similarities in the contexts of culture of two individual hospitals in different countries' to support the notion that national and institutional contexts should not be thought of as being 'in a hierarchical relationship' (1997, p. 68). Small cultures can thus run between as well as within related large cultures. Other small cultures which are not contained within large cultures are those which can be formed at the interface between older cultures. For example, 'middle cultures' can be formed across national cultural boundaries between tourists and 'local' people, teachers and expatriate curriculum developers, foreign language students and 'native-speaker' teachers, and researchers and their subjects. They are created for long or short duration to provide ground on which the dealing between the two parties takes place (Holliday and Hoose, 1996). Another example, which shall be taken up in detail below, is where people from different national groups come together to form a work or leisure small culture of their own. Multinational organization cultures would fall into this category.

Kramsch (1993, p. 235) speaks of something similar to middle cultures in the creation of 'a third culture' where people travel between or experience two cultures. However, she implies that these '"border" experiences' (ibid.) relate to the default entity of national culture, on the edge of which they form as anomalies. The 'third culture' is thus between two large cultures; and its conceptualization is large in orientation. In contrast, small cultures, no matter how temporary, are not anomalous, are not subservient to large cultures, and constitute a seamless mélange which stretches across national boundaries.

Two paradigms

The notion of small culture does not therefore relate simply to something smaller in size than large ethnic, national or international cultures, but presents a different paradigm through which to look at social groupings. The small culture paradigm, set against the large culture paradigm, is summarized in Table 13.1. The idea of small cultures (central column) is non-essentialist in that it does not relate to the essences of ethnic,[2] national or international entities. Instead it relates to any cohesive social grouping, with no necessary subordination to large cultures. Table 13.1 also distinguishes a research orientation for each paradigm. 'Research' is used here in the broadest sense, as any academic or non-academic process of learning about culture. Non-academic cultural research is naturally carried out by anyone 'approaching' an unfamiliar social grouping in the sense of Schutz's 'stranger', 'who has to place in question nearly everything that seems unquestionable to the members of the approached group' (1962, p. 96). In cultural research, small cultures are thus a heuristic means in the process of interpreting group behaviour. The idea of large cultures (right-hand column), in contrast, is essentialist in that it relates to the essential differences between ethnic, national and international entities. Because the large culture paradigm begins with a prescriptive desire to seek out and detail differences which are considered the norm, and because it aims to explain behaviour in these terms, it tends to be culturist – a notion which I shall take up later.

'Small' is therefore not just a matter of size, but of the degree of imposition on reality. Whereas the large culture notion imposes a picture of the social world which is divided into 'hard', essentially different ethnic, national or international cultures, the small culture notion

Table 13.1 Two paradigms

	Small cultures	*Large cultures*
Character	non-essentialist, non-culturist relating to cohesive behaviour in activities within any social grouping	essentialist, culturist 'culture' as essential features of ethnic national or international group
Relations	no necessary subordination to or containment within large cultures, therefore no onion-skin	small (sub) cultures are contained within and subordinate to large cultures through onion-skin relationship
Research orientation	interpretive, process interpreting emergent behaviour within any social grouping heuristic model to aid the process of reseaching the cohesive process of any social grouping	prescriptive, normative beginning with the idea that specific ethnic, national and international groups have different 'cultures' and then searching for the details (e.g. what is polite in Japanese culture)

leaves the picture open, finding 'softer' 'cultures' in all types of social grouping, which may or may not have significant ethnic, national or international qualities. In this sense, the focus of a large culture approach is what makes cultures, which everyone acknowledges as existing, essentially different to each other. In contrast, a small culture approach is more concerned with social processes as they emerge.

Large culture as reified small culture

As different paradigms, a large culture and small culture approach will not only see the social world in different ways; they will also have views about each other. Hence, the large culture paradigm will see a small, non-ethnic or non-national culture, in terms of size, as a sub-part or metaphorical derivation of large culture. This vision would be the default academic and popular position referred to above. Alternatively, there is a literature, which I classify as within a small culture paradigm, in which non-essentialist small culture is seen as the original notion, of which large culture is a reification.

The principle of reification is developed by Berger and Luckmann as a basic force in social life. It involves:

> the apprehension of the products of human activity *as if* they were something other than human products – such as the facts of nature, results of cosmic laws, or manifestations of divine will.
>
> (1967, p. 107)

This can relate to roles, identities and institutions – as in institutionalization (ibid., p. 108). In the case of culture, reification takes place where the notion of culture has been constructed for the purpose of explaining human behaviour, but is then institutionalized into something that exists over and above human behaviour. Thus, the non-essentialists argue that:

> Culture is not a real thing, but an abstract and purely analytical notion. It does not cause behaviour, but summarises an abstraction from it, and is thus neither normative

nor predictive. [. . .] The anthropologist's abstraction of a perpetually changing process of meaning-making is replaced by a reified entity that has a definite substantive content and assumes the status of a thing that people 'have' or are 'members of'.

(Baumann, 1996, pp. 11–12, citing Rothschild)

Then, after reification:

Both specialists and nonspecialists are prone to talk about 'a culture' as if it could be a causative agent ('their culture leads them to go on vision quests') or a conscious being ('X culture values individuality').

(Keesing, 1981, p. 72)

As a result of this reification:

How often, still, do I hear my colleagues and students talk as if 'a culture' was an agent that could do things; or as if 'a culture' was a collectivity of people. [. . .] I fear that our common ways of talk channel our thought in these directions. [. . .] It has passed into popular discourse. [. . .]. I recently heard a radio announcer in Australia talk about 'the different cultures living in our area'.

(Keesing, 1981, pp. 302–3)

There is thus a change in the way in which culture is used to think about human behaviour. After reification, culture appears large and essentialist, and indicates concrete, separate, behaviour-defining ethnic, national and international groups with material permanence and clear boundaries.

Although the non-essentialists may think otherwise, reification is not in any way a 'perversion' or 'a sort of cognitive fall from grace', but a natural social process common in theoretical and non-theoretical thought (Berger and Luckmann, 1967, p. 107). 'Our conception of culture almost irresistibly leads us into reification and essentialism' (Keesing, 1994, p. 302). One could say that reifying large culture from small culture comprises an inescapable occupational hazard in cultural analysis. 'Many scholars now acknowledge that *any* definition of culture is necessarily reductionist' (Sarangi, 1995, my emphasis). Furthermore, in a world in which almost all perceptions are socially constructed, the concept of 'large culture' is as real as anything else. My purpose in suggesting that large culture is a reification is not therefore to reveal it as false. It is rather to increase awareness of what its conceptualization involves, and, as will be demonstrated below, some of its ideological implications – in Fairclough's words, 'essentially making visible the inter-connectedness of things' (1995, p. 36).

The difficulty with large cultures

Having looked at the ways in which the small and large culture paradigms relate to each other, some of the more problematic aspects of the large culture paradigm will now be considered.

Nation, centres and peripheries

The notion of large culture supports various spheres of political interest. One such is the building of the concept of the material nation. European justifications of colonization through simplistic cultural definitions of subject peoples is well catalogued (Morawska and Spohn, 1994;

Comaroff and Comaroff, 1992; Asad, 1973; Nzimiro, 1979; Sarangi, 1995). 'Conventional anthropology allowed "the power of topography to conceal successfully the topography of power"' (Schudson, 1994, p. 37, citing Gupta and Ferguson). This has continued in a post-colonialist era with 'unequal narratives' creating an 'unreciprocal interpretation of other [. . .] non-Western cultures' (Sarangi, 1995, citing Asad and Said). Equating nation with homogeneous ideas of large culture also supported the conceptual development of European nations themselves. It may be true that 'most sociologists and historians do not take culture to be the central integrative mechanism for national societies' (Schudson, 1994, p. 23). Nevertheless, a 'methodological nationalist' sociology can be seen as a product of nineteenth-century nationalism (ibid., p. 21). This creation of 'national-level "imagined communities"' and attaching 'culture' to nation can also be considered as part of a process of 'modernity' (Dobbin, 1994, p. 124)[3] and to have continued and 'flourished during the conservative era of Thatcherism and Reaganism' (Keesing, 1994, p. 307). In particular, Sakamoto notes how 'Chicago school Japanologist scholars [. . .] argue that "Japan" or "the Japanese" are a social imaginary' constructed through discursive activities (1996, p. 113, citing Haratoonian and Sakai).

Essentialist large culture is however no longer a European notion. Indeed, 'others' are often more insistent in talking about 'in our culture' than 'we' are. This may be partly because it:

> has passed into the cultural nationalist discourse of Third World élites [. . .] so that the cultural heritage of a people or a postcolonial nation can be represented by its fetishized material forms and performances: 'traditional dress', dances, artifacts. So transformed, 'it' – the cultural heritage, semiotically condensed [. . .] can be deployed in rituals of state, art festivals, tourist performances, and political appearances to reaffirm that 'it' survives despite Westernisation [. . .]. The third World has inherited these European semiotic systems [. . .] The crowning irony that our own conceptual diseases should be deployed against us.
>
> (Keesing, 1994, pp. 306–7)

This may be the reason why it is sometimes very hard to discourage, e.g. English teachers from all parts of the world from talking over-simplistically about 'the situation in country X culture'. Furthermore:

> 'Culture', so essentialised and reified, can serve as an ideal symbol to deploy against foreign researchers, who can be pilloried for having stolen 'it', having sold 'it' for profit in the academic marketplace, or simply [. . .] having misunderstood and misrepresented 'it'. Is this 'culture' of cultural studies 'culture' as we anthropologists have conceptualised it?
>
> (Keesing, 1994, p. 303)

Culture has therefore become reified and essentialized as a political tool by different parties at different times 'as both dominant and dominated groups often resort to the culture card in managing their power-maintaining and power-acquiring purposes' (Sarangi, 1994, p. 416). Moeran (1996) notes how Japanese business has adopted the images of Japan projected by the West (e.g. of sumo wrestlers and geisha) to help sell its products back to the West.

Understanding the reified nature of large culture is important in evaluating a currently influential essentialist discourse in applied linguistics – the centre–periphery paradigm relating to cultural imperialism. This paradigm suggests that English, representing Western centre (large) culture, is achieving global hegemony over developing world, periphery (large) cultures. Instrumental in this process is the (large) culturally Western methodology of language education, with its 'phonocentric' orientation (Pennycook, 1994). This argument has been criticized as over-generalized (Holliday, 1997a, 1999), especially as Western education is itself significantly culturally diverse (Bloor and Bloor, 1991; Sharpe, 1993, 1995). The general centre–periphery argument is also weakened if, through reification, the 'notion of a hegemonic global culture dispensing its products to the world's peripheries' is 'more often assumed than described' (Ahmed and Donnan, 1994, p. 3). In contrast to the large culture approach, a non-essentialist small culture interpretation would support the view that:

> Even though the same cultural 'message' may be received in different places, it is domesticated by being interpreted and incorporated according to local values [. . .] Cultural flows do not necessarily map directly on to economic and political relationships, which means that the flow of cultural traffic can often be in many directions simultaneously.
>
> (ibid., citing Parkin and Featherstone)

Another criticism of the large culture paradigm is that the world is becoming an increasingly cosmopolitan, multi-cultural place where cultures are less likely to appear as large coherent geographical entities. Late modern societies become 'notable for their lack of cultural coherence or "loose boundedness"' (Crane, 1994, p. 3, citing Merelman).

Whether or not the centre–periphery argument is based on reified large cultures is perhaps immaterial, as such large cultures are perhaps as real in our socially constructed society as any other perception. If this notion of a composite, homogeneous ethnic, national or international large culture is indeed constructed for us by nationalistic governments, then the centre–periphery discourse, in attempting to reveal one cultural hegemony, is falling foul of another one. It is not therefore succeeding in seeing as critically as it claims. Indeed, the centre–periphery paradigm, because of its essentialism, may be serving to reduce rather than liberate the so-called periphery.

Reduction, the other and culturism

A significant characteristic of reification is that the concept in question becomes relatively fixed in the people's minds. Hence, the apparent 'patterns and order' of these so-called concrete groups are 'exaggerated or unduly emphasized' at the expense of the 'variations and variability' which might blur their boundaries (Vayda, 1994, p. 320). 'A culture' thus becomes the '"tagged and tied luggage of isolated groups"' (Baumann, 1996, p. 189, citing Yabsley). It:

> seems to connote a certain coherence, uniformity and timelessness in the meaning systems of a given group, and to operate rather like the earlier concept of 'race' in identifying fundamentally different, essentialised, and homogenous social units (as when we speak about 'a culture'). Because of these associations, [. . .] (it) falsely fixes the boundaries between groups in an absolute way.
>
> (ibid., pp. 10–11, citing Lutz and Abou-Lughod)

The comparison with 'race' implies the possibility of a similarly constructed *culturism*, in which the members of a group to which an ethnic, national or international large cultural label has been attached are perceived as confined and *reduced* to pre-defined characteristics. Indeed, a methodology of culturism is evident in large culture research (Figure 13.1). A prescribed, normative concern with a certain type of large cultural difference (bubble (a)) leads in stages to an exaggeration of those differences resulting in *otherization* (bubble (f)). Otherization can be defined as the process whereby the 'foreign' is reduced to a simplistic, easily digestible, exotic or degrading stereotype. The 'foreign' thus becomes a degraded or exotic 'them' or safely categorized 'other' (Holliday, 1994b, 1996b, 1997a). Said (1993) explains how such a process contributes to cultural imperialism across global society:

> Labels like 'Indian' or 'woman' or 'Muslim' or 'American' are no more than starting points. [However,] imperialism consolidated the mixture of cultures and identities on a global scale; but its worse and most paradoxical gift was to allow people to believe that they were only, mainly, exclusively White, Black or Western or Oriental. It is more rewarding and more difficult to think about others than only about *us*.

Examples of this can be seen in 'excuses' for colonialist and post-colonialist conceptualizations – hence:

> The passivity ascribed to Hindu men and egoless subjection ascribed to women under patriarchal dominance are in miniature aspects of the governability of India – two favourable conditions among others for colonial rule.
>
> (Sangari 1994, p. 54)

and in an arguably emergent Western consensus that Islam has replaced Communism as the 'Great Satan':

> phrases like 'The English' or 'The Arabs' or 'The Americans' or 'The Africans', each of them suggesting not only a whole culture but a specific mind-set. It is very much the case today that in dealing with the Islamic world – all one billion people in it [. . .] – American or British academic intellectuals speak reductively and, in my view, irresponsibly of something called 'Islam'.
>
> (Said, 1993)

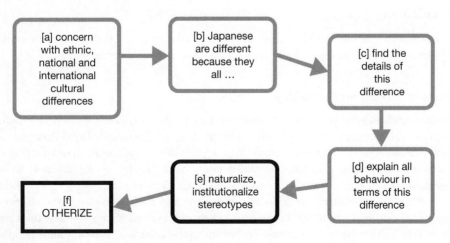

Figure 13.1 Culturist methodology

There is a parallel process of otherization and reduction at work *within* modern multi-cultural societies. It feeds 'the ideology underlying the construction of minority group cultures based on the principle of differences' (Sarangi, 1995, p. 11). In the case of ethnic minorities in Britain:

> Ethnic reductionism seemed to reign supreme [. . .] [and] whatever any 'Asian' informant was reported to have said or done was interpreted with stunning regularity as a consequence of their 'Asianness', their 'ethnic identity', or the 'culture' of their 'community'.
>
> (Baumann, 1996, p. 1)

Baumann goes on to argue that there is thus a 'dominant discourse' of 'culture' in the British government, media and popular parlance which:

> relies on equating community, culture, and ethnic identity, and its protagonists can easily reduce anybody's behaviour to a symptom of this equation. [. . .] It can even claim to speak 'for' them, 'represent' them, explain them to others.
>
> (ibid., p. 6)[4]

The notion of culture is thus hijacked by a new 'ethnopolitics' which '"stresses, ideologises, reifies, modifies, and sometimes virtually re-creates the putatively distinctive and unique cultural heritages of the ethnic groups that it mobilises"' (ibid., pp. 11–12, citing Rothschild).

It would seem that the centre–periphery argument contributes to this otherizing dominant large culture discourse, at an international rather than ethnic level. The notion of 'Western' versus, say, 'Chinese culture' succeeds not so much in an exposé of an imperialist 'linguicism' as in an otherization or tribalization of the victim 'cultures' by reducing them to peripheral, nonthinking automata (Holliday, 1994b). Again it needs to be emphasized that this does not mean that the centre–periphery protagonists *intend* to otherize the inhabitants of 'other cultures'. However, because they are caught within the natural social forces of reification, arbiters of 'culture' need to be wary of the power they wield. I shall return to the issue of dominant discourse, as it may be addressed within the small culture approach, later.

Small cultures

If large cultures are reified small cultures, what can small cultures be if they are not essentialized into descriptions of prescribed ethnic, national and international entities?

'A process of making and remaking'

Within the small culture paradigm, 'culture' refers to the composite of cohesive behaviour within any social grouping, and not to the differentiating features of prescribed ethnic, national and international entities. Distant from the large culture approach, which takes ethnic, national and international groupings as the default (Table 13.1), small cultures can be any social grouping from a neighbourhood to a work group (Beales et al., 1967, p. 8). The nature of small cultures is particularly well illustrated in Baumann's ethnography of the cosmopolitan mélange of the Southall suburb of London. A major observation in this work is the variety of ways in which 'culture' is perceived and dealt with in the suburb. On asking local people what was meant by 'culture', one group asserted that '"It depends what community you mean"'

(1996, p. 3). The Southallians use the terms 'culture' to refer to different entities at different times and, dependent on topic, to the extent that a fixed definition of anyone's notion of 'my culture' was very difficult to track down (ibid., pp. 4–5). Indeed:

> The vast majority of all adult Southallians [each] saw themselves as members of several *communities*, each with its own *culture*. The same person could speak and act as a member of the Muslim *community* in one context, in another take sides against other Muslims as a member of the Pakistani *community*, and in a third count himself part of the Punjabi *community* that excluded other Muslims but included Hindus, Sikhs, and even Christians.
>
> (ibid., p. 5, his italics)

Within this complex of social groupings, not only do individuals align themselves to different cultures at different times, there are also considerable:

> renegotiations of *culture* and *community* [. . .] [which] all form part of what anthropologists conceive culture to be in the first place: a process of making and remaking collective sense of changing social facts.
>
> (1996, p. 189, his italics)

Small culture is thus a dynamic, ongoing group process which operates in changing circumstances to enable group members to make sense of and operate meaningfully within those circumstances. When a researcher looks at an unfamiliar social grouping, it can be said to have a small culture when there is a discernible set of behaviours and understandings connected with group cohesion. The dynamic aspect of small culture is central to its nature, having the capacity to exist, form and change as required. According to Beales et al., 'the outstanding characteristic of a cultural system is that it is in process; it moves' (1967, p. 5). Small culture is thus 'the sum total of all the processes, happenings, or activities in which a given set or several, sets of people habitually engage' (ibid., p. 9). Thus, small culture constitutes a social 'tool-kit' which emerges to 'solve problems' when required (Crane, 1994, p. 11). Moreover, it involves an underlying competence in which 'people are not passive "cultural dopes"; they are active, often skilled users' (ibid., p. 11). A good example of this is the classroom group where a small culture will form from scratch when the group first comes together, each member using her or his culture-making ability to form rules and meanings in collaboration with others.

Figure 13.2 illustrates the complex factors in the formation of small culture. The bubbles in the figure are numbered for ease of reference. However, one thing does not necessarily happen before another. Bubble (i) represents the basic social and psychological function of culture as a process, which is a well-established theme running through most definitions of 'culture' and does not need to be deconstructed here (e.g. Holliday, 1994a, p. 23). Bubble (ii) represents social continuity. It needs to be remembered that although small culture may be formed rapidly:

> cultures, even in their most individualised practices, result also from validations of a past. Culture-making is not an *ex tempore* improvisation, but a project of social continuity placed within, and contending with, moments of social change.
>
> (Baumann, 1996, p. 31)

Thus, in the case of an aeroplane crew, 'the men in the crew form the group or society and the airplane constitutes a sort of combined environment' which provides a wider tradition and

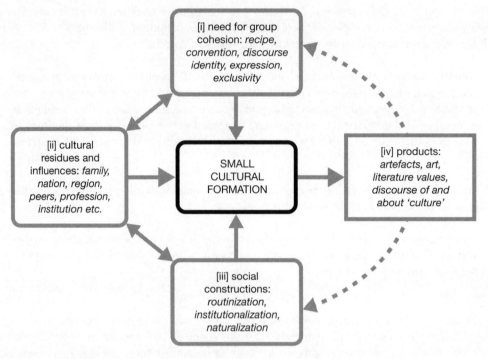

Figure 13.2 Small culture formation

history (Beales et al., 1967, p. 10). In the newly forming small culture of the classroom group, each member will bring small culture *residues* from other educational, classroom, collegial and peer experiences. Indeed, it is this characteristic of small culture which underlines its *non-essentialist, non-culturist* nature (Table 13.1). In a classroom group made up of a range of nationalities, which is common in foreign language or postgraduate English language education groups in Britain, cultural residues will be brought from many 'national' or 'ethnic' experiences; but commonalities of educational, classroom, collegial and peer experience from all these contexts will be the building blocks for the new small culture.

Implicit in bubble (ii) is an interaction with an existing environment, perhaps in a Darwinian sense, not necessarily of an ongoing improvement, but of dialogue (Coleman, 1996b). Especially in international English language education, this environment ceases to be purely national or 'ethnic', as professional–academic institutional and peer influences stretch across international boundaries (Holliday, 1994a, p. 29).

Mezzo activity

It is what the newly forming class group *does* which enables the researcher to discern the process of small culture. In one such case, a multinational group of Masters students in applied linguistics appeared to fulfil its need for cohesion (bubble (i), Figure 13.2) by creating a convention for holding birthday parties for members. Part of the recipe for doing this, which reduced the need for ongoing negotiation, was always to use the classroom as venue, invite tutors at short notice and provide inexpensive soft drinks and decorative 'party food'. The parties themselves helped to forge a very cohesive identity and enabled group expression and exclusivity by clearly defining who could come to the parties. Evidence of cultural residues and influences (bubble (ii)) was seen in the influence of various 'national' cuisines in the food provided, dominated perhaps by a Japanese orientation to tidy minimalism, a British academic informality in the fairly casual way in which tutors were invited, a definite collegiality which might have derived from notions of both close-knit studentship, evident in several of the societies represented, and a professional bond – for all were language teachers – and influence of the local institution arrangement which enabled almost all classes for this group to be held in the same room.

Small culture is thus more to do with activities taking place within a group than with the nature of the group itself:

> I have found it theoretically helpful to think of both culture and language as rooted in human activities (rather than in societies) and as pertaining to groups. [. . .] There is a different culture of the activity for each set of role performers. These differences form a part of the cultural makeup of the overall group of people who perform the activity, but there is no one culture of that activity for the group as a whole, one that all its members share. [. . .] The cultural makeup of a society is thus to be seen not as a monolithic entity determining the behaviour of its members, but a mélange of understandings and expectations regarding a variety of activities that serve as guides to their conduct and interpretation.
>
> (Goodenough, 1994, p. 266–7)

Seeing small culture as rooted in activities enables us to apply 'culture' not only to the processes that give cohesion to group behaviour, but also to the processes that give cohesion to any behaviour, as long as it involves groups. Thus, academic disciplines can be said to have small cultures (Stonequist, 1937; Kuhn, 1970; Esland, 1971; Bernstein, 1971; Tomley, 1980; Goodson, 1988; Holliday, 1994a), as can methodology. The importance of looking at classroom teaching, research and evaluation methodologies in language education as small cultures shall be seen below.

Focusing on activities places small culture research at a mezzo level. The benefits of mezzo analysis, set mid-way between the micro and macro at the level of institution, have been acknowledged in several places – Morawski and Spohn's (1994) account of the study of culture in historical sociology, Hargreaves' attention to 'intermediary processes' such as school ethos and institutional bias (1986, p. 170) and teacher cultures (1992) in education, and Holliday's (1994a) focus on professional–academic institutional conflict in international language education. In applied linguistics, Fairclough takes this direction in a substantial way when he focuses critical discourse analysis on 'the institution as a "pivot" between the highest level of social structuring, that of the "social formation" and the most concrete level, that of the particular social event or action' (1995, p. 37). Roberts, in her investigation of inter cultural understanding and European immigrants, also focuses on the institution:

> Critical and interactional sociolinguistic perspectives come together in the study of institutional discourse. For the great majority of informants [. . .] institutional encounters represent the only occasion of extended contact with the white majority.
>
> (1996, p. 230)

Also, Clark and Ivanic (1997) seem to set much of their analysis of the 'contexts of culture' surrounding writing at a mezzo level.

The process of naturalization, or routinization, in small culture formation (bubble (iii), Figure 13.2), in which behaviour which is socially constructed for the sake of group cohesion becomes routine, is perceived best at the mezzo level. In the case of the Masters group, this process can be seen as the birthday parties quickly become an institution in their own right. This process is also central to Fairclough's analysis of how ideological representations become naturalized into taken-for-granted, normal, non-ideological aspects of everyday discourse (1995, p. 28). Although he speaks primarily about the use of language, within a Marxist construct of political oppression, useful insight into the social construction of small culture is provided. Naturalization works in a similar way to reification. However, whereas reification involves forgetting the 'unreal' nature of heuristic cultural analysis, naturalization involves making a social construction 'normal' and taken-for-granted.

Small culture and discourse

The relationship between small culture and discourse is clearly strong. Fairclough's 'order of discourse' as a 'totality of discursive practices of an institution, and relations between them' (1995, p. 135) and 'genre' as 'a socially ratified way of using language in connection with a particular type of social activity' (ibid., p. 14) are clearly related to small culture dynamics. His reference to professional and organizational (small) cultural change brought about by the invasion of 'technologised discourse' (ibid., p. 100) is more obviously so.

Figure 13.2 has discourse in two of its bubbles connected with small culture formation. In bubble (i), discourse as a regulator goes along with the need for recipe and convention – underlying routine talk about birthday parties in the master group. In bubble (iv), discourse is one of the products of small culture. Thus, a technologizing discourse of language teaching methodology may not only be instrumental in the strength of the regime of the professional– academic small culture of instrumental 'ELT' (Holliday, 1999), but also a major product of this small culture represented in its stated values, literature and other forms of dissemination. Similarly, the influence of the technologizing discourse of quality control may be seen to have created discernible change in the small culture of the British university sector, or of individual institutions within it. It is also a major output, featuring strongly in its expressed values, promotional literature and educational output. Also, the academic discourse of such new disciplines as applied linguistics is both regulatory and an outward show of academic quality (Holliday, 1999). Figure 13.2 also shows that discourse in bubble (iv) has a return influence on the set of small culture needs in bubble (i), as pride of cultural product encourages cohesion, especially where the discourse is technologized, facing like Janus, as both internal regulator and proselytizer.

The precise relationship between discourse and small culture is connected to that between language and culture, which is an area in which caution must be practised. Sarangi warns against a Whorfian approach in which:

> language is contained within and reducible to culture, thus denying language its [own] reality-constructing role. [. . .] [and] 'culture' comes to be treated as the least observable category of non-behaviour [where] 'culture is that residual realm left over after all forms of observable human behaviour have been removed'.
>
> (1994, p. 410, citing Wuthnow et al.)

This is culture as the easy, default explanation for all differences. To overcome this, Sarangi, citing Sherzer, suggests a:

discourse-centred approach [. . .] [in which] discourse has to be considered as the concrete expression of the language–culture relationship because it is discourse that 'creates, recreates, focuses, modifies, and transmits both culture and language and their interaction'.

(1994, p. 414)

Thus, once again, it is at the mezzo level of discourse that cultural issues can best be untangled. Sarangi recommends Fairclough's critical discourse analysis as the ideal tool in this untangling, in that it 'pays adequate attention to the dialectic relationship between social structures and linguistic practices' at the institutional level (ibid., p. 414).

A notion which has become popular in applied linguistics, influenced partly by the sub-discipline of English for specific purposes, which incorporates many of the social attributes of discourse, is 'discourse community'. In many ways the discourse community *is* a small culture. The two concepts are not always interchangeable however. In some small cultures, e.g. the more established professional, corporate and academic cultures, that they are also discourse communities will be one of their central features. In these cases, technical, if not technologized discourses will be important regulators of thought, behaviour and expression. Also, in less-established cultures, such as that of the birthday party, discourse may play a major role. However, in other types of small culture, discourse may play a less important role, e.g. the culture of the escalators in the London Underground, where, although discourse may make occasional regulatory appearances, for much of the time, for most of the participants, standing on the right and moving on the left will be a discourse-free routine initiated and built through observation of others.

The interest of the researcher will often be instrumental in how far discourse becomes a focus for small culture analysis. Applied linguists see 'small culture' as 'discourse community' because they are primarily interested in language. In these cases, the current developing discourse in applied linguistics about discourse communities can both inform and learn from the slightly broader notion of small culture, and vice versa. For example, Roberts and Sarangi (1997), in their work on oral examinations for medical general practitioners, suggest that 'institutional', 'professional' and 'life-world' discourses interact in such a way that they can be said to 'laminate' together to form new, 'hybrid' discourses. In a very similar vein, Rogerson-Revell (1997) talks of a 'lamination of cultures' in the sense of 'groups within groups' within the inter-cultural mélange of an international airline in Hong Kong, where 'ethnic differences are only one possible factor'. Both studies are concerned with mezzo institutional settings, and I suspect that 'culture' rather than 'discourse' is used in the latter only because there is a beginning perception of large culture difference, which ironically proves a red herring. Might it be the case that 'discourse' is used by Roberts and Sarangi rather than 'culture' because there is no perception of large culture difference? A residue of essentialist onion-skin thinking (above) can be discerned in their use of 'hybrid', which implies that entities newly formed *between* established discourses, or cultures, cannot procreate.

An important aspect of bubble (iv) in Figure 13.2 is that group members' statements *about* 'culture' or 'their culture' should be seen as products or artefacts *of* the culture, expressing how they socially construct their image of their own culture, rather than a direct description of their culture. [. . .] Hence, Baumann's ethnographic interest in what Southallians *say about* and *do with* 'culture' as evidence of how 'culture' is constructed within the culture he is investigating (above). Seeing projected images of 'culture' as artefact and cultural product in this way tells us something about the way in which notions of large culture are reified, and dominant discourses of culture are set up.

A device to help us understand

It is important now to return to the important, yet complex side of the small culture paradigm in which culture is not part of the real substance of social life, but a heuristic model to help understand cohesive behaviour:

> As a deliberate abstraction it is there to help anthropologists conceptualise that ever-changing 'complex whole' through which people engage in the continual process of accounting, in a mutually meaningful manner, for what they do, say, and might think.
>
> (Baumann, 1996, p. 11, citing Tyler)

This is a difficult concept to digest because while we are told that culture is an 'abstraction', everything else that we hear, both in academic and popular parlance, suggests that cultures, whether small or large, are concrete realities. An answer to this conundrum lies partly in the way in which enthnography deals with small cultures within an interpretive paradigm.

In contrast to the large culture approach (Table 13.1), interpretive ethnography does not, positivistically, develop knowledge of the details of a prescribed culture. It describes culture (Spradley, 1980, p. 3), but this description of culture is the instrument of an interest in a particular social issue (ibid., p. 18). The first step in the ethnographic process is to locate a social situation which enables research into this social issue (ibid., p. 39). Thus, the location and boundaries of 'the culture' are instrumental to the research question. 'The culture' must thus be relevant and researchable. For example, Anderson sets out to investigate aspects of group work in language teaching. Because he wishes to look at group work within the social setting of the classroom, he chooses an ethnographic approach and, for this reason, takes the small culture of the classroom as the location (1997). To be able to do this, the classroom needs to have the social features which enable it to be a small culture; and as such, the small culture really does exist as a social fact, according to the sociological definitions of culture (embodied in Figure 13.2). It is important to note that the ethnography which selects a particular culture for study is *applied*, in that it is tuned towards understanding something specific – e.g. the factors which influence classroom group work.

Figure 13.3 illustrates this process. Initially, the social world is perceived as a seamless mélange of complex behaviours. This is perception central to interpretive ethnography. The researcher does not presume to define, a priori, the social world in one way or another, and is thus scientifically humble to its complexity. The selection of social setting ((x) in Figure 13.3) involves taking a section of this mélange and drawing an operational boundary around it. The social setting has to contain the elements of small culture ((y) in the figure). However, the grouping which makes up this small culture is essentially research-oriented (z) – picked out from many other possible small cultural groupings for the sake of the research project. In the case of Anderson's (1997) study, these might have been the small cultures of individual student groups, the student body of the institution, the teaching methodology, the professional–academic group represented by the teacher, and so on, all of which overlap and interact (cf. Holliday, 1994a, p. 29). The term 'grouping' is important, to remind the researchers that it is *they* who have grouped the individuals involved as a construction of the research. Whether or not this 'grouping' equates with the perceptions of 'group' held by the individuals within it is to be discovered rather than assumed. Small cultures do therefore exist. It is the *selection* of a specific small culture for study which is heuristic. Also, this small culture is not a 'cause of behaviour' (Baumann, 1996, p. 11, above), but a structuring within which behaviour selected for study may be understood. It is thus a means to investigation rather than an end in itself.

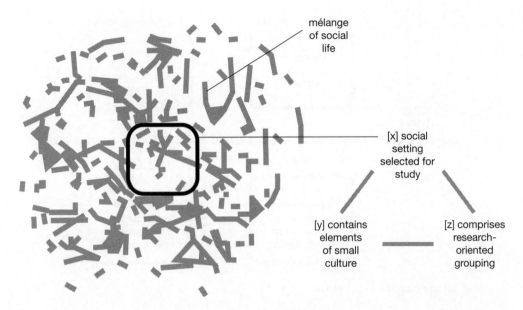

mélange
of social
life

[x] social
setting
selected for
study

[y] contains
elements
of small
culture

[z] comprises
research-
oriented
grouping

Figure 13.3 Small culture selected for ethnography

Another answer to the conundrum in which the small culture is both an abstract heuristic device as well as a real social phenomenon can be found in soft systems methodology.[5] A small culture behaves as an 'activity system', which is, on the one hand, an 'unreal world' model from which to look at the 'real world'.[6] This principle comes with a strong warning:

> Those who write about 'human activity systems' as if they exist in the world, rather than being holons which can be compared with the world, are failing to grasp [that they are] [. . .] a structured set of '*xs*' [. . .] as an *epistemology* which can be used to try and understand and intervene usefully in the rich and surprising flux of everyday situations.
>
> (Checkland and Scholes, 1990, p. 24, their emphasis)

On the other hand, activity systems are derived from real world experience:

> We perceive the world through the filter of – or using the framework of – the ideas internal to us; but [. . .] the source of many (most?) of those ideas is the perceived world outside. Thus, the world is continually interpreted using ideas whose source is ultimately the perceived world itself.
>
> (Checkland and Scholes, 1990, p. 20)[7]

This can be seen in Figure 13.4. The researcher uses real-world experience of small culture (1) to construct an unreal-world activity system (2). This activity system is then set against, and its vision of small culture *invented* in, the area of research (3). Thus:

> the anthropologist uses [her or] his own culture to study others, and to study culture in general. [. . .] We might actually say that an anthropologist 'invents' the culture

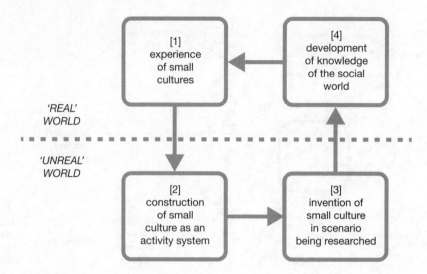

Figure 13.4 Interpreting the social world

[she or] he believes [her or] himself to be studying, that the relation is more 'real' for being [her or] his particular acts and experiences than the things it 'relates'.

(Wagner, 1981, pp. 2–3)

The 'real'–'unreal world' distinction in soft systems methodology becomes blurred at this stage, unless 'unreal' simply means 'heuristic'.

Small culture analysis

One reason for presenting small cultures as an alternative concept to large cultures is that the former is particularly useful in some of the social analysis currently important in international language education. There are two related areas I wish to look at in this regard: the cultural make-up of international curriculum scenarios in language education, and the learning of culture.

International curriculum scenarios

I take as an example a textbook project based at the University of Pune, India, in the mid 1990s (Jacob, 1996; Holliday, 1996a). The curriculum scenario was typical of many British aid projects in that it was funded by British aid and implemented by a British Council managed project involving Indian and British personnel embedded within an existing English Department. Much has been written about such scenarios; and there is now considerable sensitivity expressed regarding a potentially culturally imperialistic imposition of 'foreign' ideas and practices (e.g. Hayes, 1997; Abbott and Beaumont, 1997; Crooks and Crewes, 1995). Within a large culture approach, such scenarios are problematized on the basis that they are *international*, involving ideas, practices and expert personnel who come from other national locations – hence inter-cultural in the sense of, say, a confrontation between British and Indian ways of doing and thinking, against a potential background of Western post-colonialism. In contrast to this, a small culture approach, through an applied ethnographic analysis, demarcates social groupings which facilitate an understanding of the pertinent dynamics of a situation, whether or not it is characterized by ethnic, national or international difference. The small cultures demarked in the Pune project are presented in Figure 13.5.[8] (The black bubbles and lines represent established, and the grey bubbles and lines unestablished, small cultures and relationships.) Consonant with the discussion above, the demarcation of these particular small cultures and what is seen in them is instrumental to the research aim of understanding the curriculum project. There are many more small cultures operating in this scenario which have not been demarked because they do not *appear* relevant at the time of investigation.

The small culture view of the Pune project enables the illumination of inter cultural conflict, not between (large) British and Indian cultures, but between (small) culturally different Indian elements. This analysis is entirely my own, for which I take full responsibility, and is not meant to be critical of any of the parties concerned, but depicts an unavoidable mismatch between different types of institutional and professional–academic activity. Figure 13.5 shows the English Department faced by a very different British Council organizational culture which was characterized by a document-based discourse of budget and time lines. This was despite the fact that all the involved British Council personnel were Indian. The British Council brought with it an instrumental 'ELT' culture which seemed in natural opposition to the academic, humanities culture of the English Department. The curriculum project personnel, mainly seconded Indian academics with occasional British consultants, had to form their own new small culture between the established small cultures of the English Department, to which it had natural loyalties, and the, to them, (small) culturally strange British Council. The Indian academics within the project found themselves managed by a, to them, alien British Council line-management hierarchy. The established small culture of evaluation, brought by an Indian consultant from an élite Indian English language institution, conflicted with that grown within the project. Overall, there were the conflicting small cultures of academia and instrumental

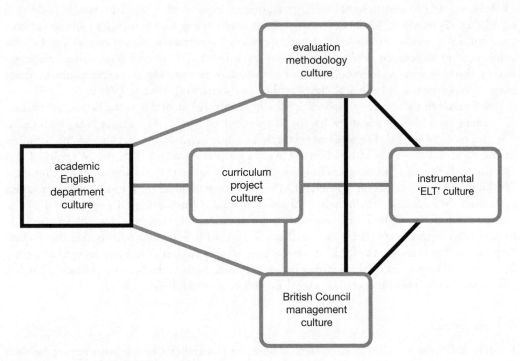

Figure 13.5 Curriculum scenario as mélange of small cultures

management between which the curriculum project was an uncertain middle culture. As in the studies of airline and medical scenarios (above) 'laminations' were very much in evidence as the small cultures within the Pune project mixed, flowed and layered around each other.

An alternative vision of cultural imperialism

This small culture interpretation also illuminates a mezzo institutional level of cultural imperialism. In the large culture version of the centre–periphery paradigm a 'professionalized' mode of English language teaching (Phillipson, 1992) is seen as part of a wider large Western culture at the centre of a global linguistic and cultural imperialism (Pennycook, 1994). However, a small cultural analysis of the Pune project reveals a small culture imperialism, instigated not by Western large culture, but by the professional–academic small culture (of instrumental 'ELT') connected with other small cultures of evaluation and the British Council. Discourse plays an important role here, with technologization of discourse (above) as the major imperialist force. The small cultures of 'ELT', evaluation and the British Council are characterized by instrumental discourses which by nature have the tacit if not overt agenda of technologizing the discourses of the project culture and the teaching of English within the academic University small culture. These small technologizing cultures gain strength from an appearance of, and claim to, being non-ideological. As Fairclough puts it:

> The projection of such context-free techniques into a variety of institutional contexts contributes to a widespread effect of 'colonisation' of local institutional orders of discourse by a few culturally-salient discourse types.
>
> (1995, p. 104)

That these claims by instrumental 'ELT' to autonomy from ideology are false is now fairly well established (Pennycook, 1989; Coleman, 1996a); and the ideological nature of all the cultures involved is illuminated by the small culture approach. Significantly, evaluation can also be seen as just another ideocentric small culture among several within the overall small culture mélange. Rather than being an autonomous engine for objectively assessing the curriculum scenario, evaluation becomes an ideological player within that scenario (Holliday, 1995a).

Returning to the centre–periphery argument, a 'centre' mentality is implicit in the notions of 'training' and 'development' which the British Council and 'ELT' cultures bring with them. The 'training' of English Department lecturers in effect involves the learning of the technical discourse of 'ELT'. It could be observed within the Pune project that, in the terms of this 'dominant discourse', the lecturers had much to learn. Similarly, in the terms of the 'dominant discourse' of the evaluation consultant, the project personnel had much to learn about evaluation. In each case, the members of the academic culture appeared peripherized by the technical culture into whose discourse they were not initiated. However, there is another side to this centre–periphery apparition. Within the terms of their own perception, the English Department lecturers see the 'ELT' discourse as periphery to *their* centre discourse of academic literature and linguistics, with its strong Indian academic basis in the broader politics of English as a post-colonial phenomenon via critical English studies (Holliday, 1996a).

Culture learning

Roberts and Sarangi's (1997) discussion of how the researcher can orientate her or his own discourse to be understood by the researched is relevant here (see also Holliday, 1997b). Once curriculum developers, evaluators, aid agencies, or whatever party entering into a mélange of new small cultures, appreciate the nature of this small cultural mix, they will also appreciate the need to monitor the ideological orientation of their *own* small culture in order to be able to accommodate and work appropriately with others (Holliday, 1995b). In the large culture approach, culture learning tends to be 'other' or 'foreign' directed. To use Schutz's terminology, the stranger focuses learning on one, predefined, 'target' ethnic, national or international culture within which she or he must operate. In contrast, in the small culture approach, culture learning will focus on searching for, demarcating and observing the interaction between several cultures within a target scenario. In this interpretive process, discovery of the stranger's own small culture, as it is aligned within the specificities of the wider mélange, will be high on the agenda. Moreover, this learning of culture will not necessarily have anything to do with ethnic, national or international difference.

At the beginning of this section and throughout the paper I have claimed impartiality to the various values implicit in the constructions and positions I have discussed. Keeping this impartiality in mind it may be observed that in the Pune project the small cultures of 'ELT', evaluation and the British Council had done insufficient culture learning, or 'research into the discursive practices' (Fairclough, 1995, p. 91) of the English Department culture to enable effective technologization in that direction. Efficient imperialism is thus thwarted by the fact that the perpetrators are 'standardly unaware' (ibid., p. 36) of the discoursal forces both surrounding them and at their disposal. In the same way, those who face the onslaught of technologizing discourse need to be aware of what is happening in case they may wish to resist. This is not to say that people everywhere are not aware of the general nature of social and political manipulation in society; but they need to understand the details of how small culture and discourse operate if they are to be truly resilient and able to make choices.

Conclusion

The small culture approach represents a different world to that of large cultures. The mezzo world of small cultures is one of institutions of work, leisure, interest and discourse which stretches seamlessly across an ongoing, multi-layered complex. It represents the coral gardens of human interaction, of which any demarcation of specific small cultures will only scratch the surface (Breen, 1986). Ethnic, national or international difference provides only one possible lamination of subtle change of shade, in some scenarios. Issues of imperialism or colonialism become matters of inter cultural confrontation and influence at the mezzo level, making such processes as the hegemonic technologization of professional and other practice (Fairclough, 1995; Usher and Edwards, 1994; Clark and Ivanic, 1997) a general conflict *within* late modern societies all over the world, rather than between global geographical cultures. On the one hand, the small culture approach is most appropriate for a world which is increasingly multi-cultural at every level. On the other hand, it is the only way to illuminate full inter cultural complexity in any world.

Notes

1   There seems to be considerable shifting between the small and large usages, even in academic discourse in which 'culture' is the focus. One such observation was in a recent conference paper by an eminent applied linguist. The paper discussed how a particular 'genre' might vary (a) in different national (large) 'cultures', and (b) according to readerships from different (small) academic or middle class 'cultures'. The distinction between (a) and (b) seemed crucial to the analysis, and yet was not addressed.

2   'Ethnic' is as troublesome as 'culture'. It can be argued that it is a product of the same essentialist discourse as large culture (e.g. Baumann, 1996; Sarangi, 1994, 1995).

3   'Imagined communities' is a term used by several writers (Gellner and Hobsbawm, cited in Sakamoto, 1996, p. 113; Anderson, 1996).
4   Baumann also maintains that '"Community" is a dishonest word . . . It is invariably party to pious fraud. Ethnic minorities are called "communities" either because it makes them feel better, or because it makes the white majority feel more secure' (1996, p. 14, citing Ignatieff).
5   Soft systems methodology is a procedure developed by Checkland to help structure problematic situations in management. Although based on systems thinking, its 'softness' enables a more appropriate application in human situations. Although not explicitly stated by Checkland, its application can be made use of to structure social problems in institutional settings in tandem with ethnographic investigation – especially necessary in international language education where such setting may not always be familiar (Holliday, 1990).
6   The activity system behaves as an 'ideal type' in the tradition of Max Weber. The difference is however that Weberian ideal types tend to refer to abstractions of character – e.g. 'learning festival' and 'teaching spectacle' (Holliday, 1994a, p. 36, citing Coleman) or 'integration' and 'collection' (1994a, p. 71, citing Bernstein) rather than abstractions of social process.
7   Checkland and Scholes place this approach within a Kantian philosophy:

> that we *structure* the world by means of already present, innate ideas, rather than the view of Locke that our minds are blank screens upon which the world writes its impressions. But it seems clear that the supposedly 'innate' ideas may have two sources. They may indeed be part of the genetic inheritance of mankind, truly innate; or they may be built up as a result of our experience of the world.
>
> (1990, p. 20, their emphasis)

8   A fuller version can be found in Holliday (1996a). There were other very important cultures within the University including administrative elements, undergraduate lecturers who were to use the textbook, who were (small) culturally very different to postgraduate lecturers in the host English Department.

References

Abbott, G. and Beaumont, M. (eds) (1997). *The development of ELT: the Dunford Seminars 1978–1993*. English Language Teaching Review. Hemel Hempstead: Prentice Hall and the British Council.
Ahmed, A. S. and Donnan, H. (1994). Islam in the age of postmodernity. In A. S. Ahmed and H. Donnan (eds), *Islam, globalisation and postmodernity* (pp. 1–20). London: Routledge.
Anderson, B. (1996). *Imagined communities*. London: Verso.
Anderson, C. (1997). Factors affecting student behaviour in group work in an EFL class: an ethnographic approach. Unpublished MA dissertation, Canterbury Christ Church University College.
Asad, T. (ed.) (1973). *Anthropology and the colonial encounter*. London: Ithaca Press.
Baumann, G. (1996). *Contesting culture*. Cambridge: Cambridge University Press.
Beales, A. R., Spindler, G. and Spindler, L. (1967). *Culture in process*. New York: Holt, Rinehart.
Berger, P. and Luckmann, T. (1967). *The social construction of reality*. Harmondsworth: Pelican.
Bernstein, B. (1971). On the classification and framing of educational knowledge. In M. F. D. Young (ed.), *Knowledge and control* (pp. 47–69). London: Collier-Macmillan.
Bloor, M. and Bloor, T. (1991). Cultural expectations and socio-pragmatic failure in academic writing. In A. Adams, B. Heaton and P. Howarth (eds), *Socio-cultural issues in English for academic purposes* (pp. 1–12). London: Modern English Publications, The British Council.
Breen, M. P. (1986). The social context of language learning – a neglected situation. *Studies in Second Language Acquisition*, 7, 135–58.
Byram, M. and Morgan, C., et al. (1994). *Teaching-and-learning Language-and-culture*. Clevedon: Multilingual Matters.
Checkland, P. and Scholes, J. (1990). *Soft systems methodology in action*. Chichester: Wiley.
Clark, R. and Ivanic, R. (1997). *The politics of writing*. London: Routledge.
Coleman, H. (1996a). Autonomy and ideology in the English language classroom. In H. Coleman (ed.), *Society and the language classroom*. Cambridge: Cambridge University Press.
Coleman, H. (1996b). Interpreting classrooms in international contexts: Darwinism and sartorial fashion. Unpublished paper, School of Education, University of Leeds.
Comaroff, J. and Comaroff, J. (1992). *Ethnography and the historical imagination*. Boulder, CO: Westview Press.

Crane, D. (1994). Introduction: the challenge of the sociology of culture to sociology as discipline. In D. Crane (ed.), *The sociology of culture* (pp. 1–19). Oxford: Blackwell.

Crooks, T. and Crewes, G. (eds) (1995). *Language and development*. Bali: IALF.

Dobbin, F. R. (1994). Cultural models of organisation: the social construction of rational organising principles. In D. Crane (ed.), *The sociology of culture* (pp. 117–41). Oxford: Blackwell.

Esland, G. M. (1971). Teaching and learning as the organisation of knowledge. In M. F. D. Young (ed.), *Knowledge and Control* (pp. 70–116). London: Collier Macmillan.

Fairclough, N. (1995). *Critical discourse analysis: the critical study of language*. London: Addison Wesley Longman.

Gelder, K. (1997). Introduction to Part II. In S. Thornton and K. Gelder (eds), *The subcultures reader* (pp. 83–9). London: Routledge.

Goodenough, W. H. (1994). Toward a working theory of culture. In R. Borofsky (ed.), *Assessing cultural anthropology* (pp. 262–75). New York: McGraw-Hill.

Goodson, I. (1988). Beyond the subject monolith: subject traditions and sub-cultures. In A. Westby (ed.), *Culture and power in educational organisations* (pp. 181–97). Milton Keynes: Open University Press.

Hargreaves, A. (1986). The micro-macro problem in the sociology of education. In M. Hammersley, (ed.), *Controversies in classroom research* (pp. 153–75). Milton Keynes: Open University Press.

Hargreaves, A. (1992). Cultures of teaching: a focus for change. In A. Hargreaves and M. G. Fullan (eds), *Understanding teacher development* (pp. 216–40). London: Cassell.

Hayes, D. (ed.) (1997). *In-service teacher development: international perspectives*. London: Prentice Hall.

Herrera, L. (1992). Scenes of schooling: inside a girls' school in Cairo. *Cairo Papers in Social Science,* 15, Monograph 1.

Hofstede, G. (1991). *Cultures and organisations: software of the mind*. Maidenhead: McGraw-Hill.

Holliday, A. R. (1990). A role for soft systems methodology in ELT projects. *System,* 18/1, 77–84.

Holliday, A. R. (1994a). *Appropriate methodology and social context*. Cambridge: Cambridge University Press.

Holliday, A. R. (1994b). Student culture and English language education: an international context. *Language, Culture and Curriculum,* 7/2.

Holliday, A. R. (1995a). Evaluation as cultural negotiation. Second PRODESS Colloquium: *Evaluation in Planning and Managing Language Education Projects* (pp. 6–11), 26–28 March. Manchester: The British Council.

Holliday, A. R. (1995b). Handing over the project: an exercise in restraint. *System* 23/1, 57–68.

Holliday, A. R. (1996a). Cultural accommodation in an 'ESL' curriculum project. Unpublished paper, Canterbury Christ Church College.

Holliday, A. R. (1996b). Otherisation in British education and media. In D. Hayes (ed.), *Debating education: issues for the new millennium?* (pp. 139–42). Department of Education, Canterbury Christ Church College.

Holliday, A. R. (1997a). The politics of participation in international English language education. *System,* 25/3.

Holliday, A. R. (1997b). Knowing what is ethical requires 'local knowledge'. In *Power, ethics and validity: issues in the relationship between researchers and researched*. CRILE, Lancaster University.

Holliday, A. R. (1999). Evaluating the discourse: the role of applied linguistics in managing evaluation and innovation. In K. Germain and P. Rea-Dickins (eds), *Managing evaluation and innovation in English language teaching: building bridges*. London: Addison Wesley Longman.

Holliday, A. R. and Hoose, J. (1996). Middle ground: collaborative research and recognition of researcher-researched subcultures. Unpublished paper, Canterbury Christ Church University College.

Jacob, P. G. (1996). Coming to terms with imperialism: safeguarding local knowledge and experience in ELT curriculum development. Unpublished paper, Department of English, University of Pune, India.

Keesing, R. M. (1981). *Cultural anthropology*. Orlando, FL: Harcourt Brace.

Keesing, R. M. (1994). Theories of culture revisited. In R. Borofsky (ed.), *Assessing cultural anthropology* (pp. 301–12). New York: McGrawHill.

Kramsch, C. (1993). *Context and culture in language teaching*. Oxford: Oxford University Press.

Kuhn, T. S. (1970). *The structure of scientific revolutions*. Reprinted and enlarged. Chicago: University of Chicago Press.

Moeran, B. (1996). The Orient strikes back: advertising and imagining in Japan. *Theory, Culture and Society,* 13/3, 77–112.

Morawska, E. and Spohn, W. (1994). 'Cultural pluralism' in historical sociology: recent theoretical directions. in D. Crane (ed.), *The sociology of culture* (pp. 45–90). Oxford: Blackwell.

Nzimiro, I. (1979). Anthropologists and their terminologies: a critical review. In G. Huizer and B. Mannheim (eds), *The politics of anthropology: from colonialism and sexism towards a view from below* (pp. 67–83). The Hague: Mouton.

Pennycook, A. (1989). The concept of method, interested knowledge, and the politics of language teaching. *TESOL Quarterly,* 23/4, 589–618.

Pennycook, A. (1994). *The cultural politics of English as an international language.* Oxford: Oxford University Press.

Phillipson, R. (1992). *Linguistic imperialism.* Oxford: Oxford University Press.

Poppleton, P. and Riseborough, G. (1990). A profession in transition: educational policy and secondary school teaching in England in the 1980s. *Comparative Education,* 26/2–3, 211–26.

Roberts, C. (1996). Taking stock: contexts and reflections. In K. Bremer, C. Roberts, M. Vasseur, M. Simonot and P. Broeder (eds), *Achieving understanding: discourse in intercultural encounters* (pp. 207–38). London: Addison Wesley Longman.

Roberts, C. and S. Sarangi. (1997). Constructing practical relevance: applied discourse analysis at work. Unpublished paper presented at BAAL 30th Annual Meeting, *Language at Work.*

Rogerson-Revell, P. (1997). Inter-cultural communication at work: developing linguistic analyses. Unpublished paper presented at BAAL 30th Annual Meeting, *Language at Work.*

Said, E. (1993). Holding nations and traditions at bay. *The Independent,* 1 July.

Sakamoto, R. (1996). Japan, hybridity and the creation of colonialist discourse. *Theory, Culture and Society,* 13/3, 113–28.

Sangari, K. (1994). Relating histories: definitions of literacy, literature, gender in early nineteenth-century Calcutta and England. In S. Joshi (ed.), *Rethinking English.* Delhi: Oxford University Press.

Sarangi, S. (1994). Intercultural or not? Beyond celebration of cultural differences in miscommunication analysis. *Pragmatics,* 4/3, 409–27.

Sarangi, S. (1995). Culture. In J. Vershueren, J. Östman and J. Blomaert (eds), *Handbook of pragmatics.* Amsterdam/Philadelphia: John Benjamins.

Schudson, M. (1994). Culture and the integration of national societies. In D. Crane (ed.), *The sociology of culture* (pp. 21–43). Oxford: Blackwell.

Schutz, A. (1962). *Collected papers 1.* The Hague: Martinus Nijhoff.

Sharpe, K. (1993). Catechistic teaching style in French primary education: analysis of a grammar lesson with seven-year olds. *Comparative Education,* 28/3, 249–68.

Sharpe, K. (1995). The protestant ethic and the spirit of catholicism: ideological and institutional constraints on system change in English and French primary schooling. Paper presented at the European Conference on Educational Research, University of Bath.

Spradley, J. P. (1980). *Participant observation.* New York: Holt, Rinehart and Winston.

Stonequist, E. V. (1937). *The marginal man, a study in personality and culture conflict.* New York: Russell and Russell.

Thornton, S. (1997). General introduction to S. Thornton and K. Gelder (eds), *The subcultures reader* (pp. 1–7). London: Routledge.

Tomley, D. (1980). The selection of curriculum content: issues and problems. In M. J. Galton (ed.), *Curriculum change: the lessons of a decade* (pp. 33–50). Leicester: Leicester University Press.

Usher, R. and Edwards, R. (1994). *Postmodernism and education: different voices. Different worlds.* London: Routledge.

Vayda, A. P. (1994). Actions, variations, and change: the emerging anti-essentialist view in anthropology. In R. Borofsky (ed.), *Assessing cultural anthropology* (pp. 320–30). New York: McGraw-Hill.

Wagner, R. (1981). *The inventions of culture.* University of Chicago Press.

Chapter 14

GABRIELE KASPER AND KENNETH R. ROSE

DEVELOPMENTAL PATTERNS IN SECOND LANGUAGE PRAGMATICS

Pragmatic and discourse ability

IN THIS CATEGORY WE encounter Schmidt's (1983) well-known study of Wes's adventures in English, as well as Schmidt and Frota's (1986) account of Schmidt's acquisition of Brazilian Portuguese. Asian languages feature prominently in the rest of the group, for example, Sawyer's (1992) study on the acquisition of the Japanese discourse particle *ne*, Ohta's (2001) report of the acquisition of alignment expressions in Japanese, work reported in Kanagy and Igarashi (1997) and Kanagy (1999) on how English-speaking kindergartners acquire Japanese classroom interactional routines in an immersion environment, and DuFon's (1999, 2000) research on the acquisition of politeness in Indonesian. Without exception, the studies in this group are longitudinal, with observational periods ranging from four months to three years, and all involve beginning learners, thus making them ideal for the observation of development over time. In discussing the findings from this body of research, we will consider first general developmental trends observed across studies, followed by a more detailed accounting of research findings, and finally note some of the unresolved issues.

Most of the studies in this category reveal a marked tendency for learners to rely on unanalyzed formulae and repetition in the earliest stages of development, which gradually gives way to an expansion of the pragmatic repertoire characterized by analyzed, productive language use. Sawyer's (1992) study of the acquisition of *ne* provides one illustration of this developmental trend. While as a marker of epistemic and affective stance, *ne* is pervasive in Japanese discourse and therefore massively available in input outside of classrooms (cf. Ohta, 1994), the Japanese as second-language learners in Sawyer's study incorporated the particle only slowly into their interlanguage discourse. Compared to the interviewers' particle use, the learners used grammatical particles more frequently, whereas the interviewers' frequency of *ne*-marked utterances was four times that of the learners. Very likely, these differences were teaching-induced, since grammatical particles are traditionally taught as obligatory grammatical markers, whereas it is doubtful whether the grammatically inconsequential but interactionally necessary sentence-final *ne* was taught at all. Although Sawyer notes that the learners' progress in the use of the marker varied individually, a common sequence observed from the first to the fourth and last interview session was for learners to start with zero-marking, followed by the formulaic expression

Source: Kasper, G. & Rose, K. (2002). Developmental patterns in second language pragmatics. Selected from *Pragmatic development in a second language* (pp. 125–57). Malden, MA: Blackwell.

soo desu ne "that's right" as a listener response, and gradually extending *ne*-marking to limited productive (non-formulaic) use. A related phenomenon that can accompany early reliance on unanalyzed formulas is the overgeneralization of one form to many functions, not all of which are appropriate. DuFon (1999, 2000) provides a good example of this. One area that DuFon examined was the acquisition of Indonesian address terms by her study-abroad participants. Indonesian has a wide range of address terms, each of which carries with it distinct politeness implications. Appropriate pronoun use, then, is a key part of Indonesian pragmatics, as indicated by a certain teacher of Indonesian DuFon mentions who actually refused to interact with foreigners who use *kamu* (the familiar "you"), rather than the more formal *anda*. DuFon notes that some beginning learners initially overgeneralized use of the more formal *anda*—including its use with the informal genitive suffix (*-mu*)—to contexts that called for the use of the informal pronoun *kamu*, thus sending a mixed social message.

Another way that the gradual move to productive use of analyzed form-function mappings shows itself is in a shift in the type of conversational contributions made by learners over time. This can be characterized as a move to higher level of involvement facilitated by grammatical as well as pragmatic development. One such case is the change in Schmidt's (Schmidt & Frota, 1986) conversational prowess in Brazilian Portuguese after just a five-month stay in Brazil. Analysis of recorded conversations between Schmidt and his co-author (a NS of Brazilian Portuguese) revealed a decrease in use of repetition (self and other), confirmation and comprehension checks, clarification requests, requests for help, and minimal responses, with an attendant increase in the use of tag questions, statements, and back-channel responses. Excerpt 14.1 illustrates Schmidt's early conversational abilities:

> (14.1) Schmidt's early conversational abilities
> S: *Como é que você se sentiu quando você sabia, soube, que vinha pro Brasil? Qual era sua idéia do Brasil?*
>   How did you feel when you knew, knew that you were coming to Brazil? What was your idea of Brazil?
> R: *Um . . . no pensia, no pensia nada, no pensia que via a América Latina mas uh . . . porque eu sei e conheço Média Este e conheço também Asia . . . uh, Japan.*
>   Um . . . I didn't think, I didn't think anything, didn't think I would go to Latin America but uh . . . because I know the Middle East and I know also Asia . . . uh Japan.
>   (S = Silvia Frota, R = Richard Schmidt. Schmidt & Frota, 1986, p. 262)

The exchange in (14.1) displays the question–answer structure commonly observed in native speaker–non-native speaker discourse with learners of lower L2 ability. S self-repairs her original question by "pushing it down" to a syntactically less complex utterance. R constructs his answer turn incrementally through successively more complex self-repairs that recycle the previously produced turn-constructional units. His answer is limited to the telling of a past (cognitive) event and an account for that event, produced as two sets of parallel constructions. Both the telling and the account center on the repeated use of the (high-frequency) cognitive verbs *pensar* "think" and *conhecer* "know." The answer turn includes no assessment of any kind. In comparison, in a later conversation, the participation structure had changed, and R's contributions became far more sophisticated (14.2):

> (14.2) Schmidt's later conversational ability
> S: *É muito comum você ver um rapaz de 30 anos morando com pai e mãe.*
>   It's very common for you to see a 30 year old guy living with father and mother.

R: *Ah, eu sei. Aos Estados Unidos se tem um rapaz de 25 anos ainda mora com os pais, ah
    . . . toda gente pensam que coisa estranha mas aqui, não, aqui talvez um cara de 25 anos
    mora sozinho a gente falam: uma coisa estranha.*
    Ah, I know. In the U.S. if there's a 25 year old guy [who] still lives with his
    parents, ah . . . everybody thinks that's a strange thing, but here no, here maybe
    a 25 year old guy lives alone and people say: a strange thing.
S: *É o opos . . .*
    It's the oppo-
R: *O oposto!*
    The opposite!
    (S = Silvia Frota, R = Richard Schmidt. Schmidt & Frota, 1986, p. 263)

The exchange in (14.2) is structured more like a casual conversation than an interview.
After a comment (rather than question) by S, R takes a fairly long response turn, starting with
an acknowledgement of S's comment (*"Ah, eu sei"*) and proceeding not only to compare common
living arrangements for single men in the United States and Brazil but also to comment on the
contrasting societal evaluations of such arrangements with great rhetorical effectiveness. The
sequence closes with an overlapping assessment, another common feature of ordinary interaction.

Similarly, although he was not able to comment on the process of Wes's conversational
development due to a lack of early data, Schmidt (1983) notes that by the end of a three-year
observational period, Wes was quite capable of engaging appropriately in small talk, and also
making use of back-channel cues differentially in Japanese and English, that is, he did not
transfer to English the generally more frequent and animated listener behavior characteristic
of Japanese conversation. Kanagy and Igarashi (1997) and Kanagy (1999) report a similar
developmental trend in their Japanese immersion kindergartners—over time, the use of formulaic
speech decreased, use of voluntary expressions increased, and use of repetition decreased.
Interestingly, they noted that the children were selective in what they chose to repeat,
hypothesizing that input was more likely to be repeated when it was consistent with the children's
pragmatic needs (e.g., use of attention getters, or asking for permission), and when it satisfied
their desires for social interaction (e.g., short commands to stand or sit). A key finding was
that "output gradually developed from the use of unanalyzed chunks, which rely on cues with
fixed verbal routines, to partially analyzed expressions used in an innovative way in new contexts"
(Kanagy & Igarashi, 1997, p. 259), which sums up well what many studies have found.

Staying with learners of JFL, Ohta (2001) is one of few researchers who have posited a
developmental sequence for a pragmatic feature. Her one-year longitudinal study looked at
the development of Japanese expressions of acknowledgment, which indicate attentiveness,
and alignment, which serve as markers of affective common ground. Given their importance in Japanese, they were well attested in the input Ohta's learners received from their
teacher. Acknowledgment expressions observed included *un, mm* (uh huh), *hai, ee* (yes), *aa soo
desu ka* (I see), and *soo desu ka* (oh really), while frequently used expressions of alignment
included *soo desu ne* (it is, isn't it), *ii desu ne* (nice, great, good), and *. . . desu ne* (that's . . .
isn't it). Ohta's participants were two American undergraduates—Candace and Rob—enrolled
in a first-year JFL course. Ohta summarizes their progress at the end of the year in a
chart listing the range of listener responses and frequency of use for the two participants
(Table 14.1).

As the table indicates, both learners made progress over time, but Candace progressed
further than Rob in her use of expressions of alignment. It is noteworthy, however, that
Candace and Rob—despite differences in their use of acknowledgment and alignment expressions

Table 14.1 Progress by the end of the academic year in the use of a range of listener responses

	Un/Mm/hai	Ao soo desu ka	Soo desu ne	~desu ne
Rob	Uses *hai* occasionally	Uses spontaneously	Misuses for *Aa soo desu ka*	Uses only when scripted
Candace	Uses all three	Uses spontaneously	Uses as a hedge, not as a listener response	Uses spontaneously

Source: Ohta (2001)

at the end of the six-month observational period—appear to have followed a similar pattern of development, which led Ohta to posit a six-stage developmental sequence in the acquisition of alignment expressions by learners of Japanese.

> Stage 1: Students ask and answer preformulated questions. There is no use of expressions of acknowledgment or alignment, in English or in Japanese, unless scripted. The follow-up turn of the IRF sequence is left unused, with speakers moving immediately, or after a pause, to a new initiation.
>
> Stage 2: Students begin to use the follow-up turn for expression of acknowledgment, such as repetition of Japanese words and laughter. Use of Japanese minimal expressions of acknowledgment such as *hai* ["yes"] is rare. Alignment expressions are used only when scripted.
>
> Stage 3: Students begin to use *Aa soo desu ka* ["Oh really?"] to show acknowledgment, particularly when prompted by the teacher, but occasional spontaneous use also emerges. Occasional use of the Japanese minimal response *hai* continues. Alignment expressions are used where scripted, and on a limited basis when prompted by the teacher.
>
> Stage 4: Students use *Aa soo desu ka* with facility, beginning to use minimal expressions of acknowledgment beyond *hai*, such as *mm* and *un*, on occasion. Alignment expressions appear when prompted by the teacher.
>
> Stage 5: Spontaneous use of a limited range of Japanese expressions of alignment emerges. Minimal response expressions occur more frequently. Expressions of alignment are limited to those commonly used by the teacher, with little or no creative expansion.
>
> Stage 6: Students use a range of expressions of acknowledgment appropriately. Alignment expressions are used spontaneously, with greater lexical variety tailored to conversational content.
>
> (Ohta, 2001, p. 117)

The use of acknowledgment and alignment expressions observed by Ohta is reminiscent of findings from other studies discussed above—from early reliance on repetition and formula (in this case scripted for classroom use) to more productive use of these expressions that serve to mark a higher level of learner involvement in the interaction, as represented in Ohta's proposed developmental sequence.

Turning from Japanese to Indonesian as the target language, DuFon (1999, 2000) reported on the acquisition of the forms *belum* and *tidak*, two ways of responding negatively to experience questions in Indonesian that pose particular problems for learners because, as DuFon explains,

The two forms are similar in scope in that they both negate non-nominal predicates, but *tidak*, which means *no* or *not*, is stronger than *belum*, which means *not yet*. The contexts of use for which *belum* is preferred over *tidak* in Indonesian, however, are broader than those for which *not yet* is preferred over *no* in English, and *tidak* is considered pragmatically inappropriate in Indonesian in many contexts where *no* or *not* would be considered appropriate in English. Consequently, second-language learners of Indonesian tend to overgeneralize the *tidak* form, using it in contexts where *belum* is more appropriate.

(DuFon, 2000, p. 77)

In addition to similarity in the semantic and pragmatic scope of *belum* and *tidak*, the choice of either element is constrained by syntactic harmony, according to which the use of a particular form in the question projects either *belum* or *tidak* in the response turn. Native speakers at times produce syntactically unharmonious responses as a means of generating the implicature that the question has "implied an incorrect assumption about the possibility of a particular experience occurring" (DuFon, 2000, p. 86). While intermediate learners' negative responses to experience questions were for the most part as clear and syntactically harmonious as native speakers' responses, beginners' responses were usually unclear and unharmonious, thus generating unintended implicatures. She posits a developmental sequence for beginners that starts with use of English *no*, followed by use of *tidak* (marked with shaking of the head and, e.g., *huhuh*), and finally the irregular introduction of *belum*, but only after additional input in the form of clarification questions, correction, and confirmation requests. Use of *belum* by intermediate-level learners was almost native-like by the end of the program. The beginner's early reliance on *tidak* across a range of contexts also illustrates the issue of overgeneralization noted above, another prominent feature of early pragmatic development.

In addition to learners' tendency to rely at first on unanalyzed formulae and later generate more analyzed, productive speech, the studies discussed here also reveal some of the problems learners encounter as their pragmatic competence develops. Returning to Schmidt and Frota's (1986) account of Schmidt's acquisition of Brazilian Portuguese, we see how grammatical competence can interact with pragmatic development, sometimes limiting what learners are able to accomplish pragmatically. In Schmidt's case, one area of difficulty was responding to Brazilian Portuguese questions in the affirmative. It appears that a simple *yes* (i.e., *sim*) is not always an appropriate response because affirmative responses often require correct marking of verbs for person and number. Thus Schmidt's inability to supply the correct verb morphology also led to the production of pragmatically inappropriate responses to questions, a problem that cannot be remedied without the requisite grammatical competence. Another problem DuFon encountered also has to do with barriers to pragmatic development, but these appear to stem more from individual learner characteristics than was the case for Schmidt's inappropriate responses to questions. DuFon (1999) found that the six learners of Indonesian changed their use of address terms over time, but they did not all follow the same development path. Two of the beginning learners initially overgeneralized use of the more formal *anda*, but only one eventually corrected this. Two other learners did not evidence any change in use of pronouns throughout the observation period, but while one relied on *anda*, the other relied almost exclusively on zero forms. Only two learners expanded their repertoire to include the familiar *kamu*. DuFon also noted that learners' journal entries showed more knowledge about address terms than was apparent from their production. Perhaps most revealing are the choices made by the two beginning learners—both expressed an awareness of their inappropriate use of address terms, but only one made the effort to remedy this. The other simply chose not to do so. This sort of interaction between pragmatic development and individual learner differences has to date received little attention in the literature.

The studies on the development of pragmatic and discourse ability that we have reviewed in this section are of particular interest because they are all longitudinal, and all involve beginning learners. This allows for development to be charted from its earliest stages. What we see across the studies is a tendency for learners to rely on routine formulas and repetition at first, which gradually gives way to an expansion of their pragmatic repertoire. We also see overgeneralization of one form for a range of functions, a potential source of pragmatic failure, as in the lack of syntactic harmony found in the use of negative markers by some beginning learners of Indonesian. In addition, certain aspects of pragmatics that are closely related to proficiency in grammar are problematic for learners without the requisite knowledge of grammar, such as Schmidt's difficulty in acquiring the ability to respond in the affirmative to questions in Brazilian Portuguese. It is also clear, however, that even lower-proficiency learners are capable of controlling what might appear to be rather challenging aspects of target language pragmatics, such as Wes's ability to vary his back-channel behavior appropriately depending on whether he was speaking Japanese or English. An issue raised by DuFon's study—facilitated by her use of dialogue journals—is the possibility that learners' pragmatic knowledge may not be accurately represented in their production. DuFon's participants indicated more knowledge of Indonesian pronouns in their dialogue journals than was present in their production, but it is not clear how much of this gap was due to their conscious decision to avoid certain forms— as in the case of the less English-like greetings in the early stages—or whether other factors were involved. To answer such questions, in addition to collecting rich production data, we also need to probe learner knowledge.

Speech Acts

Studies of the development of speech acts in a second language are the best represented in the literature, with the bulk of work centering on English requests. Longitudinal request studies include Schmidt's (1983) work on Wes, Ellis's (1992) two-year study of the requests of two primary school children in the United Kingdom, and Achiba's (2002) account of her daughter's acquisition of English requests during their 17-month sojourn in Australia. Cross-sectional studies on English requests include Scarcella's (1979) work in an ESL context, as well as studies in a range of EFL contexts—Trosborg (1995) in Denmark, Hill (1997) in Japan, and Rose (2000) in Hong Kong. A number of studies have examined the development of other speech acts as well, including Bardovi-Harlig and Hartford's (1993) longitudinal study of suggestions and refusals in an academic advising context, Takahashi and Beebe (1987) on the refusals of Japanese-speaking learners of English in Japan and the United States, and two studies of greetings—DuFon's longitudinal study of the development of Indonesian greetings and Omar's (1991) cross-sectional work on the acquisition of greetings of American learners of Kiswahili.

Requests

As was true for the development of pragmatic and discourse ability in a second language, the development of L2 requests can also be characterized generally as a move from reliance on routine formulas in the earliest stages of development to a gradual introduction of analyzed, productive language use. However, in the case of requests, a good deal more can be said about possible stages of development. Based on results from his longitudinal study of two beginning ESL learners' (whom Ellis refers to as J and R) request development in a classroom setting,

Ellis (1992) proposes a three-stage developmental sequence for requests. In the first stage of request development, learners' utterances conveyed requestive intent through highly context-dependent, minimalist realizations, expressing the intended reference and illocution but no relational or social goals. In the second stage, requests were mainly performed by means of unanalyzed routines and imperatives. The third stage brought with it the unpacking of routine formulas that then become increasingly available for productive use, and more frequent use of conventional indirectness. A somewhat overlapping analysis is provided by Achiba (2002), the only other longitudinal study of which we are aware that involved a beginning learner, in this case Achiba's daughter, Yao. However, Yao seems to have been more than an absolute beginner when observation began, and she also appears to have developed her ability to request to a greater degree than J and R. Thus, Achiba's analysis actually posits four stages of development, with Yao's earliest requests (Achiba's first stage) more reminiscent of Ellis's second stage, and her second stage analogous to Ellis's third. Achiba's third and fourth stages—characterized by what Achiba calls pragmatic expansion and fine tuning—represent levels of development not observed in J and R. We discuss each of these proposed stages in turn.

Ellis's first stage of request development is well documented in the literature and illustrates a pre-basic learner variety. In this stage, requestive intent is expressed through a "pragmatic mode," featuring highly context-dependent, minimalist realizations of illocutionary force, devoid of syntax. J and R's earliest requests were propositionally incomplete, including no more than *sir* as a request for the teacher to staple the student's card, or *big circle* as a request when the learner needed a cutout of a big circle, both of which illustrate well the entirely context-dependent nature of early requests. And once J and R began to produce propositionally complete requests, these were largely formulaic, making frequent use of imperatives, such as *leave it* and *give me*.

In Ellis's stage two (which is Achiba's stage one), requests are performed primarily through use of unanalyzed routines and continued reliance on imperatives, as the examples in (14.3) from Achiba's earliest observations of Yao's requests demonstrate:

(14.3) Yao's earliest requests
Look at the little baby./Look at this picture.
Let's play the game./Let's eat breakfast.
Do you want to play dolls?/Do you want to draw pictures?
Can I have this?/Can I have space?
Don't look./Don't push it.
Clean up.
Keep going.

(Achiba, 2002)

Achiba points out that although unanalyzed formulas and imperatives were used most frequently at this stage, Yao also made use of the full range of strategies—direct, conventionally indirect, and even hints—displaying more variety than J and R. It would appear that Schmidt's (1983) observation of Wes also began at about Ellis's second stage of development, because Wes's earliest recorded requests indicate a reliance on unanalyzed formulas and imperatives. However, like Yao, Wes's requests at this stage also included a wider range of strategies, including hints, in addition to the use of unanalyzed formulas and imperatives, as indicated in examples (14.4):

(14.4) Wes's early requests
Shall we go?

Can I have a banana spi . . . lit, please?
Please n you taking this suitcase.
This is all garbage ("Put it out").
Ah, I have two shirts upstairs ("Please get them while you're there").

(Schmidt, 1983, pp. 151–2)

It is interesting to consider why J's and R's requests at this stage were of a more restricted range than those of Wes or Yao. One possible explanation is that J and R, being absolute beginners, lacked the pragmalinguistic resources to produce more varied request forms. Another possible explanation is differences in learning context—while Wes and Yao had more varied opportunities for exposure to, and use of, the target language, and were also observed in a range of settings, it would appear that J's and R's exposure to and use of English might have been limited to the classroom, as was Ellis's observation of them. Yet another potential explanation is offered by Schmidt, who attributed Wes's early use of hints to the influence of Japanese, his—and Yao's—first language. Nevertheless, despite the more varied requests by Wes and Yao when compared with J and R, the second stage of development does appear to be dominated by formulaic requests and imperatives.

Ellis's third stage (which is Achiba's second stage) brings with it the unpacking of routine formulas that then become increasingly available for productive use, as well as more frequent use of conventional indirectness (with the concomitant decrease in directness), and the beginning of more frequent and varied mitigation of requests. For instance, Ellis notes that in this stage, J's and R's routinized conventionally indirect ability questions were now used as flexible sentence frames, shifting in perspective between speaker (e.g., "Can *I* take book with me?") and hearer focus ("Can *you* pass me my pencil?"). J's and R's relational goals (i.e., politeness) were also beginning to be overtly marked in stage three, albeit with a restricted range of strategies. Achiba's stage two very closely matches Ellis's third stage, particularly with Yao's requests shifting from formulaic to productive (i.e., analyzed) request forms, as the following examples indicate:

(14.5) Yao's stage two requests
Can you pass the pencil please?
Can you do another one for me?

(Achiba, 2002)

Schmidt (1983) also notes that Wes's directives evidenced considerable development by the end of the three-year observation period. Among the changes he noted were the productive use of formulas, use of mitigated imperatives, and more elaboration, as the following examples illustrate:

(14.6) Wes's late requests
Shall we maybe go out for coffee now, or you want later?
OK, if you have time please send two handbag, but if you're too busy, forget it.

(Schmidt, 1983, p. 154)

These last examples from Wes strike us as a good deal more advanced than the achievements of J and R (at least at the time that Ellis stopped observing them), which indicates that Ellis's three stages do not extend to later development. Achiba's discussion of Yao's stage three and four requests provides more information on development.

The final two stages of Yao's request development were from about eight months to just under a year-and-a-half. Achiba characterizes stage three as one of pragmatic expansion, that is, the addition of many new forms to Yao's pragmalinguistic repertoire for requests. These included shifts in modality (e.g., from *can* to *could*), more frequent use of mitigation (especially supportive moves), and more complex syntax with (by then) fully analyzed formulas, as seen in the following examples:

(14.7) Yao's stage three requests
Could I have another chocolate because my children—I have five children.
I don't know how to play this/can you—could you tell me how to play this?
Can I see it so I can copy it?
Can you help me to draw a donkey?
Can you put glue here and here?

(Achiba, 2002)

While noting that, by this stage, Yao had already acquired most of the pragmalinguistic features of requesting observed in the final stage, Achiba argues that, in stage four, Yao's requesting became considerably refined, particularly in her ability to fine-tune the force of her requests. Indicative of this refinement is Yao's expanded use of *could* as both an ability question and a (more subtle) suggestion.

(14.8) Yao's stage four requests
Could you please do that here and then I do the pants?
You could put some blu tack down there.

(Achiba, 2002)

Other noteworthy patterns observed are that Yao's use of conventionally indirect requests had more than doubled since the first stage, and by stage four had become the most frequent strategy used. And while hints were not used as frequently, after a slight drop in frequency from stage one to stage two, Yao's use of hints doubled with each stage. Two hinting strategies added in the final stage include "Is there any . . .?" and "Have you got . . .?", as shown below.

(14.9) Yao's use of hints
Is there any more white?
Mum have you got a lid?

(Achiba, 2002)

Taken together, then, the longitudinal studies (i.e., Achiba, 2002; Ellis, 1992; Schmidt, 1983) provide a good starting point for describing the development of requests in a second language, with Ellis's and Achiba's overlapping analyses combining into five developmental stages, summarized in Table 14.2. However, as with most longitudinal research, the database represented here is rather small—just four individuals in the case of L2 requests—so it is useful to examine what the cross-sectional request studies can contribute to this discussion.

Appeals to the cross-sectional research on L2 requests are useful because cross-sectional designs often involve significantly larger numbers of participants, making more robust generalizations possible, especially when findings from cross-sectional studies support those from longitudinal research. While none of the cross-sectional request studies represents the full range of developmental stages discussed above, several studies do offer evidence that confirms

Table 14.2 Five stages of L2 request development (based on Achiba, 2002, and Ellis, 1992)

Stage	Characteristics	Examples
1: Pre-basic	Highly context-dependent, no syntax, no relational goals	"Me no blue", "Sir"
2: Formulaic	Reliance on unanalyzed formulas and imperatives	"Let's play the game", "Let's eat breakfast", "Don't look"
3: Unpacking	Formulas incorporated into productive language use, shift to conventional indirectness	"Can you pass the pencil please?", "Can you do another one for me?"
4: Pragmatic expansion	Addition of new forms to pragmalinguistic repertoire, increased use of mitigation, more complex syntax	"Could I have another chocolate because my children—I have five children.", "Can I see it so I can copy it?"
5: Fine-tuning	Fine-tuning of requestive force to participants, goals, and contexts	"You could put some blu tack down there", "Is there any more white?"

general developmental trends. Hill's (1997) study of the requests of learners of EFL at a Japanese university showed a marked decrease in the percentage of direct requests with increasing proficiency. The distribution of conventionally indirect requests followed the opposite pattern, with advanced learners' use of this strategy approaching NS levels. Rose (2000) also found that frequency of conventional indirectness increased with proficiency among Cantonese-speaking primary-school students in Hong Kong, and that directness was most frequent among the lowest-proficiency group. Trosborg (1995) also found a preference for conventional indirectness in evidence across the three levels of Danish learners of EFL she examined, noting a slight shift from what she refers to as hearer-oriented (i.e., ability/willingness and suggestory formula) to what she calls speaker-based strategies (i.e., wishes and desires/needs) as proficiency increased. Interestingly, the use of direct requests actually increased with proficiency, while the reverse was true for hints, which runs directly counter to most studies. Trosborg suggests that the lower-proficiency learners avoided use of direct requests out of fear of sounding impolite, but it is not clear why advanced learners would not have had the same concerns. Overall, then, both longitudinal and cross-sectional research on L2 request development provides considerable evidence to support the five stages of development outlined above. Our discussion so far has focused on global strategies for requesting—two additional issues we will address are the development of mitigation in requesting, and insights from the L2 request studies concerning sociopragmatic development.

The learners in Ellis's (1992) study initially produced requests that were simple (i.e., usually consisting of a bare head act with little internal or external modification) and formulaic, but one of the first mitigating devices they introduced was *please*. This also was the case for Wes and Yao. However, it appears that *please* (particularly in early production) may best be considered a requestive marker rather than a politeness marker (see House, 1989), in which case its mitigating function might be lessened. Schmidt notes an elaboration of Wes's requests, but does not offer a detailed analysis of mitigating devices (i.e., when and how they were introduced). It is clear from the examples presented above, though, that Wes was able to use devices such as imposition minimizers (e.g., "OK, *if you have time* please send two handbag, but *if you're too busy, forget it.*") in a rather sophisticated manner. And, as noted above, Achiba found that Yao's use of mitigation increased over time, particularly during stages four and five, when supportive moves became more frequent, as did the modal shift to *could* and *would* (although *can* and *will* were still far more frequent overall). Hill (1997) found that use of downgraders per request increased with proficiency, though the advanced group still fell short of native-speaker levels. He notes that, because the Japanese NSs used considerably more internal modification than the native English speakers, the limited use of internal modification by the learners was probably not the result of first-language influence. Trosborg (1995) also reported a general increase in internal and external modification with proficiency, but differences across groups were minimal, and even learners in the highest proficiency group fell far short of the English native speakers, especially in external modification of requests. Rose (2000) observed minimal use of supportive moves (mostly grounders, e.g., "*I don't know that question. Can you teach me?*") by only the highest-proficiency group. More detailed analyses of the development of mitigation strategies are needed, and we would expect that much of the interesting development would be most evident from stage three onward.

It is worth pointing out that examining major analytical categories (e.g., directness level or use of mitigation) for developmental patterns is not without flaws. As noted above, Hill (1997) found a move toward conventional indirectness with increased proficiency among his learners. However, he points out that the global trend toward native speaker use of conventionally indirect requests concealed a number of patterns in the use of specific substrategies that did not converge toward NS norms. For example, want strategies (*I want to/I would like to*), which were hardly ever used by the native speakers of Irish-English, were overused by learners from the beginning and continued to increase as proficiency improved. The increase of ability strategies (*can/could you*) seen from low to intermediate did not continue at the advanced level; permission strategies (*may I*), though slightly on the rise, remained greatly underused; but willingness strategies (*would you*), while stable from low to intermediate, sharply increased at advanced level. So although an analysis based simply on major categories would appear to indicate that Hill's learners were moving closer to NS norms in their use of conventionally indirect requests, analysis of substrategies actually indicated the opposite. That is, the spike in use of conventional indirectness was the result of learner overuse of want and willingness strategies, actually a movement away from native speaker norms as proficiency increased. The same was true for mitigation: despite what appeared to be another developmental trend, Hill again noted patterns at the substrategy level that indicated movement away from native speaker norms, such as an overuse of syntactic downgraders (e.g., interrogative, negation, continuous, conditional) at the expense of those of the lexical/phrasal variety (e.g., politeness markers, understaters, downtoners), which were used more frequently by the native speakers. This was particularly evident in the learners' use of conditionals (e.g., *If you don't mind*), which Hill argued was transferred from very common Japanese forms such as *moshi yokattara* ("if it's okay"), and is regressive rather than developmental. The same general developmental trend was found in external modification, with the frequency of supportive moves per request increasing with proficiency, and advanced learners' use approaching native-speaker levels. Here again, despite the apparent developmental trend, Hill found regressive patterns in the use of specific substrategies, such as overuse of apology moves (e.g., *So I'm sorry very much, I'm feel bad but, Sorry to interrupt you but*) as external modifiers. One important lesson to be learned from Hill's study is that, without examining more closely the use of specific substrategies within a given strategy category, analysts may arrive at incorrect conclusions, unless the pattern displayed at the macro level reproduces the patterns of the subsumed strategies.

Our discussion so far has addressed learner development in terms of pragmalinguistics, but what about sociopragmatics? Quite early on, Scarcella (1979) argued that, "the acquisition of politeness forms appears to precede the acquisition of the sociolinguistic-interactional rules and mechanisms underlying the use and distribution of these forms" (p. 285). It would appear that this claim finds considerable support in the literature on L2 request development. Scarcella's own study—which formed the basis of her conclusion—found that, while use of indirectness by NSs on a role play task that varied the status of the hearer formed a cline across status levels, ESL learner groups at two proficiency levels varied minimally in their use of indirectness according to status. Given that adult learners bring considerable universal pragmatic knowledge to the L2 learning task, Scarcella's learners likely had knowledge of social status as a factor affecting language use (as would be evident in their L1 use), but they were not yet able to match this knowledge with the appropriate linguistic forms in the L2. Ellis (1992) noted that J's and R's requests, for the most part, were not varied according to addressee, indicating no sociopragmatic development at all, despite having displayed acquisition of a range (albeit small) of requesting strategies. Hill's (1997) participants (even the most advanced learners), who demonstrated knowledge of a wide range of request forms, showed little variation in use of direct and conventionally indirect requests and internal modification according to hearer status, indicating their inability to map target language forms to appropriate social categories. However, they did use external modification more frequently with equal-status hearers than those of higher status, showing some evidence of sociopragmatic awareness. Trosborg (1995) and Rose (2000) both reported virtually no situational variation in request strategy across all learner groups, despite having found evidence of a fairly wide range of request forms. These findings underscore the fact that, despite already possessing considerable universal pragmatic knowledge, adult L2 learners appear to require a great deal of time to develop the ability to appropriately map L2 forms to social categories. This appears to be especially true in foreign language contexts.

But not all the news is bad. Achiba (2002) noted that there were some rather interesting aspects in which Yao's requests took into account various sociopragmatic factors. For example, while Yao's use of direct requests persisted for goals such as initiation and cessation of action (e.g., "Oh just give me another story," "Here don't eat too much"), she preferred conventional indirectness in requesting goods and joint activity (e.g., "Could I please have one choc chip?", "Let's pretend this is Safeway"). There was also variation observed in requests depending on addressee, with, for example, all of the *want* statements used with adults rather than peers, the majority of requests with *let's* used with peers rather than adults, and *please* used almost exclusively to Yao's mother. Schmidt also reports some sociopragmatic awareness in Wes's responses to Scarcella's (1979) test of verbal routines, for example, on an item designed to elicit an apology for being late, Wes initially responded with "Hi! I'm sorry. Somebody call," but he then noted that, "No, this is Japan need two story. Here I'm only just say 'Hi, sorry, you waiting long time?'" (p. 154), demonstrating the level of pragmatic sophistication with concomitant grammatical infelicities that have made him famous. Thus, Wes and Yao did appear to develop some sociopragmatic competence in the target language, no doubt largely due to the fact that their learning took place in an acquisition-rich environment, with ample opportunity for input and interaction.

Summing up the request studies, perhaps the most striking finding is the proposed five-stage development sequence drawn from the work of Ellis (1992) and Achiba (2002). Stage one is a pre-basic variety, in which requestive intent is conveyed through highly context-dependent, minimalist realizations. Stage two brings with it reliance on imperatives and unanalyzed routines, which are then unpacked for more productive use in the third stage. This stage also sees a shift away from imperatives toward the use of conventional indirectness. The fourth stage involves the addition of many new forms to the pragmalinguistic repertoire for requests, and the final stage is characterized by the increasing ability to fine-tune requests for various contexts. Another obvious trend worth noting is that learners begin to gradually modify their requests, both internally and externally, as proficiency increases (particularly from stage three onward). Hill's findings, however, make a strong case for not taking the results of major category analyses at face value. Despite the move toward what appeared to be more native-like requests in terms of directness, his analysis of substrategies showed that more advanced learners were actually moving away from native-speaker norms in their choice of pragmalinguistic devices that realized conventional indirectness or modification. So while more advanced learners may have more closely resembled native speakers in using more conventional indirectness or in mitigating their requests, the ways in which they were doing so were decidedly not native-like. Concerning the sociopragmatics of request development, findings are mixed. It would be fair to say that learning context plays a key role here, with learners in second language settings (e.g., Wes, Yao) achieving some level of sociopragmatic development, and learners in foreign language contexts (e.g., learners of English in Denmark, Japan, and Hong Kong) reaching little or none. Given that the literature on requests has provided a good deal of evidence of pragmatic development, it is interesting to see whether the same will be true for studies of other speech acts, which we consider next.

Other speech acts

For research on speech acts other than requests, we start with Bardovi-Harlig and Hartford's (1993a) study of suggestions and refusals in an academic advising context, one of the first longitudinal studies of pragmatic development. Based on their earlier work on advising sessions (Bardovi-Harlig & Hartford, 1990), which indicated a number of differences in non-native speaker and native speaker use, Bardovi-Harlig and Hartford (1993a, p. 281) proposed a "Maxim of Congruence: Make your contribution congruent with your status." They note that in advising sessions, congruent contributions from the advisor include advising, recommending, and requesting information from the student, and those congruent with student status are making requests for advice, information, and permission. Incongruent acts for students include correcting the advisor and rejecting his or her advice. When congruence is not possible, a status-preserving strategy (SPS) must be employed. Bardovi-Harlig and Hartford list six such strategy types but focus on the following four (Bardovi-Harlig & Hartford, 1993, p. 281):

- Appear congruent. Use the form of a congruent speech act where possible.
- Mark your contribution linguistically. Use mitigators.
- Frequency. Avoid frequent noncongruent turns.
- Use appropriate content.

The data for this study were drawn from academic advising sessions that took place at intervals of about two months to about four-and-a-half months. Even after such a short observational period, results showed some change over time in the use of suggestions by non-native speakers. Bardovi-Harlig and Hartford (1993) identified three types of suggestion: initiated suggestions (offered by the speaker without a prompt or question), responses to prompts, and responses to questions. Of these, initiated suggestions are status-incongruent for students (and thus require SPSs), while the other two strategies are status-congruent. Both groups used suggestions with about the same frequency in the early and later sessions, but there were differences across groups in choice of suggestion type. In the early sessions, native speakers favored initiated requests, and non-native speakers relied more on responses to questions, but, in the later sessions, both groups used initiated suggestions about equally. This suggests that the non-native speakers moved from a passive to an active role in schedule building. Native-speaker suggestions were a great deal more successful (i.e., accepted by the advisor) than those of non-native speakers, with one key exception being that non-native speakers' success rate for initiated suggestions on the later sessions rose to a level approaching that of native speakers. This greater success rate of native-speaker suggestions is likely due to their more effective use of mitigators—native speakers used about twice as many mitigators as non-native speakers, who also frequently employed aggravators, as in the following examples:

(14.10) Nonnative speakers' use of aggravators
In the summer I *will take* language testing for the first summer session, the first one, the second summer session I *will take* the socio [linguistics class].
Yeah, *I'm going to* take, ah . . . applied . . . transformational syntax.
So, I, *I just decided* on taking the language structure . . . field method in linguistics.
(Bardovi-Harlig & Hartford, 1990, p. 289)

Changes were also found over time in the use of rejections. In the early sessions, non-native speakers rejected about half of their advisor's suggestions, resulting in a frequency of rejections that was almost ten times that of native speakers. However, by the later sessions, the frequency of non-native speaker rejections had decreased rather dramatically to about one-fourth the level of the early sessions, approaching native-speaker levels. The success rate of non-native speaker rejections improved somewhat, but still lagged well behind the 100 percent success rate of native speaker rejections. Another key area of change in rejections is the more frequent use by non-native speakers of what Bardovi-Harlig and Hartford call "credible content," i.e., rejecting a course for an acceptable reason such as a time conflict or having already taken it previously, rather than, say, a lack of interest (e.g., *I think I am not interested in Montague grammar*), which tended to provoke strong reactions from advisors. Bardovi-Harlig and Hartford (1993) conclude that non-native speakers "do develop competence in their handling of the advising session. What they primarily learn is the institutional rules. That is, they learn what the advising session is for and how it is generally structured" (p. 298).

Another refusal study was Takahashi and Beebe's (1987) cross-sectional study involving a standard interlanguage data set: native speakers of Japanese and English, and Japanese-speaking learners of English. The learners were divided into two groups based on location: an EFL group in Japan, and an ESL group studying in the United States. The two sets of learners were grouped into low and high proficiency. The focus of the study was on transfer, which Takahashi and Beebe expected to find in both contexts and at both proficiency levels, with more transfer occurring in the EFL setting and among higher-proficiency learners. Regarding the relationship between transfer and development, Takahashi and Beebe (1987) rather famously posited that higher levels of proficiency result in more negative first language transfer because increased fluency gives learners "the rope to hang themselves with" (p. 153). We return to this issue later in our discussion of pragmatic transfer and development. As expected, evidence of transfer from Japanese was found in the English refusals of both the EFL and the ESL groups in, for example, a preference for making a statement of philosophy (e.g., *Things with shapes eventually break*) or principle (e.g., *I make a rule to be temperate in eating*), and use of dissuading strategies (e.g., threat or statement of negative consequences, guilt trip) in a wider range of contexts. Further, more transfer was found in the EFL setting. The effects of proficiency on transfer were not so clear. It was found that lower-proficiency EFL learners marginally transferred more than those in the high-proficiency group, with the opposite pattern obtaining for the ESL learners. Takahashi and Beebe note that ESL data "weakly confirm" their hypothesis, while the EFL data "even more weakly" refute it (p. 148), and opt to argue that there were real proficiency differences only for the ESL group. However, given the lack of independent proficiency measures, this strikes us as rather unconvincing. They offer an account of the greater levels of transfer in the high-proficiency ESL group, for example, refusals of a higher formality (e.g., *I am very delighted and honored to be asked to attend the party, but . . .* and *I deeply appreciate your work*), which did not occur with lower-proficiency ESL learners.

From refusals, we now move to another speech act—greetings— which is also represented by two studies. In her account of the acquisition of Indonesian greetings by her six study-abroad learners, DuFon (1999) reports that learners were exposed to a range of Indonesian greetings. Some of these were semantically similar to English.

Halo "hello"
Selamat "happy" + time of day
Apa kabar? "What's new/How are you?"

Other greetings were not semantically similar to English.

Dari mana? "Where are you [coming] from?"
Sudah makan "Have you eaten yet?"
Sudah mandi? "Have you had your bath yet?"

When it came to their own use, learners displayed a clear preference for greetings that were semantically closest to English, and one learner even reported resistance to using the less English-like greetings because to him they didn't "seem like a greeting, but more of just a question. Almost as if they were just skipping the greeting" (DuFon, 1999, p. 303). Several learners also reported that they initially understood such greetings as information-seeking questions. For the most part, however, DuFon's account of greetings dealt with how learners were greeted, and how they responded, and she says little about development other than an initial preference for greetings semantically similar to English, with a gradual expansion of the greeting repertoire to include formulas that were initially interpreted as information-seeking questions. She does note that some learners demonstrated a rather advanced level of understanding of the politeness values of various greetings in different contexts, indicating some development of sociopragmatic awareness. One learner—a native speaker of Japanese—systematically compared greetings in Indonesian, Chinese, and Japanese in a dialogue journal entry, showing a level of metapragmatic awareness that indicates the benefits of individual multilingualism. A further study on greetings is that of Omar (1991), who conducted a cross-sectional study on the greetings of American learners of Kiswahili studying at Indiana University. Of interest to Omar was whether learners would indicate awareness of the norms governing greetings in Kiswahili, which involve more elaborated interaction than found in the rather formulaic greeting typical of American English. Kiswahili greetings typically involve a large number of turns, repetition of the same forms, and questions concerning one's family members. Omar reports that learners of Kiswahili are put off by this. Learners were classified as beginners and nonbeginners. For the most part, learners' greetings were inappropriately unelaborated, and there were few differences across the two levels. Omar notes that, if anything, it was the beginning learners whose greetings were more elaborate.

The studies of the speech acts reviewed in this section are a bit of a mixed bag. Bardovi-Harlig and Hartford's (1993) study clearly charts the progress of very advanced learners of English in negotiating their academic schedules through more appropriate use of refusals and suggestions, even over a relatively short period (as little as two months). However, their findings also show that even the most advanced learners continue to have difficulty with the finer points of mitigating their speech acts. This is not surprising, given that request studies have also shown that mitigation develops later, and studies such as Kerekes (1992) have demonstrated that learners also take time to accurately comprehend qualifiers. The two studies of greetings offer differing results as well, with Omar finding no evidence of compliance with the elaborated Kiswahili greetings, but DuFon finding that her participants relied on Indonesian greeting formulas that more closely resembled those they were familiar with from English, only slowly making use of what (to them) were more exotic greeting routines. These conflicting findings are likely explained, at least in part, by differences in learning context. DuFon's learners had the distinct advantage of residing in Indonesia when studying Indonesian, which included living with host families. Omar's participants had very different circumstances, that is, studying an uncommonly-taught language in an environment that afforded little or no intensive exposure to the target language, or opportunities to use it. Another possible explanation for the conflicting findings is individual learner differences, particularly motivation. Traveling to Indonesia to participate in a four-month study-abroad program likely indicates considerably more personal investment on the part of DuFon's learners than taking language classes most likely intended to fulfill a university foreign language requirement. DuFon's participants were also experienced second-language learners, having already learned another second language prior to learning Indonesian. Omar does not offer details on the prior second language learning of her participants, so we cannot comment on their motivation or language learning prowess. And, finally, Takahashi and Beebe's focus on transfer offers little information regarding development and does not convincingly support their hypothesis that (negative) transfer from the first language correlates positively with proficiency in the target language. It does, however, offer a nice segue into our next section, where we take up the issue of pragmatic development and transfer in more detail.

Pragmatic transfer and development

Pragmatic transfer has been attested in many of the single-moment studies comparing interlanguage performance with corresponding first language and second language data (see Maeshiba et al., 1996; S. Takahashi, 1996, for review). Here, we will consider research addressing the relationship of pragmatic transfer and development. As noted above, Takahashi and Beebe (1987) advanced the positive correlation hypothesis, predicting that second language proficiency is positively correlated with pragmatic transfer. Lower-proficiency learners, according to the hypothesis, are less likely to display pragmatic transfer in their L2 production than higher-proficiency learners because they do not have the necessary linguistic resources to do so. Higher-proficiency learners, on the other hand, do have such resources, so their L2 production will tend to reveal more pragmatic transfer. As noted above, while Takahashi's and Beebe (1987) study on the English refusals of Japanese learners of English at two different proficiency levels did not demonstrate the predicted proficiency effect, some studies have found that learners' limited second language knowledge prevented them from transferring complex first language conventions of means and form, and that increasing proficiency in the target language can apparently facilitate negative pragmatic transfer.

One such study is Cohen's (1997) account of his experience in a four-month intensive JFL course at the University of Hawai'i. His diary entries indicate that he intended to adhere to implementations of the Quantity and Manner maxims common in mainstream North American culture, which would have amounted to talking more and being more specific than was appropriate in Japanese, or, as he puts it, to "use more speech than Japanese do" (p. 150). For example, Cohen noted a specific desire to supply more than *sumimasen* in apologizing, but since his low degree of foreign language knowledge and control prevented that plan from being implemented, Japanese conversational norms were involuntarily observed. Cohen's experience lends support to the positive correlation hypothesis—despite his stated desire to violate target language norms and intentionally produce utterances in the L2 that observed pragmatic norms from his L1, he was unable to do so because he lacked sufficient Japanese resources.

Findings from Hill (1997) would also appear to support the positive correlation hypothesis. Recall that although Hill's highest-proficiency learners appeared to be moving toward native-like request production when main strategies (i.e., level of directness) and use of mitigators were considered, closer examination of substrategies for both categories turned up pragma-linguistic features that both deviated from native English speakers, and—more importantly where transfer is concerned—appeared to be the result of first language influence. For example, advanced learners' use of conditionals such as *If you don't mind* were likely a direct translation from Japanese (i.e., *moshi yokattara*, "If it's okay"), as was their overuse of apology moves (e.g., *So I'm sorry very much, I'm feel bad but,* and *Sorry to interrupt you but*) as external modifiers. It appears, then, that Hill's more advanced learners transferred these forms to English from Japanese as soon as they had the requisite linguistic skills in the target language.

But not all studies support Takahashi and Beebe's hypothesis. Maeshiba et al. (1996) carried out an apology study with intermediate and advanced Japanese-speaking ESL learners in Hawai'i. In addition to a production task, participants also completed a metapragmatic assessment questionnaire on seven contextual factors (i.e., severity of offense, offender's obligation to apologize, likelihood for the apology to be accepted, offender's face loss, offended party's face loss, social distance, and social dominance). Assessments of the various groups indicated the highest levels of agreement for status, obligation to apologize, and likelihood of acceptance, and the lowest for offender's face loss, offended party's face loss, and social distance. Maeshiba et al. (1996) predicted that transfer of apology strategies could be based on similarities and differences in assessment of contextual variables, with positive transfer occurring with similar assessments, and negative transfer where assessments differed. For the most part, these predictions were borne out. An important finding was that the advanced learners outpaced the intermediate group in both types of transfer, showing more positive transfer and less negative transfer. These results do not support the positive correlation hypothesis.

One could attempt to continue working with Takahashi and Beebe's hypothesis by looking for explanations for the conflicting findings offered by these studies. For example, one possible explanation for the different outcomes of Hill (1997) and Maeshiba et al. (1996) is that apology strategies in Japanese and English vary less in terms of syntactic complexity than request strategies do. How exactly the grammatical complexity of speech act strategies in first language and second language and pragmalinguistic transfer interrelate developmentally has not been studied thus far. Such a line of inquiry would move forward considerably the study of the relationship between pragmatic development and pragmatic transfer. In fact, it would enable researchers to explore more complex relationships than the rather facile hypothesis according to which advanced learners are prone to negative pragmatic transfer because their L2 grammar makes it possible. Although the phenomenon of pragmatic transfer is well documented, the conditions of transfer and especially its interaction with other factors are less clearly understood. Reminiscent of Kellerman's psychotypology (1983), studies by Olshtain (1983) and Robinson (1992) suggest that learners may be more prone to transfer their pragmatic first language knowledge when they hold a universalist view as opposed to a relativist perspective on pragmatic norms. To date, only one interlanguage pragmatic study (S. Takahashi, 1996) has been carried out with an explicit focus on transferability, that is, learners' perception of equivalence between conventions of means and form in first language and second language.

After reviewing the existing literature on second language pragmatic transfer, S. Takahashi (1996) argues that "in addition to product-oriented research on pragmatic transfer, we . . . need to undertake process-oriented studies of pragmatic transferability, exploring the conditions under which transfer occurs" (p. 190), and her study of the transferability of Japanese indirect request strategies to English makes a significant step in that direction. She was interested in how proficiency in the target language (i.e., English) as well as requestive imposition influenced learners' perceptions of the transferability of request strategies from their first language (i.e., Japanese). She outlined two criteria for pragmatic transferability, that is, learner assessment of the contextual appropriateness of a given strategy and their assessment of the equivalence of strategies in the first language and the target language in terms of contextual appropriateness. Based on this, Takahashi proposed a pragmatic transferability scale, which posits that strategies rated high for contextual appropriateness and viewed as contextual equivalents are more transferable, while those that are rated low for appropriateness and considered contextually different are less transferable. Participants in her study were low- and high-proficiency Japanese male undergraduates. Preliminary work was carried out to establish what Takahashi refers to as conventional equivalent pairs (CEPs) and functional equivalent pairs (FEPs). The former were basically literal translation equivalents, while the latter were equivalent in terms of their communicative effect. For example, the Japanese request form *V-te itadaki-tai-n-desu-kedo* "I would like you to VP" would have the functional English equivalent "I was wondering if you could VP," which is quite different from its literal translation. A transferability judgment questionnaire was constructed to measure perception of the contextual appropriateness of five Japanese indirect request strategies and their contextual equivalence vis-à-vis their CEP counterpart. Scores from these two were then used to compute pragmatic transferability rate. It was found (among other things) that CEPs were rated higher in terms of equivalence than FEPs, with no differences across the two proficiency groups. Takahashi (1996, pp. 209–10) noted that her "Japanese learners of English could not identify the English requests that were the real functional equivalents of the Japanese request strategies," no matter what their level of proficiency, indicating that both groups "equally relied on their first language request conventions or strategies in second language request realization." By examining the cross-linguistic correspondences of a specific subset of first and target language pragmatic features, Takahashi's study represents a more sophisticated approach to pragmatic transfer and development.

[. . .]

References

Achiba, M. (2002). *Learning to request in a second language: child interlanguage pragmatics*. Clevedon, England: Multilingual Matters.

Bardovi-Harlig, K. and Hartford, B. (1990). Congruence in native and nonnative conversations: status balance in the academic advising session. *Language Learning*, 40, 467-501.

Bardovi-Harlig, K. and Hartford, B. (1993). Learning the rules of academic talk: a longitudinal study of pragmatic development. *Studies in Second Language Acquisition*, 15, 279–304.

Cohen, A. D. (1997). Developing pragmatic ability: insights from the accelerated study of Japanese. In H. M. Cook, K. Hijirida & M. Tahara (eds), *New trends and issues in teaching Japanese language and culture* (Technical Report No. 15, pp. 133–59). Honolulu: University of Hawai'i, Second Language Teaching and Curriculum Centre.

DuFon, M. A. (1999). The acquisition of linguistic politeness in Indonesian as a second language by sojourners in a naturalistic context (Doctoral dissertation, University of Hawai'i). *Dissertation Abstracts International*, 60, 3985.

DuFon, M. A. (2000). The acquisition of negative responses to experience questions in Indonesian as a second language by sojourners in naturalistic interactions. In B. Swierzbin, F. Morris, M. Anderson, C. A. Klee & E. Tarone (eds), *Social and cognitive factors in second language acquisition* (pp. 77–97). Somerville, MA: Cascadilla Press.

Ellis, R. (1992). Learning to communicate in the classroom: a study of two learners' requests. *Studies in Second Language Acquisition*, 14, 1–23.

Hill, T. (1997). The development of pragmatic competence in an EFL context (Doctoral dissertation, Temple University Japan). *Dissertation Abstracts International*, 58, 3905.

House, J. (1989). Politeness in English and German: the functions of please and bitte. In S. Blum-Kulka, J. House & G. Kasper (eds), *Cross cultural pragmatics: requests and apologies* (pp. 96–119). Norwood, NJ: Ablex.

Kanagy, R. (1999). Interactional routines as a mechanism for L2 acquisition and socialisation in an immersion context. *Journal of Pragmatics*, 31, 1467–92.

Kanagy, R. and Igarashi, K. (1997). Acquisition of pragmatics competence in a Japanese immersion kindergarten. In L. F. Bouton (ed.), *Pragmatics and language learning* (monograph series vol. 8, pp. 243–65). Urbana-Champaign, IL: Division of English as an International Language, University of Illinois, Urbana-Champaign.

Kellerman, E. (1983). Now you see it, now you don't. In S. Gass & L. Selinker (eds), *Language transfer in language learning* (pp. 112–34). Rowley, MA: Newbury House.

Kerekes, J. (1992). Development in non-native speakers' use and perception of assertiveness and supportiveness in mixed-sex conversations (Occasional Paper No. 21). Honolulu: University of Hawai'i at Mānoa, Department of English as a Second Language.

Maeshiba, N., Yoshinaga, N., Kasper, G. and Ross, S. (1996). Transfer and proficiency in interlanguage apologizing. In S. M. Gass & J. Neu (eds), *Speech acts across cultures: challenges to communication in a second language* (pp. 155–87). Berlin: Mouton de Gruyter.

Ohta, A. S. (1994). Socialising the expression of affect: an overview of affective particle use in the Japanese as a foreign language classroom. *Issues in Applied Linguistics*, 5, 303–26.

Ohta, A. S. (2001). A longitudinal study of the development of expression of alignment in Japanese as a foreign language. In K. R. Rose & G. Kasper (eds), *Pragmatics in language teaching* (pp. 103–20). New York: Cambridge University Press.

Olshtain, E. (1983). Sociocultural competence and language transfer: the case of apology. In S. Gass & L. Selinker (eds), *Language transfer in language learning* (pp. 232–49). Rowley, MA: Newbury House.

Omar, A. (1991). How learners greet in Kiswahili: a cross-sectional survey. In L. F. Bouton & Y. Kachru (eds), *Pragmatics and language learning* (monograph series vol. 2, pp. 59–73). Urbana-Champaign, IL: Division of English as an International Language, University of Illinois, Urbana-Champaign.

Robinson, M. (1992). Introspective methodology in interlanguage pragmatics research. In G. Kasper (ed.), *Pragmatics of Japanese as native and target language* (Technical Report No. 3, pp. 27–82). Honolulu: University of Hawai'i at Mānoa, Second Language Teaching and Curriculum Centre.

Rose. K. R. (2000). An exploratory cross-sectional study of interlanguage pragmatic development. *Studies in Second Language Acquisition*, 22, 27–67.

Sawyer, M. (1992). The development of pragmatics in Japanese as a second language: the sentence-final particle ne. In G. Kasper (ed.), *Pragmatics of Japanese as a native and foreign language* (Technical Report No. 3, pp. 83–125). Honolulu: University of Hawai'i at Mānoa, Second Language Teaching and Curriculum Centre.

Scarcella, R. (1979). On speaking politely in a second language. In C. A. Yorio, K. Peters & J. Schachter (eds), *On TESOL '79: The learner in focus* (pp. 275–87). Washington, DC: Teachers of English to Speakers of Other Languages.

Schmidt, R. (1983). Interaction, acculturation and the acquisition of communicative competence. In N. Wolfson & E. Judd (eds), *Sociolinguistics and second language acquisition* (pp. 137–74). Rowley, MA: Newbury House.

Schimdt, R. and Frota, S. N. (1986). Developing basic conversational ability in a second language: a case study of an adult learner of Portuguese. In R. Day (ed.), *Talking to learn* (pp. 237–326). Rowley, MA: Newbury House.

Takahashi, S. (1996). Pragmatic transferability. *Studies in Second Language Acquisition*, 18, 189–223.

Takahashi, T. and Beebe, L. M. (1987). The development of pragmatic competence by Japanese learners of English. *JALT Journal*, 8, 131–55.

Trosborg, A. (1995). *Interlanguage pragmatics*. Berlin: Mouton de Gruyter.

Chapter 15

ANNA MAURANEN

SIGNALING AND PREVENTING MISUNDERSTANDING IN ENGLISH AS LINGUA FRANCA COMMUNICATION

Introduction

MISUNDERSTANDING ARISES IN any communication, and natural languages tend to be well equipped with means for signaling as well as resolving it. What kinds of misunderstanding take place in lingua franca communication and what strategies develop for resolving and preventing misunderstanding are less clear. We might assume, on the one hand, that lingua franca communication is particularly susceptible to misunderstanding, because the participants' command of the language is imperfect, there is little intersubjectivity, or certainty about sharedness, and the speakers' linguistic imperfections are likely to diverge from each other's. On the other hand, it is perhaps equally plausible that not much is misunderstood, since interlocutors tend to maximize simplicity in their expression, because their command of the vehicular language is far from perfect, and because they can expect the same from their inter-locutors. It is also the case that, although non-native speakers' productions deviate from native speaker standards, this does not necessarily hamper interaction.

It is the former view which appears to be the general expectation: it is not uncommon to see offhand remarks in linguistic publications suggesting that it is clear there will be more comprehension problems in communication where at least one of the parties is not speaking their mother tongue. This, however, is above all a commonsense assumption. We might then assume that speakers engaged in intercultural communication anticipate such difficulties, and attempt to offset this by working harder toward mutual understanding. What actually happens in lingua franca discourse, and how speakers deal with the misunderstandings that arise—or how they might seem to be anticipating and subverting the possibility—is largely still an open question.

Misunderstanding has been studied widely in native–non-native communication, and it seems that while it does arise, in real-life situations native speakers tend to manifest their cooperation by orienting toward the contents and the flow of the interaction rather than the defective form of their non-native interlocutors (Kurhila, 2003b). In studies of L2 acquisition, the focus has often been on the inadequacy of linguistic form. Lack of pragmatic or discourse competence in L2 users, for instance the infrequent use of modals or hedges, has been assumed to generate communicative misunderstanding between native and non-native speakers in both

Source: Mauranen, A. (2006). Signaling and preventing misunderstanding in English as lingua franca communication. *International Journal of the Sociology of Language*, 177, 123–50.

spoken (Nikula, 1996) and written (Ventola and Mauranen, 1990) discourse. But it is important to note that the native vs. non-native situation, especially as concerns the L1 speaker vs. the L2 learner, is not really comparable with two individuals communicating via a vehicular language: the native–non-native (L1–L2) situation is asymmetrical with respect to command of the target language, while in non-native–non-native (L2–L2) interaction this is not so, and in this respect the interactive mechanisms in these conversations could well be more similar to the symmetry of native speaker (L1) conversations.

Findings from lingua franca research either seem to suggest that misunderstandings are not very frequent (Firth, 1990; Meierkord, 1998) or, on the contrary, that quite a few of them occur (Bae, 2002). Earlier findings on conversational data (Lappalainen, 2001) also suggest that important means of signaling nonunderstanding include confirmation checks, repair requests, and requests for clarification. This would seem to reflect a tendency toward self-regulation in English as a lingua franca (ELF), as speakers aim at mutually acceptable and comprehensible ways of expressing their intended meaning. However, research in the field has not been very extensive yet, and the findings come from different social and linguistic situations.

The present paper is an exploration into the use of English as lingua franca in a situation which in these days is familiar around the globe: spoken academic discourse in international degree programs in countries where English is neither the local language nor that of most of the international students. In such institutional encounters, the speakers and the discourse demands are fairly sophisticated compared with survival-level talk, tourism, or casual conversations in fleeting encounters. The paper reports on a larger research project seeking to discover and describe characteristic features in ELF discourse and the ways in which, and the extent to which, it might differ from comparable L1–L1 discourse and from L2–L1 discourse. The paper is primarily an empirical analysis of instances where either genuine misunderstandings were signaled by at least one of the interlocutors, or a noticeable effort was detected in attempts to avoid misunderstanding.

Background

In lingua franca research, the English language seems to have been virtually ignored until relatively recently (but see e.g. Knapp and Meierkord, 2002), and most of the research that has been carried out has had fairly clear applicational goals (e.g. Jenkins 2000). Some applied linguists have seen a clear need for research in this field (e.g. Seidlhofer, 2002). In scholarship on the English language, there has been little research, and even scholars genuinely interested in variation and change have tended to dismiss lingua franca use of English as of trivial interest (e.g. Trudgill, 2002). In corpus linguistics it has been ignored or put aside as just not worth serious attention (e.g. Hunston and Francis, 1999). International English has been seen in terms of "World English," that is, established vernacular varieties in postcolonial contexts (e.g. the ICE corpus project; Trudgill and Hannah, 1994), or as learner English (from a corpus perspective, e.g. Altenberg and Granger, 2001; Granger, 1998; Römer, 2003). This is a strange situation in view of the fact that most of the use of English today is by non-native speakers, and people speaking it as a foreign or second language have outnumbered its native speakers (cf. e.g. Crystal, 1997; Graddoll, 1997).

The study of English as lingua franca

Investigating English as lingua franca serves many kinds of research interest, not least because it has spread on such an unprecedented scale, but also because it has certain special features:

its speakers come from highly diverse linguistic backgrounds, and consequently the ensuing language contact is not restricted to two, as is characteristically the case in language contact studies. Moreover, all communicating parties have usually received formal instruction in English at some point. ELF is thus a "distant" contact language for many speakers, that is, adopted via foreign language instruction rather than personal contact.

Insofar as ELF is seen as a form of language contact, we can assume that similar mechanisms are at work, as have been discovered in language contact situations generally, such as, for example, "negotiation." Negotiation, that is, speakers changing their language to approximate what they believe to be the patterns of another language or dialect (Thomason, 2001; Winford, 2003), is likely to be at work also in ELF. Since ELF users have highly diverse backgrounds, their guesses about that which is shared are likely to be most accurate in the case of features which are most widely shared and least marked across languages. As these features tend to be generally the easiest to learn as well, we might predict that most pervasive ELF features are likely to be among the most widespread unmarked features of language.

Linguistic features which are regarded as universal discourse level phenomena but which are commonly thought to be hard for learners should find expression in ELF in one way or another, given that the communicators already are competent speakers of at least one natural language. Examples of such presumably universal discourse features would be making a distinction between information as either being "referred to" or "proclaimed" (Brazil, 1985), or discourse marking, which McCarthy (2001) claims is universal. Aijmer (2002) points out the centrality of discourse particles to language, and the fact that non-native speakers tend to get them wrong. It is generally known that discourse markers vary in scope and realization across languages (recent examples in, e.g., Altenberg, 2002; Behrens and Fabricius-Hansen 2002); what is not known is how the different ways of usage come together in lingua franca communication.

ELF can be expected to manifest features which arise from what can be called "variable learning" (cf. Mauranen, 2003), similar to contact-induced changes, commonly known as "imperfect learning" (cf. Thomason, 2001; and criticism of this term in Brutt-Griffler, 2002). Despite the often-heard claim that EFL textbooks present a very uniform picture of English, it is likely that local differences in teaching materials (locally produced in e.g. Europe), teaching practices, teacher qualifications, and ideologies of learning cause variation in learners' EFL repertoires, which are not points on a unidimensional scale, as "imperfect learning" might imply. Nevertheless, what is commonly called imperfect learning has been observed to cause structural or phonological rather than lexical changes in the target language, and more often than not, to lead to simplification of the target language structure. It is reasonable to assume that also ELF tends toward structural simplification. Simplification is far from a straightforward issue in linguistic analysis, and therefore empirical evidence from different kinds of discourse where it can be expected, such as ELF, will make valuable contributions to understanding it better.

In brief, we could depict ELF as being characterized by (1) varying degrees of bilingualism; (2) "dialectal" contact, in that speakers come from varying first language backgrounds, which can be seen as representing dialectal differences from the target language as well as each other; and (3) as language shift, "group second language acquisition," of a particular kind, namely one in which speakers shift languages in certain domains of use (e.g. the academic domain, which for many entails using English).

Lingua franca English in academic discourse communities

For many ELF speakers in academic contexts, English is a language of secondary socialization into the discourse community: many of these speakers have a domain-specific English repertoire which they may not even possess (or need) in their L1.

The academic community is a particular kind of discourse community (Swales, 1990, 1998), in other words, a social formation with its own discourses which serve both as resources and products of the community. The discourses of academic communities serve a gatekeeping function (Bourdieu and Passeron, 1977), bring cohesion to the community, and mark its identity. They thus serve to draw a line of demarcation between insiders and outsiders, "us" and "them." In brief, the discourses are category markers. Academic discourse communities exist both in local form, consisting of members who habitually interact, and as global communities, defined by a commitment to particular actions and discourses (Killingsworth, 1992). With ELFA (English as Lingua Franca in academic settings; see section 3 below) discourse communities, the local community is relevant as the scene for the spoken interaction, which needs to be performed and negotiated in the immediate context, whereas the global community is relevant as the general backdrop and the eventual target community for the participants. That which is global in the academic world, is already presumed or shared by participants in an international encounter, although the precise degree and nature of the shared elements are elusive, and need to be renegotiated with each encounter (for unexpected differences within European university communities, cf. Mauranen and Markkanen, 1994). It is membership in the international discourse community that is presumably the ultimate goal of those who participate in international programs. It is to be expected, then, that the primary identity constructed with the use of English is international, with its diverse associations. The linguistic form of such an identity is likely to be lingua franca English.

Clearly, the academic setting differs in many ways from the casual conversations that have been studied in some earlier ELF research, not to speak of simulated conversations or other simulated dyadic speech. These discussions have institutional communicative goals to achieve, which are not transactional in the traditional sense (as opposed to service encounters), nor are the participants gathered together to socialize (as in casual conversation), and finally, the speech events are not dyadic but multiparty discussions. Although the present data may look rather different from standard English, the speakers nevertheless manage to get demanding communicative business done, negotiating meanings, arguments, and alternative viewpoints. The speakers manage to engage in high-level and often abstract discussion, and to carry out the kinds of discourses which constitute the institutional settings they are in. This is no "survival English," it is using English for sophisticated professional purposes.

Misunderstanding

The default assumption in conversation is understanding, and normally understanding is not signaled; the smooth progression and expected turns in themselves indicate comprehension of previous turns. A misunderstanding is a potential breakdown point in conversation, or at least a kind of communicative turbulence. Misunderstandings may arise despite participants' communicative and interactive skills. Some can be traced back to linguistic causes, that is, a lack of shared expressions, which means that the interlocutors fail to assign a satisfactory interpretation to an expression. Yet not all misunderstandings need be based on gaps in the shared code. They may also relate to pragmatic matters in the discourse, such as the intended illocutionary force of a speech act, or to its relevance, or else a more "procedural" confusion about the progression of the discourse situation.

The discourses investigated here can be characterized as academic, with the dialectical global–local identity that this involves, as multicultural, since the actual face-to-face encounters involve engaging in cross-cultural interaction, and as international, with no clear or defined national anchorage.

Data and methods

Making sense of lingua franca English requires a good database. A corpus of spoken discourse is being compiled at the English department of the University of Tampere (cf. Mauranen, 2003). The ELFA corpus (English as Lingua Franca in academic settings) is being recorded in international degree programs and other university activities which are regularly carried out in English, such as international conferences and workshops, thesis defenses with international examiners, etc. Both universities involved in the recordings (the University of Tampere and the Technological University of Tampere) offer degree programs for international as well as Finnish students, which are conducted entirely in English. These include masters' and doctoral programs; and students as well as some of the staff come from a variety of countries, mostly European.

The approach toward data collection is comparable to that adopted in two US corpora, the Michigan Corpus of Academic Spoken English (MICASE, cf. Simpson et al., 1999) and the T2K-SWAL corpus at Northern Arizona (cf. Biber et al., 2001) in taking one university as a point of departure for corpus compilation, even though each of these corpora have their own characters, and are not built on exactly the same principles.

The social context in international academic settings is complex, and the data must reflect the social parameters involved. As a general principle, the data in the corpus are authentic in that they are not elicited but recorded in their normal use. They consist of complete individual speech events. Compilation criteria are "external," that is, determined by socially based definitions of the prominent genres of the discourse community, not linguistic register features. In practice, the "folk genres" of the discourse communities involved are given prominence, such as seminar, lecture, plenary talk, etc. Sessions with speakers who all share a L1 and foreign language courses are excluded. Native English speakers are not completely excluded; their presence in multiparty dialogic events is accepted, because it is in the nature of things in ELF discourses that L1 speakers mix with L2 speakers. But L1 speakers are excluded if they are speakers in monologic events, such as lectures.

The principal selection criteria for genres reflect their perceived importance in one way or another: (1) prototypicality, or the extent to which genres are shared and named in different disciplines; for example, lectures, thesis defenses, conference presentations; (2) influence: genres that affect a large number of participants; for example, introductory lecture courses, obligatory courses; (3) prestige: genres with high status in the discourse community; for example, guest lectures, plenary presentations in conferences. The criteria converge in some genres, others fulfill only one. In practice, the selection is limited by a number of contingencies—for instance, sometimes courses are attended by Finnish students only, and the language gets switched to Finnish.

The present data are taken from an early stage of the ELFA: the first five hours of recordings were available for the analyses at hand. Four seminar sessions were recorded and transcribed, and one conference discussion. All situations included speakers with different language backgrounds, of different ages, and both genders. One senior faculty member was present in each session, the rest were senior undergraduates, that is, third- or fourth-year students. The seminar participants' backgrounds are summarized in Table 15.1 for those who actually spoke during the session.

Of the conference participants, it was harder to obtain detailed information on all who spoke. The total number of participants was 29, of whom the nine who spoke are included. Their details are presented in Table 15.2.

Together with my research assistant, Sari Lappalainen, we each searched the data separately, picking up instances of misunderstanding, then compared our results. I then went on to distinguish types of signaling, and finally looked briefly into the kinds of things that were misunderstood.

Table 15.1 Seminar participants in terms of first language, gender, and age

L1		Gender		Age	
Finnish	9	male	14	17–23	14
Polish	4	female	12	24–30	7
Lithuanian	3			31–50	2
English	3			51+	3
Dutch	1				
Russian	1				
German	1				
Slovak	1				
Somali	1				
Arabic/English	1				
Japanese	1				
Total	26		26		26

Table 15.2 Conference participants in terms of first language, gender, and age

L1		Gender		Age	
English	4	male	4	17–23	–
German	1	female	5	24–30	2
Finnish	1			31–50	7
Turkish	1				
Unknown	2				
Total	9		9		9

One of the first observations that struck both initial analysts about the data was the infrequent occurrence of misunderstandings. However, it is hard to think of a clear norm against which to compare this, apart from an intuitive expectation. It is true that frequent misunderstandings in L1–L2 conversations have sometimes been reported, which may raise expectations concerning ELF usage as well, but given that the situations are not directly comparable, hypotheses of highly frequent misunderstandings based on this analogy appear too hasty—and, as it turns out, not confirmed.

How did misunderstanding take place, then, and, in particular, since it seemed to be rare, what happened instead of overt misunderstanding? At the outset, it is clear that if we restrict misunderstandings to cases where one is explicitly recognized by at least one of the interlocutors, this is already limiting attention to "retrospective" misunderstanding only. If the interactive situation is to be captured more fully, we should also include "prospective" behavior. From this perspective, the speakers' proactive behavior is equally relevant. Clearly, including advance prevention of misunderstanding makes bolder guesses about speaker behavior than limiting attention to overtly marked misunderstandings, but since preventive strategies by L2 speakers have been observed before, the bold guess seems motivated. Thus it was decided to look for communication strategies observed earlier in similar circumstances, such as repetition, explication, and overexplicitness (cf. Tarone and Yule, 1987). Transcripts from comparable discourses in the MICASE corpus were consulted to throw light on interaction between native speakers. The findings are presented below in the following way: first, an overview is given of the kinds of signaling found, followed by strategies of preventing misunderstanding. The third phase illustrates the objects of misunderstanding, and finally some borderline cases are briefly discussed, so as to make clearer what was excluded from the analysis, despite the inevitable fuzziness of the borders.

Signaling misunderstanding

Straightforward misunderstandings were not very many: the researchers independently identified six clear cases among the 29 that were agreed on for inclusion as misunderstandings or their active prevention. They were signaled by direct questions or repetition of the troublesome item. It was more common to treat misunderstanding indirectly, mostly by clarifying or preventive action, which was jointly constructed by the participants. As the most typical behavior, this deserves a section of its own (see below).

Specific question

To start with the clear cases, direct, focused questions on an expression or its meaning are perhaps the easiest to detect and also the most unequivocal signs of lack of understanding. Four instances of this kind were found in the data. In the first, fairly straightforward example (example (1)), the lack of comprehension concerns an individual lexical item.

(1)
S1:   yeah well i tried to explain this by centre periphery
S1:   yeah you tried [yeah]
S6:   [but it's] i mean i'm not a Finn so i (xx) so much insight that's the problem
S3:   but that's an asset
S1:   hm?
S3:   that's an asset that you're not a Finn in this in this topic i think
S1:   what does an asset mean?
S3:   it's an advantage
S1:   ok yeah (.) well (.)

After S3 has used the word asset, S1 first tries to express his lack of understanding with a minimal, unfocused signal (hm?). This elicits a repetition of the utterance by S3, with some expansion. Presumably S3 takes the minimal signal to indicate mishearing or insufficient specificity. Such requests were classified as "minimal incomprehension signals" in the analysis. As S3's response proves to be of little help, S1 elaborates his request by expanding it into a direct question, a specific request for clarification. S3 then glosses the problematic word asset as advantage, which S1 then accepts (ok yeah), and goes on to discuss the issue. Signaling comprehension is made explicitly, which was also found by Kurhila (2003a) in L1–L2 conversations. This seems to indicate an enhanced cooperative effort toward ensuring continued communication.

Repetition of problematic items

The second type of signaling misunderstanding also concerns an individual linguistic item, the meaning of which is unclear to the speaker. Instances in the sample were rare: only three cases. The strategy of repeating the source of the problem is more informative than the vague minimal incomprehension signal exemplified in (1), as it indicates the source of the problem. It is, however, also a minimal response in that it is a single-word utterance.

(2)
S1: mean the Turkish immigrant community would naturally congregate and that's the whole cause is that right?
S2: *eh congregate?*
S1: they would naturally form some of the groups and that's the only requirement
S2: oh that that that is another contradiction actually [Turkish people]
S1:   [sounds a bit difficult to believe]
S2: are never able to do work together so we already have eh (.) only in Helsinki there are let's say about a thousand Turkish people and we have six seven different associations and which fight with each other and (. . .) so that is another aspect to it so one association doesn't mean doesn't eh represent the whole

Difficulty is signaled here by a simple repetition of the problematic item. After S1 provides a paraphrase, S2 goes on to respond to the question. The minimal signal seems to work reasonably well with many individual lexical items, but sometimes simple repetition leaves too much space for alternative interpretations, and what gets offered as clarification may not match the need, as can already be seen in the next section. In the exchange, one of the interactants (S1) happens to have English as L1, but the exchange is similar to purely non-native interaction. Native English speakers were not excluded from the data in multiparty events, as will be remembered from above.

Indirect signaling of misunderstanding

The third category in signaling comprehension problems is what I would like to call "indirect" on the grounds that, although some signaling of problems takes place, it is unfocused and gives little indication of what is unclear to the speaker. The minimal incomprehension signal (hm?) in example (1) was one such instance. Example (3) below is similar, even though it ostensibly involves the repetition of a single item, as was the case in example (2). Yet it is obvious that the repetition in this case cannot indicate ignorance of a lexical meaning, and therefore interpreting it as a request for further information is the only option left to the interlocutors. But the kind of information called for is open. Assigning relevance to the repetition must thus work on other grounds than an explicit demand for clarification.

(3)
S1: and one question when you say that eh (.) that when European allies prefer to spend money on social welfare at home than on the military confirms the rule that democracies at the time of peace are hardly motivated to spend money on the military do you think that this this applies to the United States for?
S2: *United [States]*
S1:   [it's] a demo- democracy and still spends a lot of money on on the mil-
S2: yeah but i think that and this is a personal conception and eh i think that a super power /. . ./

In example (3), S2 responds to S1's question by repeating United States, which S1 takes as a clarification request, and responds by offering an explanation of the connection implied in his question. Since S2's repetition is not a sign of misunderstanding the proper noun itself, it is interpretable either as indicating puzzlement over the comparison requested, or a way of gaining a little time for considering the answer. S1 seems to interpret it in the former way. S2 acknowledges the clarification (yeah), but goes on to contest the interpretation offered by S1 (but I think . . .). The heavy hedging that S2 prefaces the answer with (I think that and this is a personal conception and I think) would point to the second possibility above, that the repetition of the item was to gain time; all this hedging is also seemingly redundant, in view of S1's original formulation of the question, which already asks for the speaker's personal view (do you think that this applies . . .).

Occasionally, even questions which are direct in their form are quite unspecific; they leave the focus of the query for the interlocutor to interpret, as in example (4).

(4)
S1:   maybe that's why
S2:   [yeah]
S3:   [maybe] there's barriers
S2:   *what?*
S3:   [they] are language barriers
S2:   [yeah]
S1:   yes
S2:   yeah yeah okay

S2's question (what?) is unfocused, but S3 takes it up and responds by an expansion of the first message. It is possible that S2 misheard the first time, since S3 intervened in the dialogue between S2 and S1. S2 and S3 overlapped when S3 asked the question, and it is possible that S2 was not paying attention; the yeah she uttered could have been intended as prefacing a turn. S3 nevertheless appears to interpret the question to concern the clarity or relevance of his suggestion.

In this section we have dealt with cases where misunderstanding has occurred and has been recognized, and action has been taken to remedy the problem in an effort to secure continued discourse progressing on the lines of the purpose of the setting. The misunderstandings were typically signaled by questions of some kind. Whether focused or not, these questions constituted an important means of not letting vague or potentially incorrect understanding pass; the participants cooperated toward achieving a sufficient basis in their mutual understanding to continue the discourse. The seemingly redundant signaling of comprehension also seemed to reflect a heightened awareness of a need for cooperation.

Preventing misunderstanding

The prevention of misunderstanding, or proactive work in talk, appeared as a striking feature of this ELF interaction. Speakers were requesting clarification or confirmation frequently, and subsequently rephrasing their utterances or providing additional explanations. In these proactive instances, no overt marker of a misunderstanding is in evidence other than seemingly spontaneously arising additional checks, explanations, or clarifications. Or alternatively, there is active co-construction of expressions which the current speaker seems to be lacking, that is, participants other than the current speaker initiate the production of an expression that is acceptable. Acceptability is here understood in terms of whether an expression or repair allows the discourse to proceed, and judged by how the discourse moves on—with further clarifications or searches, or with apparent satisfaction with the degree of shared understanding.

Confirmation checks

The first kind of speech act that seems to be in active use to guard against misunderstanding is a confirmation check. This often takes the form of a minimal check, as in examples (5) and (7), but can be more explicit, too, as in example (6). Especially the more explicit kind of question is also in use in L1 seminar discourses, but often in argumentative contexts it takes the form "*are you saying*" (cf. Mauranen, 2002).

> (5)
> S1: /. . . / eh (.) then there are how to convince your reader? and this is also i-
> this is now kind of a (.) eh (.) i- is included in the first part of the pap- of this
> (.) paper eh using authorities data data can be also own experiences and
> observations, theories, concepts, methods, previous studies, also morals, values,
> and ethics (.) as i think we see in Renata's paper (.) *yeah?* (.) one part
> S2: *yeah*

Example (5) is a typical case where a speaker inserts a confirmation check (yeah?) in his or her turn, and somebody responds to it, as S2 does here by a minimal acknowledgment (yeah). A specific, explicit request for clarification is illustrated by the following example (6), where the request "*did i understand right?*" is followed by a confirmation response (yeah) by S2.

> (6)
> S1: so this is i i think this is an interesting question because this goes back to eh my
> question about the eh nature of of NATO is it a political or military organisation
> you you say that it is about security and i think you are imply that it is when
> talking about security is about eh military security or or it is that just that that's
> the core of of security as such and and this being eh transformed to mo- a more
> political organisation is somehow eh counterproductive from that viewpoint *did
> i understand right?*
> S2: yeah from from point of view of my country i think it is

Minimal confirmation checks clearly have many uses in ELF communication, as in example (7), where the original signaling of disagreement by S2 is followed by S1's query as to whether this was indeed meant as a disagreement. After a couple of repetitions the interlocutors seem to accept that S2 disagrees with S1's understanding of the point, and S1 yields the floor to S2. Again it looks like the repeated "*no*" signals comprehension, not necessarily disagreement.

> (7)
> S1: yeah but the only thing i probably would like to answer you that you you (.)
> ok the people are there now so you have try to deal with them if we all s- start
> like to remember or like you know start suddenly thinking so how actually
> Swedes co- like come up to be in Finland so you can also think about this maybe
> occupants roots in a way [so]
> S2: [no] no
> S1: *no?*
> S2: no
> S1: *no?* [ok]
> S2: [no] it's not really that there were Swedes or /. . ./

It seems from this example that ELF speakers can make good use of small linguistic devices. The negotiation with the seemingly minimal "no" here achieves a communicative purpose which accomplishes a turn change and takes the argumentation forward.

Interactive repair

Speakers in multiparty encounters often engage in co-construction of expressions, just as people do in dyadic interaction. Such co-constructive behavior occurs relatively often (in the present sample, about a third of the selected cases). It is useful to distinguish between "retroactive" (backward-looking) and "proactive" repairs (those prospecting ahead). Although most repairs play a prospective role in that their major goal is to enable continuation of the discourse, self-repairs in particular are strongly proactive as opposed to interactive repairs, which tend to take place when a problem has been recognized. Example (8) serves as an illustration of retroactive co-construction; it is relatively long, because it contains two interactive repair sequences.

(8)
S1:   eh if you think eh that NATO has a future it doesn't [(xxxx)]
S2:   [we need it or we don't]
S1:   *we need it or we don't thank you*
S2:   we need it or we don't (.) according to your opinion
S3:   my country eh we came (xxx) and eh we wanted eh to access NATO because eh we felt that eh we would more secure more secure and eh i think eh now if it is transforming into this political organisation with with Russia is on i don't think that Polish people will promote it because it was eh just we wanted eh somehow protection against Russia even now eh so we m- may not approve this k- this eh direction of transformation eh but i think that still it is important for us eh to have this i don't know con- consciousness that eh (.) eh this eh idea of collective defence is works still now so i think eh it is eh it it has left eh
S2:   *sense of security (.) feel sense of security*
S3:   *yeah but eh on the other hand this sense* eh can be a truly a real a real *not only a sense* it should be some real eh basis for that . . .

In this sequence, the current speaker (S1), who is trying to ask a question of S3, appears to be lacking a suitable expression, and a third participant (S2) comes to assistance. This exchange differs from those above with signaled misunderstanding (cf. the section on "Signaling misunderstanding") in that there is no question or repeated item to prompt help from other participants, only a search for an expression. S2 provides help by suggesting a formulation for part of the question, which S1 seems to accept by repeating it and thanking S2. S2 then takes the floor and rephrases the whole question, apparently to S3's satisfaction, since she begins to answer it. However, in the course of her answer she in turn seems to run into problems, or appears to be searching for an expression, and at this point S2 offers his help again. Although S3 recognizes the help (*yeah*), this seems to confirm understanding, but clearly it was not quite what she was looking for, and she goes on ("*but on the other hand*") to produce a different view from S2's suggestion ("*not only a sense it should be some real basis*"). It looks like S3 in fact did not intend to say what S2 finished for her as he completed her turn. This latter co-construction therefore appears less happy than the first one.

Self-repair

Monologic self-repair is very common in these data, and works proactively. There is little point in trying to count sequences with self-repairs, because they take place so frequently, so I just illustrate them here. Quantitative comparison with L1 data must remain impressionistic; it seems, however, by going through several seminar discussion transcripts from both the MICASE corpus and the present data that, although there is considerable individual variation in the tendency to self-repair, virtually all ELF speakers engage in rephrasing their own speech to a considerable extent, while some native speakers do it relatively little. Example (9) is a fairly typical, longish ELF turn:

(9)

S1: /. . ./ conditions for minorities ah then it will be no questions eh it will be no conflicts between the ethnic people and eh minorities Russian minorities (.) so eh in Lithuania there is no such question about these in eh uhm i about *Letvi-Latvia* i'm not sure because i'm not very familiar with the situation but i know that in Estonia still exist eh a lot of problems between local government and eh minorities (.) and what about a another part of your question eh it's eh about *a general position of Balti- general Baltic states' eh position* in world yes in just ah (.) as it was a t- (.) is it *okay*

S3: yeah

S1: *okay* @ as it was told before eh that eh as you (x) you (x) told before that *main roles eh the main roles* are in uhm in France, German uhm (.) in NATO i i'm talking about NATO ah in France, German, Great Britain and another big countries' hands so and in other small countries it's like the Baltic states they only can eh follow them (.) because *they will eh at f- maybe at first they will not have any eh eager and any important eh ah any (.) they will not be allowed it (. . .) to have a big influence to make big influence* to all this politic so eh and eh i would i mentioned in my presentation that eh now (.) Baltic states want to eh uhm (. . .) mm to define them like eh European countries and they want to improve their eh (.) uhm image that is @ i- image not like not as eh a former Soviet Union's eh state but like a independent and European countries so it's my point

In this extract, the speaker makes several false starts. There is one clear comprehension check (S1: *is it okay*; S3: *yeah*; S1: *okay*), apparently relating to whether it is all right to go on to answer a second question, that is, checking the appropriateness of a speech act function within the context rather than appropriateness of a word choice. The repairs include many proper names, but also rephrasing the content (*"between the ethnic people and eh minorities Russian minorities"*) or wording (*"then it will be no questions eh it will be no conflicts"*), or grammar (*"main roles eh the main roles; to have a big influence to make big influence"*). The grammar type did not come up in the MICASE seminars, but adding hedges on the second round, like here (*"they will eh at f- maybe at first they will"*), also appeared in those data. Interestingly, Kurhila (2003a) also found that non-native speakers often initiated grammatical self-repairs, even though native speakers did not respond to ungrammaticality in their speech, but rather to the meaning and successful interaction.

Self-repairs are not often highly explicit in their attempts to secure comprehension, but occasionally speakers seem to show a high level of language awareness. In example (10), the speaker goes to some length to explain her choice of language usage.

(10)

S1:   /. . ./ what was done in different chapters? if you have this kind of i call chapter also this one little part of eh eh i mean there can be different chapters in in one page they are perhaps subchapter- chapters really yeah (.) eh (.)

It appears that the speaker lacks the word *paragraph* in this case, and shows some awareness of a missing term ("*I call chapter also this one little part*"), along with some awareness of her choice not being entirely satisfactory ("*they are perhaps subchapter- chapters really*"). This explanation seems to function to prevent misunderstanding, and at the same time to indicate her awareness that this is likely to be an unorthodox use and therefore unfamiliar to others.

This section has focused on means of preventing incomprehension, reflecting the participants' self-regulatory discourse strategies. Frequent comprehension checks and responses to them suggest both willingness to cooperate toward comprehension and an awareness of its precariousness. Repair work also indicates the salience of comprehension and the potential problems related to it in these encounters. Both interactive, that is coconstructed repairs, and self-repairs are highly cooperative means of ensuring the flow of intelligible and mutually satisfactory discourse.

What was misunderstood

It is generally assumed that misunderstandings arise from matters relating to the language code between L1 and L2 speakers—mainly on account of the latter having a defective command of the target language. In addition, culture-specific misunderstandings are often reported. The ELF situation might not be similar to L1–L2 encounters in this respect, but since so little ELF research has been carried out, this is hard to predict. In any case I felt the contents of misunderstandings would be worth a look in addition to the signaling and prevention tactics. I therefore considered the kinds of misunderstanding that occurred: whether and what kinds of linguistic categories would be involved (e.g. lexical, grammatical, speech act), whether culture-specific misunderstandings would occur, or whether there would be problems in grasping matters of propositional content, or procedural conventions, for example.

The type that first comes to mind is the linguistic. As we already saw in the section on signaling misunderstanding, queries about the meanings of individual lexical items are made now and then. But an obvious misunderstanding can also arise from apparent mishearing. In example (11), the misheard utterance is given a relevant interpretation and treated seriously.

(11)

S1:   /. . ./ but the (.) eh designing or definite factor was that South African army was beaten in two battles (.) eh then (.) in fact what you ask about Finnish role in peacekeeping operations eh that is also an interesting thing in the Finnish history (.) eh

S2:   s- something to do with importing cars?

S1:   *yeah important class but*   [i-]

S2:   [importing] it

S1:   *importing? no but it's im- it's important* in a way that if one looks who had been on the field got some field experience those are also those officers who will be in the highest ranks in the Finnish army afterwards so /. . ./

In this case, it is very difficult to see the relevance of S2's question. S1's preceding turn is long and deals with different matters in UN and Finnish foreign policy, but even taking all of it into account, neither cars, imports, nor even generally economic matters are mentioned at all. It is therefore relatively easy to understand S1's mishearing what S2 says more in accordance with what S1 actually has been saying—and to continue a train of thought that was triggered off by this interpretation of the mishearing. The dissonant *importing* is simply cast aside quickly, even after S2 has ventured to repeat it. S1 insists on his interpretation and maintains a consistent perspective despite S2's correction. Misunderstanding of this kind probably takes place in L1–L1 speech as well (even though I did not find examples in the MICASE): a turn is misheard in a way which renders it relevant or meaningful to the hearer. It requires special action (like repetition here) to bring the original utterance to attention so as to ensure its correct hearing. The assignment of a meaningful interpretation reflects the principle of charity, a kind of suspension of disbelief, which characterizes cooperative discourse generally. It may be particularly salient in communication between speakers who are aware of their different linguistic and cultural origins.

In some instances, uncertainty concerned the interpretation of a speech act rather than linguistic form or individual items, as is the case in example (12).

(12)
S1: @ basically is this in some way really? i mean that's of course we've we have all seen this question of apartheid thing in South Africa
S2: in what in [South yeah]
S1: [in South Africa] apartheid is it in some way comparable or not to that (x)?
S2: no (.) *you mean why did i refer to that?* i was more like when i was defining why why minority should be minority not by the amount but rather by what po- kind of power they have /. . ./

Here S1 starts by asking a question of S2, who first replies with a request for clarification ("*in what in South*"), thereby eliciting a reformulation of the question from S1. After S1's rephrasing, S2 first gives a short answer ("*no*"), but then seems to move on to a new interpretation: S1 was really after the relevance of her earlier reference to South Africa in the first place. This exchange is therefore about the function of a particular earlier stretch in the ongoing discourse, and resembles ordinary L1 discourse. Example (13) is more complicated and shows a clearer misunderstanding, not just an alternative interpretation of the intended speech act.

(13)
S1: about Stalin i heard i heard that eh during the seventies they had a vote in the city council that should they tear this old (x) castle (.) @ away and build a new techno city and it was like one or two votes that @ that saved it so it was pretty close that that @ those castles wouldn't be there anymore
S2: why should they be?
S1: but but somehow i [think]
S2: [if you go] to Turku you can see that many old places have been put down and new buildings (.) valueless buildings have been build instead on places and this you could do the same for the dooming cathedral in Turku
S1: *yes but i i meant that it was pretty close* that
    [if you are a tourist what you go to Tallinn to see (.) and]
S2: [yeah yeah i unders- yeah yeah yeah yeah that that] that's the reason why many tourist go to Tallinn yeah (. . .) and it was pretty close here in Tampere that this old city hall (.) mustn't be p- put down (.) that was also depending on just

a couple of votes (. . .) *so we we shouldn't blame socialism or it's it's in ev- every system the same* modern is more valuable than the past

In example (13), S1 first takes S2's "why" question to be challenging his point. He then starts defending himself, but S2 intervenes with a comparable example from a different situation; S1 then begins again to defend his original idea ("*but i i meant that it was pretty close*"), not having seen the function of the counterexample as S2 appears to have intended it. S2 then comes in again, now laying down his intention in more detail: he spells out what he agrees about with S1, bringing in another analogous example, and finally explicitly saying what it was he had intended to challenge ("*so we shouldn't blame socialism it's in every system the same*"), that is, the generalization he was illustrating in his first turn. Speaker intentions can be misunderstood, but when it becomes evident that there has been a misunderstanding, interpretations can subsequently be revised and a new response sequence begun, as in example (14).

(14)

S1: ok but what can we do if we say Estonian citizen citizenships who studies in in Estonia at school but teaching in Russian? is it ok in Russian? i know some

S2: no ok they because they they have a law on minority you ki- you you you have a right to to have your school and language but it's i mean how i understand this problem it's it's kind of like the the whole policy it's just like to to wait to somehow to put Russian on the back and maybe it's fair i don't know but like for example they have a school but they there is no fund from government so people can't really eh

S1: so there is another problem how to integrate such kind of people who who who are Estonian but they don't speak [Estonian?]

S2:   [oh you] mean Estonian?

S1: yeah i mean [e- e-] Estonian citizenships they are they are Estonian

S2:   [oh]

S2: but they study in school in Russian and teaching is in the Russian /. . ./

Here S1 reformulates ("*so there is another problem . . .*") his original question after he has received an unsatisfactory answer from S2 to his first formulation. By reformulating he seems to indicate that he believes S2 would have answered differently had she understood the question as intended. The next turn ("*oh you mean Estonian?*") from S2 confirms this interpretation. S1 starts again: he reformulates the question and the question–answer sequence starts from the beginning.

Finally, sometimes apparent mismatches in the estimated level of explicitness appeared in connection with conventions or procedures. This is perhaps the closest that we come to culture-specific misunderstandings, but it is virtually impossible to separate academic culture from local culture in these cases, which emerged in their overlap areas, as in example (15).

(15)

S1: /. . ./ this was the this was the reason why there was made eh apart from all the concessions were made one demand that was a fifteen years transition-transitional period for the for the so called arctic farming and eh

S2: five

S1: *five?*

S2: *minutes left*

S1:   ok @ five minutes five minutes ok eh about fifteen years not far eh (.) eh (.)
        eh so this was the only demand because to /. . ./

S1 is a student, whose presentation is interrupted by the teacher's (S2) comment on time.
The student repeats the item, which S2 takes as a request for clarification, and expands on his
original signal. S1 acknowledges this ("*ok*"), and then repeats the phrase "*five minutes*" a couple
of times, apparently to gain time to assess the need to reorganize the rest of his presentation.
Clearly, in this example we have moved quite far from understanding linguistic surface forms.

Problems of comprehending linguistic, procedural, or propositional meanings were
discernible in this material, but I found no clear evidence of culture-based comprehension
problems, at least not in the traditional sense of "national culture." Apart from the most surface-
level misunderstandings concerning the linguistic meaning of items, the other types are not
specific to lingua franca communication, but likely to occur elsewhere independently of the
speakers' native languages.

It is perhaps interesting to note that the communicative turbulence caused by misunderstanding was eventually overcome in every case. It seems a remarkable achievement in view
of the demanding situation. The kinds of misunderstanding that occurred reflected the strong
orientation toward content that characterizes these encounters. The same is true of the strategies
for coping with misunderstanding as well as those of preventing them—the participants seem
concerned that shared meanings are achieved to a degree that they can accept. To this end,
they are willing to regulate and modify their discourse, seeking and offering alternative expressions as well as assurances of continued comprehension.

[The author discusses several borderline examples to clarify the criteria of data selection.]

Conclusion

Misunderstandings in ELFA communication were not as common as originally expected, not at
least in their overt expressions. Whether they are frequent or not, however, seems to depend
on what they are compared with: in L1–L1 data, overt misunderstandings of linguistic expressions
seem to be less frequent than here. What appeared to characterize ELF was the considerable
effort invested in preventing misunderstanding—there were frequent self-repairs, in fact in almost
every turn, and there were several instances of co-construction of expressions and seemingly
unsolicited clarifications and repetitions, which appeared to arise from a perception of the speaker
in need of help. Some misunderstandings were of a kind that could be related to gaps in the shared
language code, but not all. Many misunderstandings that arose were related to discourse pragmatics.
Speaker intentions with respect to speech act functions were misunderstood, and relevance was
assigned incorrectly (albeit charitably) to interlocutors' utterances.

No interactive grammatical correction occurred. In contrast, self-repairs often involved
grammatical reformulations, which did not seem to be the case in the MICASE data, where
native speakers' self-repairs tend to deal with paraphrasing longer stretches of meaning rather
than local choices of syntax, or with reformulating the level of certainty by adding or removing
hedges. Grammatical self-repairs, that is, speakers' initiations of grammatical reformulations
in their own speech before closing their turns, thus appeared to distinguish the ELFA data
from native speakers' and resemble L2 speakers' behavior: similar observations were made by
Kurhila (2003a) in L1–L2 conversations of Finnish. In her conversations, non-natives often
resorted to grammatical self-repairs, although their native speaker interlocutors were not
concerned with un-grammaticality, and never indicated grammatical incomprehension. Kurhila
suggests the non-native speakers' orientation to grammatical correctness and their desire to

elicit help from the L1 speakers as one possible explanation for this. However, in the context of solely non-native speakers, the emphasis may be less on anticipated help; the grammatical searches may derive from a faith in the positive role of grammatical correctness in facilitating mutual intelligibility.

The function of the frequent repetitions and self-repairs was not always easy to determine, since their primary motive could be either making meanings clearer, or interaction smoother, but also gaining more planning time. Sometimes there are other indicators in favor of one interpretation or the other, but it is also thinkable that several purposes are simultaneously served by the same behavior.

The most straightforward signals of misunderstanding were direct questions and item repetitions. In addition, active co-construction of expressions was taken to indicate a perceived communication problem. Mishearing or misunderstanding was treated gently by participants, and the principle of charity seemed to be strong in making sense of interlocutors' speech. The previously reported "let it pass" strategy was not observed here. It is possible that it is not a feasible option in academic discussions—but it is also possible that it simply does not manifest itself in a multiparty discussion. After all, if some participants do not follow everything, they may remain silent and leave the active participation to others.

Frequent signaling of comprehension occurred, often with minimal responses (*yes, yeah, ok*), which is in accordance with Kurhila's (2003a) findings on L1–L2 conversations. This may thus be a strategy adopted by speakers without a shared native language, rather than be a special characteristic of L2 speakers interacting with native speakers.

In all, these conversations manifested a strong orientation toward securing mutual intelligibility: frequent confirmation checks, self-repairs which include grammatical self-correction, and signaling of comprehension are all indications of attempts to ascertain a smooth flow of interaction, which is a prerequisite for a successful management of the discourse goals of the community. Lingua franca speakers thus appear to work hard to achieve mutual understanding, quite possibly on the basis of the natural commonsense assumption that it is not easy to achieve without special effort.

This study shows some of the potential of ELF data in making sense of English as it is used today. We need to break out of the confines of accepting only the native speaker as worth investigating, and above all stop considering second and foreign language users as eternal "learners" on an interminable journey toward perfection in a target language. Speakers may opt out of the role of learner at any stage, and take on the identity of language users, who successfully manage demanding discourses despite imperfections in the code. As we saw here, lingua franca speakers show considerable awareness of the requirements of the communicative situation in which they find themselves, and are able to regulate their language and interaction accordingly. A distinct orientation toward content allows minor imperfections to pass, but only as long as they do not hamper intelligibility; maintaining a sufficient level of intelligibility is constantly monitored in cooperative interaction. The relatively strong orientation toward grammar, manifested in the self-repairs, is probably also best understood as a self-regulatory mechanism rather than an unspecific desire to approach some linguistic ideal such as standard English.

Appendix: transcription conventions

The transcription is broad, that is, minor pronunciation deviations are not transcribed, because the data are intended to be suitable for corpus searches, and the soundtrack will be available to researchers.

The speakers in each extract have been labeled as S1, S2, etc., in the order in which they appear in the extract.

(.)	pause of up to five seconds
(. . .)	pause longer than five seconds
@	laughter
[ ]	overlapping speech
(x)	transcription not possible; each x roughly standing for a word
?	question intonation
/. . ./	speech not included in the example
italics	used here to highlight parts of the transcript discussed in the text

References

Aijmer, K. (2002). *English discourse particles*. Amsterdam: Benjamins.

Altenberg, B. (2002). Concessive connectors in English and Swedish. In H. Hasselgard, S. Johansson, B. Behrens, and C. Fabricius-Hansen (eds), *Information structure in cross-linguistic perspective* (pp. 21–44). Amsterdam: Rodopi.

Altenberg, B. and Granger, S. (2001). The grammatical and lexical patterning of make in native and non-native student writing. *Applied Linguistics*, 22(2), 173–89.

Bae, J. H. (2002). Discourse strategies solving trouble in German lingua franca communication. In K. Knapp and C. Meierkord (eds), *Lingua franca communication* (pp. 195–216). Frankfurt: Lang.

Behrens, B. and Fabricius-Hansen, C. (2002). Connectives in contrast: a discourse semantic study on elaboration based on corpus research. In H. Hasselgard, S. Johansson, B. Behrens, and C. Fabricius-Hansen (eds), *Information structure in cross-linguistic perspective* (pp. 45–62). Amsterdam: Rodopi.

Biber, D., Reppen, R., Clark, V., and Walter, J. (2001). Representing spoken language in university settings: the design and construction of the spoken component of the T2K-SWAL corpus. In R. C. Simpson and J. M. Swales (eds), *Corpus linguistics in North America* (pp. 48–57). Ann Arbor: University of Michigan Press.

Bourdieu, P. and Passeron, J. C. (1977). *Reproduction in education, society and culture*. London: Sage.

Brazil, D. (1985). *The communicative value of intonation*. Birmingham: English Language Research, University of Birmingham.

Brutt-Griffler, J. (2002). *World English. A study of its development*. Clevedon: Multilingual Matters.

Crystal, D. (1997). *English as a global language*. Cambridge: Cambridge University Press.

Firth, A. (1990). "Lingua franca" negotiations: towards an interactional approach. *World Englishes*, 9(3), 269–80.

Graddoll, D. (1997). *The future of English?* London: The British Council.

Granger, S. (ed.) (1998). *Learner English on computer*. London: Longman.

Hunston, S. and Francis, G. (1999). *Pattern grammar*. Amsterdam: Benjamins.

Jenkins, J. (2000). *The phonology of English as an international language*. Oxford: Oxford University Press.

Killingsworth, M. J. (1992). Discourse communities local and global. *Rhetoric Review*, 11, 110–22.

Knapp, K. and Meierkord, C. (eds) (2002). *Lingua franca communication*. Frankfurt: Lang.

Kurhila, S. (2003a). *Co-constructing understanding in second language conversation*. Helsinki: University of Helsinki.

Kurhila, S. (2003b). Kakkoskielistä vuorovaikutusta [Second-language interaction]. *Virittäjä*, 2003(4), 580–4.

Lappalainen, S. (2001). English as lingua franca. Towards fluent communication. Unpublished MA thesis, University of Turku.

McCarthy, M. (2001). *Issues in applied linguistics*. Cambridge: Cambridge University Press.

Mauranen, A. (2002). "one thing I'd like to clarify . . ." Observations of academic speaking. In A. Nurmi (ed.), *Helsinki English Studies, vol. 2: Corpora in Today's English Studies*. Available online at www.eng. helsinki.fi/hes.

Mauranen, A. (2003). The corpus of English as lingua franca in academic settings. *TESOL Quarterly*, 37(3), 513–27.

Mauranen, A. and Markkanen, R. (eds) (1994). *Students abroad. Aspects of exchange students' language*. Jyväskylä: The Language Centre for Finnish Universities.

Meierkord, C. (1998). *Lingua franca English: characteristics of successful non-native–non-native speaker discourse.* Erfurt Electronic Studies in English, 1998. Available online at http://webdoc.sub.gwdg.de/edoc/ia/eese/eese.html

Nikula, T. (1996). *Pragmatic force modifiers. A study in interlanguage pragmatics.* Jyväskylä: University of Jyväskylä.

Römer, U. (2003). Looking at "looking"—functions and contexts of progressives in spoken English and "school" English. Paper given at the ICAME Conference, Guernsey, April 23–27.

Seidlhofer, B. (2002). Closing a conceptual gap: the case for a description of English as a lingua franca. *International Journal of Applied Linguistics,* 11(2), 133–58.

Simpson, R. C., Briggs, S. L., Ovens, J., and Swales, J. M. (1999). *The Michigan corpus of academic spoken English.* Ann Arbor: The Regents of the University of Michigan.

Swales, J. (1990). *Genre analysis. English in academic and research settings.* Cambridge: Cambridge University Press.

Swales, J. (1998). *Other floors, other voices. A textography of a small university building.* Mahwah, NJ: Erlbaum.

Tarone, E. and Yule, G. (1987). Communication strategies in east–west interactions. In L. Smith (ed.), *Discourse across cultures: strategies in world Englishes,* (pp. 49–65). New York: Prentice Hall.

Thomason, S. G. (2001). *Language contact.* Edinburgh: Edinburgh University Press.

Trudgill, P. (2002). *Sociolinguistic variation and change.* Edinburgh: Edinburgh University Press.

Trudgill, P. and Hannah, J. (1994). *International English: a guide to varieties of standard English.* London: Arnold.

Ventola, E. and Mauranen, A. (1990). *Tutkijat ja englanniksi kirjoittaminen* [Researchers and writing in English]. Helsinki: Helsinki University Press.

Winford, D. (2003). *An introduction to contact linguistics.* Oxford: Blackwell.

PART IV: NOTES FOR STUDENTS AND INSTRUCTORS

Study questions

1 According to Holliday, what are the differences between small culture, sub-culture, and large culture? What problems are inherent in the large culture and sub-culture approaches? What benefits can a 'small culture' approach bring to language education?
2 What is the relationship between small culture and discourse? Holliday argues that, 'In many ways the discourse community is a small culture'. Do you agree?
3 What are the general developmental trends in the study of pragmatic and discourse abilities of second-language learners? What role does grammatical knowledge play in the development of pragmatic skills?
4 What are the general stages in the development of a speech act such as a request? Does the learning context, for example, second-language learning vs. foreign language learning, make a difference, and why?
5 What is pragmatic transfer? How does it impact on pragmatic development?
6 What strategies do lingua franca speakers use to signal, prevent and repair misunderstanding?
7 According to Mauranen, how does lingua franca communication differ from interaction between native speakers? Do you agree?

Study activities

1 Find a language textbook (in any language you can read) and explore how culture and intercultural differences are represented and approached in the book. Do you think it has limitations in the way it treats culture? If yes, why? Can you propose any alternative approach to offset the limitations?
2 There are a number of language learner corpora available online, such as CHILDES Talkbank, French Learner Language Oral Corpora, Cambridge Learner Corpus, Longman Learners Corpus, International Corpus of Learner English, Antwerp Corpus of Institutional Discourse, Japanese EFL Learner Corpus, Estonian Interlanguage Corpus, etc. Explore a corpus and identify any interlanguage features in the selected data sample. Discuss whether any interlanguage features identified can be explained in terms of 'pragmatic transfer'.

3   The ELFA corpus (English as a Lingua Franca in Academic Settings (www.eng.helsinki.fi/elfa), the Vienna–Oxford International Corpus of English (www.univie.ac./voice/page/index.php) and the Michigan Corpus of Academic Spoken English (MICASE at http://micase.elicorpora.info/) are major lingua franca databases. Explore one database and identify significant features of lingua franca communication. Discuss what resources lingua franca speakers employ in the following situations:

(a) when there is mis/non-understanding;

(b) when a speaker makes a mistake in grammar, choice of words or pronunciation;

(c) when a speaker is struggling to find a word;

(d) when there is disparity among speakers' language proficiency.

Further reading

On language teaching and learning, see:

Byram, M., Morgan, C. *et al.* (1994). *Teaching-and-learning Language-and-culture.* Clevedon: Multilingual Matters.

Hinkel, E. (ed.) (1999). *Culture in second language teaching and learning.* Cambridge: Cambridge University Press

Kramsch, C. (1993). *Context and culture in language teaching.* Oxford: Oxford University Press.

Kramsch, C. (1998). *Language and culture. Oxford introductions to language study.* Oxford: Oxford University Press.

Valdes, J. M. (ed.) (1986). *Culture bound.* Cambridge: Cambridge University Press.

On second-language pragmatic development, see:

Bardovi-Harlig, K. (1999). Exploring the interlanguage of interlanguage pragmatics: a research agenda for acquisitional pragmatics. *Language Learning, 49*(4), 677–713.

Kasper, G. & Blum-Kulka, S. (1993). *Interlanguage pragmatics.* Oxford: Oxford University Press.

On lingua franca communication, see:

House, J. (ed.) (2009). The pragmatics of English as a lingua franca. A special issue of *Intercultural Pragmatics,* 6(2).

Firth, A. (2009). The lingua franca factor. *Intercultural Pragmatics,* 6(2), 147–70.

Jenkins, J. (2007). *English as a lingua franca: attitude and identity.* Oxford: Oxford University Press.

Knapp, K. & Meierkord, C. (eds) (2002). *Lingua franca communication.* Frankfurt: Peter Lang.

On Internet-mediated language teaching and learning, see:

Belz, J. & Thorne, S. (eds) (2006). *Internet-mediated intercultural foreign language education.* Boston, MA: Thomson Heinle.

O'Dowd, R. (ed.) (2007). *Online intercultural exchange: an introduction for foreign language teachers.* Clevedon: Multilingual Matters.

PART V

Interculturality

Introduction to Part V

Zhu Hua

TRADITIONAL INTERCULTURAL communication studies are predominantly concerned with providing a cultural account for mis- or non-understanding in interaction or different styles of communication. These studies often assume that, in intercultural interaction, cultural values determine speakers' discourse strategies, and cultural differences are a source of intercultural miscommunication. In contrast, interculturality, as an emerging research paradigm, represents a line of investigation that departs from these traditions. It problematises the notion of cultural differences by asking the following questions:

- What is culture?
- What is the nature of cultural differences?
- Are cultural differences a given fact?
- Who attributes cultural differences to the participants under investigation?
- Are 'cultural differences' always relevant to, or the source of, mis- or non-understanding in intercultural interaction?
- What analytical method is most suitable for analysing mis- or non-understanding in interaction?
- What interactional resources do participants in intercultural interaction make use of in establishing and negotiating their sociocultural identities and how?

In essence, the interculturality approach advocates that 'being culturally different' is a socially constructed phenomenon and needs to be studied through a fine-grained analysis of interaction on a case-by-case basis. Studies following this line of approach argue that an individual may simultaneously belong to several different categories, and not all the categories are equally relevant or salient at a given point in real-life encounters. Echoing those sociolinguistics and cultural studies scholars who have argued the fluidity and multiplicity of social identities, researchers of interculturality believe that participants' sociocultural identities are neither a priori (something knowable independent of experience; for example, the assumption that a Westerner tends to be direct in making a request, while an East Asian person tends to be indirect), nor static. Instead, participants' sociocultural differences are constructed and negotiated through interaction. Therefore, they see the cultural differences as a process rather than an end-product and emphasise the emergent, discursive and dynamic nature of cultural differences.

The three articles reprinted in this part of the *Reader* address the above questions with different focuses. Sarangi (Chapter 16), in his agenda-setting article, offers a critical review of the concept of 'culture' in intercultural communication analysis carried out from cultural–anthropological, sociolinguistic and pragmatic perspectives. He argues that existing intercultural studies often take an essentialist and unified view of 'culture' by creating hypothetical individuals who represent their respective 'cultures'. He calls for a non-essentialist and dynamic perspective on culture and suggests a discourse-analytic approach to the study of intercultural communication, as such an approach allows us to see the 'shifting' nature of culture and what people do with cultural difference in interactions.

Similar to Sarangi, Nishizaka (Chapter 17) challenges the practice of using cultural categories such as 'East', 'West', 'Indian', 'European' etc. as independent variables and argues that whether a person is 'culturally different' or not is something achieved in the actual course of the interaction. Using conversation analysis as an analytic tool, Nishizaka studies the conversation between a Japanese journalist and a foreign student living in Japan on a radio programme. During the interview, which is aimed at finding out 'the foreigner's' view on living together with Japanese people, the interviewer, a Japanese himself, does not make his Japanese-ness relevant to the interaction. Rather, he deliberately distances himself from 'Japanese people' by repeatedly referring to them as 'Japanese people' or 'they' in the conversation. Similarly, the interviewee, a non-Japanese himself, also takes care not to align himself as a foreigner. He uses the word 'foreigners' as if he were talking about a group of people not involving himself. The study convincingly demonstrates that cultural categories (being Japanese) are not always relevant to intercultural interaction, and it is participants who make (some) cultural categories relevant through the actual process of interaction.

In establishing and constructing interculturality, various linguistic and non-linguistic means can be employed by conversation participants. Apart from reference terms as demonstrated in Nishizaka's chapter, other devices include turn-taking, topic management, prosody, nonverbal behaviour, choice between T-type and V-type address terms, laughter, language alternation etc. Higgins (Chapter 18) provides a specific example on how language alternation (also known as code-switching), together with teasing and pronoun usage, is employed by Tanzanian journalists to establish their own and others' membership categories. The study provides rich data on a group that has hitherto received very little attention in intercultural communication. It reveals how participants use linguistic resources to align or realign themselves as co-members of the same group and how the previously established and shared insider identity can be challenged and re-oriented in the subsequent talk-in-interaction. In doing so, the study highlights the emergent, discursive and ever-changing nature of sociocultural identities and shows that the idea of interculturality can be applied to the analysis of a group of the 'same' people, therefore extending interculturality beyond ethnic and cultural boundaries.

Studies of interculturality question the validity of defining culture solely in terms of nationality, treating cultural values as something shared homogeneously among a group, and the practice of applying national character to the interpretation or prediction of behaviour of an individual coming from that culture. Cultural differences cannot be assumed to be relevant to, or the cause of, all the mis/non-understanding in intercultural interaction. Participants in intercultural communication can make use of a range of interactional resources to establish and negotiate their sociocultural identities and, in some cases, to create a sense of common ground among the participants.

Chapter 16

SRIKANT SARANGI

INTERCULTURAL OR NOT?
Beyond celebration of cultural differences in miscommunication analysis[1]

Introduction

THE BASIC QUESTION this paper addresses is: What should be the underlying purpose of intercultural analysis? Is the purpose to explain conversational mismatches in terms of cultural differences in an abstracted way? Or is the purpose to make an attempt to understand the complex institutional processes in which the shifting nature of 'culture' is embedded? As the main title suggests, I primarily address these issues by focusing on what characterises intercultural communication as '(not) intercultural'. The subtitle – 'celebration of cultural differences in miscommunication analysis' – applies to two aspects of intercultural analysis: (i) how 'culture' is used as an analytic construct to study miscommunication, and (ii) how certain researchers indulge in the 'analytic stereotyping' of intercultural encounters as mainly characterised by the cultural differences present.[2]

The first part of this paper offers a by no means exhaustive critical review of two specific types of intercultural communication analysis, i.e. one that can be situated within cultural anthropology and another with a more sociolinguistic and pragmatic orientation. By pointing at a dominant trend of 'thematisation of cultural differences', I offer a critique of an essentialist view of 'culture' in these types of intercultural analysis, thus extending a position taken earlier (Roberts & Sarangi, 1993). The second part of the paper starts with a call for a discourse orientation to the analytic concept of 'culture', which is followed by an analysis of situated intercultural data in the gatekeeping situation of selection interviews. This leads me to revisit the notion of 'interculturality' from a cultural–theoretic perspective, with particular reference to migrants' experience in contemporary multicultural societies.

Miscommunication and culture as represented in two traditions

Intercultural analysis from a cultural–anthropological perspective

'Intercultural communication' is the preferred term among some cultural anthropologists to describe the study of interaction – generally in the face-to-face informal setting – between

Source: Sarangi, S. (1994). Intercultural or not? Beyond celebration of cultural differences in miscommunication analysis. *Pragmatics*, 4, 409–27.

individuals representing different 'cultures' (e.g. Asante & Gudykunst, 1989; Brislin, 1981; Casmir, 1978; Condon & Yousef, 1975; Gudykunst, 1983, 1991; Gudykunst & Kim, 1984, 1988; Prosser, 1978a, 1978b; Samovar & Porter, 1991; Samovar et al., 1981). Asante et al. (1979) divide this tradition into two categories on the basis of the preferred research goals. The first group of researchers, whom they label 'cultural dialogists', emphasise the need to develop a humanistic view of communication theory and practice that would promote world understanding. The second school, referred to as 'cultural criticism', is guided by the principle of conflict and tries to identify points of conflict between individual cultures as researchable issues. These two schools, in my view, are not exclusive to one another, as both of them share an interest in the study of 'differences across cultures'. Although these studies acknowledge the role of language in the manifestation of cultural differences, the underlying assumption is that cultural problems are more significant than linguistic problems. As Prosser (1978a, p. 102) maintains:

> Actually, though the individual language and culture are tightly linked, and therefore do cause important barriers for intercultural communication and for cultural spokespersons, the language problems may be less severe than other cultural barriers; for example, perceptions, attitudes, stereotypes, prejudices, beliefs, values, and thought-patterning itself.

This view suggests, on the one hand, that there is a link between culture and language in a Whorfian sense, but on the other hand, that 'language' is to be kept analytically separate from 'culture'. These two assumptions amount to saying that language is contained within and reducible to culture, thus denying language its reality-constructing role (as will also be made clear in the section on 'A discourse orientation to the analytic concept of "culture"').

Moreover, individual 'cultures' are seen as unified and homogeneous entities, and, by extension, communicative difficulties are invariably explained in terms of cross-cultural differences. By equating 'culture' with thoughts, feelings, values and beliefs of individuals, and by assuming that it exists in the heads of individuals, this notion of culture misses the dynamics of social life. According to Wuthnow et al. (1984, p. 4), in this tradition of analysis, 'culture' comes to be treated as the least observable category of non-behaviour:

> Culture is that residual realm left over after all forms of observable human behaviour have been removed. It consists of the inner, invisible thought life of human beings either as individuals or in some difficult-to-imagine collective sense, as in notions of 'collective purpose', 'shared values', and 'intersubjective realities'. What people actually do, how they behave, the institutions they construct [. . .] however, are not a part of culture.

This tradition can thus be said to neglect the complex and multilayered 'cultural' outlook of individual interacting participants. Also, with its heavy reliance on examples drawn from hypothetical contact situations, it can offer very little insight into what really goes on in the context of situated discourse. Although these studies claim to be concerned with interactions at the situated level, they themselves rather run the risk of giving rise to cultural stereotypes by overlooking individual differences and other situational variables surrounding the intercultural communication event. In other words, in these studies the individual participants are considered to represent their respective 'cultures' and thus cease to be individuals in their own right.[3] Consequently, while the analysis of the intercultural event is made on a collective scale, the creation of a hypothetical individual is a means toward arriving at generalisations about 'cultures'.

Intercultural analysis from sociolinguistic and pragmatic perspectives

THE INTERACTIONAL–SOCIOLINGUISTIC PERSPECTIVE

Works by, among others, Gumperz (1978, 1982), Gumperz & Tannen (1979) and Scollon & Scollon (1980, 1983) can be seen as a reaction to the above-mentioned cultural–anthropological tradition which pays very little attention to linguistic and interactional data. Two of the key assumptions which underlie the interactionalist research tradition are: (i) ethnicity and different cultural backgrounds determine speakers' discourse strategies (different ways of speaking, different ways of structuring information etc.); (ii) different discourse strategies and communicative styles can lie at the heart of interethnic misunderstandings.

With regard to these key assumptions, we notice strong resonances between this tradition and the cultural–anthropological tradition reviewed above, as they continue to share a belief that communicative problems can be accounted for in terms of cultural differences. But unlike the cultural–anthropological tradition, which hypothesises about potential problems on the basis of cross-cultural differences, the interactional–sociolinguistic tradition locates communicative problems in observed linguistic data. This tradition thus deserves credit for having produced fine-grained analyses of naturally occurring intercultural encounters.

It is beyond the scope of this paper to review the accusations of ethnocentric analytic bias hurled against the Gumperzian analysis of miscommunication.[4] What concerns me more is the way in which this framework overemphasises the explanatory power of 'contextualisation cues' in relation to understanding 'culture'. Consider what Gumperz (1992, pp. 51–2) writes in a recent paper titled 'Contextualisation revisited':

> The notion of contextualization has significant implications for our understanding of what culture is. Traditionally, anthropologists speak of culture in terms of shared meaning or shared interpretive practices or shared cognitive structures. Our discussion points to the importance of shared typifications that enter into the signaling and use of activity types in interaction, as well as systems of contextualization conventions. In contrast to the established, commonly accepted idealizations, such interactively defined notions of culture can be studied by empirical means [. . .].

This view no doubt highlights the importance of framing encounters through 'contextualisation cues' on the one hand, and the fluid nature of social/cultural identity in discoursal settings on the other. While not denying the significant role contextualisation cues play in the construction of an interactional context, I envisage insuperable problems in assigning contextualisation cues an overpowering explanatory value when it comes to interpreting participants' cultural identities in an intercultural encounter. The problem stems from the fact that there is more to 'contextualisation cues' than 'culture'. As Shea (this volume) shows, inferences and contextualisation strategies are also mediated by situational and societal structures, and this makes it particularly difficult to isolate the 'cultural' in contextualisations.

THE CROSS-CULTURAL PRAGMATIC PERSPECTIVE

Staying close to the contrastive–linguistic tradition, studies such as Blum-Kulka & Olshtain (1984), Brown & Levinson (1987) and Blum-Kulka et al. (1989) focus on how normative patterns for linguistic activities contrast across cultures. These cross-cultural comparisons have been carried out in two ways. First, some authors investigate how a specific linguistic activity is carried out in culturally different speech communities. Brown & Levinson's (1987) comparative account of how politeness strategies are realised differently in different languages is a classic example of this kind of cross-cultural enquiry.[5] Secondly, some studies look at the different realisations of, for example, a particular speech act in a second language by learners with different mother tongues. The Cross-Cultural Study on the Speech Act Realization Patterns project, as reported by Blum-Kulka & Olshtain (1984), is a case in point as it attempts to establish the similarities and differences between native and non-native realisation patterns of 'requests' and 'apologies'. The problem is that dealing with cultural differences in doing cross-cultural comparisons does not get one nearer to the point of 'intercultural contact'. Moreover, such a comparative analysis does not help to explain potential sources of 'intercultural miscommunication'.

Outside the realm of contrastive pragmatics is the work by Thomas (1983), who suggests that mismatches in intercultural settings can be categorised as either 'pragmalinguistic' (the inappropriate transfer of speech act strategies from first to target language) or 'sociopragmatic' (cross-culturally different assessments of social parameters affecting linguistic choice). These categories are self-explanatory and therefore helpful, but a pragmatic analysis of this kind, in much the same way as interactional–sociolinguistic analyses, takes 'culture' for granted, forges a strong link between 'language use' and 'culture' and therefore pays little attention to individual variations.[6]

The burden of 'cultural differences' in miscommunication analysis

Wittgenstein once said, when put on an unbalanced diet of examples, philosophy suffers from deficiency diseases. This medical metaphor can be extended to describe quite aptly the deficiency syndrome in the types of intercultural research reviewed above. The deficiency I allude to relates to these analysts' preoccupation with diagnosing and treating miscommunication among individuals in 'cultural' terms. In the remainder of this paper my main concern will be with what particular goals this type of analysis of miscommunication serves, and with suggesting possible alternatives.

In communication research generally, there seems to be some agreement among researchers that it is through the study of communicative breakdown that we understand how successful communication happens (Gumperz & Tannen, 1979; Stubbs, 1983). Indeed, in a recent volume titled *'Miscommunication' and problematic talk,* Coupland et al. (1991, p. 2) undertake to 'rescue "miscommunication" from its theoretical and empirical exile, and explore its rich explanatory potential in very diverse contexts'.[7] Applied to the context of intercultural miscommunication, however, this heuristic value attached to miscommunication seems to take on a peculiar shape. Rather than studying miscommunication in its own terms or for the undoubtedly valuable sake of coming to grips with communicative success, studies of the type identified in the previous subsections use 'miscommunication' to reify cultural differences. Put very strongly, it is through the occurrence of miscommunication that cultural differences become real and take on a life of their own. This leads to what I call 'analytic stereotyping' of intercultural events. Analysts operate with a prior definition of the situation and its participants as (inter)cultural and subsequently play upon a principle of cultural differences in accounting for instances of miscommunication.[8] The risk of circularity attached to this analytic practice should be clear: If we define, prior to analysis, an intercultural context in terms of 'cultural' attributes of the participants, then it is very likely that any miscommunication which takes place in the discourse is identified and subsequently explained on the basis of 'cultural differences'.[9] This mode of analysis, which forces an analytic separation between language and culture, also presupposes that there are clearly demarcated boundaries which divide one homogeneous cultural group from another. Such a unified, monolithic view of 'culture' goes hand in hand with the thematisation of cultural differences.

Rethinking 'culture' in multicultural societies

A discourse orientation to the analytic concept of 'culture'

The discussion in the foregoing section makes clear the need for an orientation that can overcome the analytic separateness between language and culture. In this respect, Sherzer's (1987) discourse-centred approach to language and culture is a very appealing alternative. As he points out, discourse has to be considered as the concrete expression of the language–culture relationship, because it is discourse that 'creates, recreates, focuses, modifies, and transmits both culture and language and their interaction' (1987, p. 295). Sherzer's view is able to offer serious advantages if applied to analysing intercultural encounters. It allows one to move away from the tradition of 'identifying' miscommunication at the 'linguistic' level, and then 'explaining' the phenomenon of miscommunication at the 'cultural' level.

Critical discourse analysis (Fairclough, 1985, 1988) seems very apt to offer the tools for implementing the discourse-centred approach in the context of intercultural studies. Critical discourse analysis pays adequate attention to the dialectic relationships between social structures and linguistic practices. It holds that discourse has effects upon social structures, and is at the same time determined by them. This has implications for the study of encounters in multicultural settings in the sense that these settings are a typical locus where the micro and the macro levels intersect. Critical discourse analysis also draws attention to how actual discourse is determined by 'orders of discourse' (Foucault, 1984), which are ideologically shaped by power relations in social institutions and society as a whole. Consider, for instance, any modern Western society with its unique history of the migrant phenomenon and the accompanying discourses of 'racism' and 'discrimination' to mark the changing nature of social relationships between members of the minority and majority groups. In the context of intercultural analysis, then, one will be able to address the question as to how issues like 'racism' and 'discrimination', which are connected to such institutionalised orders of discourse, can become conversational topics in situated talk between members of minority and majority groups. For the purposes of analysing my intercultural data in the institutional setting (see the section on 'Intercultural miscommuncation analysis' below), I shall adopt an integrated framework which brings together the micro–macro concerns of critical discourse analysis and Sherzer's view about the language–culture relationship.

From 'what is culture' to 'what we do with culture'

Next to overcoming the culture–language analytic separateness and being aware of the significance of the structure–agency relationships, we are now faced with tackling an essentialist view of 'culture'. The conceptualisation of culture as people embodying a unified belief or value system is increasingly being regarded as a myth, since it misleadingly portrays social groups as 'ideational islands'. Partly fuelled by a sociological critique, there is now a sense of uneasiness among some contemporary anthropologists regarding 'what culture is', addressing the related problem 'of whether the concept has any real analytic importance, and of how to recognise the existence and boundaries of distinct cultures' (Drummond 1986, p. 215). Clifford & Marcus (1986, p. 19), for instance, point out that 'culture' cannot be represented as a 'unified corpus of symbols and meanings that can be definitely interpreted'.[10] Implied here is a critique of the traditional anthropological preoccupation with searching for cultural shared-ness at the expense of diversity and contradictions within a given society. Barth's (1989, p. 122) recent study of Bali 'culture', which exposes the 'multiplicity of partial and interfering patterns', raises fundamental questions about the nature of cultural coherence:

> Instead of trying to make our theories embrace what is there, we are led to picking out some small, distinctive pattern in this confusing scene, and applying our ingenuity to salvaging a (functionalist) holism by constructing (structuralist) isomorphies and inversions of this randomly chosen pattern, as if it encoded a deeper connectedness.

Barth hereby warrants that anthropology needs to reshape its assumptions about 'culture', particularly in response to recent reflexive and deconstructionist critiques.

A promising alternative lead comes from Thornton (1988, p. 26) who, likewise rejecting the notion of a fixed inheritance of shared meanings, suggests to ask not 'what culture is' but 'what culture does':

> Part of the problem that besets our current efforts to understand culture is the desire to define it, to say clearly what it is. To define something means to specify its meaning clearly enough so that things which are like it can be clearly distinguished from it.

Taking this line of thinking further, Street (1993, p. 25) treats 'culture' as a 'verb' and points out how people put 'culture' to different uses:

> Indeed, the very term 'culture' itself . . . changes its meanings and serves different often competing purposes at different times. Culture is an active process of meaning making and contest over definition, including its own definition.

In a similar vein, Eisenstadt (1989) addresses the issue of the mutual determination of 'culture', 'social structure' and 'social behaviour'. This view opposes the 'order-maintaining' and 'order-transforming' functions of culture. Eisenstadt quotes Peterson (1979, p. 159):

> While it [culture] was once seen as a map of behaviour it is now seen as a map for behaviour. In this view, people use culture the way scientists use paradigms [. . .] to organise and normalise their activity. Like scientific paradigms, elements of culture are used, modified, or discarded depending on their usefulness in organising reality [. . .] as nearly equivalent to the term ideology, but without the latter's pejorative connotations [. . .] Sociologists now recognise that people continually choose among a wide range of definitions of situations or fabricate new ones to fit their needs.
>
> (original emphasis)

A non-essentialist and action-oriented perspective on 'culture' enables analysts interested in intercultural miscommunication to take on board the complexities related to the uses and functions of 'culture' in contemporary societies (cf. discussion in Hall, 1981, 1990). The notion of 'culture' is very much a contested one in many modern societies, as both dominant and dominated groups often resort to the culture card in managing their power-maintaining and power-acquiring purposes. So, in analysing encounters between the dominant and dominated groups in a multicultural society, we need to subscribe to a dynamic view of 'culture'. Rather than attribute communicative breakdown to cultural differences in an unproblematic way, the analysis of intercultural encounters should aim at coming to grips with the workings of 'culture' in individuals' discourse practices, as will be attempted in the data analyses in the following section.

Intercultural miscommunication analysis: towards a dynamic model

In this section I shall illustrate the discussions in the preceding sections by presenting some situated data and by evaluating competing lines of explanation. The data I analyse below concern gatekeeping situations of selection interviews. The interviewees can be characterised as younger Asian migrants who are typically different from the 'first' or 'second' generation migrants in terms of socio-educational background, professional ambitions etc. The first example is taken from a selection interview for a motor mechanics training course. The interviewer (I) is British, and the interviewee (R) is of Asian origin. What I have just provided is an identification of the context in terms of its intercultural dimension, highlighting the different cultural attributes of the participants. But such a characterisation of this discourse situation is selective since the participants' identities are fundamentally multifaceted. The interviewee is not only a member of the minority culture, he also enjoys less situational power as far as the 'interview game' is concerned, and, moreover, as a non-native speaker of English, he may be lacking in linguistic knowledge. By contrast, the interviewer is not only a native speaker of English, he is also a member of the majority culture, and has the situational power in the interview context. Thus, an alternative to the intercultural characterisation of this discourse setting is a characterisation which foregrounds the linguistic and situational asymmetries. Let us now consider example (1), and assess the different lines of explanation these alternative characterisations of the setting can offer.[11]

Data example 1

```
01  I:   right mhm hm what kind of driving have you been doing in England
02  R:   uhm [long pause] it's very good
03  I:   what kind of what kind of driving though big truck or small
         | truck in factories
04  R:   | eh no no no I have licence only car
05  I:   you have a car licence
06  R:   licence right
```

What would a 'cultural' explanation accounting for R's minimal response in turn 2 look like? Bringing R's ethnic and cultural origin to the forefront of analysis, it would invoke the cultural stereotype of Asians as submissive and non-confrontational. But such a reading is difficult to justify when the question to which turn 2 responds is itself not confrontational. An alternative line of explanation, looking at the linguistic and situational asymmetries, is certainly more sophisticated. We could attribute R's failure to understand the force of I's question in turn 1 to his inadequate linguistic knowledge. This seems convincing as, in turn 2, we see R providing a minimal response which is punctuated with a long stretch of silence. This response is judged unsatisfactory by the interviewer, as can be noticed in turn 3 where the question is paraphrased for the benefit of R. This suggests I recognises that R's problem is a linguistic one, and this is confirmed later as R offers an acceptable answer in response to the reformulated question.

Should we decide to take our analysis of 'miscommunication' a bit further, it is possible to argue that the communicative problem does not squarely lie with R. I can be held partly responsible for the way he phrases the question. The ambiguity surrounding the question relates to driving, which occupies the subject position. It could therefore be taken to mean either 'quality of driving' or 'driving certain types of vehicle' – the latter being the most preferred reading under the circumstances. Is this failure on the part of the interviewer to disambiguate the force of his question also a matter of linguistic incompetence? Perhaps the choice of the term 'type', rather than 'kind', could have made it comprehensible. Perhaps an alternative phrasing such as 'what kind/type of vehicle have you been driving?' would have been more straightforward.

We know that in the context of selection interviews questions often have a hidden purpose which the candidate has to work out for him/herself. Under such an assumption, the present interviewer's 'indirect' questioning behaviour can be legitimated or at least apprehended. But given that R has problems with decoding the linguistic structure in this instance, why does he go on to provide an answer instead of making a request for clarification? There are several competing explanations. In situational terms, it means that all interview settings are marked by a procedural power differential, where to ask questions of the powerful participant can be seen as face-threatening. Additionally, because it is an interview situation involving a non-native speaker of English, to indicate non-comprehension can potentially lead to a negative evaluation of R.

At another level, it is theoretically viable to assume that an interviewee in fact understands the question but decides to 'flout' (in the Gricean sense) the conventions of the interview game. This explanation is not tenable in the case under discussion, however, as two turns later (in turn 4) R does provide an 'acceptable' response. The point I want to make is that if a member of the majority group were to provide a response similar to that of R, this would most likely be interpreted as 'flouting' rather than as evidence of linguistic incompetence or unfamiliarity with interview norms. This begs the question: why should an instance of mis-communication, when it involves participants from different ethnic/cultural backgrounds, be treated as resulting from culture-specific behaviour, whereas the same instance of mismatch, when it involves participants from the same 'culture', becomes labelled as a challenge? The problem, as I see it, is not just related to the relative weighting of one framework over another, it also concerns the set of explanatory presumptions which researchers entertain when dealing with monocultural and intercultural communicative settings.

Let me take this issue further by re-interpreting a familiar case study (example 2) taken from Gumperz et al. (1979), followed by a comparison with a parallel situation in my own data (examples (3) and (4)). Example (2) involves Sandhu (SN), who arrived in Britain in the early sixties and had several manual jobs in factories, worked as a bus conductor, and at the time of the interview is working in a training resource centre. He has now applied for a post of assistant librarian and in the interview is asked what his present job is about. Apart from the interviewee Sandhu, the extract represented here involves two interviewers, I2 and I3.

Data Example 2

01 I2: You say you're very busy eh in your present job [pause] what exactly do you do [pause] I mean what are your duties day by day

02 SN: Well we've to eh receive the visitors [pause] show them around and then we have to go out eh to the factories you know [pause] eh sometimes to attend the classes [pause] eh how to do erm cataloguing classification

03 I2:   Erm what are you familiar within the field of cataloguing and classification
04 SN: Well it it depends on what sort of eh classification college is using and [pause]
          I'm sure erm this Middleton College will be using the decimal classification
          uhm which I've done you know in the college
05 I3:   Can I move on to the question of handling er library users [pause] this is
          mentioned little bit in the job description erm [pause] how well do you get
          on with people mister Sandhu [pause] I mean how much experience have
          you got of getting on with people generally
06 SN: Well I I think I'm very good so far as getting with the other people I'm
          very very good particularly with the students [. . .]

Following Gumperz et al., one could account for the miscommunication in turn 2 in terms of culture-specific ways of structuring information. I would like to suggest looking at it as a case of 'activity-specific' mismatch in the sense that interview talk can go wrong, whether or not participants are culturally different. This is not to deny that interviews are shaped and influenced by culture-specific preferences, but it is possible to argue that, even in cases where interviewee and interviewer have the same cultural background, perceptions about what is (not) 'acceptable' in the interview context may differ. What Sandhu does, it seems to me, is follow the rules of the interview game, as he presents himself favourably both in relation to how knowledgeable he is with regard to cataloguing and classification and in relation to how good he is in human relationships.

As in example (1), we should recognise how this instance of mismatch in example (2) is jointly constructed. For instance, we could point at the lack of clarity in the manner in which the interviewer conflates two different questions (turns 1 and 5), which results in Sandhu supplying incomplete responses. The first question (turn 1) has a twofold function, but Sandhu chooses to focus on one aspect – 'what exactly do you do' – while answering the second aspect of the interviewer's question – 'what are your duties day by day' – only marginally. In turn 3, the question about cataloguing and classification is asked in order to enable Sandhu to display his technical knowledge about the job of librarianship. Given this hidden purpose, the question – 'what are you familiar with' – is fairly general and is open to several interpretations. Again, Sandhu answers the question marginally and it is not clear why he starts his answer by saying 'it depends'. In turn 5, the question about handling library users again has two aspects: 'how good' he is and 'how much experience' he has. Sandhu's answer is partial in that his answer is about 'how good' he is, completely overlooking the other aspect of the question. Even in answering the first part, he makes no reference to his actual experience.

Let us now consider an excerpt from my own data which involves a situation parallel to example 2. Samal (SL) is interested in joining the British Social Security department as a clerical assistant. Before arriving in Britain he worked in Bangladesh as a school teacher and as an assistant clerk in an insurance firm. His previous employment in Britain includes twelve years in the Bradford City Transport Company and, subsequently, a job as a machine operator. The excerpt begins with the interviewer (I1) asking the candidate a question about the present job.

Data Example 3

01 I1:   Erm you worked as an assistant clerk for a few months in an insurance
          | company
02 SL: | Yeah yes I did

03 I1:   What did that job entail

04 SL: Erm [pause] I had to copy sometimes er eh the letters sending somewhere
           [pause] and also quite a bit er eh records and so on [pause] sometimes I
           work in wages department

05 I1:   Yes I see [pause] did you do that job after the school teaching

06 SL: Eh yes | after teaching

07 I1: | Yes erm did you find anything in about the job particularly interesting

08 SL: Erm in my that job

09 I1:   Mhm hm

10 SL: Well eh job yes [pause] the clerical job was very interesting [laughs] but in
           education department [pause] eh is is also inte interesting [pause] but clerical
           job was more interesting than the teaching

11 I1:   What was it about the clerical job that you found interesting

12 SL: Erm to [pause] eh almost everything I did er interesting

13 I1:   You found the the whole job interesting itself

14 SL: Yeah

15 I1:   Right then I would like to introduce you [. . .]

We can notice the casual-conversational style of the interview, manifested in the turn-taking
system, interruptions initiated by SL and the use of back-channelling. This conversational style
overlaps with the content of Samal's response. Instead of providing a specific judgemental
answer when asked about which of the two previous jobs he liked most and why, Samal
responds with a factual account which offers no comparative evaluation of the two jobs.
Maintaining that he liked both jobs equally well, he gives the impression that it was not a
dissatisfaction with teaching which led to a shift in career. In turns 11 and 13, the interviewer
tries to delve into the actual nature of the clerical job, but in both cases SL provides minimal
responses. In both examples (2) and (3), questions about the current job are asked. In the
context of selection interviews in general, an interviewer expects the candidate to offer a
response which includes those bits of work from among the host of other things, which are
not only 'interesting' but also 'relevant' to the prospective job in question. At a less abstract
level, there is the expectation that the candidate will touch upon the transferable skills s/he
could bring to the new job. Both SN and SL do not offer 'satisfactory' responses to these
expectations, which can be partly seen in the way the interviewers in both cases stay on the
topic for a while and make the implicit expectations transparent.

Let us now turn to another focal aspect of job interviews, i.e. how candidates' profiles
can be constructed negatively. In example (4) below, which also involves Samal (SL), the
interviewer (I2) asks a question of the following type: 'Why did you do "x" before and why
do you want to do "y" now?'.

Data Example 4

01 I2:   Well mister Dixon started talking to you about jobs [pause] what I would
           like to ask you is some questions relating particularly to this job that you've
           applied for [pause] so the first question I would like to ask you is [pause]
           why have you applied for this job when when previously as I understand
           (unclear) you've been doing manual work for the last well for few years

02 SL: Yeah er [pause] I came to almost it's not particularly myself I have seen
           some of my friends also in in similar situation [pause] erm I did try myself

so so many places to get similar job in clerical or in office job or anything like that [pause] but could not succeed in [pause] and you know after all I applied in Bradford city transport and got a job and I was there about eleven twelve years I think [pause] and in sixty nine I had to go to Bangladesh and I left the job [pause] erm when I came back erm I registered myself in the job centre and they erm send me a letter to go to (unclear) because I had a bit experience about the machine operating so I went there and I had a job you know and it was a very good job

03 I2:   Oh yes but

04 SL: In er something else beside is [pause] while there applied and the the factory you know international factory is closed at eighty two

05 I2:   Mhm

06 SL: Close down so I had no job so this in eh (unclear) there is community college and they are running the course [pause] A B L E course access to bilingual employment [pause] which means already you know no eh eh two languages they will improve ehm your skill [pause] and I applied there and I was eh er I almost almost finish [pause] the course is almost finished [pause] so I have got some weeks more extra experience to getting a new job you know

07 I2:   Having been to (unclear) you say you're bilingual erm is there a particular skill that you feel would help you in the job and if so how

08 SL: Ehm [pause] they they teach there er about about various organisation [pause] how does it run and so on you know (unclear) [pause] and also er teach English [pause] I think my English has erm improve a lot than I have before [pause] and also how to do the er from English to Bengali [pause] Bengali to English [pause] and how to er translate and everything [pause] they do try to develop [coughs]

Rather than giving a profile of himself to show convincingly how he would fit into the job he is applying for, SL offers a narrative of past experience. He opts for 'telling' – not 'selling' – the story of his work life, even to the extent of interrupting the interviewer (turns 3–4). The interviewer takes on the role of a passive listener until turn 7, where he dismisses the story-telling and reasserts his authority to ask questions 'relevant to the interview situation'. Once again, though, in turn 8, SL resorts to the story-telling mode as he offers a somewhat detailed description of the course content, instead of specifying a set of 'learned' skills which are transferable.

The above analysis, in sum, shows that, although these interview situations can from one analytic angle straightforwardly be labelled and interpreted as intercultural, many of the communicative difficulties that occur in these situations do not easily lend themselves to an explanation exclusively based on the principle of cultural differences. A situational reading of the data seems to capture more closely the complexities – institutional and otherwise – involved in these contact situations.

Migrant 'culture' in multicultural societies: from problem of 'difficulty' to politics of 'difference'

The institutional and other complexities of the contact situations analysed above can at the societal level be traced in the discursive performances of first generation younger migrants such as the ones involved in the data. External forces such as underemployment among minority groups, perceived and real discriminatory tendencies in the job market etc. seem to have partially shaped migrants' life experiences in multicultural societies. In light of this, rather than treat mismatches as exclusively resulting from 'cultural differences' or 'linguistic inadequacies', we need to consider how they reflect, following Bourdieu (1991), a kind of 'habitus' which is rooted, generally, in these life experiences. This comes out in the way the interviewees in my corpus choose to narrate believable stories in preference to conforming to the norms of the job interview format. As Bourdieu (1976, p. 654) points out:

> A speaker's linguistic strategies (tension or relaxation, vigilance or condescension, etc.) are oriented (except in rare cases) not so much by the chances of being understood or misunderstood (communicative efficiency or the chances of communicating), but rather by the chances of being listened to, believed, obeyed, even at the cost of misunderstanding (political efficiency or the chances of communicating).

If some migrants share the features of a life history, having been through similar discontinuities in their employment patterns, it is quite possible that they will draw on their life histories in such gatekeeping encounters. So, when we detect a pattern in their talk, it may not simply be a question of structuring of information according to culture-specific norms, but rather a matter of what Raymond Williams (1981) calls 'structures of feeling' – how people narrate lived experiences. In my analysis, this type of explanation takes into account the potential structuredness of interindividually similar experiences, but at the same time reaffirms individual diversities.

It also leads us to move away from homogenising the migrant communities in terms of the significant 'other'. Some accounts of migrants do problematise the representation of migrant communities as homogeneous entities, but they do so along hypothetical lines. Cicourel (1982), for instance, takes it as a general characteristic of the situation of migrant workers that they have to live in two cultures. The resultant strain between the 'old self' and the 'new' is said to be manifested in problems of identity, social ambivalence, alienation and rejection. In this respect, Cicourel describes their situation as a 'no man's land' which is neither that of the migrant's country of origin nor that of his/her country of employment or residence. Similarly, Parris (1982, p. 4) summarises the migrant worker's position as follows:

> On the whole his (sic) existence is organised around two poles: his family and fellow countrymen, in a cultural environment resembling that of the country of origin; and his work and public life, in a culture unfamiliar to him or her.

This, for me, is an unsatisfactory account of a migrant's life world. The actual dichotomy between these two cultural environments is much more complex than what Parris seems to suggest. Only from an essentialist viewpoint can the two 'worlds' be held separate for one particular group of migrant workers. In addition, the interrelationship between these two 'worlds' will vary from one group to another. Moreover, the problems of identity, social ambivalence, alienation and rejection are just as well problems of the non-migrant population. In this sense the analytic concept of a homogeneous 'culture' is just as perilous for the non-migrant population, which in intercultural studies tends to feature as 'culturally integrated individuals', and thereby often simply remains unnoticed.

It is worth pointing out that different notions developed within the existing literature on migrant communities are inadequate in their attempt to describe the situation of many different categories of migrants in a relatively similar way. Ekstrand et al. (1981), for instance, propose the notion of 'interculture' to refer to an intermediate culture which shares properties of both home culture and host culture, independent of whether those properties are shared between the cultures-in-contract. This notion of 'interculture' is very similar to the linguistic notion of 'interlanguage' (as proposed by Selinker, 1972) referring to shared features of a speaker's native and target languages. But, as Skutnabb-Kangas & Phillipson (1983, p. 71) point out, while 'interlanguage' can be typically seen as a transitory state with the target language as a goal, the notion of 'interculture' implies a rather stable state with none of the cultures in contact as a goal.

Neither of the above constructs – 'living in two cultures' or 'interculture' – is powerful enough to capture the migrants' fluid identities. I hope my analyses have shown that it may however be possible to reconceptualise the notion of 'interculture', not alongside the concept of 'interlanguage', but in a way which captures the multifaceted identities and diversified lived experiences of specific migrant groups. In order not to fall prey to the binary bias and the homogenisation of a group's 'cultural' practices, we need to take into account further markings within 'intercultures' such as 'urban youth culture', 'younger migrant culture' etc. The interviewees in the data presented in this paper, in this sense, share a 'migrant outlook', but this outlook (values, interactive styles etc.) cannot be captured by reference to either their 'culture of origin' or the 'culture of non-migrants'.

Conclusion

In this paper I have raised questions about the 'cultural' emphasis in intercultural miscommunication analysis. Through analyses of intercultural data, I have shown how a selective characterisation of a communicative situation on the basis of different cultural attributes of the participants can only serve to reify cultural differences in an essentialist way. As an alternative, I have argued in favour of a discourse-analytic approach to the study of intercultural miscommunication as it allows us to interpret specific discursive practices of individual interactants both in terms of their cultural attributes and in the context of their societal and institutional role-relationships. One consequence of this is that intercultural analysis should not only aim at explicating the role which cultural differences play in intercultural miscommunication, but also at tackling the shifting nature of 'culture' in contemporary societies and what people actually do with cultural differences in real-life encounters. To conclude, the use of a unified view of 'culture' and, correspondingly, the thematisation of cultural differences in accounting for instances of 'intercultural miscommunication', both run the risk of stereotyping the field of intercultural communication research.

Notes

1   A condensed version of this paper was first presented at the fourth International Pragmatics Conference, Kobe, July 1993, under the title 'Beyond celebration of miscommunication: critical perspectives on intercultural communication'. I am very thankful to Jan Blommaert, Michael Meeuwis and Stef Slembrouck for their suggestions on an earlier draft.
2   Elsewhere (Sarangi 1992) I elaborate this notion of 'analytic stereotyping' with reference to the study of native–non-native discourse, where misunderstandings are explained by appealing to the linguistic deficiency on the part of the non-native speakers.
3   A related paradox arises, however, as these studies lead to a proliferation of 'how to' literature emphasising 'intercultural adjustment', 'adaptation through awareness' etc. aimed at real-life individuals.
4   Singh et al. (1988) and Kandiah (1991) allege that there is a strong ethnocentric bias in the interactional-sociolinguistic tradition. My impression, however, is that these critics' alternative explanations from the viewpoint of the 'cultural other' maintain a generic 'cultural principle' (for a fuller discussion, see Sarangi (1994)).

5   It is worth pointing out that 'cross' often presupposes an oppositional trend. It asks the question as to how x differs across cultures, i.e. how x is manifested in a number of separate cultures with n number of differences and n number of similarities.

6   A possible alternative (suggested in Sarangi 1994) focuses on Levinson's (1979) notion of 'activity type' in order to show how the existence of layers of normative rules in gatekeeping situations makes communicative breakdowns possible, whether or not participants share the same 'cultural' norms. This implies a shift from 'culturally-determined' discourse strategies (in the heads of people) to 'socio-culturally' governed 'activity types'.

7   For a detailed discussion of several interpretations of the notion 'miscommunication' and its many variants, see Coupland et al. (1991).

8   Consider here the analytic basis of intercultural studies carried out in the workplace setting (for example, Moran & Harris (1991) and Moran & Riesenberger (1994)). Unlike in the anthropologically oriented work reviewed, the focus is on the denial of a problem by claiming that cultural differences do not necessarily mean barriers; they can become bridges to understanding and to the enrichment of our lives. By contrast with its metaphorical use in this paper, these workplace studies realise the 'celebration of cultural differences' in a literal way.

9   This line of critique has also been taken up by Blommaert (1991), and it is similar to what Henley & Kramarae (1991) refer to as the 'two cultures' approach to language and gender studies. For Henley & Kramarae, such an approach explains away the inherent power struggle in cross-gender communication as 'mere' communicative differences.

10 Gramsci (1981, p. 193) has drawn our attention to the danger inherent in a view of 'culture' as 'memory' when he says:

> We need to free ourselves from the habit of seeing culture as an encyclopaedic knowledge, and men [sic] as mere receptacles to be stuffed full of empirical data and a mass of unconnected raw facts, which have to be filed in the brain as in the columns of a dictionary, enabling their owner to respond to the various stimuli from the outside world.

11 In the data represented here, the following transcription conventions are used:

    ()   inaudible speech
    []   extralinguistic details such as 'laughter', 'pause' etc.
    | overlaps
    |

References

Asante, M. K., Newmark, E. and Blake, C. A. (eds) (1979). *Handbook of intercultural communication*. Beverly Hills: Sage.

Asante, M. K. and Gudykunst, W. B. (eds) (1989). *Handbook of international and intercultural communication*. London: Sage.

Barth, F. (1989). The analysis of culture in complex societies. *Ethnos*, 54(3/4), 120–42.

Blommaert, J. (1991). How much culture is there in intercultural communication? In J. Blommaert and J. Verschueren (eds), *The pragmatics of intercultural and international communication*. Amsterdam: John Benjamins.

Blum-Kulka, S. and Olshtain, E. (1984). Requests and apologies: a cross-cultural study of speech act realisation patterns (CCSARP). *Applied Linguistics*, 5(3), 196–213.

Blum-Kulka, S., House, J. and Kasper, G. (eds) (1989). *Cross-cultural pragmatics: requests and apologies*. Norwood, NJ: Ablex.

Bourdieu, P. (1976). The economics of linguistic exchanges. *Social Science Information*, 16(6), 645–68.

Bourdieu, P. (1991). *Language and symbolic power*. Edited and introduced by J. B. Thompson; translated by G. Raymond and M. Adamson. Cambridge, MA: Polity Press.

Brislin, R. (1981). *Cross-cultural encounters*. New York: Pergamon.

Brown, P. and Levinson, S. (1987). *Politeness: some universals in language use*. Cambridge: Cambridge University Press.

Casmir, F. L. (ed.) (1978). *Intercultural and international communication*. Washington D.C.: University Press of America.

Cicourel, A. C. (1982). Living in two cultures: the everyday world of immigrant workers. In *UNESCO: Living in two cultures: the socio-cultural situation of migrant workers and their families* (pp. 17–66). Paris: The Unesco Press.

Clifford, J. and Marcus, G. E. (1986). *Writing culture*. Berkeley, CA: University of California Press.

Condon, J. C. and Yousef, F. (1975). *An introduction to intercultural communication*. Indianapolis, IN: The Bobbs-Merill Company.

Coupland, N., Giles, H. and Wiemann, J. (eds) (1991). *'Miscommunication' and problematic talk*. Newbury Park: Sage.

Drummond, L. (1987). Are there cultures to communicate across? An appraisal of the 'culture' concept from the perspective of anthropological semiotics. In S. P. X. Battestini (ed.), *Georgetown University Roundtable on Languages and Linguistics* (pp. 215–25). Washington, D.C.: Georgetown University Press.

Eisenstadt, S. N. (1989). Introduction: culture and social structure in recent sociological analysis. In H. Haferkamp (ed.), *Social structure and culture* (pp. 5–11). Berlin: Walter de Gruyter.

Ekstrand, L. H., Foster, S., Olkiewicz, E. and Stankovski, M. (1981). Interculture: some concepts for describing the situations of immigrants. *Journal of Multilingual and Multicultural Development*, 2(4), 269–93.

Fairclough, N. (1985). Critical and descriptive goals in discourse analysis. *Journal of Pragmatics*, 9, 739–93.

Fairclough, N. (1988). *Michel Foucault and the analysis of discourse*. CLSL Research Paper No. 10. Lancaster University.

Foucault, M. (1984). The order of discourse. In M. Shapiro (ed.), *Language and politics*. London: Basil Blackwell.

Gramsci, A. (1981). Culture. In T. Bennett, G. Martin, C. Mercer and J. Woollacott (eds), *Culture, ideology and social processes* (pp. 193–97). London: Batsford (in association with The Open University Press).

Gudykunst, W. B. (ed.) (1983). *Intercultural communication theory*. Beverly Hills, CA: Sage.

Gudykunst, W. B. (1991). *Bridging differences: effective intergroup communication*. Newbury Park, CA: Sage.

Gudykunst, W. B. and Kim, Y. Y. (1984). *Communicating with strangers: an approach to intercultural communication*. New York: Random House.

Gudykunst, W. B. and Kim, Y. Y. (eds) (1988). *Theories in intercultural communication*. Newbury Park, CA: Sage.

Gumperz, J. (1978). The conversational analysis of interethnic communication. In E. Lamar Ross (ed.), *Interethnic communication* (pp. 13–31). Proceedings of the Southern Anthropological Society. Athens, GA: The University of Georgia Press.

Gumperz, J. (1982). *Discourse strategies*. Cambridge: Cambridge University Press.

Gumperz, J. (1992). Contextualisation revisited. In P. Auer and A. Di Luzio (eds), *The contextualization of language* (pp. 39–54). Amsterdam: John Benjamins.

Gumperz, J. and Tannen, D. (1979). Individual and social differences in language use. In C. Fillmore, D. Kempler and W. Wang (eds), *Individual differences in language ability and language behaviour*. London: Academic Press.

Gumperz, J., Jupp, T. and Roberts, C. (1979). *Crosstalk*. Southall: National Council for Industrial Language Training.

Hall, S. (1981) Cultural studies: two paradigms. In T. Bennett, G. Martin, C. Mercer and J. Woollacott (eds), *Culture, ideology and social processes* (pp. 19–38). London: Batsford (in association with The Open University Press).

Hall, S. (1990). Cultural identity and diaspora. In J. Rutherford (ed.), *Identity: community, culture, difference* (pp. 222–37). London: Lawrence and Wishart.

Henley, N. and Kramarae, C. (1991). Gender, power and miscommunication. In N. Coupland, H. Giles & J. M. Wiemann (eds), *'Miscommunication' and problematic talk* (pp. 18–43). Newbury Park: Sage.

Kandiah, T. (1991). Extenuatory sociolinguistics: diverting attention from issues to symptoms in cross-cultural communication studies. *Multilingua*, 10(4), 345–79.

Levinson, S. (1979). Activity type and language. *Linguistics*, 17, 365–99.

Moran, R. T. and Harris, P. (1991). *Managing cultural differences*. Houston, TX: Gulf Publishing Co.

Moran, R. T. and Riesenberger, J. R. (1994). *Making globalization work*. London: McGraw Hill.

Parris, R.G. (1982). General introduction. In *UNESCO: living in two cultures: the sociocultural situation of migrant workers and their families* (pp. 1–14). Paris: The Unesco Press.

Peterson, R. (1979). Revitalising the culture concept. *Annual Review of Sociology*, 5, 137–66.

Prosser, M. H. (1978a). Intercultural communication theory and research: an overview of major constructs. In B. D. Ruben (ed.), *Communication yearbook*, Vol. II. New Jersey: ICA-Transaction Books.

Prosser, M. H. (1978b). *The cultural dialogue: an introduction to intercultural communication*. Washington: Houghton Miflin Company.

Roberts, C. and Sarangi, S. (1993). 'Culture' revisited in intercultural communication. In T. Boswood, R. Hoffman and P. Tung (eds), *Perspectives on English for professional communication*. Hong Kong: City Polytechnic.

Samovar, L. A. and Porter, R. E. (eds) (1991). *Intercultural communication: a reader*. Belmont, CA: Wadsworth.

Samovar, L. A., Porter, R. E. and Jain, N. (1981). *Understanding intercultural communication*. Belmont, CA: Wadsworth.

Sarangi, S. (1992). Power asymmetries in the study of NS-NNS discourse. Paper presented at PALA Conference, University of Gent, Belgium.

Sarangi, S. (1994). Accounting for mismatches in intercultural selection interviews. *Multilingua*, 13(1/2), 163–94.

Scollon, R. and Scollon, S. B. K. (1980). *Linguistic convergence: an ethnography of speaking at Fort Chipweyan*. New York: Academic Press.

Scollon, R. and Scollon, S. B. K. (1983). Face in interethnic communication. In J. C. Richards and R. W. Schmidt (eds), *Language and communication* (pp. 157–88). London: Longman.

Selinker, L. (1972). Interlanguage. *International Review of Applied Linguistics*, 10, 209–31.

Shea, D. (1994). Perspective and production: structuring conversational participation across cultural borders. *Pragmatics*, 4(3), 357–90.

Sherzer, J. (1987). A discourse-centered approach to language and culture. *American Anthropologist*, 89, 295–309.

Singh, R., Lele, J. and Martohardjono, G. (1988). Communication in a multilingual society: some missed opportunities. *Language in Society*, 17, 43–59.

Skutnabb-Kangas, T. and Phillipson, R. (1983). Intercommunicative and intercultural competence. Rolig-Papir 28. Roskilde Universitets Center.

Street, B. V. (1993). Culture is a verb: anthropological aspects of language and cultural process. In D. Graddol, L. Thompson and M. Byram (eds), *Language and culture* (pp. 23–43). Clevedon, UK: BAAL and Multilingua Matters.

Stubbs, M. (1983). *Discourse analysis: the sociolinguistic analysis of natural language*. Oxford: Basil Blackwell.

Thomas, J. A. (1983). Cross-cultural pragmatic failure. *Applied Linguistics*, 4(2), 91–112.

Thornton, R. (1988). Culture: a contemporary definition. In E. Boonzaier and J. Sharp (eds), *Keywords* (pp. 17–28). Cape Town: David Philip.

Williams, R. (1981). The analysis of culture. In T. Bennett, G. Martin, C. Mercer and J. Woollacott (eds), *Culture, ideology and social processes* (pp. 43–52). London: Batsford (in association with The Open University Press).

Wuthnow, R., Hunter, J. D., Bergesen, A. and Kurzweil, E. (1984). *Cultural analysis: the work of Peter L. Berger, Mary Douglas, Michel Foucault and Jurgen Habermas*. London: Routledge and Kegan Paul.

Chapter 17

AUG NISHIZAKA

THE INTERACTIVE CONSTITUTION
OF INTERCULTURALITY
How to be a Japanese with words[1]

Interculturality as a phenomenon to be investigated in its own right

ONE KIND OF COMMUNICATION between two or more people is called "intercultural." For sociologists or anthropologists it is a type of communication in which participants have culturally different backgrounds. However, the fact that the participants are "culturally different" is usually taken for granted, as it is treated as a parameter rather than a topic of investigation. The "interculturality" of the participants tends to be referred to as an independent variable with which to explain the observable features of the communication in question.

There are some illuminating studies in intercultural communication. For example, J. J. Gumperz (1982, Chapter 5) observes that when "Indian" and "Western" students have a discussion in an anthropology class, "Western" students tend more often to start talking before "Indian" students finish (i.e., the "Western" tend more often to interrupt the "Indian") than the other way around. He attributes this observation to the fact that the intonation of "Indian" students' speech, because their English is influenced by Hindu, is different from that of "Western" ones. The intonation "Indian" students use to punctuate an utterance in its course is very similar to what "Western" students use at the end of their talk. Another example is K. Liberman's (1985, 1990) studies of communication between Aborigines and Europeans in Australia. He reports that Aborigines tend to put themselves into a disadvantageous position in a classroom or in court, because their way of conversation is quite different from that of Europeans. Aborigines usually avoid asserting themselves and try gradually to produce agreement by repeating the same phrases together, so that, even when cross-examined in court, they tend just to say, "yes," in order to let conversation go smoothly, rather than answering the question. Aborigine children, when asked to voice their opinions in a classroom, tend to be hesitant to speak out, avoiding self-assertion, so that a European teacher may consider them to lack understanding.

F. Erickson and J. Shulz (1982) follow a similar procedure. They find "that *situationally emergent* rather than *normatively fixed* social identity had the strongest influence on the character and outcome of interview" (p. 181, emphasis in original). They reach this conclusion by

Source: Nishizaka, A. (1995). The interactive constitution of interculturality: how to be a Japanese with words. *Human Studies*, 18, 301–26.

identifying the troubles ethnically different participants get into, with differences between communicative patterns of different ethnic groups, and then proceeding to argue that:

> If a student is ethnically different from the counselor and wants special help and friendliness, he or she must *make up for* ethnic differences by establishing some other form of co-membership. For example, if a student is Polish–American and the counselor is Italian–American, it helps if they both happen to be wrestlers and reveal themselves as such.
>
> (p. 176, emphasis added)

I would not deny that studies like these are valuable from various points of view. However, what I want to do is to show how it is that *the fact of being* intercultural is organized as a social phenomenon. In the following, I want to treat this as a phenomenon to be investigated, instead of using interculturality—the fact that the participants come from different cultures—as a given fact from which the argument should start.

In the studies just mentioned, it is the authors, and *not the participants themselves*, that attribute cultural differences to the participants. The authors explain the features of the communication by reference to behavioral patterns, independently identified from an outside observer's perspective. The participants themselves must be ignorant of these patterns, for otherwise they could manage to do away with troubles they come across. These explanations are really good sociological ones in the usual sense. The authors explain what they observe by means of hypothetical devices independently constructed for just that purpose. This cannot but remind me of a complaint Harvey Sacks made about the procedures of traditional sociology: It has not dealt with "real phenomena." In order to approach such "real phenomena," I want to show how it is that interculturality—cultural differences between the participants—is relevant to or in the very communication that can be called "intercultural." I also intend to show how it is that this relevance of interculturality is relevantly consequential for some observable features of the communication in question.[2]

Some "traditional" sociologists might say that the real social phenomena really worth investigating lie beyond immediate interaction; each interaction, or communicative situation, they would say, cannot but be influenced by those structural features related to such attributes as "Japanese," "Sri Lankan," "male," "female," etc., which are hidden behind that interaction itself and outside its relevances. However, I would say, if so, the question should be rather: How do we, not only as professional sociologists but also as "well-informed" citizens, get a sense of hidden structure, although it is hidden? I will not answer this question directly, but I believe that the answer, whatever it may be, must be searched for in the talk-in-interaction.[3]

In the following, I wish to show that what is assumed to be simply a given fact and used as an explanation for some observed phenomena can be an interactive phenomenon to be investigated in its own right. The fact of being culturally different is also an achievement in and through talk-in-interaction.

"Japanese" and "Foreigners"

The materials I will analyze in the following are transcribed fragments of radio program interviews conducted with "foreign students"[4] in Japan. I will present only their English translation in the text, to avoid unnecessary complexity. [. . .] The materials are not necessarily translated in natural English, because the translation is just a supplementary means by which to show how I analyze the original Japanese materials; the translation is not in any sense the materials

I analyze.) I want to show, first, how it is that the cultural difference between the participants is made relevant to the interaction they participate in, through and as an arrangement of their linguistic, and other vocal, conduct. (A is the interviewer; B the interviewee.)

(1) (9/23/ 1992: 115)

```
 1    A:  One thing I want to ask you is: when Japanese people talk in
 2         Japanese, they are sometimes only diplomatic,
 3    B:  Yes.
 4    A:  [they] are just apparently sociable,
 5    B:  Yes.
 6    A:  [they] are sometimes so, aren't//[they]?
 7    B:  Yes.
 8    A:  For example, "Well, Shiri-san, come to my home uh next holiday,"
 9         say [they] very easily.
10    B:  Yes.
11    A:  If you actually go there on the next holiday, [they] will say, "Oh?
12         For what have you come here," ma(h)//y(h)be(h).//.hhhh
13    B:  hhhhhhhhhhhh
13a        Yes.
14    A:  I mean, what [they] say and
15    B:  Yes.
16    A:  what [they] mean seem different,
17    B:  Yes
18    A:  this way Japanese often
19    B:  Yes.
20    A:  talk,//don't [they]. [they] often talk so.
21    B:  Yes.
21a        Yes.
22    A:  How about this.
23    B:  This is a little troublesome to foreigners, //[they] th-
24    A:  It's troublesome, isn't it.
25    B:  Yes, wrongly, [they] will take what is said for what is meant,
26         everyone thinks so, //I think.
27    A:  That's exactly what I was thinking.
28    B:  Yes.
29    A:  U:::n, but in case Japanese talk among themselves,
30    B:  Yes.
31    A:  "That must be just diplomatic," an//d
32    B:  Uh h//uh
33    A:  "This must be different from what is meant," – this way [they]
34         understand what's meant, //you know
35    B:  Yes.
36    A:  Uh, without any special effort.
37    B:  Yes.
38    A:  It's exactly this "without any special effort" that is troublesome, isn't
39         it.
```

40   B: Ye(hhhhh)s, that's a little, uh troublesome.=not a little: but u::/ /:h
41   A: u(hhhhhhhh)h ve(h)ry(h) trou(h)ble(h)/ /so(h)me(h)
42   B: troublesome.

The interviewer does not introduce himself as a Japanese, nor is he called a Japanese by the interviewee. In this interview, however, he is neither more nor less than a Japanese. Indeed, when listening to the (tape recorded) interview, not only do I have no doubt that he is a Japanese, but also his Japanese-ness is constitutive for my activity of listening to, and understanding, the interview. The interviewer is relevantly a Japanese in and to that interview (i.e., both for the participants and for an overhearing analyst), even though independent of the correctness of his being a Japanese. This Japanese-ness consists in the way in which the interaction between the participants goes on in the interview; i.e., it is interactively constituted.

Harvey Sacks may have been the first sociologist to pay serious attention to the distinction between the "correctness" and the "relevance" of applications of categories (see Schegloff, 1972). For instance, that I am a Japanese is correct, but the category "Japanese" is not always relevantly applicable to me; whether I am a Japanese or not might be irrelevant when I talk to students about Structural-Functionalism in a sociology class. One of the most important implications of what Sacks (1972a, 1972b etc.) says about the relevance of categories is that when one relevantly uses a category this makes a *collection* of categories relevant. For example, if you apply the category "fathers" to someone, it is relevant to use "mother" to refer to another one insofar as she is the mother in the family in which the former person is the father. Using the category "father" makes relevant the category collection "family." Some categories belong to more than one collection. For example, the category "children" is a member of the collections "family" as well as "stages of life."

Another important implication of Sacks' argument is that within each collection there are some normatively expected relationships between its categories. Sacks observes that some activities are bound to categories: e.g., babies will cry, Japanese university students will play a lot, etc. Such category-bound activities are often, expectedly, directed to other categories of the same collection to which the category those activities are bound to belong; e.g., a mother or father will pick up their baby when it cries.[5] As to this, I happened to find a nice example in the (very) American film, *The Sound of Music*. A nun, called Maria, came to a captain's house as a private tutor of his children, to find the strictly disciplined children in uniform. One day, when her request to give them play suits was refused by the captain, she said to him, "But they are children." Then he says in response, "Yes, I *am* their father." The category "children" used by Maria belongs to the collection "stages of life." The category now relevantly applicable to Maria and the one to the captain are both "adult." Accordingly, the normative expectation is invoked that adults should be lenient towards children. On the other hand, the captain treats the category "children" as a member of the collection "family." By referring to himself as "father," he has made the collection "family" relevant, instead of "stages of life." Exploiting the fact that the category "children" happens to belong to two collections, he deprived Maria of the legitimate position she could otherwise have held in relation to the children; she does not have any position in their "family." That is to say, now Maria is an "outsider" or "stranger" rather than "adult" to them. The expectation invoked by his utterance is that outsiders or strangers should not have any rights to the family affairs, while the father has the right and obligation to take care of his children; he is saying to her, "That's none of your business."

In the above material, A (the interviewer) often uses the category "*nihonjin* (Japanese)," although not referring to himself with this category. He speaks only generally of Japan and the Japanese people. Nevertheless, as I said, he is relevantly a Japanese. How?

It is true that the category "Japanese" is a member of the collection "nationalities," to which "Sri Lankan," "French," "American," etc. also belong. We notice, however, that B uses the category "*gaikokujin* (foreigner)," although, again, he speaks only generally with this category, not referring to himself. That is, the category "Japanese" used by A is not a member of "nationalities" but rather of the pair "'Japanese'/'foreigner (non-Japanese)'." "Japanese" is not just a member of a collection whose members stand side by side, but rather, together with "foreigner," co-constitutes a pair whose members are contrasted to one another and related asymmetrically. Indeed, in the above material, we see that "Japanese" and "foreigner" are contrasted, such that what the Japanese understand easily "without any effort" (36) is "troublesome" (40) to the "foreigner" or the non-Japanese precisely because of its easiness for the Japanese. Generally speaking, cultural differences are a matter of of relativity. For example, depending upon what criteria are to be used, the Sri Lankans and the Japanese may not be any more culturally different than Bostonians and New Yorkers are, and those living in Boston and those living in Cambridge may be as culturally different as the Sri Lankans and the Japanese. The Sri Lankans are only culturally different from the Japanese through being "foreigners" or the non-Japanese. It is the pair "'Japanese'/'foreigner'" that makes "interculturality" relevant to and in the interaction in which those categories are used.

The categories "Japanese" and "foreigner" are mutually exclusive; i.e., the one and same person cannot be a Japanese and foreigner (in Japan) at the same time. This has a consequence for the normatively expected relationships between the Japanese and foreigners. Although A has not referred to himself, nor has he been referred to by B, as a Japanese, while B was introduced as a Sri Lankan by A at the beginning of the program, A is *relevantly* a Japanese by locating himself in a relationship of this kind with B. It is normatively expected that the Japanese should be more entitled to report anything "usual" and "ordinary" in Japan than foreigners, and that foreigners should be more entitled to report any troubles that result from unfamiliarity with Japan than the Japanese. This does not mean that the Japanese *really* know what is usual and ordinary in Japan better than foreigners, nor that foreigners *really* know what troubles the non-Japanese may encounter better than the Japanese. Indeed, many non-Japanese know about what the Japanese usually and ordinarily do much more than do many Japanese. There is even no guarantee that the interviewer (A) knows about such things more than the interviewee (B). In fact, I am very doubtful that what A says about the Japanese people is true, and I believe that there are other peoples much more diplomatic than the Japanese.

The point is that it is normatively *expected* that the relative entitlements should be systematically distributed between the Japanese and foreigners. Indeed, the expectation of this systematic distribution of entitlements is observably embodied in the interaction in question. A introduces what the Japanese people usually do without any trouble (1 through 20), and as to troubles resulting from unfamiliarity with this, he asks B for confirmation (29 through 39). For his part, B answers A's question on behalf of the foreigner (23 through 26 and 40 through 42). Thus, I want to argue, "interculturality" or a cultural difference is accomplished, as relevant to and in the interaction, through its participants putting themselves in a relationship normatively expected to obtain between incumbents of the categories "Japanese" and "foreigner," using this category pair in that interaction.

Interactive constitution of interculturality

In the preceding section, I tried to show that what makes the interaction relevantly intercultural is neither those features outside the interaction that are observed by the observer in reference to attributes selected by him or her, nor what each participant thinks about themselves behind the interaction (i.e., inside their heads); rather, it is a form of exchange in the interaction itself. As matter of fact, the above fragment is located in a dramatic context, looking at which will help show the point more clearly.

Note that the above fragment starts with the phrase uttered by the interviewer (A) "*Hitotsu ukagaitainowa ne* (One thing I want to ask you is)." This phrase acts as a preface to a question that the speaker has wanted to ask but has not found any chance to ask until now, and it implies that this is the first time in this interaction to ask such a question. If he had asked another such question at an earlier point sufficiently close to here, it would be natural to say, "*Moohitotsu ukagaitainowa* (Another thing I want to ask you)" or "*Tsugini ukagaitainowa* (A second thing I want to ask you)." However, we find the following fragment immediately before the above one.

(2) (9/23/ 1992: 107)

1	A:	Well, what I definitely want to ask is:
2	B:	Yes.
3	A:	u::h Studying Japanese, alright?
4	B:	Yes.
5	A:	and speaking to Japanese people, //alright?
6	B:	Yes.
7	A:	then, sometimes don't you find what they are saying difficult to
8		understand? //I wonder.
9	B:	Yes, I do.
10	B:	Yes, I do. Sure, I do.
11	A:	Yes.
12	B:	That is, in my company I work for, and I work //now.
13	A:	Yes, yes.
14	B:	In that company, that is a construction company,
15	A:	=Yes.
16	B:	there are used many technical words.
17	A:	=O, technical terms. //( ), right?
18	B:	Technical terms ( )
19	B:	Then, I come across a non-understandable [for me] wo- thing,
19a		// sometimes.
20	A:	U:::::::::h
21	A:	Yes.
22	B:	Not just sometimes, but r//::- r//::-
23	A:	m:: m::
24	B:	m::
25	?:	hhhhhhhh
26	A:	so(h)me(h)ti(h)mes(h), you(h) do(h).
27	B:	Yes
28	A:	But anyway you couldn't avoid it. To learn them one by one is the
29		only way, //I think, //yeah.
30	B:	Yes. Yes.
31	A:	One thing I want to ask you is: . . .

The very last utterance is the first one of fragment (1). We notice that the phrase is very similar to the first one in this fragment (2), which is *also* a preface to a question that the speaker has wanted to ask but has not had a chance to ask until now. Taken literally, the utterance at 1 in (2) contradicts the implication of the first one in fragment (1) (i.e., the last one in (2)), because it turns out that the question prefaced by the first utterance in (1) (i.e., the last one in (2)) may not be the first question of this kind (i.e., an askable-but-not-yet-asked question). Then, to dissolve this apparent contradiction, those questions prefaced by both of the prefatory utterances, the first in (2) and the first in (1), should be considered the same one. Indeed, the question at the start of fragment (1) can be regarded as a reiteration of the one at the start of (2), because its content can be heard to be just more specific. In fragment (1), A refers not just to the Japanese language, as in (2), but the Japanese mode of linguistic behavior. He appears to be reiterating the preceding question by repairing, or clarifying, it (see Schegloff et al., 1977). Certainly, the fact that A is trying to repair his former question seems to be concealed in a subtle fashion; he seems to keep the talk on the topic occasioned by his question until its possible termination point, without interrupting it by saying something like: "Excuse me, I mean . . ." However, what is important here is the *fact* of the repair. What is its consequential significance?

In fragment (2), the interviewer (A) also uses the category "Japanese" in his question, but this category does not become relevant to this part of the interaction. B mentions "technical terms" or "technical words" in answering the question. The category collection which can be made relevant by the phrase "technical terms" is not "'Japanese'/'foreigner'," but rather "'specialist'/'lay person'"; and a normatively expected relationship bound to this collection is that the "specialist" should be more entitled to talk about technical terms than "lay persons." If so, then in our case, it is not A, who is a "Japanese," but B, who works for a "construction company," who should be more entitled to talk about technical (even though Japanese) terms. This expected relationship goes against the one bound to the collection "'Japanese'/'foreigner'." Indeed, at lines 28 and 29, A makes only an unspecified, general comment about difficulties of (Japanese) technical terms, without going into details. Although, as the title of the program suggests, A and B might have been arranged to be relevantly a Japanese and a foreigner beforehand, they cannot necessarily keep being so successfully throughout the interaction. Their being a Japanese and a foreigner successfully is contingent on the actual development of the interaction.

The same uncertainty of communication being successfully intercultural can be seen in the following fragment, which is taken from another interview of the program series. (Again, A is the interviewer and B the interviewee.)

(3) (9/24/1992: 379)

```
1    B:   . . . U::h for example, in Japanese- Japanese history,
2    A:   Yes.
3    B:   mountains are important. Import- mountain
4    A:   Mountains.
5    B:   Uh
6    A:   Yes.
7    B:   .hh But .hh in this respect, in Tokyo, about mountains, uh like
8         Mt. Takao ( ) u//::
9    A:   Mt.(h) Takao(h) is the only one, //isn't it, in the neighborhood.
10   B:   Yes.
11   B:   .hh only few, so //( )
12   A:   m
```

13   B: in the Kansai area
14   A: m
15   B: uh natural verdure and //then rivers a::nd mountains a//nd
16   A: m:::n
16a   ri:ght, //ri:ght
17   B: Yes. .hhh b- //boundary ( )
18   A: In Kyoto, like Mt. Arashi and //that Katsura river,
19   B: Yes
20   A: .hhh a lot of rivers and mountains and nature //are there, //aren't there.
21   B: .hhhhhhhhh
21a   Yes, this makes:: (.) .hhh boundary, the notion of boundary
22   very //c- cl//ear.
23   A: U:::::
23a   yes, yes, yes, o::::::h I see:::::::.

Before this fragment, B cites the Kansai area as the one most interesting of those he has visited in Japan. When B mentions mountains at line 3 and names Mt. Takao at 8, A says that there are only few mountains around Tokyo at 9. Then, B, agreeing with A, mentions "natural verdure and then rivers and mountains" (15) in the Kansai area (i.e., the midwestern area in Japan; Tokyo is in the eastern area). In response to this, A, citing proper names (Mt. Arashi and the Katsura river), says at 20 that Kyoto (an ancient city located in the Kansai) is very natural, as compared with Tokyo. So far, "mountains" and "rivers," along with "natural verdure" and even "nature" itself, appear to be members of the category collection "nature." Nature in Japan can be a topic that the "Japanese" are normatively expected to be more entitled to talk about than "foreigners"; indeed, A can be heard to make such a claim by displaying his ability to go into details about nature in Japan, citing proper names at line 18. Again, it is not relevant to this point whether what A says is true and whether the Japanese people *really* have a better knowledge about nature in Japan than foreigners. In any event, thus far, the collection "'Japanese'/'foreigner'" could be relevant in and to the interaction.

It turns out, however, that "mountains" and "rivers" mentioned by B are members of the collection "*sakai* (boundary)," not "nature" (21a and 22); what B has been saying is that Kyoto has a lot of nature, and that therefore it has also a lot of mountains and rivers, which used to be used as boundaries. At the very beginning of the program, B was introduced by the interviewer as a French student of Japanese history. Now it is obvious that when he starts with saying, "In Japanese history mountains are important," he is explaining the importance of mountains and rivers as boundaries in Japanese history. If so, "boundary" mentioned by B can be a topic that again makes the collection "'specialist (in Japanese history)'/'lay person'" relevant, instead of "'Japanese'/'foreigner'"; and it is B who can be an incumbent of the category "specialist" and can be more entitled to talk of that topic. This again contradicts the normative expectation bound to the collection "'Japanese'/'foreigner'."[6] When A understands that B is talking about boundaries, not nature, he marks that he has discovered something in B's talk (23a), uttering, "*A, sooka* (Oh I see)," especially using the so-called discovery marker ("*A* (oh)"). It is not clear *what* he has actually discovered, nor even what he is *claiming* he has discovered. However, what is obvious is that claiming that he now has something new, whatever it may be, he succeeds in bringing the topic to close, without any efforts to develop it. After the claim of a discovery, he introduces another topic (see Note 6). Of course, A *may* know something about the significance of boundaries in Japanese history and he *may* be even less knowledgeable about nature, especially natural geography, in Kyoto than B. However, the point is the *fact* that he goes into some details about the latter by citing proper names, while he does not do this about the former.

So far I have argued that interculturality is organized in and through an actual development of interaction. It may be noted that, after A asks a repaired question in fragment (1), immediately following B's answer, i.e., "This is a little troublesome to foreigners" (23), A repeats that part of B's utterance, which makes prominent the contrast involved in the pair "'Japanese'/ 'foreigner'," i.e., "troublesome" (24). What each participant is thinking inside his "head", that, for example, he has a special feeling of being a Japanese or foreigner, that he is strongly conscious of his being a Japanese or foreigner, that he wants to be just like a Japanese or foreigner—all this is completely irrelevant to the *fact* of being a Japanese or foreigner. This fact is interactively achieved through and as a sequential arrangement of the participants' (vocal) conduct. It is social in the strongest sense of the word.

Ownership of the Japanese language

In this section, I want to show that the ownership[7] of the Japanese language is embodied in a form the interaction takes in its actual course, and that through this, we can perceive the interaction to be one between a "Japanese" and a "foreigner." What is here meant by the ownership of the Japanese language is, again, a normatively expected relationship between the Japanese people and foreigners, or a normatively expected distribution of entitlements. That is not (just) to say that the Japanese are generally expected to speak and understand Japanese better than foreigners. As matter of fact, it is the case that some non-Japanese people speak Japanese better (grammatically more properly; with a more refined vocabulary etc.) than the average Japanese. The fact that they really speak Japanese better than many Japanese people, however, does not let them have, or share, that expected ownership of the language. The ownership of the language is the normative expectation that the Japanese should be able not only to understand better, but to evaluate the understandability of the Japanese language used by the non-Japanese, and that they should be entitled to give advice about how to speak Japanese, appraise a foreigner's Japanese and so on. For example, it would sound unnatural, although not impossible and maybe even reasonable, if a non-Japanese, whose mother tongue is not Japanese but who speaks Japanese at least as fluently as a native Japanese, were to say to the latter, "You speak Japanese very well." On the contrary, however poor a speaker a native might be, he or she should be able to use the compliment when speaking with the non-Japanese (at least more) naturally. Note that I am not saying that only the Japanese have the exclusive right to use the Japanese language in an authentic way. The ownership of the language is a normative expectation, which is used by the participants as a resource for organizing their interaction.

What I want to emphasize here is a prominent pattern observable in the materials. That is, the interviewer (A) often starts to talk before the interviewee (B) finishes. For example:

(4) (9/24/ 1992: 352)

```
1    A:   . . what is the most impressive to you.
2    B:   .hh uh it's the Kan(h)sai(h), I think.
3    A:   Huh?
4    B:   Of the Kansai, u:://::m Kyoto=
5    A:   the Kansai,
6    A:   =Kyoto.
```

7   B: Kyoto //and Nara::::::::::: .hhhh
8   A: What is the most interesting in Kyoto.

At lines 5 and 8, A's voice overlaps B's, not just starting before B's sentences are finished. Is he interrupting B? Is this an expression of his arrogance and rudeness, or his friendliness? I am not here interested in answering these questions. What I want to do here is to show what expected relationship is embodied in a form of interaction, even if it may be the case that one participant is arrogant or rude to the other. Fragment (4) is a fairly complicated one. To see what is happening in it, it will help to examine some other fragments.

   (5) (9/23/ 1992: 100)

   1   B: . . . [I] talked to those people, and //then, when anything I couldn't
   2   A: Right, right.
   3   B: understand, learned from them,
   4   A: Yes.
   5   B: This way, urn like rapidly? //like one by one?
   6   A: U::::h hu::::: O:::h I see:::::://:::
   7   B: um I have come to be able to understand many things.

   (6) (9/23/1992: part of (2))

   16   B: there are used many technical words.
   17   A: =O, technical terms, //( ), right?
   18   B: Technical terms ( )
   19   B: Then, I come across a non-understandable wo- thing (.) //sometimes.
   20   A: U:::::::::h Yes.

   (7) (9/24/1992: 223)

   1   A: Then, when for the first time in France you heard and learned of
   2   Japanese Shintoism, Buddhism or culture,
   3   B: Ye//s
   4   A: how did you feel?
   5   B: .hhhhhh Ye::.hhah, m:: .hhhh //uh
   6   A: "In more detail,
   7   B: Uh, in mo//re-
   8   A: I feel like study//ing::"
   9   B: Yes, so:: //so did I feel.
   10   A: U:::h hu:::h, then at last you came to Japan u(hhhhhhhh)h, I see (h)

A's last utterances of these fragments (6 in (5), 20 in (6), 10 in (7)), which all overlapped B's preceding utterance, include a grasp claim. Saying "I see" or "Uh huh" in an exaggerated mode, A claims that the point of each utterance of B's has been grasped. Generally, such an expression is also used to claim that the utterer of it understands what the co-participant has just said. In particular, in the environment like those observable in fragments (5) through (7), the claim of an understanding of the preceding talk is enhanced in a significant way. In all the above fragments, immediately prior to the markers in question, there are slight perturbations on B's side. In (5), not only is the expression, "-mitai (like)," unnatural in Japanese together with "*dondon* (rapidly)." Because of its upward intonation contour, it even sounds like an invitation to A to check what he has just said. In (6), B cuts off a word he has started and replaces another one ("wo- thing . . ."). In addition, just before that, A corrects B's phrase "*senmonno kotoba* (technical words)" (17), and B accepted the correction "*senmon yoogo* (technical terms)" (18). In (7), not only is a perturbation observable at line 5, but also after that, A answers his own question on B's behalf. Grasp claims put in the troublesome environment may suggest, not simply an understanding of what has been said, but rather, "I know you are getting in trouble, but don't worry; that doesn't matter, I understand." This suggestion is related to the evaluation, and acceptance, of the understandability of the utterance just made by the co-participant and the latter's ability to use the language. Such a suggestion should be supposed to be made by those who own the language, when the participants' languages are different. (Note that this suggestion exempts the speaker of the original utterance from responsibility for the possible misunderstanding, which, in turn, implies that the speaker *could* be responsible for it; the usual claims of understanding may imply the responsibility on the hearer's side.) Thus, in those troublesome environments, insofar as A presumes the expected entitlement to evaluate the understandability of B's utterances, it should be appropriate for A to propose as soon as possible that B's utterances are understandable, even if A's utterance ends up overlapping B's (here, too, it is irrelevant whether A does *really* understand them). Otherwise B's ability might be dubious, which could be in turn another (more serious) obstacle to the current interaction. That is to say, in those environments it should be preferred that A's voice overlap with B's rather than that he delay proposing B's understandability.

The same thing can be said about the last part of fragment (1):

(8) (9/23/1992: last part of (1))

```
38   A:  It's exactly this "without any special effort" that is troublesome, isn't
39       it.
40   B:  Ye(hhhhh)s, that's a little, uh troublesome.=not a little: but u:://:
41   A:  u(hhhhhhhh)h ve(h)ry(h) trou(h)ble(h)//so(h)me(h)
42   B:  troublesome.
```

Here, just after an noticeable perturbation ("u:::") on B's side, A comes in to fill out the slot which has been opened by B's utterance, "*chottoja nakute* (not a little but)," responding to B's laughing voice with his own, upgraded one. In this way, he demonstrates that the point of B's utterance can be grasped even though this has not been completed, and, with his upgraded laughing voice, he seems to propose that B's utterance is understandable and that therefore B has the sufficient ability for the Japanese language.

Now we can see what happens in fragment (4). In response to B's answer at 2 to his first question, A asks B to clarify by saying "Huh?" This clarification request is not necessarily clear at this point; it may be directed to the propriety of B's utterance at 2 as an answer to A's first question, or it may have something to do with problems in A's listening. If the propriety of B's answer is questioned, it means that B's ability to speak Japanese may be dubious. That is, in this case, "Huh?" constitutes a possible troublesome *environment* in the sense that it *may* unsettle a basis of the communication. If so, it is appropriate for A to get rid of the possible suspicion about B's ability, insofar as A is expected to be in a relationship to B which is bound to the ownership of the language. Indeed, after B repeats "the Kansai," which is part of the original answer, A immediately repeats the same word again. A treats B's repetition of the word as a possible proper answer to his "Huh?", and through this, he makes observable that his "Huh?" was directed to some unhearable part of B's utterance; A makes it clear now that the problem he detected in B's first answer is not about the propriety of that answer, but about a word that was unclear. Here, again, insofar as he has the expected entitlement to approve the understandability of B's utterances and B's linguistic ability, it should be appropriate for him to do away with any possible suspicion about B's ability as soon as possible, so that A's utterance ends up overlapping B's.

Note that the possibility of "Huh?" being directed to the impropriety of B's answer is not arbitrary. In his first question A says not "*doko* (where)" but "*nani* (what)"; moreover, just before this fragment B mentioned three ancient cities he visited, of which two are in the Kansai area, and A's question seems to be based on this. He can be heard to ask, "what is the most impressive in those cities?" However, B answered this question by citing a place name. What A is doing at lines 5 through 8 to prevent this possible impropriety of B's first answer is to treat that answer as a preparatory section for answering A's first question. In other words, A treats B's mentioning the Kansai as though it further specifies the area where B found the most impressive thing. Just when the area is even further specified as Kyoto, A asks B a modified version of the first question, using the phrase, "in Kyoto." That is to say, by treating B's first answer as a further specification of the area, i.e., a preparatory work for answering the question, instead of treating it as the answer itself, A shows that he accepted B's utterance as a properly understandable one. Here, again, insofar as A is expected to dispose of the problem about B's ability, he is supposed to do it as soon as possible, at least soon enough to prevent B from possibly going so far as to finish an inappropriate answer, and, again, his modified question ends up overlapping B's preceding utterance.[8]

In this section, I have shown that interaction takes a particular form as a consequence of the embodiment in it of an expected relationship between the participants, i.e., a relationship bound to the ownership of the language, and therefore bound to the category pair, "'Japanese'/'foreigner'." In other words, one party's claim for the ownership of Japanese in relation to the other is ratified through and as a form of interaction. That is, it is ratified through its being consequential for formal features of the interaction without being denied or canceled in the natural course of the interaction (and even through the fact that the interaction in which it is embodied was broadcast without being checked).[9] This may seem tautological, but this seeming tautology is not any problem insofar as I am not engaged in any sociological explanations in the traditional sense. The expected relationship is ratified through a form the interaction takes in its actual course, while the form of the interaction is a consequence of this ratified relationship. That is to say, being relevantly a Japanese or a foreigner is constituted and reproduced in and through the actual course of the interaction.

Notes

1   I wish to thank George Psathas and Jeff Coulter for their helpful comments and encouragement. I am also grateful to Michael Lynch for his very detailed comments on an earlier draft of this paper. Thanks also to Tom Conroy for his remarks and for providing an opportunity for me to present an earlier version of the paper at a graduate student colloquium at Boston University.

2   I am going to follow the program E. A. Schegloff (1991) proposes for dealing with what he calls "talk-in-interaction." He points out two problems to take into consideration when analyzing the data of talk-in-interaction:

> There is . . . the problem of showing from the details of the talk or other conduct in the materials that we are analyzing that those aspects of the scene [on which we are focusing] are what the parties are oriented to. For that is to show how the parties are embodying for one another the relevancies of the interaction and are thereby producing the social structure.
>
> (p. 51)

And:

> . . . there remains another problem, that is to show the context or the setting (the local social structure), in that aspect, is procedurally consequential to the talk. How does the fact that the talk is being conducted in some setting (say, "the hospital") issue in any consequences for the shape, form, trajectory, content, or character of the interaction that the parties conduct? And what is the mechanism by which the context-so-understood has determinate consequences for the talk?
>
> (pp. 52–3. See also Schegloff (1987, p. 215)).

3   With the later Wittgenstein, I doubt the assumption that there is always something essential, hidden behind appearances. Wittgenstein (1953) says: "The strict and clear rules of the logical structure of propositions appear to us as something in the background—hidden in the medium of the understanding. I already see them (even though through a medium); for I understand the propositional sign, I use it to say something" (§102). "If it is asked: 'How do sentences manage to represent?'—the answer might be: 'Don't you know? You certainly see it, when you use them.' For nothing is concealed" (§435).

4   The title of this program series (broadcast by NHK from 21 through 25 September in 1992) is: *Ganbare, Ryugakuse*, or Hang in there, foreign students!

5   Sacks (1972a) points out that some "standardized" relationships are expectable between the incumbents (whoever they are) of categories in the special collection he calls R, i.e., the collection of pair relations such as "wife–husband," "friend–friend," etc. I argue that some relationships, even though not so strong as those, are expectable between category members in other collections.

   Incidentally, when I use the phrase "normatively expected," I follow N. Luhmann's definition of "normative expectation." Luhmann (1980, 1984, etc.) defines this as expectations which resist learning (even) when breached, as opposed to what he calls "cognitive expectation," defined as expectations subject to learning when breached. However, what I have in mind may be slightly different from what Luhmann must have had in mind when he formulated this definition. He would call cognitive, rather than normative, such an expectation as: Japanese university students do not study hard; because if all Japanese university students one met studied hard it would be reasonable to change one's expectation. However, as Sacks (1966) observes, even this kind of expectation will resist change. In this sense, such expectations should be also normative. In Sacks' term, they are "protected against induction."

6   What topic can be a technical one which the specialist is expected to be more entitled to talk about is not definitely determinable, especially independent of the context. "Nature in Japan" could be such a topic. Following fragment (3), A and B are discussing a Japanese ethnologist, Shinobu Origuchi. Although this topic may be a technical one, they can be heard to talk in such a way as to make the collection "'Japanese'/'foreigner'" relevant, rather than "'specialist'/'lay person'." This is made possible by, for one, A's mentioning Origuchi as "famous" (A calls him "*taito*," or great authority). Here, too, it is not relevant whether he is *really* so famous as to be generally known to the Japanese people. This may sound tautological. It should be noted, however, that what I want to do is not to give an explanation in the usual sense, nor to specify what provides conditions for what. The relevances of a category collection and a normatively expected relationship elaborate each other in H. Garfinkel's (1967, p. 78) sense.

7   W. W. Sharrock (1974) discusses owning knowledge in an insightful way.

8   The fact that the materials here analyzed are taken from a radio program must be consequential to how the interaction in question unfolds. I will not go into the matter here. Only a couple of words are in order. In news interviews, it is generally observed, the interviewer tends to repeat the points made by the interviewee in a version designed for the audience that is supposed to lack some background knowledge (see Heritage, 1985). It seems that this tendency in news interviews may encourage the interviewer to initiate and/or correct the interviewee's utterances. This general tendency might seem to be able to account for the pattern observed in the materials here. However, it is compatible with another tendency in news interviews which is often pointed out; i.e., the interviewer and the interviewee tend to refrain from starting to speak until the interviewee makes his or her points and the interviewer asks main questions (see Heritage and Greatbatch, 1992; Schegloff, 1988/89, etc.). This also seems to have something to do with the fact that news interviews are designed for an overhearing audjence. So, in this respect, the argument in this paper does not have to be modified by the fact that the materials are a radio program.

   The interviewer in these materials may be the more obliged to show the understandability of the interviewee's utterances because the interview is also designed for an audience; he may be the more solicitous of the interviewee's understandability in order to sustain the stability of the interview. Moreover, for the same purpose, the interviewer may have an additional task to display the understandability of the interviewee's utterances to an (especially native) audience, even if there is no necessity to show it to the interviewee. In any event, although the tendency I have shown in the text may be enhanced in a radio program, this does not contradict my argument.

9   The concept of "ratified" is elaborated by J. Coulter (1989).

Symbols used in transcripts

?	indicates upward intonation.
//	indicates point at which following line starts.
(.)	indicates very brief, but observable pause.
( )	indicates something said but not transcribable.
:::	indicates stretching of sound immediately preceding.
wo-	indicates broken word.
=	indicates observable absence of interval between two parts of talk.
hhh	indicates voiced sound of expiration.
.hh	indicates sound of inhalation or voiceless sound of expiration.

References

Coulter, J. (1989). *Mind in action*. Cambridge: Polity Press.

Erickson, F. and Shulz, J. (1982). *The counselor as gatekeeper: Social interactions in interview*. New York: Academic Press.

Garfinkel, H. (1967). *Studies in ethnomethodology*. Engelwood Cliffs: Prentice Hall.

Gumperz, J. J., (1982). *Discourse strategies*. Cambridge: Cambridge University Press.

Heritage, J. (1985). Analyzing news interviews: Aspects of the production of talk for an "overhearing" audience. In T. van Dijk (ed.), *Handbook of discourse analysis*, 3: *Discourse and dialogue* (pp. 95–119). London: Academic Press.

Heritage, J. and Greatbatch, D. (1992). On the institutional character of institutional talk: The case of news interview. In D. Boden and D. Zimmerman (eds), *Talk and social structure: Studies in ethnomethodology and conversation analysis* (pp. 93–137). Cambridge: Polity Press.

Liberman, K. (1985). *Understanding interaction in Central Australia: An ethnomethodological studies of Australian Aboriginal people*. London: Routledge.

Liberman, K. (1990). Intercultural communication in central Australia. In E. Carbaugh (ed.), *Cultural communication and intercultural contact* (pp. 177–83). Hillsdale: Lawrence Erlbaum.

Luhmann, N. (1980). *Rechtssoziologie*, 2 Auflage. Opladen: Westdeutcher Verlag.

Luhmann, N. (1984). *Soziale Systeme*. Frankfurt a.M: Suhrkamp Verlag.

Sacks, H. (1966). Lectures. In Harvey Sacks, *Lectures on conversation*. Edited by G. Jefferson. Oxford: Basil Blackwell, 1992.

Sacks, H. (1972a). An initial investigation of the usability of conversational data for doing sociology. In D. Sudnow (ed.), *Studies in social interaction* (pp. 31–74). New York: Free Press.

Sacks, H. (1972b). On the analyzability of stories by children. In J. J. Gumperz and D. Hymes (eds), *Directions in sociolinguestics* (pp. 325–45). New York: Holt, Rinehart and Winston.

Schegloff, E. A. (1972). Notes on conversational practise: Formulating place. In D. Sudnow (ed.), *Studies in social interaction* (75–119). New York: Free Press.

Schegloff, E. A. (1987). Between micro and macro: Context and other connections. In J.D. Alexander, B. Giesen, R. Muench and N. J. Smelser (eds), *The macro-micro link* (207–34). New York: Columbia University Press.

Schegloff, E. A. (1988/89). From interview to confrontation: Observations on the Bush/Rather encounter. *Research on Language and Social Action*, 22, 215–40.

Schegloff, E. A. (1991). Reflections on talk and social structure. In D. Boden and D. Zimmerman (eds), *Talk and social structure: Studies in ethnomethodology and conversation analysis* (pp. 44–70). Cambridge: Polity Press.

Schegloff, E. A., Jefferson, G. and Sacks, H. (1977). The preference for self-correction in the organisation of repair in conversation. *Language*, 53, 361–82.

Sharrock, W. W. (1974). On owning knowledge. In R. Turner (ed.), *Ethnomethodology*. London: Penguin Books

Wittgenstein, L. (1953). *Philosophical investigations*. London: Macmillan.

Chapter 18

CHRISTINA HIGGINS

CONSTRUCTING MEMBERSHIP IN THE IN-GROUP

Affiliation and resistance among urban Tanzanians

Introduction

THIS ARTICLE INVESTIGATES whether and to what degree language alternation[1] is used as a tool for constructing social identity categories in and through conversation. Specifically, the article examines how multilingual Tanzanians use the resource of language alternation in collusion with *membership categories* to establish their own and others' social identities. The analysis presented here contributes to studies of talk-in-interaction that show the complex ways in which speakers use categorial language to construct identities for themselves and for their co-participants (e.g., Antaki and Widdicombe, 1998; Hansen, 2005; Maynard and Zimmerman, 1984). Categorization involves the positioning of speakers with various *discursive identities*, such as hearer, speaker, and ratified overhearer, and also with a variety of *social identities*, such as woman, professor, and American (Goffman, 1981; Zimmerman, 1998). Within Sacks's (1972, 1979) framework of *membership categorization analysis* (MCA), these identities are established in part through *categorization sequences* that serve to characterize a participant as a member of a certain social group, and through *category-activity sequences*, which categorize participants indirectly by indexing typical activities bound to categorizations (Maynard and Zimmerman, 1984; Sacks, 1972).

This study investigates how speakers use language selection and alternation to order the world into *collections of things* (Sacks 1972, 1979, 1992). In examining several excerpts of bilingual English–Swahili conversation, the analysis will rely heavily on Sacks's *membership categorization analysis* (MCA), and it will also incorporate Antaki and Widdicombe's (1998) conceptualization of identity as *identities-in-practice*, or speakers' dynamic production of themselves and others. The studies of identities-in-talk that draw on Sacks's work have yielded many insights into the nature of identity, but few studies have been conducted on bilingual conversation within this framework, as far as I know. Only Gafaranga (2001) and Torras and Gafaranga (2002) have treated language selection as a way to index membership in social categories, and namely, the social category of "doing being bilingual." In his work on multilingual Rwandans living in Belgium, Gafaranga (2001, p. 1916) treats language choice as practical social action, "not in terms of the identities society associated with the languages involved, but

Source: Higgins, C. (2007). Constructing membership in the in-group: affiliation and resistance among urban Tanzanians. *Pragmatics*, 17(1), 49–70.

rather in terms of the locally relevant linguistic identities participants have adopted." In his research, the focus is on how speakers negotiate the medium of talk as they perform their multilingual linguistic identities through language selection and language alternation.

In a similar vein, this article examines how Swahili–English bilingual speakers employ language alternation as one resource among many for constructing their identities-in-talk. I will illustrate how, in conjunction with other resources, the participants use two different forms of language alternation as a strategic device to propose, display, accept, resist, and reject membership in certain categories. [. . .]

Conceptual framework

Interculturality

I follow Nishizaka's (1995) and Mori's (2003) use of the term *interculturality* to mean cultural affiliations that produce cultural differences which are made relevant through conversation. As Nishizaka (1995, p. 302) proposes, we should not take different cultures for granted when analyzing talk, but rather, explicate "how it is that the fact of being intercultural is organized as a social phenomenon." Nishizaka's research examines the ways that "being a Japanese" is achieved interactively in the same way that "being a foreigner" is achieved through talk. Nishizaka (1995, p. 305) explains, "For instance, that I am a Japanese is correct, but the category 'Japanese' is not always relevantly applicable to me; whether I am Japanese or not might be irrelevant when I talk to students about Structural-Functionalism in a sociology class."

Mori (2003) continues this line of research, examining question–answer sequences in a study of participation frameworks. She focuses on the description of interculturality by examining moment-by-moment shifts of participation structures for the next-speaker selection, and she also shows that interculturality is treated as irrelevant for some interactions altogether. By examining talk based on the membership categories displayed and made relevant by participants, both Nishizaka and Mori are interested in examining sequences of talk to see how the participants show whether or not their cultural differences are salient. Many other researchers have examined intercultural communication from a social constructivist perspective, including Cheng (2003), Gumperz (1982), and Scollon and Scollon (2001), but perhaps because none of these researchers has used MCA as the primary framework for analysis, their work tends to take cultural difference as a starting point, rather than a phenomenon which remains to be empirically located in talk.

Membership categorization

Sacks's (1972) interest in how members categorize themselves is rooted in the traditions of ethnomethodology, an approach to sociology most often associated with Garfinkel (1967) which was established to investigate people's methods for accounting for their own actions and the actions of others. [. . .] Sacks drew on Garfinkel's interest in understanding when and how members describe their activities, and he extended the study of members' productions of their activities to the study of talk. Sacks was interested in formulating descriptions of people's actions, not from relying on his own perspective as the analyst to describe the activity, but by seeing how the members themselves described the activity. His interest in the ways that people use language to arrange and rearrange the objects of the world into *collections of things* formed the basis of MCA, or the ways that members organize activities and actions in their talk.

Sacks's collections of things are what he calls *membership categorization devices* (MCDs). He describes MCDs as "any collection of membership categories, containing at least a category, which may be applied to some population containing at least a member, so as to provide, by the use of some rules of application, for the pairing of at least a population member and a categorization device member" (Sacks, 1972, p. 332). Examples of MCDs include "the family," in which the categories might be mother, father, and child; "middle-class occupations," in which the categories might be teacher, lawyer, banker; or "woman," which might include the categories mother, grandmother, niece, and sister. Of course, a person can be correctly described as being a member of different categories. From the set of applicable categories, a particular category may be selected as relevant by an individual or by his or her co-participants in the course of a developing interaction.

[The author briefly discussed the significance of MCA drawing from Sack's and Silverman's work.]

BEING ASCRIBED AND RESISTING MEMBERSHIP IN INTERCULTURALITY

The idea that ethnic identity is dynamic, rather than static, has a long tradition in critical studies rooted in the frameworks of post-modernism, post-colonial studies, and cultural studies. The notions of race and ethnicity, among other categories, have been illustrated to be dynamic, shifting, and dependent on perspectives and context. Similar to MCA, these approaches to categories such as ethnicity take the view that all identities are performed, rather than fixed (Bhabha, 1994; Butler, 1999; Hall, 1997; Kristeva, 1974; Rampton, 1995). To illustrate, Ibrahim (2003, p. 172) explains his own personal experience with shifting ethnic/racial categories, based on his different affiliations and self-conceptualization as a 'Black' person:

> As a continental African, for example, I was not considered "Black" in Africa; other terms served to patch together my identity, such as tall, Sudanese, and basketball player. In other words . . . my Blackness was not marked, it was outside the shadow of the Other—North American whiteness. However, as a refugee in North America, my perception of self was altered in direct response to the social processes of racism and the historical representation of Blackness whereby the antecedent signifiers became secondary to my Blackness, and I retranslated my being: I became Black.

Studies of face-to-face interaction within ethnomethodological approaches have shown that categories such as ethnicity are made relevant among speakers by way of explicit category naming, and through CBAs (category-bound activities; see e.g. Hansen (2005)). However, the naming of these categories alone does not make them "real" for all parties. For example, a person may be categorized as "White" or "African American" by another, but the person initially categorized that way may react against such membership altogether, or as relevant for the immediate conversation. Moreover, the person may react against the categorization altogether, since these categories and who they apply to are contestable in themselves. [The author reviews Day's work on the relevance of ethnic group categorisation (1998).]

Identities-in-practice

In recent work on MCDs, Antaki and Widdicombe (1998) establish five principles for the analysis of identities in practice (Table 18.1). My own analysis makes use of these principles in determining whether the participants employ language alternation to help produce, accept, and/or reject MCDs.

Table 18.1 Five principles for the analysis of identities-in-practice (Antaki and Widdicombe, 1998)

---

1. For a person to "have an identity"—whether he or she is the person speaking, being spoken to, or being spoken about—is to be cast into a *category with associated characteristics or features*;
2. such casting is *indexical and occasioned*;
3. it *makes relevant* the identity to the interactional business going on;
4. the force of "having an identity" is in its *consequentiality* in the interaction; and
5. all this is visible in people's exploitation of the *structures of conversation*.

The first principle is based on Sacks's idea that categories are bound together as belonging to *collections of things*, or categories which are grouped together because of associated characteristics. Antaki and Widdicombe (1998) give the example of a "flight cabin crew," with the categories "bursar," "first-class steward," and "flight attendant" as the associated features of the MCD "cabin crew." These categories may be enacted through explicit reference to the MCD, or to CBAs, the actions which indirectly group categories into MCDs. Using Antaki and Widdicombe's example of a flight crew as a MCD, CBAs might be "being knowledgeable about aircraft safety," "being polite," and "well-traveled." For the flight crew, however, is important to realize that this very same group of people could be classified under various MCDs, such as "British," "Caucasian," or "female" (Principle 1). Antaki and Widdicombe (1998, p. 4) emphasize that the converse is also true since CBAs can also imply the categories; they write, "if you look and act a certain way, you might get taken to be a flight attendant; if you have certain legal documents with certain appropriate authorizations, you can be taken to be British". In this view, one can do "being a flight attendant" while in one's own home, perhaps for charades, and the actions will be recognizable as such even if the person doing "being a flight attendant" is not really in that line of work. The MCD "British" might be *indexed* when passing through immigration checks, when the crew files to the counter labeled "domestic" rather than "foreign arrivals" while in the U.K., and *occasioned* by the context of the immigration procedures (Principle 2). In another context, their status "female" might be *occasioned* by which bathroom they enter in the public domain, or when they are referred to as "ladies" by a fellow co-worker, and their "female" MCD becomes marked through the use of the gender-specifying label.

MCDs are made *relevant* (Principle 3) because they are *oriented* to by the participants themselves, rather than the analyst. In the cabin crew scenario, for example, the crew may orient to one another as "good friends" while off the job, but as "formal colleagues" while passing one another while moving down the aisle of the plane, or during a work meeting. In work meetings, we can see the "formal colleagues" identity only if it has *procedural consequentiality* (Principle 4) for the speakers. In other words, the identity is real only if it has a visible effect on the interaction. Finally, the above four principles are made visible in *structures of conversation* (Principle 5), the locus of interaction where participants produce and display their interpretations of one another's identities moment-by-moment.

By making reference to the above principles, I will first show the MCDs which participants can be seen as making relevant through their conversational structures, either through explicit reference or through CBAs. I will then show how language alternation, one of the *structures of conversation* (Principle 5), is employed by participants as a means to produce identities-in-practice.

Data analysis: interculturality among the "same" people

The data presented here are drawn from a larger study of Swahili–English conversation that took place in a newspaper office in Dar es Salaam, Tanzania (Higgins, 2004). Sixty hours of data were recorded, and 53 workers participated in the original study. All of the participants may be considered bilingual in Swahili and English, as their work at an English-medium newspaper office requires that they be able to attend press conferences, carry out interviews, and read documents in both Swahili and English. Most of the participants speak at least one ethnic community language as well, such as Chagga, Nyakyusa, Haya, or Iraqw. While many Tanzanians who have graduated from high school have quite limited English proficiency, the participants in this study can be described as highly proficient in English and Swahili and of a relatively affluent socioeconomic status. All of the participants in the data presented have obtained a post-secondary degree in which English is the medium of instruction, and all of them use English in their daily work.

In this section, I will present two excerpts of talk-in-interaction which reveal how participants at the newspaper office constructed MCDs concerning interculturality through explicit mention of particular categories as well as CBAs indexing these categories. The transcripts follow conversation analytic conventions (e.g. Atkinson and Heritage, 1984) and are produced so that the first line represents the actual utterance, the second line is a morpheme-by-morpheme translation, and the third line is a gloss in conversational English (see Appendix for abbreviations).

The data show how the participants employ MCDs to establish "insider" and "outsider" groups, but in this case, this dichotomy is established to first construct a shared culture among the journalists. This shared culture is based on the journalists' rejection of "uncritical Westernization," which contrasts with what they name as "traditions." Their shared membership is then disrupted by the instantiation of interculturality minutes later, however, when CBAs not associated with the culture of "doing being journalists" are carried out by one of the participants.

Westernized and traditional identities in talk

In the first excerpt, the participants use MCDs and the conversational structure of *insertional codeswitching* (Muysken, 1995), a very hybrid code involving English and Swahili, to align themselves as members of the same group. Insertional codeswitching is akin to borrowing in that it involves the insertion of a lexical or phrasal category into the matrix language.[2] Using this code, the journalists make interculturality relevant in the first excerpt, but only as a means for drawing a boundary between themselves and those Tanzanians who they identify as "outsiders" through their talk. Interculturality is thus established between the speakers in the newspaper office and those Tanzanians who follow Western ways uncritically, such as the Tanzanian youth who dress like rap singers. In the excerpt, the participants are discussing the phenomenon of young Tanzanians who follow fashion trends that they see on television without consideration of how the trends might be inappropriate due to their local tropical weather. Through the talk, an "insider" MCD becomes established through CBAs which organize all those present in the office within the same group. The journalists achieve "insider" membership by jointly criticizing the youth that enthusiastically follow these styles, and they tease one another for not being fashionable since they do not follow the hip-hop trends. Prior to the excerpt, the participants have been looking at a photo of a popular soccer team. The photo has prompted a contentious debate in which the journalists argued whether a team of Tanzanian soccer players were wearing their cleats while boarding a plane. The journalists had been disagreeing with one another over whether or not the cleats are visible, and also over who is to blame for the soccer team's ignorance regarding appropriate footwear on planes. The conversation continues in this theme, and Leonard's first line below refers to people such as these soccer players:

(1a)

1 Leonard: *Sasa unajua   wanavyoona   kwenye television   yule   kwa vitendo*
now you-pres-know they-pres-see on   television that-person by act
"Now you know that when they watch television and see a person doing something"

2   *hawamwelewi   hh. wanasema   nini kwa hiyo hao wakimwona mtu*
they. neg-obj-understand hh. they-pres-say what   for that they they- if-obj-see person
"that they don't understand and they say what, therefore, they when they see someone"

3   *amevaa   gloves anafikiri   hh. ni   style kumbe wale wamevaa gloves s/*
he-has-wear gloves s/he-pres-think hh. it.is style wow they-there they-have-wear gloves
"wearing gloves, they think that it's a style to follow, and all of a sudden they decide to wear gloves too".

4   *wakati wa wakati ..hh bari- wa winter kule kuna   baridi hh.*
time   of time   cold- of winter over.there.is cold
"During, during the cold peri- during winter it is cold there (in Europe)."

5   ((Everyone laughs; everyone is smiling))

6   *Sasa mchezaji wetu hapa akija   hh. uwanja wa kimataifa   na jua*
now player our here s/he-if-come hh. field   of dj-countries and sun
"Now our player here, when he comes out onto the international field and the sun"

7   *linawaka   degree thelathini na mbili hh. anavaa   gloves,*
it-pres-blaze degree thirty   and two hh. s/he-pre-wear gloves
"is blazing at thirty two degrees (Celsius) and he's wearing gloves,"

8 Fikiri: *Anapachika   daluga.*
S/he-pres-pierce spikes
"He's sticking the spikes in (to the ground)." ((F is examining the photo))

9 Leonard: *Yeah.*
"Yeah."

In lines 1–7, Leonard is criticizing Tanzanian soccer players for what he characterizes as their provincial nature. On lines 1–7, he expresses his disdain for how members on the team apparently misunderstand Western soccer players' need to wear gloves during winter as a fashion statement. Using the journalists' unmarked hybrid code involving insertional codeswitching, he says, "*wakimwona mtu amevaa gloves anafikiri ni style kumbe wale wamevaa gloves*" ("when they see someone wearing gloves, they think it's a style, and all of a sudden they wear gloves too"). Leonard is laughing and smiling throughout these turns, but it is clear that he is being critical of the soccer players' gullibility or ignorance. The laughter on line 5 marks the others as sharing the same understanding, and their laughter indicates that it is comical for this group of educated and well-traveled journalists to imagine misunderstanding gloves as a fashion statement instead of a means to keep warm during European winters.

The conversation had already covered the topic of the players' wearing cleats while boarding a plane, so Fikiri's comment about the matter again on line 8 marks his preoccupation with the choice to do so as particularly ignorant or foolish. Leonard, Fikiri, and others had already shared many minutes discussing whether the shoes were cleats or running shoes, and at this point, Fikiri's comment indicates his continued incredulity towards the idea that anyone could ever make the conscious decision to wear cleats on a plane. Leonard's "yeah" on line 9 confirms this incredulity, and groups Leonard and Fikiri together as people who share the same sentiments.

In the remainder of this excerpt, we see how the other participants engage collaboratively in the conversation while using insertional codeswitching, thus ratifying their membership in the group of "insiders," or people who do not blindly follow Western ways.

(1b)

10 Peter: *Hilo   wala si   kwa wachezaji tu   sema majority wa Tanzania.*
             it-dem nor neg for players   only say majority of Tanzania
             "This isn't for sports players only; admit it, it's the majority of Tanzania."

11 Leonard: *Ni wengi yes mpaka   vijana unakuta   wana   wanafanya.*
             it.is many yes including youths you-pres-find they-pres they-pres
             "It is many, yes, even the youth. You will see them doing, doing it (too)."

12 Frankie: *Mbona wale (.) wanaoimba   rap wanavaa   makofia ya winter yale:,*
             Why they (.) they-pres-sing rap they-pres-wear pl-hat of winter dem
             "Why do those people who sing rap wear winter hats (and)"

13   *yale majacket.*
             dem pl-jacket
             "those jackets?"

14 Peter: *Hiyo ni kwa Watanzania   wengi .Isipokuwa Mosi.*
             dem is for pl-Tanzanian many except   Mosi
             "That (style) is most Tanzanians. Except Mosi."

15 Frankie: *Mosi yeye ameamua   kubakia   traditions.*
             Mosi he   he-pfc-decide to-remain traditions
             "Mosi has decided to remain in the traditions."

16 Jongo: *Mo:si::.*

17 Peter: *Mosi n [(circumstance tofauti) xxx.*
             Mosi is circumstance different
             "Mosi is in a different circumstance."

18 Frankie: *[Kuna vijana (.) wachache born with their traditions first.*
             There-are   youths   pl-few born with their traditions first
             "There are few youths these days born with their traditions first."

19 Peter: Traditions first.

20   *Eh, umema ↑liza.* ((to another journalist, Noreen, regarding the computer))
             hey you-have-finish
             "Hey, are you done?"

On line 10, Peter confirms this insider–outsider grouping and further clarifies the members of both groups, and, making use of the hybrid English–Swahili insiders' code, he declares the outsiders to be "*majority wa Tanzania*" ("the majority of Tanzanians"). Leonard's confirmation of his statement on line 11 jointly constructs Leonard, Peter, and Frankie as people who are not of "the majority." The CBAs of being "Westernized" here involve "dressing according to outsiders' standards," and "being unduly influenced by cultures outside of Tanzania."

The MCD of "Westernized" becomes more clear when the journalists polarize it with what they explicitly call "traditions" later in the excerpt. In lines 12–13, Frankie asks about the practice of youth who wear winter hats and coats in Tanzania while rapping, which can be taken as another critique of youth culture which does not examine the appropriateness of winter clothing (and hence, Western ideals) for the Tanzanian context in which a Northern type of "winter" does not exist. On line 14, Peter marks his understanding of this "insider" group identity of which he is a member by teasing another journalist, Mosi, for not being like the majority of Tanzanian youth who embrace Westernization, at least in terms of fashion. By teasing him, Peter places Mosi into the "insider" group, i.e., those who are "traditionalists," when he says "That (style) is most Tanzanians, except Mosi." The tease is actually a compliment, based on the pejorative comments that have been made about the soccer players who blindly follow the Western trends they see on television.

Peter's comment on line 14 can be taken as praise for Mosi's (and by group-association, his own) resilience which rejects Western fashion trends and, thereby, promotes Tanzanian values instead. These positive sentiments are echoed by Jongo and Frankie (line 15). Interestingly, Frankie uses the English word "traditions" in his hybrid code, even though the Swahili choices such as *mila* ("custom"), *desturi* ("tradition"), or *kienyeji* ("indigenous") would have been available to him, as these words are very common lexical items. Frankie's next turn in line 18 makes use of "born with their traditions first," which contrasts with the medium of the surrounding talk. Unlike the previous turns of talk that involve hybrid language mixing, this turn is comprised of *alternational codeswitching* (Muysken, 1995). Unlike insertional codeswitching, alternational codeswitching typically involves the use of a different code at levels higher than the morpheme or word boundary. This type of language alternation is starker than insertional codeswitching, and it appears to have a much more clearly pragmatic function in talk.

This contrast seems to emphasize traditions or Tanzanian life as different from the surrounding talk's content (CBAs involving "Westernized" activities). Furthermore, the English word "traditions" arguably takes on the voice of the *other* (Said, 1978; Spivak, 1987), as it categorizes traditional ways as noticeably different or marked, in reference to modern (or Westernized) ways. In other words, cultural practices only become traditions when perceived through the eyes of the other.

At this point in the conversation, the group shares "insider" status through their mixed code, and through sharing the MCD "traditionalists," marked by the CBAs "dressing appropriately for their local context," "rejecting Western trends," and "critiquing other Tanzanians for their provincial ways." In terms of conversational structures, the use of Swahili–English establishes an insider group in collusion with these MCDs. It is relevant to note that these English insertions index normative speech among these journalists. In my six month period of field work, I observed that Swahili–English talk was their regular mode for communicating with one another, and it was clear that their daily language practices rarely involved either "pure" English or "pure" Swahili.

Doing (and not doing) being a journalist

The second excerpt, taken from moments later in the talk, demonstrates how this recently-established shared culture is re-analyzed by the group when Mosi, who has just been praised for his insider-status, is removed from this status and re-oriented to as an outsider. Throughout the talk, CBAs deemed appropriate for the identity of "doing being a journalist" emerge, and Mosi's activities are characterized as inappropriate and uncooperative for this categorization through the use of alternational codeswitching.

At the start of Excerpt 2a, Peter asks Mosi (who is working on a project with Jongo, an intern) whether he is writing a story or doing some other kind of work. Peter has been waiting for a computer to become free for quite a while at this point:

(2a)

75 Peter:	*Aah nyie mnaandika stori au mnafundishana?*	
	ah you-pl you.pl-pres-write story or you.pl-pres-teach-each.other	
	"Ah, are you writing stories or are you teaching each other?"	
76 Mosi:	*Ah ah,*	
	"no,"	
77 Peter:	*Sisi tunataka kompyuta bwana.*	
	we we-pres-want computer sir/friend	
	"We want the computer, buddy."	
78 Mosi:	*Aisee uta- tutaenda wapi?*	
	I-say you-will we-will-go where	
	"Hey, you'll- where will we go?"	
79 Peter:	t! ((alveolar tongue click, indexing aggravation))	
80 Frankie:	*Wewe kama nanii: hiyo page unamali- umeshamaliza kutype*	
	you like um this page you-pres-fin- you-presperf-finish to-type	
	"Um, when you fin-, once you have finished typing that page,"	
81	*mwambie Peter akusaidie kuondoa ile [pale.*	
	him-tell Peter he-you-help to-remove that there	
	"tell Peter to help you to take it out there."	
82 Peter:	[This is not a computer lesson.	
83 Mosi:	*Nimeshamaliza.*	
	I-pres.pfc-cpl-finish	
	"I have already finished."	

In line 75, Peter uses the journalists' hybrid code of insertional codeswitching when he asks Mosi and Jongo whether they are engaged in what he characterizes as "legitimate journalism activity," with his question, "Are you writing a story or are you teaching each other?" Mosi responds minimally, choosing neither option, which prompts Peter to complain, "We want the computer, buddy." At this point in the conversation, Peter has been waiting for a computer to become available so that he can write up his news story. His choice of *"sisi"* ("we") in line 77 is interesting, since he is the only one on queue for a computer. However, what this pronominal choice may be doing is marking him as one of the people with a legitimate activity, i.e., the activity of typing a story for the newspaper. Mosi's response on line 78 concedes his activity as outside the bounds of "writing stories," as he asks where he and Jongo will go to finish their task of creating forms. Peter responds with an alveolar tongue click, which, in Tanzania, indicates disdain for what someone has just said.

Frankie joins the conversation on line 80, confirming Peter's characterization of Mosi's activity as inappropriate for the setting, and tells him to hurry his task. Peter interrupts in line 82, declaring in English, "This is not a computer lesson," a turn which clearly labels the activity that Mosi and Jongo are engaged in as outside the boundaries of what journalists should be doing in the office. This turn marks their activity as belonging to "others," those who are not engaged in journalism, and its medium of expression, English, helps to construct the "otherness" of the activity by virtue of its disjunction with the previous talk. The stark use of alternational codeswitching here contrasts greatly with the prior use of insertional codeswitching and consequently becomes a forceful way to contest Mosi's activities. Mosi complains that he is about finished on line 83, but he remains in his chair, continuing with his action of "not doing being journalist."

In Excerpt 2b, the conversation continues, and Frankie repeats his advice to Mosi to hurry up by asking Peter to help him edit the forms so that he can free up the computer for Peter.

(2b)

84 Frankie: *Kweli> mwambie   jamaa   akusaidie   kurekebisha forms na*
              really   him-tell person   he-you-help   to-adjust   forms and
              "Really, you should tell the guy to help you to correct the forms and"
85   *kufanya virekebisho vingine<. (.) uondoke.*
              to-do   corrections other   you-sbj-leave
              "to do other corrections so that you can leave."
              ((omitted talk: Mosi and Frankie discuss how Mosi might do the alterations on his form, and whether or not Fikiri is coming back to use the computer that Mosi is using))
91 Mosi: *Sasa   unasema (.)   unapiga   kelele.*
              Now   you-pres-say   you-pres-hit noise
              "Now you say, now you're making racket (complaining)."
92   (1.0)
93   *Kama utakuwa   mstaarabu   unakuja   kukaa hapa lakini kama*
              if   you-fut-be peaceful.person you-pres-come to-sit here but   if
              "If you are reasonable/decent, then you'll get to sit here, but if"
94   *utaamua   kuforce   mambo ndiyo   hivyo.*
              you-fut-decide to-force things indeed are-this-way
              "you decide to force things, then that's it."

Between lines 85 and 91, Mosi responds to Frankie's advice with a complaint, and he mentions that another journalist had told him that the person previously using the computer was finished, therefore providing a rationale to his rights to the computer. Peter did not agree with this logic, probably because Mosi's activity has been characterized by several people as outside the bounds of writing a story, which is what this group of journalists orients to as the priority activity for the computers. On line 91, Mosi orients to Peter's disdain as a complaint, and he characterizes Peter as "making racket."

In lines 93–94, Mosi offers his perception of legitimate activity and behavior in the room, as he explains *"kama utakuwa mstaarabu unakuja kukaa hapa"* ("If you are reasonable/decent, then you'll get to sit here"), but continues, *"lakini kama utaamua kuforce mambo ndiyo hivyo"* ("but if you decide to force things, then that's it"). Here, Mosi's strategic juxtaposition of *"mstaarabu"* and *"kuforce"* creates a disjunction with how he views Peter's behavior, and the way that his own behavior is being treated by others in the office such as Frankie and Peter. *"Mstaarabu"* means "civilized person," and is a term which would not be grouped with the activity of being "forceful," as in *"kuforce."* Moreover, the language choice indexes opposition, as Mosi's pairing of these two words shows the discontinuity between his desires and those of Peter, and also shows his view of Peter's actions as negative. While such language use might be categorized as insertional codeswitching, I propose treating it as alternational for the way in which it establishes a clear contrast in the interpretation of activities among the participants.

After line 94, Peter turns his attention to the whereabouts of Fikiri, the person responsible for handing over the computer to Mosi in the first place. His effort to resolve the problem this way does not succeed, however, and another journalist who has been sitting in the office the entire time, Mbwilo, joins the conversation. Mosi's activities continue to run counter to the on-task journalist identity, and Mbwilo names his ethnicity as the source of his inability to work with his colleagues in a suitable manner. Hence, by way of association, his ethnicity becomes one of the features of the MCD "doing being uncooperative" or "being off-task in the office." His status as an outsider becomes made real through explicit categorization of him as culturally marked, and his response shows his rejection of this ethnic marking.

(2c)

98 Mbwilo: *Sasa wewe maliza acha [uone   atakayekaa   au ataxxx.*
now   you   finish   leave   you-sbj-see   he-will-who-sit   or   he-will-xxx
"Now, you finish and leave, and see who will sit there or who will"

99 Frankie: [*Wewe maliza uondoke   uende   zako=*
you   finish   you-sbj-leave   you-sbj-go   yours
"You just finish and get on your way"

100 Peter: =*Kwa hiyo wewe huondoki   mpaka [Fikiri aje.*
for   that   you   you.neg-leave   until   Fikiri   comes
"So you aren't leaving until Fikiri comes?"

101 Mbwilo: [*Kwa yeye ataruhuswa-*
for   him   he-fut.allow-psv
"For him to be allowed (to use the computer)"

102 Frankie: *Huyo nani yuko   nani (.) hamna   monitor.*
he   who   he-loc   who   neg.loc   monitor
"That guy, um, he's um. There's no monitor there."

103 Mosi: *Wala haitoki.*
nor   it.neg-go.out
"And it doesn't work."

104 Mbwilo: *Wewe unaleta   mambo ya Kikurya   huku.*
you   you-pres-bring   things   of   adj-Kurya   here
"You bring this Kurya stuff here."

In line 98, Mbwilo tells Mosi in no uncertain terms to leave the computer and to hand it over to Peter. Frankie's voice becomes part of the directive on line 99, where he uses the expression "*uende zako*" ("get on your way", or even, "get lost"). Everyone in the office (Peter, Frankie, and Mbwilo) is telling Mosi that his activities are not legitimate, and that he needs to abandon his computer. He is characterized as not behaving appropriately, and his activities are not oriented to as belonging to "doing being a journalist" in this context. Peter asks him to leave again (line 100), and Frankie looks around to find another computer that Mosi might use for his non-journalistic task (line 102). Still, Mosi remains seated at the coveted computer, and this appears to prompt Mbwilo to say "you bring this Kurya stuff here," on line 104, referring to Mosi's ethnic group, a Bantu group in Northern Tanzania that is often portrayed in the media as stubborn and hostile, with a preference for careers in the police and military. Mbwilo's line 104 groups Mosi outside the boundaries of the "insiders," those who are engaged in journalistic tasks, as it makes salient his ethnicity, which is not shared by any other member of the group. His use of the word "here" marks the context as one in which "being Kurya" is inappropriate since it creates obstacles for the other journalists to do their job. In other words, being an outsider here is evaluated negatively. In excerpt 2d, we then see how everyone orients to the disturbance that this othering creates in the office, and we see various efforts to reenlist Mosi as an insider who is "doing being a journalist":

(2d)
105 Frankie: *Halo njoo wewe njoo ukae   hapa. Usipoteze   muda wa*
               mwenzio.
               hello come you come you-sit-sbj here you.neg.sbj-lose time of your.colleague
               "Hey, come, you, and sit here. Don't waste your colleague's time."
106   (.)
107   *Njoo.=*
               "Come here."
               ((Mosi stands up but remains at the computer))
108 Mosi: *=Sasa unanilazimisha.*
               now   you-pres-me-force
               "Now you are forcing me."
109 Frankie: *Haya   ma- nanii madiskette mabovu   haya. Hallow nanii, (.)*
               enough pl.- um   pl-diskette pl-corrupt dem hello   um
               "Okay, these, um these disks are bad, these (ones). Hey there, um,"
110   *>Kijana<njoo:e*
               young.person come
               "Youngster, come here."
               ((Mosi moves towards the seat Frankie offers))
111 Mosi: *Kijana   wa hapo xxx wana   tabia.*
               young.person of here xxx they-have (bad) characters.
               "The young people here have bad attitudes."
               ((creaky voice mimicking an elder))
               ((Peter takes Mosi's seat))

Frankie echoes Mbwilo's sentiments on line 105 by saying "Don't waste your colleague's time," clearly marking Mosi's activities as illegitimate and contrary to what "colleagues" should be doing for one another. At the same time, his turn on this line attempts to return Mosi back to the "insider" group, as it asks for cooperation. Frankie tells him "Come here" and politely requests that he sit next to Frankie using subjunctive, rather than imperative form.

At this point in the interaction, Mosi stands up and says "*Sasa unanilazimisha*" ("Now you are forcing me"). By moving out from behind the computer, and allowing Peter to use it (line 111), Mosi becomes a cooperative member of the insider group of journalists once again, and his utterance in line 108, in "pure" Swahili this time (as opposed to "*kuforce*", line 94), marks the end to the disjunction created earlier in the conversation. Mosi moves towards Frankie in line 110, and in a creaky voice mimicking an *mzee* ("elder"), he says "The youth here have bad attitudes," and then smiles. Through *crossing* (Rampton, 1995) into the voice of the *mzee*, he rectifies the discord which he has created, and he displays his interest in cooperating with the group so that he can be treated as an insider once again. Through crossing, he takes up the categorization he has been offered—not a Kurya person, but rather, a *kijana* ("a young person") whose bad manners might be excused by his youth. In other words, through this language alternation into the voice of another (but not into another language), he resists the identity selected for him as a Kurya person, and he asserts his primary identity as that of a young person, rather than remaining in the "outsider" position of a Kurya. In doing so, he rejoins the group as an "insider," making the interculturality which emerged irrelevant for any activities that follow. Table 18.2 summarizes these moves.

Discussion

This article has examined the ways that participants use bilingual conversation to produce and resist MCDs which are contingent upon the notion of interculturality. Data analysis has shown that interculturality can be used as a means to achieve shared experience through participants' alignments or disaffiliations as "insiders" and "outsiders." In the data examined, participants were seen to employ a variety of strategies, including two forms of codeswitching, to create disjunction between participants deemed "insiders" and those who they characterized as "outsiders."

In examining extended excerpts, it was possible to see how participants employed language alternation as a means to align themselves and others with specific MCDs. In the first excerpt, the participants used the discursive practice of language alternation in a very hybrid fashion to mark off identities-in-practice which aligned the entire office as "insiders" in their rejection of

Table 18.2 Mosi's transformation from insider (4) to outsider (2a–c) back to insider (2d)

Identity-in-practice	CBA/MCD
Excerpt 1b: Insertional CS 15 *Mosi has decided to remain in the traditions.*	insider: 'not a Westernized youth'
Excerpt 2a: Alternational CS 82 *This is not a computer lesson*	outsider: not doing being a journalist
Excerpt 2b: Alternational CS 93 *If you are reasonable/decent, then you'll get to sit here* 94 *but if you decide to force things, then that's it.*	resistance to others' CBAs of how to be a journalist; "force" in English
Excerpt 2c: Ethnification 104 *you are bringing Kurya stuff here*	not doing being an insider through ethnicity
Excerpt 2d: Crossing 105 *don't waste your colleague's time* 108 *now you are forcing me ((co-occurs with getting up from seat))* 110 *Youngster, come here* 111 *The young people here have bad attitudes*	not doing being an insider by not being empathetic/cooperative with insiders' work move towards cooperation with insiders; "force" in Swahili re-instituting "insider" membership disalignment with self as "Kurya" in favor of alignment with self as "young person"; doing being a journalist

"uncritical Westernization." Here, a code described best as either insertional code-switching (Muysken, 1995) or *language mixing* (Auer, 1999) was used to emphasize the differences between the insider and outsider groups, thereby creating a shared culture among the hybrid-language using journalists in the office. Minutes later in the conversation, however, that very same shared culture, or shared "insider" status, was reanalyzed when Mosi's activities were evaluated as "outsider" activities by the other participants. This reanalysis became apparent due to language alternation of a different sort, alternational code-switching (Muysken, 1995), when Peter used a purely English utterance to challenge the legitimacy of Mosi's activities (line 82, "This is not a computer lesson").

Interculturality became salient for the participants in the second data set when the CBAs which Mosi was engaged in were evaluated by the rest of the office as being an uncooperative journalist. Through alternational codeswitching, Mosi resisted this characterization through positioning his colleagues as people who were forcing him (line 94) to act in certain ways. In response, his fellow journalists used the category of ethnicity to construct an intercultural and tense social order. The Kurya ethnicity became part of the MCD of "outsider" when it was used in association with the MCD "off-task journalist." Mosi's subsequent use of Swahili in "*unanilazimisha*" ("you are forcing me"), along with his physical movement away from the computer, marked his re-entry into the "insider" group, the MCD of "doing being journalists." This language alternation signaled Mosi's own self-positioning as a cooperative member, and it had the effect of "erasing" his previous language alternation ("*kuforce*") along with his previously antagonistic stance. Mosi further identified with the in-group by crossing, when he took on the identity of an elder Swahili in order to critique his own behavior.

Finally, it is possible to link the journalists' use of language alternation and their establishment of interculturality to more macro level observations about the divisive effects that English has had on Tanzanians. As Blommaert (1999) has argued, in spite of Tanzania's radically socialist past which eschewed the formation of social classes, the use of English-interfered Swahili among educated elites in Tanzania has created sociolects by which socioeconomic classes have become apparent. Those who are able to mix English into their Swahili index their social positioning among one another, thereby reifying and reinstating their identities as educated, white-collar workers through talk. In making use of this and other varieties of speech in the newspaper office, the journalists establish cultural sameness and difference with one another through constructing membership categorizations along linguistic lines. Moreover, in using these varieties of langauge, they instantiate intercultural difference among themselves and others in Tanzania who have not experienced the same degree of access to English, and therefore, remain in the outgroup.

Appendix

Transcript symbols

.	falling intonation
,	continuing intonation
?	rising intonation
underline	emphasis
[	overlapping talk
:	sound stretch
hh.	outbreath/laughter
.hh	inbreath

(.)	micropause
talk-	cut-off
TALK	loud volume
((comments))	transcriber's description of events

Abbreviations

adj	adjectival marker
cpl	completed action marker
dem	demonstrative
fut	future tense
loc	locative
neg	negative marker
pfc	perfective tense
pl	plural marker
pres	present tense
pst	past tense
psv	passive voice
sbj	subjunctive mood

Notes

1   I use the term *language alternation* instead of the more common term *codeswitching*, as *codeswitching* typically carries the implication that a switch in language has taken place. Conversation analytic studies of language alternation (e.g. Auer, 1998, 1999; Li Wei, 1995, 2002) have shown clearly that not every case of language alternation is indeed oriented to by participants as a switch in language.

2   Examples of insertional CS are more like borrowings than cases of codeswitching that have any pragmatic function. In the examples provided, the instances of insertional CS are very similar to what Auer (1999) calls *language mixing*, the ungrammaticalized use of alternate languages which yield no pragmatic effect at the sequential level. In the transcript, I have chosen not to format the instances of insertional CS as a distinct language from Swahili because these "insertions" do not represent another language, but rather, index the use of a mixed code as a legitimate language in its own right.

References

Antaki, C. and Widdicombe, S. (eds) (1998). *Identities in talk*. Thousand Oaks, CA: Sage.

Atkinson, J. M. and Heritage, J. (1984). *Structures of social action: Studies in conversation analysis*. Cambridge: Cambridge University Press.

Auer, P. (ed.) (1998). *Code-switching in conversation: Language interaction and identity*. London: Routledge.

Auer, P. (1999). From codeswitching via language mixing to fused lects: Toward a dynamic typology of bilingual speech. *International Journal of Bilingualism, 3*(4), 309–32.

Bhabha, H. (1994). *The location of culture*. London and New York: Routledge.

Blommaert, J. (1999). *State ideology and language in Tanzania*. Cologne: Köppe.

Butler, J. (1999). *Gender trouble: Feminism and the subversion of identity*. New York: Routledge.

Cheng, W. (2003). *Intercultural conversation*. Amsterdam: John Benjamins Publishing Company.

Day, D. (1998). Being ascribed, and resisting, membership of an ethnic group. In C. Antaki and S. Widdicombe (eds), *Identities in talk* (pp. 151–170). Thousand Oaks, CA: Sage.

Gafaranga, J. (2001). Linguistic identities in talk-in-interaction: Order in bilingual conversation. *Journal of Pragmatics, 33*(12), 1901–25.

Garfinkel, H. (1967). *Studies in ethnomethodology*. Englewood Cliffs: Prentice Hall.

Goffman, E. (1981). *Forms of talk*. Philadelphia, PA: University of Pennsylvania Press.

Gumperz, J. (1982). *Discourse strategies*. Cambridge: Cambridge University Press.

Hall, S. (1997). *Representation: Cultural representation and signifying practices*. London: Sage.

Hansen, A. D. (2005). A practical task: Ethnicity as a resource in social interaction. *Research on Language and Social Interaction,* 38(1), 63–104.

Higgins, C. (2004). Swahili-English bilingual conversation: A vehicle for the study of language ideology. Unpublished doctoral dissertation, University of Wisconsin-Madison.

Ibrahim, A. (2003). "Whassup homeboy?" Joining the African disaspora: Black English as a symbolic site of identification and language learning. In S. Makoni, G. Smitherman, A. F. Ball, and A. K. Spears (eds), *Black linguistics: Language, society, and politics in Africa and the Americas* (pp. 169–85). London & NY: Routledge.

Kristeva, J. (1974). *Revolution in poetic language.* Paris: Lautreament et Mallarme.

Li Wei (1995). Code-switching, preference marking and politeness in bilingual cross-generational talk: Examples from a Chinese community in Britain. *Journal of Multilingual and Multicultural Development,* 16(3), 197–214.

Li Wei (2002). "What do you want me to say?" On the conversation analysis approach to bilingual interaction. *Language in Society,* 31(2), 159–80.

Maynard, D. and Zimmerman, D. (1984). Topical talk, ritual and the social organization of relationships. *Social Psychological Quarterly,* 47(4), 301–16.

Mori, Junko (2003). The construction of interculturality: A study of initial encounters between Japanese and American students. *Research on Language and Social Interaction,* 36(2), 143–84.

Muysken, P. (1995). Codeswitching and grammatical theory. In L. Milroy and P. Muysken (eds), *One speaker, two languages* (pp. 177–98). Cambridge: Cambridge University Press.

Nishizaka, A. (1995). The interactive constitution of interculturality: How to be a Japanese with words. *Human Studies,* 18(2–3), 301–26.

Rampton, B. (1995) *Crossing: Language and ethnicity among adolescents.* New York: Longman.

Sacks, H. (1972) On the analyzability of stories by children. In J. Gumperz and D. Hymes (eds), *Directions in sociolinguistics* (pp. 325–45). New York: Holt, Rinehart, & Winston.

Sacks, H. (1979) Hotrodder: A revolutionary new category. In G. Psathas (ed.), *Everyday language: Studies in ethnomethodology* (pp. 7–14). New York: Irvington.

Sacks, H. (1992) *Lectures on conversation,* G. Jefferson (ed.) 2 vols., Oxford: Blackwell.

Said, E. (1978) *Orientalism.* New York: Random House.

Scollon, R. and Scollon, S. W. (2001) *Intercultural communication: A discourse approach* (2nd edn). Malden, MA: Blackwell.

Spivak, G. (1987). *In other worlds: Essays in cultural politics.* New York: Metheun.

Torras, M.-C. and Gafaranga. (2002). Social identities and language alternation in non-formal institutional bilingual talk: Trilingual service encounters in Barcelona. *Language in Society,* 31(4): 527–48.

Zimmerman, D. (1998). Discourse identities and social identities. In C. Antaki and S. Widdicombe (eds), *Identities in talk* (pp. 87–106). Thousand Oaks, CA: Sage.

PART V: NOTES FOR STUDENTS AND INSTRUCTORS

Study questions

1 According to Sarangi, what should be the purpose of intercultural analysis and why?
2 How does a dynamic model of intercultural miscommunication analysis as presented by Sarangi approach intercultural miscommunication differently from other models such as cross-cultural pragmatics and interactional sociolinguistics?
3 Why is interculturality a phenomenon to be investigated in its own right, according to Nishizaka?
4 Both Nishizaka's and Higgins' main arguments rest upon Harvey Sacks' ideas of membership categorisation devices (MCDs). What are the key components of Sacks' concept of MCDs? Explain how the concept can be applied to studies of interculturality.
5 Higgins argues that the idea of interculturality applies not only to participants of different cultures, but also to the 'same' group of people. What interactional resources do the participants in her study use to ascribe to or resist group membership?

Study activities

1 How do studies of interculturality answer the following questions? Do you agree with their views?
   • What is culture?
   • What is the nature of cultural differences?
   • Are cultural differences a given fact?
   • Who attributes cultural differences to the participants under investigation?
   • Are 'cultural differences' always relevant to or the source of mis- or non-understanding in intercultural interaction?
   • What analytical method is most suitable to analysis: mis- or non-understanding in interaction?
   • What interactional resources do participants in intercultural interaction make use of in establishing and negotiating their sociocultural identities and how?
2 What does the interculturality approach tell us that the traditional cultural-value approach cannot?

3   Choose an excerpt of the conversation transcribed in Chapter 19 and discuss: (a) What 'cultural differences' are brought into the conversation and how? (b) Do you think cultural differences are brought into the conversation intentionally? Relate your discussion to the notion of 'interculturality'.

Further reading

Key publications on interculturality include:

Mori, J. (2003). The construction of interculturality: a study of initial encounters between Japanese and American students. *Research on Language and Social Interaction*, 36(2), 143–84.

Higgins, C. (ed.) (2007). A closer look at cultural difference: 'Interculturality' in talk-in-interaction. A special issue of *Pragmatics*, 17(1).

Zhu Hua (2010). Language socialisation and interculturality: address terms in intergenerational talk in Chinese diasporic families. *Language and Intercultural Communication*, 10(3), 189–205.

The following article discusses the reason why intercultural discourse should be analysed from the perspective of the participants:

Koole, T. & ten Thije, J. D. (2001). The reconstruction of intercultural discourse: methodological considerations. *Journal of Pragmatics*, 33, 571–87.

The following articles provide the key conceptual frameworks from which interculturality draws:

Sacks, H. (1972a). An initial investigation of the usability of conversational data for doing sociology. In D. Sudnow (ed.), *Studies in social interaction* (pp. 31–74). New York: Free Press.

Sacks, H. (1972b). On the analyzability of stories by children. In J. J. Gumperz & D. Hymes (eds), *Directions in sociolinguistics* (pp. 325–45). New York: Holt, Rinehart and Winston.

Antaki, C. & Widdicombe, S. (eds) (1998). *Identities in talk*. Thousand Oaks, CA: Sage.

Intercultural communication in a professional context

Introduction to Part VI

Zhu Hua

A S THE LAST SECTION OF the *Reader*, Part VI includes a selection of papers on intercultural communication in various professional, linguistic and cultural contexts. A common thread underlying the chapters in this part, with the exception of Chapter 19, is the cross-cultural and cross-linguistic comparative approach. In some papers, such as Chapter 20 and Chapter 22, more differences than commonalities are highlighted, whereas in Chapter 21 the two cultures under study are found to be more similar in terms of specific speech acts, which may be attributable to the constraint of the generic type of discourse under investigation.

As one of the earliest studies in intercultural communication at work, Chapter 19 investigates the interaction among non-native English speakers at workplaces in Melbourne, Australia. It closely examines turn-taking behaviours in the realisation of apology and complaint routines and attempts to account for communication breakdown in terms of discrepancies in cultural expectations.

Chapter 20 studies the pragmatics of advertising and compares the way suggestions are made in television commercials from the United States, Japan, China and South Korea. The speech act of suggestion as mediated in television commercials, according to the authors, differs from other speech acts in that its persuasive goal or illocutionary force is explicit to television viewers; the discourse in commercials is scripted, and the conventional notions of speaker and hearer do not apply any more. The value of this study lies not only in its rich data and systematic and highly applicable approach, but also the way its findings are accounted for in a plethora of factors including universal pragmatic principles, cultural norms, economic systems, regulations of the advertising industry and the medium of television.

Moving on to business management meetings, Chapter 21 investigates what counts as interruption and the pragmatic functions of 'interruptive' strategies in task-oriented multiparty conversations in British and Italian management meetings. The authors argue that, contrary to the common 'negative' association with this speech act, most of the interruptions in management meetings are supportive in nature and are used to facilitate group dynamics in multiparty speech as a means of reaching agreement. By looking at native speakers' turn-taking behaviour, Chapter

21 can be used as an extension to the discussion in Chapter 19, which investigates turn-taking patterns among non-native English speakers. The study also reveals a number of extra-linguistic factors that impact on turn-taking dynamics, including the genre of the discourse, the expertise of the speaker, the task of the meeting, and the power and status of the speaker. Again, this can be read in connection with a discussion on the findings in Chapter 19.

Language use varies from one culture to another. This not only applies to situations where different languages are used, but also to the same-language situation. Chapter 22 reports an empirical investigation of the language of service encounters in two cities where the same language (i.e. Spanish) is spoken, but there are many sociocultural differences underlying the language use owing to historical, political and social development. Significant differences are found between the two cities in terms of turn sequences, selling strategies and the styles of interactions: whereas the Montevidean participants prefer informality and closeness, their Quiteño counterparts attempt to maintain the social distance boundary. By examining cross-cultural differences in the use of the same language, the study highlights the sociocultural variations in language use.

Chapter 19

MICHAEL CLYNE, MARTIN BALL, AND DEBORAH NEIL

INTERCULTURAL COMMUNICATION AT WORK IN AUSTRALIA
Complaints and apologies in turns

Introduction

THE INTERCULTURAL STUDY of discourse has made substantial advances in recent years through the marrying of discourse analysis with contrastive pragmatics and interlanguage pragmatics. In the 1960s and early 1970s, syntactic, phonological and semantic studies contrasting languages claimed to be able to predict learners' errors. Contrastive pragmatics and discourse analysis, however, are more oriented toward linguistic description. Interlanguage pragmatics and discourse analysis (like other interlanguage research; Selinker, 1972; Corder, 1981) examine L2 discourse, which differs from L1 discourse in the language, regardless of whether the deviations are due to interference, hypercorrection, simplification, generalization or other causes (see, for example, Kasper, 1981, 1989; Hüllen and Lörscher, 1989; Riley, 1989). Some of these studies are based on interaction between native and non-native speakers (Bremer et al., 1988; Faerch and Kasper, 1983; Perdue, 1982).

This paper is a progress report of research exploring interaction in English between immigrants from different non-English-speaking backgrounds. The study is prompted by the challenges and exigencies of multiculturalism and multilingualism in Melbourne, Australia. According to the 1986 Census, about 100 languages other than English are in daily use in this city. Nine languages other than English are spoken in the home by more than 20,000 speakers. They are (in order)—Italian, Greek, Serbo-Croatian, Chinese, Maltese, German, Arabic, Vietnamese, Macedonian, and Polish. People from ethnolinguistic groups which have no previous history of contact and with vastly different cultural expectations of communication have co-settled and are working together, for example: Turks and Vietnamese, Greeks and Chinese, Maltese and Ukrainians. In some industries, the majority of workers are from non-English speaking backgrounds. These immigrants have little opportunity to communicate with native English speakers, but habitually use English as a lingua franca amongst themselves in the workplace. Such situations offer potential for interlanguage intercultural pragmatics and discourse research which could contribute a new perspective to language contact studies, long dominated by preoccupation with code-switching, lexical, and syntactic interference, and grammatical simplification.

Source: Clyne, M., Ball, M. & Neil, D. (1991). Excerpt from Intercultural communication at work in Australia: complaints and apologies in turns. *Multilingua*, 10, 251–73.

Intercultural communication breakdown has both social and economic consequences (for example, a decline in work satisfaction, interpersonal conflict, racial tension, a drop in productivity, even retrenchment). Intercultural communication research in the work domain may therefore have some significance for both labor and management, especially in the push towards industrial democracy. We would hope that this research would contribute also to policy and curriculum decisions in the educational domain (including English as a second language).

The multicultural nature of Australian society is widely recognized in a number of areas, including educational curriculum policy, languages in education policies, the media, and interpreting/translating. Australia has a national policy on languages, a telephone interpreter service functioning in over fifty languages, a state-run television network transmitting in languages other than English (with English sub-titles), government-supported radio stations broadcasting in over sixty languages, and commercial bilingual radio stations. Melbourne state primary schools currently teach a total of seventeen languages, and thirty-two languages are examined at the end of secondary school. Yet Australian rhetoric still presupposes a trichotomy of "Anglo-Celtic," "Aboriginal," and "Ethnic," where "ethnic" dictates exclusion from "mainstream Anglo-Celtic culture." Adult and child immigrants are taught to communicate with and like native speakers of Australian English in English as a Second Language classes (including English in the Work Place programs). This reflects two general assumptions: firstly that there is no need for English speakers to learn how people of other cultural backgrounds communicate; and secondly that there is little potential for communication breakdown where "ethnic Australians" of different cultual backgrounds interact.

In this paper we shall ouline the ctriteria for our data collection, the methodology of field work, and data analysis. We will discuss some data pertaining to apology and complaint routines, focusing on intercultural issues, demonstrating the value of this type of research and some of the theoretical assumptions in pragmatics. The relationship between turn-taking and discourse sequencing on the one hand and speech acts on the other will also be considered.

Description of project

Four workplaces were selected in Melbourne: one from the public sector and four companies. Consideration was given to industry type, locality and whether the companies were purely domestic or multinationals. [. . .] The workplaces chosen were:

A. An electronics manufacturer in the eastern suburbs which is a subsidiary of a West German company. Many of the upper and middle management are native German speakers, who often use German in social conversation: official policy is for English to be used whenever a non-German-speaker is present. Data have been collected using many informants in the electronic assembly building, where the workforce comprises some central Europeans and many South-East Asians.
B. A textile manufacturer in the western suburbs. The workforce consists of mainly older Southern European immigrants and their children, with some newer, mainly Vietnamese, immigrants. Research has centered on areas in the plant such as spinning, warping, fabric finishing and dyeing, as well as the comprehensive employee participation program.
C. A car manufacturer in the northern suburbs which is a subsidiary of an American company. This is a very large plant, with a substantial personnel on site, including a large Middle-Eastern complement, as well as many Southern Europeans, and some South-East Asians. Research has centered on the production line, where workers perform mainly routinized jobs within specific areas of the line, and in employee participation groups.

D. A car manufacturer in the south-eastern suburbs which is a subsidiary of a Japanese company. The workforce comprises a high percentage of East and South-East Asian workers, as well as Central Europeans. Data have been collected on the production line (similar to C above), and in a neighboring plant where door trims are manufactured.

At each workplace, specific sites for research were selected with the assistance of staff. Our requirements were a communication-rich environment with a relatively low noise level, and a breadth of ethnolinguistic and cultural diversity. The choice of research-sites followed lengthy discussion with management, personnel officers, supervisors and leading hands, shop stewards, and trades union officials. Through these discussions, the researchers gained the confidence and support of people whose co-operation was essential and were able to obtain insights into the communication situations.

Data collection

Much of the existing literature on intercultural studies in discourse is based on role-play (for example, Blum-Kulka et al., 1989; Kasper, 1981; Bremer et al., 1988). This has frequently been challenged on the grounds that people do not always behave in role-play as they would in real-life situations (ideal versus reality) and, in fact, do not always perceive their own behavior (see, for example, Blum-Kulka et al., 1989; papers in Olesky, 1989; Heidelberger Forschungs-projekt, 1975). Other methods that have been used are participant and nonparticipant observation, interviews and recording of spontaneous communication (Gumperz, 1982; Milroy, 1987). The relative merits of these data gathering methods have been discussed elsewhere (see, for example, Labov, 1970; Heidelberger Forschungsprojekt, 1975; Milroy, 1987).

We decided to employ three methods in this project: observation, recording spontaneous communication, and (at a later stage) tests of perception. Thus far, data have been gathered through participant observation in the work setting, by recording certain selected key people wearing a lapel microphone, and audio- and video-taping (and observing) meetings of employee participation groups. Key informants were chosen in observation sessions on the basis of:

(a) their willingness to participate,
(b) their non-English-speaking background,
(c) their frequent need to communicate at work with people from differing non-English-speaking backgrounds, and
(d) the range of their communication acts, including receiving and/or making complaints and requests, giving advice, asking questions, expressing approval/disapproval, which should go beyond the formulaic level.

(It should be stressed that recording only proceeds with the full awareness and agreement of the workers at the research site. The microphone used is visible but unobtrusive.)

We initially selected key informants in powerful positions, for example: supervisors, foremen, leading hands. Such people are generally involved in much interaction, and perform a wide variety of speech acts. More recently, we have approached process workers, in order to appreciate the complete spectrum of the communicative environment. We intend to find pairs or groups of interlocutors with matching ethnolinguistic/cultural backgrounds in inverse power relationships (for example, Chinese and Central Europeans each in H and L positions). Follow-up interviews with interlocutors assist in the interpretation of the data (cf. Neustupny, 1985). By recording spontaneous speech in work situations, we have been able to collect instances of pragmatic success and failure in intercultural contexts. Complementing these naturalistic data are audio- and video-recordings of meetings in which interaction is of a more formal nature. Later in the project, we intend to test informants' ability to decode both information and attitude in intercultural communication situations, through reactions to a film of a role-play based on data we have collected (cf. Perdue, 1982). In this sense, role-play is not used as a substitute for naturalistic data, rather as a useful attitudinal complement.

[The authors briefly discuss the discourse and pragmatic approaches in intercultural communication studies.]

The speech acts

Communication breakdown in interethnic situations is very often a result of the hearer's failure to understand the speaker's communicative intent because of culture-bound differences in rule variants. Much of the literature on contrastive pragmatics contrasts direct and indirect single-utterance realizations of speech acts in different cultures. Our data suggest, however, that the illocutionary force is achieved through a complex of realizations over a more extensive stretch of discourse. Often there are recurring scripts or schemata (Schank and Abelson, 1977; Rumelhart, 1975) featuring a particular speech act. We shall discuss instances of two speech acts—complaints and apologies, illustrated by examples from our recordings.

The connection between speech acts such as complaints and apologies in a multiple speech act discourse goes far beyond the adjacency pairs described in most of the literature on pragmatics and ethnomethodological conversation analysis (Henne and Rehbock, 1982; Sacks et al., 1974; Kasper, 1981). This connection has been presented in the flow charts of Ehlich and Rehbein (for example, Ehlich and Rehbein, 1972; Rehbein, 1977). Nevertheless, it must be acknowledged, that, where the complaint is being made about the addressee, (s)he is required to make an apology. Where the complaint is unjustified, the person making the complaint is required to apologize.

Apologies (and justifications) can be performed differently across cultures:

(a) formulaically,
(b) creatively,
(c) with or without honorifics.

In different cultures, people might lose face—in Brown and Levinson's (1978, 1987) sense—by

(i) apologizing,
(ii) not apologizing,
(iii) not apologizing in the appropriate way,
(iv) not successfully soliciting a particular reassurance.

Turns

In the data interpretation section, we shall give evidence that it is in both the differences in discourse rhythm (turns) and the relation between speech acts and length of turn that some communication breakdown has its origin. We are expanding the terminology adopted widely since the seminal paper of Sacks et al. (1974) in order to cater explicitly for all the possibilities in our data.

Turn terminating   A's turn comes to an end, giving others the option (or the responsibility) to take it up.

Turn receiving   A gives turn to B, B accepts turn from A: B wants the turn, A does not.

Turn keeping   A wants to keep turn, B does not want it. *or* A wants to keep it, B wants it too.

Turn appropriating   A wants to keep turn, but B takes it.

Turn change   Any instance of turn receiving or appropriating.

Turn appropriating can be achieved by increase in the volume of speech or simultaneous speech; turn keeping is aided by speeding up utterances and increasing volume. Eye gaze movements play a substantial part in turn changes and their prevention.

Turn length varies widely between cultures. For instance, turns are longer in Japanese than in English (Elzinga, 1978) and in Turkish than in German (Barkowski et al., 1976). Finns make long pauses, whereas Germans "think aloud" and do not tolerate silent periods (see Lenz, 1990). Turns may be measured through (filled and unfilled) pauses, length of utterances or in other ways (see below). In cross-cultural discourse, markers used to indicate turn terminating may not be recognized by interlocutors. Similarly, markers used to signify intention of turn appropriation may pass unnoticed. Examples of this, and its consequences, will be discussed in the data.

Marking communication breakdown

Intercultural communication depends on a maxim of mutual intelligibility: Make sure that the other person understands.

Communication breakdown can take two main forms:

(i) Noncommunication, where no message is communicated; and
(ii) Miscommunication, where an unintended message is communicated.

The latter is perhaps the more serious, firstly because often it can pass without either of the interlocutors grasping that it has occurred, and secondly as it can be at the root of intercultural communication conflict in which dignity or trust are threatened.

Where either noncommunication or miscommunication is recognized, different cultural groups (and individuals) have different ways of coping, as we shall discuss below. These include:

1. Ignoring that communication breakdown has occurred.
2. Admitting it has occurred according to particular rules of politeness.
3. Admitting it has occurred while flouting the rules of politeness.
4. Blaming the other party for the communication breakdown.
5. Marking the communication breakdown with a solidarity marker such as laughter.

Where negotiation of meaning takes place, repetition and paraphrase have proved the most usual and culturally universal means in our corpus of addressing this problem (cf. Perdue, 1982).

Discussion of some data

In the following section, we shall discuss texts illustrating apology, complaint, a combination of apology and complaint, and some in which the focus is on turn changes. We have given our informants pseudonyms according to Table 19.1.

Table 19.1 Details of workplaces and work-sites

Pseudonym	Age	Sex	Country of birth	L1	L2	Position in Company
Inge	45	F	Germany	German	English	Process Worker
Slobodan	45	M	Yugoslavia	Croatian	German, English	Supervisor
Celia	25	F	Philippines	Tagalog	English	Process Worker
Krysztina	45	F	Poland	Polish	English	Process Worker
Jennifer	35	F	Malaysia	Hokkien, English	Malay, Cantonese	Leading Hand
Marianne	40	F	Germany	German	English	Process Worker
Dulip	40	M	Sri Lanka	Sinhalese	English	Super-intendent
Liesl	50	F	Austria	German	English	Parts Distributor
Hoa	35	F	Vietnam	Vietnamese	English	Process Worker

Samples of transcripts follow; see the appendix for transcription conventions.

Transcript A1. *Workplace A(i)*

1 Jennifer   yes krysztina
2 Krysztina   jennifer   now i can see you because everything is fixed up
3 Jennifer   yes
4 Krysztina   so i can tell you
....
5 Jennifer   fixed up what   yeah
6 Krysztina   i # + yesterday   the incident with xxxx ++ i
....
7 Krysztina   was probably. it was my fault alright i don't know whose
....
8 Krysztina   fault but i take + my ++   yes i blame myself
9 Marianne   you blame yourself for it
....
10 Jennifer   why Krysztina just for ↑ get it
11 Krysztina   for it   it was to make the conn. the +++ the #
12 Marianne   the transistors
....
13 Jennifer   ↓oh
14 Krysztina   transistors # +++   alright ++++ and that was the
15 Marianne   <xxx transisors>
....
16 Krysztina   reason i don't want to give.give xxxxx the job + alright +
....
17 Krysztina   because i find that in the middle of the job was.accidentally i
....
18 Krysztina   find oh # what's going wrong and after all i. check every part
....
20 Jennifer   oh

21 Krysztina i put in but. i didn't know how many had done it and on the
....
22 Jennifer   look
22 Krysztina end i just check that and was nine wrong + alright
....
23 Jennifer   krysztina + ← for me ++ is nothing worrying me → it's just
24 Krysztina   <xxxxxxxxxxxx>
....
25 Jennifer   that if
26 Krysztina i thought she was so angry so upset when she said "you
....
27 Jennifer   for me if there's problems just have to
28 Krysztina are worst person' ++++ <xxxxx> it's just.
....
29 Jennifer discuss and sort it out that's all
30 Krysztina it's just <xxx> hong told me not to tell
....
32 Jennifer   ← these things
33 Krysztina anyone it was # # it was mixed up and # ++
....
34 Jennifer   happen these things happen kryszteiner # ↓d don't worry ++
35 Krysztina # you.
....
36 Krysztina you know I'm very sensitive
37 Marianne   when i have trouble with jennifer
....
38 Marianne   i tell her her off and she tells me off and then we're right
....
39 Krysztina and i said to my husband you know + that's
40 Marianne   again aren't we [laughter]
....
41 Krysztina life and everything and # and he said "oh you should leave
....
42 Krysztina that job' huh
43 Jennifer   is your husband back. back from atlantic
44 Krysztina everytime
....
45 Krysztina i just find something out he says you should leave that job
....
46 Krysztina you should stay et home
47 Marianne   so you can't even talk about it at
....
48 Marianne   home
49 Krysztina no i can't even talk you know can't even talk to anyone
50 Marianne   mm
....
51 Jennifer   Krysztina look sometimes people do have i understand
52 Krysztina ++

53 Marianne #
....

54 Jennifer   these things ## it just do happen sometimes people just
....

55 Jennifer   overlook yes it's just overlook like they did it's just
....

56 Jennifer   overlook +++++
57 Krysztina do you know yesterday it was their + boards
....

58 Krysztina i didn't want to <xxxxxx> the reason was because was
....

59 Krysztina was mixed up the components + alright and i want to fix it
....

60 Krysztina myself because that was my fault alright i.i got nothing
....

61 Krysztina against you or i.i didn't want to <give> you because i don't
....

62 Krysztina like your company so it's the only reason i can't give you the
....

63 Jennifer   oh krysztina don't worry
64 Krysztina boards alright yeah but it's.it's so. i
....

65 Jennifer   oh! don't worry i'll fix it up for you
66 Krysztina feel so. so bad y'know
....

67 Jennifer   §   ↑good morning elisabeth

In this first example, Krysztina is "apologizing" to her superior, a Chinese–Malyasian woman, that is, she wants to be freed from her "guilt" for she fears the consequences of an error she committed in her work. Jennifer tries to calm her:

(i)   by multiple use of the Australian routine "don't worry",
(ii) by expressing her understanding ("I understand these things," "these things happen"),
(iii) through diversion ("is your husband back. back from atlantic?")

Krysztina repeatedly expresses her anxieties and guilt feelings. This extends the length of her turns beyond the expectations of her interlocutor who tries to draw the exchange to a close. She introduces a number of schemas to achieve the leading hand's reassurance:

(a) It was really Hong's fault.
(b) I'm very sensitive.
(c) My husband won't talk to me about it.

The extract highlights some radical differences in turn-changing behavior. There are several instances where Krysztina terminates her turn, and there is a considerable delay before it is received by Jennifer, whereas Marianne seems to pick up the cues more quickly. On the other hand, when Jennifer ends her turn, Krysztina is quick to receive it. Jennifer's median length of utterance[1] is 4.5 seconds (twelve words), whereas Krysztina's turns are more commonly

8 to 10 seconds (25 words), and up to 22 seconds (65 words) and 25 seconds (68 words). In this conversation with three interlocutors, Krysztina commands 60 percent of the floor-time. Eventually, the desired reassurance ("I'll fix up for you") is reached after a very long exchange, but Jennifer, not taking any more chances, turns to another worker and starts a new conversation ("good morning").

Two other texts in our corpus demonstrate the close nexus between complaint and apology. In the first exchange (CA1), a Croatian male supervisor (Slobodan) is interacting with two women younger than himself, a Chinese–Malaysian leading hand (Jennifer) and a Filipina worker (Celia). He begins by marking the intended speech act (laughingly) in order to demonstrate his authority ("ah ha, complaint again"). There are two sub-routines in the stretch of discourse:

(i) It is the responsibility of all of you to work hard and well.
(ii) This is not the most wonderful job, but we all have to do unpleasant work.

Whether he is complaining to Jennifer about allowing untrained persons to do particular jobs or whether he is complaining to the workers themselves, his turns are very long and he completely dominates the exchange. When it turns out that he has wrongly accused Celia, he apologizes in such a way as to not lose face—for example, through the use of the first person plural and a shift from the indicative (real) to the conditional (hypothetical):

"whatever happened if we blame you for the things what you didn't done we apologize on it but anyway it would happen"

Similarly, later in the exchange:

"I'm sorry, we apologize for this mistake and that's it okay everybody can make mistakes"

In the other exchange (CA2), the same Croatian supervisor is interacting with a German woman worker (Inge). It should be noted that they are employed by a German company. Slobodan had himself been a guest worker in Germany prior to migrating to Australia and had been employed in German companies in Australia ever since. He is complaining about the absence of some parts, again using long turns. Although he does not ask any questions—he is merely compalining—the request for an explanation is inherent in a number of his statements:

"there is supposed to be the five seven ones what you already did I think yesterday or then"
"yeah but I saw it in there they already had it in here"
"and we don't need them"

The German woman shows that she had not received the parts by answering his implied questions with reasons:

"*because* no I haven't anything"
"*because* I haven't got anything"
"*so* you don't need them at all today"
"*because* whatever A. got, I haven't got anything yet"
"*because* you have eight twenty five here"
"*because* it's still there you know"

She understands perfectly what he is after and gives him the appropriate response.
He simply apologizes, giving an explanation:

"I'm sorry I'm sorry oh sorry I thought xxx I didn't er look for in the (pause) on the
paper just by (pause) on the board yeah"

There is no toning down of the apology as in CA1 where he is interacting with people whose
communicative styles are rather different to his and who may be perceived as being lower on
the ethnocultural power hierarchy. The above episodes demonstrate culture-bound variation
in turns as well as the relation between status, gender, culture, and speech act realizations.

C4 (below) is an instance of complaint where cultural variation in turn lengths effects a
communication breakdown between Slobodan and a number of South-East Asian women,
including Jennifer, the Chinese–Malaysian leading hand.

Transcript C4. *Workplace A(i)*

1	Slobodan	jennifer listen you now and all you people here you
		....
2	Slobodan	know how much we need the soldering ++++ we desperately need
		....
3	Slobodan	soldering people to do ericson or to do any # job on soldering in
	. .	the area # from now on i don't want to sec anybody who is
4	Jennifer	yeah yeah
		....
5	Slobodan	competent with solder to do the cleaning +++ alright and only
6	. .	one things i don't understand why every ten or twenty minutes
7	. .	people who are nominated to clean those boards alright are off
8	. .	from this shop ++ i don't understand the one things how peoples
9	. .	are not ← ashamed to sitting doing nothing alright +++ doing
10	. .	nothing and # # in.instead # to.to. give us something to. to
11	. .	produce something +++ that is really. well it is embarrassing
12	. .	+++ keep it under control look nominate the people who are
13	. .	waiting time to clean these boards there the job has to be done i
14	. .	know it's # not # it's not ++++ easy job but i don't know is it
15	. .	right word to say easy or hard job we don't select in job here in
16	. .	our area ah that's hard that's easy you know the all job are
14	. .	practically the same though sometimes we prefer one job than
15	Slobodan	the other but +++ we may not do it like that
16	Jennifer	okay slobodan
		....
17	Slobodan	alright <look> we need output from that area and i see people
18	Jennifer	yeah xxxxxxxxxxxxx xxxxxxxxx
		....
19	Slobodan	who are soldering then cleaning the boards but we can't do that
20	Jennifer	okay
		....
21	Slobodan	+++ # and people are here sitting doing nothing +++++
22	. .	what's the reason +++ if they go there and they sit there ten

```
23  ..        minutes and after that they just disappear ++++ i would like to
24  ..        see what's the reason is there any reason for that tell me ++++
25  Jennifer  the
    ..................................................................................................
    Jennifer  rea. you want a ↑ reason
26  Slobodan  yeah ............................. yeah i would like to have a reason
    ..................................................................................................
27  Jennifer  oh                     okay
28  Slobodan  alright then i. i'll take people that are confident alright
```

Turn lengths are markedly unequal in this exchange. Slobodan's monolog continues for 2 minutes 35 seconds (c. 300 words), with only four attempts at turn appropriation by Jennifer (lines 4, 16, 20, 25). A number of variables, such as gender, power hierarchy and cultural background, may account for this.

Slobodan's main sub-routine (schema) in the extract is: People are not working hard enough, for example:

"I don't understand the one things how people are not ashamed to sitting doing nothing alright"

Jennifer makes three attempts to terminate his turn and the speech act, taking advantage of a pause, by saying:

"okay, Slobodan" . . . "yeah'" . . . "okay"

but this is of no avail.

Slobodan then challenges them to give the reason why they sit around and disappear instead of soldering:

"what's the reason"
"I would like to see what's the ↑reason↓ is there any ↑reason↓ for that ↑tell me!"

When asked for confirmation of the request, he gives this but continues his very lengthy turn. Our Serbo-Croatian speaking resource person informed us that the speaker's intonation and lexis would be rhetorical if based on L1 interference (repetition, "tell me"; Croatian *recite mi*). The Chinese-speaking interlocutors were confused because they were receiving two different inputs:

I want you to tell me (Verbal)
I don't want you to tell me (turn behavior).

It is not the case, however, that it is impossible for a person of South-East Asian background to negotiate meaning and resolve a communication breakdown with the Croatian supervisor. In C3, the Chinese–Malaysian leading hand is on her own with him. There is a potential conflict when the supervisor expresses his disapproval and his authority through interrogatives, imperatives, and modals:

"what do you stop ↑changing these things"
"tell me how many connectors you changed hundreds of it"

"you may not you may not destroy these connectors"
"you may not put them in the rubbish"
"you can keep them separate and count them you know that"

As will be seen in the transcript, every accusation, every question, every reproach is answered immediately, and the supervisor is not given a chance to maintain his turn indefinitely (as is the case in C4).

Transcript C3. *Workplace A(i)*

 1 Slobodan ah here you are i'm looking for you + what you do stop
 ....
 2 Slobodan   changing these things
 3 Jennifer   these are all from last week one
 ....
 4 Jennifer +++++++ <.......> monday all good ones ++++
 5 Slobodan   ai ai ai
 ....
 6   tell me how many
 7 Jennifer   these are all from last week ones +++
 ....
 8 Slobodan   connectors you changed hundreds of it ++++ maybe
 ....
 9 Slobodan   petersons accept it but i don't know
10 Jennifer   i have asked them to
 ....
11 Slobodan   sss.some but how many some
12 Jennifer   send some extra connectors but
 ....
13 Jennifer   they
14 Slobodan   # you may not, you may not destroy these connectors you
 ....
15 Slobodan   may not put them in the rubbish you can keep them
 ....
16 Slobodan   separate and count them +++ you know that ++ know any
 ....
17 Slobodan   components you change they be scrap +++
18 Jennifer   and then # but
 ....
19 Jennifer   monday we have already started with the new carrier and
 ....
20 Jennifer they're all very good no rejects ++ the new carrier
21 Slobodan   yeah well
 ....
22 Slobodan   the people who are cleaning there should be aware about that
 ....
23 Slobodan   ++ those people + who are cleaning now did you told them
24 Jennifer   yeah I

....

25 Jennifer did told them
26 Slobodan did you show, show them that yeah you sh.
27 Jennifer yes i did show them

....

28 Slobodan you <x>   yeah when is not enough then
29 Jennifer how to handle that ++++ and

....

30 Slobodan you should +++ i show them a sample what's been happen

....

31 Slobodan if they are not handled properly or if they push them +++
32 Jennifer

....

33 Jennifer told them not. ++++ anyway i knew <xxxxxxx> to clean
34 Slobodan   #

....

35 Jennifer   them and they are very good
36 Slobodan   please jennifer aware them what

....

37 Slobodan and how to handle this connector tell them look if that's

....

38 Slobodan happened the board or connector is scrap it is too much

....

39 Slobodan time to <xxxxxx> +++++ they learn by examples
40 Jennifer   yeah #

Here Jennifer makes a determined effort to interrupt Slobodan, mid-utterance if necessary, in order to take the floor and present her case. The attempts at appropriation do not coincide with turn-terminating markers from Slobodan. At the same time, he takes little notice of her desire to gain the floor: significantly, he still controls 70 percent of the conversation.

Slobodan likes to use what could be interpreted as an apology as an authority marker to give him the final say, for example,

"sorry, girls, that's the way it is."

But, as we have pointed out, the authority marker comes sometimes in the form of a performative verb or its derivative, for example,

"complaint again!" (as conversation opener)

The dynamics of turn-taking as an indicator of communication control are illustrated in the videos of employee participation groups. Present in T1 are eight males: a Ukrainian (the circle leader), a Sinhalese (superintendent), a Northern Italian (foreman), two Maltese (foreman and leading hand), an Australian of Greek background (leading hand), and an Australian of British descent (management representative) and the field worker. In the first half of this discourse, initiated by the Italian in a somewhat theoretical but not very conclusive manner, there is a rather heated discussion on the function of the meetings with many short turns and most members participating. Half way through the discussion, the Sinhalese (Dulip) takes control of the meeting and maintains his turn until the resolution of the issue under discussion. Interjections cease; he even receives an apology for one, from the circle leader. He keeps his long turn due to his perceived articulate skill at formal meetings, his use of repetition, and authoritativeness indicated by falling tone, for example,

> "up to there toni, it's a general thing, up to ↓there number four, that's the project choices ↓there ↑right up to there everything was ↓general"

Dulip is not nearly so effective in a small group situation on the factory floor—with the Maltese and a Croatian leading hand also present. On three occasions within an exchange of 3 minutes 20 seconds, he is not allowed to complete his turn. Twice his turn is appropriated. Another time, he tries to take over but is ignored. The fact that others take far less notice of him in informal settings than in formal meetings may be due to sub-cultural and individual rather than cultural factors: for instance, Dulip is more educated than his workmates. It is for this reason that we are attempting to replicate different cultural dyads.

Small talk on the factory floor can, however, also be a cause of intercultural communication breakdown, as in CB1, where an Austrian female leading hand (Liesl) is approached at her desk by a Vietnamese woman worker (Hoa) for some requisite parts. It is the Thursday before Easter, and Liesl begins with some phatic, rather than work-related communication:

> "now you get five days off [ov] what're you going to do"

This question leads to noncommunication marked by a long period of silence. Even after the question is repeated in paraphrased form, the connection between the personal question and the purpose of the interaction remains a puzzle to Hoa.

Liesl has commented that she never had any problems communicating with Southern Europeans but there was considerable communication breakdown with the Asians. This is one of the key issues in this study; European migrants of different backgrounds perceive similarities in their communication patterns. However, they sense (sometimes erroneously) that their patterns are closer to those of Anglo-Australians than of Asian-Australians (especially those from South-East Asia). This, together with their longer period of residence, makes them believe that their own patterns of communication are more "correct." Among other things, Central and Southern Europeans view the issue of face in a way which is vastly different to that of South-East Asians.

Concluding remarks

Most of the intercultural communication breakdown we have examined from our corpus so far is due to pragmatic and discourse rules, and not to grammatical or phonological problems. In cross-cultural interactions, the maxim of mutual intelligibility—make sure that the other person understands—is approached from different angles, highlighting the culture-bound differences in rule variants. Where culture-based communication patterns are less distant, implications are more often understood and communication more successful. This project looks beyond simple comparisons of communicative rules among L1 speakers to the interaction between interlanguages in cross-cultural discourse. Turn length and sequencing are largely culture-bound, and such variation is the cause of much frustration in intercultural communication. Most speech acts are realized, not through single utterances, but in a complex way through a series of schemata and embedded in culture-specific discourse with multiple speech acts. This may need to be addressed in theoretical studies of pragmatics.

Appendix: legend for transcriptions

#	filled pause	<xx>	unrecognizable speech
↑, ↓	rising, falling intonation	→, ←	acceleration, deceleration
+	unfilled pause—no verbal communication		

Note

1   Note we use median as distinct from mean (MLU).

References

Barkowski, H., Harnisch, U. and Krumm, S. (1976). Sprechhandlungstheorie und Gastarbeiterdeutsch. *Linguistische Berichte,* 45, 42–56.

Blum-Kulka, S., House, J. and Kasper, G. (1989). *Cross-cultural pragmatics.* Norwood: Ablex.

Bremer, K., Broeder, P., Roberts, C., Simonot, M. & Vasseur, M.-T. (1988). *Ways of achieving understanding: communicating to learn in a second language.* Strasbourg and London: European Science Foundation.

Brown, P. and Levinson, S. (1978). Universals in language usage: politeness phenomena. In E. Goody (ed.), *Questions and politeness* (pp. 56–289). Cambridge: Cambridge University Press.

Brown, P. and Levinson, S. (1987). *Politeness: some universals in language usage.* Cambridge: Cambridge University Press.

Corder, S. P. (1981). *Error analysis and interlanguage.* Oxford: Oxford University Press.

Ehlich, K. and Rehbein, J. (1972). Zur Konstitution pragmatisches Einheiten in einer Institution. In D. Wunderlich (ed.), *Linguististische Pragmatik* (pp. 209–54). Frankfurt: Athenäum.

Elzinga, R. H. (1978). Temporal organization of conversation. *Sociolinguistics Newsletter,* 9(2), 29–34.

Faerch, C. and Kasper, G. (1983). *Strategies in interlanguage communication.* London: Longman.

Gumperz, J. J. (1982). *Discourse strategies.* Cambridge: Cambridge University Press.

Heidelberger Forschungsprojekt. (1975). *Sprache und Kommunikation ausländischer Arbeiter.* Kronberg: Scriptor.

Henne, H. and Rehbock, H. (eds) (1982). *Einführung in die Gesprächsanalyse.* Berlin: Walter de Gruyter.

Hüllen, W. and Lörscher, W. (1989). On describing and analyzing foreign classroom discourse. In W. Olesky (ed.), *Contrastive pragmatics* (pp. 169–88). Amsterdam: Benjamins.

Kasper, G. (1981). *Pragmatische Aspekte in der Interimsprache.* Tübingen: Narr.

Kasper, G. (1989). Interactive procedures in interactive discourse. In Olesky, W. (ed.), *Contrastive pragmatics* (pp. 189–229). Amsterdam: Benjamins.

Labov, W. F. (1970). The study of language in social context. *Studium generale,* 23, 30–87.

Lenz, F. (1990). *Der wortkarge Finne und beredte Deutsche? Oder Die Angst des Geschäftsmanns vor dem Muller sprachler.* (Työpapereita F. 244.) Helsinki: School of Economics.

Milroy, L. (1987). *Observing and analysing natural language.* Oxford: Blackwell.

Neustupny, J. V. (1985). Language norms in Australian-Japanese contact situations. In M. Clyne (ed.), *Australia meeting place of languages* (pp. 161–70). Canberra: Pacific Linguistics.

Olesky, W. (ed.) (1989). *Contrastive pragmatics.* Amsterdam: Benjamins.

Perdue, C. (ed.) (1982). *Second language acquisition by adults. A field manual.* Strasbourg: European Science Foundation.

Rehbein, J. (1977). *Komplexes Handeln.* Stuttgart: Metzler.

Riley, P. (1989). "Well don't blame me." On the interpretation of pragmatic errors. In Olesky, W. (ed.), *Contrastive pragmatics* (pp. 231–44). Amsterdam: Benjamins.

Rumelhart, D. E. (1975). Notes on a schema for stories. In D. G. Bobrow and A. Collins (eds), *Representation and understanding.* New York: Academic Press.

Sacks, H., Schegloff, E. and Jefferson. G. (1974). A simplest systematics for the organisation of turn-taking for conversation. *Language,* 50, 696–735.

Schank, R. C. and Abelson, A. P. (1977). *Scripts, plans, goals and understanding.* Hillsdale: Erlbaum.

Selinker, L. (1972). Interlanguage. *International Review of Applied Linguistics,* 10, 209–31.

Chapter 20

RICHARD SCHMIDT, AKIHIKO SHIMURA, ZHIGANG WANG, AND HY-SOOK JEONG

SUGGESTIONS TO BUY
Television commercials from the U.S., Japan, China, and Korea

Introduction

THIS CHAPTER DEALS WITH television commercials as suggestions to viewers to buy consumer products, comparing television commercials from the United States, Japan, the People's Republic of China, and South Korea from this perspective.[1] It is intended to complement and augment other studies of differences in the realization of speech acts across cultures, but is different from most other studies in several respects.

1. It is often assumed that the most problematic issue both in speech act theory and in cross-cultural communication is the determination of what is meant by what is said. It is commonly pointed out that our goal in conversation is to convey our intentions in socially appropriate ways (Aston, 1993; Grice, 1975; Searle, 1969, 1976) and that failure to convey or interpret intentions may be the most important source of cross-cultural communication breakdown (Gumperz, 1982).

However, the goal of a television commercial is obvious: it is to persuade consumers to buy a specific product. Successful communication is less a matter of getting television viewers to recognize this illocutionary force (indeed, advertisers may attempt to mask this goal) than a function of the persuasive impact of the commercial, including the linguistic and nonlinguistic strategies used to persuade.[2]

2. Speech act analyses have been based on several kinds of data, including native speaker intuitions, interviews, naturally occurring utterances in face-to-face interaction, role play, spoken or written language elicited through discourse completion tests, and various perception tests such as card sorts, paired comparisons, and rating scales (see Kasper & Dahl (1991) for review). However, we are unaware of any other study of speech acts in different cultures that is based on data from television commercials. Our data are not just unique but also represent artful rather than naturally occurring discourse, carefully scripted by professional writers, although the television commercial is naturally occurring language in another sense, not experimentally elicited for the purpose of linguistic analysis.

Source: Schmidt, R., Shimura, A., Wang, Z. & Jeong, H. (1995). Suggestions to buy: television commercials from the U.S., Japan, China, and Korea. In S. Gass & J. Neu (eds), *Speech acts across cultures: challenges to communication in a second language* (pp. 285–316). Berlin: Mouton de Gruyter.

3. Very useful work has been done in the cross-cultural comparison of speech act behavior by focusing on patterned variation in speech act realizations. The distribution of linguistic strategies for performing particular speech acts has been matched with speaker and hearer variables such as age, sex, social distance, and relative power, together with the degree of imposition of the speech act involved, factors which are, according to the theory of politeness (Brown & Levinson 1987), the primary determinants of linguistic choices in speech act realization. In the case of the television commercial, we might expect similar variation in speech act realization when characters on screen talk to one another or when particular segments of the viewing audience are targeted (e.g., children, adolescent males, etc.), but the central notions of speaker and hearer are problematic when applied to the language of advertising.

Goffman (1981) has criticized the commonsense notion of *speaker*, pointing out that a speaker may be the one who speaks the message, the one who has encoded it, or the one who is committed to the beliefs expressed. In ordinary conversation, these three typically coincide; in role play, there may be no committed speaker; and in commercials, these roles are distributed among actors, copywriters, producers and directors, and the product manufacturer. As for the *hearer*, Lakoff suggests that, in advertising language and in persuasive language in general, there is no addressee, but only an audience (Lakoff, 1982, p. 31). In addition, while commercials may use a particular kind of language in order to influence specific target audiences and may exploit such roles as celebrity/fan, these devices are often used strategically, creating situations and relationships rather than being sensitive to them.

4. Many studies of cross-cultural variation in speech act realization have direct relevance for second-language learners, whose goal is to interact effectively with native speakers of the target language under different social constraints. We do not claim such implications for our work, but we do see this study as basic research for the teaching of language in business contexts, a field for which there is great demand and little empirical research (Johns, 1986).

Television commercials as suggestions

Television commercials provide easily obtainable data that are relevant for a number of sociolinguistic concerns. Commercials have been analyzed as expressions of cultural codes and mythologies (Barthes, 1972; Hall & Saracino-Resh, 1979; Mueller, 1987; Sherry & Camargo, 1987); as a medium-specific example of the register of advertising language with a focus on novel uses of language (Agoston & von Raffler-Engel, 1979; Bhatia, 1987; Leech, 1966; Masavisut et al., 1987; Moeran, 1985; O'Barr, 1979); as manipulative or deceptive language (Bolinger, 1973, 1980; Coleman, 1990; Harris, 1983; Vestergaard & Schrøder, 1985); and as an exemplar of the broader category of persuasive discourse (Lakoff, 1982; Schmidt & Kess, 1985, 1987). Geis (1982) has perceptively analyzed a number of the pragmatic aspects of American television commercials, including the ways in which product claims are interpreted through reference to conversational maxims, but no study to date has dealt with television commercials from a speech act perspective.

As a speech act, the television commercial is clearly some sort of directive (Searle, 1976) or impositive (Leech, 1983). The essential point of a television commercial, the reason an advertiser purchases time, is that it is an attempt to get some hearer or audience, viewers in their role as consumers, to perform some future action, that is, to buy a product. We propose that television commercials are best viewed as *suggestions* to buy, however, rather than some other species of directive, such as request, orders, or hints. Commercials do not seem to be requests, because they rarely attempt to engage the hearer's compliance on the ground that the speaker wants or needs the act to be done. They are not orders, because advertisers cannot expect consumers to buy a product as a consequence of the advertiser's or manufacturer's authority. They are not hints, because their illocutionary force is transparent (Weizman, 1993). A commercial can only suggest or recommend, persuading the viewer "to consider the merits of taking the action in virtue of the speaker's belief that there is sufficient reason to act" (Fraser, 1983, p. 40). Geis has argued that syntactic imperatives, observed to be common in advertising (Leech, 1966), are to be viewed as suggestions rather than orders (Geis, 1982, p. 19). However, in analyzing commercials as suggestions, we are somewhat hampered by the lack of detailed studies of this speech act, particularly from a cross-cultural perspective. Requests have been investigated extensively (see Blum-Kulka et al., 1989, for summary), but the speech act of suggestion, a cousin of the request, has been much less studied. We have located only two data-based cross-cultural studies, Rintell's (1979) brief comparison of suggestions in Spanish and English and Banerjee and Carrell's (1988) comparison of suggestions by native and non-native speakers of English.

Although our discussion of television commercials so far has assumed that a commercial as a whole is a speech act with a unifying illocutionary point, it may be preferable to view the commercial as a whole as a speech *event*, the internal structure of which consists of a sequence of utterances that may differentially support such functions as suggesting, informing, entertaining, and the like. Our analysis will be based on a distinction between *head acts* within the discourse of television commercials, those utterances or parts of utterances that directly realize the act of suggesting, and various *supporting moves* that provide grounds or reasons for something to be done or remove objections to the proposed action (Blum-Kulka et al., 1989; Blum-Kulka & Olshtain, 1984; Edmondson & House, 1981). We view the underlying discourse structure of a commercial as in example (1).

(1) Head act +   Supporting moves
    Consumer should buy, because Product is effective, stylish (etc.)
    use (etc.) the product Product will make consumer
                          happy, healthy, young (etc.)

Commenting on the application of the distinction between head act and supporting moves to data derived from discourse completion tests, Blum-Kulka and Olshtain (1984) and Edmondson and House (1981) have observed that distinguishing between the two is difficult and subjective, because what may be a supporting move in one case may function as the head act elsewhere, for example when a hint does not preface a request but by itself conveys the force of requesting. We have attempted to minimize this problem by providing as strict a separation as possible between head acts and supporting moves or reasons. Operationally, we have defined the head act of suggestion in television commercials as any utterance or part of an utterance that linguistically refers to the viewer or some other consumer buying an advertised product or interacting with the product in some other way, such as using it or enjoying the benefits of owning it.

We therefore allow the possibility of commericals that have more than one utterance classified as a head act, as well as commercials that have no head act as we have defined it, while admitting that much of the remaining language in a commercial may be suggestive in a broader sense. Even this relatively strict definition, however, does not result in the exclusive assignment of each turn or utterance to only one category, either head act of suggestion or supporting move. Consider, for example, E37 from our sample of English commercials:

E37 I'm gonna take what doctors would take, wouldn't you?

In this example, the only linguistic material that directly refers to a desired action to be taken by the viewer is the question tag *wouldn't you?* However, by our definition, there are two, other utterance parts we identify as additional head acts. The actor uttering the lines of the commercial, acting as a surrogate consumer, states that he is going to take the product (*I'm gonna take*) and will presumably have to buy it in order to do so. He also asserts that other consumers would do the same (*what doctors would take*). These different strategies for suggesting are common in our data, and we therefore code for three instances of the head act in this case, although the claim that doctors would use the product is also clearly presented as a reason (supporting move) for the viewer to act.

The study

In this chapter, we look at American television commercials and compare them with commercials from three Asian countries. Japan, the People's Republic of China, and South Korea. There are reasons to think that a comparison of American and Asian commercials may uncover some interesting differences. A great deal of advertising research supports the claim that American advertising (in all media) is primarily persuasive rather than informative (Dowling, 1980; Hong et al., 1987; Hunt, 1976; Kaynak & Mitchel, 1981; Laczniak, 1979; Madden et al., 1986; Resnik & Stern, 1977; Stern et al., 1981). But the view from Asia is rather different.

In China, advertising was banned during the Cultural Revolution (1966–1976), and a modern advertising infrastructure has been developed only since 1978, as part of a rapid shift from Marxist socialism to market socialism (Rice & Lu, 1988; Tse et al., 1989). The official view is that the functions of advertising are to promote production, invigorate the economy, increase consumer convenience and guide consumption, develop international economic activities, and promote socialist moral standards (Central Administration for Industry and Commerce, cited in Rice & Lu, 1988). Ho and Sin (1986) found that Chinese managers hold that the main purpose of advertising is to inform.

In both Japan and Korea, Miracle (1987) claims that advertisers rely on a *feel–do–learn* strategy, in which the primary goal of advertisers is to entertain and establish feelings and moods that are transferred to the product, as opposed to the predominant Western *learn–do–feel* sequence, in which advertising presents reasons for buying, with positive feelings the result rather than the precursor of purchase. Japanese advertising practices have been quite thoroughly studied, and from a number of impressionistic studies (Fields, 1983; Miracle, 1985, 1987; Yamaki, n.d.) a consistent picture has emerged. Japanese television commercials are said to be evocatively filmed, but extremely indirect in approach. In a study of print advertising, Sherry and Camargo report that most Japanese ads "neither preach, promise nor praise; some don't even portray product attributes" (Sherry & Camargo, 1987, p. 181).

Based on the literature on advertising in the U.S., China, Japan, and Korea, our initial hypothesis was the following:

H1   Suggestions will be more frequent in commercials from the U.S. than in those from any of the three Asian countries.

[. . .]

H2   Imperatives will be the most frequent form used to realize suggestions in American television commercials, but not in any of the three Asian languages.

Method

DATA

The data for this study consist of one full evening of television broadcasting in Honolulu (NBC), Tokyo (Fuji), Seoul (Korean Broadcasting), and Beijing (CCTV) during the first week of March, 1988. Commercials were recorded from the most watched station in each location at peak audience times.

These video types yielded slightly more than one hour of commercials in each language, from which a sample of 50 commercials was drawn for each country. Our original intent was to balance the samples for products advertised, but this proved impossible, because the most commonly advertised products are not the same in each country. The Chinese data contained numerous advertisements for washing machines and television sets, not found in any of the other language databases. The English and Japanese tapes both contained a high proportion of automobile ads (March is the traditional season for car sales in both countries), while the Korean database contained fewer commercials for consumer durables of all types than the other three language samples (Keown et al., 1992). Because we were interested only in consumer product advertising, the sample analyzed in this chapter consists of the first 50 commercials from each database, after elimination of repeats, public service announcements, commercials clearly of local rather than national origin, film trailers, and promotional spots advertising other television programming. We also eliminated from the Chinese sample a number of commercials showing heavy industrial equipment, on the grounds that few viewers could be considered potential consumers of such products.

The samples also vary in length. Commercials in the U.S. vary between 10 and 30 seconds (occasionally longer), in five second increments. Japanese and Korean commercials tend to be shorter than those from the U.S., while Chinese commercials are longer than those from the U.S. and more than twice as long as those from Japan. For the samples analyzed here, the mean length of commercials for each language was as follows: Japanese, 13 sec.; Korean, 18 sec.; English, 22 sec.; Chinese, 28 sec.

We believe that our samples are reasonably representative of prime-time consumer advertising on major channels in the four countries, but do not claim that our sample is representative of all television advertising in any of them. For example, we would expect some important differences in the language of American television commercials broadcast at different times of the day, such as Saturday mornings or late at night. We would also expect differences in commercials that are not nationally distributed (e.g., local used-car commercials) and for products sold through mail-order and advertised primarily on cable stations.

ANALYSIS

All commercials were transcribed, including spoken, printed and sung language, and three translations were produced: a morpheme-by-morpheme translation, a literal translation into English, and an idiomatic or free translation. Except in cases where linguistic form is at issue, examples are presented only in romanized transcription and free translation.

Each of the four authors of this chapter was responsible for the analysis of commercials in his or her native language and the initial assignment of utterances to categories, after which the examples were discussed by all four researchers until consensus was reached on each categorization.[3]

Chi-square analysis was used to test hypotheses, and the alpha level for significance was set at .05. Reported frequencies represent the number of instances of a category in the whole set of 50 commercials for each language (which may include more than one instance from a single commercial), not the number or percentage of commercials in which utterances of a particular type occurred. In addition to results addressing our specific hypotheses, we will also present a number of post-hoc and qualitative analyses, together with examples illustrating the tone of commercials from each country.

Results and discussion

As indicated in Table 20.1, the hypothesis that suggestions would be more common in American commercials than in those from any of the three Asian countries was supported. Considering all types of suggestions coded from our data—including suggestions made to either viewers or on screen characters, testimonials and reported behavior referring to other consumers—the set of English commercials contained a significantly higher number of suggestions than the Japanese, Chinese, or Korean samples. Korean commercials contained more suggestions than either Chinese or Japanese commercials.

The distribution of linguistic forms in suggestions is shown in Table 20.2, comparing imperatives (including those with *please* or a tag question appended) to all other forms, but only including those suggestions addressed directly to the viewer. We expect that suggestions addressed by on-screen characters to one another might exhibit some interesting differences, possibly varying as a function of speaker and hearer sex, age, status, and role, but suggestions to on-screen characters occurred too infrequently in our data to permit meaningful analysis. Some types of suggestion (reports of what other consumers have done) would not permit the imperative at all.

Table 20.1 Frequency of suggestions in the four language samples

				Eng	Jpns	Chns	Kor
Total number of suggestions:				78	35	35	53
All:	$X^2 = 24.73$	df = 3	p < 0.05				
E × J	$X^2 = 15.86^*$	df = 1	p < 0.05				
E × C	$X^2 = 15.86^*$	df = 1	p < 0.05				
E × K	$X^2 = 4.27^*$	df = 1	p < 0.05				
J × C	$X^2 = 0.00$	df = 1	n.s.				
J × K	$X^2 = 4.18^*$	df = 1	p < 0.05				
C × K	$X^2 = 4.18$	df = 1	p < 0.05				
Suggestions to viewer only:				54	27	26	30
All:	$X^2 = 15.44$	df = 3	p < 0.05				
E × J	$X^2 = 8.50^*$	df = 1	p < 0.05				
E × C	$X^2 = 9.30^*$	df = 1	p < 0.05				
E × K	$X^2 = 6.36^*$	df = 1	p < 0.05				
J × C	$X^2 = 0.52^*$	df = 1	n.s.				
J × K	$X^2 = 0.66^*$	df = 1	n.s.				
C × K	$X^2 = 0.78^*$	df = 1	n.s.				

* Corrected value, because df = 1 (Hatch & Lazaraton, 1991, pp. 405–06)

Table 20.2 Suggestions to the viewer, imperatives vs. other forms

				Eng	Jpns	Chns	Kor
Imperatives				33	3	11	10
Other forms				21	24	15	20
Total				54	27	26	30
Imperatives, All:	$X^2 = 19.25$	df = 3	$p < 0.05$				
Imperatives, E × J	$X^2 = 24.50*$	df = 1	$p < 0.05$				
Imperatives, E × C	$X^2 = 10.50*$	df = 1	$p < 0.05$				
Imperatives, E × K	$X^2 = 10.80*$	df = 1	$p < 0.05$				
Imperatives, J × C	$X^2 = 4.07*$	df = 1	$p < 0.05$				
Imperatives, J × K	$X^2 = 4.27*$	df = 1	$p < 0.05$				
Imperatives, C × K	$X^2 = 0.55*$	df = 1	n.s.				

* Corrected values

As shown in Table 20.2, the hypothesis that imperatives would be the preferred form for suggestions in American television commercials and would be used less frequently in commercials from the three Asian commercials was also supported. Japanese commercials also contained significantly fewer imperatives than either Chinese or Korean, which were not significantly different from each other.

These two measures indicate that American television commercials are more overtly suggestive than commercials from Japan, Korea, and China. One measure, the overall frequency of suggestions of all types (Table 20.1), indicates that Korean ads are somewhat more suggestive than commercials from Japan or China, whereas the frequency of imperatives (Table 20.2) indicates that Japanese commercials are the least suggestive in that respect. One possible interpretation of these findings is that the persuasive function of television is emphasized in American ads, whereas other functions are emphasized in Asian commercials, such as simply providing information to consumers. Another possible interpretation is that the function of suggestion is accomplished just as effectively though less directly in Asian commercials.

A caveat must be raised regarding the identification of syntactic imperatives as a basic measure of directness in suggestions. Although the syntactic imperative is the most direct possible way to make suggestions in each of the four languages, we cannot assume functional equivalence across languages; in fact, we know that the Japanese imperative is virtually a tabu form. Moreover, indirection in suggestions is not one-dimensional. While attempts have been made to rank directive utterances along a single scale of directness or politeness (Takahashi, 1987), we find that in television commercials there are at least four ways in which suggestions can be conveyed indirectly. We have already recognized that what we consider supporting moves (reasons to buy, such as product attributes) can function indirectly as suggestions in a broad sense, just as hints function as indirect requests in face-to-face interaction. In addition, we find examples in our data of what we will call indirection by participant shift, indirection by action shift, and linguistic indirection.

INDIRECTION BY PARTICIPANT SHIFT

Suggestions in commercials that are addressed directly to the viewer as a potential consumer and that refer to the desirability of the viewer buying the product or doing something with it (direct) can be distinguished from suggestions that are directed at some other addressee or simply report what other consumers have done (indirect). As already indicated (see Table 20.1), suggestions to the viewer were the most common type in our samples. In each language, we find suggestions addressed to the viewer such as in samples E49, E36, J40, J8, C23, C31, K16, and K42.

E49   *Consider the Acura Legend Coupe.* (male announcer)

E36   *So don't get confused. Shop where you like, but start at your Buick dealer.* (on screen actor, female)

J40   *Ima, Pipp Erekiban o kau to, 18-kin to daia de dekita sutekina puchi pendanto ga chuusen de atarimasu.*
"If you buy Pipp's Erekiban now, you may win a petite pendant made of 18K gold and diamonds." (male announcer)

J8   Gankai no shiji ni shitagai tadashiku goshiyoo kudasai.
"Please follow your eye doctor's directions and use them properly." (printed message)

C23   *Xinqiu yinxiang, nin de lixiang.*
"Xinqiu stereo system, your ideal choice." (male announcer)

C31   *Qing nin fuyong tongrentang shengchan de kanglaoyannianwan.*
"Please use the Kanglao Yannian produced by Tongrentang Medicine Factory." (female announcer)

K16   *Hyokwalul senthaykhaseyyo.*
"Choose the effect." (on screen actor, female)

K42   *Philyohal ttayman cokumssik ccaseyyo.*
"When needed, press a little." (on screen actor, male)

It is interesting to note who makes the suggestion to the viewer. In English, such suggestions may be made by an on-screen character, through printed messages, or through song lyrics, but the most frequently used strategy by far is the device of using the voice of an off-screen announcer to make the suggestion (34 of 54 suggestions to viewers). Overwhelmingly (in 33 of 34 cases), the off-screen announcer is an adult male. Although the observed frequencies are too small to permit tests of statistical significance, interesting patterns can be seen in each of the other languages. Only the commercials from China are like the American ones in strongly preferring the off-screen announcer as the primary source of suggestions (18 of 26 suggestions), and in the Chinese commercials two-thirds of those suggestions were made by female announcers. In the Japanese commercials, the most common way to present suggestions was through printed rather than spoken messages (13 of 27 suggestions to the viewer). On-screen actors made suggestions to the viewer as often as did an off-screen announcer (7 cases each). However, when an off-screen announcer makes the suggestion, Japanese commercials are just as gender-biased as American ones. All off-screen voices except two were male in our Japanese sample. One was a child's voice, and one commercial used a female off-screen voice to represent the thoughts of a character. The Korean commercials did not use printed messages for any suggestions, used an off-screen announcer for just over half of all suggestions (16 of 30), and—like the Chinese commercials—did not show gender bias; 9 off screen announcers were female and 7 were male. The remaining suggestions to the viewer in the Korean commercials were either spoken by on-screen actors or presented in song lyrics.

A less direct way to make a suggestion is to make it to an on-screen character, an actor appearing as a surrogate consumer. Such suggestions might be made by an off-screen voice, but we found no examples of this strategy in any of our language samples. In each of the language samples, there are examples of actors making suggestions to other actors, such as samples E42, J2, C33, and K11.

E42   *Here, try this one.* (male actor to female actor)

J2   *Ojii-chan, Tansu ni gon katte kite kudasai na?*
     "Grandpa, please go and buy Tansu ni Gon, won't you?" (daughter-in-law to father-in-law)[4]

C33   *Ni chi dian jianpixiaoshi wan jiu hao le, haoma?*
      "You will feel better after taking Jianpi Xiaoshi Wan, OK?" (mother to son)

K11   *Enni twuthongyakul tusil ilici.*
      "Sister, why don't you take a headache medicine?" (female actor to female)

It would be interesting to compare commercials from these different countries to see which role relationships are used most often in such cases and who gives advice to whom, but it would take a larger sample than ours to identify patterns.

Alternatively, still in their role as surrogate consumers, on-screen actors can indirectly convey a suggestion to the viewer or another on-screen actor by reporting that they have used a product and benefited from it. We found examples of such testimonials from each country, such as in E36, J37, C1, and K32.

E36   *Thank goodness for Pine Sol.* (female actor)

J37   *Boku wa itsumo hakuchuu doodoo suwan nan desu yo.*
      "I always drink Swan boldly in broad daylight." (male celebrity)

C1   *Wo young guo, xiaoguo hai bu chuone.*
     "I've tried it and found its effects not bad." (female actor)

K32   *Yocum daewoo patko salayo.*
      We live now receiving good treatment" (male actor)

Finally, instead of having an on-screen character report his or her purchase or satisfaction with the product, advertisers may suggest indirectly by reporting what other consumers have done. Again, we find examples in each language sample, as in E17, J41, C7, and K23.

E17   *Since the Johnsons got their Mitsubishi Mirage, they've been driving a lot more.* (male announcer)

J41   *Katakori no tonari no Gen-san Pipp katte, nonde, kiita.*
      "Gen-san, our next door neighbor with the stiff shoulder, bought Pipp and took it." (on screen male actor to female)

C7   *Luotuo jin wanjia, wan ja huanle duo.*
     "Camel comes to thousands of families and brings them more happiness." (female announcer)

K23   *I taykeyto ce taykeyto soykoki Masna.*
      "At this home and that home too, Soykoki Masna." (song lyrics)

Between-language differences in the distribution of suggestions to the viewer, suggestions made to on-screen characters, testimonials, and reports were not significant. However, there is one additional strategy for conveying suggestions indirectly that we have found only in the U.S. commercials, a variant of the testimonial. This is modeled behavior, in which the on-screen "consumer" does not report past actions but is shown purchasing the product or indicates that he or she is going to buy or use the product. Five U.S. commercials used this strategy, as in samples E6 and E25.

> E6 *Oh! I'll take it home now.* (female actor)
> E25 *Wear-dated, please.* (female actor)

INDIRECTION BY ACTION SHIFT

Any suggestion involves some threat to an addressee's face, because people do not, in general, want to be told what to do. The suggestion to buy involves a literal cost as well. In advertising, various strategies are used to present messages that emphasize the benefits and minimize the costs to the buyer. Price may or may not be mentioned. If it is, the price may be presented as a reason for buying, either because the price is lower than that of the competition or because it will be higher after a limited offer expires. Other strategies involve the formulation of price ($39.95 instead of $40.00) or stating a base price in large print while mentioning restrictions and exclusions in small print. (Both of these strategies were found only in the U.S. commercials.)

The suggestion that the consumer is to buy something, i.e., part with money, can also be conveyed less directly by referring to consumer actions other than buying itself. This is done in commercials from all four countries. We identified the following categories of suggested action:

Suggestion to buy: An utterance that lexically refers to buying, selling, or ordering the product, or a related financial transaction, as in samples E25, J5, C38, and K20.

> E25 *If you're one of the thousands of people who asked for a free sample of Wear-Dated carpet with Stainblocker and tried it, you'd probably like to know what steps to take to buy it.* (male announcer)
> J5 *Nyuu konseputo gokoinyuu no kata ni Goto Kumiko orijinaru terehon kaado purezento chuu.*
> "Giving away original Kumiko Goto telephone cards to those who purchase New Concept." (printed message)
> C38 *Dianhua dinghu, shonghuo shangmen.*
> "Order by phone, delivered to your home." (printed message)
> K20 *Ne Jin Ramyon hana te saollay?*
> "Would you go buy one more Jin Ramyon?" (on-screen actor, father to daughter)

Suggestion to get: An utterance that lexically refers to some action which implies the possibility or likelihood of purchase, for example, going to a store or calling for information, as in samples E25, C9, and K44.

> E25 *Call for the dealer near you.* (male announcer)
> C9 *Quing jizhu wo de shangbiao, weili pai xiyiji.*
> "Please remember my brand, Weili washing machine." (cartoon character)
> K44 *Niksaykpyengul chacuseyyo.*
> "Look for the green bottle." (female announcer)

Suggestion to use: An utterance that refers to a consumer using the product in some way, as in samples E25, J39, C1, and K12.

E25   *Throw in your dirtiest clothes, then toss in a Fab 1-Shot pack.* (male announcer)

J39   *Poora no Dei-ando-dei, Massaaji Kuriimu wa mizu de arainagaseru kara kantan ni tsukaemasu.*
"As Pola's Day And Day massage cream can be washed off with water, you can use it easily." (off-screen voice of female character)

C1   *Ni key fangxin de yong.*
"You can use it without worry." (on-screen female actor, to female)

K12   *Wuli emanun Heinz.*
"Our mother uses Heinz." (song lyrics)

Suggestion to enjoy benefits: An utterance that refers to the consumer experiencing the benefits of owning or using the product, as in samples E43, J13, C35, and K24.

E43   *Instead of spending your evening creating a classic, you can spend it enjoying one.* (male announcer)

J13   *Saa, hajimemasen ka, ii iki no shuukan?*
"Let's start the habit of new breath, shall we?" (on-screen male celebrity)

C35   *Ji jiang jianmei you xiang koufu.*
"You can keep fit and enjoy gourmet's luck at the same time." (male announcer)

K24   *Santtushan masulo kiekhaseyyo.*
"Remember as a fresh taste." (female announcer)

Suggestion with unspecified action: An utterance that implies that a viewer will interact with the product in some way, but leaves the desired action unspecified or makes a metaphorical suggestion, as in samples E41, J17, and K27.

E41   *Listen to the heartbeat of America.* (song lyric)

J17   *Kotoshi wa fain na nama biiru.*
"For this year, fine draft beer." (on-screen male celebrity and printed message)

K27   *Memohaseyyo.*
"Do the Memo." (female announcer). [Note: the product name is "Memobis"]

Table 20.3 shows the distribution of suggestions to buy versus all others. Explicit references to buying (ordering, purchasing, etc.) or to selling (the reciprocal of buying) are not favored in any of the four languages investigated. In each sample, reference to other actions such as getting, using, or benefiting from owning the product are emphasized. Korean television commercials appear to represent the extreme in avoiding mention of buying and selling, while Japanese commercials are apparently the least reluctant to mention financial transactions. However, between-language differences in the frequencies of suggestions to buy are not statistically significant. It is also worth noting that all but one of the Chinese ads in this category simply referred to where products are sold, which might be taken as a simple statement of availability rather than a suggestion to buy.

LINGUISTIC INDIRECTION AND POLITENESS PHENOMENA

As was indicated in Table 20.2, syntactic imperatives were the most common form of suggestions in the American television commercials but were uncommon in Japanese, Chinese, and Korean commercials. Table 20.4 presents an expanded tabulation of linguistic forms found

Table 20.3 Content of suggestions

	Eng	Jpns	Chns	Kor
Suggestions to buy	7	10	7	2
All other actions	71	25	28	51
Total	78	35	35	53
Category × Language, All:	$X^2 = 14.18$	df = 3	p < 0.05	
Category × Language, English	$X^2 = 52.05*$	df = 1	p < 0.05	
Category × Language, Japanese	$X^2 = 5.92*$	df = 1	p < 0.05	
Category × Language, Chinese	$X^2 = 12.10*$	df = 1	p < 0.05	
Category × Language, Korean	$X^2 = 44.80*$	df = 1	p < 0.05	

* Corrected values

Table 20.4 Linguistic form of suggestions to viewer

	Eng	Jpns	Chns	Kor
Bare imperative	33	0	7	9
Imperative + *please* or tag	0	3	4	1
Elliptical imperative (no verb)	4	14	0	11
Negative question	1	2	0	0
Nominalization	4	4	3	0
Embedded suggestion	4	1	0	0
Conditional	2	1	1	0
Consumer as object	3	0	6	0
Ability/possibility statements	1	2	1	0
Passive	0	0	4	0
Propositives (e.g., let's go)	0	0	0	4
Other forms	2	0	0	5
Total	54	27	26	30

in our data, again limited to suggestions directed at the viewer. The observed frequencies are too small to permit statistical analysis and are reported here simply to illustrate the range of forms found. We were also interested in seeing whether television commercials contain other suggestion forms such as those identified for face-to-face communication in English by Edmondson and House (1981), as in example (2).

(2)   *Why not . . .?*
      I suggest that you . . .
      You should/ought to/must . . .
      Maybe you could . . .
      The thing to do is . . .

No examples of expressions such as *you should, you ought to*, or *I suggest that* were found in any of the four language samples, though in American commercials a number of somewhat similar forms were found:

E21   *Why not the best?*
E16   *Why cook in oil, margarine, or butter?*
E43   *. . . you can spend it enjoying one.*
E25   *You'd probably like to know . . .*
E13   *Isn't it nice to know . . .*
E9   *It's a good time for the great taste at MacDonald's.*
E5   *It's gotta be a Dodge.*

Other forms found in our data that have not been previously identified in the literature as forms for suggestions included E17 and E30.

E17   *Suddenly, the obvious choice.* (nominalization)
E30   *This one's gonna turn your head around.* (consumer as object).

We suspect that a larger sample of commercials would yield more suggestion forms. American commercials occasionally contain need-statements, both those referring to hearer-need (*If you're a frequent flyer, maybe you need a new credit card* [hypothetical example]) and speaker-need (*At Friendly Auto Sales, we have to get rid of 200 cars and trucks this weekend* [hypothetical example]), neither of which were found in our sample. As indicated in Table 20.4, a range of suggestion forms was also found in each of the other languages investigated, and presumably a larger sample would also increase these inventories.

There are some major problems in attempting to compare the incidence of such forms across languages. We think it unlikely that an etic grid could be devised that would include all forms and provide a universally valid ranking of forms by level of directness and politeness. However, three minimal assumptions seem reasonable: (1) imperatives are more direct and less polite than all other forms; (2) imperatives with tag questions or overt politeness markers such as *please* or polite address forms are more polite (though no less explicit) than bare imperatives; and (3) suggestions in which the addressee is the linguistic subject and in which the verb represents the action recommended are more direct than those in which the recommended action is omitted or nominalized or suggestions cast as passives. These assumptions are insufficient to rank commercials from the four languages in terms of directness or politeness in a completely precise way, but some interesting patterns do emerge for each language.

American television commercials are, as we have already noted, most direct according to principle (1) and are also (as seen in Table 20.4) the least polite by principle (2). English advertising is alone in its extreme preference for bare imperatives, with no mitigating devices. However, our English commercials also contain less explicit forms such as those mentioned in principle (3) and (as discussed previously) often make suggestions less explicit through participant shift and action shift, so it is not the case that the U.S. commercials are unremittingly aggressive. There is also an apparent interaction in the U.S. commercials between these different ways of being indirect. Although English prefers the bare imperative for suggestions in commercials, and although nearly 10 percent of all suggestions are suggestions to buy, we do not have a single case in which either the viewer or an on-screen character is bluntly told to *buy the product*. Explicit mention of the exchange of money appears to require either participant shift (actors as surrogate consumers may say that they bought a product or some other consumer did) or linguistic indirection (viewers may be told that a product is a *better buy* or told *what steps to take to buy it*.[5]

This trade-off between the different dimensions of indirectness in the U.S. commercials was not found in our samples from Asia. The Chinese and Korean commercials in our sample contained few suggestions to buy (regardless of the type of linguistic encoding), and the Japanese sample contained very few imperatives of any sort. However, it is interesting to note that one of the two examples of imperatives in the Japanese sample was an imperative to buy:

> J9   *Minna katte ne?*
> "Everybody buy, won't you." (child's voice)

However, this utterance occurred in a commercial directed at children, and a child's voice was used to make the utterance, conveying an intimate, cute tone in Japanese.

In the Chinese television commercials, the most striking aspect of the form of suggestions is the use of *please* and polite pronouns. In Chinese, the tone of an imperative may be softened by adding particles *ba, le,* or *la* at the end of a sentence (none of which is found in our data), using verbs with less directness of action (as discussed under indirection by action shift), or by adding *please* to the imperative. Our Chinese sample contains four instances of imperative plus *please*, of which C33 is typical.

> C33   *Nin yao xiangyao nin de xiao baobao huobokeai ma? Na qing nin gei tamen fuyong tongrentangzhiyaochang shenchan de jianpixiaoshiwan.*
> "You want your children to be as healthy and lovely [as these]? Please give them Jianpi Xiaoshi Wan produced by Tongrentang Medicine Factory." (female announcer)

Pronouns of address also indicate politeness in Chinese. For the addressee, there is a choice between *ni* (regular, informal) and *nin* (polite, honorific). In our data, *nin* is always used when the suggestion is addressed to the viewer (as in C33 above, for example), although the sample contains several commercials in which on-screen actors use the *ni* form to each other. The use of polite pronouns gives suggestions in Chinese commercials a polite and formal tone.

Korean commercials do not favor imperatives with *please*, but Japanese commercials do. Of the three imperatives in our Japanese sample, one uses a question tag, and the other two are printed messages with *kudasai* "please", again sounding more like requests (by English norms) than suggestions. Suggestions in Japanese commercials also contain negative questions (two to the viewer and two to on-screen actors), which have been identified as preferred Japanese request forms (Takahashi, 1987).

For both Japanese and Korean, the most interesting finding with respect to linguistic form is the very high incidence of elliptical imperatives, related to the strategy of indirection through action shift. Several examples of elliptical imperatives also occur in English, as in E16 and E24.

> E16   *Pam cooking spray, because how you cook is as important as what you cook.* (male announcer)
> E24   *Pine Sol, because you care about clean.* (male announcer)

Elliptical imperatives have been noted for English requests, e.g., *salt*, meaning "pass the salt" when said at a dinner table, and are generally considered to be at the explicit, direct end of the continuum of directive types (Ervin-Tripp, 1976). Elliptical imperatives such as those in

E16 and E24 are not direct in this context, however, but are ambiguous. The utterance *Pine Sol, because you care about clean* could be paraphrased as "We created Pine Sol because you care about clean" or as "Buy Pine Sol, because you care about clean."

What is a relatively minor suggestion strategy in English commercials turns out to be a major strategy in Japanese and Korean. Examples from the Japanese sample include J14, J16, and J43.

> J14   *Kondo no do nichi wa ochikaku no matsuda e.*
>   "Next Saturday and Sunday, to Mazda (stores) near (you)." (male announcer)
> J16   *Odekake mae ni ichi kapuseru.*
>   "Before going out, one capsule." (printed message)
> J43   *Migaki-arai wa Kaneyon.*
>   "For polishing, Kaneyon." (female actor and printed message)

Korean examples include K9, K25, and K40.

> K9   *Ttenaki cen nal pamey Kwimitheytlul.*
>   "At night before leaving, Kwimithey." (male announcer)
> K25   *Iceypwuthen, Shiny Fresh Brown.*
>   "From now on, Shiny Fresh Brown." (song lyrics)
> K40   *Ismomi nappulttayn, Insatol.*
>   "When gums are bad, Insatol." (male announcer)

Native speakers of Japanese and Korean judge most of the examples of elliptical imperatives in our data to be typical of advertising language, not language that would be used in face-to-face interaction. What is interesting about this is that there is a connection between this conventionalized use of language in advertising and grammatical and pragmatic principles that function more generally in these languages. Both Korean and Japanese are discourse-sensitive languages that permit the deletion of any constituent if it is recoverable from context, although verbs are less likely than nouns to be deleted. Takahashi (1987) has reported that Japanese subjects produced directives in discourse completion tasks that did not refer explicitly to the action to be taken, making the recipient of the directive responsible for guessing what was wanted.

Conclusions

Previous studies of cross-cultural advertising practices have reported that American advertising is essentially persuasive in nature, while Asian advertising emphasizes other functions, informativeness in the case of Chinese advertising, and entertainment value and the establishment of positive feelings in the case of Japanese and Korean advertising. Advertising research of this type is typically based on the intuitive reactions of native speaker judges, and results are reported without reference to the language used in commercials or other forms of advertising. This study has shown that prime-time consumer product advertising on television in the U.S. *is* more overtly persuasive than similar advertising in three Asian countries in terms of the frequency of suggestions and the frequency with which imperatives are used to make such suggestions. Indeed, as Leech has pointed out, statements such as "Asian advertising is less persuasive than American advertising" only make sense if they can be relativized in terms of the pragmalinguistic strategies used in different communities and situations (Leech, 1983, p. 231). We have provided some pragmalinguistic evidence that Japanese advertising practices are at the opposite pole from those in the U.S. with respect to the speech act of suggesting, while Korean and Chinese commercials are nearer the middle of a continuum.

This study has uncovered a number of other intriguing facts about the ways suggestions are made in television commercials in these four countries. Perhaps the most interesting general question that can be asked is whether the language of advertising is a function of universal pragmatic principles, a reflection of cultural norms, the result of the requirements of selling in a market economy (Hall & Saracino-Resh, 1979), or just a reflection of arbitrary conventions established by the advertising industry.

While our evidence is fragmentary, we have reason to think that each of these forces plays a role and that no one of them is entirely responsible. Our hypotheses were based on the assumption that general cultural norms regarding directness in language would be reflected in advertising language. At the same time, these cultural differences are manifested against a background of universal principles. The suggestion to buy implies a cost to the viewer, and we find that Leech's maxim of tact, to minimize cost and minimize benefits to a hearer (Leech, 1983, p. 132), is reflected in commercials from all four countries. Suggestions referring to purchase are less common than those that stress benefits to the consumer and avoid mention of the actual exchange of money for goods. In the U.S. data, we also found an apparent trade-off between the use of the imperative, the most direct linguistic form, and the choice of the action recommended, a nice illustration of one of the corollaries of Leech's tact maxim, that the more transparent the cost to the hearer in terms of prepositional content, the greater will be the need for optionality and indirectness in expression of the impositive (Leech, 1983, p. 126).

There are a number of ways in which the commercials in our samples reflect the economies in which they are embedded, most obviously in the distribution of products that are advertised. Other differences among the commercials from the four countries that we have not mentioned so far in this chapter reflect governmental regulation. These differences are less noticeable with respect to the head act of suggestion than to the types of supporting moves used, the *reasons* presented to the viewer to buy a product. One example is the use of comparative advertising, which is proscribed (more by culture and tradition than by law) in both Japan and Korea, but not in China. Only the U.S. sample contained comparative statements in which competing brands were mentioned by name (in 6 of 50 commercials). However, a wide variety of other comparative devices was found, including strategies that can be paraphrased as *better than others* (unspecified), *the best, nothing better, unique,* and *winner.* Only the Japanese commercials are non-comparative in this wider sense, while Chinese commercials are quite comparative, frequently mentioning the number of prizes a product has won in government-sponsored quality competitions (14 out of 50 commercials). Another aspect of commercials subject to governmental supervision is the type of claims allowed. In the U.S., FTC regulations prohibit the making of statements that cannot be substantiated (Geis, 1982). This may account for the fact that U.S. commercials make very few explicit claims and are full of puffery, statements that sound important but that actually make few if any claims. Chinese commercials, by contrast, make very strong claims that would not be allowed under U.S. advertising regulations (e.g., promising that a particular medicinal product will cure a long list of diseases, restore youth, and bring the user success and prosperity). By this measure, Chinese advertising is much more direct than advertising in the U.S., Japan, or Korea. However, the language of advertising cannot be completely a function of the requirements of selling in a particular economy under a particular set of government regulations. The U.S. and Japanese commercials were most different with respect to the aspects of language examined in this chapter, although the economies in which they are situated are the most similar in many respects.

There are several ways in which the realization of suggestions to buy in commercials reflects the potential of the medium of television. The clearest example of this is the use of indirection by participant shift, making suggestions directly to a viewer through an off-screen voice, printed message, or song lyric, having on-screen actors make suggestions to each other, and so forth. The technique of having on-screen characters directly model the action of purchase, found only in the U.S. commercials, may be simply an innovation in the use of the medium which may spread across national and linguistic borders in time. In commercials from each country, we also find some apparent examples of register-specific conventionalized language. For U.S. advertising, the high frequency of imperatives may be partly viewed as a convention of advertising, since it cannot be attributed to universal requirements of selling (imperatives are infrequent in commercials from the other countries) or the function of suggesting versus requesting (imperatives are not the most common form for suggestions in face-to-face interaction). The finding that the formal pronoun *nin* is used to address the viewer in Chinese commercials conflicts with the claim of Fang and Heng (1983) that *nin* has been replaced almost completely by *ni* since the Cultural Revolution, so this may be a Chinese advertising convention. (Alternatively, the claim by Fang and Heng, for which no empirical sources were cited, may be incorrect.) Probably the best example of conventionalized language in advertising we have found in our data is the use of elliptical imperatives in Korean and Japanese commercials, though as we have noted, this draws upon both the linguistic resources of those languages (topic-comment structure, with optional deletion of constituents) as well as the pragmatic preference in commercials for avoiding reference to the desired action.

One of the most interesting issues for continued cross-cultural study of the pragmatics of advertising and the language of business in general is the need to further elucidate relationships among the language used, universal pragmatic principles, cultural norms, and the more strictly conventionalized aspects of advertising register. Another line of fruitful inquiry raised by the data examined here concerns the nature of speech acts such as suggestions and requests. We do not have a fully satisfactory explanation for the occurrence of request-like forms in commercials from China, Japan, and (to a lesser extent) Korea, especially those with *please* and formal politeness markers that are not found in U.S. commercials at all. One possible line of explanation could be that requests and suggestions may be less differentiated speech act categories in Japanese and Korean than in English. An analysis along these lines is suggested by Coulmas' (1981) observation that apologies and expressions of gratitude are less differentiated as speech act categories in Japanese than in many other languages. Banerjee and Carrell (1988) reported that their non-native speakers of English (of Chinese and Malay language backgrounds) sometimes used requesting strategies inappropriately for suggestions in English. However, even in English there is great overlap among the linguistic forms used for requesting and suggesting, and these categories of speech acts are not completely distinct at a conceptual level. There are clear cases of requests directed at actions desired by a speaker with no benefits for a hearer, as well as suggestions in cases where only the hearer's benefit is at issue and the speaker making the suggestion has no interest at all in whether or not the hearer carries out the action. However, the business concept of a free transaction between a willing seller and a willing buyer implies a balance between the costs and benefits accruing to both parties. Perhaps our initial analysis, that commercials should be understood as suggestions, was incorrect. If commercials are more properly analyzed as hybrids containing elements of both request and suggestion, then the U.S. preference for the linguistic forms typical of suggestions and avoidance of those typical of requests might be seen, not as a reflection of the fact that commercials are suggestions in essence, but as another manifestation of the maxim of tact, a manipulative strategy designed to minimize apparent costs by using linguistic forms that are appropriate when recommending actions that are clearly to a hearer's benefit.

Notes

1   The videotapes of Chinese, Korean, and Japanese commercials used in this research were provided by Charles Keown and Lawrence Jacobs. Initial transcription of the English commercials was done by Johanna Guth. An information content analysis of a larger sample of commercials drawn from the same database appears in Keown et al. (1992). Useful comments on an earlier draft of this paper were provided by Carl James, Gabriele Kasper, Rajendra Singh, Peter Schmidt, and Keiichi Morita, none of whom are responsible for any weaknesses.

2   We do not discuss visual strategies in this chapter. While television is often considered to be primarily a visual medium in which language plays only a secondary role, Geis (1982) has provided ample evidence that television is no less an auditory medium than is radio.

3   An alternative to using consensus among the authors for coding decisions would have been to have more than one rater categorize examples from each language and compute inter-rater reliability coefficients. While this would enhance confidence in the analysis of each individual language sample, this method would not guarantee comparability of coding across languages, which we believe was achieved better using discussion and consensus.

4   It is common for a Japanese women to address her father-in-law as *ojiichan* "grandpa," especially in front of her children. He is not her grandfather, but he is grandfather to her children, and grandfather is seen as his primary role with respect to the family unit.

5   An exception to the generalization that imperatives are not used in U.S. advertising with explicit reference to the exchange of money occurs in advertisements for mail-order products (none in the sample analyzed in this chapter), at the end of which a viewer might be told: *Call 1–800-xxx-xxxx, Have your credit card ready, Or send $9.95 plus $3 shipping and handling to . . .* [hypothetical example]. A possible explanation for these forms may be that, unless the viewer takes note of the address or phone number when the commercial is being broadcast (or, as a minimum, is primed to do this when next hearing the same commercial), the commercial will not fulfill its goal.

References

Agoston, T. & von Raffler-Engel, W. (1979). A linguistic analysis of some commercial television advertisements. In Robert St. Clair (ed.), *Perspectives on applied sociolinguistics* (pp. 224–42). Lawrence, Kansas: Coronado Press.

Aston, G. (1993). Notes on the interlanguage of comity. In Gabriele Kasper & Shoshana Blum-Kulka (eds), *Interlanguage pragmatics* (pp. 224–50). New York: Oxford University Press.

Banerjee, J. & Carrell, P. L. (1988). Tuck in your shirt, you squid: Suggestions in ESL. *Language Learning,* 38, 313–64.

Barthes, R. (1972). *Mythologies.* New York: Hill and Wang.

Bhatia, T. K. (1987). English in advertising: Multiple mixing and media. *World Englishes,* 6, 33–48.

Blum-Kulka, S., House, J. & Kasper, G. (eds) (1989). *Cross-cultural pragmatics: Requests and apologies.* Norwood, NJ: ABLEX.

Blum-Kulka, S. & Olshtain, E. (1984). Requests and apologies: A cross-cultural study of speech act realization patterns (CCSARP). *Applied Linguistics,* 5, 196–213.

Bolinger, D. (1973). Truth is a linguistic function. *Language,* 49, 539–50.

Bolinger, D. (1980). *Language: The loaded weapon.* London: Longman.

Brown, P. & Levinson, S. C. (1987). *Politeness.* Cambridge: Cambridge University Press.

Coleman, L. (1990). The language of advertising (review article). *Journal of Pragmatics,* 14, 137–45.

Coulmas, F. (1981). Poison to your soul. Thanks and apologies contrastively viewed. In Florian Coulmas (ed.), *Conversational routine* (pp. 69–91). The Hague: Mouton.

Dowling, G. R. (1980). Information content in U.S. and Australian television advertising. *Journal of Marketing,* 44(Fall), 34–7.

Edmondson, W. & House, J. (1981). *Let's talk and talk about it.* Munich: Urban & Schwarzenberg.

Ervin-Tripp, S. M. (1976). Is Sybil there?: The structure of some American English directives. *Language in Society,* 5, 25–66.

Fang, H. & Heng, J. H. (1983). Social changes and changing address norms in China. *Language in Society*, 12, 495–507.

Fields, G. (1983). *From bonsai to Levi's*. New York: New York Library.

Fraser, B. (1983). The domain of pragmatics. In Jack C. Richards & Richard W. Schmidt (eds), *Language and communication* (pp. 29–59). London: Longman.

Geis, M. (1982). *The language of television advertising*. New York: Academic Press.

Goffmann, E. (1981). *Forms of talk*. Philadelphia: University of Pennsylvania Press.

Grice, H. P. (1975). Logic and conversation. In Peter Cole & Jerry L. Morgan (eds), *Speech acts (Syntax and semantics 3)* (pp. 41–58). New York: Academic Press.

Gumperz, J. J. (1982). *Discourse strategies*. Cambridge: Cambridge University Press.

Hall, D. R. & Saracino-Resh, L. (1979). Advertising as cultural language. In Robert St. Clair (ed.), *Perspectives on applied sociolinguistics* (pp. 191–211). Lawrence, Kansas: Coronado Press.

Harris, R. J. (ed.) (1983). *Information processing research*. Hillsdale, NJ: Erlbaum.

Hatch, E. & Lazaraton, A. (1991). *The research manual: Design and statistics for applied linguistics*. New York: Newbury House.

Ho, S.-C. & Sin, Y.-M. (1986). Advertising in China: Looking back and looking forward. *International Journal of Advertising*, 5, 307–16.

Hong, J. W., Muderrisoglu, A. & Zinhan, G. M. (1987). Cultural differences and advertising expression: A comparative content analysis of Japanese and U.S. magazine advertising. *Journal of Advertising*, 16, 55–68.

Hunt, S. D. (1976). Informational vs. persuasive advertising: An appraisal. *Journal of Advertising*, 5(Summer), 5–8.

Johns, A. M. (1986). The language of business. *Annual Review of Applied Linguistics*, 7, 3–17.

Kasper, G. & Dahl, M. (1991). Research methods in interlanguage pragmatics. *Studies in Second Language Acquisition*, 13, 215–47.

Kaynak, E. & Mitchel, L. A. (1981). Analysis of marketing strategies in diverse cultures. *Journal of Advertising Research*, 213, 25–32.

Keown, C. F., Jacobs, L. W., Schmidt, R. W. & Gymn, K.-I. (1992). Information content of advertising in the United States, Japan, South Korea, and the People's Republic of China. *International Journal of Advertising*, 11, 257–67.

Laczniak, G. R. (1979). Information content in print advertising. *Journalism Quarterly*, 56, 324–27, 345.

Lakoff, R. T. (1982). Persuasive discourse and ordinary conversation, with examples from advertising. In Deborah Tannen (ed.), *Analyzing discourse: Text and talk, Georgetown University round table on languages and linguistics* (pp. 25–42). Washington DC: Georgetown University Press.

Leech, G. (1966). *English in advertising*. London: Longman.

Leech, G. (1983). *Principles of pragmatics*. London: Longman.

Madden, C. S., Caballero, M. & Matsukubo, S. (1986). Analysis of information content in U.S. and Japanese magazine advertising. *Journal of Advertising*, 15(3), 38–45.

Masavisut, N., Sukwiwat, M. & Wongmontha, S. (1987). The power of the English language in Thai media. *World Englishes*, 5, 197–207.

Miracle, G. E. (1985). Advertising regulations in Japan and the USA: An introductory comparison. *Waseda Business and Economic Studies*, 21, 335–69.

Miracle, G. E. (1987). Feel-do-learn: An alternative sequence underlying Japanese commercials. In F. Feasely (ed.), *Proceedings of the 1987 conference of the American Academy of Advertising* (pp. R73–R78).

Moeran, B. (1985). When the poetics of advertising become the advertising of poetics. Syntactical and semantic parallelism in English and Japanese advertising. *Language and Communication*, 5, 29–44.

Mueller, B. (1987). Reflections of culture: An analysis of Japanese and American advertising appeals. *Journal of Advertising Research* (June/July), 51–9.

O'Barr, W. M. (1979). Language and advertising. In James E. Alatis & G. Richard Tucker (eds), *Georgetown University round table on languages and linguistics 1979* (pp. 272–86). Washington, DC: Georgetown University Press.

Resnik, A. & Stern, B. L. (1977). An analysis of information content in television advertising. *Journal of Marketing*, 41, 50–3.

Rice, M. D. & Lu, Z. (1988). A content analysis of Chinese magazine advertisements. *Journal of Advertising*, 17(4), 43–8.

Rintell, E. (1979). Getting your speech act together: The pragmatic ability of second language learners. *Working Papers on Bilingualism*, 17, 97–106.

Schmidt, R. & Kess, J. F. (1985). Persuasive language in the television medium: Contrasting advertising and televangelism. *Journal of Pragmatics*, 9, 287–308.

Schmidt, R. & Kess, J. F. (1987). *Television advertising and televangelism: Discourse analysis of persuasive language.* Amsterdam: Benjamins.

Searle, J. R. (1969). *Speech acts*. Cambridge: Cambridge University Press.

Searle, J. R. (1976). A classification of illocutionary acts. *Language in Society*, 5, 1–23.

Sherry, J. F. & Camargo, E. G. (1987). May your life be marvelous: English language labeling and the semiotics of Japanese promotion. *Journal of Consumer Research*, 14, 174–88.

Stern, B. L., Krugman, D. M. & Resnik, A. (1981). Magazine advertising: Analysis of its information content. *Journal of Advertising Research*, 21(2), 39–44.

Takahashi, S. (1987). A contrastive study of indirectness exemplified in L1 directive speech acts performed by American and Japanese. Unpublished Master's thesis, The University of Illinois at Urbana-Champaign, Urbana IL.

Tse, D. K., Belk, R. W. & Zhou, N. (1989). Becoming a consumer society: A longitudinal and cross-cultural content analysis of print ads from Hong Kong, the People's Republic of China, and Taiwan. *Journal of Consumer Research*, 15, 457–72.

Vestergaard, T. & Schrøder, K. (1985). *The language of advertising*. Oxford: Basil Blackwell.

Weizman, E. (1993). Interlanguage requestive hints. In Gabriele Kasper & Shoshana Blum-Kulka (eds), *Interlanguage pragmatics* (pp. 123–37). New York: Oxford University Press.

Yamaki, T. (n.d.). International comparison of television commercials [Unpublished MS].

Chapter 21

FRANCESCA BARGIELA-CHIAPPINI
AND SANDRA J. HARRIS

INTERRUPTIVE STRATEGIES IN BRITISH
AND ITALIAN MANAGEMENT MEETINGS

Introduction

I T IS INTERESTING—but perhaps not altogether surprising—that the recent public controversy (April 1995) over the way BBC interviewers behave towards Conservative politicians should have centered on interruptions.

Jonathan Aitken, a leading minister in the Conservative government, initiated the attack on the BBC by claiming that John Humphreys of the radio program *Today* interrupted the chancellor, Kenneth Clarke, thirty-two times in a ten minute interview. Such behavior, said Aitken, was not only inappropriate and rude but was also indicative of a negative bias toward Conservative politicians which undermined the obligatory neutrality of the BBC.

When taxed with this accusation (i.e. thirty-two interruptions of Kenneth Clarke), John Humphreys responded that it all depends on what you mean by "interruption"—probably a more interesting question than Humphreys realized. Indeed, it would appear that, even from a common sense and folklorist perspective, what counts as an interruption is not easy to determine.

The literature on interruptions is now very considerable and has come a long way in the twenty years since Sacks et al. (1974) first proposed their rules on turn-taking, and Zimmerman and West (1975) correlated, controversially, interruptive behavior with gender and power. In the meantime, a great deal of research on simultaneous speech has been done, and several trends are apparent.

Firstly, much of the past research has been focused on interruptions as they reflect either gender relationships or power relationships of both. This has proved a controversial area of investigation, with some conflicting evidence (e.g., Marche and Peterson, 1993; Chambliss and Feeny, 1992; Talbot, 1992; LaFrance, 1992; Smith-Lovin and Brody, 1989; Dindia, 1987). Secondly, some of the conflicting evidence emanates from the difficulty of devising a precise and generally acceptable definition of what counts as an interruption or even, more recently, the question as to whether a stable phenomenon of "interruption" as a subclass of speech overlap exists at all (Hopper, 1992; Drummond, 1989). What is an interruption has proved extremely difficult to agree on, especially since the term has negative connotations which, for some

Source: Bargiela-Chiappini, F. & Harris, S. (1996). Interruptive strategies in British and Italian management meetings. *Text*, 16(3), 269–97.

researchers, have confused the issue still further and made it essential to distinguish interruptive behavior from other types of overlapped speech (Talbot, 1992; Goldberg, 1990; Kennedy and Camden, 1983). Thirdly, recent work has recognized that interruptions (and other types of overlapped speech) are more complex than was initially realized and that much, if not most, overlapped speech is not actually dysfunctional or an indication that the turn-taking system has broken down (e.g., Makri-Tsilipakou, 1994; Murata, 1994; Goldberg, 1990; Kennedy and Camden, 1983). Ulijn and Li (1995), on the basis of Chinese–Western and other business encounters, suggest that the overwheling majority of interruptions in such encounters are not viewed by participants as impolite, though there are significant differences in interruptive behavior between cultures.

This paper examines interruptive strategies in Italian and British business meetings, where the constraints imposed by generic conventions and the variable degree of asymmetry within the interactions (generated by individuals commanding differing degrees of power) create an unusually challenging linguistic environment that calls into question some of the current research findings in the light of influencing contextual factors. There is now a need to move beyond the notion of interruptions as primarily conversational "accidents" with local causes and consequences, and toward a more holistic perspective which views interruptions not only as possible indicators of power (Hopper, 1992)[1] but also, we will argue, as necessary functional devices indicative of interactional aims.

Functional "usefulness" also characterizes interruptions in one other type of business interaction, i.e., in service encounters, where "interruptions seem to have the same function and the same position in both British and Italian data [where] a request is interrupted only if it is not being understood or if it is highly predictable" (Zorzi Calò, 1990, p. 104, our translation). In order to appreciate the complex interactional environment in which interruptions take place, Bazzanella (1990) advocates a polyedric approach to their study, which takes into account both objective and subjective contextual factors, such as the degree of formality, participant roles, topic, and the presence of recording apparatus and/or of a researcher. Bazzanella claims that the type of interruption and its effects on interpersonal relationships must be determined on the basis of the presence (or absence) and degree of influence of the various parameters and their interplay (Zorzi Calò, 1990, p. 90, our translation). In this paper, we will consider some of these factors and their influence on our data.

Background

Much of the work on interruptions has been done by conversation analysts, who propose, at least initially, that conversation is best approached as a locally managed activity consisting of loosely defined units identifiable on the basis of the prosodic and/or syntactic criteria. Each unit is thought to define a point where speakers may, but are not compelled to, change: a Transition Relevance Place (TRP). According to Levinson's (1983) useful summary of turn-taking rules, Rule 1b proposes that if C [current speaker] does not select N [next speaker], then any (other) party may self-select, first speaker gaining rights to the next turn (adapted from Levinson, 1983, p. 298).

The situation described above creates a linguistic environment potentially conducive to Simultaneous Speech (SS), or in the terminology of Sacks et al., "overlap," which may occur in the form of (a) "competitive first starts," (b) "inadvertent overlap" (in the case of systematic unpredictability of the unit's end), or (c) "violative interruption" (Levinson, 1983, p. 299).

Only (c) represents what we consider clear cases of interruption since in this paper we will argue that violation at the semantic level, i.e., that of intentional disregard of, or conflict with, propositions in a previous turn, is one of the possible criteria for identifying interruptive behavior. Therefore, while some notion of the Transitional Relevance Place (TRP) seems not only useful but also essential to any analysis which involves turn-taking, there is a need to refine the definition (and categorization) of "interruptions" by paying more attention to the functions of semantic and pragmatic devices activated by speakers within and between turns.

In his discussion of telephone conversations, Hopper (1992) reminds us that most overlaps take place at moments of possible completion, but also echoes Jefferson's (1986) conclusion that "there is no consistent pattern of who drops out, or who 'wins' an overlap" (Hopper, 1992, p. 123). While Hopper provides an alternative definition of overlap as "a clash, or a contention for finite floor time"—thus emphasizing the competitive nature of discourse—he also warns that merely counting overlaps presents a misleading picture of interruptive behavior.

A further complication is introduced by the multiparty nature of management meetings, where several speakers compete to gain access to the floor against specific time constraints and a set agenda. This alternative scenario is a potentially fertile ground for competitive turn-taking, since "contention for the floor may be an environment for accomplishing power" (Hopper, 1992, p. 127). It is quite possible to envisage a speaker who takes a dominant role by not respecting TRPs and thus causing an "interruptive speech overlap" (Hopper, 1992, p. 127), although Drummond (1989) found that most overlaps in his study of business talk are in fact supportive statements, or, in Hopper's words, "facilitative overlaps". West and Zimmerman (1983, p. 104) consider that interruption occurs, firstly, if the second speaker's turn begins more than two syllables from a TRP point and, secondly, if the overlapping turn is not supportive or facilitative of the first turn. The extension of this category of overlaps to include turns which are unambiguously supportive in terms of propositional content and yet violate the two-syllable rule does not "water down" the concept of interruption, or make it "less related to speaker power and competition" as Hopper fears. The likely outcome of the application of the highly selective set of qualifying criteria can ultimately only lead to a more robust and precise notion of interruption. This may also involve looking beyond the adjacency pair construct, since an apparently successful interruption can be negated by a power move in a subsequent turn. Like some of the earlier findings on the subject (e.g., Zimmerman and West, 1975), Roger et al.'s (1988) outcome-based classification of interruptions is therefore seriously flawed in its simplicity. Pragmatic features such as topic shift or prosodic strategies like irony and sarcasm may sometimes be interpreted as interruptive behavior.

Similarly, Bazzanella (1990) in her investigation of interruptions in Italian points to prosody and topic shift as two of the "objective parameters" that identify interruptions, the remaining being the length of the overlap, insistence and persistence, presence or absence of politeness markers. It is interesting that she also lists six "contextual parameters" (status,[2] individual style, set and acknowledged aim of the interaction, gender, "psychological urgency," and *force majeure*), the first three of which appear to be particularly relevant to management meetings.

Given the diverse nature of past work on interruptions, our own research is distinguished primarily in the following ways:

1. *Concern with multiparty speech.* Most, though by no means all, work on overlapped speech and interruptions has been based on dyads (but see: Murray, 1985). Multiparty speech (involving more than two interacting speakers) is particularly appropriate and interesting to look at in conjunction with interruptive strategies, since it tends to accentuate the complexities of turn-taking behavior and the skills of speaker contention for the floor, as anyone knows who has participated in group discussion. Some of our conclusions may relate directly to the fact that we are dealing with multiparty speech, which also imposes

serious problems of transcription. Identifying different voices and disambiguating overlaps when more than two speakers are present is often a considerable challenge, since there appear to be points in most multiparty situations where speakers converge in such a way that all speech becomes unintelligible.

2. *Emphasis on natural language data.* By this we mean recording speech events which would have occurred anyway, i.e., they are not contrived to enable the research to take place. Nor have we made use of simulations. Much previous work has been done on groups organized for research purposes, and a disproportionate amount of work, understandably perhaps, has used students as subjects.

3. *Use of data relating to a specific generic type: management meetings in British and Italian companies.* Most research in the past on interruption (though again, not all) has focused on ordinary conversation. The use of data relating to management meetings has several advantages. (*a*) It permits the analysis of entire texts in a holistic way, not merely isolated pairs of overlapping utterances. This is an important point which several recent researchers have made, i.e., that one cannot view "interruptive strategies" in isolation from what happens in the text as a whole. (*b*) Meetings as a generic type most often have highly visible status and power relationships. Because of the corporate context, hierarchical status is easily identifiable and not usually ambiguous. Investigating dominance and power as variables should be easier, though again our data reveal interesting results in this area.[3] (*c*) A final advantage is the task-oriented nature of management discourse, in which participants are constrained not only by the topic of the meeting but also by the fact that decisions must be reached and actioned. Speakers need to cooperate, not simply, as Grice would maintain, because the cooperative principle underlies all conversation, but because they have to work together interactively to produce a collective outcome.

4. *Interest in cross-cultural comparison.* Increasing interest in the nature of "politeness" has significantly altered the original Anglo-centered perception of interactional concepts such as the perception of self and other, face-work, conflict avoidance, etc. (Janney and Arndt, 1993). This, in turn, has led to a critique of concepts such as "interruption" being "culture-free". It is against this backdrop that our work poses a comparison between British and Italian management meetings, with a view to highlighting both differences and similarities in selected types of linguistic behavior which together generate management style.

Data and methodology

From an archive of English and Italian business texts, two meetings have been selected in each language, one formal and one informal. Formal meetings differ from informal ones in several ways, i.e., having an official written agenda circulated beforehand to participants, a designated chair, formal minutes, and usually a set meeting time and place on a regular basis.

These particular data were collected in two multinational companies, one British and one Italian, which produce comparable products. The meetings cited as data involved groups of staff at similar levels of seniority and a generally comparable mix of executive, managerial, and more junior staff in both multinationals. All of the meetings in both cultural settings were task-oriented, and in both countries the formal meetings were interdepartmental and the informal meetings were intradepartmental. Perhaps most important, all of the meetings involved the discussion of controversial topics and some challenging decision making. Both companies were going through difficult periods at the time of the recordings, with staff being asked to consider potentially divisive and threatening policies. This has produced data which are not only particularly interesting but also more obviously comparable considering their multinational origins.

The British meetings

The informal meeting consists of seven individuals, three males and four females at various hierarchical levels (including a personal assistant and a senior manager), all but one belonging to the personnel department. The group was set up on a voluntary basis to look into the issue of how to design and administer a company-wide questionnaire on performance-related pay (RPR). Personnel was aware that the issue of performance-related pay had not been well received by nonmanagerial staff, and before introducing it to middle and senior managers, a working group was asked to test initial reactions through a questionnaire. This is the second in a series of meetings which take place, in turn, in the office of each participant who leads the proceedings on a rota basis. An informal written agenda and synoptic minutes are produced.

The formal meeting consists of eight male participants, three at executive level, three at managerial level, and two young assistants, who meet to discuss the implementation of a new computing systems technique for manufacturing and stock control called masterscheduling, which the company is keen to introduce. This is the second time the group has met, after a training session during which they were briefed on the nature of the project. The meeting is a scheduled, periodic event that takes place in a seminar room and for which a written agenda and minutes are made available to all participants.

The Italian meetings

The informal meeting is a one-hour long interaction between three male members of the quality assurance department. All three hold posts at executive level, but the most senior acts as a chair, though in an informal fashion. He has the task of communicating to his colleagues the outcomes of a meeting in which he and their common boss participated and which will affect the quality assurance staff directly in the form of extra workload. The meeting takes place in a small seminar room in the quality assurance department.

The formal meeting is a quality review of a new product before its launch and is chaired by an executive from the quality assurance department. Nineteen people (eighteen males, one female) take part, of various status (executives to technical assistant), representing all the main functions of the company, i.e., operations, planning, research and development, marketing, etc. (Interestingly, the young woman was there to represent one of the least "powerful" departments of all, i.e., "documentation".) This is a periodic event with a formal, written agenda that the chairman follows quite closely. It takes place in a large seminar room outside the quality assurance department.

Criteria and analytical framework

The first stage of the analysis was to establish criteria for identifying different types of overlapped speech. It soon became very clear that overlap was a complex phenomenon, serving different functions at different points in the meeting and utilized by speakers in different ways. Since our primary interest was in interruptive strategies, there was a need for an analytical framework which would identify instances of overlap that were clearly interruptive and interpreted as such by participants.

Using a modified version of the work of West and Zimmerman (1983), we devised the following criteria to identify types of overlapped speech and the functions that they serve in multiparty discourse:

(1) The relationship to a TRP (Transition-Relevance Place):

a. The second speaker overlap is at or near a TRP, including initial overlaps = *facilitative overlap* or *inadvertent overlap*.

b. The second speaker overlap is not at or near a TRP, excluding initial overlaps = *interruptive overlap*.

(2) The nature of the proposition, in terms of its pragmatic features and/or semantic content:

a. The second speaker's overlapping proposition is supportive; high semantic convergence; topic continuity, including back channeling = *facilitative overlap*.

b. The second speaker's overlapping proposition is competitive or conflictual; low semantic convergence; topic shift = *interruptive overlap*.

Criterion (2) appears to take precedence over Criterion (1) in determining whether overlapped speech is interpreted by participant speakers as facilitative or interruptive. For example, in the following extract the overlapped speech is clearly facilitative, though it does not occur at or near a TRP.

(1) R: but as to your knowledge—sorry—that was
part of the—er trial discussion ⌈ about restaurants
C: ⌊ right

Supportive back-channelling utterances, e.g., "right," "yes," "okay," are very frequent in meetings and are often overlapped outside TRP boundaries. Conflictive prepositions or topic shifts, even if overlapped at or near a TRP, are more likely to be interpreted as interruptive.

These criteria are not entirely without problems. Firstly, no very precise definition of a TRP has yet been formulated. The difficulties in defining a TRP in general terms arise mainly from its inherently multidimensional nature. The listener is cued in by prosodic, syntactic, semantic, and nonverbal indicators which may include features such as the semantic completeness of the utterance, syntactic predictability, intonational contour, speed of delivery, and gaze orientation. Moreover, not all of these are accessible to researchers working from audio-tapes. Yet some notion of a TRP is crucial to understanding and interpreting interruptive behavior.

For the British data, we adopted West and Zimmerman's two-syllable rule, i.e., "near a TRP" is defined as being within two syllables of a TRP judged by semantic, syntactic, and prosodic criteria (with the latter taking precedence in cases of conflict.) The Italian data proved somewhat more problematic. We experienced difficulty in a relatively small number of cases in identifying the boundaries of the overlapped turns with accuracy, particularly when a crucial portion of the turn was unintelligible, thus making it impossible to retrieve lexical (and therefore prosodic) elements that could have assisted our interpretation. This situation arises most frequently in the Italian formal meeting, where, because of the high number of participants (19), the meeting sometimes splits into parallel conversations, making it extremely difficult for the listener to identify interweaving turn-taking patterns.

A second problem is that supportive and competitive/conflictive overlaps can be difficult to distinguish in certain cases. However, task-oriented business discourse, where participants are most often working toward a previously specified goal, facilitates such distinctions being made, especially in formal meetings where topic shifts are constrained by a formal agenda.

The selected criteria generate the following analytical framework.

Types of overlapped speech

Type 1
Criterion (1) 1. At or near TRP   } facilitative or
Criterion (2) 2. Supportive proposition, etc. } inadvertent overlap

Examples:

   (2)   (Facilitative overlap, British informal meeting)
        C: but if people have dogmatic reasons rather than lack of understanding—
                we've eliminated—the communication aspect of it—so we can say people
                do understand it—⌈just don't like it
→   H: ⌊they still don't like it
   (3)   (Inadvertent overlap, British informal meeting)
        S: I'd be happy with—the eight
        H: yeah
        S: ⌈we get continuity
→   J: ⌊what was the   what was the initial purpose of having sort of—a fair
                proportion of people from outside the function involved

Type 2
Criterion (1) 1. Not at or near TRP   } facilitative
Criterion (2) 2. Supportive proposition, etc. } overlap[4]

Examples:

   (4)   (Facilitative overlap, British formal meeting)
        F: but assuming that the information is held in a central core as we're
                suggesting it should be— we can get
                ⌈all the information—and it can
→   CH: ⌊it can actually be assessed
        F: be assessed by others as well
        CH: it—it can be assessed—yes—yeah—absolutely

Type 3
Criterion (1) 1. At or near TRP   } competitive[5] or
Criterion (2) 2. Competitive proposition, etc. } inadvertent overlap

Examples:

   (5)   (Competitive overlap, British informal meeting)
        H: right—can't do consecutive meetings
        C: that's a new rule   ⌈is it
→   H: ⌊Friday afternoon
        S: it is at the moment—Colin
        C: all right—well—Friday afternoon—we'll all feel pretty relaxed

Type 4
Criterion (1) 1. Not at or near TRP   } interruption
Criterion (2) 2. Competitive proposition, etc. }

Examples:

   (6)   (Interruption, British informal meeting)

        S: I think the other   ⌈important—

→   C: ⌊you're a bit quiet John—aren't you

        J: no I understand

        C: oh good—good

        S: I think the other important point that came out was also er—the fact
of when we contact people, etc.

   (7) (Interruption, British formal meeting)

        D: they can try to influence a change—and this is why this master scheduler
has got to be a real hard man because he has to reconcile the
                       ⌈the the dichotomy between commercial

→   G: ⌊this is what I'm saying—you can't

        D: need   ⌈and business planning and manufacturing

        F: ⌊yeah

This framework provides an interesting way forward. Types 1 and 4 are clearcut, i.e., both criteria are either facilitative (Type 1) or interruptive (Type 4). More problematic are Types 2 and 3, where the criteria conflict, and Criterion (2) takes precedence over Criterion (1). However, because we are concerned with interruptions in this paper, our analysis will focus primarily on Type 4, which provides a clear working definition of an interruption. Example (6) involves a topic shift, and example (7) a conflicting proposition. What counts as an interruption in the analysis of both the British and the Italian data is defined as Type 4.

Discussion of British data

Since both the British and the Italian data involve certain clear power indicators, interruptive behavior cannot be interpreted in isolation from other aspects of turn-taking behavior, such as length and number of turns and other types of overlap. Such behavior establishes the context for highlighting differences between informal and formal meetings and for facilitating the cross-cultural comparison (see Tables 21.1–21.3.)

The length and number of turns are clearly related to power and status in both the informal and formal British meetings. Even allowing for a margin of error, given the difficulty of transcription of multiparty speech, this seems undeniably the case. Those participants with highest status talk most and take the longest turns.

However, both the topic of the discussion and the task set also have a bearing on turn-taking behavior. This is clearly evidenced by the participation of Dave, who is the information technology manager, in the formal meeting (see Table 21.3). Since the topic is expert systems and the task is how to implement "master-scheduling," the discussion is very technical. Dave, as the participant with the greatest subject expertise in this area, plays a role which is far more dominant than that of the other nonexecutive speakers. Knowledge and expertise as well as status govern turn-taking behavior and are related to power. There is no obvious relationship between gender and the length and number of turns in the informal meeting (see Tables 21.4–21.6). Both the interrupters and the interrupted are the three participants of managerial status.

Table 21.1 British meetings: general quantitative profile[6]

	Formal meeting	Informal meeting
Number of words	17,200	4,240
Number of participants	8	7
Duration of meeting	1 hour 30 minutes	41 minutes
Number of turns	780	331
Number of turns longer than 50 words	74	12
Number of overlaps	219	47
Number of interruptions	34	3

Table 21.2 British meetings: Analysis of turn-taking behaviour—informal meeting

Participants	Number of turns	Turns of more than 50 words
Colin (chair and most senior)**	105	8
Helen (personnel manager)*	86	2
Sarah (personnel manager)*	80	1
Hazel (personnel officer)	16	1
Audrey (outside personnel)	8	—
Robin (trainee)	29	—
John (junior personnel officer)	7	—
Totals	331	12

Notes:
Instances of overlapped turns: 47
* Seniority
** Seniority plus Chair

Table 21.3 British meetings: Analysis of turn-taking behavior (formal meeting—in two parts)[7]

Participants	Number of turns		Turns (50 words +)	
	Part A	Part B	Part A	Part B
Chairman (executive)**	85	157	10	9
Aubrey (executive)*	28	172	3	11
Frank (executive)*	57	77	12	2
Graham (manager)	18	26	5	—
Dave (manager)	35	80	9	7
Howard (manager)	18	9	3	—
David (assistant)	6	5	2	—
Mike (course arranger)	4	—	1	—
Totals	254	526	45	29

Notes:
Instances of overlapped turns: 219
* Seniority
** Seniority plus Chair

Table 21.4 British informal meeting: interruptions

Participants:	7 (3 male, 4 female)
Instances of overlapped speech:	47
Number of interruptions:	3 (6% of overlapped speech)

2nd speaker (interrupter)	1st speaker (interrupted)
Colin* 2	Colin* 1
Helen* 1	Helen* 1
	Sarah* 1

Success rate

1 interruption	2nd speaker completes
	1st speaker recycles later
1 interruption	2nd speaker fails to complete but later recycles
	1st speaker completes
1 interruption	both speakes complete

Table 21.5 British formal meeting: interruptions

Part A

Participants:	8** (all male)
Instances of overlapped speech:	71
Number of interruptions:	8 (11% of overlapped speech)

2nd speaker (interrupter)		1st speaker (interrupted)	
CH*	2	CH*	2
Dave	4	Dave	1
Graham	1	Aubrey*	3
(?)	1	Frank*	1
		Graham	1

Success rate

In all interruptions, both speakers complete their utterances.

Part B

Participants:	8** (all male)
Instances of simultaneous speech:	148
Number of interruptions:	26 (17.5% of overlapped speech)

2nd speaker (interrupter)		1st speaker (interrupted)	
CH*	13	CH*	8
Aubrey*	8	Aubrey*	10
Frank*	2	Frank*	2
Dave	2	Dave	4
Graham	1	Howard	2

Success rate

22 interruptions	both speakers complete
2 interruptions	2nd speaker completes
	1st speaker doesn't complete but later recycles
1 interruptions	2nd speaker completes
	1st speaker doesn't complete
1 interruption	2nd speaker doesn't complete
	1st speaker completes

* Participants of executive status

** Aubrey is present for only eight minutes of the meeting.

Table 21.6 British meetings: interruptions (relative to power indicators)

		Informal Meeting		
Participants	Power indicators	Interruptions		
	Status	Turns (50 words+)	Interruptor	Interrupted
Colin (Chair)	managerial	8	2	1
Helen	managerial	2	1	1
Sarah	managerial	1	—	—
Hazel	personnel officer	1	—	—
Audrey	nonmanagerial	—	—	—
Robin	trainer	—	—	—
John	junior officer	—	—	—
		Formal Meeting		
Byron (Chair)	executive	19	15	10
Aubrey	executive	14	8	13
Frank	executive	14	2	3
Dave	managerial	16	6	5
Howard	managerial	3	—	—
Graham	managerial	5	2	1
David	assistant manager	2	—	—
Mike	course manager	1	—	—

Turning explicitly to interruptions identified on the basis of Type 4 overlaps, the data reveal several interesting features:

1. *The number of interruptions as a proportion of simultaneous speech is generally low overall.* It is, however, somewhat higher in the formal meeting (11 percent in Part A and 17.5 percent in Part B) than in the informal meeting (at six percent) (see Table 21.5). This difference may be related to the gender mix; it may also be related to the fact that the topic of the formal meeting is much more technical and that this group is under more pressure to produce a very specific outcome.

2. *In the informal and the formal meetings, the participants with the highest status and power both interrupt and are interrupted.* Indeed, there are only two instances of a nonexecutive speaker interrupting in the formal meeting (except for Dave, who has specialist expertise) and no instances of nonmanagerial interruption in the informal meeting.

3. *Less powerful speakers do not, by and large, have their turns interrupted.* This is an interesting finding which may well conflict with research making use of ordinary conversation as data. Speakers with power and status in a clearly hierarchical context interrupt each other most often in both meetings.

4. *The majority of interruptions in both meetings are neither successful nor unsuccessful.* Success is determined by (*a*) whether a speaker completes his/her overlapped utterance, or (*b*) whether the uncompleted utterance is later recycled. In the informal meeting, all utterances are eventually completed. In the formal meeting, there are only two utterances which are not

either completed or recycled. This is, again, an interesting finding undoubtedly related to the fact that high status participants are predominantly interrupting other high status participants.

Clearly, there are a range of ways by which the "outcomes" of interruptive talk can be measured. A further criterion for determining the success of an interruption might be whether the overlapped talk is taken up and addressed by other speakers. It might also be useful to consider whether the topical development of subsequent talk has been influenced by the interruption. For example, in example (6) (see p. 353), C interrupts S in order to address J on his lack of participation in the meeting thus far. According to the criteria, this is a successful interruption, in that the interruptive utterance is completed. It is taken up by J, who interprets C's question as an accusation that he hasn't been following the meeting. C then acknowledges J's response, after which S recycles her initial interrupted utterance. However, C's interruption does not succeed in eliciting J's more active participation during the remainder of the meeting, as it is probably intended to. It does manage to shift the topic but only momentarily. Success in this more holistic sense is clearly harder to determine.

Example (7) is also interesting, when success is judged from a more holistic perspective. The question at issue here is the role of the "masterscheduler." G's interruption is successfully completed, though D (the interrupted) also completes his utterance. However, since G's conflicting proposition is actually uttered at the same time as D's proposition, it is difficult to determine precisely what is being negated. Moreover, later in the meeting, the Chair states:

(8)   CH: yeah—so that's—I think all these arguments all support the view that
              in fact not to give the master-scheduler access (1) or rather not to give
              the customer access to the master-scheduler

Thus, what appear to be conflicting propositions are summarized as a consistent view, and the notion that the master-scheduler should not have to reconcile commercial interests and business planning directly (G's point) appears to have been accepted.

Finally, perhaps the most important feature of interruptive behavior in the British data is that:

5. *Interruptions are not necessarily dysfunctional in management meetings which are task oriented.* They do not in either meeting result in explicit acknowledgment, apology, or breakdown of the turn-taking system. Interruptions do tend to cluster around talk involving propositional disagreement. But it is quite possible to argue that, far from being dysfunctional, interruptions of the type identified in these data are actually a necessary part of the process of reaching agreement. Certainly, all meetings do involve some form of argument, i.e., the expression of divergent views. The interruptions which arguments generate appear to be accepted by participants as a feature of business discourse. There is no indication that they are regarded as rude behavior or damaging to relationships. As in the Italian data, stretches of argumentative talk (with high levels of overlapped speech, including interruptions) merge with more convergent stretches of speech. Indeed, as in the following example, interruptive behavior is quickly followed by agreement.

(9)   (British formal meeting)
      A: well the customer focus group will tell you it's on time and deliveries
      CH: no no—you—we're talking totally different purposes here—you're t—

you're trying to say—well what—what what—how should it be used—
I'm saying—what I'm asking—what is the unit of measurement (4)

    A: I don't believe it then

    H: you're you're looking from a different ⎡point of view—

→   CH: ⎢you you

                                                  ⎣no no we're

talking at cross purposes

    H: yours is a measurement of how well you've satisfied the customer ( )
the plan

    A: but isn't that the most important thing

    CH: no no—I'm not talking ⎡about that—no no no

→   A: ⎣the most important thing is if

look at that family of products—whatever it could be—matchsticks in
matchboxes—as far as I'm concerned

    CH: you're right—I don't disagree with what you're saying

This stretch of speech contains two clear Type 4 interruptions (neither is near a TRP, and both involve competitive propositions). Yet they seem to lead to agreement rather than to breakdown. This extract also contains competing propositions which are not overlapped and thus emphasizes the complexity of determining what should ultimately count as interruptive behavior in an holistic approach to the data. Indeed, one might contend, as Hopper does, that interruptive behavior transcends overlapped speech. Our own view is, however, that it is not ultimately productive to extend the definition of interruptions in such a way as to categorize all counter propositions as interruptive and thus to de-emphasize the commonsense perception of interruptions as inherently involving a breach of turn-taking rules.

Discussion of the Italian data

In a radical critique of the turn-taking tradition initiated by Sacks et al. (1974), O'Connell et al. (1990) remark that the (pseudo) economy of time that regulates (allegedly) optimal turn-taking practices in conversation does not take into account the variety of communicative purposes that motivate interactants. The positive value attributed to time and the efficient organization of turns has given rise within the conversation analytical tradition to the negative connotation of terms such as "gap," "overlap," and, of course, "interruption." These have tended to become prescriptive terms that language analysts have used to categorize what can go wrong in interactions instead of concentrating on what can, and does, go on when participants use language interactionally in social situations (O'Connell et al., 1990).

Zorzi Calò, in her 1990 study of interruptions in Italian and British service encounters, stresses the difficulties in defining the boundaries of conversational turns since, as she remarks, there are no watertight intonational or syntactic criteria. Even more relevant to our generic data type is her observation that, besides the overlaps already identified by conversation analysts as dysfunctional, there may be other forms of overlap which are not accidental "but [. . .] determined by the development of the conversation, and therefore subject to different rules from those of turn-taking" (Zorzi Calò, 1990, p. 89, our translation). Indeed, Testa (1988, p. 291) claims that "an interpretation of interruption is crucially dependent on the particular turn-taking procedures deployed in the event being analysed."

These insights have important implications for the analysis of interruptions in task-oriented discourse, such as management meetings, which develop along outcome-led interactional paths, regularly signposted by the items on the official (and hidden) agenda. Their nature is therefore quite different from everyday, spontaneous conversation.

Although it may be common for meeting outcomes to be pre-empted at least in part by decisions already taken somewhere else in the organization, it is still unlikely for such a meeting to be reduced to mere rubber-stamping. In the case of the Italian informal meeting, for instance, the awareness of their relatively small influence on their boss's decision does not deter the participants from engaging in an animated discussion which discloses all the complexities of organizational life, with its group alliances, personality contrasts, shifting loyalties, and struggles for dominance. Verbal interaction is perhaps the most powerful method that organizational members have at their disposal to make sense of all this, particularly in meetings. Our meetings show that the process of sense-making, if not decision-making, through discourse involves adapting and even breaking the rules of turn-taking to accommodate different interactional strategies and objectives.

The high occurrence of overlaps is likely to be one of the visible consequences of this underlying tension, and, as in the British meetings, in most cases the completion of the first turn is unaffected by the overlapping second turn, regardless of the point where the overlap begins. A general overview is provided in Table 21.7.

As in the British meetings, we have identified "contextual factors" (Bazzanella, 1990) which contribute to an increased incidence of interruptive behaviour, i.e., status and the length of turns—see Table 21.8.

Table 21.7 Italian meetings: General quantitative profile

	Formal meeting	Informal meeting
Number of words	19,800	7,550
Number of participants	19	3
Duration of meeting	2 hours 40 minutes	45 minutes
Number of turns	738	286
Number of turns longer than 50 words	81	33
Number of overlaps	251	99
Number of interruptions	37	19

Table 21.8 Italian meetings: Interruptions (relative to power indicators)[8]

Power indicators	Participants					
Status	Formal meeting			Informal meeting		
	CH executive	A senior manager	Others Manager plus senior manager	C senior executive	DR executive	G executive
Number of turns longer than 50 words	28	21	25	18	12	3
Interruptions	13	10	14	11	5	3

As might be expected, chairmanship entails privileged access to the floor in both meetings that we have analyzed and is a factor that may override, or combine with, personal status, particularly when the chairman represents a less influential department such as quality assurance (in the formal meeting).[9] The case of speaker A in the formal meeting (see example (10)) is an excellent example of a senior manager who combines personal status and influence deriving from the prominent role of his department, operations, with a high degree of self-confidence and, possibly, self-awareness.[10] (See the appendix for a translation of examples (10) and (11).)

(10)

	CH:	ok va be' direi che va fatta l'analisi su	*proposes*
		questa roba qua e poi ⌈ vediamo *action*	
	D:	⌊ puo'essere il	*suggests*
		bios puo' essere la modifica puo' er	*cause*
		non lo so	
	A:	R[surname] come almeno da quello	*explains*
		che abbiam visto in prima battuta	
		siccome vengono toccate er 16	
		chip 16 ⌈ resistenze (4)	
	?:	certo	*supports*
→	D:	puo' anche darsi	*suggests*
			cause
→	CH:	no ma direi che (.) puo' darsi che ci	*continues*
		sia anche un problema di⌈ ( )	*suggestion*
→	A:	⌊ puo'darsi che	*echoes*
		ci sia qualche problemino lo vediamo	*suggestion*
	CH:	( ) ⌈dico va fatta l'analisi poi decidiamo	*proposes*
			action
	D:	⌊appunto appunto pero' essendo	*justifies*
		⌈ oggi la quality review (.) non posso	*objection*
		fare a meno *supports*	
→	CH:	no no ma no no	*objects*
→	?:	⌊ ma quale problema	*(speaker 4)*
	D:	di dirlo questo non non ⌈ mi sta er be	*continues*
			justification
	CH:	va benissimo	*supports*
		lanzi	
→	A:	che abbiano	*suggests*
		sbagliato	*cause*
		a cambiare ⌈la resistenza nell'intervento	
	CH:	⌊nell'intervento ah non avevo	*echoes*
		capito non aveva capito (.) chiedo⌈scusa	*suggestion*
	CH:	⌊no no	*proposes*
		ma scusa dico va fatta ⌈ va fatta l'analisi	
→	A:	e'un problema di	*suggests*
		(.) modifica	*cause*
		diciamo del	
	D:	del ⌊ del manuale	
		stanno lavorando	

```
?:        nell'arco della riunione quando  ⎡ avranno
                                           ⎣ come si
          chiama er notiva' hanno          ⎡ l'incarico di
                                           │ chiamarmi qui
A:                                         ⎣ ( )
CH:       va bene senti intanto nei manuali qua davanti
          ci sono delle cose da osservare  ⎡ poi      initiates
C:                                         │          new topic
                                           ⎣ si' io avrei un paio di cose
          sul bios ⎡ ehm                        first
CH:                │                             contribution
                   ⎣ si'
```

Example (10) (from the formal meeting) contains several Type 4 interruptions, yet interruptions appear to be used here as devices available to speakers to make a substantive contribution to the discussion by supplying technical details, suggestions, or suppositions that assist in the identification of the causes of a problem, in this case a mechanical fault in a new product. Despite the formal nature of the meeting, the role of the chairman (CH) is reduced to an attempt to control the direction of the interaction rather than imposing one. The urgency of the problem raised overrides concern for smoothly running proceedings and, during the debating phase, at least six individuals out of the nineteen are actively involved in complex verbal problem-solving routines. It is hardly surprising, then, that overlaps abound and that, relatively speaking, interruptions are frequent.

The important question, however, is whether such apparently disorganized turn-taking sequences, where conversational rules are repeatedly broken, are detrimental to the achievement of the aim and objectives of the meeting, two of which we have envisaged to be the discussion of technical problems on the agenda and the gathering of technical information that will eventually lead to their solution. The proceedings suggest that progress is made on both these counts, despite the high number and different types of overlaps which characterize them. It follows that the orderly alternation of turns does not guarantee the communicative success of multiparty interaction, or indeed any interaction, and in this sense, we need to look beyond the "messy" surface of overlapped speech, and beyond adjacency pairs, in order to understand what speakers are trying to achieve.

For example, in example (10), the chairman (CH) invites contributions on a specific item on the agenda, which produces a lengthy sequence of turns and no apparent conclusion. In an attempt to bring the discussion on this item to a close, he suggests that an analysis should be carried out on the findings currently available "and then we'll see".

Besides the chairman, three speakers intervene on the question and do so in an apparently uncooperative manner, i.e., by continuously overlapping the preceding turn. A closer look at the content of their utterances, however, led us to conclude that their contributions are in fact purposeful in that they supply new technical details and possible suggestions as to the causes of the problem. Overlaps are not detrimental to local development of the meeting, so much so that the chairman takes up A's interruption ("e' un problema di (.) modifica diciamo del del manuale") in order to introduce a new topic ("va bene senti intanto nei manuali qua davanti ci sono delle cose da osservare poi"), which consequently opens a new sequence of exchanges.

When discussion turns into disagreement, the tendency is for interruptions, rather than other types of overlap, to appear more often, as illustrated in example (11) from the informal meeting. When the Chairman announces a "proposal" (*la proposta*), a euphemism for more work to be carried out with the same resources, G's negative reaction is immediate and strong:

(11)

    C: il secondo step potrebbe invece vederci
           crescere er il know-how su questi temi per
           poter poi entrare nel merito dei processi
           commerciali (.) questo pero' come farlo
           come non farlo non lo so (.) io l'ho gia'
           detto a C[boss name] ieri che (.) e' un
           lavoro in piu' che voi dovete fare
                ⌈e che

→   G: ⌊inoltre al lavoro in piu' c'e'un   *expands on*
           altro discorso quando tu arrivi alla quality   *previous*
           review finale (.) i soliti processi (.)   *turn*
           commerciali che non sono ( ) perche' tu li
           vai a vedere ( ) (.) no quindi quando ti
           dicono il la marketing news sara' pronta tra
           un mese tu ti fidi (.) e fra un mese non vai
           piu' a controllare che sia veramente pronte e
           che   ⌈esca (. . . . .)

→   C: ⌊scusami questa e' e' la fase finale   *object to*
           dello sviluppo del prodotto no quello nella   *previous*
           quality review quello che stiamo mettendo a   *turn*
           punto sempre nello stesso team e' la fasatura
           fra tutte le documentazioni ufficiali la fasatura
           fra i processi no industriali e commerciali che
           sicuramente non devono avvenire a valle
           della quality review ma devono avvenire a
           monte (.)   ⌈della   *Turn 1*

→   G: ⌊si' pero   *overlap 1*
           preparazione del mondo ⌈commerciale   *end turn 1*

→   G: ⎪sai be che piu'   *overlap 2*
                          ⌊volte

     C: eh lo so   *reply to*
                                              overlap 2

     G: la marketing news la fai sulla base   *end turn 2*
           dei risultati . . .

However, G's objections do not lead to a break down in communication. On the contrary, a few turns later, both he and the chairman switch to the less conflictual, ordinary mode of overlapping turns with which example (11) ends.

    This local pattern of conflict solution is repeated throughout both meetings, where it is possible to find, in alternating order, long, mainly facilitative overlap sequences which culminate in a series of interruptions only to revert back to more facilitative overlap. In all meetings, the final outcome, i.e., common agreement, is always reached, at least on the surface.

    Besides contextual factors shared with the British meetings, a possible explanation of the interruptions and other types of overlap in the Italian meetings is to be found in a "subjective factor" identified by research on Italian debates. Bazzanella (1990) calls it "sense of urgency", to which we would add a high degree of personal involvement as a feature characterizing the (more animated) Italian meetings. Italian speakers are known to engage in intricately argued, long turns as if they were verbal crusades waged ultimately in defence of personal beliefs. Whether this is attributable to the "dramatic sensibilities" of the popular stereotype of Italians which persists both in the popular and academic press is not certain but should not be dismissed either. As Saunders (1985, p. 174) writes of Italian contexts, "where you see emotion, there is emotion but the emotion you see is not always the emotion that is there".

Conclusions

This study of a selection of British and Italian management meetings contradicts some of the findings from the existing literature on interruptions while supporting others in the following ways.

1   Bearing in mind the task-oriented nature of this form of multiparty talk, facilitative speech behavior is far more common than interruptive behavior, even within the high-pressured, technical debate of the British formal meeting or the conflictual discussion of the Italian informal meeting.
2   With regard to their discursive functions, the majority of overlaps that we have identified in both sets of data are supportive ones in such a way as to (a) facilitate group dynamics in multiparty speech, and (b) extend, reinforce, or elaborate the positions of other speakers.
3   The positioning of simultaneous speech is also of some interest. Our data show that interruptions and inadvertent overlaps can occur very close together or even (possibly) simultaneously. So, for instance, one second speaker can facilitate almost simultaneously as another interrupts.
4   In both formal and informal meetings, turn-taking dynamics (in terms of both length and number of turns) are clearly related to the status of the individuals, and they are therefore taken to be indicators of power. Expertise in the topic or task of the meetings is also a highly influential factor on frequency of turns and may or may not be related to status and power.
5   With regard to interruptions, the relationship to power and status is weaker and more complex. On the basis of the data analyzed, we are able to conclude that those participants with explicit and visible power and status both interrupt and are interrupted more frequently. Participants with lower status rarely interrupt and are rarely interrupted.[11]

Interruptions, especially in formal British meetings (and in all Italian meetings), tend to coincide with portions of the interaction where conflicting propositions are put forward. However, unlike most research based on ordinary conversation, the majority of interruptions in our data are neither successful nor unsuccessful, i.e., both participants finish their utterances and neither gives way. Even where one speaker does give way, his/her utterances are often recycled later.

Our data suggest that interruptions in management meetings are not usually dysfunctional for the participants. Indeed, they would seem often to function as a taken-for-granted means of reaching agreement in task-oriented discourse, characteristic of both the British and Italian data. On a final, contrastive note: with the focus on interruptions, British and Italian managers and executives are perhaps more similar than they are different. On the basis of our findings, the generic type of discourse is obviously a powerful determinant.

Appendix: English translation of Italian extracts

(10)

CH: OK well I'd say that this stuff should be analysed and then

                                   [we'll see

D: [it may be the bios it may be the modification

    it may ehm I don't know

A: R [surname] from what we have seen in the first instance,

    since 16 chips are touched 16   [resistors (4)

?:   D: | quite

→   [it may be

→   CH: no but I'd say that (.) there may also be a problem with

    ( )

→   A: there may be a little problem we'll see

    CH: behind   [I'm saying an analysis should be done and then

                                                we'll decide

D: quite quite but today being quality review (.)

→   CH: no no but no no

→   ?:   [but what is the problem

D: I cannot help saying   [I don't like it as it is

CH: | on the contrary that's fine

→   A: [might it be that they were mistaken

    in replacing the resistor during the operation

C: during the operation oh I misunderstood I misunderstood

    (.) I beg your   [pardon

CH: [no no but sorry I'm saying that an analysis

    should be   [should be done

                          [it's a matter of (.) altering say the

→   A: [manual . . .

D: [they're working [on it] whey they've finished they're to contact me

    here

A: ( )

CH: OK listen in the meantime in these individuals here there

    are things to be discussed   [then

C: [yes I have

    a couple of things on the bios   [er

CH: [yes

(11)

C: the second step could instead see us developing ehm the know-how on these matters so as to be able to tackle the commercial process (.) this how to do it I don't know (.) I already told C[boss's name] yesterday that (.)

    it's extra work that you have to do   [and that

→   G: [besides the extra work there

    is another side to it when you reach the final quality review (.) the usual commercial processes (.) which aren't ( ) because you look into them ( ) (.) don't you therefore when they tell you the marketing news will

be ready in a month you trust them (.) and after a month you don't go
and check whether it is really ready and [is going out ( )

→   C: excuse me this is the final stage of product development isn't it the
quality review what we are setting up with the same team is the alignment
of all the official documentation the alignment of industrial and
commercial process which must not take place after the quality review
but

ahead   ⌈of the
→   G: ⌊yes but

C: preparation of the   ⌈commercial world
→   G: ⌊yes do know that often

C: yes I do

G: you do the marketing news on the basis of results . . .

Notes

1 According to Hopper, interruptions are not only the visible structural phenomena highlighted by conversation analysts (e.g., competitive simultaneous starts and deep overlap) but may also take place at the level of suprasentential strategies (e.g., through topic shifts and prosodic features).

2 Status is defined here as "the degree of deference, esteem and power to influence others" (Ridgeway, 1983, p. 160, quoted in Smith-Lovin and Brody, 1989, p. 424).

3 The influence of gender has not been considered in this initial study, given the limitations of the present data sample.

4 Criterion (2) takes precedence over Criterion (1).

5 Criterion (2) takes precedence over Criterion (1).

6 A *turn* is pragmatically defined here as any individual verbal contribution to the interaction that constitutes a meaningful propositional unit which is audible and therefore retrievable for transcription.

7 The formal meeting was divided into two parts. Part B begins with the use of a flip chart and involves a much more technical discussion. Aubrey is present for all of Part B but only eight minutes of Part A.

8 Legend: CH—Chairman and executive; A—senior manager; "others"—unidentifiable speakers; C—Chairman and senior executive; DR and G—executives.

It has not been possible to compile a more detailed account of the quantitative findings for the Italian formal meeting since the high number of participants made turn attribution an impossible task, even with professional-quality audio equipment. Hence the category "others" that refers to a the group of "active" participants, varying in number from six to eight.

9 Smith-Lovin and Brody (1989, p. 424) claim that literature on conversational dyads and families shows that "high-status actors talk more, are more successful in introducing topics, interrupt more and receive more positive feedback from their listeners." The implication, then, is that people who talk more are also more at risk of being interrupted.

10 Unlike the British meetings, we have no evidence of the effect of the recording equipment and of the researcher's presence on the interaction except a revealing, post-event comment by the only (other) woman present, from the documentation department, who remarked on the "remarkably clean" language of this meeting. It is therefore possible that there might have been even more overlaps and interruptions had the meeting not been recorded and observed. On the other hand, one could argue that, on a self-conscious, boisterous individual such as senior manager A, the presence of an academic observer from Britain could have acted as an incentive to raise the quantity and variety of his verbal performance.

11 This may of course be partially a consequence of the discrepancy in the number and length of turns between high- and low-status participants.

References

Bazzanella, C. (1990). Le interruzioni "competitive" e "supportive". In S. Sati, E. Weigand and F. Hundsnurscher (eds), *Dialoganalyse III. (Referate el 3. Arbeitstagung Bologna 1990)* (pp. 283–92). Max Niemeyer Verlag: Tubingen.

Chambliss, C. and Feeny, N. (1992). Effects of sex of subject, sex of interrupter, and topic of conversation on the perceptions of interruption. *Perceptual and Motor Skills,* 75(2): 1235–41.

Dindia, K. (1987). The effect of sex of subject and sex of partner on interruptions. *Human Communication Research,* 13(3), 345–71.

Drummond, K. (1989). A backward glance at interruptions. *Western Journal of Speech Communication,* 53, 150–66.

Goldberg, J. A. (1990). Interrupting the discourse on interruptions. An analysis in terms of relationally neutral, power- and rapport-oriented acts, *Journal of Pragmatics,* 14, 883–903.

Hopper, R. (1992). *Telephone conversation.* Bloomington, IN: Indiana University Press.

Janney, R. W. and Arndt, H. (1993). Universality and relativity in cross-cultural politeness research: a historical perspective, *Multilingua,* 12(1), 13–50.

Jefferson, G. (1986). Notes on "latency" in overlap onset. *Human Studies,* 9, 153–84.

Kennedy, C. W. and Camden, C. T. (1983). A new look at interruptions. *Western Journal of Speech Communication,* 47, 45–58.

LaFrance, M. (1992). Gender and interruptions: individual infraction or violation of the special order? Issue: women and power. *Psychology of Women Quarterly,* 16(4), 497–512.

Levinson, S. C. (1983). *Pragmatics.* Cambridge: Cambridge University Press.

Makri-Tsilipakou, M. (1994). Interruption revisited: affiliative vs. disaffiliative intervention. *Journal of Pragmatics,* 21, 401–26.

Marche, T. A. and Peterson, C. (1993). The development and sex-related use of interruption behavior. *Human Communication Research,* 19(3), 388–408.

Murata, K. (1994). Intrusive or co-operative? A cross-cultural study of interruption. *Journal of Pragmatics,* 21. 385–400.

Murray, Stephen O. (1985). Toward a model of members' methods for recognizing interruptions. *Language in Society,* 14, 31–40.

O'Connell, D., Kowal, S. and Kattenbacher, E. (1990). Turn-taking: a critical analysis of the research tradition. *Journal of Psycholinguistic Research,* 19(6), 345–73.

Roger, D., Bull, P. and Smith, P. (1988). The development of a comprehensive system for classifying interruptions. *Journal of Language and Social Psychology,* 7(1), 27–34.

Sacks, H., Schegloff E. and Jefferson G. (1974). A simplest systematics for the organization of turn-taking for conversation. *Language,* 50, 696–735.

Saunders, G. R. (1985). Silence and noise as emotion management styles: an Italian case. In D. Tannen and M. Saville-Troike (eds), *Perspectives on silence* (pp. 165–83). Norwood NJ: Ablex.

Smith-Lovin, L. and Brody, C. (1989). Interruptions in group discussions: the effects of gender and group composition. *American Sociological Review,* 54, 24–435.

Talbot, M. (1992). "I wish you'd stop interrupting me!" Interruptions and asymmetries in speaker-rights in equal encounters. *Journal of Pragmatics,* 18, 451–66.

Testa, R. (1988) Interruptive strategies in English and Italian conversation. *Multilingua,* 7(3), 285–312.

Ulijn, J. and Li, X. (1995) Is interrupting impolite? Some temporal aspects of turn-taking in Chinese-Western and other intercultural business encounters. *Text,* 15(4), 589–630.

West, C. and Zimmerman, D. (1983). Small insults: a study of interruptions in cross-sex conversations between unacquainted persons. In B. Thorne, C. Kramarea and N. Henley (eds), *Language, gender and society* (pp. 102–17). Rowley, MA: Newbury House.

Zimmerman, D. and West, C. (1975). Sex role, interruptions and silence in conversation. In B. Thorne and N. Henley (eds), *Language and sex* (pp. 105–29). Rowley, MA: Newbury House.

Zorzi Calò, D. (1990). *Parlare insieme. La co-produzione dell'ordine conversazionale in italiano e in inglese.* Bologna: CLUEB.

Chapter 22

ROSINA MÁRQUEZ REITER AND
MARÍA E. PLACENCIA

DISPLAYING CLOSENESS AND RESPECTFUL DISTANCE IN MONTEVIDEAN AND QUITEÑO SERVICE ENCOUNTERS[1]

Introduction and aims

THIS ARTICLE REPORTS THE results of a preliminary pragmatic contrastive study on the language of service encounters (SEs hereafter) in Montevideo (Uruguay) and Quito (Ecuador). Based on data gathered in clothing and accessories shops in lower-middle class areas in both capitals, this study attempts to characterise the interactional style of participants in SEs (salespersons in particular) in the two cities.

SEs, understood as everyday social interactions between a service provider and a customer who are in some service area (Merritt, 1976), were chosen as the focus of examination since they represent everyday social activities characterised by socially shared, regular patternings (Ventola, 1987; Kuiper & Flindall, 2000). Through the study of the linguistic elements that constitute these encounters, cultural patterns can emerge and preferred communicative styles can be established.

The motivation for this study comes from the findings of previous pragmatic studies carried out on these varieties in other contexts (cf. Placencia, 1994, 1996, 1997, 1998, 2001a; Márquez Reiter, 1997, 2000, 2002a, 2002b, 2003). Even though Spanish is spoken in both Montevideo and Quito, sociocultural differences underlying language use are to be expected given that Uruguay and Ecuador have experienced different historical, political, and social developments, which permeate institutional and other types of interactions. In this respect, this study forms part of a recent trend of contrastive studies into Spanish pragmatic variation (cf. Fant, 1996; Puga Larraín, 1997; Curcó, 1998; García, 2004), that is to say, how different varieties of a language, in this case Spanish, vary in their use of language in context. These studies have highlighted possible communication problems and misunderstandings between speakers of different varieties of Spanish due to differences in the cultural norms underlying their communicative style.

Source: Márquez Reiter, R. & Placencia, M. (2004) Excerpt from Displaying closeness and respectful distance in Montevidean and Quiteño service encounters. Selected from R. Márquez Reiter and M. Placencia (eds), *Current trends in the pragmatics of Spanish* (Chapter 7, pp. 121–55). Amsterdam/Philadelphia: John Benjamins.

Background

SEs have been examined from different perspectives in different languages. There have been single language/culture studies, contrastive, and intercultural studies. Among the most important studies is Ventola's (1987) within the British systemics tradition. Ventola's work is a proposal for a *generic structure* for public SEs. George's (1990) is an ethnomethodological ethnography of requests and complaints in Naples with the aim of uncovering the underlying interactional norms necessary for successful intercultural communication with Neapolitans. Scholars on the PIXI (Pragmatics of Italian/English cross-cultural interaction) project, on the other hand, have carried out contrastive studies of bookshop SEs in English and Italian mostly within the conversation analytic tradition, thus focusing on different aspects of the local organisation of these interactions (cf. Aston, 1995, 1998; Gavioli, 1997). These studies highlight, for example, differences in interactional style in English and Italian through an analysis of the way in which elements of the SE are sequenced. More recently, *small talk* in different types of SE (and other kinds of interaction) has been the object of analysis, as in McCarthy's (2000) and Kuiper and Flindall's (2000) studies. These scholars, as others in Coupland's (2000) collection of studies, emphasise the significance of small talk not only for the marginal sections of SEs, but for the entire interaction. In the same vein, in the present study we stress the function of *phatic* (Malinowski, 1972 [1923]; Laver, 1975) and other relational talk (e.g. the use of address forms) in the opening section of SEs as setting the tone for the entire interaction. However, we also show how some Montevidean participants in the study, in contrast with the Quiteño participants, make attempts to renegotiate the degree of closeness they established at the beginning, or we show how Montevidean participants attempt to reinforce the 'closeness' created at the beginning, in other stages of the interaction.

In addition to the works so far mentioned, two studies of particular relevance to the present study are Bailey (1997) and Traverso (2001). The former focuses on contrasting interactional practices in interethnic SEs between Koreans and African Americans, as a reflection of a different conception of the customer–salesperson relationship held by members of these two ethnic groups. Like Bailey's, the present study is also contrastive though cross-cultural, and its main aim is to discover similarities and/or differences in the customer–salesperson relationship in Montevideo and Quito, as reflected in the interactional style of Montevidean and Quiteño speakers. Traverso's work, on the other hand, is of interest to us given that she examines service encounters of a similar nature to ours and like Bailey she also focuses on the construction of the interpersonal relationship in the (re)negotiation of the exchange.

Concerning Spanish, there are a few studies on SEs. Ciapuscio and Kesselheim (1997) examine how immigrants and representatives of a public institution in Buenos Aires construct their respective identities and the institutional context through talk. Placencia (1998) investigates similarities and differences in the realisation of requests for information and services at hospital information desks in Madrid and Quito. Placencia (2001a), on the other hand, examines aspects of politeness in service encounters in a public institution in Quito; Placencia (2001b) focuses on address behaviour in service encounters in public institutions in La Paz, and Placencia (2004) looks at a range of interactional activities carried out in corner shop encounters in Quito. Finally, Chodorowska-Pilch (2002) examines offers in travel agencies in Spain with data from the Comunidad de Madrid and Galicia.

In the present study, drawing from pragmatics and conversation analysis, we examine similarities and differences in the *overall organisation* of SEs, that is, how these interactions are organised section by section (Schegloff, 1972; Schegloff & Sacks, 1973). We look at how SEs in both cultures are opened and closed and the types of selling strategy shop assistants employ to carry out the business exchange.[2] Owing to the type of data collected (see the section on methodology below), the emphasis will be on the language of service providers only. Through the analysis of features of the overall organisation and linguistic realisations we examine similarities and differences regarding the type of interaction/relationship buyers and salespersons seek to construct in Montevideo and Quito. In Montevideo, the encounters examined display participants' preference for a 'friendly' interaction, with a blurring between the public and the private, whereas in Quito participants appear to value distance-maintenance, with little or no blurring between the public and the private.

Methodology

The data for this study consist of 56 audio-recorded SE interactions in clothing and accessories shops collected *in situ*; namely, 28 in Montevideo and 28 in Quito. As indicated earlier, the data were gathered from lower-middle class areas in both cities. Lower-middle class shopping areas were chosen in order to ensure sameness of situational context in both cultures and as a consequence of the steady increase of Western-like malls, where the ethos of multinational chains can pervade in selling–purchasing encounters. In this sense, the shops selected for this study represent a more traditional Montevidean and Quiteño style of shopping experience where employees tend to receive very little training, if any.

Also to ensure sameness of situational context, shops corresponding to the *closed* only rather than the *open* setting type (Traverso, 2001) were selected. As some studies have shown, spatial (and other) features of the encounter may constrain the type of talk that takes place (McCarthy, 2000). An additional feature shared by the shops examined is that they can be characterised as *non-self-service* (Traverso, 2001), in that customers need to interact with a salesperson in order to examine or try on the goods and find out about their characteristics (material or origin) and price. As such, both Montevidean and Quiteño encounters in this study constitute a kind of personalised shopping experience for customers which stands in contrast with the impersonal shopping experience that international chains in modern malls offer, where customers have free access to the goods and whose only interaction is often with the cashier when the payment for the goods needs to be effected. In this respect, the interactions examined correspond to what Traverso (2001, p. 424) refers to as *speech-intensive* encounters. The encounters in the present study thus provide rich data for examination.

The selection criterion for the choice of clothing and accessories shops over other types of shop was mainly based on the greater availability of these in comparison with others in the areas where the data were collected. Also, the rationale for collecting data in clothing and accessories shops only, as opposed to in a variety of shops is threefold: firstly, to ensure cross-cultural comparability, as remarked earlier; secondly, because some of the selling strategies employed will depend on the type of product being sold. Thus, the selling/purchasing of a sports car is likely to involve a higher incidence of certain strategies than the selling/purchasing of a pair of jeans; and thirdly, because in these types of SE private and/or personal information is unlikely to emerge. Both researchers, with the aid of friends who agreed to go into the above-mentioned shops and simulate a shopping experience, collected the data. Although the research collaborators were not prompted at all as to what was expected from them and were asked to be as natural as possible, in other words, to shop as they would usually do, the fact that in some cases they did not need the item(s) they were inquiring about might have had an effect on their interactional behaviour. This is a point we shall return to during the analysis of the results.

While the research collaborators knew beforehand that the interactions were being audio-recorded by the researchers, the service providers were not informed about this until after the interaction had taken place. It was then that permission to use the recordings was sought from them. Permission to record was not sought in advance since this might have affected the language of the service providers and since this kind of interaction is neither intimate nor private and thus permission to record is fairly easily obtainable (Ventola, 1987).[3]

In Montevideo, a random sample of 35 SEs was employed, whereas in Quito, due to a smaller number of clothing and accessories shops in the selected area, SEs were audio-recorded in every clothing and accessories shop in that particular area, amounting to 32 SEs altogether. Owing to background noise which made some recordings inaudible, and owing to the fact that permission to keep the recordings made was not granted in all cases, seven interactions in Montevideo and four in Quito had to be discarded.

In order to counterbalance the limitation of customer-simulated scenarios, the analysis will focus on the language of the salespersons and will only use the language of the customers as reference when and if necessary. Another reason for this is that the customers in this study correspond to four participants only (two in Montevideo and two in Quito) so, unlike Traverso (2001), whose data also come from the interaction of two participants – friend and friend's mother – with 17 service providers, we do not think it is appropriate to focus on their style, as any patterns found could represent their idiolect.

The results

The analysis of the data reveals that the most prominent differences between Montevideans and Quiteños relate to the way in which the speakers position themselves within the interaction, with the former employing strategies that seek involvement or closeness between the interlocutors and the latter employing respectful distance-keeping strategies. This difference in the interactional orientation of the SEs is reflected firstly, by the overall organisation of the interaction in Montevideo and Quito, that is to say, in the number and type of turns and turn sequences that occur; secondly, by the type and frequency of the selling strategies employed and their actual linguistic realisation showing differences at the level of (in)directness and tentativeness; and thirdly, by the stylistic (in)formality of the language employed mirrored by the choice of address forms, discourse markers, and other related linguistic features. Owing to the scope of this paper we will only discuss in detail the similarities and differences in terms of the overall organisation of the interactions and in their stylistic (in)formality as reflected throughout the interaction.

The overall organisation of the interaction

One of the main differences in the overall organisation of the SEs in Montevideo and Quito can be found in the actual length of the interactions. Montevidean interactions have more and longer turns than Quiteño ones; more specifically, the former have a mean of 47.43 turns per interaction and a median of 41 against a mean 43.71 and a median of 36 for the latter.[4] This would, at first glance, give the impression that all in all Montevideans are more verbose than Ecuadorians; however, a closer examination of the turn sequences found in the data indicate that, while the above characterisation would accurately describe the business exchange and closing sections of the interactions, including the use and frequency of the selling strategies employed, as well as the closings sequences, Ecuadorian openings are longer: they are realised over three to four turns, unlike Montevidean ones which are generally realised over two turns and sometimes over three.

Openings

In both Montevidean and Quiteño SEs, openings are realised by (paired) greetings, summons-response and summons, and offers to help. Quiteño openings, unlike Montevidean ones, also display invitations to come in.

Greetings are defined by Goffman (1971) as *access rituals* and as such they mark the transition to a period of interpersonal access. Along the same lines, Firth (1972) suggests that a central function of greetings is to reduce uncertainty in social contact, particularly between persons not previously known. So using Firth's words, greetings in SEs can be said to provide 'a framework within which individuals can identify each other as preliminary to further action' (1972, p. 30).

In the context of service encounters, greetings can also function as summons to direct the salesperson's attention to the customer. In both cases, the linguistic realisation of the greetings helps to construct the interpersonal relationship between the interactants (also see Goffman, 1971; Firth, 1972).

Table 22.1 illustrates first and second pair parts of greetings, as employed in the interactions. Within the types of greeting available, most of the Montevidean ones (19 out of 28) correspond to *Hola – Hola* 'Hi – Hi' and *Hola – Buenas tardes* 'Hi – Good afternoon' while most of the Quiteño ones (20 out of 28) are realised by *Buenos días – Buenos días* 'Good morning – Good morning', thus showing differences in the degree of (in)formality, with Montevideo speakers exhibiting a preference for informality and Quiteño speakers, for formality. Such choices of greeting initially signal the closeness or distance that the interlocutors are likely to adopt in the course of the interaction, a point we shall refer to throughout the article.

Summons *per se* had a very low incidence, with only 2 out of 28 in each language. The physical presence of the customer constitutes a summons in itself and is responded to by the salesperson with an offer to help such as *sí, en qué te/le puedo ayudar* 'yes, how can I help you[T]/you[V]'. These responses also help to establish the degree of closeness between the conversational participants in the service encounter, through the choice of address forms. Montevidean speakers employ T forms, in contrast to the Quiteño interactants who employ V, thus showing a preference for closeness and respectful distance, respectively.[5]

Although offers to help were present in both samples, with 2 out of 20 in Montevideo and 16 out of 28 in Quito, Quiteño speakers employed a wider range of formulae such as *en qué le puedo ayudar* 'how can I help you[V]' or *a la orden* 'at your service'. As in the previous cases, Quiteño speakers show a preference for formality as expressed in the choice of V and formulaic expressions. While both types of formula explicitly state the sales provider's willingness/obligation to help, the second formula also suggests an asymmetrical relationship between the interlocutors.

In the same vein, it is interesting to note that invitations to come in, such as *siga no más,* 'come on in', which only occur in the Quiteño data (5 out 28), also function as expressions of willingness to help while seemingly granting the customer permission to enter the realm of the salesperson. None of the Montevidean interactions had any incidences of such an opening, and thus Montevideans seem to be less affected by space boundaries in relation to their Quiteño counterparts. However, more data would be necessary in order to substantiate this point.

With respect to the number of turns that comprise the opening sequence, while Montevidean openings are normally realised in two turns, with the second turn generally constituting the main request for service by the customer, Quiteño openings are carried out in two to three turns, with the main request for service occurring in the third or fourth turn, as shown in examples (1) and (2) below.

Table 22.1 Type and frequency of greetings

	Type of greeting		Frequency	
First pair	Second pair		Mdeo N: 28	Qto N:28
Hola 'Hi'	*Hola* 'Hi'		8	
Hola qué tal 'Hi how are you'	*Hola* 'Hi'		4	
Hola 'Hi'	*Buenas tardes* 'Good afternoon'		7	1
Hola buenas tardes 'Hi good afternoon'	*Buenas tardes* 'Good afternoon'		3	
Buen día 'Good day'	*Buen día / Buenas tardes* 'Good day'/'Good afternoon'		2	
Buenos días/Buenas tardes 'Good morning'/'Good afternoon'	*Buenos días/Buenas tardes* 'Good morning'/'Good afternoon'			1
Buenos días 'Good morning'	*Buenas* 'Morning'			2
Muy buenos días 'A very good morning'	*Buenos días* 'Good morning'			2
Buenos días 'Good morning'	*Cómo está buenos días* 'How are you^V good morning'			1
Buenos días Good morning'	*Siga no más buenos días* 'Do come in good morning'			1
Buenos días/Buenas tardes 'Good morning'/'Good afternoon'	*0 greeting*			3
0 greeting	*0 greeting*			6
(Summons) *Sí/45* 'Yes'/'45'*	(Summons response) *Acá* 'Here'		2	
(Summons and offer to help) *Sí en qué te puedo ayudar* 'Yes how can I help you^T',	*Hola buenas tardes* 'Hello good afternoon'		2	
(Response to nonverbal summons) *Sí buenos días* 'Yes good morning'	*Buenos días* 'Good morning'			1
Buenos días 'Good morning'	*Sí a la orden* 'Yes at your service'			1

* 45 is the customer's ticket number.

(1) [Mdeo.][6]
    S: *hola*
            'hi'
    C: *hola mirá estoy buscando camisa para mi marido*
            'hi look^T I'm looking for a shirt for my husband'

(2) [Qto.]
    S: *buenos días*
            'good morning'
    C: *buenos días*
            'good morning'
    S: *en qué le puedo ayudar*
            'how can I help you^V'

C: *verá ando buscando una chaqueta de cuero*
        'look[V] I am looking for a leather jacket'

The length of the openings together with the use of formulae in Quito, in contrast with the shortness and the more limited number of formulae exhibited in the Montevidean data, constitute another feature of the formality of Quiteño interactions against the informality of Montevidean ones, thus ensuring respectful distance or closeness between the interactants. Moreover, the fact that Montevidean customers produce the main request for service immediately after the exchange of greetings and do not wait to be invited in or offered help, unlike most Quiteño interactions, would seem to indicate differences in space boundaries between Montevidean and Quiteño speakers. Montevideans appear to take for granted that service providers are there to help them, whereas Quiteño participants seem to be less certain and thus wait until they are offered help. This waiting could be interpreted as seeking permission to engage in the business exchange. According to Laver's work on access routines, 'maximum risk leads to maximum routine, and, conversely, maximum routine reflects higher risk' (1981, p. 290). In other words, the length and formulaic nature of Quiteño openings in relation to Montevidean ones could be taken as an indication that the Quiteño interlocutors of this study are more bothered about considerations of *negative face* (Brown & Levinson, 1987) than the Montevidean ones.

Closings

This section examines the procedures that participants in SEs in Montevideo and Quito employ to bring the SE to an end by means of pre-closing (*warrants* and offers) and other closing devices (e.g. promises to come back to the shop or to think about the purchase, expressions of gratitude and their corresponding replies, apology and leave-taking utterances).

As in telephone conversations (Schegloff & Sacks, 1973), the majority of closings in SEs in both data sets start with the production of a pre-closing device in the form of a *warrant* by one of the participants, the customer in this case. *Warrants* are utterances such as 'okay' and 'well', which signal the speaker's desire to end the interaction. These utterances allow for the other participant to agree to proceed with the closing or to introduce a new topic. Common realisations of warrants in Montevidean closings are *bueno entonces/ta*, 'okay then', and in Quiteño closings, *ya/bueno*, 'okay'. It is interesting to note that the range of warrants available for Montevidean speakers appears to include forms such as *bueno* as well as intensified expressions such as *ta bárbaro*, 'okay excellent', or *muy bien*, 'very well', whereas Quiteño speakers limit themselves to the 'unemotional' forms *bueno*, 'okay', and *ya*, 'okay'. Intensified forms can be regarded as *positive statements* of the encounter (Albert & Kessler, 1978) signalling that the customer found the experience enjoyable. As such, the use of these forms could be interpreted as Montevidean speakers displaying a higher degree of involvement and investment in the interaction than Quiteño speakers.

Another utterance that appears to function as a pre-closing device, and which was found in the Montevidean data only, is an offer by the salesperson for an additional purchase, as in the following example.

(3) [Mdeo.]
     S: *algo más?*
             'anything else?'
     C: *no nada más*
             'no nothing else'

> S: *bueno pasar por aquí*
>   'okay come this way'

Utterances of this type could be said to correspond in some way to Schegloff and Sacks's (1973) *offerings* (e.g. *are you busy?*), which, nevertheless, occur at the beginning of conversations. In both cases, however, the reply by the other participant determines whether the conversation/interaction develops further or draws to a close. The occurrence of this particular pre-closing device, however, is tied to whether a customer has made any purchases or not.

Going back to warrants, in Montevidean SEs only, salespersons are given the opportunity to display agreement or not after the initial warrant, as in example (4) below. The closing is thus prolonged, as the salesperson's agreement can also include the first part of a new adjacency pair (a display of willingness to help) to which the customer needs to respond, generating in turn another sequence (a thank you – rejection of thanks sequence).

(4)   [Mdeo.]
      C: *bueno entonces*
            'okay then'
      S: *bueno cualquier cosita a las órdenes*
            'okay if there is anything[D] I am at your service'
      C: *bueno muchas gracias*
            'okay many thanks'
      S: *de nada por favor*
            'don't mention it please'
      C: *chau*
            'bye'
      S: *chau*
            'bye'

However, in the majority of cases in both data sets, warrants do not normally occur on their own but are accompanied by another closing device, which is the use of formulae involving a promise to come back or to think about the purchase, as in (5) and (6) below. These formulae would roughly correspond to Schegloff and Sacks' (1973) *arrangements*.

(5)   [Mdeo.]
      C: *bueno ta voy a ver entonces*
            'okay then I'll see then'

(6)   [Qto.]
      C: *bueno voy a darme una vueltita después de clases*
            'okay I'll have a look[D] around and come back after school'
      S: *ya*
            'okay'

Participants in SEs, salespersons in this case, can agree with the arrangement proposed and proceed with the closing or use the opportunity to reintroduce a sales topic. In the Quiteño interactions, salespersons tend to agree to proceed with the closing, as in example (6) above. In contrast, in the Montevidean interactions, although salespersons may initially display agreement, they will more often attempt to reintroduce a sales topic, as in (7), and even offer an apology in the absence of the garment requested, as in (8) below.

(7) [Mdeo.]
  C: *bueno ta (.) voy a ver entonces muchísimas gracias*
     'okay okay (.) I'll see then many[A] thanks'
  C: *no por nada (.) no hay de qué*
     'not at all (.) don't mention it'
  C: *bueno entonces*
     'okay then'
  C: *bueno a las órdenes (.) mi nombre es Diego*
     'okay I'm at your service (.) my name is Diego'
  C: *bueno muy bien*
     'okay very well'
  S: *cualquier cosa lo reservás porque es el único que me queda*
     'just in case you[T] will have to reserve it because it is the only one left'

(8) [Mdeo.]
  C: *y no van a recibir de niños*
     'and will you[P] not get children's'
  S: *no en bermudas por ahora nada (.) tenemos mercadería vieja*
     'no in shorts nothing for the moment (.) we only have the old stock'
  C: *y sí (.) ya se termina la temporada (.) bueno (.) entonces*
     'that's right (.) the season is about the finish (.) okay (.) then'
  S: *bueno (.) perdoná que no te pueda ayudar*
     'okay (.) sorry that I cannot help you[T]'
  C: ( )
  S: *remeras no querés (.) de niño*
     'don't you[T] want t-shirts (.) for children'

In (7) above, the use of a self-identification can be noted. This personalizes the interaction and as such it can be seen as an attempt by the salesperson to reduce the distance between the service provider and the consumer.

  (Dis)agreement to end the encounter can also happen after expressions of gratitude by customers, which in both data sets accompany warrants and promises to come back or to think about the purchase, as in (9) and (10).

(9) [Mdeo.]
  C: *ta bárbaro bueno muchas gracias*
     'excellent okay many thanks'

(10) [Qto.]
  C: *bueno gracias*
     'okay thank you'

In Quito, the expression of gratitude and its corresponding reply in most cases constitutes what Schegloff and Sacks (1973) refer to as the terminal exchange, that is, the adjacency pair that brings the interaction to a close, as in (11):

(11) [Qto.]
    C: *bueno voy a ver si le traigo le agradezco*
            'okay I'll see whether I can bring him thank you[V,]
    S: *ya mi señora*
            'yes Ma'am'

Le agradezco in this example appears to function both as an expression of gratitude and as the first part of the terminal exchange; the reply the salesperson gives can be interpreted as both an acceptance of thanks and an agreement to end the interaction.

In the Montevidean interactions, on the other hand, one can observe that expressions of gratitude do not necessarily function as the terminal exchange; leave-taking utterances, as in (4) above, can be employed instead.

Clark and French (1981), in relation to telephone closings, propose that the occurrence of leave-taking utterances is related to the degree of involvement between the participants, as these utterances are geared towards reaffirmation of acquaintance rather than contact termination. Thus, the use of leave-taking utterances in the Montevidean SEs could be interpreted as a reflection of the closeness achieved during the interaction (cf. Aston, 1988). This would also be in line with Goffman's (1971, p. 65) suggestion that *supportive interchanges*, of which leave-taking utterances are an instance, are apparently 'more important for relations between persons who know each other . . . than for anonymous ones'. Participants in SEs in Montevideo appear to interact as if they knew each other, thus they need to part as if they knew each other.

This stands in sharp contrast with the Quiteño data, where there is only one occurrence of leave-taking utterances, therefore showing the distance maintained throughout the encounter.

As can be seen from the examples provided so far, a larger variety of turns appear to occur in Montevidean SE closings; this results in longer closings. In fact, the number of turns that constitute the closing in Montevideo varies from 3 to 9, with closings of 5 and 7 turns being the most common: there are 10 instances of 5-turn closings and 6 instances of 7 turns. In contrast, in Quito, the number of turns ranges from 2 to 6, with closings of 2 and 4 being the most common: there are 15 and 6 instances of each, respectively.

It was noted in the previous section that openings in Quito, as compared with Montevideo, stretch over a larger number of turns, so it is surprising at first glance that closings do not mirror openings in this respect. Closings, nevertheless, appear to reflect other aspects of the interaction such as the 'verbosity' encountered in the business exchange section of Montevidean interactions, as opposed to the 'restraint' found in Quiteño interactions, with more salespersons in Montevidean SEs seeking opportunities to restart the business exchange in the closing. Longer Montevidean closings also possibly reflect the closer relationship Montevidean participants seem to aim to pursue from the beginning of the interaction, as opposed to the respectful distance Quiteño participants appear to want to keep throughout. In other words, closings are orientated to what preceded them and as such they not only reflect but also ratify the nature of the interaction.

While Quiteño openings reflect certain apprehensiveness on the part of the customer who, through the opening sequences, seeks (re)assurance from the service provider to proceed with the business exchange, the briefness of the closings appears to be directly related to the lack of closeness evidenced throughout the interaction. In other words, owing to the fact that Quiteño participants maintain distance in the interaction, closings can be briefly effected. On the other hand, the briefness of Montevidean openings reflects the 'confidence' customers have that their request for service will be attended to. Such 'confidence' could derive from the belief that salespersons are there to provide a service for customers.

Type and frequency of selling strategies

Interestingly, the negotiation of the business exchange was done in pragmatically similar, albeit non-identical, ways. Both Montevidean and Quiteño salespersons made use of a largely similar range of strategies to attend to their customers. There were a total of nine selling (sub)strategies identified in the Montevidean data, seven of which were also found in the Quiteño data (see below). Strategies relating to the provision of product-related information are the most common type within both data sets. However, within these strategies, a number of similarities and differences were identified in the amount and type of information given.

1. *Disclosure of personal information*: the salesperson volunteers information of a personal nature:
    yo nunca he tenido problemas con esta marca [Mdeo.]
    'I've never had any problems with this brand'
    mi nombre es Diego, cualquier cosita a las órdenes [Mdeo.]
    'my name is Diego I'm at your service for whatever you might need'
2. *Anticipating customer's experience of the product*: the salesperson comments on the (un)suitability of the product according to the customer's needs before the latter tries the product on or makes any comments to that effect:
    viste que no te lastima el pie [Mdeo.]
    'you^T see that it does not hurt your^T foot'
    vas a ver que esas van a andar bien [Mdeo.]
    'you'll^T see that those will go well'
    usted le siente suavecito el zapato [Qto.]
    'the shoe will feel soft for you^V,'
3. *Product explanation*: the salesperson volunteers information of an allegedly non-evaluative/factual nature about the product:
    C: *¿a cuánto están estas botas?* [Mdeo.]
        'how much are these boots?'
    S: *a 2500 y ésta es más cara pero sino la bota de dama, la de dama es ésta, lo que pasa es que traen diferentes numeraciones para, o sea para marear al cliente*
        '2500 and this one is more expensive otherwise there are the lady's boots, this one is the lady's, what happens is that they have a different numbering so as to, to confuse the customer'
    C: *es de cuero* [Qto.]
        'is it leather'
    S: *es cuero cuero es cuero pulat que es lo ( ) mejor que tenemos aquí en cueros sí y ese cuero es trabajado en aceite quemado? entonces el color es natural*
        'it is leather leather it is pulat leather which is ( ) the best we have here in leather yes and we treat that leather with burnt oil? so the colour is natural'
4. *Product attribute enumeration*: the salesperson positively comments on some aspects of the product:
    éstas son lindas [Mdeo.]
    'these are nice'
    éstos están en plena moda
    'these are very fashionable'
5. *Intensified product attribute enumeration*: the salesperson makes intensified positive comments on some aspects of the products. The intensification is realised through the mere repetition of qualifying adjectives, the use of superlatives and adverbs:

la tela es buena buena [Mdeo.]
'the fabric is good good'
éstas son las más cómodas [Mdeo.]
'these are the most comfortable'
ésas lo que tienen es que son comodísimas [Mdeo.]
'what those have is that they are extremely comfortable'
. . . es bien suavecito ese zapato [Qto.]
'. . . that shoe is very soft[D]'

6. *Disclosure of restricted salesperson's information*: the salesperson volunteers information about business transactions in his/her shop and/or other shops:
    no sé si queda porque, o nos olvidamos de pedirlo o porque no le queda a ella [Mdeo.]
    'I don't know if we have any left, either because we forgot to order it or because she has none left'
    vas a ver que en todos lados te pasa lo mismo, los números grandes no hay nada porque este año se vendió mucho el número más grande y otra que las fábricas a su vez hicieron menos, muy pocas fábricas hicieron hasta 40 [Mdeo.]
    'you'll[T] see that wherever you go the same happens, there isn't anything in large numbers because this year we sold a lot of large numbers and the other thing is that the factories made fewer, very few factories made up to (size 40)'

7. *Suggestions aimed at cornering the customer*: the salesperson volunteers information aimed at making the customer buy the product:
    te hago una atención igual (referring to the product price) [Mdeo.]
    'I give you[T] a complimentary gift anyway'
    cualquier cosa la reservás porque es el único par que me queda [Mdeo.]
    'just in case reserve[T] it since it's the only pair that I've got left'
    lléveselo después se lo llevan [Qto.]
    'take[V] it otherwise someone will take it'

8. *Solicited product explanation*: the salesperson complies with the customer's request for product explanation:
    C: *de qué material es?* [Mdeo.]
         'what's the fabric'
    S: *de seda*
         'silk'
    C: *éstos qué son de qué son?* [Qto.]
         'these what are these what are they made of'
    S: *( ) gamuza*
         '( ) suede'

9. *Offers*: the salesperson offers other related products, which might interest the customer, or discounts:
    S: *después tenés el modelo que salió ahora para dama* [Mdeo.]
         'then you[T] have the lady's model which has just come out'
    S: *pero sí le damos un buen descuentito para que se anime a llevarse* [Qto.]
         'but we will give you[V] a discount[D] to encourage you[V] to take it'

Despite the fact that both data sets exhibit a similar variety of strategies across all the interactions, more differences than similarities were found in the frequency with which some of the strategies are employed, as can be seen in Table 22.2.[7]

Table 22.2 Frequency of use of selling (sub)strategies

Selling (sub)strategy	Number of occurrences	
	Montevideo	Quito
1. Disclosure of personal information	12	—
2. Anticipating customer's experience of the product	14	5
3. Product explanation	41	11
4. Product attribute enumeration	64	59
5. Intensified product attribute enumeration	12	18
6. Disclosure of restricted salesperson's information	16	—
7. Suggestions aimed at cornering the customer	12	4
8. Solicited product explanation	67	19
9. Offers	36	34

As can be seen in this table, the sub-strategy that figures most prominently in both data sets is attribute enumeration (including intensified product attribute enumeration), showing a similar incidence across the 28 SE interactions, 64 and 12 times, respectively, for the Montevideans, and 59 and 18 times, respectively, for the Quiteño salespersons.

The second most salient sub-strategy in the Montevidean data is solicited product explanation, with 67 instances, followed by product explanation, with 41 instances, closely followed by offers, with 36 occurrences. The Quiteño data, on the other hand, show a preference for offers, with 34 instances, followed by solicited product explanation, with 19 occurrences, and then product explanation, with 11 instances.

The remaining strategies found in both data sets, namely anticipating the customer's experience of the product and making suggestions aimed at cornering the customer, exhibit a lower incidence in both languages, with the Montevidean data showing an incidence of 14 for the former and 12 for the latter, and the Quiteño data exhibiting an incidence of 5 and 4, respectively.

Finally, the disclosure of personal information and the disclosure of restricted salesperson's information, as indicated earlier, were only found in the Montevidean data. These strategies show a similar incidence to anticipating the customer's experience and to making suggestions aimed at cornering the customer in the Montevidean data, 12 and 16 times, respectively.

[The authors provide a statistical analysis of the sample and description of sub-strategies.]

The stylistic (in)formality of the interactions

While Quiteño interactions show a preference for formality in their interactions, Montevidean ones reflect a preference for informality. This (in)formality is not only evidenced by contrast to the formulaic nature of the Quiteño opening sequences, but also by the choice of forms of address, the use of titles, discourse markers and even humour by the interlocutors.[8]

FORMS OF ADDRESS AND TITLES

Before we start discussing the findings under this sub-section, it should be borne in mind that our aim is to provide an analysis of the results in line with the overall linguistic behaviour of the participants discussed so far. In other words, our objective here is not to present an exhaustive analysis of the choice and use of address forms between the two data samples since, firstly, this is not the main purpose of the paper and, secondly, the type of data collected for this study would not render itself for such purposes owing to the unequal numbers of female and male interactants, among other reasons.

Montevidean and Quiteño interactions can be sharply contrasted with each other in terms of the choice of address forms. Unlike Quiteño interlocutors, who show an absolute preference for the formal pronoun of address, *usted*, in all their SEs, Montevidean interactional participants exhibit a preference for informality in their exchanges.[9] This informality is realised through the choice of *tú* and *vos* in preference to *usted*.

More than a third (20/28) of the Montevidean Ses, whether initiated by the customer or the salesperson, employed *tú/vos* in preference to *usted*.[10] Four out of the 28 SEs were initiated with *usted* by the salesperson and then negotiated to *tú/vos*. In only two out of the 28 interactions was *usted* employed by both salespersons and consumers, and, in 2 out of 28 SEs, the interlocutors code-switched between *tú/vos* and *usted* throughout the interactions. It should be noted that, in these four interactions, either the salesperson or the customer were in his/her fifties, and this could have influenced the choice of pronoun of address. However, owing to the small number of interactions where *usted* was employed, such comments should only be taken speculatively.

Whereas *usted* appears to be the only appropriate socio-pragmatic choice available to Quiteños in these types of interaction, Montevidean interactional participants appear to be able to fluctuate along the (in)formality continuum, despite showing a clear preference for informality. Thus, in 6 out of 28 interactions, Montevidean conversational participants were able to negotiate the preferred form of address, unlike their Quiteño counterparts who appear to follow a socially pre-patterned or fixed choice. From this linguistic behaviour, it could be argued that the Montevidean interlocutors of this study seem to have room for negotiation, in contrast to the Quiteños whose role-relationships in this type of social context appear to be pre-established. In other words, while Quiteños appear to be recreating the existing *status quo* by conforming to the socially expected form of address, hence maintaining distance between the salesperson and the consumer, Montevideans seem to (re)define it in their interactions, in favour of shortening the distance between the conversational participants.

With respect to the use of titles, these were not very prominent in either data set. Montevideans employed three titles in 28 interactions. The title employed is *señora* and it was used in those interactions where *usted* was the preferred form of address. In the Quiteño data, there were a few more occurrences (eight altogether), with a larger range of formal forms: *señora*, 'Mrs/Madam', *señorita*, 'Miss/Madam', and the deferential form *mi señora*. The occurrence of these forms would display once again the higher degree of formality in Quiteño SEs in relation to Montevidean SEs. One exception, however, was the occurrence of the familiar form *mija*, 'my daughter'. The use of this form would constitute one of the few instances of involvement strategies in the Quiteño SEs examined.

The Montevidean overall orientation towards closeness in their interactions is also evidenced by the use of *viste* in more than half of the SEs.

VISTE, VERÁ

The Montevidean data contain a number of *interpersonal* discourse markers such as *mirá*, 'look[T]', *sabés*, 'you know[T]', and *viste*, 'you see[T]/you know[T]'.[11] Whereas the first two markers have a very low incidence, the latter is employed by the salespersons in more than half of the SEs.

The use of *viste* as an interpersonal discourse marker follows the conjugation of the informal second person singular with *vio* as its formal counterpart. Both markers are only employed in the preterite and could be translated as 'you see' or 'you know' in British English.

Viste occurs in initial, middle and final utterance position, as illustrated below:

(12) [Mdeo.]
    C: *. . . para que veas la calidad (.) viste que el otro era más finito*
              'for you[T] to see the quality (.) you see[T] the other one was thinner'

(13) [Mdeo.]
    C: *si fuese cuerina viste que te lastima*
              'if it were PVC you see it would hurt'

(14) [Mdeo.]
    C: *son perlas españolas viste*
              'they're Spanish pearls you see'

In all three positions, *viste* is employed as a way of involving the hearer, that is to say, assuming the hearer agrees or is aware of what the speaker is saying. In other words, when employing *viste,* the speaker does not provide the hearer with new information but makes reference to something already known and/or shared by both interlocutors. Thus, in using *viste,* the speaker seeks to engage the hearer further by making him/her share the responsibility of what is being or has been said (Carranza, 1998). As such, the employment of the marker by the Montevidean salespersons could be interpreted as an involvement substrategy.

In the Quiteño data, the interpersonal discourse markers that were found are *verá*, 'look' (literally, 'you will see'), *vea/vea usted,* 'do you realise it?', *no/no es cierto,* 'isn't that so?', and *sí,* 'are you with me/is that clear?'. The form with the highest incidence is *verá*, with 17 instances, whereas there are only a few occurrences of the other forms.

Verá, as opposed to the Montevidean *viste,* occurs in initial position only, as in the following examples:

(15) [Qto.]
    S: *verá éste le cuesta 550*
              look this is 550'

(16) [Qto.]
    S: *ya le voy a indicar (.) verá (.) ésta es la 6 de Diciembre sí*
              'I'll show it to you straight away (.) look (.) this is 6 of December yes'

This marker seems to be used to preface explanations, as a way of ensuring and focusing the hearer's attention. Its use seems to constitute an attempt to draw the hearer towards the speaker's space/position; however, it does not seem to imply the same degree of involvement that *viste* appears to create. A key difference in function is possibly related to the use of a past or a future form. The use of the past form *viste,* in contrast with the future of *verá,* seems to convey that the speaker assumes the other person shares his/her point of view, whereas *verá,* as remarked earlier, appears to constitute a request to the hearer to share his/her view. In any case, it has to be stressed that the majority of occurrences of *verá* and other interpersonal discourse markers in the Quiteño data were found in two interactions only. These were interactions with a larger number of turns that did not follow the pattern of briefness that characterised most of the Quiteño interactions.

Conclusions

The analysis of the interactions shows that, overall, the Montevidean participants of the study are more 'verbose' than Quiteños. With the exception of the opening sequences, this verbosity is manifested through a larger number of turns, a higher frequency of selling strategies, which in the vast majority are characterised by their informativeness, in contrast to the briefness and less frequent use of the same strategies by the Quiteño speakers in this study. Furthermore, Montevidean salespersons, unlike Quiteños, also employ personalisation strategies. The features described for Montevidean SEs can be associated with interactional proactiveness, and those of Quiteño speakers, with interactional reactiveness. However, it should be noted that these are tendencies observed in one specific context and cannot be generalised to all Montevidean and Quiteño salespersons.[12]

The findings also reflect that Quiteño speakers prefer formality in their interactions. This is shown in the formulaic nature of some of the sequences, in particular in their openings and in their absolute preference for a V form of address, in contrast to the Montevidean preference for informality as reflected by a lesser use of formulae and the preference for T forms of address. These features seem to be geared towards maintaining or shortening the distance between the interlocutors, respectively. All in all, the differences found in terms of the different sequences and the selling strategies employed, together with the (in)formality exhibited throughout the encounters, would seem to indicate that the Montevidean and Quiteño participants of this study have different conceptions of their space and that of the other. While Montevidean speakers use strategies, which are orientated towards closeness thus 'erasing' the social distance boundary between the consumer and the service provider, Quiteño participants tend not to make any attempts to trespass over this boundary.

With respect to the generalisability of the research findings, it should be noted that, owing to unequal numbers of female and male service providers, as well as age differences between them, the results cannot be generalised to all Montevidean and Quiteño salespersons' linguistic behaviour in clothes selling/purchasing interactions in lower-middle class areas. The collection of this kind of data would involve considerably more time and resources, and this is not necessary for the purposes of a preliminary study of pragmatic variation. Also, while focusing on clothes selling/purchasing interactions in both capitals helps comparability, it may also restrict the generalisability of some of the observed regularities, in that they could respond to the specific setting in question and/or to the idiosyncrasies of the interlocutors involved (Aston, 1998).

Another limitation of the study is that it does not include the perspective of the customers or salespersons. For a future study, semi-structured interviews would need to be employed for triangulation purposes. It would be useful to examine, for example, how customers rate the interactions in which they take part in terms of the treatment they received in a shop encounter, the amount of information they were given and their degree of satisfaction with the service overall. Such interviews would provide access to customers' expectations, which can be cross-culturally variable. It would also be useful to find out about the type of training salespersons receive (if any) in terms of 'appropriate' selling strategies, use of address forms and other linguistic behaviour, as well as how shop owners assess the interactional performance of their salespersons. Such information would be needed to determine perhaps how much of a salespersons' behaviour is a reflection of the ethos of the company or of the social group (i.e. salespersons in a lower-middle class shopping area).

Appendix

Transcription conventions

:   signals vowel lengthening
?   marks rising intonation
(.)   marks a short pause measured impressionistically
^T indicates the use of a T-form of address in the singular (i.e., familiar address)
^V indicates the use of a V-form of address in the singular (i.e., formal address)
^P indicates the use of the only second person plural form of address available in the two varieties, which is an unmarked form in terms of familiarity/formality
^D indicates the use of a diminutive
^A indicates the use of an augmentative

Notes

1 We are grateful to Helen Spencer-Oatey for her useful comments on an earlier version of this paper.
2 In the analysis of the overall organisation of conversation, conversation analysts refer to conversations as having beginnings, middles and ends (see Benson & Hughes, 1983). In SE studies, different terms have been proposed to refer to the middle section, i.e. the section where the SE transaction is carried out. Bailey (1997), for example, refers to it as the *negotiation of the business exchange/transaction*, from which the term employed here derives, and Kuiper and Flindall (2000) as the *matrix interchange*.
3 For a different approach to recording without informants' prior permission, see Lamoureux (1988/89).
4 A turn in this paper is understood as the holding of the floor with the intention of making a contribution. Backchannel items were not counted as turns.
5 It should be noted that, in Montevideo, there are two familiar forms in the singular: *tú* and *vos*, and that their use is not uniform, in that speakers tend to employ *tú* with the conjugation corresponding to *vos* (cf. Pederetti de Bolón, 1983).
6 See the Appendix for the transcription conventions employed.
7 The frequency of use of each sub-strategy was treated nominally, that is to say, every time an occurrence of a sub-strategy was found in a SE interaction, a value of 1 was assigned; likewise, when no occurrences of a sub-strategy were found, a value of 0 was assigned. Hence, if different explanations were given about a particular product, each explanation (i.e. the origin of the product, the product make, its uses, etc.) was assigned one point; similarly, if four product attributes were mentioned by the shopkeeper in an interaction, then a value of 4 was assigned.
8 Humour was mostly employed by the customers.
9 This finding is in line with the results of a previous study of public SEs in Quito in the context of hospital information desks, where such usage was also found (cf. Placencia, 1998).
10 It should be noted that, in Uruguay, as in many other Latin American countries, there is an alternative pronoun which expresses solidarity: *vos*, which has almost replaced *tú* in Montevidean Spanish.
11 Chodorowska-Pilch (1999) distinguishes in her study *interpersonal* discourse markers such as *vamos* from other discourse markers that have been examined where the focus is on the propositional content and the role of the speaker in the coherent expression of an utterance, rather than on the speaker's motivation to exert influence upon the hearer.
12 For example, in the context of corner shop interactions in Quito, where participants are familiar with each, most of the behaviour Placencia (2004) describes for shopkeepers would fall under the category of *interactional proactiveness*.

References

Albert, S. & Kessler, S. (1978). Ending social encounters. *Journal of Experimental and Social Psychology*, 14, 541–53.

Aston, G. (1995). Say 'Thank you': Some pragmatic constraints in conversational closings. *Applied Linguistics*, 16(1), 57–86.

Aston, G. (ed.) (1998). *Negotiating service. Studies in the discourse of bookshop encounters.* Bologna: CLUEB.

Bailey, B. (1997). Communication of respect in interethnic service encounters. *Language in Society*, 26, 327–56.

Benson, D. & Hughes, J. A. (1983). *The perspective of ethnomethodology.* London: Longman.

Brown, P. & Levinson, S. (1987). *Politeness. Some universals in language usage.* Cambridge: Cambridge University Press.

Carranza, I. (1998). *Conversación y deixis de discurso.* Córdoba: Universidad Nacional de Córdoba.

Chodorowska-Pilch, M. (1999). On the polite use of *vamos* in Peninsular Spanish. *Pragmatics,* 9(3), 343–55.

Chodorowska-Pilch, M. (2002). Las ofertas y la cortesía en español peninsular. In M. Placencia & D. Bravo (eds), *Actos de habla y cortesía en español* (pp. 21–36). Munich: Lincom Europa.

Ciapuscio, G. & Kesselheim, W. (1997). 'Usted, qué es?': Categorizaciones y contexto institucional. In K. Zimmerman & C. Bierbach (eds), *Lenguaje y communicación intercultural en el mundo hispánico* (pp. 105–30). Frankfurt: Vervuert.

Clark, H. H. & French, J. W. (1981). Telephone goodbyes. *Language in Society*, 10, 1–19.

Coupland, J. (ed.) (2000). *Small talk.* London: Longman.

Curcó, C. (1998). 'No me harías un favorcito?': Reflexiones en torno a la expresión de la cortesía verbal en el español de México y el español peninsular. In H. Haverkate, G. Mulder & C. Fraile (eds), *La pragmática lingüística del español. Recientes desarrollos* (Diálogos Hispánicos 22) (pp. 129–71). Amsterdam: Rodopi.

Fant, L. (1996). Regulación conversacional en la negociación: Una comparación entre pautas mexicanas y peninsulares. In T. Kotschi, W. Oesterreicher & K. Zimmerman (eds), *El Español hablado y la cultura oral en España e Hispanoamérica* (pp. 147–85). Frankfurt: Vervuert; Madrid: Iberoamericana.

Firth, R. (1972). Verbal and bodily rituals of greeting and parting. In J. S. La Fontaine (ed.), *The interpretation of ritual: Essays in honour of A. I. Richards* (pp. 1–38). London: Tavistock.

García, C. (2004). Reprendiendo y respondiendo a una reprimenda: Similitudes y differencias entre peruanos y venezolanos. *Spanish in Context*, 1, 113–47.

Gavioli, L. (1997). Bookshop service encounters in English and Italian: Notes on the achievement of information and advice. In F. Bargiela-Chiappini & S. Harris (eds), *The languages of business. An international perspective* (pp. 136–56). Edinburgh: Edinburgh University Press.

George, S. (1990). *Getting things done in Naples. Action, language and context in discourse description.* Bologna: Cooperativa Libraria Universitaria Editrice.

Goffman, E. (1971). *Relations in public.* New York: Harper Torchbooks.

Kuiper, K. & Flindall, M. (2000). Social rituals, formulaic speech and small talk at the supermarket checkout. In J. Coupland (ed.), *Small talk* (pp. 183–207). London: Longman.

Lamoureux, E. L. (1988/89). Rhetoric and conversation in service encounters. *Research on Language and Social Interaction*, 22, 93–114.

Laver, J. (1975). Communicative functions of phatic communion. In A. Kendon, R. M. Harris & M. Ritchiekey (eds), *Organization and behaviour in face-to-face interaction* (pp. 215–38). The Hague: Mouton.

Laver, J. (1981). Linguistic routines and politeness in greeting and parting. In F. Coulmas (ed.), *Conversational routine: Explorations in standard communication situations and prepatterned speech* (pp. 289–304). The Hague: Mouton.

Malinowski, B. (1972 [1923]). Phatic communion. In J. Laver & S. Hutcheson (eds), *Communication in face-to-face interaction* (pp. 146–52). Harmondsworth, Middlesex: Penguin.

Márquez Reiter, R. (1997). Politeness phenomena in British English and Uruguayan Spanish: The case of requests. *Miscelánea*, 18, 159–67.

Márquez Reiter, R. (2000). *Linguistic politeness in Britain and Uruguay.* Amsterdam: John Benjamins.

Márquez Reiter, R. (2002a). Estrategias de cortesía en el español hablado de Montevideo. In M. E. Placencia & D. Bravo (eds), *Actos de habla y cortesía en español* (pp. 89–106). Munich: Lincom Europa.

Márquez Reiter, R. (2002b). A contrastive study of conventional indirectness in Spanish: Evidence from Uruguayan and Peninsular Spanish. *Pragmatics,* 12(2), 135–51.

Márquez Reiter, R. (2003). Pragmatic variation in Spanish: External request modification in Uruguayan and Peninsular Spanish. In R. Núñez-Cedeño, L. López & R. Cameron (eds), *A romance perspective on language knowledge and use* (pp. 167–80). Amsterdam: John Benjamins.

McCarthy, M. (2000). Mutually captive audiences: Small talk and the genre of close-contact service encounters. In J. Coupland (ed.), *Small talk* (pp. 84–109). London: Longman.

Merritt, M. (1976). On questions following questions in service encounters. *Language in Society*, 5, 315–57.

Pederetti de Bolón, A. (1983). *El idioma de los uruguayos. Unidad y diversidad*. Montevideo: Ediciones de la Banda Oriental (Temas del Siglo XX).

Placencia, M. E. (1994). Pragmatics across varieties of Spanish. *Donaire*, 2, 65–77.

Placencia, M. E. (1996). Politeness in Ecuadorian Spanish. *Multilingua*, 15(1), 13–34.

Placencia, M. E. (1997). Address forms in Ecuadorian Spanish. *Hispanic Linguistics*, 9, 165–202.

Placencia, M. E. (1998). Pragmatic variation: Ecuadorian Spanish vs. Peninsular Spanish. *Spanish Applied Linguistics*, 2(1), 71–106.

Placencia, M. E. (2001a). Inequality in address behavior in public institutions at la Paz, Bolivia. *Anthropological Linguistics*, 43(2), 198–217.

Placencia, M. E. (2001b). Percepciones y manifestaciones de la (des)cortesía en la atención al público: El caso de una institución pública ecuatoriana. *Oralia*, 4, 177–212.

Placencia, M. E. (2004). Rapport-building activities in corner shop interactions. *Journal of Sociolinguistics*, 8(2), 215–45.

Puga Larraín, J. (1997). *La atenuación en el castellano de Chile: Un enfoque pragmalingüístico*. Universitat de Valencia: Tirant lo Blanch Libros.

Schegloff, E. A. (1972). Sequencing in conversational openings. In J. J. Gumperz & D. Hymes (eds), *Directions in sociolinguistics: The ethnography of communication*. New York: Holt, Rinehart and Winston.

Schegloff, E. A. & Sacks, H. (1973). Opening up closings. *Semiotica*, 7, 289–327.

Traverso, V. (2001). Syrian service encounters: A case of shifting strategies within verbal exchange. *Pragmatics*, 11(4), 421–44.

Ventola, E. (1987). *The structure of social interaction*. London: Pinter.

PART VI: NOTES FOR STUDENTS AND INSTRUCTORS

Study questions

1   What issues have Clyne et al. considered in their study design and selection of the subjects in Chapter 19 and why? In what way are these issues relevant to your own interests and experience?

2   Clyne et al. argue that turn-length and sequencing are largely culture-bound. Can you give examples from the transcripts in the study to show how they are culture-bound?

3   What is unique about television commercials as a speech act or event of suggestion? Can you list the key differences in the way persuasion is achieved in television commercials in different countries?

4   Schmidt et al. state that, 'As Leech has pointed out, statements such as "Asian advertising is less persuasive than American advertising" only make sense if they can be relativized in terms of the pragmalinguistic strategies used in different communities and situations'. Explain what the authors mean and justify the argument with the findings from this study. Do you agree?

5   What counts as 'interruption' in sequences of conversation, according to Bargiela-Chiappini and Harris? What are the pragmatic significances of interruptive strategies in British and Italian management meetings? What factors impact on turn-taking dynamics? In the light of the findings in Chapter 21, can you re-interpret the findings in Chapter 19?

6   What are the main features of the interactional styles of salespersons in Montevideo and Quito (Chapter 22)? What interactional strategies do the salespersons use to negotiate their relationships with the buyers? Are there any differences between the two places and why?

Study activities

1   Clyne et al.'s study (Chapter 19) uses the data collected through participant observation and recorded discourse. Read the section on data analysis and discern what arguments are drawn from which type of data. Comment on the advantages of using the mixed method of data collection.

2   Record five television commercials, either in English or any other languages you are familiar with. Analyse them following the procedure and the framework in Chapter 20. How is the speech act of persuasion achieved in these commercials? Are there differences between your findings and the findings reported in Chapter 20?

3   Watch a broadcaster's or journalist's interviews with politicians on television or YouTube. Analyse the interactional features in these interviews. What strategies are used by the interviewer and the interviewees? Are they successful?

4   Chapter 22 examines the sociocultural variations in the use of Spanish in service encounters. Team up with other colleagues and select a language that is shared by two or more countries or regions. This could be, for example, English (American English, British English, Australian English, Singapore English, etc.); Chinese (Putonghua in Mainland China, Guoyu in Taiwan, and Huayu in Singapore, etc.); French (French spoken in Paris, Swiss French, Belgian French, Quebec French, Acadian French, Haitian French, Moroccan French, etc.); Portuguese (Portuguese spoken in Brazil, East Timor, Macau, Portugal, etc.). Are there sociocultural variations in the language interactions in service encounters in these places? If yes, why?

Further reading

Samovar, L. A., Porter, R. E. & McDaniel, E. R. (2007). *Communication between Cultures* (7th edn). Boston: Wadsworth. (This contains separate chapters on cultural influences on business, education and health care settings.)

Pan, Y., Scollon, S. W. & Scollon, R. (2002). *Professional communication in international settings.* Malden, MA: Blackwell. (This contains separate chapters on the telephone call, the résumé, the presentation and the meeting.)

Bargeiala-Chiappini, F. (ed.) (2009). *The handbook of business discourse.* Edinburgh: Edinburgh University Press.

Kotthoff, H. & Spencer-Oatey, H. (eds) (2007). *Handbook of intercultural communication.* Berlin: Mouton. (This contains a section on intercultural communication in different sectors of life, including health care, business management, legal contexts, media and intercultural marriage.)

ZHU HUA

CONCLUSION

Studying language and intercultural
communication: methodological considerations

Introduction: two frequently asked questions

WHILE SUPERVISING STUDENTS' dissertation projects, I have frequently been asked two questions by them. The first one, usually asked at the start of the project, is *Where/How do I start?* This question requires a long answer. Identifying and formulating a workable research question requires a critical understanding of the themes and issues of the field of interest and a good knowledge of the research methodology relevant to the field. Rather than answering it directly, I normally ask my students to think about the following questions instead:

- What is the issue that you are interested in? What real-life problem would you like to solve?
- Why are you interested in it? What is its significance to you? Does it have any significance to other people? Will other people be interested in the same issue/problem?
- Can the issue be investigated or the problem solved by any of the research that you have read or heard about? Has anyone else asked the same question? If yes, how is the question asked? Will the answer tell you and other people anything that you don't know already?
- What theoretical model, approach or framework can be applied to the issue or problem that you intend to investigate, and why?
- Can the issue/problem be investigated with empirical evidence? What evidence would you need, and how and where do you obtain that evidence?
- Is the research doable within the resources and time you have?

These questions bring together the key issues in designing a research project and help students to make an informed choice. Starting from a real-life problem or issue will help students to see the relevance of research to everyday life and practice. But the problem or issue needs to have broader significance, not just to the student but also to other people, as well as theoretical significance. Linking up with theoretical models or frameworks will transform a practical, personal-interest question to a research question that is theoretically motivated and can generate new knowledge. The last two sets of questions not only serve as a reality-check to see whether the process of investigation is achievable, but also offer an opportunity to adjust the focus and scope of the investigation. In addition to these essential questions, students also need to think about ethical issues (see the section on ethical considerations below). Once the student has thought through these questions, they can start by finding out whether anyone else has done similar investigations before and what methods have been used by other researchers, and identify any gaps in the literature.

The second frequently asked question is more practical: *How many questionnaires do I need to distribute?* Or: *How many people do I need to interview*? It is usually asked when students have formulated a research question. Although such questions are often asked innocently, they tend to ring alarm bells for me. Practical responses – 150 copies or 40 people – are not actually very helpful, as the students need to understand the logic of research – in particular, the link between a research question and data collection methods. They also need to have a good awareness of the strengths and weaknesses of a particular study design and data-gathering technique. Methods must be chosen because they can provide the right and best evidence to answer the research questions. Different methods serve different purposes, and every method has its pros as well as cons in different contexts. In terms of research design, for instance, if the research question is about the relationship between culture and cognition, an experimental design may be the most appropriate; if the research question is about changes in cultural beliefs, values and behaviours over a period of time, a longitudinal design may be more appropriate.

The main purpose of this chapter is to help the students to understand the logic of research methodology and gain a general idea of various study designs and data collection methods for the study of language and intercultural communication. It should be pointed out that the field of language and intercultural communication is highly multi- and interdisciplinary. Researchers have borrowed a range of different methods from different research traditions in their empirical work. In what follows, I will discuss a number of research designs first, followed by a brief account of the main data collection methods relevant to the field of language and intercultural communication. For the purpose of clarity, I divide data collection methods into two sections: one for non-interactional data and the other for interactional data. I will use the study design and data collection methods adopted in the articles in this Reader as examples wherever appropriate and possible. Some additional examples are used.

Key issues in research design

Research design is a critical first step of a project. It differs from data collection method in that it deals with the logical structure of the research and asks the question, 'given this research question (or theory), what type of evidence is needed to answer the question (or test the theory) *in a convincing way*?' (de Vaus, 2001, p. 9, original emphasis). Using an analogy, de Vaus compares the role and purpose of a research design in a project to knowing what sort of building (such as an office building, a factory for manufacturing machinery, a school, etc.) is being constructed before ordering materials or setting critical dates for completion of the project stages.

A number of research designs have been used in the study of language and intercultural communication. These are:

1   The number of cultures involved: Is the primary aim of the study to compare two or several cultures or languages or to focus on one particular culture? Or does it go beyond cultural membership (etic vs. emic)?

2   The type of data: Are the data collected and analysed in numerical form or not (quantitative vs. qualitative)?
3   The collection of data: Are the data collected under controlled conditions or not (experimental design vs. non-experimental design)?
4   The duration of the study: Is the study conducted over a period of time or at one point in time (longitudinal design vs. non-longitudinal design)?
5   The number of participants to be included: Does the study involve one single participant, a small group of participants or a large number of participants (case study vs. cross-sectional)?

Etic vs. emic

Two general approaches have been used in studies on human behaviours and language use across cultures. One is called *etic* and is often known as a comparative study, which involves comparing one culture with another. All cross-cultural studies, by their nature, belong to this type of study design.

A number of chapters in this Reader have adopted this design. For example:

- the CCSARP project in Blum-Kulka and Olshtain's chapter (Chapter 9);
- Schmidt *et al.*'s comparison of television commercials across four cultures (Chapter 20);
- Bargiela-Chiappini and Harris's study on interruptive strategies in British and Italian management meetings (Chapter 21);
- Márquez Reiter and Placencia's comparative study on service encounters in two varieties of Spanish (Chapter 22).

The challenge facing an etic design is the issue of comparability when several cultures are studied together. Ideally, comparison should be made on a 'like for like' basis, but in reality, comparative studies often encounter practical difficulties. For example, in Schmidt *et al.*'s study, the original plan was to compare the use of persuasive language for similar products advertised on television during peak time in different countries. However, as the authors found out, this was impossible, as the products advertised in each country differed in type and frequency.

The other approach is what has been referred to as *emic*, whereby researchers use local cultural terms to interpret a cultural phenomenon and explore and discover the indigenous culturally based meanings. Li Wei (1996) has argued for two principles guiding the emic study: one is 'holism', which requires that issues concerning communication patterns of a specific group are not divorced from the historical development, social experience, cultural beliefs and values of that group; the other is the principle of 'emergence', which requires that structure and meaning are discovered rather than predetermined and assigned.

Among the articles collected in this Reader, several have adopted the emic approach. For example:

- Ide's analysis of honorifics in the Japanese culture (Chapter 6);
- Katriel's discussion of *dugri* speech in Israeli Sabra culture (Chapter 10).

In both studies, the researchers examine and interpret the language use and communication patterns within the context of local cultures. Other examples of emic approach can be found in the key word approach advocated by Wierzbicka (1997), who believes key concepts, expressed in key words in a language, are indices of the core values of a given culture to which the words belong.

Emic and etic designs provide different perspectives, but they are neither exclusive of each other nor irreconcilable. Instead, they are often taken as interdependent stages of an academic enquiry and a 'continuous circle of research activity' (Berry, 1999, p. 12). At the starting point, a researcher may set out to test whether an argument or observation true to one culture applies to another culture. This may then set the agenda for an in-depth study from within that culture. When ample and extensive studies on several cultures have been carried out separately, a researcher may attempt to compare and integrate what has been learned about a common phenomenon in different cultures. An example of a combined emic and etic design can be found in Wierzbicka (2003).

Recent years have seen some studies (such as those following the interculturality approach in Part V in this Reader) that go beyond cultural boundaries. The conventional emic or etic divide does not apply to these studies, which take cultural membership as socially constructed and emerging from interaction rather than something prescribed.

Quantitative vs. qualitative

One key difference between quantitative and qualitative research is the use of numerical data. Quantitative research is essentially about explaining phenomena and identifying trends and patterns by collecting and analysing data numerically, whereas qualitative research is an umbrella term that covers a variety of approaches that focus on the meaning of the phenomenon being investigated and do not involve numerical data.

Although people generally think of intercultural communication research as largely qualitative, quantitative research is in fact widely used in specific sub-areas such as cultural-value studies (e.g. Hofstede, 2001) and intercultural communicative competence (ICC) assessment (e.g. Hammer *et al.*, 2003). Questionnaires are often used in quantitative studies to collect numerical data. Some studies in cross-cultural pragmatics also compare the frequency of occurrence of various speech acts and linguistic strategies in different languages, contexts or cultures. The main advantages and disadvantages of quantitative research areas follows:

- Advantages:
  - Statistical analysis can give research findings additional confidence and help to discover the relationship between variables (e.g. whether two variables are causal or correlational).
  - It can handle a large quantity of data, and therefore the findings can be more representative.
  - It appears to be scientific with the help of mathematics and probability.
- Disadvantages:
  - By reducing data to numbers, it may decontextualise patterns and meanings.
  - Individual differences and richness of data may be overlooked.

Qualitative research in the area of language and intercultural communication takes many forms; for example, the discourse approach in Clyne, Ball & Neil's article (Chapter 19), the interculturality perspective in Nishizaka's (Chapter 17) and Higgins' (Chapter 18) articles, and ethnography in Katriel's study (Chapter 10). It very often involves coding, categorising and transcribing data. But the focus is very much on the interpretation of the meaning of the phenomenon under study. Compared with quantitative research, qualitative research has the following advantages and disadvantages:

- Advantages:
  - It offers an opportunity to carry out in-depth analysis of data.
  - The data may be richer and more detailed.
  - Special cases or individual differences can be highlighted.
  - Interpretation can be more nuanced.
- Disadvantages:
  - The data may be less representative, and generalisations may be less clear.
  - Data collection and interpretation may be subject to researchers' positions and backgrounds.

Quantitative and qualitative can be combined in mixed-method designs. Márquez Reiter & Placencia's article (Chapter 22) is an example of how these designs are used together to provide a relatively comprehensive and in-depth analysis.

Experimental vs. non-experimental design

Experimental studies collect data under controlled conditions. The purpose of the 'control' is to keep everything, except for the variables under investigation, as similar or comparable as possible, so that the experimental results can be reliably attributed to the changes in variables. Among variables under investigation, a distinction is usually made between dependent and independent variables. Independent variables are those that have an effect on other variables, and a change in their value or state would lead to a change in other variables, whereas dependent variables are those that change as a result of changes in other variables (see an example of independent and dependent variables in the example discussed below).

In a typical experimental design, a researcher starts by formulating a hypothesis between the dependent variable and independent variables and then decides on subject sampling criteria, instrument, treatment and procedures. There are many variations of experimental designs, depending on how many groups of subjects are involved, whether the groups are identical or different, whether the groups are doing different things or doing the same thing under different conditions, and how many times data will be collected from each group.

Several experimental studies are discussed in Nisbett's investigation of the relationship between language and cognition (Chapter 2). In the study by Li-jun Ji, Zhiyong Zhang and Nisbett (2002), two groups of subjects are used: American students vs. Chinese students from mainland China and Taiwan. Both groups are presented with a number of sets of three words (e.g. panda, monkey and banana) and then asked to indicate which two words among each set are most closely related. The results are compared between groups. In this study, the independent variable is the language background, as the change in the language background may affect the dependent variable. The dependent variable is patterns of thinking, which depends on the language background as hypothesised.

Some researchers refer to the type of experimental design in which subjects are not randomly allocated as quasi-experimental design. This type of experimental design is often used in evaluation studies in which random assignment is neither possible nor practical. For example, to evaluate the effectiveness of AFS (an international organisation) Study Abroad programme, Hammer (2005) administrated questionnaires to a total of 1,500 students and a control group consisting of 600 friends or acquaintances who were nominated by the students and who were not involved in AFS Study Abroad programmes. The questionnaires were collected at pre-departure, immediately after the experience and five months after departure.

The main advantages and disadvantages of experimental design are:

- Advantages:
    - It is easy to discover the relationship between variables.
    - The results are easier to process and interpret.
- Disadvantages:
    - Behaviours under experimental conditions may not be the same as those in naturally occurring social contexts.
    - The 'control' over the variables can be difficult.

In non-experimental design, researchers do not manipulate conditions. This design is suitable for research questions that aim to explore the phenomena in a more natural manner, such as spontaneous interaction, to find out opinions, attitudes or facts or to assess current conditions or practice. Most of the existing studies in language and intercultural communication and most of the selected articles in this Reader belong to this type. The main varieties of non-experimental design in language and intercultural communication include a descriptive or exploratory survey using questionnaires or interviews (e.g. Hofstede's survey in Chapter 3), ethnography of communication (e.g. Katriel's study of Israeli Sabra culture in Chapter 10) and conversation and interactional analysis (e.g. Higgins' conversation analysis in Chapter 18). The advantages and disadvantages associated with non-experimental design are:

- Advantages:
    - can afford to sample a larger population;
    - can collect a large amount of data efficiently, hence can be more representative or in-depth.
- Disadvantages:
    - unable to establish the causal link between variables;
    - data can be difficult to process and analyse.

Longitudinal vs. cross-sectional vs. case study

Longitudinal study refers to studies in which data are collected from a small number of subjects over a period of time. Longitudinal studies are suitable for answering research questions that aim to explore changes and development over time or to evaluate the effectiveness of a training programme or the impact of an experience. The main advantages and disadvantages of longitudinal study design include:

- Advantages:
    - sensitive to sequential development and changes;
    - offers an opportunity to examine individual differences;

    −   allows for a large amount of data to be collected from every participant over time and hence provides detailed information.
- Disadvantages:
  - time-consuming;
  - vulnerable to participants' attrition;
  - subject to practice effect (the more times a participant is observed over the same task, the better or worse they would become) and inconsistency between each data collection.

Cross-sectional study design refers to the types of study in which data are collected at one point in time from a large number of subjects grouped together according to either age or other variables, such as length of stay in a new country. Cross-sectional studies can be used to explore the relationship between various variables: for example, the correlation between the degree of cultural appropriateness in use of the speech act of greeting and the length of stay in an English-speaking country; or to describe the developmental pattern of a particular feature or skill, such as development of intercultural communicative competence. The main advantages and disadvantages of this design are:

- Advantages:
  - a large quantity of data can be collected over a short period of time;
  - multiple subjects can be sampled and then be more representative;
  - relationships between variables can be established more clearly.
- Disadvantages:
  - not sensitive to developmental patterns and changes;
  - not sensitive to individual differences;
  - demand consistency in data collection from different subjects.

Case study design is an in-depth investigation of a single subject or a small group of subjects. It can be used to describe linguistic or communicative behaviour of an individual member of a group, to refute a generalisation as counter-evidence, or alternatively to show what is possible as positive evidence. The main advantages and disadvantages of this design are:

- Advantages:
  - providing rich and in-depth data;
  - allowing for close observation and intensive study.
- Disadvantages:
  - limitations in generalisability due to a small sample;
  - susceptible to practice effect, which occurs when subjects are asked to perform a similar task again in a longitudinal study;
  - demand on consistency between each data collection.

Longitudinal, cross-sectional and case study designs are not exclusive of each other. They are very often combined together in research projects. For example, both case study and cross-sectional study can be conducted longitudinally. In fact, a longitudinal case study is very common in studies of interlanguage pragmatics. The results from cross-sectional studies and longitudinal case studies complement each other. This is well demonstrated in Kasper and

Rose's proposal of the five-stages model of the developmental sequence of the speech act of request in English as a second language (L2) (Chapter 14). Kasper and Rose first base the five-stages model on the findings of two longitudinal studies and then look into a number of cross-sectional studies on L2 requests, which corroborate the validity of the model.

So far we have reviewed a number of study designs. The choice of a study design depends on considering the number of cultures concerned, the type of data to be collected, the conditions under which data are to be collected, the duration and the size of the population.

Data collection methods and techniques for non-interactional data

There are a number of data collection methods and techniques that are used to find out people's attitudes, opinions and behaviours regarding intercultural communication. This section reviews some of them, with a focus on collecting non-interactional data.

Questionnaires and surveys

Questionnaires collect data by asking people to respond to a set of predesigned questions. They are often used as part of a survey to collect descriptive and explanatory data about opinions, behaviours and attitudes. The data collected can be coded and analysed by computer. Questionnaires can be administered to a large number of people at multiple sites by a variety of means, ranging from the most common type, pencil-and-paper questionnaires, to telephone or face-to-face interviews, from postal to online survey. There are a number of web-based survey tools, such as *SurveyMonkey*, which can facilitate the distribution of questionnaires and data analysis.

The main advantage of questionnaires is that they can collect a large quantity of data within a short period of time, and it is relatively easy to analyse the answers quantitatively, provided the questions are set out in a clear and structured way. The weakness, however, is that questionnaires do not normally give room for in-depth exploration. A good questionnaire also takes time to develop.

There are a number of question types that can be used in a questionnaire. Open-ended questions (or open questions) give respondents the freedom to respond in their own way. They are easier to design and can be used in exploratory research. But they are difficult to analyse, because the answers tend to vary from one person to another. Multiple-choice questions ask

---

An example of a combined use of open-ended questions and multiple-choice questions (Source: INCA at www.incaproject.org/tools.htm)

- How many friends from abroad do you have?
- How many languages do you speak well?
- Where and how did you learn these languages?
- How often have you dealt with people from other countries in your professional life?
- Have you ever worked in a work group with members from various cultures?
- How often do you read books that are written in foreign languages?
- How often have you been abroad?

the respondents to choose one or several from a list of options. They are more difficult to design, as an informed prediction on the possible answers is required. However, they are easier and quicker to answer and therefore save time for the respondents. They are also suitable for quantitative analysis.

An example of a rating question (Source: Goodman, 1994, p. 45)

Cross-cultural awareness:

Please indicate the degree to which you would answer the questions listed below. There is no passing or failing answer. Please use the following scale, recording your score in the space before each question.

1 = definitely no   2 = not likely   3 = not sure   4 = likely   5 = definitely yes

___ 1   I can effectively conduct business in a language other than my native language.
___ 2   I can read and write a language other than my native language with great ease.
___ 3   I understand the proper protocol for conducting a business card exchange in at least two countries other than my own.

. . .

An example of ranking questions

Please number each of the qualities in a good leader listed below in order of importance to you. Number the most important 1, the next 2 and so on. If a quality has no importance at all, please leave blank.

Quality	Importance
Flexibility/adaptability	[ ]
Mindfulness	[ ]
Creativity	[ ]
Tolerance for differences	[ ]
Patience	[ ]
Vision	[ ]
Popularity	[ ]
Good listening skills	[ ]
Good communication skills	[ ]
A good role model	[ ]
Experience	[ ]

A variation of the multiple-choice question is a *rating question,* in which a rating device, such as the Likert-style rating scale, is used to record response. A respondent is asked how strongly she or he agrees or disagrees with a statement or series of statements, usually on a 4, 5, 6 or 7-point rating scale.

Similar to rating questions, *ranking questions* ask respondents to place things in a rank order to discover their relative importance to the respondent.

Standardised assessments

There are a number of standardised assessment tools in evaluating ICC. Most of the assessments, such as intercultural development inventory (Hammer *et al.,* 2003), take the form of multiple-item questionnaires, through which respondents are asked to rate various components of ICC.

An assessment tool that departs from the multiple-choice format is the Autobiography of Intercultural Encounters (AIE) designed for the Council of Europe. As a way to encourage intercultural learners to reflect critically on their own intercultural experience, AIE takes the form of a series of questions and prompts carefully designed to guide the learner's reflections on his or her intercultural encounters. It provides the learner with a structure to analyse an incident and consider what they have learnt from it. Two versions (one for older learners or adults and the other for younger learners or children who need help from adults with reading, writing and thinking back over their experience) are available at (www.coe.int/t/DG4/AUTOBIOGRAPHY).

INCA (Intercultural Competence Assessment) is a comprehensive assessment consisting of three different types of test, including questionnaires, scenarios and role plays, to test intercultural competence. More information can be found at the assessment website (www.incaproject.org/index.htm) or in Prechtl & Lund (2007). Information on other types of standardised instrument in the field of intercultural communication and related areas can be found in a comprehensive review by Spencer-Oatey & Franklin (2009, pp. 311–91).

Self-reports of critical incidents

The questions in AIE are essentially self-report of critical incidents, i.e. keeping notes of the incidents that are meaningful and noticeable in the format of journals or questionnaires. Self-report is a useful data collection method to capture incidents that are difficult to predict and observe. It also offers an opportunity to reflect on one's own behaviour. Spencer-Oatey (2002, reproduced in this Reader) uses this method to collect rapport-sensitive data. A copy of the record sheet can be found at the end of her article. The record sheet documents information on the context of the incident, such as setting, age, gender, nationality and relationship of the people involved, the incident itself and one's own reactions to the event. Spencer-Oatey & Franklin (2009, pp. 272–9) discuss the generic issues concerning self-report data.

Interviews and focus group interviews

An interview is a purposeful conversation conducted between the researcher and one or several interviewees, often with the aid of a set of predesigned questions. In a typical interview, the interviewer will lead the discussion by asking the questions. The interview is usually audio- or video-recorded and then transcribed for analysis. It is used to obtain information and find out opinions. In some studies, interviews can also be used as a means of eliciting interactional data (see below).

The main advantage of interviews, compared with written questionnaires, for example, is the degree of flexibility: an interviewer can decide on site whether to explore an issue further or to offer the interviewee an opportunity to elaborate. It is sensitive to individual differences, and the data are likely to be more in-depth. However, the interview and transcription processes can be very time-consuming. Therefore, interviews are more suitable for small-sample studies. Another disadvantage of interviews is the interviewer/interviewee relationship effect. The following factors very often have an impact on the responses:

- Who is doing the interview and who is being interviewed? Is the interviewer known to the interviewee beforehand?
- How is the interviewer presenting him/herself?
- What are the interviewer's expectations?
- Are there variations between interviewers or between sessions?

Focus group interviews involve interviewing a selection of people at the same time. The emphasis is on obtaining several perspectives about the same topic. It is often used at the preliminary or exploratory stages of a study to generate hypotheses for further research, to develop new ideas and creative concepts, or to diagnose the potential problems with a new programme, service or product. In recent years, a focus group is also used to explore the dynamic interdependences and co-construction effects whereby participants, very often occupying diverse and heterogeneous positions, mutually monitor each other's exchanges and co-construct meaning (see Markova *et al.*, 2005).

The interviewees are often carefully selected to represent different sectors of a community. Problems may arise when attempting to differentiate an individual's view from the group's view, as well as with the practical, logistical difficulties of conducting focus group interviews. The invited interviewees will all need to be at one location at the same time, rather than doing the interview at a place and time of the interviewee's choice. The interviewer (referred to as the *moderator* in focus group interview) plays a key role in moderating the group discussion. An example of focus group interview can be found in Nakane (2007), who uses both interviews and focus group interviews to find out the interviewees' opinions towards their own language use and practice in the classroom.

Ethnography and observation

It is probably true to say that no other research method has been used more in the study of language and culture than ethnography. As a research strategy, ethnography is used in a range of social sciences, particularly in anthropology and some branches of sociology. It is a holistic approach to human behaviour and social phenomena that are believed to be best understood in the fullest possible context. The best known example of the ethnographical approach to language and culture is Dell Hymes' SPEAKING model (1972), which laid the foundation for the so-called ethnography of communication.

The key idea behind the model and ethnography of communication is that, in order to use a language competently, one needs not only to learn its vocabulary and grammar, but also the context in which linguistic structures are used. The SPEAKING model consists of sixteen components that can be applied to many sorts of discourse: message form; message content; setting; scene; speaker/sender; addressor; hearer/receiver/audience; addressee; purposes (outcomes); purposes (goals); key; channels; forms of speech; norms of interaction; norms of interpretation; and genres. Hymes grouped the sixteen components within eight divisions:

- (S) setting and scene, both physical and psychological;
- (P) participants;
- (E) ends: purposes, goals and outcomes;
- (A) act sequence or form and order of the event;
- (K) key, i.e. tone, manner or spirit of the speech act;
- (I) instrumentalities or forms and styles of speech;
- (N) norms, including social rules governing the event and the participants' actions and reaction;
- (G) genre, or the kind of speech act or event.

Hymes' model and ethnography of communication generally have been used in a variety of empirical studies of intercultural communication in contexts such as the language classroom, health and medical communication, the courtroom, Internet and digital media. For advice on how to apply ethnography, see Saville-Troike (1989) and Madden (2010). Examples on applying ethnography to language learning and teaching can be found in Roberts et al. (2001) and Starfield (2010).

Ethnography requires rich data, often collected through a combination of different means including recordings, interviews and questionnaires. But the key data collection method for ethnography is *in situ* observation. Observation enables the investigator to describe events, actions, behaviours, language use, etc., in detail and to interpret what has happened in context. During observation, researchers make field notes of what they see in as much detail and as objectively as possible. There are different types of observation, depending on the researcher's role and visibility in the event under study. Researchers can either actively take part in observation and have maximum contact with the people being studied, or remain as unintrusive as possible. Katriel's monograph of *Talking straight: dugri speech in Israeli Sabra culture*, one chapter of which is reprinted in this Reader, is an example of an ethnographic study involving observation. Clyne et al.'s article (Chapter 19) provides an example of combining observation with recorded interactional data. Researchers can also collect interactional data through observation, and this will be discussed in the next section.

The main advantages of observation are that it allows the researcher to uncover information previously unknown, to gain an in-depth description and to capture a series of events and processes over time. The challenges of observation are several: researchers may have biases in selecting what to note down; it is difficult to differentiate describing from interpreting what has happened; documenting an event while observing and participating in activities can be a demanding task. Silverman (1993), Mack et al. (2005) and Denscombe (2005) offer practical advice on the techniques of taking field notes. Examples of how the researcher's perspective can make a difference to what is observed can be found in Creese et al. (2008).

Matched guise technique

The Matched guise technique (MGT) is an experimental data collection method that aims to investigate participants' language attitude. In a typical MGT, a recording is made with a number of different voices, all talking about the same subject matter with more or less the same content. Two of the voices are actually the *same person*, impersonating two different speakers (e.g. British and American English speakers). This is often done by an actor, to ensure that the guises are believable. Without being told about the speakers, participants are asked to rate the recording in terms of social attributes such as solidarity or status (how friendly, intelligent, rich etc.), purely on the basis of what they hear. Because MGT controls for voice quality, age, gender etc., the differences in the ratings (if any) would, in theory, reveal differences in the participants' attitudes towards different accents or languages being represented in the recording.

In rating the voices, a semantic differential scale is often used. Participants are asked to rate a number of pairs of opposite adjectives. An example of the semantic differential scale is provided in Wray & Bloomer (2006, p. 156).

Your impressions of voice A on the tape:								
Friendly	–	–	–	–	–	–	–	unfriendly
Unintelligent	–	–	–	–	–	–	–	intelligent
Inactive	–	–	–	–	–	–	–	active
Reliable	–	–	–	–	–	–	–	unreliable

Data collection methods and techniques for interactional data

Interactional data consist of a continuum with elicited conversation and naturally occurring conversation at either end, according to the degree of naturalness. Conversation can be elicited through a range of methods and techniques, such as discourse completion tasks, recall protocols or role play. The key issue for the interaction obtained through elicitation is its comparability with naturally occurring interaction. For naturally occurring conversation, the key issue is how to capture it (using observation sheet vs. audio-visual recording, for example) and how to strike the balance between details and analytical approach (interactional or conversation analysis). In addition to elicited and recorded conversation, conversation data are also available from a number of other sources, such as data bank, the Internet and other mass media. Some of the methods of collecting interactional data are discussed below.

Discourse completion task

A discourse completion task (DCT, sometimes also referred to as discourse completion test) elicits discourse data from participants by asking them to note down what they would say or how they would react in a given situation. This technique is very often used in comparing how the same speech act is realised in different contexts. An example can be found in Blum-Kulka

& Olshtain's study (Chapter 9), in which this technique is used to elicit the speech act of apology.

DCT has many advantages. It allows researchers to control certain variables, for example, the age or status of the speakers involved, and the location and the situational context of the speech act. A large amount of data can be collected within a short period without any need for transcription. It is easy to compare responses from people of different backgrounds, e.g. native vs. non-native speakers, men vs. women, the young vs. the elderly etc. To make the discourse data more 'naturalistic', researchers can provide more contextual information or orally administer DCT. The potential problem of this technique is that the data collected via DCT do not always correspond to natural data. What one *thinks* is said is not the same as what is actually said. It, at best, only reveals a participant's accumulated experience with language. Golato (2003) compares German speakers' compliment responses collected through DCT and those in natural conversation and finds that many DCT participants choose to accept the compliments with *danke* ('thank you'), whereas such an appreciation token is never found in naturally occurring data in her study.

Recall protocols

In recall protocols, participants are asked to recall the exact wording of a speech act to describe the context in which it has occurred. For example, Knapp *et al.* (1984) use this method in their study of the form and content of compliments and ask their participants to recall a recent compliment they have given or received. This method, similar to DCT, lacks comparability with naturally occurring conversation. Respondents may remember the propositional content of an utterance, but they may not be able to remember the precise form of utterance, which may be crucial for the analysis and interpretation.

Role play

Role play is widely used in research on interlanguage pragmatics. In role play, participants are asked to act out specified roles within a context, and the conversation is recorded for transcription later. There are two types of role play, i.e. open and closed role play, depending on how prescribed and standardised the course and the outcome of the interaction are, and how much freedom the participants are allowed in acting out. Compared with DCT and recall protocols, the conversation data collected through role play are relatively more comparable with naturally occurring conversation, because they are produced orally and more spontaneously. It is rich with features of naturalistic data such as hesitation, negotiation of turns and topic management and allows for control of variables such as power, distance, degree of imposition etc. For a review on the available studies that compare the data collected through DCT and role play, see Kasper (2008), Kasper & Rose (2002) and Golato (2003).

The main challenge of role play is that, though the conversation data collected through role play resemble naturally occurring data, they are not the same. Factors that contribute to the differences between naturally occurring conversation and role play data include: first, in role play, participants need to imagine the context and their roles, and therefore it is likely that they produce the conversation according to what they think should occur; second, what occurs in role play would not bear real-life consequences for participants, and this may impact on the content of the role play; and, third, role play is very often watched and recorded, and the presence of the audience and the recording equipment might impact on the acting. Kasper & Rose (2002, p. 87) list a few studies that use role play to collect conversation data on various speech acts such as request, complaint, apology, greeting, response to question, etc., and other discourse features such as gambits, routine formulae, pragmatic fluency, etc.

Observation sheets

Interactional data can also be collected through observation sheets. Informants are given an observation sheet in advance and asked to note down the sequence and content of an exchange or an event as faithfully as possible, as well as information about the time and location of the exchange, the participants (such as their age, gender, occupation, relationship etc.). For an example of an observation sheet, see Zhu Hua *et al.* (2000). This data collection method is particularly useful when it is difficult to make recordings of a particular speech event over a large sample of population. However, the interactional data documented by informants, usually after the event, at best represent what has been said, not how it was said. The data collected may be sufficient for the analysis of the sequence of the exchange and communication breakdown in broad terms, but not detailed and naturalistic enough for studies of the features of conversation such as hesitation, discourse makers, overlapping of turns etc.

Recorded, naturally occurring talk

Audio- or video-recording of naturally occurring conversation has been an important data collection method in the study of language in interaction in various fields. The process of recording is fairly straight-forward: seeking consent from the speakers; setting up equipment in advance before the recording; and transcribing conversation, following transcription conventions, after the recording (see Clemente (2008) for the advantages and procedures of recording). Technology changes are rapid; new equipment for recording conversational interaction becomes available all the time.

Recorded, naturally occurring talk is essential to any study that aims to investigate how an interaction is conducted and negotiated between speakers in detail. Depending on the research question and the analytical framework, the amount of detail in transcription varies, and one can spend a substantial amount of time processing the data. In transcription, various features of speech delivery, such as turn overlapping, length of pause in seconds, intonation, pitch, sound quality, etc., are noted using a variety of punctuation marks. For an example, see Nishizaka (Chapter 17) or Higgins (Chapter 18).

There are two main approaches in the analysis of naturally occurring talk in the study of language and intercultural communication. One is interactional sociolinguistics. As briefly discussed in the Introduction, interactional sociolinguistics is mainly concerned with interpreting misunderstandings in interaction in terms of differences in discourse strategies and styles among speakers of diverse cultural backgrounds. An example of interactional sociolinguistics can be found in Clyne *et al.* (Chapter 19) and Gumperz (1982). The other approach is conversation analysis, which studies how meaning is produced, interpreted and negotiated in conversation through an analysis of linguistic features such as sequential organisations, repairs and topic management, and extralinguistic features such as pause, intonation, eye gaze, etc. Conversation analysis differs from interactional sociolinguistics in its insistence that meaning is locally created through interaction and it therefore pays less attention to the speakers' backgrounds. It appeals to, and is well integrated into, the interculturality approach, which argues that cultural differences are constructed and negotiated through interaction (see the Introduction). For differences between conversation analysis and interactional analysis, see Hall (2002). For an example of applying different analytical approaches to the analysis of the same conversation, see Sarangi & Roberts (1999).

Data bank as a source of language in interaction data

There are now a number of corpora available that provide conversational data of multilingual speakers, learners of English or lingua franca speakers of English. The last section in the Resource list at the end of this Reader includes some of the major corpora. Most of the corpora are transcribed using a standard coding system. More information on the use of data banks and corpora can be found in Wray & Bloomer (2006), Backus (2008) and Stubbs (2004). Generally speaking, researchers use existing corpora for comparison with data that they have collected themselves, rather than conducting their research entirely on corpora that are constructed by other people. Corpora can be used as a major resource in teaching language and intercultural communication.

Other sources of language in interaction data

In addition to existing corpora, there are other sources of interaction data that are readily accessible. For example, a vast amount of video clips of speeches, interviews and live shows are available on YouTube, a video-sharing website. Television, radio, webcast and other media output are a useful source for political debates and speeches, court hearings, live shows etc. Online, real-time text chat rooms, which use typed messages, are a source for a hybrid of spoken, written and electronic discourse (Jepson, 2005). However, extra care should be taken with regard to copyright and ethical issues in accessing this type of interaction data. Some data might have been edited, and a decision needs to be made on the authenticity of the data and how to use them for analysis.

Ethical considerations

Research involving human subjects must be carried out in accordance with accepted ethical standards, and studies in language and intercultural communication are not an exception. The key considerations are:

(a) Justification: the proposed research will achieve worthwhile objectives and the time and resources needed for the research are justifiable. Participants' welfare and public responsibility are paramount. Where the project may potentially put the participants at risk, either physically or psychologically, care must be taken to ensure that the benefits of the project outweigh the risks. Appropriate support mechanisms need to be provided to minimise any potential risk. Where there is possible conflict of interest (e.g. the work is to be carried out in the same organisation or sponsored by an organisation), again a case must be made.

(b) Access to participant(s): this includes issues of participants' privacy, the need to reduce invasiveness of the presence of researchers, and issues of confidentiality and anonymity etc.

(c) Informed consent: when seeking consent, participants need to be fully informed about the aim and nature of the project and any potential risks. They should be made aware of their rights in the project, such as the right to withdraw anytime, the right to refuse to answer any question, the right to ask any question etc. With young and school-age children and vulnerable populations such as patients, consent must be sought from their parents, guardians, carers or schools (if the research is carried out on the school premises or with assistance from the school).

Other ethical concerns relevant to studies in language and intercultural communication include:

(d) Participants' language ability: whether participants' language ability is sufficient for them to understand the informed consent form.
(e) Cross-cultural differences in ethics: there may be differences in the ethical considerations between the culture in which the research is carried out and the culture from which participants come. This issue is particularly relevant to studies on study abroad and intercultural interactions. It is important to anticipate any potential differences and clarify any misunderstandings.

Most universities and institutes have an ethics committee that oversees ethical approval and a set of ethical approval procedures. Students must check with the procedure and seek approval before carrying out data collection. In addition, ethical guidelines are provided by some professional bodies or research journals. For example,

- *TESOL Quarterly* research guidelines are available at: www.tesol.org/s_tesol/seccss.asp? CID=476&DID=2150
- BERA (British Education Research Association) ethical guidelines are available at www.bera.ac.uk/ethics-and-educational-research-philosophical-perspectives/

Wray & Bloomer (2006) also provide useful information on the differences between confidentiality and anonymity and data protection laws.

Conclusion

This chapter reviews some of the key issues in conducting research projects on language and intercultural communication. It is important to remember that the study design and data collection methods are determined by the research questions, and not the other way round. Language and intercultural communication, being a very inter- and multidisciplinary field of enquiry, benefits from a variety of study designs and data collection methods. However, each design or method has its own strength and weakness, and may be more suitable for some types of research question than others. A good empirical study very often uses a mixed study design to maximise the strengths of the data collection methods and keep limitations to the minimum. When a mixed study design is not feasible, a nuanced interpretation of the research findings would help to reduce the risk of over generalisation.

References

Backus, A. (2008). Data banks and corpora. In Li Wei & M. Moyer (eds), *The Blackwell guide to research methods in bilingualism and multilingualism* (pp. 232–48). Malden, MA: Blackwell.

Berry, J. W. (1999). On the unity of the field of culture and psychology. In J. Adamopoulos & Y. Kashima (eds), *Social psychology and cultural* context (pp. 7–16). London: Sage.

Clemente, I. (2008). Recording audio and video. In Li Wei & M. Moyer (eds), *The Blackwell guide to research methods in bilingualism and multilingualism* (pp. 177–91). Malden, MA: Blackwell.

Creese, A., Bhatt, A., Bhojani, N. & Martin, P. (2008). Fieldnotes in team ethnography: researching complementary schools. *Qualitative Research*, 8(2), 197–215.

de Vaus, D. (2001). *Research design in social research*. London: Sage.

Denscombe, M. (2005). *The good research guide for small-scale social research projects* (2nd edn). Maidenhead: Open University Press.

Golato, A. (2003). Studying compliment responses: a comparison of DCTs and recordings of naturally occurring talk. *Applied Linguistics*, 24(1), 90–121.

Goodman, N. (1994). Cross-cultural training for the global executive. In R. Brislin & T. Yoshida (eds), *Improving intercultural interactions. Modules for cross-cultural training programmes* (pp. 34–54). Thousand Oaks: Sage.

Gumperz, J. (1982). *Discourse strategies*. Cambridge: Cambridge University Press.

Hall, J. K. (2002). *Teaching and researching language and culture* (pp. 125–98). London: Longman. (This book provides an introduction to general issues in researching language, culture and learning.)

Hammer, M. R. (2005). *Assessment of the Impact of the AFS Study Abroad Experience*. Retrieved from AFS Intercultural Programmes website: http://74.52.0.194/downloads/files/Educational-Results-Report-Final.pdf.

Hammer, M. R., Bennett, M. J. & Wiseman, R. L. (2003). Measuring intercultural sensitivity: the intercultural developmental inventory. *International Journal of Intercultural Relations*, 27, 421–43.

Hofstede, G. (2001). *Culture's consequences: international differences in work-related values* (2nd edn). Beverly Hills, CA: Sage.

Hymes, D. (1972). Toward ethnographies of communication. In P. P. Giglioli (ed.), *Language and social context* (pp. 21–44). Harmondsworth: Penguin.

Jepson, K. (2005). Conversations and negotiated interaction in text and voice chat rooms. *Language Learning & Technology*, 9(3), 79–98.

Kasper, G. (2008). Data collection in pragmatics research. In H. Spencer-Oatey (ed.), *Culturally speaking: culture, communication and politeness theory* (pp. 279–303). London: Continuum.

Kasper, G. & Rose, K. R. (2002). *Pragmatic development in a second language*. Malden, MA: Blackwell.

Knapp, M. L., Hopper, R. & Bell, R. A. (1984). Compliments: a descriptive taxonomy. *Journal of Communication*, 34(4), 12–32.

Li Wei (1996). Chinese language, culture and communication. A non-contrastive approach. *Journal of Asian Pacific Communication*, 7(3&4), 87–90.

Madden, R. (2010). *Being ethnographic: a guide to the theory and practice of ethnography*. Thousand Oaks: Sage.

Mack, N., Woodsong, C., MacQueen, K. M., Guest, G. & Namey, E. (2005). *Qualitative research methods: a data collector's field guide*. Research Triangle Park, North Carolina: Family Health International.

Markova, I., Linell, P., Grossen, M. & Salazar-Orvig, A. (2005). *Dialogue in focus groups: exploring socially shared knowledge*. London: Equinox.

Nakane, I. (2007). *Silence in intercultural communication: perceptions & performance*. Amsterdam: John Benjamins.

Prechtl, E. & Lund, A. D. (2007). Intercultural competence and assessment: perspectives from the INCA project. In H. Kotthoff & H. Spencer-Oatey (eds), *Handbook of intercultural communication* (pp. 467–90). Berlin: Mouton.

Roberts, C., Byram, M., Barro, A., Jordan, S. & Street, B. (2001). *Language learners as ethnographers*. Clevedon: Multilingual Matters.

Sarangi, S. & Roberts, C. (1999). *Talk, work and institutional order: discourse in medical, mediation, and management settings*. Berlin: Mouton de Gruyter.

Saville-Troike, M. (1989). *The ethnography of communication: an introduction* (2nd edn). Oxford: Blackwell.

Silverman, D. (1993). *Interpreting qualitative data. Methods for analysing talk, text and interaction*. London: Sage.

Spencer-Oatey, H. & Franklin, P. (2009). *Intercultural interaction. A multidisciplinary approach to intercultural communication*. Basingstoke: Palgrave.

Starfield, S. (2010). Ethnographies. In B. Paltridge & A. Phakiti (eds), *Continuum companion to research methods in applied linguistics* (pp. 50–65). London: Continuum.

Stubbs, M. (2004). Language corpora. In A. Davies & C. Elder (eds), *Handbook of applied linguistics* (pp. 106–32). Malden, MA: Blackwell.

Wierzbicka, A. (1997). *Understanding cultures through their key words*. Oxford: Oxford University Press.

Wierzbicka, A. (2003). *Cross-cultural pragmatics: the semantics of human interaction* (2nd edn). Berlin: Mouton de Gruyter.

Wray, A. & Bloomer, A. (2006). *Projects in linguistics. A practical guide to researching language*. London: Hodder Arnold.

Zhu Hua, Li Wei & Qian Yuan (2000). The sequential organisation of gift offering and acceptance in Chinese. *Journal of Pragmatics*, 32(1), 81–103.

CONCLUSION: NOTES FOR STUDENTS AND INSTRUCTORS

Study questions

1   What is a study design? Can you give as many types of study design as you can? What are the main features of each study design? What kinds of research question is it suitable for?
2   What are the main data collection methods for studying people's attitudes, opinions, experiences or language use in intercultural contexts? What are their main features?
3   What are the main data collection methods for interaction data? What are the main features of these methods?

Study activities

Select an empirical study published in a journal article and discuss the research questions, the research design and data collection methods used in the study. In your opinion, is the study well-designed, and why? Are there limitations in the study, and how does the author address any limitations?

Further reading

The following are some generic research skills guides and textbooks:

Denscombe, M. (2005). *The good research guide for small-scale social research projects* (2nd edn). Maidenhead: Open University Press. (This book contains three parts, including strategies for social research, methods of social research and analysis, and is suitable for beginners.)
Silverman, D. (1993). *Interpreting qualitative data. Methods for analysing talk, text and interaction*. London: Sage. (This book focuses on qualitative research design suitable for the study of talk, text and interaction.)
Muijs, D. (2004). *Doing quantitative research in education*. London: Sage. (This book offers a clear and jargon-free guide to the conduct of quantitative research and analysis of quantitative data.)

Other more discipline-specific but equally recommendable research method books are:

Wray, A. & Bloomer, A. (2006). *Projects in linguistics. A practical guide to researching language*. London: Hodder Arnold. (A special feature of this book is its over 300 practical project ideas.)

Li Wei & Moyer, M. (eds), *The Blackwell guide to research methods in bilingualism and multilingualism.* Malden, MA: Blackwell. (This book is a comprehensive guide to research methods and approaches in bilingualism.)

Hall, J. K. (2002). *Teaching and researching language and culture* (pp. 125–98). London: Longman. (This book provides an introduction to general issues in researching language, culture and learning.)

Saunders, M., Lewis, P. & Thornhill, A. (2007). *Research methods for business students.* Essex: Prentice Hall. (This book is an essential guide to researching business. The companion website provides additional learning materials at www.pearsoned.co.uk/saunders.)

Shiraev, E. & Levy, D. (2004). *Cross-cultural psychology: critical thinking and contemporary applications.* Boston: Pearson. (This book, as its title suggests, critically reviews the practice and methodology in cross-cultural psychology. It is suitable for advanced level and experienced researchers.)

Paltridge, B. & Phakiti, A. (eds) (2010). *Continuum companion to research methods in applied linguistics.* London: Continuum. (This book is designed to be the essential resource for students in applied linguistics. It contains overviews on research methods and techniques as well as areas of research.)

Resource list

Key textbooks

Bowe, H. & Martin, K. (2007). *Communication across cultures*. Cambridge: Cambridge University Press.

The book provides an introduction to linguistic issues that either result from or impact on cultural differences. It is written primarily from a cross-cultural comparison perspective.

Jandt, F. E. (2010). *An introduction to intercultural communication: identities in a global community* (6th edn). Thousand Oaks: Sage.

An introductory textbook covering a wide range of issues in communication and culture. There is a wealth of examples, case studies and cultural features to aid classroom use. The book has various editions. There is an accompanying reader, *Intercultural communication: a global reader,* by the same author.

Holliday, A., Hyde, M. & Kullman, J. (2004). *Intercultural communication: an advanced resource book*. London: Routledge.

A resource book written from a cultural studies perspective. It is built around three themes – identity, otherisation and representation – and follows the format of a three-tiered discussion, from introduction to extension and exploration, with essential readings.

Kotthoff, H. & Spencer-Oatey, H. (eds) (2007). *Handbook of intercultural communication.* Berlin: Mouton.

A handbook covering various issues and aspects of intercultural communication.

Neuliep, J. (2009). *Intercultural communication: a contextual approach* (4th edn). Thousand Oaks: Sage.

An intermediate-level textbook on the general issues of intercultural communication. Using a contextual model, the book brings together various factors of intercultural communication and illustrates how these factors interact with each other.

Samovar, L. A., Porter, R. E. & McDaniel, E. R. (2006). *Communication between cultures* (6th edn). Belmont: Wadsworth.

An intermediate-level textbook providing an overview of the issues and theories in intercultural communication.

Scollon, R. & Scollon, S. W. (2001). *Intercultural communication*. Malden, Massachusetts: Blackwell.

A research monograph written from a discourse analysis perspective, with a specific focus on the discourse of East Asians, especially Chinese.

Key book series

Pragmatics & Beyond New Series, published by John Benjamins and edited by Andreas Jucker.
Language for Intercultural Communication and Education, published by Multilingual Matters and edited by Michael Byram and Alison Phipps.
International and Intercultural Communication Annual, published by Sage. With the first volume published in 1983, it is the earliest and longest series on intercultural communication.
Intercultural Press has published many books on intercultural communication, including practical guides and videos for intercultural training and learning.

Key journals

Journal of Pragmatics (Elsevier) is a long-established international journal published monthly. Pragmatics is defined broadly as language use in context. Many frequently cited articles on language and intercultural communication have appeared in this journal.
Multilingua (Mouton) is a journal dedicated to cross-cultural and interlanguage communication.
Language and Intercultural Communication (Routledge) publishes articles that investigate the intercultural dimension of language learning and teaching and the implications of linguistic and intercultural issues for workplaces.
Intercultural Pragmatics (Mouton) publishes theoretical and applied pragmatics research from an intercultural perspective.
Pragmatics (quarterly publication of International Pragmatics Association, IPrA) publishes on a spectrum of subfields and disciplines in pragmatics.

The following journals very often publish articles on intercultural communication:

- *Applied Linguistics*
- *Business Communication Quarterly*
- *Communication Monographs*
- *Communication Reports*
- *Communication Studies*
- *Cross-Cultural Management: An International Journal*
- *Cross-Cultural Psychology Bulletin*
- *Cross-Cultural Research*
- *Discourse and Society*
- *Discourse Processes*
- *Discourse Studies*
- *ELT Journal*
- *European Journal of Cross-Cultural Competence and Management*
- *Howard Journal of Communications*
- *Human Communication Research*
- *Intercultural Education*
- *International Journal of Applied Linguistics*
- *International Journal of Cross-Cultural Management*

- *International Journal of Cross-cultural Research*
- *International Journal of Intercultural Relations*
- *International Journal of Multicultural Education*
- *International Journal on Multicultural Societies*
- *Journal of Asia-Pacific Communication*
- *Journal of Communication*
- *Journal of Cross-Cultural Psychology*
- *Journal of Intercultural Communication* (free online)
- *Journal of Intercultural Communication Research*
- *Journal of International and Intercultural Communication*
- *Journal of International Business Studies*
- *Journal of International Management*
- *Journal of Language and Social Psychology*
- *Journal of Multicultural Counselling and Development*
- *Journal of Multicultural Discourses*
- *Journal of Multilingual and Multicultural development*
- *Journal of Politeness Research*
- *Language and Communication*
- *Language in Society*
- *Language, Culture and Curriculum*
- *Language, Learning & Technology*
- *Research on Language and Social Interaction*
- *TESOL Quarterly*
- *Text*
- *Text and Talk*
- *The Journal of Business Communication*
- *Western Journal of Communication*

Websites, electronic mailing lists and other resources

Dialogin (The Delta Intercultural Academy)
www.dialogin.com
A networking site and information portal for intercultural trainers and students.

Intercultural-crosscultural-communication.com
www.intercultural-crosscultural-communication.com
Provides a directory of intercultural trainers.

Intercultural Communication and Translation News
www.kwintessential.co.uk/cross-cultural/intercultural-communication-translation-news/2009/11
Publishes intercultural news or anecdotes.

Kwintessential
www.kwintessential.co.uk
An information portal on intercultural communication, translation, interpreting and multilingual design.

Emerald

www.emeraldinsight.com/Insight/menuNavigation.do?hdAction=InsightHome

A publisher specialised in research in management. The website provides learning and teaching resources in management (such as interviews with experts, case studies etc.), conference information and research networking facilities.

Global people

www.globalpeople.org.uk

The website provides resources on research and a toolkit on the effectiveness of working across cultures.

Intercultural dialogue and Council of Europe

www.coe.int/t/dg4/intercultural/default_en.asp

The website highlights the activities of the Council of Europe, in particular, policies and practices to promote intercultural dialogue within Europe and between Europe and its neighbouring regions. Some examples of good practice are available.

Intercultural insights

http://finance.groups.yahoo.com/group/interculturalinsights

A networking and discussion website on intercultural business, training, education, and research and consultation, supported by Yahoo Group.

Global Excellence

www.global-excellence.com

A cross-cultural and global mobility services provider. The website hosts resources on cross-cultural coaching and training as well as cultural quizzes.

Inter/cross-cultural communication professional bodies and organisations

SIETAR (Society for Intercultural Education, Training and Research)

www.sietar.org

One of the world's largest interdisciplinary networks for professionals working in the intercultural field. Its purpose is to encourage the development and application of knowledge, values and skills and to develop effective intercultural and interethnic relationships at individual, group, organisation and community levels.

SCCR (Society for Cross-Cultural Research)

An interdisciplinary organisation for scholars from a wide variety of approaches to cross-cultural and comparative research. Its official journal, *Cross-cultural Research,* is published by Sage.

IPrA (International Pragmatics Association)

http://ipra.ua.ac.be

An international organisation dedicated to the study of language use. Established in 1986, it now has over 1,200 members in more than 60 countries worldwide. It publishes a quarterly journal, *Pragmatics,* and organises a conference biannually. Intercultural communication research is well represented both in the journal and at the conference.

International Association of Language and Intercultural Communication
www3.unileon.es/grupos/ialic/index.html
A forum for academics, practitioners, researchers and students who are interested in the interplay between language and intercultural communication. Its official journal, *Language and Intercultural Communication*, is published by Routledge.

International Society for Language Studies
www.isls-inc.org
An interdisciplinary association of scholars who investigate language in historical, political, social and cultural contexts. Its official journal, *Critical Inquiry in Language Studies: an International Journal* (CILS), is published by Routledge.

TESOL
www.tesol.org
An international professional organisation of language teachers and educators. Its mission is to develop and maintain professional expertise in English language teaching and learning for speakers of other languages worldwide. There is an intercultural communication interest group within TESOL.

AILA (International Association of Applied Linguistics / Association International de Linguistique Appliquée)
www.aila.info
A professional body for applied linguists. It runs several research networks and organises a world congress every three years. It promotes coordination among its regional affiliates through activities and networks such as the Network of European Applied Linguists (AILA-Europe). It publishes an academic journal, *AILA review,* and a book series called AILA Applied Linguistics Series (AALS), published by John Benjamins.

AAAL (American Association for Applied Linguistics)
www.aaal.org
US affiliate of the International Association for Applied Linguistics (AILA). Its official journal is *Annual Review of Applied Linguistics,* published by Cambridge University Press.

BAAL (British Association of Applied Linguistics)
www.baal.org.uk
UK affiliate of the International Association for Applied Linguistics (AILA). In collaboration with Cambridge University Press, it sponsors BAAL-CUP seminars.

NIC (Nordic Network of Intercultural Communication)
www.ling.gu.se/projekt/nic
The purpose of NIC is to promote cooperation in the Nordic countries (including the Baltic countries) between researchers and practitioners interested in intercultural communication. The main activities supported by NIC are the annual conferences on intercultural communication. The conferences are open to scholars and practitioners throughout the world.

IACCP (International Association for Cross-Cultural Psychology)

www.iaccp.org

Founded in 1972, it has a membership of over 800 in more than 65 countries. Its aim is to facilitate communication among persons interested in a diverse range of issues involving the intersection of culture and psychology. IACCP is affiliated with the International Union of Psychological Science (IUPsyS).

NCA (National Communication Association)

www.natcom.org

Formerly known as the Speech Communication Association, it is a major professional association for Communication Study.

ICA (International Communication Association)

www.icahdq.org

A major professional association for communication study, it has an intercultural communication division and interest group that promotes research and studies in intercultural communication.

WCA (World Communication Association)

http://wcaweb.org

A major professional association for communication study, it publishes the *Journal of Intercultural Communication Research*.

IAIE (International Association for Intercultural Education)

www.iaie.org

An international association for professional educators interested in intercultural education, multicultural education, anti-racist education, human rights education, conflict-resolution, multilingualism issues, etc. It publishes an academic journal, *Intercultural Education*.

IAIR (International Academy for Intercultural Research)

www.interculturalacademy.org/index.html

A professional association dedicated to research in intercultural relations. Its official journal is the *International Journal of Intercultural Relations*.

Two websites that contain guidelines on research ethics:

TESOL Quarterly Research Guidelines

www.tesol.org/s_tesol/seccss.asp?CID=476&DID=2150

BERA (British Education Research Association) ethic guidelines

www.bera.ac.uk/ethics-and-educational-research-philosophical-perspectives

Corpus

General Corpus

Interculture project database: student accounts of Residence Abroad

www.lancs.ac.uk/users/interculture/index.htm

A good collection of students' account about their experiences during study broad gathered from diaries and through interviews.

Talk bank

http://talkbank.org

An interdisciplinary project, containing a number of sample databases within each of the subfields of communication, such as aphasiabank, CHILDES, BilingBank, CABank, DementiaBank and PhonBank. Its primary aim is to set up a system for sharing and studying conversational interactions.

CHILDES

http://childes.psy.cmu.edu

The child language component of the TalkBank system. It contains transcript and media data collected from conversations between young children and their playmates and caretakers.

Bank of English

www.titania.bham.ac.uk/docs/svenguide.html#Getting%20Connected

A corpus collected at the University of Birmingham, currently containing a 450-million-word corpus of present-day English and a subcorpus aimed at teaching consisting of 56 million words. The COBUILD series of dictionaries and grammars is built on this corpus.

British National Corpus

http://corpus.byu.edu/bnc

A corpus collected by Oxford University Press, Longman, Chambers, the British Library and the Universities of Oxford and Lancaster. It contains both spoken and written British English.

The Corpus of Contemporary American English (COCA)

www.americancorpus.org

The largest corpus of American English. It contains over 400 million words.

Language learner and Lingua Franca corpus

Cambridge Learner Corpus (CLC)

www.cambridge.org/elt/corpus/learner_corpus2.htm

As part of the Cambridge International Corpus, CLC has been compiled by Cambridge University Press and Cambridge ESOL. It contains a large collection of examples of English writing from anonymised exam scripts written by students taking Cambridge ESOL English exams around the world. It currently contains over 30 million words from over 95,000 students, speaking 130 different first languages.

Cambridge International Corpus (CIC)

www.cambridge.org/elt/corpus/international_corpus.htm

A very large collection of English texts, compiled by Cambridge University Press over the last ten years, with the primary purpose for writing language textbooks for learners of English. It has a number of subsets of corpora on spoken English in the UK and in North America, business English, legal English, financial and academic English.

Longman Corpus Network

www.pearsonlongman.com/dictionaries/corpus/index.html

A database of 330 million words from a wide range of real-life sources, such as books, newspapers and magazines. Longman dictionaries are compiled using the database.

International Corpus of Learners' English

http://cecl.fltr.ucl.ac.be/Cecl-Projects/Icle/icle.htm

One of the first learners' English corpora, currently containing over 3 million words of writing by learners of English from twenty-one different language backgrounds.

French Learner Language Oral Corpora

www.flloc.soton.ac.uk

A comprehensive list of French learner corpora, including Linguistic Development Corpus, Progression Corpus, Salford Corpus, Brussels Corpus, Reading Corpus, Newcastle Corpus, UEA Corpus, etc.

English as a Lingua Franca in Academic Settings (ELFA)

www.uta.fi/laitokset/kielet/engf/research/elfa

A joint research project between University of Tampere and University of Helsinki in Finland. The project has compiled a corpus of spoken academic English in intercultural contexts.

Vienna–Oxford International Corpus of English (VOICE)

www.univie.ac.at/voice/page/index.php

A database containing 1 million words of spoken ELF interactions among speakers from fifty different first languages (mainly, though not exclusively, European languages).

Michigan Corpus of Academic Spoken English (MICASE)

http://micase.elicorpora.info

A collection of nearly 1.8 million words of transcribed speech (almost 200 hours of recordings) at the University of Michigan in Ann Arbor. It contains data from a wide range of speech events, such as lectures, classroom discussions, lab sections, seminars and advisory sessions and locations across the university.

Glossary

Acculturation the process whereby someone new to a culture learns to adapt to the host culture.

Address terms terms used by speakers to address each other or to refer to other people.

Adjacency pairs a unit of conversation that contains two utterances by two speakers, one after the other. The two utterances are functionally related to each other, and the first utterance requires a certain type of second utterance.

Affective style of communication a communication style in which speakers are primarily concerned with developing and maintaining social relationships, rather than the goal or outcome of communication (cf. instrumental style of communication).

Anxiety/Uncertainty management (AUM) theory the theory developed by Gudykunst (2005, *Theorizing about intercultural communication.* Thousand Oaks, CA: Sage) to explain and improve interpersonal and intergroup communication effectiveness by using uncertainty and anxiety reduction.

Assimilation the process whereby someone new to a culture becomes integrated into the host culture.

Autobiography of Intercultural Encounters (AIE) an assessment tool of intercultural communicative competence that takes the form of a series of questions and prompts designed to guide the learner's reflections on his or her intercultural encounters.

Back-channelling a conversational behaviour showing that one is following the conversation, such as the use of interjections ('uh-huh', 'mm') in English.

Back-translation a method of checking the reliability of a translation by translating from one language to another and then translating back into the original.

Biculturalism the state in which an individual has successfully integrated skills and norms from another culture.

Bilingual speaker a speaker who can use two languages in interaction.

CCSARP (Cross-cultural speech act realisation patterns) project the project set up by a team of experts, including Shoshana Blum-Kulka, Julianne House and Gabriele Kasper etc., to investigate cross-cultural and sociolinguistic variations in two speech acts, requests and apologies.

Chronemics   the study of how people structure, interpret and perceive time and the subsequent impact on the way they communicate.

Co-construction   the joint creation of meaning or identity between individuals.

Co-culture   the term to describe the coexistence of cultural groups.

Collectivism   a cultural orientation that promotes interdependence between members of groups and emphasises priority of group goals over those of individuals.

Communication breakdown   difficulty with communication due to misunderstanding, non-understanding or problems with the channel of communication.

Communication style   the way individuals or a group of individuals communicate with others.

Communicative effectiveness   the degree to which people achieve their communicative goals.

Community of practice   a group that shares a common identity and comes together for shared purposes.

Conflict management   the knowledge, skills and actions to identify, handle and solve conflict.

Contact theory   the theory put forward by Allport (1954, *The nature of prejudice*. Reading, MA: Addison-Wesley) which specifies four conditions for optimal intergroup contact: equal group status within the situation, common goals, intergroup cooperation and authority support.

Conversation analysis   an approach to studying natural conversation. It involves a close examination of participants' turn-taking, sequences, identifying and repairing problems, etc.

Cooperative principle   a term used by Grice (1975, in P. Cole & J. Morgan (eds), *Syntax and semantics 3: Speech acts* (pp. 41–58). New York: Academic Press) to describe the principles guiding the conversation participants, such as cooperative efforts, on how much, when and how to contribute to the conversation.

Corporate culture   the set of values, goals and priorities shared by, and encouraged through, the policies and procedures of an organisation.

Critical discourse analysis   a discourse analytical approach that is primarily concerned with the relationship between language use and power and ideologies.

Cross-cultural communication   studies that compare patterns of communication in different cultures.

Cross-cultural pragmatics   studies that compare patterns of language use, in particular, speech acts, in different cultures.

Cultural artefact   thing that represents a culture significantly and meaningfully.

Cultural dimensions   a term to refer to the key features or characteristics that differentiate various cultural groups.

Cultural fundamentalism   the view that people have innate cultural traits.

Cultural iceberg model   an analogy of what culture is by comparing visible and invisible aspects of culture, as well as the interrelationship between these two parts, to an iceberg.

Cultural identity   one's sense of belonging to a culture.

Cultural key words   words that describe the main characteristics of a culture.

Cultural norms   the collective expectations shared by a cultural group on what constitutes proper or improper behaviour in a context.

Cultural onion model   an analogy of what culture is by comparing the various internal levels and layers of culture to those of an onion.

Cultural pluralism   an ideology that calls for cultural groups to maintain separate and distinct entities.

Cultural relativism the principle that one's beliefs and behaviours must be understood in the context of one's own culture.

Cultural representation a set of meanings, beliefs, intentions, etc., shared by a cultural group.

Cultural schema one's knowledge about one's cultural experiences or expectations towards other cultures.

Cultural script a term used by Anna Wierzbicka and her colleagues (2004, reprinted in this Reader, see Chapter 8) to refer to the way of formulating cultural norms, values and practices using a clear, precise metalanguage.

Cultural values shared assumptions or beliefs about how things are, or ought to be, in the group.

Culture adaptation the process whereby one adjusts one's behaviour to meet the needs of the host culture.

Culture shock negative reaction, such as a feeling of anxiety or loss, experienced by some people when living in a new culture.

Cultures within a culture a phrase to describe the fact that there are many smaller cultures within a dominant culture.

Culturism the practice whereby members of a group are reduced to the predefined characteristics of a cultural label.

Diaspora a general term to refer to people who disperse from their home countries and become residents in areas often foreign and distant to their close relations.

Direct speech act the type of speech act in which the speaker communicates the literal meaning that the words conventionally express.

Direct style of communication a communication style in which overt expression of intention is preferred (cf. indirect style of communication).

Discourse analysis a general term for a number of approaches to study spoken or written discourse.

Discourse completion task a data collection method whereby participants are asked to write down what they are going to say in a specific context.

Discursive practice the process by which meanings, as well as participants' sociocultural identities, are created and negotiated through discourse.

Dugri style of communication a communication style of straight talk, originally found among Israelis. *Dugri*, originating from Turkish, means 'straightforward, direct'.

Elaborated code a speech system in which there are a variety of linguistic options as to what speakers can say or do, verbally and explicitly (cf. restricted code).

Emergent view a view that treats cultural difference as something that comes into existence through interaction rather than something given.

Emic an approach in studies of human behaviour across cultures whereby a researcher uses local cultural terms to interpret a cultural phenomenon.

Essentialist view of culture an approach that believes that people from a cultural group share the same characteristics, and misunderstanding in intercultural interactions can largely, if not completely, be attributed to group differences.

Ethnic identity one's sense of belonging to an ethnic group.

Ethnocentrism the belief that the views and practices of one's own group are much more important or correct than those of any other groups.

Ethnography of speaking the field of study that is concerned with the way speech communities communicate.

Ethnography the field of study in which a researcher employs field work or observation to describe the practice of a group.

Etic an approach in studies of human behaviour across cultures that involves comparing one culture with another using culture-general constructs.

Experiential learning the learning-by-doing approach proposed by Kolb in his book, *Experiential learning: experience as the source of learning and development* (1984, New York: Prentice Hall).

Face a term used in politeness theory to refer to the public self-image a person affectively claims for himself.

Face-negotiating theory the theory proposed by Stella Ting-Toomey (1988, Intercultural conflicts: a face-negotiation theory. In Y. Kim & W. Gudykunst (eds), *Theories in intercultural communication* (pp. 213–35). Newbury Park, CA: Sage) to explain face concerns, conflict styles and facework behaviour.

Face-threatening acts a term used in politeness theory to refer to acts that challenge the face want of conversation participants.

Facework the communicative strategies to manage one's own and others' face wants.

Femininity a cultural orientation in which caring and nurturing behaviours are preferred.

Grice's maxims the four maxims proposed by Grice in his article 'Logic and Conversation' (1975, in P. Cole & J. Morgan (eds) *Syntax and semantics 3: Speech acts* (pp. 41–58). New York: Academic Press) as part of the Cooperative Principle. It includes the Maxim of Quantity, Maxim of Quality, Maxim of Relation and Maxim of Manner.

Haptics the study of the meaning and functions of the behaviour of touching.

High context a communication style in which speakers rely on factors such as setting or shared knowledge, rather than explicit speech, to convey their messages (cf. low context)

High involvement a conversational style in which speakers demonstrate one or several of the following features: a faster rate of speech, faster turn-taking, avoidance of inter-turn silence, collaborative overlap, participatory listenership etc.

High-power-distance a cultural orientation in which differences in power and status are accepted and respected in communication.

High uncertainty avoidance a cultural orientation in which people try to avoid uncertainty and ambiguity in communication and practice.

High-contact cultures a cultural orientation in which individuals interact in closer proximity to each other, such as more eye contact, more touching.

Hofstede's value dimensions the model proposed by Geert Hofstede in his book *Culture's consequences: comparing values, behaviours, institutions and organisations across nations* (first in 1980 and then updated in 2001, Thousand Oaks, CA: Sage) to differentiate between various cultures. It includes individualism vs. collectivism, high vs. low uncertainty avoidance, high vs. low power distance, masculinity vs. femininity and long-term vs. short term orientation.

Honorifics affixes, words and formulaic phrases that show the speaker's respect when addressing or referring to other people.

Horizontal collectivism a cultural orientation that emphasises and promotes interdependence between members of groups and assigns equal status to all the group members (cf. vertical collectivism).

Horizontal individualism a cultural orientation that emphasises personal independence within a group and assigns equal status to all the group members (cf. vertical individualism).

Indirect speech act the type of speech act in which the speaker communicates a different meaning from the apparent surface meeting.

Indirect style of communication a communication style in which speakers' intentions are implicit (cf. direct style of communication).

Individualism a cultural orientation that emphasises personal independence and the priority of an individual's goal over that of the group.

Ingroup the group to which one feels emotionally close and a sense of belonging (cf. outgroup).

Instrumental style of communication a communication style in which speakers are primarily concerned with the goal and outcome of the communication (cf. affective style of communication).

Intercultural awareness knowledge or understanding of cultural norms and differences.

Intercultural communication a situation where people from different cultural backgrounds come into contact with each other; or a subject of study that is concerned with interactions among people of different cultural and ethnic groups and comparative studies of communication patterns across cultures.

Intercultural conflict a type of conflict in which one's cultural membership becomes a factor in how conflict is perceived, managed and resolved.

Intercultural mindfulness one's awareness and sensitivity towards intercultural differences.

Intercultural sensitivity the ability to understand, appreciate and accept cultural differences.

Interculturality a process whereby people from different cultures interact with each other; or a research paradigm in which cultural differences are studied as a social phenomenon and discursive practice rather than something given.

Interlanguage pragmatics the study of the development of pragmatic knowledge and skills by non-native speakers.

Internationalisation the process of incorporating an international perspective into activities and practices.

Kinesics the study of posture, body movement, gestures and facial expressions.

Language socialisation the dual process of learning to speak the language in a way appropriate to the community and adapting to the beliefs and norms associated with speaking that language.

Lingua franca communication the type of communication in which at least one conversation participant interacts in his or her non-native language.

Linguistic determinism a version of the Sapir–Whorf hypothesis of the relationship between language and culture that speculates that language structure controls thought and cultural norms (cf. linguistic relativity).

Linguistic relativity a version of the Sapir–Whorf hypothesis of the relationship between language and culture that argues that thought is influenced by language, and at the same time it also influences language (cf. linguistic determinism).

Long-term orientation a cultural orientation that focuses on traditions (cf. short-term orientation).

Low context a communication style in which speakers rely on explicit speech rather than setting, shared knowledge etc. to convey their messages (cf. high context).

Low uncertainty avoidance a cultural orientation in which people accept uncertainty and ambiguity.

Macroculture a term to refer to the higher-level or dominant culture (cf. microculture).

Masculinity   a cultural orientation in which ambition, achievement, money and signs of manliness are favoured.

Matched guise technique   a research method whereby participants are asked to rate speakers on various traits after listening to different recordings of the same speakers. This method is very often used to investigate participants' intergroup attitude.

Microculture   a term to refer to the smaller cultural units within a larger culture (cf. macroculture).

Monochronic time   a cultural orientation in which people prefer one thing at one time.

Multiculturalism   the state in which various cultures co-exist and complement each other.

Natural semantic metalanguage (NSM)   the approach developed by Anna Wierzbicka and her colleagues (2002, C. Goddard & A. Wierzbicka (eds), *Meaning and universal grammar: theory and empirical findings* (2 volumes). Amsterdam/Philadelphia: John Benjamins) to describe a culturally salient event or act in simple, clear words which are universal in meaning across languages.

Negative face   a term in Brown and Levinson's politeness theory (1987, *Politeness: some universals of language use.* Cambridge: Cambridge University Press) to refer to the desire to be unimpeded in one's actions.

Nonverbal communication   a way of communicating using nonverbal stimuli either intentionally or unintentionally. It includes body movement (such as posture, gestures, facial expressions etc.), paralanguage, personal space, silence etc.

Norms of interaction   rules of interaction regarding appropriateness and effectiveness in communication shared by members of a community.

Norms   rules or expectations of behaviour or practices shared by a group.

Olfactics   the study of smell and scent and their associated meetings.

Outgroup   a group to which one feels no emotional ties or sense of belonging (cf. ingroup).

Paralanguage   the nonverbal element of speech such as volume, pitch, rhythm, laughing, crying, etc., used to complement or modify the verbal message and convey emotion.

Participant observation   a data collection method in which the researcher observes practices of an activity while being a participant.

Politeness theory   the study of linguistic behaviours that address each other's face wants in conversation, proposed first by Brown & Levinson (1987, *Politeness: some universals of language use.* Cambridge: Cambridge University Press).

Polychromic time   a cultural orientation in which people prefer multitasking.

Positive face   a term used in Brown and Levinson's politeness theory (1987, *Politeness: some universals of language use.* Cambridge: Cambridge University Press) to refer to the desire to be approved of.

Pragmatics   the study of language use in context. It covers topics such as conversation implicature, speech act, conversation structure etc.

Prejudice   an individual's negative feelings and predispositions towards outgroup members.

Proxemics   the study of personal space.

Racism   negative feelings towards other ethnic groups.

Rapport management   an approach proposed by Spencer-Oatey (2000, *Culturally speaking: managing rapport through talk across cultures.* London: Continuum) to take motivational concerns of participants, such as face wants and rapport building, into account in interpreting interactions.

Re-entry shock   the anxiety and negative feelings experienced by individuals when they return to their native cultures.

Reification the process of imagining something to be real when it is not.

Restricted code a speech system in which there are a limited number of linguistics options as to what speakers can say or do verbally owing to the restriction of the social system, such as status orientation (cf. elaborated code).

Sapir–Whorf hypothesis Sapir and Whorf's observations on the interrelationship between language and culture, which were interpreted later as either linguistic relativity or linguistic determinism.

Schwarz's value orientations the classification scheme of human values shared across cultures proposed by Shalom Schwarz (1992, Universals in the content and structure of values: theoretical advances and empirical tests in 20 countries. In M. Zanna (ed.), *Advances in experimental social psychology*, Vol. 25 (pp. 1–65). New York: Academic Press). It includes benevolence, tradition, conformity, security, power, achievement, hedonism (the need or motivation for pleasure), stimulation, self-direction and universalism.

Self-reflection the ability to reflect on one's own practice or behaviour.

Short-term orientation a cultural orientation that emphasises the present (cf. long-term orientation).

Small culture the term used by Holliday (1999, reprinted in this Reader, see Chapter 13) to refer to an approach in language education in which the emphasis is on the process of interpreting commonalities shared by a small social grouping through activities rather than prescribing groupings at the start.

Small talk the informal conversation aimed to establish rapport between the participants.

Social construction the process or practice of creating and perceiving reality or phenomenon in its social context.

Social identities one's sense of belonging to a social group such as family, gender, age, profession, ethnic communities and cultural groups.

Socialisation the process of learning to adapt to a new culture or a community.

Sociocultural language learning theory the approach that regards language learning as a social activity in which the learner not only learns how to take actions with words, but also acquires the knowledge needed to be a full participating member.

Sojourners people who live abroad for a short period of time.

SPEAKING the analytic framework proposed by Dell Hymes (1972, *Toward ethnographies of communication*. In P. P. Giglioli (ed.), Language and social context (pp. 21–44). Harmondsworth: Penguin) to describe the components of a communicative event. The letters stand for Setting and Scene, Participants, Ends, Act Sequence, Key, Instrumentalities, Norms and Genre.

Speech act the performance of certain kinds of act in speaking, such as requesting, apologising etc.

Speech community a group of individuals who share norms and rules regarding communication.

Speech event an activity in a speech situation in which a number of speech acts are performed to achieve communicative goals.

Speech situation the context of communication.

Speech/communication accommodation the way one adjusts one's speech style to either converge with, or diverge from, that of other conversation participants.

Stereotypes over generalisation about the characteristics of a cultural group.

Subculture the term referring to a social group that is different from the dominant cultural group, or a small social group within a large cultural group.

Third culture   a term to describe shared meaning and mutual understanding developed during the interaction between people from different cultures.

Third space   a term proposed by Homi K. Bhabha in his book *The location of culture* (1994, London: Routledge) to describe the possibility for a negotiated and constructed cultural identity.

Translation equivalent   the corresponding word or expression in another language.

Trompenaars and Hampden-Turner's cultural dimensions   the model developed by Fons Trompenaars and Charles Hampden-Turner (1997, *Riding the waves of culture: understanding cultural diversity in global business.* Nicholas Brealey Publishing) to describe and differentiate various cultures. It includes universalism vs. particularism, individualism vs. collectivism, neutral vs. emotional, specific vs. diffuse, achievement vs. ascription, sequential vs. synchronic and internal vs. external control.

Turn   the basic unit of conversation consisting of what one speaker utters at one time.

Turn-taking   the alternation of turns between speakers.

U-curve of culture shock   a model that describes the stages of culture shock for people leaving their home culture for a foreign one. In the model, people start with high expectations, sink to disappointment and frustration and then experience satisfaction again.

Vertical collectivism   a cultural orientation that emphasises and promotes interdependence between members of groups, but there are status differences among all the group members (cf. horizontal collectivism).

Vertical individualism   a cultural orientation that emphasises personal independence, but there are status differences among all the group members (cf. horizontal individualism).

W-curve of culture shock   a model that describes the stages of culture shock for people leaving their home culture for a foreign one, and then returning home. In the model, upon returning home, people repeat the U-curve sequence – the high expectations, the shock and the readjustment.

Index

Index of languages and cultures

Intercultural Communication
2nd edition
An advanced resource book
for students

Adrian Holliday, John Kullman and Martin Hyde

Part of the Routledge Applied Linguistics series,
edited by Ronald Carter, University of Nottingham, UK and
Christopher N. Candlin, Macquarie University, Australia.

'This book helps the reader to gain a greater understanding of intercultural communication, of their own culture and of themselves. It does so by presenting engaging case studies of problematic intercultural 'events', by providing enlightening explanations and by inviting the reader to connect these cases to their own thinking and their lives.'

Brian Tomlinson, Leeds Metropolitan University, UK

The 2nd edition of Intercultural Communication:

- Updates key theories of intercultural communication.
- Explores the ways in which people communicate within and across social groups around three themes. These include identity, Othering, and representation - which are developed through the book's three sections.
- Contains new examples from business, healthcare, law and education.
- Presents an updated and expanded set of influential readings including James Paul Gee, James Lantolf, Les Back, Richard Dyer, Jacques Derrida and B Kumaravadivelu, with new critical perspectives from outside Europe and North America.

Written by experienced teachers and researchers in the field, Intercultural Communication is an essential resource for students and researchers of English Language and Applied Linguistics.

ISBN13: 978-0-415-48941-6 (hbk)
ISBN13: 978-0-415-48942-3 (pbk)

Available at all good bookshops
For further information on our English Language and Linguistics series,
please visit http://www.routledgelinguistics.com/

For ordering and further information please visit:
www.routledge.com